INTERNATIONAL BUSINESS

THEORY AND MANAGERIAL APPLICATIONS

Robert Grosse is Chairman of the World Business Department at the American Graduate School of International Management (Thunderbird). He received his Ph.D. in International Economics from the University of North Carolina and his bachelor's degree in Economics and French from Princeton University.

Dr. Grosse has published widely in the academic literature, including articles in the *Journal of International Business Studies,* the *Journal of Banking and Finance, Management International Review, The World Economy,* and the *Journal of Global Marketing.* His recent books include *International Business and Governments* (with Jack N. Behrman, University of South Carolina, 1990), and *Government Responses to the Latin American Debt Problem* (North/South Center, 1994). He is a member of the editorial review boards of the *Journal of International Business Studies* and the *North American Review of Economics and Finance.*

Professor Grosse is active in international business through work with multinational organizations such as the United Nations Center on Transnational Corporations, the InterAmerican Development Bank, and the Organization of American States. He also consults with many U.S. and Latin American multinational firms and banks, principally in Latin America. He teaches regularly in executive programs in Argentina, Colombia, Chile, Ecuador, Mexico, Peru, Uruguay, and Venezuela.

Duane Kujawa received his doctorate in Business Administration from the University of Michigan in 1970. Prior to his doctorate, Dr. Kujawa earned an MBA at the University of Santa Clara, where he had a dual major in Management and Economics, and a bachelor's degree in Electrical Engineering from the University of Detroit. He is presently Director of the International Business Center at the University of Miami, where he is also a professor in the Department of Management. Dr. Kujawa's teaching interests include Japanese Business, the Management of Multinational Enterprises, and Business Strategy.

Dr. Kujawa's publications have appeared in the *Journal of International Business Studies, Labor and Society,* the *British Journal of Industrial Relations,* the *Academy of Management Journal* and other journals. In addition to this text, he is the author of *Japanese Multinationals in the United States* (Praeger Publishers, 1986).

Professor Kujawa is a fellow and past president of the Academy of International Business and a fellow of the International Academy of Management. He has also served as a consultant to the Academy for Educational Development (Peru Project), universities, and private companies. He is also a member of the EuroBank Board of Directors.

THIRD EDITION

INTERNATIONAL BUSINESS

THEORY AND MANAGERIAL APPLICATIONS

ROBERT GROSSE
AMERICAN GRADUATE SCHOOL OF
INTERNATIONAL MANAGEMENT

DUANE KUJAWA
UNIVERSITY OF MIAMI

IRWIN

CHICAGO • BOGOTÁ • BOSTON • BUENOS AIRES • CARACAS
LONDON • MADRID • MEXICO CITY • SYDNEY • TORONTO

To Alan, Amanda, David, Laura, and Matthew

© RICHARD D. IRWIN, INC., 1988, 1992, AND 1995

Senior sponsoring editor:	Craig Beytien
Associate editor:	Karen Mellon
Senior marketing manager:	Kurt Messersmith
Project editor:	Lynne Basler
Production manager:	Bob Lange
Graphics supervisor:	Heather D. Burbridge
Cover Designer:	Annette Spadoni
Compositor:	Carlisle Communications, Ltd.
Typeface:	10/12 Garamond Light
Printer:	Buxton Skinner Printing Co.

Library of Congress Cataloging-in-Publication Data

Grosse, Robert E.
    International business : theory and managerial applications /
Robert Grosse, Duane Kujawa. — 3rd ed.
        p.   cm.
    Includes bibliographical references and indexes.
    ISBN 0-256-14175-4
    1. International business enterprises—Management.   I. Kujawa,
Duane.   II. Title.
HD62.4.G77 1995
658'.049—dc20   94–5433

Printed in the United States of America

1 2 3 4 5 6 7 8 9 0 **BX** 1 0 9 8 7 6 5 4

Preface

International business is the field of study that focuses on business activities that cross national boundaries. It includes exports and imports—the subject of traditional international trade discussions—as well as foreign direct investment, international banking, and international transfer of technology, global business strategy, and many more topics. Our concern is to present a panorama of the most important activities in international business and to offer a framework for thinking about them from the perspective of the company manager.

As countries enter into more highly-linked regional blocs (such as the European Union and the North American Free Trade Area), the analytical techniques and strategies presented here can be applied to inter-regional business. Similarly, as some countries become more decentralized in their power structures (Such as Canada with the isolationism of Quebec, or several Eastern European countries with their multi-ethnic divisions—or even in the United States, with its huge Latin American population today), the thinking learned in international business will apply in inter-province or inter-state or inter-cultural business contexts as well.

In fact, what distinguishes international business from its domestic counterparts is not so much the analytical techniques, since most of them can be applied at both domestic and international levels, but rather the context itself. That is, at the international level the key variables that a manager must cope with include different *currencies* whose values change, and different *government policies* (e.g., taxes, antitrust rules, financial controls)—along with the variables that exist in any domestic context, such as competition, cost conditions, and customer characteristics. In addition, different *cultures* exist in different countries, although cultures within individual countries also often differ importantly, as well.

Analysts of international business have developed some perspectives that are uniquely international—such as Vernon's international product cycle (discussed in Chapter 3), Dunning's eclectic theory of international production (discussed in Chapter 4), and all analyses of currency exchange rates (discussed in Chapter 6). Nevertheless, much of what is used in marketing, finance, strategy, and other business functional areas can be applied to international business phenomena. Indeed, the basic analytical perspective used in this book is the competitive advantage view of business strategy, which was developed in the domestic context and can be readily applied to international business as shown throughout the text.

There are many important challenges and problems that face firms that do business outside of their home countries. How can you handle business in different currencies? What are the ways of dealing with governments and operating effectively in diverse legal environments? Is it possible to avoid some of the business problems that arise due to cultural differences among people from different countries? What strategies will enable a firm to compete successfully against rivals from other countries? All of these questions and many other key concerns of decision-makers operating in international business are treated in this book. Conclusive answers are not always possible, but logical methods for dealing with the questions are developed and analyzed.

Many of the concerns of decision-makers in international business have to do with environmental (as opposed to company-specific) factors such as government policies and economic conditions in different countries. Such issues as the oil crisis of the 1970s, the international debt crisis of the 1980s, and the opening of Eastern Europe in the 1990s have forced companies in all industries to come to grips with higher and more volatile inflation and interest rates, greater risks in less developed countries, and possible opportunities or challenges from a much stronger, larger Europe. The evolution of international firms has pushed older, largely ethno-centric, multinationals from North America and Europe to cope with newer rivals from Asia. At the same time, competitive pressures from all sides are pushing firms to become at once global and multi-domestic, that is, to create global strategies to try to maximize efficiency and to be responsive to domestic demand pressures in each major national market served.

These conditions really go to the core of business at the end of the 20th century. Whether a firm is international or not, its competitors may come from different countries, its suppliers likewise may be domestic or foreign, and the environment in which it operates may depend on activities of foreign governments and firms.

It is in this context that the present book has been written. Although its focus is international, the decision-making methods and considerations presented in the book generally apply to domestic firms as well. From another perspective, it is our hope that the content of this book will be developed further in the traditional courses in finance, marketing, strategy, etc. There can be no doubt that business around the world has become open to foreign competitors, foreign markets, and foreign supply sources; so any manager should understand the implications of these phenomena for the firm.

Purpose and Organization

The text was designed for a survey course in international business at the undergraduate or MBA level. It is a comprehensive text, intended to be used in a one-semester course, with the selection of chapters left to the instructor's discretion. It should also prove useful as a reference source both in subsequent courses and in business practice.

The material is organized into five sections. The first section introduces the subject of international business and explores the scope of the field. It also presents the central conceptual base of the text, the theory of competitive advantages. The second section treats the "environment" that faces decision-makers in international business. The basic economic fundamentals that affect trade, investment, and other business activities between countries are presented in this section, along with a description of the institutional structure of the international economy. Part 3, provides in-depth coverage of functional areas of business administration and other broad managerial concerns, at the international level. In addition to chapters on international marketing and international finance, etc., this section examines cultural issues, transfer of technology, and export/ import management. Part 4 is a particularly distinctive aspect of the book; it looks at international business activities and government policies in three major kinds of countries: the industrial nations, the less developed countries, and the formerly-communist countries. The last section presents some thoughts about where multinational firms—or *international contractors* as we call them—are headed in the 21st century. An appendix presents detailed studies of international business in four industries—oil, banking, autos, and telecommunications.

This text is distinctive from others in the field because of its unifying theme of "competitive advantages," which gives continuity to what are all too often studied as free-standing topics. Also, throughout the text, real-life business situations are cited to clarify the material being discussed and to make it more exciting and interesting. The cases presented at the end of each chapter give further opportunity for understanding the material in its practical aspects and applications.

New sections called "IB Illustrations" and "Added Dimensions" are used to provide more detailed discussion of some topics and to illustrate the ideas with current examples of international business activities. The "Added Dimensions" are used to cover topics that appear in the text in more depth, when that kind of coverage could detract from the flow of the main text. The "IB Illustrations" are used to separate examples that apply concepts from the text, so that the analytical logic and clarity are maintained, and the examples can be used to reinforce the reasoning in the text.

Based on evaluations from many of the users of the first and second editions of the book, several structural changes have been made. Chapter 2 on "Competitive Advantages" has been thoroughly revised to present the key analytical tools more clearly. Chapter 11 on the "Effects of Culture and Ethics" has been revised to better deal with this important aspect of international business. The number of chapters has been reduced to focus more closely on the current key issues in international business. And finally, more cases and examples have been added to both illustrate the concepts and update the application of ideas to current international business activity.

Changes in the Third Edition

The world has experienced a huge upheaval since the first edition of this book was published. The fall of the Berlin Wall in 1989 signaled the end of the Cold War, which had been a primary feature of international politics and a limitation on international business since 1945. When the Soviet Union under President Gorbachev chose to open its economy to private-sector business and to pursue a more market-based set of policies, this dramatic change eliminated the communist alternative as a major challenge to the global market system. While the former members of the Soviet bloc are still economically weak, these countries constitute a major new business opportunity for international firms today and a potential source of new challengers to competitors in Europe and elsewhere in the future. The text discusses these major changes in detail in the rewritten Chapter 21, along with the "Skoda" case and text references in other chapters.

Along with the disintegration of the communist bloc has come renewed effort at integration within several regions of the world. The European Union and its "Europe 1992" and Maastricht initiatives figure centrally in this picture. The nations of the European Union have dropped literally hundreds of barriers to business among the members—and additional countries are pushing for membership in the group. Similarly, the United States and Canada formed a free trade area in 1988, and Mexico joined what is now called NAFTA in 1993. The North American Free Trade Area, even as it begins operation, is receiving requests from Latin American countries for membership, toward a free trade area of the Americas. These important shifts and other inter-country cooperative efforts are discussed in the rewritten Chapter 10 on "Economic Integration."

The world economy continues to become more dominated by service-sector activities (e.g., financial services, consulting, computer programming, hotels and restaurants, transportation service, telecommunications service, etc.) in the 1990s. This reality is reflected in the greater number of examples and cases related to service industries throughout the text. The increasingly cost-driven competition in manufacturing worldwide is emphasized in the discussion of offshore assembly and foreign sourcing of production in several chapters. And the undiminished centrality of key raw materials industries such as oil is emphasized in the Appendix as well as elsewhere through the text.

The increasing use of inter-company alliances (strategic alliances) in domestic and international business is discussed especially in Chapter 5 and 12, but also throughout the book in new examples and new cases. These alliances were first seen extensively in the auto industry, with all of the major multinational manufacturers forming joint ventures and other partnerships with their rivals. The "NUMMI" case in Chapter 11 presents a detailed look at the Toyota-General Motors joint venture plant in California.

As with the prior editions, an instructor's guide and a computerized test bank are available to accompany the text. These supplementary materials provide the instructor with suggestions for presentation of the chapters and cases, additional readings, and more than 2,000 test questions based on the text.

ACKNOWLEDGMENTS

We would like to thank the many people who contributed their time, talents, and efforts toward the completion of this book. Most importantly, Patricia Olney, Adolfo Chiri, Jeff Life, Achim Fehlker, Emanuela Allgood, Sivakumar Venkataramany, and Sylvia Lima, graduate students at the University of Miami, all worked diligently and carefully to gather information and check the facts that appear in these pages. In addition, our Assistant Director, Ron Rodgers, very capably helped to coordinate the project and keep track of our communications with the publisher and business people who gave inputs into the book.

There are more than 100 business people who provided information and interpretations about their firms' international business activities that are incorporated in the book. Those with whom we worked most closely are the several senior executives in multinational firms and international banks who are also members of our International Business Center's Board of Advisors. They are: Gene Rostov, Gonzalo Valdes-Fauli, Clovis Estorilio, Pedro-Pablo Kuczynski, Juan Yañes, Eduardo Masferrer, Burt Landy, Ralph Llop, and Enrique Arias. In addition, we would like to thank Steve Vogel, Jim Widmer, David Friedson, Jerry Brock, John Hume, Ernesto Garuolis, Jose Muzuarieta, and Yves Bobillier. Others assisted in various important ways that we truly appreciate.

Our intellectual debts are to many scholars, but we would like to mention specifically Jack Behrman, whose views and encouragement stimulated this project. Others have also substantially influenced us in our own professional development, and their influences are reflected in this book. These scholars include: Vern Terpstra, Bob Hawkins, Ingo Walter, Gunter Dufey, Steve Robock, Alan Rugman, David Ricks, Jeff Arpan, Bill Ogram, Jim Goodnow, Hans Scholl-hammer, John Daniels, Jose de la Torre, Larry Franko, Raj Aggarwal, Bal Bhatt, Steve Kobrin, Ivan Vernon, Brian Toyne, Riad Ajami, Rosalie Tung, Dick Moxon, Mike Czinkota, Subhash Jain, Arvind Phatak, Phil Grub, Russ Root, Laurent Jacque, John Dunning, Irene Lange, Moises Naim, Jean-Francois Hennert, Ian Giddy, Jerry Watzke, Bob Vichas, John Weber, George Tesar, Jim Sood, Ken Simmonds, Bill Renforth, David Rutenberg, Alex Murray, John Ryans, Attilla Yaprak, and Joe Azel.

Our colleagues who read all or some of the manuscript and offered very valuable comments include: J. Frederick Truitt, David Hopkins, Ellen Cook, Chong S. Lee, Jose Azel, Filemon Campo-Flores, Evangelos S. Djimopoulos, Patricia Tansuhaj, James D. Goodnow, M. Raquib Zaman, and James C. Baker.

While this book reflects valuable inputs and influences from all of these people, we want to note that we alone take responsibility for its contents. In closing, we invite you—professor or student—to share your thoughts on this book with us. A good text is one that lives and that reflects the needs and interests of both professors and students as they and the field evolve over time. We think that this is a good text, and we would value your comments to make it even better.

Robert Grosse
Duane Kujawa

Contents
in Brief

Contents

INTRODUCTION

1

Issues and Concepts

In some ways international business is an extension of domestic business; in other ways it is quite distinct. This chapter describes the scope and context of international business in the 1990s, aiming primarily to:

1. Illustrate important differences between international business and domestic business.

2. Identify the entities involved in international business.

3. Illustrate how important business functions vary firm by firm internationally and discuss why this occurs.

4. Present the organization of this book.

Young children in a small town of Soviet Latvia Republic, which had declared independence, touch a statue of Lenin that once stood as a symbol of communist control in the region.

AP/Wide World Photos

INTRODUCTION

What is international business? To some people, it means "big business." These people see international business as dominated by giant corporations whose economic power is so great that it may even compromise the political autonomy of nation-states. Other people equate international business with international trade, thinking only in terms of exports and imports. Some of these people may work for firms that sell products to overseas markets; others may work for firms that are battling foreign-made products right in their home markets. For such people, international business can mean either big opportunities or big problems.

Figure 1–1 shows a variety of international business examples. Let's look briefly at a few of them to get a better idea of what international business is.

Exports: Exports are products and services a company in one country sells to customers in another country. To illustrate, Canadian Eskimo art is exported to customers in San Francisco, California.

Direct investment: When the German company Volkswagen, AG puts up an assembly plant in Brazil, the investment is termed *direct.*

Imports: Imports are products or services a customer in one country buys from a supplier in another country. For example, a Japanese consumer buys Scotch whisky from a distillery in Great Britain.

Licensing: When Germany's Volkswagen, AG transfers robotics technology to its Brazilian plant, it licenses the Brazilian plant (i.e., a subsidiary company) to use the robotics technology. It may also license the Brazilian company to use the VW trademark.

Portfolio investment: When Fidelity, the large US mutual fund company, buys stock in British Telecom, a portfolio investment occurs.

FIGURE 1–1

Examples of International Business Activities

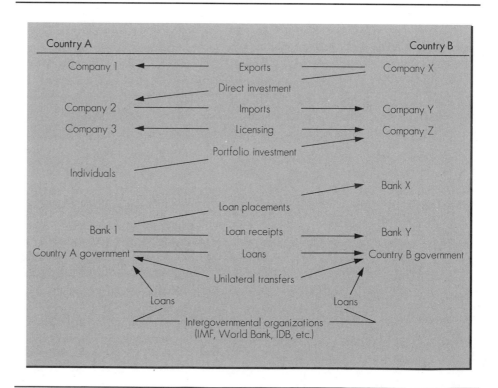

Loans: Loans arise when a borrower in one country becomes indebted to a lender in another country. Chase Manhattan Bank's loan to the government of Hungary is a cross-border loan.

Unilateral transfers: When one receives a gift from someone from another country, a unilateral transfer occurs. The US government's food aid to less developed countries is a type of unilateral transfer.

In addition to the activities shown in Figure 1–1, there are a few others, such as turnkey projects, management contracts, franchising, and so on. An example of a turnkey project occurred when Italy's Fiat built a truck plant for a Russian state-owned enterprise. Management contracts, which are common within multinational companies, involve charging an overseas subsidiary for services provided by the parent company, or they can involve a foreign firm managing operations for local investors, such as Hilton Hotels in France. International franchising, which can be viewed as a licensing and management contract "package," involves a franchisor contracting with franchisees in foreign countries, such as Blockbuster Video contracting with a franchisee in Chile.

But there are considerably more dynamics to international business than the activities in Figure 1–1 portray, especially for students who want to learn about business administration. Let's look at a few real-life cases to appreciate better what international business is all about.

INTERNATIONAL BUSINESS HIGHLIGHTS: COCA-COLA, CITICORP, DOW, AND HONDA[1]

Coca-Cola

The Coca-Cola Company is the world's largest producer and distributor of soft drinks. Its lead brand, Coca-Cola, is undeniably a global product. In 1992, Coca-Cola marketed soft drinks, juices, and food products to customers in over 195 countries. Its global revenues totaled more than $13 billion. At the close of the 1980s, Coke, the company's lead product, commanded a 48.5 percent international market share and was outselling its closest competitor by nearly four to one.

Unlike some "high-tech" companies whose products come and go, Coke has been around for over 100 years since its beginnings in Atlanta in 1886. A product that old should be about as mature as a product can be; at least, that's the conventional wisdom. But not so in Coke's case! In the 1980s, the company introduced several variations of the basic product, including Diet Coke (a product marketed under the "Coke Lite" brand in Japan, where consumers are not so weight conscious), which resulted in new growth as new market segments were identified and served. Moreover, its international markets are growing at rates beyond that of its traditional home market, the United States. For these reasons, Coca-Cola plans to focus even more heavily on international markets in the future. The explanation is really quite simple. Sales of soft drinks are income driven. As societies' incomes grow, so also will their consumption of soft drinks, and Coke is a big player in the soft-drink market. Why is Coke a big player? The answer is Coke's "secret" formula and its "system," the global production and distribution network kept vibrant by Coca-Cola's global expertise in management and marketing.

Coca-Cola concentrate is made in several key countries strategically located around the globe. This concentrate is sold to bottlers and/or distributors in just about every country. Coca-Cola also supplies bottlers with marketing support and production and water purification technologies based on parent company–provided research and systems designs. Bottlers conduct local market research, provide for sales financing, and handle distribution and promotion. Coke may well be a global product, but it takes a well-organized team effort to deliver it to customers around the world.

Citicorp

One of the world's largest financial services institutions, Citicorp operates in 39 states in the United States and in 89 other countries. It has a customer relationship with one out of every five US households, and its assets totaled $213.7 billion at the end of 1992. Citicorp is headquartered in New York City, but 48 percent of its 86,000 employees and nearly two-thirds of its offices were located overseas in early 1992. Citicorp, which calls itself a "global financial services company," is organized at the top into two major business units: Global Consumer and Global Finance. It is diversified by customer base, geographic presence, and product line. As might be expected, considerable coordination exists among the different customer and product-oriented operating units both within each country or region and among countries and regions.

The financial services industry is becoming increasingly competitive, and Citicorp's competitive strategy is based on innovation, customer orientation, and management decentralization. Citicorp notes, for example, that a key support element cutting across its major business units is its advanced information-processing and transmission capabilities. Coming into the 1990s, Citicorp world-wide operates 160 data centers working through 20,000 terminals, 7,000 of which are located in its customers' facilities. In the past several years, the company has spent over $500 million in developing and implementing electronic information-handling technologies, and it contends that it is now the world leader in electronic banking for commercial applications. It also contends that these technologies give it special capabilities for generating new products in an industry in which old-line, mature products are no longer very profitable. Cases in point here include the establishment of "Citifunds," an Asian-based cash management account marketed to non-US customers with high net worth, and the revitalization of its Diners Club and other travel and entertainment–related businesses by enabling more efficient, lower-cost operations. In addition, Citicorp sells its funds transfer service to some 7,000 financial institutions located around the world.

Dow

A globally integrated producer of chemical, health care, and other consumer and industrial products, Dow Chemical Company is headquartered in Michigan and has numerous facilities in the United States, Canada, Europe, the Orient, and Latin America. Dow's foreign operations range from wholly owned subsidiaries such as those in Canada, the Netherlands, Italy, Greece, Germany, Mexico, Argentina, and Colombia to joint ventures such as those in the United Kingdom, Spain, the Netherlands, France, Italy, Germany, Argentina, Ecuador, Colombia, Chile, Mexico, Japan, India, Australia, New Zealand, and Malaysia. In 1992, Dow's sales revenues totaled $19 billion. About 50 percent of Dow's sales are outside the United States, as are nearly half of its 61,000 employees. At the end of 1992, Dow Chemical Company (US) had equity investments in approximately 155 companies located in 32 countries.

Dow's top-level organizational operating structure is geographically divided into five regions: the United States (Dow Chemical USA), Canada, Europe, Latin America, and the Pacific. The president of Dow Chemical Europe, for example, has operations responsibility for the entire European region. Management and technical personnel at various organizational levels within the regional divisions coordinate with their counterparts in other divisions on major investment, production allocation, and similar decisions. About one-sixth of Dow Chemical USA's production is exported to customers in the other four regions.

Dow's mainstream production is in chemical intermediates, and over the years the company has been especially successful in developing families of products around a common product core, such as with styrene plastic. Dow is deliberately expanding its presence in specialty chemicals, pharmaceuticals, and other health and consumer products that are less capital intensive and less sensitive to cyclical declines than chemical intermediates. The company conducts its basic R&D in the United States but conducts applications research, which focuses on adapting products to meet the capabilities and needs of local users, in both the United States and the foreign divisions. The overseas subsidiaries, whether wholly or partially owned by Dow, produce under licensing agreements with the parent company.

Honda

Honda Motor Company, Ltd., manufactures and sells motorcycles, automobiles, and power products (e.g., portable generators, outboard motors, and lawn mowers). It is headquartered in Tokyo and operates several factories in Japan as well as at wholly owned subsidiaries in Belgium, Canada, France, Italy, Mexico, New Zealand, the United Kingdom, and the United States. Honda performs additional overseas production at minority-held subsidiaries and 50-50 joint ventures in Indonesia, Iran, Nigeria, Peru, Taiwan, Thailand, and the Philippines. Honda's fiscal year 1993 worldwide sales were 4,132 billion yen (about US $35.5 billion using an exchange rate of approximately 116 yen per dollar, the rate on March 31, 1993). Over half of the company's revenues come from overseas markets. Direct exports from Japan represent approximately one-sixth of total Japanese production. (Data on domestic and overseas employment are not routinely made available by the company.)

Honda eschews formal organization structures. Functionally, however, the parent maintains direct responsibility for the manufacture and sale of all products in Japan. Honda Research & Development Company, Ltd. (a Japan-based subsidiary), provides product R&D and product designs, and Honda Engineering Company, Ltd. (also a Japan-based subsidiary), performs process-related R&D and manufactures production tooling and equipment for Honda plants worldwide. The situation of the US subsidiary illustrates organizational relationships internationally. The president of Honda of America is also a managing director and member of the board of directors of the parent company. Operational coordination is achieved via varied contacts involving managerial and technical personnel at the parent and subsidiary in the product divisions and specialty areas (e.g., Honda Engineering for use of production technology and equipment).

Honda Motor Company's growth has traditionally been production driven. The company has had to develop markets as outlets for its continuously expanding, low-cost production capabilities. Large markets, which include domestic and foreign segments, enable Honda to take advantage of its large-scale production facilities for certain parts and components, such as motorcycle engines, and to put such low-cost production to its competitive advantage. This was the situation, for example, when Honda first established motorcycle production at its US plant in

**IB
ILLUSTRATION**

Honda Motor Company

As the world's leading motorcycle manufacturer for over two decades, Honda is maintaining its commitment to expanding the worldwide market for motorcycles by expanding in existing markets and entering new country markets. For example, Honda began producing in Pakistan in 1992, expanded production in Malaysia by 27 percent in 1993 (to 926,000 units), and will increase production in China by 20 percent in 1994 (to 450,000 units). ■

Source: Honda Motor Company, Ltd., 1993 Annual Report.

Ohio in 1979. Engines were imported from Japan until sales in the US market grew large enough (in 1984) to justify producing engines in Ohio.

Production R&D, conducted at Honda Engineering in Japan, is heavily oriented toward robotics and automated production equipment that have general applicability in Honda plants worldwide. Product R&D, such as that for motorcycle models, is less monolithic. In this case, the company uses market-generated information from both foreign and domestic operations and technical design expertise housed at Honda Research & Development Company in Japan. Through wholly owned subsidiaries, joint ventures, and licensing arrangements, Honda products are manufactured in 40 countries.

THE CONDUCT OF INTERNATIONAL BUSINESS

Coca-Cola, Citicorp, Dow, and Honda have a lot in common. They export something of value from their home countries and also produce abroad. They implement overseas activities via wholly owned foreign subsidiaries, joint ventures, franchising, and licensing arrangements that display obvious dependence on the parent company. They generally center their R&D at home. But Coca-Cola, Citicorp, Dow, and Honda differ in important ways too. Dow produces abroad to export back to the US market in some cases. At both Dow and Coke, R&D is centered in the home market, while Dow, Citicorp, and Honda conduct product application and consumer research in foreign markets. The four companies exhibit very different organization structures at the top: The divisionalizing of Coca-Cola is on a geographical basis; that of Citicorp and Dow is on a hybrid product, customer, and/or geographic basis; and that of Honda is on a functional basis. Let's explore the implications of these observations for managers.

Product Impact

Product variations are required to accommodate different technical considerations, such as the electrical characteristics of Citicorp's information-processing equipment; different use conditions, such as with the chemicals used in agricultural applications; and different consumer preferences, such as the infatuation of Americans with powerful, heavy-duty motorcycles (compared, for example, to the smaller, scooter-type motorcycles preferred in some European countries). Product design for different markets also incorporates cost considerations related to scale economies in production, the use of standardized components on a global basis, and the production skills available in the work force at the foreign plant.

For some of the same reasons, the use of certain kinds of production processes, machinery, and equipment may vary between domestic and foreign operations. These are *process* variations. The level of production at a domestic plant may vary with demand conditions in a foreign country or with interruptions of production (caused by a strike, for example) at a foreign plant.

Marketing Impact

Marketing is similarly complicated. Market research must now be coordinated among the different countries served, not only to determine product needs but also to arrive at product sales estimates used in setting production and inventory levels and purchasing and staffing needs. Pricing and promotional strategies must be determined for geographically segmented markets with different competitive characteristics. Successful marketing also requires understanding country-specific distribution systems, packaging preferences and standards, and so on.

IB ILLUSTRATIONS

Dow Chemical Company

Behind Dow's international growth is a global network. As early as the mid-1960s, Dow recognized that global success means competing effectively in local markets. Thus, while it pursues worldwide economies of scale, the company also strives for close ties with customers. Local managers, often working in their native countries, adapt products and strategies to their markets' particular requirements. Yet whether it's purifying water in Brazil or developing a joint venture in China, Dow answers each market's demands with a worldwide leader's resources. People, plants, and products are linked to combine a local touch with a global perspective. ■

The Coca-Cola Company

Price inflation is a factor in many markets around the world and consequently affects the way a company operates. In general, Coca-Cola management believes the company is able to adjust to counteract the effects of increasing costs and generate sufficient cash flows to maintain its productive capability. In highly inflationary countries, the company has benefited from its net monetary liability position. This position is viewed as a hedge against the effects of high inflation, since net liabilities will ultimately be paid with devalued currency. ■

Citibank

Citibank's foreign exchange revenues of $1,005 million in 1992, from both customer transactions and interbank trading, increased by $296 million, or 42 percent, from 1991, a year also noted for its strong performance. The momentum in foreign exchange revenues continues due to global volatility of foreign exchange and financial markets, increased customer transactions, and Citibank's success in identifying trends and prices. Foreign exchange revenues include activities in the spot, forward, futures, and options markets. ■

Sources: Dow Chemical Company, *1992 Form 10-K* Annual Reports; The Coca-Cola Company, *1992 Form 10-K* Annual Report; Citicorp, *1992 Form 10-K* Annual Report.

Financial Impact

Finance is concerned with handling cash flows and funding needs in both domestic and foreign operations in home country and foreign country currencies. Dow Chemical, for example, uses a capital budgeting procedure to evaluate a plant investment proposal in Germany characterized by cash flows denominated in both deutsche marks and US dollars. Moving funds internationally and having the right amount of funds in the right currencies are also major concerns. Coca-Cola needs French francs to pay the wages of its workers at its concentrate plant in Signes; Dow wants to bring home its profits from its Dutch subsidiary and Honda the licensing fees from its Costa Rican licensee. The currency denominations of assets and of debt funds are also important. What happens, for instance, to Citicorp's loans denominated in the Peruvian currency (soles) if that currency cannot be converted to dollars, or what happens to the US dollar value of Dow's Canadian dollar debt if the relative value of the Canadian dollar climbs? Can Citicorp and Dow somehow protect themselves against the risk involved here?

Personnel Impact

Personnel concerns also differ when a company deals with foreign operations. Honda uses Japanese nationals in managerial and technical positions at its US subsidiary; Coca-Cola uses some Americans at its German subsidiary. How are these parent-company employees in turn managed? What career paths do they tread? Do they mix well with local nationals?

Another concern is the management of workers at the foreign plant. The industrial relations environment must be analyzed in terms of several issues,

---

**IB
ILLUSTRATIONS**

Citicorp

The consolidated financial statements include the accounts of Citicorp and its wholly owned subsidiary, Citibank, N.A., and their majority-owned subsidiaries, after the elimination of all material intercompany transactions.

Affiliates which are 20 percent to 50 percent owned are carried under the equity method of accounting and the pro rata share of their income (loss) is included in other revenue. Income from investments in less than 20 percent-owned companies is recognized when dividends are received.

As a U.S. corporation, Citicorp is subject to domestic taxation currently on all of its foreign pretax earnings if earned by a foreign branch or when earnings are effectively repatriated if earned by a foreign subsidiary or affiliate. In addition, certain of Citicorp's domestic income is subject to foreign income tax where the payor of such income is domiciled overseas. ■

Honda Motor Company, Ltd.

The consolidated financial statements are expressed in yen. However, solely for the convenience of the reader, the consolidated financial statements of and for the year ended March 31, 1993, have been translated into United States dollars at the rate of Y116 = US$1, the approximate exchange rate prevailing on the Tokyo foreign exchange market on March 31, 1993. This translation should not be construed as a representation that all the amounts shown could be converted into U.S. dollars. ■

Source: Citicorp, *1992 Form 10-K Annual Report*; Honda Motor Company, Ltd., 1993 Annual Report.

including the wage determination process, the implementation of technological change, the propensity for industrial conflict, and the composition, magnitude, and determination of nonwage compensation.

Accounting Impact

Financial accounting systems must be developed to reflect operations consolidated on a global basis. Dow Chemical presents a dollar-denominated, consolidated financial report on its worldwide activities, even though its foreign subsidiaries deal in and report their own operations in their own currencies. How is this accomplished? How can managerial accounting systems be designed to convey meaningful information to parent company management when operations cross a variety of national environments?

Tax Impact

Coca-Cola, Citicorp, Dow, and Honda operate internationally but within various national tax jurisdictions. Most governments, the United States and Japan included, like to collect taxes. Operating entities, such as parent companies and subsidiaries, generate profits (or losses) and are taxed. Profits can be moved around, however, between parent and subsidiaries depending, for example, on what the latter pay for imported components, management fees, and royalties. Nonetheless, the US Internal Revenue Service reserves the right to determine these charges (for tax purposes) for firms operating in the United States, including foreign-owned subsidiaries such as American Honda Motor Company, Inc.

Certainly we could say more about the differences between operating solely domestically and operating internationally. In fact, that is what this book is all about. Table 1–1 summarizes the differences noted above. Later in the book, each

TABLE 1–1

How the Management Functions Differ in International Business

Management Topic	Selected Highlights of International Business Dimensions of Operations
Product	Adaptive to differences in technical requirements, use conditions, scale economies, consumer preferences, available production skills, and available materials.
Process	Adaptive, as noted above, with emphasis on scale economies and available production skills and materials.
Marketing	Marketing research—decentralized, market specific, yet coordinated across different countries to identify commonalities. Distribution, packaging, promotion, etc. usually market specific. Pricing set via competitive conditions in geographically segmented markets.
Finance	Concerned with cash flows and funding needs in both domestic and foreign currencies, capital budgeting for foreign operations and currency denomination of debt. Focus is on the financial and business risks associated with such activities and on the methods available for reducing or offsetting these risks.
Personnel	Selecting, motivating, and rewarding personnel on foreign assignments. Justification for using expatriate personnel. Managing industrial relations internationally.
Accounting	Accounting for foreign transactions and consolidating financial statements at the multinational level. Developing and implementing informative managerial accounting systems internationally. Minimizing taxes on a global corporate basis.

of these traditional functional areas of management, as put into practice in the international business setting, is discussed in substantial detail.

LEVELS OF ANALYSIS

This text incorporates two levels of analysis. The first level deals with *awareness*, the second with *understanding*.

From a management perspective, the differences between operating domestically and operating internationally are substantial. Being aware of these differences constitutes the first level of analysis. But what accounts for these differences? Answering this question gives rise to the second level of analysis: understanding and appreciating the environmental and institutional peculiarities that uniquely affect international business and influence the nature of the management functions. Included in the second level are knowledge of the pressures resulting in international trade and investment, operation of the foreign exchange markets, cultural environments, and the politically determined presence of trade and investment barriers and incentives. The chapters that follow address these issues.

The second level of analysis, understanding, also involves explanations of the differences in how companies operate internationally. Look at how Coca-Cola, Dow, Citicorp, and Honda differ. Why do these differences exist? The analysis here focuses on how each company operates within a specific competitive and technological setting and within its own corporate culture and on how this situation may either expand or constrain its options. Honda, for example, can produce components or subassemblies offshore or purchase from offshore manufacturers for consumption in the United States due to labor cost differences; Dow cannot. Honda assembles and markets heavy-duty motorcycles in the United States, as does its main competitor, Harley-Davidson. Honda imports lighter-weight vehicles that cater to other market segments in which there is no domestic competition. Why? Coca-Cola, with its global product, is not routinely concerned with product modifications; Dow is, to some extent. Citicorp has identified global customers with global needs. Honda is very market sensitive in its product planning. Why? All four companies view international operations as important to their success strategies, yet their strategies vary considerably.

The following chapters focus heavily on this second level of analysis. They deal with environmental differences, the impact of such differences on managerial decisions, and the variations in managerial decisions that arise from companies' differing approaches to operating internationally.

TOPICS OTHER THAN THE MULTINATIONAL CORPORATION

Thus far, our discussion has focused solely on the multinational corporation (MNC). But international business involves a much more diverse set of actors than multinational corporations alone.

Governments and International Organizations

As implied earlier, governments are also highly relevant to international business. They usually implement their policies via specific agencies, and these policies and agencies are certainly appropriate subjects for this text. In addition, governments even yet often own companies that compete with private sector firms; thus, these companies will be discussed. International institutions, typically constituted via government action, help define the environment within which international business functions. The International Monetary Fund, the World Bank, and the International Labor Office are examples of such institutions.

Culture

As noted earlier, culture is also an important variable in international business, where firms operate cross-culturally. People are products of specific cultural settings, and international business is conducted through people. Culture affects values, communications, institutions, and so on. Most often it is seen as being national or subnational in character. But there is also the "corporate culture." People in firms are groups too, and they often share common values, interests, hierarchies, and the like. International business deals with home country and host country cultures within a corporate culture. Finding commonalities across cultural groups often facilitates successful operations. The topic of culture is addressed specifically in Chapter 11. The influences of culture, however, will be addressed in other chapters, especially those dealing with international business operations in the functional areas.

Exporting/Importing Activities

The four companies presented above are all quite large. International business, however, is also relevant for small and medium-size firms. Today many of these firms are involved in exporting and in foreign sourcing of materials or parts. For example, RECO International, BV, a Dutch-owned food and beverage processor and distributor with $12 million in sales, operates four factories in Europe and has recently begun exporting processed bananas from an Ecuadoran plant to the United States. The Ecuadoran plant, built with World Bank funds and utilizing automated processing equipment provided by an Australian firm, is government owned. Like the Ecuadoran government, many other governments, including that of the United States, do much to promote exports—providing tax breaks, special foreign marketing assistance, and so forth. These activities are usually fairly well publicized. Some governments also have special policies designed to encourage imports. These policies often take the form of special tariff reductions on goods imported from selected countries. A case in point is the duty-free import into the United States of many manufactured goods under the Generalized System of Preferences (GSP) and the Caribbean Basin Initiative (CBI) and of numerous goods, and services under the North American Free Trade Agreement (NAFTA). Export/import management is the subject of Chapter 18. Government activities pertaining to international trade are also discussed in that chapter and in other chapters as appropriate.

WHY STUDY INTERNATIONAL BUSINESS?

The answer to this question should be fairly obvious by now. We need to study international business because

1. Almost all of the large enterprises in the United States, Western Europe, and Japan are multinational in character.
2. Many small and medium-size firms also operate internationally. This may take the form of export or import operations, support activities directly related to international trade (e.g., freight forwarders, customs brokers), professional services pertaining to international trade or multinational operations (e.g., accounting/auditing, banking, legal counsel), and so on. Some of these firms are also involved in overseas plant investment or licensing arrangements with foreign firms.

   The Agro-Dominicana Group case at the end of this chapter illustrates some of the complexities involved when even a small company does business internationally. When you first read the case, try to get a feeling for what is really different because the company operates internationally.

Answering the questions at the end of the case should help you appreciate why it is important to study international business. International business *is* different!

3. Competitive environments are typically industry specific, and industries today very often compete internationally. Overseas investment, incidentally, is not a requirement for international competitiveness. International trade, or the potential for it, can also link markets. A popular case in point here is the US steel industry, which has contracted considerably in the face of expanding imports.

4. Today more and more personal investments are being placed internationally. The Japanese have been big buyers of US Treasury bills; Americans are increasingly investing funds in European, Latin American, and Pacific-Basin mutuals. International financial markets are increasingly behaving as a single market. Your parents' retirement investments, and maybe even your own, are often buffeted by events in foreign markets. The Tokyo exchange's downfall sours the mood on Wall Street and may cause London's markets to tumble. We had all better understand what is going on in our world!

5. Public policy issues often relate to international trade, investment, and finance. Today any country's economic policies must consider the foreign sector. These policies are directly concerned with structuring business-to-government and business-to-business relationships in ways consistent with national interests. Many domestic public issues and policies also have important spillover effects for international business. For example, the British manufacturer of Austin-Healey sports cars abandoned exporting to the United States when it realized it could not meet US auto safety requirements and remain competitive. What have air quality standards done to the competitiveness of domestic versus imported steel in the US market? The number of examples here is endless!

The next three chapters present specific information on the scope and magnitude of international trade and investment and on the form and extent of multinational corporate activity. Public policy issues are analyzed in several of the chapters that follow.

Clearly, international business is important to managers. *The Wall Street Journal, Business Week, Forbes,* and other business periodicals typically include articles and commentary on global business activities and on how the changing global environment is affecting business. The academic world also recognizes the importance of international business. To ensure that people study international business, the US business school accrediting agency, the American Assembly of Collegiate Schools of Business (AACSB), now requires that all bachelor's- and master's-level degree programs include a "worldwide business component." From the student's personal perspective, however, the study of international business should also be important. Many business school graduates are or will be employed by firms engaged in international business. Even more business school graduates are or will be employed by firms in industries characterized by, or at least influenced by, international trade or investment. All business school graduates, as business practitioners, will be influenced by public policies pertinent to national interests and the dynamics of a world economy. Business practitioners have a responsibility to operate in a manner consistent with these policies and to work constructively to influence them. "Good citizenship," when viewed in this perspective, means good business too!

CONTENT AND ORGANIZATION OF MATERIALS PRESENTED IN THIS BOOK

Introduction

As is evident from the preceding discussion, the multinational corporation or, as it is often called, the multinational enterprise (MNE), is the key figure in international business, especially for students of business administration. The MNE is also the key figure in this text. The focus is not exclusive, however. Other forms of international business and other issue areas are also discussed. The next chapter presents the operational concepts that affect decision making in the MNE. That chapter and this one constitute the introductory materials.

Manager in the World Economy

Part II, "Manager in the World Economy," provides a thorough discussion of the environments and the institutional and theoretical frameworks within which international business is conducted. The topics covered in Part II include international trade and foreign direct investment patterns and theories, with additional commentary on their relevance to business decisions; international financial markets and how firms dealing in these markets operate; and the more important business-government issues, such as trade and investment barriers (e.g., tariffs, quotas, exchange restrictions), and the partial elimination of these barriers via economic integration.

Managing the MNE

Part III, "Managing the MNE," deals with the challenges and opportunities of multinational operations and the means by which MNEs develop and sustain a competitive presence. The first chapter focuses on culture. The other chapters cover the traditional, and not so traditional, management decision-making areas of organization structure and business strategy, marketing, accounting and taxation, finance and control, industrial relations, personnel, export/import management, and technology transfer.

Doing Business in . . .

Part IV consists of three chapters that focus on selected, fairly distinctive environments within which international business functions. These are the developed countries, the less developed countries (LDCs), and the emergent Eastern European democracies that once constituted the "communist bloc."

A Look to the Future

The final two chapters take a look at the future. The commentary is structured around analyses of several industries and around political developments affecting the MNE.

CONCLUSIONS

This chapter presented international business as being the domain of multinational enterprises and smaller firms that engage in export/import activities or provide related support functions and of political activities that directly and indirectly influence international trade and finance. International business is implemented via management functions that have to account for different and compelling environmental circumstances and that are unique unto themselves in some instances, such as those concerned with foreign exchange markets and host country assessments of the desirability of foreign direct investment.

Coca-Cola, Citicorp, Dow Chemical, and Honda were cited as examples of international businesses that operate in ways common to all and in ways unique to each. Different aspects of each company's situation were highlighted and subsequently categorized by management function. The result was fairly distinctive descriptions of differences in management functions consistent with the international (versus purely domestic) content of the operational environment.

The chapter introduced the idea of "level of analysis" and identified two levels: (1) analysis of the differences between operating domestically and internationally ("awareness") and the environmental circumstances that give rise to these differences and (2) analysis of the rationales for making management decisions in international business in light of these differences ("understanding").

The importance of studying international business was discussed. Business today is truly international! Almost invariably, firms and industries are internationally involved. Business school graduates may find themselves working for an MNE or dealing with management problems arising from competition from foreign companies in their industries. Public policy issues, including those often identified with ostensibly domestic problems, strongly influence international business activities.

Finally, the chapter presented a general outline of the text. Its five parts were identified: "Introduction" (including the concept of the MNE), "Manager in the World Economy" (analyzing the more significant environmental influences), "Managing the MNE" (focusing on the management functions), "Doing Business in . . . " (covering developed countries, LDCs, and the emergent democracies of Eastern Europe), and "A Look to the Future" (examining industry and political trends). We believe this five-dimensional format covers all of the topics necessary for a thorough introduction to international business. For many students, the topics covered in this text will constitute their only academic experience with international business. Other students will use this text as an introduction to later courses in international management, marketing, finance, and other areas. The text has been designed to serve the needs of both groups.

QUESTIONS

1. What is "international business"?
2. How important is international business to the economic and political development of the emergent democracies in Eastern Europe?
3. How important is international business to Coca-Cola? Citicorp? Dow? Honda? Is the domestic competitiveness of these firms in any way affected by their international business success?
4. How might the four firms be different or similar in international business, especially in the areas of product design, marketing, finance, industrial relations, personnel, and accounting and taxation?
5. Why is it important to study international business?
6. What are the differences between the two levels of analysis? Is there a logical progression through the levels?
7. Judging from your general knowledge, how important is international business to IBM, Exxon, Sears, Burger King, Holiday Inns, and General Motors? How do their international business activities differ?
8. How would you differentiate between international business and international trade?
9. Identify a current public policy issue related to international business. How is that issue important to you as a consumer or a citizen? How would it be important to you if you were a business manager? What do you think the government should do in this case? Why?
10. Why do you think a small or new firm would get involved in international business? Would your answer differ if the firm were in, say, Belgium rather than the United States?

REFERENCES

Annual reports. Select a company. Study its annual reports for the past five years. Note how "international" fits into its business strategy. Identify the relationships between its domestic business and its international business.

Business Week. Feature articles often refer to international issues or analyze the corporate strategy of an MNE.

The Economist. Especially strong on environmental analysis, economic and political issues, and non-US MNEs.

Fortune. In-depth analyses and presentations of the Fortune 500 and other companies.

International Business. Published monthly. Articles are more practice oriented and often report on what firms and management are doing to compete successfully internationally. Also includes articles on important aspects of the political and technological environments affecting international business.

Investing Licensing, and Trading Conditions. Annually updated reports on regulatory policies relevant to foreign companies and business conditions from more than 60 countries around the world published by the Economist Intelligence Unit.

Journal of Commerce. Published daily. Focuses heavily on international trade activities and issues.

Journal of European Business. Published bimonthly. Topical, practical orientation like *International Business*, but exclusively European.

The Nikkei Weekly. Reports on political, economic, business, and financial events in Japan. Similar in coverage style and topics to *The Wall Street Journal*.

The Wall Street Journal. Keep current on daily issues related to international business and the activities of MNEs. Read the international section especially. See also the *Asian Wall Street Journal Weekly*.

NOTE

[1]The information presented in this section is based on company interviews conducted by the authors and/or annual reports published by the companies.

The Agro-Dominicana Group, Inc.

The Agro-Dominicana Group, Inc., is engaged in the commercial cultivation and wholesale marketing of cantaloupe and honeydew melons for importation to the United States. Through its Dominican project company, the Group maintains controlling interest in its operations from seed to harvest.

Group History and Background

Agro-Dominicana was established in 1983 and is owned and controlled by three private investors. Two of the Group's shareholders are corporations with specialized prior experience in wholesale agribusinesses. Controlling interest of the Group is held by the Ricardo family, which also owns Ricardo Foods, a Group affiliate. Through Ricardo Foods and other, related companies, the family has engaged in the domestic production and wholesale distribution of produce throughout the United States and Canada for 20 years.

The Ricardos emigrated from Cuba in the 1950s after a successful export produce and cattle business on the Isle of Pines was confiscated by the Cuban government. Subsequently they purchased some 1,500 acres of farm land in Orange County, Florida, at an estimated cost of $750,000. Its appraised value is now about $30 million. Cultivation on this land is gradually being phased out. Tree nurseries have been planted, and it is anticipated that the land will eventually be sold and/or developed as commercial property. According to the Group, its primary objective was to reduce the dependence of domestic agro-based production on this increasingly valuable property. The Group identified offshore agricultural production as an alternative given the market opportunities for growth of nontraditional winter crops, especially melons.

The Market for Melons

Prices for melons in the United States are highly volatile and dictated virtually exclusively by supply factors. They typically range from a low of US $8 per 50-pound box, the US standard, to US $25 over the course of a year. The Group looks for an average price range of US $12 to US $14 and peak prices of US $25 during the winter months. Industry sources indicate that in the latter 1980s, only 15 to 20 percent of the US winter demand for melons was met. Winter production has increased in the last several years, but it is still a sellers' market.

The "winter window" opens between November and April, when no melons are produced on the US mainland. Hawaii produces melons, but Hawaiian

This case was developed and written by Professor Duane Kujawa with research assistance from MBA students Anthony Abitbol, Guillermo Castro, and Kevin Kendall and from company representatives. Company names, dates, and other selected information have been changed to preserve anonymity.

melons cannot be shipped economically beyond the Rockies. Melons from Mexico and Florida usually come into the market in late February. There is either too much rain or cold for earlier winter production in either area. Production from Mexico or Florida benefits from cheaper transportation costs that, by ship or truck, allow for a 50-pound box of melons to be sold at wholesale for US $7 to US $8. If a box of melons can be brought to market *before* mid-March, however, the seller can command a price of $15 to $25. By targeting delivery of a winter melon harvest, the Agro-Dominicana Group planned to carve itself a niche for a product with a seasonal but virtually unlimited demand and substantial profits often approaching 50 percent of gross sales. Agro-Dominicana estimates it can bring melons to market at an all-inclusive cost of just under $8 per box.

Selecting a Project Site   The Group first embarked on a nine-month mission to find the "ideal" farm site. The cultivation of melons requires very specific natural climate and soil conditions. The production cycle for winter consumption is from August to April. A semiarid climate, hot and without humidity, with no rainfall from October to April is essential. However, sufficient fresh water availability is just as crucial. Several potential sites had to be discarded in coastal Puerto Rico because not enough water for irrigation was available.

Land tracts of sufficient size for efficient irrigation and cultivation took St. Kitts out of the picture. The country's infrastructure, available refrigeration facilities, and infrequency of refrigerated ship sailings further shortened the prospect list, eliminating sites such as Aruba and Antigua in the eastern Caribbean.

Two project sites were initially identified. The first was in the Sacapa region of east-northeastern Guatemala and the other in the fertile Azua Valley region in the southwest section of the Dominican Republic. Much development has centered in the Dominican region since 1980. In fact, the Group's decision was "encouraged" by the presence of similar foreign-owned and operated projects in the valley. This, together with other shareholder business contacts in the Dominican Republic, led to the selection of the Azua Valley.

Government Incentives   The Dominican government has targeted the development of export agriculture as a top priority. Agriculture is the most important sector of the Dominican economy in terms of employment and export earnings. It represents 25 percent of gross domestic production and accounts for 70 to 80 percent of export earnings. It employs 45 percent of the labor force. Within the agricultural sector, raw sugar production has traditionally been the most important industry. In light of the world depression of sugar prices, the government has made a concerted effort to foster an environment for economic development in other areas, such as nontraditional crop production. The Group's management viewed this development as critical in terms of providing a favorable working/investment environment.

In 1982 the government enacted Law 409, the agroindustry law that offers benefits to agribusiness investors consisting primarily of tax remissions. Pursuant to meeting the law's prerequisites, the Group was granted a 15-year federal tax holiday and 100 percent exemption from all import duties on machinery and equipment. (The Caribbean Basin Initiative abolished a 35 percent US import tariff as well.) In addition, the Group was allowed to repatriate 100 percent of its earnings in dollars (to be converted at the official rate at the time of repatriation.)

Organization and Operating Structure

The Group set up a Dominican corporation, Agro-Azua, SA, as "the project company." The project company is the company of record and, on behalf of the Group, contracts for the land, hires the farmhands (*campesinos*) to prepare the land, and is responsible for harvesting, processing, and packing the crop. The project company is also the exporter of record. It sells the crop to the Group's marketing company, Ricardo Foods. The Group establishes a *transfer price* on the cost-plus basis. The profits of the project company show a 5 to 10 percent profit margin on sales. In addition, Ricardo Foods charges the project company 5 to 10 percent of gross sales for marketing and distribution expenses. These are included in Agro-Azua's cost base.

Most notably, the upside profit potential benefits Ricardo Foods. This is due to the fact that product market prices are variable and are highly influenced by supply factors, while costs of production are invariant. The Agro-Dominicana Group, Inc., is considered "the management company," and 5 to 10 percent of gross sales for export management and technical assistance is billed to the project company. (This too is included in Agro-Azua's cost base.) Technical assistance consists primarily of supervision from farmers brought in from Florida and the use of university-trained local agronomists, mostly on a consulting basis. Since 1985, the project company has sold 50 percent of the crop to a Channel Island company that is well regarded for its tax haven status. This "paper transaction" involves invoicing the sale to the Channel Island company and consigning the shipment to Ricardo Foods. The physical shipment of the crop is made directly to Ricardo in the United States. The Channel Island company, in turn, invoices Ricardo at a predetermined, marked-up price. In this manner, some of the profits avoid US income taxes. This intricate approach is predicated on management's strategy to control and protect the flow of funds (profits) by minimizing taxes.

Due to Ricardo's well-established market contacts, the crop is practically presold. Ricardo very seldom takes possession of the crop. Once the shipment leaves the Dominican port, supermarket and wholesale buyers are contacted and arrangement is made with the buyer for pickup at the port. Ricardo sells to major supermarket chains such as Publix and Winn–Dixie. In addition, the Group sells to food brokers in the Northeast and Canada. According to the Group, the primary concern of the buyers is the grade, quality, and reliability of delivery to market. Usually a supermarket chain like Publix will know its demand estimate for any winter crop by the preceding fall or by late summer, about three months before harvest begins. If the market is "hot" with extra demand, especially toward the end of harvest, melons can be sent up to a week early in what is called "half-slip" condition, a little less ripe than the "full-slip" condition in which the produce is usually sent.

Agro-Dominicana has grossed millions of US dollars each harvest since the project was initiated. Production expanded from an initial 600 acres in 1983–1984 to a 1,000-acre planting farm in 1985–1986. The Group expanded production to 2,000 acres in 1988. (Estimated annual production of melons in the Dominican Republic is 12 million, 90 percent of which are cultivated in the Azua Valley. The secretary of agriculture reports that 9,000 acres are now cultivated for melons in the valley by four different concerns.)

The Melon Patch

The minimum size of a commercially tenable melon patch is 200 acres. Though not the case here, much of the land in the Dominican Republic promoted for such production is land once used for sugar cane production and is cleared and ready to fill. Typically each acre yields 450 to 500 boxes of melons. The box's weight, depending on the grade of the crop, is 40 to 60 pounds.

Due to the natural climate and soil conditions, the production cycle time for melons is shorter in the tropics than in the United States. In the tropics, the time from seed to harvest is 65 days, compared to 90 days in US subtropic regions. This natural phenomenon facilitates crop turnover and enhances the producer's planting flexibility.

A farmer's workday is about 12 hours, from sunrise to sunset. In a highly labor-intensive process such as the cultivation of melons, cheap labor is essential for effective competition. Farm wages in the Dominican Republic are considerably lower than in the United States. There are no labor unions, and government interference is minimal. The government prescribes the minimum wage and an additional month's pay at year's end. Due to the seasonal nature of the work, government requirements regarding "layoff benefits" are not applicable. The minimum wage for the *campesino* is $1,456 pesos per month (the exchange rate was 12.75 peso per US dollar at the end of 1992). As is the case with most foreign investors, Agro-Azua generally pays slightly in excess of the daily minimum. It also provides transportation to and from the farm, as well as food and medical services to both field laborers and harvest processors. The variety of export products grown in the valley and the staggered harvest times for the different crops ensure that locals will have longer work seasons and steadier incomes than what a single crop would provide. As a result, average *campesino* income in the valley has risen 300 percent in four years. In addition, four agribusiness firms there have contributed to the building of a hospital and two schools in the area.

Labor is employed in three stages of production: land preparation, crop growing, and crop harvesting. Land preparation entails clearing the acreage and leveling the field. Six to seven tractor drivers and their helpers are employed in this process. Land preparation begins early in the year and continues up to seeding time.

The crop-growing stage requires approximately 30 to 40 laborers per acre. It requires irrigation every 7 to 10 days and periodic planting and fertilizing. The fertilization formula is dependent on soil conditions, and a knowledgeable, on-site agronomist is essential. Agro-Azua employs a staggered planting procedure whereby plots are brought to harvest in a time-staggered sequence.

Technical assistance is in the form of US-trained agronomists, one of whom resides at the project site during crop growing and harvesting. Other agronomists provide assistance on a consulting basis. Three or four local agronomists are employed on a permanent basis. Total employment varies depending on the stage of production and size of the crop. A permanent labor force is composed of eight or nine individuals, mainly the agronomists and a small staff of farm hands. Seasonal farm labor consists of approximately 200 to 250 *campesinos* from September to April. They are dispatched in teams of various sizes depending on the task: 20 to an acre to lay irrigation pipe, 12 to 15 if weeding and cultivating or doing pest control work, and only 7 or 8 to an acre when planting and fertilizing. The Group estimates labor costs in 1992 reached DR $2,000,000. These costs represent a 2,000-acre crop and do not include technological assistance charged to the project company.

Bringing Melons to Market

Once picked, a melon has an average shelf life of 7 to 10 days. State-of-the-art packing processes extend the shelf life to 17 to 21 days. Agro-Azua set itself apart from the other producers in the region by investing in timely process technology. This "hydrocooling" equipment costs approximately US $250,000. When the harvested melons are brought in from the field, their temperature is the same as the outside air, usually about 90 degrees Fahrenheit. When the melons are put in refrigerated storage, the fruit does not chill to the center for approximately 36 hours. Just as warmth accelerates its growth, so too does it speed up spoilage. With hydrocooling, melons are instead immersed in a frigid water bath that reduces their temperature inside and out to 44 degrees in 30 minutes. Once cooled, the melons are stored in a 10,000-square-foot refrigerated storage facility until shipping. Bringing to market a crop with extended shelf life is a key ingredient to buyer acceptance and satisfaction. Moreover, it affords Agro-Azua longer storage flexibility in the face of production and shipping uncertainties.

At times, Ricardo Foods has gone to extra expense to air freight produce by charter when necessary. (It is indicative of the large profit margin that produce can be shipped by air at 11 to 12 cents a pound instead of by ship at 5 to 6 cents a pound, and a profit can still be made.) Even so, in its first three years, the company reduced its reliance on air freight from 30 percent of the total crop to almost zero.

The hydrocooler was part of a larger investment made in 1984. A packing plant was built on a 45-acre lot purchased with a US $500,000 OPIC (Overseas Private Investment Corporation) direct loan. OPIC made the loan for a 10-year term, with two years' grace on both principal repayment and interest, collateralized by the equipment, land, and building.

The company had been using a government-owned processing facility and worried about the risk of keeping produce there. The US holding company and the individual investors guaranteed the loan. According to the Group, the ability to defer principal payments for two years was helpful, but not critical, in terms of managing the project's cash flow. The Group also purchased an apartment in the capital city of Santo Domingo for prolonged stays by the US staff.

Lack of transportation infrastructure has been a well-noted barrier to business in the region. The Azua Valley is surrounded by five active ports. However, the closest ports, in Barahona and Haina, are 40 and 60 miles, respectively, from the plant. Local roads and rail methods of transportation have been developed to the point where transportation by truck or rail car is used interchangeably depending on the size of the shipment. Local transportation in this regard has not been a problem.

Transportation to the United States is by refrigerated ships to South Florida ports. Presently three carriers service traffic between these ports twice a week: Seaboard Marine into Palm Beach, CCT into Fort Lauderdale, and Concord/NOPAL into Miami. In contrast, in the early 1980s, only two shipping lines serviced the Dominican ports twice every two weeks. Transit time is usually four days. Since 1987, the entire crop has been shipped by sea freight.

The Ricardo Family's Present Concerns

At the present time, the Ricardo family has decided to review the activities of the Agro-Dominicana Group, Inc. Agro-Dominicana has proven itself to be reasonably profitable, especially since 1988. But there is always concern that one of the operation's success factors may be eliminated or turn negative. This concern underscores the family's desire to review the entire situation. Stated somewhat differently, what could happen to injure Agro-Dominicana's fundamental business strategy and prevent profitability? What can Ricardo do now to prevent such events or their negative effects?

2

The International Contractor and Competitive Advantages

This chapter introduces the International Contractor (INC) as the key actor in international business. The main goals of the chapter are to:

1. Define *international contractor (INC)* and show how the term can be used to describe both large and small firms.

2. Describe the *multinational enterprise (MNE)* and illustrate this concept with a number of firms whose names will recur throughout the book.

3. Recognize the growing importance of nonownership forms of international involvement of firms, such as international licensing, international franchising, turnkey contracts, and other strategic alliances.

4. Explain the theory of *competitive advantage* and show how firms can use these advantages to benefit from doing international business.

5. Describe the concept of *internalization* and how it helps explain why MNEs act as they do.

6. Provide examples of how competitive advantages are used in international business (such as in the Caterpillar case) to shed more light on the concepts and on their applications in actual business situations.

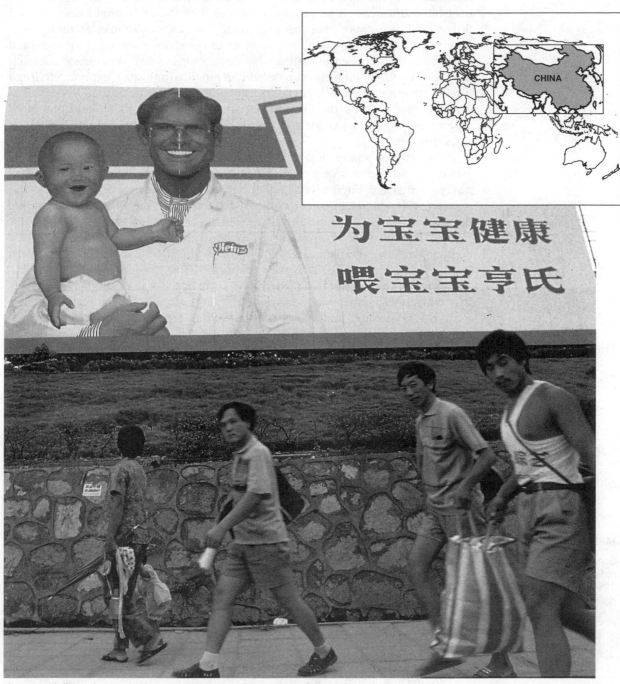

This Heinz billboard in Guangdong, China, attracts the attention of passersby.
© Greg Girard/Contact Press Images

INTRODUCTION

The central focus of international business is on the **multinational enterprise (MNE)** or, more accurately, on the **international contractor (INC).** The multinational enterprise is defined as a firm with subsidiaries, branches, or other controlled affiliates in three or more countries. The INC is a more broadly defined firm, with business activities that may range from exports to manufacturing in at least two countries. The minimum number of countries involved in international business is two; hence the international contractor is a firm that carries out such business. This definition encompasses firms ranging from small exporters to huge foreign investors such as Exxon and IBM, with affiliates in dozens of countries. This chapter focuses on the international contractor and its relations with customers, suppliers, competitors, and governments in the countries where it does business.

Although *companies* undertake international business, the national *governments* that set the rules of the game in business are clearly important, as are local governments and international organizations that likewise pose barriers and incentives for international companies. Also important are the noninternational firms that function as competitors, suppliers, and customers of the INC. Since our interest is to explore the particular problems and opportunities that arise for companies at the international level, we will deal primarily at that level and with local firms and governments as they relate to INCs.

Before examining the INC in detail, let us review some of the main activities that constitute international business. Table 2–1 shows that international trade (that is, exports and imports) is the largest category of international business activity, followed by international bank lending, foreign direct investment, and other contractual agreements, such as international licensing and franchising. Exports and imports alone accounted for close to $US 4 trillion of business during 1992, while international lending reached about one-fourth of that. The values for foreign direct investment and the other contractual forms should be interpreted carefully, since the investment (or the license) implies only the price paid for ownership or control of some business activity; the actual value of sales of a foreign factory or a franchised hotel is generally several times greater. The table does not include intergovernment transactions, which are much smaller in total than the trade or banking values but also contribute to the total amount of international business.

TABLE 2–1

Some Estimates of the Size of International Business, 1992 (billions of US dollars)

	World	US
Exports (1992)	$3,647.7	$448.164
Foreign direct investment		Stock: $486.67
		Flow: $ 25.72
Licensing		
Of affiliates		$ 15.467
Of nonafiliates		$ 4.159
Other contractual dealings		
With affiliates		$ 16.093
With Nonaffiliates		$ 34.377
International commercial bank lending (value of loans outstanding)	$ 689.4	

Sources: *International Financial Statistics*, September 1993; *Survey of Current Business*, March, July 1993; Bank for International Settlements, *Maturity Distribution of International Bank Lending* July 1993.

The bulk of the **value** of international business transactions comes from activities of large multinational firms. These firms export and import through their own affiliates and via unrelated firms; they move funds internally through loans, payments for use of technology, overhead, and so on; they borrow from, and lend to, unrelated parties; they exchange ownership of assets across national borders; and they pass uncountable amounts of information internationally among their affiliates and to and from unrelated parties. By definition, multinational enterprises carry out foreign direct investment, which they use to set up and expand their overseas affiliates. In addition, most international lending (in terms of the value of the loans) is done by large multinational banks that possess sufficient information about foreign clients to justify the banks' participation in such business. On the other hand, only about one-third of the total value of exports and imports is transacted by MNEs, with the rest spread among hundreds of thousands of smaller firms that do not operate overseas subsidiaries or branches. In terms of total transactions, non-MNEs constitute the majority of the actors in international business. Together, these various actors and activities are the essence of international business.

Figure 2–1 presents another view of international business, with the INC as the central actor. The INC is a central organizing institution for international transactions involving money, goods, and information. The INC not only seeks to earn profits for its owners but also generates income for suppliers in more than one country, provides outputs for customers in more than one country, poses additional competition for firms in each country, and operates under the rules set by governments in each jurisdiction involved.

This chapter explains what an international contractor is, what kinds of activities it undertakes, and why it undertakes them. The aim of this discussion is to get the reader to think about the kinds of problems and decisions an INC manager faces.

The next section defines the INC and MNE in more detail. The following section identifies a number of large, visible international firms and discusses some of their attributes. By using the theory of competitive advantage (described in the second half of the chapter), a manager can decide what information to gather and how to use that information to make decisions about INC activities

FIGURE 2-1

The International
Contractor in International
Business

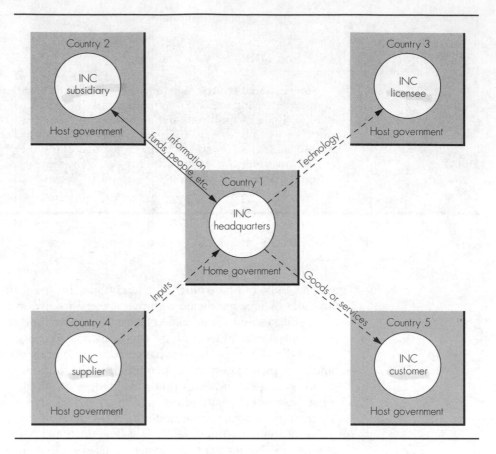

ranging from capital budgeting to market positioning to dealing with governments. Competitive advantage is used throughout the text as a general
framework for thinking about the issues the INC manager faces and for defining
the basic rationales for key decisions that INC managers must make. The chapter
concludes with an extended example of one international contractor—
Caterpillar, Inc.—and its competitive situation with respect to key rivals around
the world.

CHARACTERISTICS OF THE INTERNATIONAL CONTRACTOR

The term *international contractor* covers large firms that have been called
multinational enterprises and smaller firms with fewer overseas commitments that
may be simple exporters or contractors selling some service such as the use of
proprietary technology or management skills. During the 1980s, the range of
contracting activities international firms used to pursue their competitive objectives grew substantially. It now includes activities such as joint ventures that are
used to market products for two otherwise competing firms, coproduction
agreements under which two firms share a factory to produce their separate
products, and other so-called strategic alliances.

Due to the limitations many countries impose on foreign ownership of local
firms, firms that carry out substantial international business are finding more and
more nonownership forms of activity to undertake (e.g., licensing, franchising,
turnkey ventures, and other, more complex contracting arrangements in addition

to simple exporting). Also, small firms often discover that international business can be carried out through nonownership forms that do not require the large amounts of resources necessitated by operation of subsidiaries. Even large MNEs may find it useful to join with another firm(s) in a research project, marketing venture, or other alliance to reduce their costs and risks. Thus, both for competitive reasons and due to regulatory requirements, international firms are finding that contractual agreements help them achieve more and more of their goals. (This issue is discussed again in Chapters 5, 11 and 22.)

International contracting has become quite common in raw materials industries and in public utilities such as telephone and electric power companies. Firms such as Exxon, Texaco, AT&T, and GTE are making fewer simple foreign investments in oil wells or telephone operating companies and entering into more technical consulting agreements, joint ventures, coproduction agreements, etc. International banking has traditionally relied on correspondent relationships among banking firms in different countries to provide international services. Even in manufacturing, contracting out to provide managerial or technical services has become very common for large as well as small firms in international business. All of the world's major auto firms contract out extensively to obtain components such as tires, glass, accessories, and other parts, in addition to cooperating with each other in joint ventures in the United States and other countries.[1]

Strategic alliances other than traditional wholly owned foreign direct investment are becoming very common among multinational enterprises.[2] This phenomenon demonstrates MNEs' realization that contractual strategies offer such benefits as pooling scarce resources, sharing risks, and other positive features that cannot be obtained by going it alone. Hence, the concept of the international contractor emphasizes the new perspective of decision makers that a variety of means can be used to serve the end of international competitiveness.

CHARACTERISTICS OF THE MULTINATIONAL ENTERPRISE

No single definition of the MNE has received wide acceptance at this time. Some analysts view large, dominant firms that do at least some international business (such as those listed in the Fortune 500) as the relevant ones. Others include only firms that have owners from more than one country. Even the label is arguable; the United Nations calls the firms **transnational corporations,** and the AFL-CIO calls them **multinational companies.** While no definition can be completely objective, Vernon and Wells have offered a view that covers the concept fairly well. Their view is that multinational enterprises are companies made up of a cluster of affiliated firms [that], although in different countries, nevertheless share distinguishing characteristics as follows:

1. They are linked by ties of common ownership.
2. They draw on a common pool of resources, such as money and credit, information systems, trade names and patents.
3. They respond to some common strategy.[3]

In this view, the MNE may be privately or governmentally owned; it may be very large or relatively small; its ownership may be held by investors from any number of countries; and it may engage in any number of forms of international business—as long as it possesses owned affiliates in more than two countries. This may be called a *functional* definition of the MNE, since it focuses on the functioning of the firm and not on its ownership structure or other characteristics. The one necessary function of an MNE is foreign direct investment, through which the firm obtains or creates affiliates in at least three countries.

Typically, the firms discussed in this book not only have affiliates in three or more countries but also possess the other characteristics of multinational ownership and large size, as discussed in the next section. The key point of our definition is that firms need *not* possess these latter characteristics to use the strategies and organization structures discussed in later chapters. The ability to use more than one country as the firm's market or production site (and to face the concomitant opportunities and constraints) is the distinguishing feature of the MNE. From this arise the competitive advantages peculiar to multinational firms.

EXAMPLES OF MNES

The list of multinational enterprises according to our definition would number in the thousands. Instead of trying to create such a list, we consider a small number of very successful MNEs and a few of their competitive characteristics. Our purpose is to discover not only which companies are multinational but also to see what enables them to operate successfully at the international level. Table 2–2 lists 36 large US-based multinationals that a study by Peters and Waterman (1982) found to be highly successful from 1961 to 1980, and shows some of their current characteristics.

Notice that the vast majority of these firms spend much more on research and development (R&D), and thus are more technology intensive, than the US industry average of 3.7 percent of sales spent on R&D. Also, most of them possess affiliates in far more than the three countries needed to be considered a multinational enterprise. Finally, notice that the group is spread over a wide variety of industries, despite their similarity of above-average commitments to technology and international diversification.

A similar listing of non-US MNEs cannot be as detailed, because far less information is available on those firms. By ranking firms according to size (defined as annual sales converted into US dollars), however, a listing can be created. Table 2–3 presents the 40 largest non-US MNEs, which appear in the *Fortune* list of the 500 largest non-US industrial companies. These companies are classified by profitability (defined as gross profits divided by total assets), size, country of parent company, industry, and capital intensity (defined as total assets divided by total employees).

Despite the proliferation of countries represented, the industrial concentration of these large non-US firms is striking: Over half are in the petroleum and automotive industries. Most of the firms are in European countries, but Japan has more entries (13 companies) in the list than any other single country.

What can account for the uneven distribution of MNEs across countries and industries? Certainly no single factor is the key. The next section presents a viewpoint that offers both an understanding of some of the important factors involved and ways for managers to use these factors in operating their own companies.

THE THEORY OF COMPETITIVE ADVANTAGE

The theory of **competitive advantage** is a perspective on business strategy that offers the analyst a simple framework for studying a firm's competitive environment. It helps in decision making on key issues such as choosing which markets to serve, selecting sources of supply, and deciding whether to carry out activities within the firm or to contract out for them. The theory is presented here as a sequential process in which the firm must

1. Define its competitive advantages and disadvantages, as well as analyze the importance of each in its competition with the relevant rival firms.
2. Choose how to obtain those advantages viewed as crucial in a particular competitive context (and how to minimize the negative impact of competitive *disadvantages* that cannot be eliminated).
3. Decide how to capitalize on the firm's competitive advantages through international business activities such as exports, direct investment, and strategic alliances.[4]

The rest of this section describes the process of strategy formulation using competitive advantages in an international firm.

Defining Competitive Advantages

Studies of successful large firms in industrial countries during the 1970s and 1980s have shown that these firms typically compete in domestic and foreign markets on the basis of competitive advantages that are based on company-specific characteristics. That is, these firms usually possess some **proprietary asset**—a new production process, a superior sales location, facilities that realize economies of scale in production or distribution, and so on (or a combination of such assets)—that allows them to achieve lower costs, higher revenues, or lower risk than their competitors.[5]

For example, Pfizer Corporation discovered it could successfully transfer product differentiation strategies developed in one country to other countries in which it does business in pharmaceuticals. The company managed its internal resources to obtain economies of scale in advertising and physical distribution for its differentiated products. Westinghouse Electric Corporation has demonstrated an ability to negotiate contracts to provide major power-generating facilities with governments in less developed countries (LDCs) and Eastern Europe. It now possesses a competitive advantage in government contracting and a protected business position in several national markets. Mobil Oil, Caterpillar, and several other firms have developed internal "codes of conduct" that they publicize widely and use to convince governments and social pressure groups that the company is acting in the interest of the country involved. This is a kind of competitive advantage in social goodwill, since it is expected to result in more favorable treatment of the company by each government or social pressure group. Hewlett-Packard, IBM, and many Japanese companies have corporate philosophies that are passed on to employees and substantially followed by the companies' executives, leading to internal labor and personnel relations superior to those in many other firms. LM Ericsson, the Swedish telecommunications manufacturer, has developed small electronic switching systems that suit many customers that need less extensive, less costly telephone systems than those produced and sold by its major rivals in international business. Ericsson has developed a market niche advantage. Each of these examples of competitive advantages enables the company to outcompete its rivals in a particular business situation.

Many of these proprietary characteristics are not limited to international firms; in fact, most of them pertain to successful domestic firms as well. Table 2–4 lists a number of commonly cited attributes that create competitive advantages for international firms. Advantages that exist for both domestic and international firms are discussed in this section; specifically international advantages are discussed in the following section.

TABLE 2-2

Characteristics of
Top-Performing US-Based
MNEs (1992)

Company	Technology Intensity* (R & D as % of sales)	Sales† ($mil.)	Countries with Affiliates‡	(Assets) Capital§ per Worker‖ ($thou./empl.)
Electronics				
Amdahl	5.25	7,086.5	17	305
Data General	9.97	1,115.9	36	132
Digital Equipment	12.59	13930.8	43	97
Emerson Electric	3.17	7,706.0	27	116
Hewlett-Packard	9.87	16,410.0	20	155
IBM	7.88	64,523.0	46	302
Intel	13.35	5,844.0	19	314
National Semiconductor	11.18	1,717.5	13	49
Raychem	10.75	1,296.3	18	121
Texas Instruments	6.31	7,440.0	17	87
Wang Labs.	6.95	1,896.2	25	55
Eastman Kodak	7.86	20,183.0	32	189
Cosmetics and Health Care Products				
Avon	0.77	3809.09	31	61
Johnson & Johnson	8.19	13753	54	140
Bristol-Myers Squibb	9.70	11156	51	318
Procter & Gamble	2.93	29362	36	141
Chemicals				
Dow Chemical	6.79	18,971.0	39	413
Du Pont	3.43	37,208.0	34	311
Merck	11.50	9,662.5	17	289
Electrical Appliances				
Maytag	NA	3,041.0	7	117
Industrial Machinery				
Caterpillar	3.04	10,194.0	17	275
Dana	2.05	5,036.1	19	118
3M	7.25	13,883.0	53	108
Oil				
Amoco	1.18	25,280	24	605
Project Management				
Boeing	6.11	30,184.0	8	128
Fluor	NA	6,847.0	15	54
Services				
Delta Air Lines	NA	11,579.0	4	130
Walt Disney	NA	7,979.0	12	207
Kmart	NA	38,124.0	3	59
Marriott	NA	8,722.0	19	33
McDonald's	NA	7,133.0	9	71
Wal-Mart	NA	55,484.0	1	48

*,†"R & D Scoreboard," *Business Week,* June 28, 1993.
‡Moody's 1993 *Industrial Report.*
§"The 1993 Business Week 1000," *Business Week,* June 28, 1993.
‖Moody's 1993 *Industrial Report.*

TABLE 2-3   Characteristics of the Largest Non-US Multinationals (1991)

Rank/Company	Profits/ Assets	Annual Sales ($mil.)	Industry	Country	Assets per Employee ($thou./empl.)
1 Royal Dutch/Shell	0.040	103,834.8	Petroleum	UK/Netherlands	791
2 Toyota Motor	0.048	78,061.1	Motor vehicles	Japan	636
3 IRI	NA	64,095.5	Petroleum	Italy	NA
4 British Petroleum	0.013	58,355.0	Petroleum	UK	530
5 Daimler-Benz	0.023	57,321.3	Motor vehicles	Germany	131
6 Hitachi	0.027	56,053.3	Electronics	Japan	196
7 Matsushita Electric Industrial	0.029	48,595.0	Electrical appliances	Japan	296
8 Fiat	0.013	46,812.0	Motor vehicles	Italy	242
9 Volkswagen	0.014	46,042.2	Motor vehicles	Germany	174
10 Siemens	0.027	44,859.2	Electronics	Germany	104
11 Samsung Group	0.008	43,701.9	Electronics	South Korea	231
12 Nissan Motor	0.007	42,905.7	Motor vehicles	Japan	332
13 Unilever	0.072	41,262.3	Foods, soap, cosmetics	UK/Neth.	85
14 ENI	NA	41,047.3	Petroleum, chemicals	Italy	NA
15 Elf Aquitaine	0.037	36,315.8	Petroleum, chemicals	France	536
16 Nestlé	0.059	35,583.7	Food, beverages	Switzerland	143
17 Toshiba	0.021	33,232.5	Electrical appliances	Japan	243
18 Honda Motor	0.025	30,567.3	Motor vehicles	Japan	246
19 Philips Electronics	0.022	30,217.6	Electronics	Netherlands	121
20 Renault	0.013	29,432.4	Motor vehicles	France	281
21 ABB (Asea Brown Boveri)	0.019	28,883.0	Specialty transformers	Switzerland	143
22 Hoechst	0.028	28,468.2	Chemicals	Germany	131
23 Peugeot	0.041	28,403.3	Motor vehicles	France	150
24 Alcatel Alstham	0.024	28,390.7	Electronics	France	209
25 BASF	0.025	28,130.4	Chemicals	Germany	190
26 NEC	0.013	26,675.4	Electronics	Japan	237
27 Sony	0.025	26,581.5	Electronics	Japan	290
28 Bayer	0.044	25,581.3	Chemicals	Germany	152
29 Daewoo	NA	25,362.6	Electronics	South Korea	NA
30 Total	0.047	25,361.7	Petroleum	France	391
31 PDYSA	NA	24,000.0	Petroleum	Venezuela	269
32 Mitsubishi Electric	0.024	23,976.3	Electronics	Japan	243
33 Nippon Steel	0.020	23,141.6	Metal manufacturing	Japan	580
34 Thyssen	0.020	22,465.0	Metal manufacturing	Germany	96
35 Imperial Chemical Industries	0.046	22,339.4	Chemicals	UK	160
36 Fujitsu	0.021	21,226.2	Electronic computers	Japan	182
37 Robert Bosch	0.018	20,271.5	Motor vehicles	Germany	90
38 Mitsubishi Motors	0.013	20,109.9	Motor vehicles	Japan	360
39 Mazda Motor	0.017	19,321.5	Motor vehicles	Japan	371
40 Pemex (Petroleos Mexicanos)	0.013	19,165.2	Petroleum	Mexico	304

Source: "The Global 500," *Fortune*, July 27, 1992.

Historically, 20th-century multinational enterprises began primarily in extractive industries, ranging from oil to bananas to copper.[6] These multinationals competed on the basis of their access to supplies of natural resources and to substantial markets. By the advent of World War II, many of these advantages had been partially or completely competed away, and thus the firms were vulnerable to competition from other firms and to greater regulation by governments.

Analysis of the competitive advantages of large firms in the period after World War II has focused on the idea of *barriers to entry*. Bain (1956) defined these characteristics as arising from **absolute cost advantages** (such as proprietary production techniques and control over limited resources by established firms),

TABLE 2-4

Competitive Advantages of
Multinational Enterprises

Advantage	Description
General Competitive Advantages	
Proprietary technology	Product, process, or management technology held by a firm that others can obtain only through R&D or contracting with the possessor
Goodwill based on brand or trade name	Reputation for quality, service, etc. developed through experience
Scale economies in production	Large-scale production facilities that lower unit costs of production
Scale economies in purchasing	Lower costs of inputs through purchasing large quantities
Scale economies in financing	Access to funds at a lower cost for larger firms
Scale economies in distribution	Shipments of large quantities of products/inputs to necessary locations, lowering unit shipping costs
Scale economies in advertising	Sales in several markets, allowing somewhat standardized advertising across markets
Government protection	Free or preferential access to a market limited by government fiat
Human resource management	Skill at fostering teamwork among employees and optimizing productivity
Multinational Competitive Advantages	
Multinational marketing capability	Knowledge of and access to markets in several countries
Multinational sourcing capability	Reliable access to raw materials, intermediate goods, etc. in several countries that reduces single-source costs
Multinational diversification	Operations in several countries so that country risk and business risk are reduced
Multinational access to technology	Ability to find and assimilate technological advances in different countries through presence in these countries.
Managerial experience in several countries	Skill for managing multicountry operations gained through experience in different countries (learning curve gains)

from **product differentiation** advantages (such as an established brand name or a patented product), and from **economies of scale** (in areas such as production, advertising, and purchasing).

Studies of multinational enterprises likewise have focused on barriers to entry. The initial investigations (for example, Vernon, 1966) found that **proprietary technology** is a fundamental basis for competitiveness for many such firms. Indeed, many of the most successful US-based MNEs in the 1950s and 1960s produced high-tech products in such industries as pharmaceuticals (Pfizer, Johnson & Johnson, Merck), data processing (IBM, Burroughs, Honeywell), telecommunications (ITT, GTE) chemicals (Dow, Du Pont, Monsanto), and electronic instruments (Eastman Kodak, Texas Instruments). The competitive advantage came from some technology created or purchased by the firm that the firm was able to utilize in production to generate better or less expensive products than those produced by its competitors. For example, Du Pont created distinctive products such as nylon, rayon, and more recently Kevlar; IBM was a leader in moving data processing from electromechanical computations to electronic processing; and Eastman Kodak created a higher-quality paper for photographs than its rivals offered.

Early analyses also focused on the marketing advantages possessed by MNEs (e.g., Vernon, 1966; Caves, 1971). Particularly important in this case is the firm's ability to differentiate its product from others. By establishing a respected **brand or trade name,** the firm may be able to attract additional buyers due to name recognition and trust. Examples of industries in which firms possess this type of advantage include electrical appliances (General Electric, Maytag, Sunbeam), health care products (Bristol-Myers Squibb, Colgate-Palmolive, Procter & Gamble), foods (Coca-Cola, Kraft, RJR Nabisco), and pharmaceuticals. In this case, the advantage arises from the firm's developing a reputation for high-quality products, good service after the product has been purchased, and/or good value relative to competitors' products. These characteristics become identified with the brand or trade name, enabling the firm to sell more output or charge higher prices than competitors.

More recent analysts have looked at multinational firms as holders of a variety of such competitive assets, no one of which is necessary by itself. A fairly extensive list of those advantages appears in Table 2–4. Let us consider the rest of the advantages listed.

Scale economies in production exist when a firm is able to operate a production facility that attains lower costs per unit at large levels of output than the costs competitors incur in production facilities that have lower output capacities. That is, as the scale (volume) of production is increased by increasing the size of the production facility, unit costs can be decreased at higher levels of output. Scale economies in production are important in many industries, especially those that are heavily capital intensive, such as the automotive, airframe manufacturing, industrial chemical, and oil industries. General Motors, for example, is able to achieve substantially lower production costs for its cars than Isuzu or Chrysler, each of which produces in smaller facilities and at lower volumes of output.

Scale economies in purchasing can be attained by firms that are able to buy inputs in large quantities and thus reduce their unit costs. This competitive advantage is usually available to larger firms, which are able to purchase larger quantities than their rivals. It also tends to arise for firms with more standardized production as the selection of inputs becomes more predictable and larger stocks become justifiable. By contracting to buy millions of pounds of beef on a regular basis, such companies as Burger King and McDonald's reduce their hamburger cost far below that of local, single-location restaurants.

Scale economies in financing exist for firms that are able to borrow large sums of funds and thus can obtain quantity discounts. Because of its very large size (and also because of its extremely good creditworthiness), IBM can borrow at interest rates similar to those paid by the largest commercial banks for their own funds. A small computer manufacturer or component maker will pay far higher rates. By borrowing in the Eurocurrency markets (which are restricted to fairly large-scale transactions, as discussed in Chapter 6), IBM or another large firm may find even lower rates than those available to smaller firms.

Scale economies in distribution arise when the firm is able to contract for shipping to several destinations and for large quantities of products to serve its several markets. The per-unit cost of distributing products often falls when the selling firm can contract for multiple shipments and high volumes. (The firm may even purchase its own distribution system, if the cost of so doing is lower than the cost of contracting with outside distributors.)

Scale economies in advertising may be attainable when a firm sells products in several countries and can standardize its promotion across countries.

In industrial countries, adjusting for language differences, such standardization can often be carried out, and advertising costs can thus be reduced. On the contrary, when products are introduced into very different countries (e.g., less developed nations), the promotion and even the product often need to be adapted to local conditions, and these scale economies cannot be realized. Exxon successfully used its "Put a tiger in your tank" promotional campaign around the world in the late 1980s. Campbell Soup Company and Johnson & Jonhson use different promotional methods and messages in different countries due to varying customer and regulatory characteristics.

Government protection is another source of competitive advantage. This type of advantage is often ignored, since it is based not on the firm's activities in the market but on the legal framework and negotiations with government regulators and government customers. Nevertheless, managers should be aware that in every country, temporary or permanent protection from competition may be obtained from the government. Whether it be operation of the national telephone company (which AT&T monopolized in most of the United States until 1984) or establishment of an import-replacing plant that receives tariff protection, the firm may obtain exclusive rights or other protection from competitors by the host government. Such protection precludes other firms from competing or makes their entry and operations far less profitable than the protected firm's activities. The disadvantage of government protection is that it may be lost when the government decides to alter the protection—for example, to create competition or assist another company—and the company may not be able to build or obtain another competitive advantage to replace the one lost.

It should be noted that government protection advantages arise from two distinct kinds of relationship. First, the direct protection given to favored firms in the form of tariffs or subsidies clearly can enable a firm to carve out a successful competitive position. Second, dealing with the government as its supplier of products or services can generate a protected environment for the firm, since governments tend to stay with reliable suppliers without switching frequently. Thousands of firms in the United States earn all or most of their income from selling to the US government. Such relationships tend to be fairly stable, and they are common in other countries as well.

Human resource management has proven a very important advantage for Japanese firms competing with US-based competitors in recent years. When the firm's managers are able to create a working environment that stimulates employee productivity, the firm can lower its unit costs and improve the quality of the product. Countless stories have been told (e.g., William Ouchi's *Theory Z*) about Japanese firms' greater success at managing people than their US rivals'. Of course, many successful US firms have achieved superior human resource management as well (see Table 2–2).

Multinational Competitive Advantages

All of the advantages already discussed can be used at the international level as well as domestically. Scale economies in purchasing, production, distribution, or financing may be even greater for a firm that is able to spread its sales over several countries rather than just one. A technological lead can be exploited in many countries without reducing its value. Similarly, the other domestic competitive advantages can be extended to include foreign business. This section examines five competitive advantages that are primarily limited to MNEs, though some of them can be attained by domestic firms that contract with foreign firms.

Perhaps the most important multinational competitive advantage is **multinational marketing capability,** which enables the firm to sell its products in many national markets simultaneously. Compared to competitors that operate in only one national market, the MNE gains a key advantage in being able to sell its excess production in other markets due to its sales affiliates in those markets. The affiliates function as gatherers of information about market demands, regulatory conditions, and other business intelligence that could benefit the firm, and this enables the firm to quickly take advantage of markets for selling its output. The wider the firm's net of affiliates, the greater its possibility of maximizing its revenues. From another perspective, shortfalls in demand in one country can be remedied by sending excess output to other countries where the firm encounters an excess demand beyond the ability of the local affiliate to supply.

Another fundamental multinational competitive advantage is **multinational sourcing** of production, which enables the firm to minimize production costs by using facilities in low-cost countries. This advantage enables the MNE to reduce its costs relative to local competitors in any one country. Very frequently in the 1980s and 1990s, firms set up offshore production facilities in Asian countries (such as Singapore, South Korea, and Taiwan) or Mexico, where labor costs are low, to assemble machinery, clothing, or other products for sale in the United States or Europe. (In some cases, the MNE could realize this advantage through contracting with a local Korean or Mexican firm to do the assembly rather than through investing in local production.)

A third multinational advantage is the risk-reducing benefit of **multinational diversification.** Many MNEs use facilities in several countries to produce the same products for several markets. That way, if a strike, natural disaster, or just a machine breakdown occurs in any one country, markets can be served from the other production sites. Major chemical companies produce the basic petrochemicals, such as ethanol, polyethylene, and butyl rubber, in a "portfolio" of countries, so their supply is assured in the event of a nationalization, a work stoppage, or the like in any one country. Similarly, they try to establish multiple sources of raw materials, such as oil and metals, and even of other inputs, such as labor, to avoid dependence on one supplier country. Thus, by operating multiple sourcing and marketing affiliates, the MNE gains this important risk-reducing capability.

A fourth multinational competitive advantage is **multinational access to technology,** the ability of a firm with affiliates in several countries to learn new technology developed in any of those countries and transfer it to the rest of the MNE. This is similar to the multinational sourcing advantage, since it means that firms operating in a given country may be able to benefit from the same technology developments (or low-cost opportunities in the sourcing instance) as other firms operating there. In fact, since technology is such an important competitive advantage, some firms even establish overseas operations expressly to be located where technological advances are occurring. Many foreign electronics firms have established activities in Silicon Valley in California, and IBM moved its laptop PC facility to Tokyo, both locations where new technology has been introduced recently and frequently.

Finally, **managerial experience in several countries** gives the firm the advantage of know-how in dealing with business situations in different countries. This advantage generally helps the MNE that possesses experienced managers relative to other MNEs without such people. The managers learn how to cope with business conditions and regulatory environments in different countries; then they

ADDED DIMENSION

Sources of Competitive Advantages

A basic framework of competitive strategy, and one used fairly widely by business analysts, views companies as organizations that carry out a set of economic activities. Let us define the economic activity of the firm as essentially production, subdivided into obtaining necessary inputs, actually producing goods or services, distributing them to points of sale, and marketing them to customers. Figure 2–2 sketches the basic aspects of production in which competitive advantages may arise.

At purchasing, the first stage, inputs are assembled for production of the product or service. Then, either in that location or after transferring the inputs elsewhere, basic production is carried out. If additional assembly is needed, it may be done in the same location or at one or more assembly or finishing facilities. Finally, the product or service is marketed to customers in the same location and/or other locations. In some businesses, after-sale service adds one more step to the process. Research and development may also be undertaken as part of the firm's total activity.

Notice that at each step of the production process, the firm must choose combinations of inputs—manpower, physical capital, financial capital, and information—that will generate the output. It must decide how to organize them and how to deal with the risks involved. Managers should do this to minimize the cost of completing the economic activity. So, for example, if it is less expensive to buy components than to produce them internally, the firm should contract out for the components. Similarly, if the firm chooses to bear the risk of losses rather than contract with an outside insurance provider to cover that possibility, it is providing "self-insurance." In all, the firm can be viewed as a value-maximizing organization that decides on optimal combinations of inputs at each stage of the production process to generate its output and thus profit. Two key points here are that (1) the firm must attempt to evaluate the impact on profits of not only its own activities but also the activities of its rivals and of other outside actors (e.g., governments) and (2) the firm must consider the functioning of its own internal market, including the "people problems" of labor/personnel relations that must be solved to achieve optimal outputs. From this scheme, we can derive the main competitive advantages that have been noted elsewhere (e.g., Porter, 1980, 1990; Grosse, 1984) and identify many additional areas in which advantages may arise. ■

can bring that experience to bear on situations in the current country and gain an advantage over rival managers who lack such experience. By choosing the most capable and experienced local managers, the MNE may even gain an advantage over host country firms. Skill in managing a multicountry operation is itself a scarce factor of production, and firms with managers who possess such a skill will presumably obtain better results than firms without them.

Managers of international contractors and potential competitors seek to obtain and benefit from these competitive advantages. While firms can generally either create such advantages from their own activities or buy them from other firms or individuals, we will consider throughout the book many specific ways firms can obtain and benefit from proprietary assets. The key point of this section has been to identify the main sources of competitive advantage. It is up to the manager to then evaluate the importance of each advantage and decide which ones are needed to compete successfully.

FIGURE 2–2

Competitive Advantages in the Production Process (or Value-Added Chain)

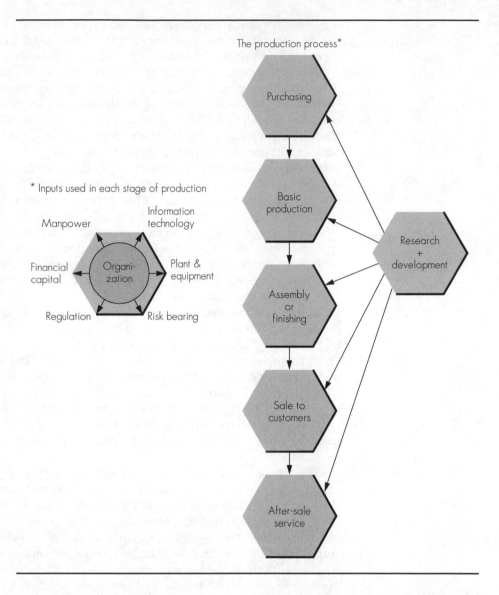

The goal of competitive strategy is to obtain, utilize, and sustain competitive advantages to the optimal level. Given the advantages discussed above and others that may be uncovered, the manager needs to see how the firm can obtain these advantages and when it is desirable to do so. Of course, in simple economic terms, it will be best to obtain each competitive advantage up to the point where the additional economic benefit gained is just equal to the additional cost of obtaining or extending that advantage. (The decision is complicated, however, by uncertainty about future conditions, difficulties in valuing the advantages, and the unclear accessibility of some of them.)

The challenge to managers is to carve out competitive positions based on these advantages; thus, their potential values must be measured. Perhaps the best way to begin any such evaluation is to consider the possibility of purchasing a competitive advantage from another firm as opposed to creating it internally within the firm. This "make-versus-buy" decision can be made on the bases of expected revenues, expected costs, and expected risks, just as with the purchase of production inputs. For example, the managerial experience gained from operating in a particular country can either be produced internally through the company's business over time or purchased in the market by hiring a manager from the outside. A distribution system can be constructed by the firm itself or purchased from another firm, as Nestlé did with its purchase of Carnation, as Imperial Chemicals (a British firm) did with its purchase of Atlas Chemicals (a US firm with many affiliates in the United States and Latin America), and as Mitsubishi did with its partial purchase of Chrysler. Technology may be purchased through a licensing agreement or developed within the firm. It can even be obtained by buying another company, as in the 1991 purchase of NCR (a computing equipment manufacturer) by AT&T and the purchase of Zenith Data Systems by the French computer firm Bull. Even a brand name can be obtained without spending many years to develop goodwill in dealings with customers for a particular product. The firm seeking a brand name advantage can simply buy a branded line from another company, or even buy the whole company–an acquisition strategy followed very successfully in food products by Nestlé and Heinz during the past twenty years.

In each of the above examples, the firm seeking to obtain a competitive advantage must evaluate the costs and benefits expected from that advantage in terms not only of the firm's own activities but also of the responses it may expect from its important competitors at home and abroad. The competitive gains from achieving scale economies in production may be zero if all important competitors build large-scale plants too. Thus, while the make-versus-buy view can be applied by the firm to each competitive advantage, the ultimate decision to pursue an advantage depends on the expected reaction of competitors, the firm's own activities, and the amount of time competitors need to duplicate the advantage.

The choice to even consider making or buying a particular competitive advantage rests on the assessment of how important that advantage is (or will become) in competition. Economies of scale in distribution, for example, may offer an advantage to firms possessing their own distribution channels, but the advantage may be so slight compared to the costs other firms using outside suppliers of distribution face that the benefits may not warrant investment in the channels. Instead, the key competitive factor in that industry may be proprietary technology or advertising effectiveness. So rather than focus efforts on accruing as many competitive advantages as possible, the manager should assess the relative importance of each advantage in the industry (and country) and then pursue those that offer the greatest benefits—usually those that create the greatest barriers to entry to and exit from the industry. (Exit barriers are those difficulties faced by firms trying to leave a business, such as the problem of selling machinery or other assets specific to that business.)

INTERNALIZATION

Perhaps the most useful concept to employ in studying the strategies (and also the regulation) of INCs is **internalization.** This term, popularized by Buckley and Casson (1976), and Rugman (1981), refers to the extension of ownership by a firm to cover new markets, new sources of materials, and new stages of the production process.[7] Internalization covers many of the same ideas that horizontal and vertical integration do, as discussed in the economics literature related to industrial organization.

Briefly, **horizontal integration** is the expansion of a firm to carry out the same activity in a market other than the one in which it originally operated. Every time Sheraton Hotels builds a new hotel in another city, that company has integrated horizontally. On the other hand, **vertical integration** is the expansion of a firm into a stage of the production process other than that of its original business. A company that manufactures wood furniture can integrate vertically by expanding its activities upstream to include lumber production or downstream to carry out the sale of the furniture through its own stores rather than through furniture stores belonging to others. (The firm could also do both.)

The key differences between integration and internalization are that (1) *internalization emphasizes the strategic choices* of the firm in deciding whether to buy inputs or buy suppliers and whether to sell to other firms or buy those firms and deal with their customers directly and (2) *internalization covers transactions outside the scope of horizontal or vertical integration*, such as the purchase of labor, capital, and technology.

To better understand this idea, consider a company whose only business is petroleum refining. This firm may choose to buy or build another oil refinery located in another market. This would be horizontal integration, that is, entry into a similar business and stage of the production process in a different location. As a second strategy, the oil-refining firm may choose to buy a chain of gasoline stations to extend its sales downstream to final customers. Alternatively, the firm may choose to buy into oil exploration and producing (either through acquisition or creation of a new firm), in this case integrating vertically in the upstream direction. Either of these two cases of vertical integration is also a form of internalization, in which additional levels of the production process are brought into the same firm. Finally, the firm may choose to hire a scientist(s) or engineer(s) involved in oil-refining research so that it can gain a new, low-cost processing technology. By internalizing this research, the firm avoids the need to rely on an outside supplier of the R&D. In all of these examples, the firm internalizes additional transactions; when a firm does this across national borders, it becomes multinational. Figure 2–3 illustrates this idea. Hence, just as in the cases of most of the competitive advantages discussed previously, internalization may be either domestic or international; it does not exist solely in the province of MNEs or INCs.

Other classic examples of vertical integration include most mineral and metal industries, in which a few firms have succeeded in creating huge structures that stretch from mining or drilling all the way to sales to final consumers. Exxon, Texaco, Shell, and British Petroleum exemplify international internalization in the oil industry,[8] Kennecott and Anaconda in the copper industry, Reynolds and Kaiser in the aluminum industry, and so on. In each case, the firm owns some of the natural resource, explores for and produces some of the metal or mineral, and then processes and distributes the downstream products, often all the way to final consumers in many national markets.

Firms may choose to take advantage of their competitive advantages through internalization when the gains from buying or establishing the new operation outweigh the costs and risks of doing so. For example, it does not necessarily make sense for McDonald's to integrate upstream into cattle raising to service its restaurants if contracting with cattle ranchers or slaughterhouses proves satisfactory. (Typically, the benefits of internalization are lower when there is a large number of such suppliers than when there are only a few, powerful suppliers.) On the other hand, it may make economic sense for a steelmaker to integrate

FIGURE 2-3

Internalization in the Oil
Industry

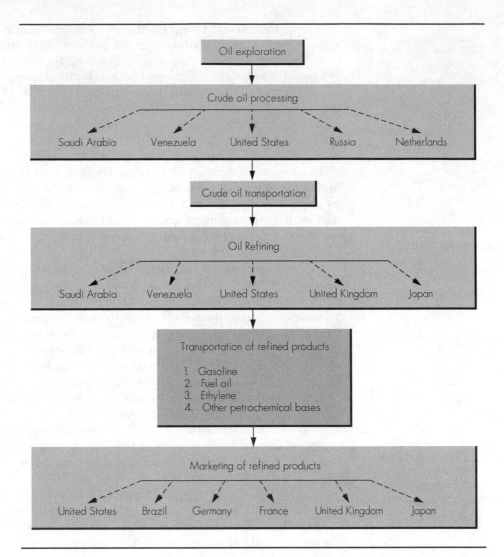

backward into the mining and production of iron ore or for a lumber company to
internalize the growing and cutting of timber. In each of these cases, the firm
faces a limited number of suppliers that can virtually hold it hostage for higher
prices, unless the firm owns the raw materials supply itself.[9]

Internalization is a powerful concept that instructs the firm's decision makers
on how to proceed in maximizing the gains from its competitive advantages.

Internalization applies to domestic or international business, but it is especially
vital at the transnational level. In the case of horizontal international integration,
the firm gains

1. A diversified portfolio of markets, including the home country and the
   countries where affiliates are located.

2. Multiple sources of output, which conceivably can be shipped to any
   markets that require it.

3. New opportunities to achieve scale economies and learn about new markets
   (learning curve effects).

In the case of vertical international integration, the firm gains

1. New or multiple sources of raw materials, which preclude events in any one country from interrupting the full range of the firm's activities (backward integration).
2. New market outlets, which preclude any one country's economic condition from limiting the firm's sales (forward integration).
3. Experience in new markets (learning curve effects).

Taking Advantage of Competitive Advantages

The final step for the manager in creating a competitive strategy is to determine how to benefit from and sustain the firm's accumulated competitive advantages. The solution depends, of course, on the specific set of advantages the firm obtains and on the competitive conditions in the industries and countries in which it competes. A natural resource company will be very limited in its ability to own mines, wells, land, or other sources of raw materials in many countries today. Instead, raw materials must often be purchased through long-term contracts or in spot markets—and a key advantage may accrue to firms that have multiple suppliers. Manufacturers of mature industrial products may need to reduce costs by seeking low-cost assembly locations, perhaps in newly industrializing countries such as Mexico, Taiwan, or Malaysia. Manufacturers of military goods may need to produce some of their components and/or products in other countries to comply with government restrictions in the (foreign) purchasing countries, regardless of cost conditions that favor other sites.

This section considers only *international* business strategies based on the competitive advantages. An array of vehicles for doing business in various national markets is sketched in Table 2–5, which also suggests several criteria for choosing among the alternative methods of exploiting competitive advantages. Notice that the "bottom line" is not a simple cash flow analysis of market-serving alternatives; rather, it is a strategic evaluation of how the method fits into the firm's full global organization and strategy. For example, a project in Japan whose net present value is lower than that of an alternative project in France may be accepted if the impact of the project in Japan is to reduce the profitability of a competitor in Japan and thus limit the competitor's ability to compete in other

TABLE 2–5 Methods for Exploiting Competitive Advantages through Foreign Involvement

Form of Foreign Involvement	Decision Criteria*						
	Added Income	Capital Commitment	Management Commitment	Technology Commitment	Political Risk	Flexibility	Impact on Rivals
Exports[†]	?	Low	Low	Low	Low	High	?
Contracting[‡]	?	Low	Possibly high	Possibly high	Low	?	?
Partially owned direct investment[§]	?	?	Possibly high	High	Medium	Low	?
Wholly owned direct investment[‖]	?	High	High	Low	High	?	?

* Each column represents a dimension for decision making that should be considered when choosing a method to use in exploiting a competitive advantage. The rankings will differ from company to company and also across countries.

† Examples: (a) direct, (b) through a distributor, (c) through a trading company.

‡ Examples: (a) licensing technology, (b) franchising, (c) management contracting, (d) turnkey venture, (e) joint marketing agreement.

§ Examples: (a) joint venture with local company, (b) joint venture with foreign company, (c) joint venture with government.

‖ Examples: (a) assembly plant for local sales, (b) basic manufacturing, (c) raw materials extraction, (d) offshore assembly plant.

markets as well.[10] Similarly, a project with a lower net present value than that of some other alternative should be chosen if the more profitable project demands too much of the firm's scarce management time or presents too great an exposure to economic, political, or foreign exchange risk. All in all, market-serving alternatives should be chosen on the basis of their total impact on the global corporation and not just on the basis of their expected returns as independent activities.

Notice that the *exports* form of foreign involvement may be carried out through several different channels. First, exports may be sold directly to foreign customers, without employing a middleman firm. This alternative often arises when a firm receives an unsolicited export order from a foreign buyer specifying the quantity of goods and other particulars for the transaction. A second possibility for exporting is for the initial firm to sell to a distributor that in turn seeks buyers in foreign markets. In this case, the distributor may buy the goods from the exporter for delivery overseas, the distributor may arrange to sell on consignment without taking title to the goods, or some other arrangement may be made. A third possibility is for the exporter to sell to a trading company that in turn looks for foreign sales opportunities in general, functioning like a distributor but without limiting sales to a single market.

The *contracting* form of foreign involvement can be used in many and often creative ways. One typical contractual form is **licensing,** in which the initiating firm contracts to have a foreign firm produce and sell its product in return for a licensing fee (and according to terms that attempt to ensure quality control and protection of the technology involved). This kind of venture is common in high-tech businesses, where the technology is proprietary and the initiating firm chooses to avoid investing overseas because of the expense or other limitations.

Another contractual form is **franchising,** in which the initiating firm sells the use of its name to a foreign franchisee, who in turn sells the product or service to customers overseas. This is very common for hotel chains such as Hilton, Marriott, and Sheraton and restaurants such as McDonald's and Burger King.

A third contractual form is the **turnkey venture,** in which the initiating firm agrees to bring into operation a factory, mine, or other capital project, then manage it for a specified time period, and finally "turn over the keys" to a host country firm or government. Turnkey ventures are common in large electric power plant projects in less developed countries and in Eastern Europe. A company such as General Electric or Westinghouse contracts with the host government to construct the power plant and operate it for three to five years. During that period the company trains local managers, scientists, and workers to operate the plant, so that they can run it independently after the turnkey period ends. (Exxon's coal mine in Colombia, currently in the middle of a 30-year contract period, is a good example of a turnkey venture.)

The third category of foreign involvement is the *joint venture,* a form of direct investment in which the initiating firm shares ownership with one or more partners. This partner(s) may be another international contractor, a local firm in the host country, or even the host government. Joint ventures are the most common ownership form for foreign ventures in Eastern Europe, and they are also common in less developed countries where the host government demands local participation in ownership. During the past decade, joint ventures have become a frequent form of strategic alliance (see page 47) between firms in industrial countries, too.

The final form of foreign involvement is *wholly owned direct investment*, in which the initiating firm establishes an affiliate overseas and owns the entire venture. The investment may take place through establishment of a new business in the host country, or it may involve the purchase of an existing business there.[11] This topic is the subject of Chapter 4.

The international contractor may exploit its competitive advantages through multiple vehicles in various markets, ownership of a factory or office in each country is unnecessary. Hilton Hotels earns a substantial return on its business activities in different countries, even though most of the hotels in the chain worldwide are franchised out to independent hotel owners. Similarly, pharmaceuticals manufacturers routinely contract with other firms in their industry to produce their drugs under "tolling" agreements, which are essentially licenses to manufacture ethical drugs using the proprietor firm's name. The Dow Chemical pharmaceuticals plant in Argentina formulates drugs for Eli Lilly, Brazil's Astra, and other multinational drug companies; in other countries, Dow contracts out to other firms to produce its products in the same manner. The correct strategy depends on the company's overall competitive position in all of its markets.

Generally, the firm needs to take stock of its own competitive advantages, plus those of its competitors, and select a strategy that emphasizes its strengths and minimizes its weaknesses. The multinational firm must consider the strategies of its competitors not only in its home market but also in every relevant foreign market. Finally, managers must realize that no matter how strong the competitive advantage, other firms are likely to chip away at it, so that ultimately the advantage will disappear.[12] To be competitive in the long run, a firm must regularly review its competitive position in its various markets and products and then adjust its strategy to take advantage of environmental and internal changes.

Example: Caterpillar, Inc.

Consider Caterpillar, Inc. (or Cat), the world's leading manufacturer of earthmoving machinery, the second largest producer of diesel engines, and a major competitor in other construction equipment markets. Because of the major decline in growth of its main business segments during the 1980s, the firm's recent performance has been very shaky. Over the period 1982 to 1984, Caterpillar lost almost $US 1 billion and also lost market share in most key countries to its primary competitor, Komatsu. Cat's $9.8 billion of sales in 1991 still place the firm at the top of its industry, but 1991 nevertheless produced losses of $US 404 million. The competitive challenge of Komatsu and the stagnant market for construction equipment around the world (due to an estimated 40 percent greater production capacity compared to worldwide demand in 1989) have both created conditions that require a well-planned corporate strategy for Cat. This section describes how Caterpillar could utilize the competitive strategy approach detailed above.

First, Cat needs to take stock of its competitive advantages and those of its major competitors. Table 2–6 shows estimated global market shares of the main earthmoving equipment manufacturers in 1988–91. Although other firms have significant market shares, Komatsu clearly is Caterpillar's main competitor, and our discussion focuses only on that rivalry.

From the list of competitive advantages presented in Table 2–4, Caterpillar is generally perceived to possess a highly respected brand name due to its long history of providing the industry's *highest-quality equipment* and offering the *best*

TABLE 2–6   Sales of 11 Largest Construction Machinery Producers, 1988–1991* (millions of US dollars)

	1988	1989	1990	1991	1989–91 Average Annual Growth (%)
Caterpillar	8,206	8,478	8,735	7,397	
Caterpillar-Mitsubishi	2,110	2,561	2,642	2,627	
	10,316	11,039	11,377	10,024	-0.6
Komatsu	4,260	4,223	4,684	4,355	
Komatsu-Dresser[†]	395	1,363	1,300	936	
	4,655	5,586	5,984	5,291	5.2
Dresser[†]	864	352	311	279	-27.1
Case	2,068	2,129	2,158	1,780	-4.4
Deere	1,162	1,310	1,348	1,014	-3.1
Clark-Volvo[‡]	1,084	1,177	1,325	1,368	8.1
Clark-Melroe	288	346	382	345	7.0
Ingersoll-Rand	1,140	1,328	1,445	1,363	6.5
Fiat-Allis[§]	707	734	676	620	-4.1
Total	22,284	24,001	25,006	22,084	0.06
Year-to-year growth	24.9%	7.7%	4.2%	-11.7%	

*Based on construction machinery segment reporting. Results are measured in dollars and reflect changes in prices, exchange rates, and unit volume. Komatsu 1988–91 results are for fiscal years ending March 31, 1989–92, respectively.

[†] Results reflect Dresser deconsolidation of construction machinery business from September 1, 1988.

[‡] 1991 results reflect acquisitions, which added $277 million to sales.

[§] Merged with Fiat farm equipment business and Ford Tractor to form NH Geotech (80 percent owned by Fiat) in 1991.

Source: Stephen Allen, "Caterpillar and Komatsu in 1992," Bobson College case # 393-070-1 (1992).

after-sale service.[13] Relative to multinational competitors such as Komatsu, Fiat-Allis, and J. I. Case, it does *not* possess any particular economies of scale in production, financing, or other areas that the other competitors lack. (However, relative to smaller competitors in many countries, Cat does possess some of these advantages.) Caterpillar's long experience in international business may give its managers an advantage over rivals in dealing with problems in a wide variety of countries.

Technology is considered to be fairly standardized in this industry as it is in its sister automotive industry. However, both Komatsu and Caterpillar are investing hundreds of millions of dollars each year in factory automation, flexible production facilities, and new-product generation. Caterpillar calls its efforts to upgrade manufacturing activities the Plant with a Future (PWAF) program. This program seeks not only to achieve just-in-time inventory control and employ robots where appropriate but also to provide worldwide information within the company about product and parts availability and feedback from customers. Komatsu has moved aggressively into overseas production, including factories in the United States, as well as into industrial partnerships with many foreign firms (especially with Dresser in North America) for the purpose of developing new products via licensing and coproduction. Thus, among the relevant competitors, Cat and Komatsu each have some technological advantages based on their new products and processes that are continuing to evolve.

Given Caterpillar's much greater international business volume, with 30 plants in a dozen countries and sales offices and distributors in most of the rest of the

ADDED
DIMENSION   Strategic Alliances

Strategic alliances became very popular vehicles for pursuing domestic and international business among large international contractors during the late 1980s and early 1990s. These alliances range from simple licensing agreements to complicated coproduction ventures with management contracts and cross-licensing accords tied together. A strategic alliance is any cooperative agreement between firms that results in some continuing business link between them—for example, a joint venture (such as the NUMMI project owned by General Motors and Toyota described later in this book) or simply a joint marketing agreement in which each partner agrees to sell the other firm's products in its own market (as in the discontinued venture between AT&T and Olivetti, in which AT&T agreed to sell Olivetti's personal computers in the North American market and Olivetti agreed to sell AT&T's telephone switching gear in the European market).

Strategic alliances generally are formed when each partner has a weakness in its own ability to carry out a specific business activity and the partner firm can compensate for that weakness. For example, General Electric Corporation formed a joint venture to produce aircraft engines with the French company Snecma. This alliance enabled Snecma to obtain state-of-the-art technology and ongoing access to GE innovations, while permitting GE to obtain access to European government-owned airlines (such as Airbus Industrie) that otherwise would have purchased their engines from local suppliers.

Very often the weakness that leads a company to join in a strategic alliance is insufficient capital. The fixed costs of undertaking many high-tech industrial projects in the 1990s are so great that individual firms have been seeking partners to share R&D costs as well as operating costs for large production facilities. The European computer consortium Esprit was formed so that the eight member companies could pool their financial resources and achieve a level of investment needed to compete with IBM and other non-European giants.

Strategic alliances are not a panacea for international contractors, since such cooperative agreements open the firm's management skills and technology to the partner to some degree—and the partner is generally a competitor in other contexts. Thus, the agreement between AT&T and NEC in 1990 to exchange some of AT&T's computer-assisted design technology for NEC's advanced logic chips established a base of cooperation between these two firms, which are and will remain competitors in other key computer and telecommunications products. The agreements among various major auto producers around the world do not preclude intense competition among them. The wisdom of sharing key technology or management skills must be evaluated carefully, or the partner may later outcompete its former ally in another important market. ■

world, the firm undoubtedly has a competitive advantage based on *international distribution*.[14]

Finally, some outside observers (e.g., Peters and Waterman, 1982) believe that Cat maintains a significantly better internal work environment and a harmony between blue- and white-collar workers that leads to greater productivity than in other firms. This may be true relative to US-based competitors, but with respect to

Komatsu, "people management" probably is not a significant strength for Caterpillar, and it may even be a disadvantage.

The main competitive disadvantages Cat faces may be the firm's large investments in inventory and in plant and equipment, which continue to weigh down its financial position during the protracted slump in the global construction industry. The firm has cut back on physical facilities, eliminating almost a dozen plants during the 1980s, and also on manpower, to a work force of about 54,000 people in 1991. This is a disadvantage particularly relative to Komatsu, which contracts out for about 70 percent of its parts and components, while Cat makes about two-thirds of such inputs within the firm. The slump in worldwide growth does not pressure Komatsu to cut its own production so much as to cut purchases from outside suppliers.

Having weighed the competitive advantages and disadvantages in this context, Cat next must decide which competitive strengths it wants to obtain. According to company statements in the early 1990s, the desired key advantages are more flexible manufacturing and more offshore production (to reduce exposure to exchange rate fluctuations and reduce vulnerability to US conditions in general).

The first goal is being pursued through the PWAF program, in which Cat invested almost $US 2 billion from 1986 through 1992. The new technology that has been developed is enabling Cat to achieve just-in-time inventory management and to track parts, inventories, customer demands, and other crucial information worldwide. The second goal is also being pursued, with a consistently increasing willingness to contract out for components and to source offshore.

After analyzing competitive advantages and disadvantages and obtaining the additional advantages that appear most crucial to success, Caterpillar must decide how to utilize its advantages in the markets where it competes. Large possibilities still exist to reduce production costs by moving parts of the production process offshore to low-wage countries.

In each aspect of the new-strategy development, Cat needs to judge the likely reactions of its rivals to estimate the effectiveness of its own steps. If Komatsu is able to compete with low prices and high-quality products because of the dollar's appreciation relative to the yen, Cat may choose to compete more strongly in the Japanese market (where it already has a large joint venture with Mitsubishi). If American rivals face even greater difficulties than Caterpillar does, perhaps some of their complementary operations can be acquired at very low prices. If Eastern Europe develops into a major new market, Cat needs to try to beat Komatsu into that market at the outset.[15]

This sketch (developed by the authors) of possible alternatives for Caterpillar is intended simply to illustrate the use of the proposed analytical framework. Similar reasoning could be used for any large or small firm competing at the international level; the framework used here provides an approach to strategic decision making.

CONCLUSIONS

The international contractor is unquestionably the central actor in international business today. International firms function as major vehicles for transfer of technology and other knowledge, international financial flows, and exports and imports of goods and services. These firms include huge manufacturers such as IBM and Dow Chemical, but they also include service sector companies such as Hilton Hotels, Citibank, and Merrill Lynch. In addition, many smaller firms are

INCs in the sense that they export, contract with overseas partners, and sometimes even own affiliates in other countries. Much of the strategy designed for the large multinationals is relevant for these smaller firms as well.

The theory of the international contractor is being advanced by analysts along many lines. Competitive advantage and internalization are two concepts that have been widely discussed in the recent literature. Both concepts recognize the highly imperfect competition that characterizes international (and domestic) business throughout the world. Both offer the manager perspectives for capitalizing on the firm's competitive strengths relative to rival firms. Although this is not the only view of the INC that has merit, it does offer decision makers a wide range of applications.

Given the perspective outlined in this chapter, we can analyze decisions made in international business as part of the competitive strategy of the firm. In the next few chapters, we will consider some of the environmental conditions firms in international business face. Then we will look at competitive strategies for decision makers in the various functional areas.

QUESTIONS

1. What are the important differences between a multinational enterprise and a domestic company? Why are these differences important?

2. Explain the competitive advantages of Caterpillar, Inc. What strategy do you think the company should follow during the continued severe downturn in farm and construction equipment sales?

3. Why are the largest multinational enterprises concentrated in only a few industries such as petroleum and motor vehicles? Why are the most profitable MNEs (measured in terms of, for example, profits per share) *not* concentrated in any one or two industries?

4. How can a company such as Apple Computer Corporation best take advantage of its competitive advantages in foreign markets? Discuss opportunities in both developed countries and LDCs.

5. Should a chemical company such as Dow Chemical Company internalize its supply of oil for making petrochemicals by entering the oil business? What other choices does Dow have to ensure competitive access to the raw materials it needs for production around the world?

6. What competitive advantages does Citibank possess? How can it use those advantages in international banking competition?

7. Perez Trading Company is a small Los Angeles–based firm that serves as an exporter for several small US manufacturing companies and as an importer for several more US firms. Almost all of the firm's business is done with Latin American customers or suppliers. The only foreign activities Perez has are sales offices in Mexico and Peru. Is this a multinational company? What do you think are Perez's competitive advantages? Do you regard its 20 years' experience in this business as a competitive advantage?

8. Why are about half of the world's largest multinational enterprises based in the United States? Does this country possess some advantage that its companies obtain automatically? Is that advantage changing over time?

9. What characteristics enable companies such as Sheraton Hotels and Holiday Inns to compete in foreign markets? Do you regard these companies as MNEs?

10. What is Ford Motor Company's competitive situation in the international auto industry? What are Ford's key competitive disadvantages relative to Toyota and Honda? How can Ford compete successfully in the North American market?

REFERENCES

Alchain, Armen, and Harold Demsetz. "Production, Information Costs, and Economic Organization." *American Economic Review,* December 1972.

Allen, Stephen. "Caterpillar and Komatsu in 1992." Case published by Babson College, Wellesley, MA 1992.

Bain, Joe, *Barriers to New Competition.* Cambridge, MA: Harvard University Press, 1956.

Bartlett, Christopher, and Susan Ehrlich. "Caterpillar Inc.: George Schaefer Takes Charge," Harvard Business School case #9-390-036 (April 23, 1990).

Buckley, Peter, and Mark Casson. *The Future of the Multinational Enterprise.* London: Macmillan, 1976.

Buckley, Peter, and Mark Casson. *The Economic Theory of the Multinational Enterprise.* London: Macmillan, 1985.

Caves, Richard. "International Corporations: The Industrial Economics of Foreign Investment." *Economica,* February 1971.

Davidson, William, and José de la Torre. *Managing the Global Corporation.* New York: McGraw-Hill, 1989.

Dunning, John. "Trade, Location of Economic Activity, and the Multinational Enterprise: A Search for an Eclectic Approach." In *The International Allocation of Economic Activity,* ed. Bertil Ohlin. New York: Holmes & Meier, 1977.

Grosse, Robert. *Competitive Advantages and Multinational Enterprises.* University of Miami Discussion Papers in International Business, no. 84-7, November 1984.

———. "An Imperfect Competition Theory of the MNE." *Journal of International Business Studies,* Spring 1985.

Hennart, Jean-François. *The Multinational Enterprise.* Ann Arbor, MI: University of Michigan Press, 1982.

Hout, Thomas; Michael Porter; and Eileen Rudder. "How Global Companies Win Out." *Harvard Business Review,* September-October 1982.

Lall, Sanjaya. "Monopolistic Advantages and Foreign Involvement by U.S. Manufacturing Industry." *Oxford Economic Papers,* March 1980.

Ouchi, William. *Theory Z.* New York: Basic Books, 1979.

Peters, Thomas J., and Robert H. Waterman. *In Search of Excellence.* New York: Harper & Row, 1982.

Porter, Michael. *Competitive Strategy.* New York: Free Press, 1980.

———. *The Competitive Advantage of Nations.* New York: Free Press, 1990.

Prahalad, C. K., and Yves Doz. *The Multinational Mission.* New York: Free Press, 1987.

Rugman, Alan. *Inside the Multinationals.* London: Croom Helm, 1981.

Vernon, Raymond. "International Investment and International Trade in the Product Cycle." *Quarterly Journal of Economics,* 1966.

———. *Storm over the Multinationals.* Cambridge, MA: Harvard University Press, 1977.

Vernon, Raymond, and Louis T. Wells, Jr. *Manager in the International Economy.* Englewood Cliffs, NJ: Prentice Hall, 1986. (5th ed.)

Watson, Craig. "Counter-Competition Abroad to Protect Home Markets." *Harvard Business Review,* January-February, 1982.

Williamson, Oliver. *Markets and Hierarchies: Analysis and Antitrust Implications.* New York: Free Press, 1975.

NOTES

[1]See, for example, US International Trade Commission, *The Internationalization of the Automobile Industry and Its Effects on the U.S. Automobile Industry* (Washington, DC: USITC, June 1985), p. 5.

[2]Some of these ventures are discussed in Kenichi Ohmae, "The Global Logic of Strategic Alliances," *Harvard Business Review* (March–April 1989), and in Lewis Jordan, *Partnerships for Profit: Structuring and Managing Strategies Alliances* (New York: Free Press, 1990).

[3]Raymond Vernon and Louis T. Wells, Jr., *Manager in the International Economy,* 5th ed. (Englewood Cliffs, N.J.: Prentice Hall, 1986), p. 2.

[4]Of course, the firm should periodically review performance and revise its com

petitive strategy when appropriate. This iterative process of strategy formulation is discussed in Chapter 5.

[5]Some competitive advantages are not *firm specific* but general to firms of some particular type. For example, MNEs based in the United States had a competitive advantage in the 1960s, when the US dollar was overvalued, because they had access to cheaper financing than foreign firms. Also, firms from Switzerland have been relatively unharmed by world wars, since Switzerland has been consistently neutral in wartime. Along another dimension, very large firms realize many economies of scale; such economies are not limited to just one firm in an industry or country.

[6]M. Wilkins, *The Emergence of Multinational Enterprise* (Cambridge, Mass.: Harvard University Press, 1970).

[7]Internalization also refers to bringing an "externality" that markets fail to price from the outside into the firm. For example, governments try to force pollution control costs, previously an externality, onto polluting firms. The firm may use internalization to bring market power within its command by acquiring competitors and then raising prices to monopolized customers. Thus, internalization does not always connote improvement of economic welfare or efficiency.

[8]It is interesting to note that the widespread vertical integration of the oil industry has been reduced by the participation of OPEC countries at the oil-producing stage; those countries are integrating downstream into processing and into the marketing of final products.

[9]Conceivably, the use of long-term contracts, if they are enforced, could offer the firms the same level of assurance of supply and negate the need for ownership of the raw material (i.e., internalization of the source of supply).

[10]Watson (1982) discusses this idea of challenging international competitors in their home markets as a competitive strategy. He concludes that forcing your competitors to compete actively in their home markets will reduce their ability to put resources into competing in your home market.

[11]Generally, direct investment is discussed as meaning investment in production of a product or service in the host country. However, investment in a sales office in the host country through which products imported from the home country are sold also constitutes direct investment.

[12]Following the international product cycle for any product demonstrates the stages during which proprietary technology, strong advertising and effective distribution channels, and low-cost production are the key competitive advantages. See, for example, Vernon and Wells (1986).

[13]This view appears repeatedly in the literature, such as in the three-case sequence by Stephen Allen, "The Construction Machinery Industry"; "Caterpillar and Komatsu in 1987," in Davidson and de la Torre (1989), pp. 69–107; and "Caterpillar and Komatsu in 1992" (Babson College, 1992).

[14]This argument is made, for example, in Hout et al. (1982).

[15]Caterpillar had beaten its competitors into contracting for construction of the Soviet natural gas pipeline from Siberia to Western Europe in 1981. When the US government revoked Cat's export license, about $200 million of sales were lost directly and an estimated additional $500 million of follow-on sales were lost—all to Komatsu. This "political risk" may continue to haunt Caterpillar in its efforts to build business in Eastern Europe.

Mom & Pop's Restaurants, Inc.

Introduction

Sitting at his personal computer one evening in 1994, Pop Westerfield was thinking about the growing food business that he had built up over the past 10 years and that constantly seemed to present him with new, major problems. Just last week, the Burger King restaurant chain had introduced stuffed potatoes and a new salad bar in all of its restaurants throughout his territory of Illinois, Indiana, and southern Michigan. McDonald's was likewise expanding its menu to compete increasingly with traditional restaurants such as Mom & Pop's. Pop was beginning to think he should consider entering some new areas that were not as highly competitive for restaurant business, such as nearby Canada.

The Existing Business

The Westerfields had entered the restaurant business with a small, unassuming operation in Homewood, Illinois, in 1986. Pop, at age 33, had decided he was unwilling to continue at his job with a large automotive parts firm in Chicago, given the unabated crisis in the auto industry since 1977. Even while growing up, he had had the desire to open a small business, and restaurants looked like a suitable environment for his easygoing manner and his enjoyment of good food. Every day, while commuting to work in the early 1980s, Pop had passed an attractive family restaurant at the corner of Halsted Avenue and Third Street in Homewood. When a For Sale sign appeared in the window one day in 1984, Pop began to consider the possibility of taking over the business. In early 1985, he finally decided to jump at the opportunity. After a few weeks of fact finding concerning the owner's asking price, suppliers, the costs of the foods needed to supply his restaurant, taxes, and so forth, Pop made an offer for the building, which was accepted.

The initial "strategy," if it can be called that, was to serve very good meals in traditional American style at reasonable prices. No advertising was undertaken, except for installing the new sign proclaiming "Mom & Pop's Restaurant" (Mrs. Westerfield had agreed to join him in this entrepreneurial venture). Even in the first few months, business picked up enough to pay the bills and generate a small operating profit for the firm. When construction of a new roadway nearby took place in 1986, Mom & Pop's found itself the beneficiary of twice as much traffic on Halsted Avenue and twice as many customers. By the end of 1988, Mom suggested that they look into the possibility of opening up another restaurant to

This case was written by Professor Robert Grosse in 1987 as a basis for class discussion (revised 1994).

take advantage of their apparently successful formula of simple, home-cooked meals, moderate prices, and quiet atmosphere.

After deliberating on this suggestion for a few weeks, Mom and Pop decided to pursue the expansion. Pop hired a realtor friend to check out the availability of corner properties within 10 miles of the initial building, to either buy or rent. Then, armed with a list of four possible locations, the Westerfields chose the one that offered the fewest commuting problems from their home and from the existing business. The second venture followed the same path as the first, with almost immediate moderate success. By 1991, Mom and Pop had opened three more restaurants—one near their son's college in South Bend, Indiana, and the other two through an arrangement with a trusted friend who lived in Detroit (both restaurants were located in the suburbs of Detroit).

In early 1994, the Westerfields owned six restaurants using the Mom & Pop name, all of which were in the three locations noted above. The last one was started in late 1993, located in a new shopping center just off Interstate 94 near Skokie, Illinois. (Another start-up had failed due to last-minute difficulties in agreeing on the rental space in a new building in Chicago.) At this point, the firm employed 9 full-time salaried staff members and about 40 wage-earning servers, cooks, busboys, and other helpers. (The firm's financial statements appear at the end of the case.)

Luckily, Pop had found a capable office manager to keep his books and watch over the daily activities of the restaurant chain. He himself therefore had more time to think about the future of the business and about the problems and opportunities that arose frequently. The threat of increased competition from the large, well-financed hamburger chains struck him as serious enough to look into alternative markets for long-run survival. The near failure of the second restaurant when road construction almost eliminated customers' access to the building also made him realize the desirability of diversifying into more locations. While neither of the Westerfields was willing to move far from home, both thought that southern Canada, along the border with Michigan, would provide a possible starting point for expanding into that country. Pop's main concern was choosing a method of dealing with one or several restaurants that were so distant from the existing businesses and—another important factor—so expensive to open and operate.

The Canadian Situation   At the time Pop Westerfield began to look seriously into a Canadian venture, that country's government had recently reversed its policy toward foreign firms. During the previous decade, Canada had required that all foreign direct investment projects obtain permission from the Foreign Investment Review Agency. This agency was charged with evaluating the impact of proposed investments on Canadian income, employment, and ownership of the Canadian economy. A number of projects were rejected during that period. After several years of serious recession in the early 1980s, Canada's government decided to switch its policy in favor of an open attitude, seeking to attract foreign direct investment and stimulate economic growth. As part of the new strategy, the agency itself changed its name to Investment Canada. All of this meant that Pop Westerfield discovered a very responsive Canadian government when he inquired about Canadian laws and rules pertaining to the opening of a new restaurant.

Given the liberal government policies, Mom & Pop's needed primarily to decide on the type of venture to establish and on a location for it. The range of possibilities included a new restaurant, set up in a new location; purchase of an existing restaurant; creation of a joint venture with a local partner who knew the market; franchise of the firm's name and use of proprietary food preparations; and some combination of these choices. A sketch of the costs and benefits of each choice is given below.

A *green field* (or *de novo*) *investment* would require site selection, major financing, legal assistance to comply with local laws, and employment of basically all-new staff. From his previous experiences, Pop knew the start-up cost of the restaurant would be in the neighborhood of $150,000. The Canadian location might offer somewhat lower costs, but dealing with unknown contingencies arising from the new environment would probably leave the total cost about the same. None of the current employees were willing to move to the Windsor, Canada, area (across the river from Detroit), although the Westerfields' oldest son would be a possibility after his college graduation in another year. There appeared to be no significant limitations on importing any needed equipment or food into Canada, though this point needed to be checked in more detail once the specific location was chosen. The tax situation really confused Pop Wester-field, but he had heard repeatedly that Canadian taxes were similar to US taxes and that the US government would not double-tax his Canadian earnings.

An *acquisition* of an existing Canadian restaurant would cost somewhat less than the new venture, but it still involved many of the other problems. The lower financial cost and the potential availability of existing staff were very attractive to Pop. However, the purchase of an existing facility would bring with it the problems as well as the benefits of the previous business. Given their experience with acquisitions in the past, neither of the Westerfields was overly concerned with the problems likely to be involved.

A *joint venture* was an approach they had never tried. By finding a local partner, the Westerfields could reduce all the costs of doing business in Canada. The drawbacks of this strategy are that there is a real risk that the partner will not be a good or reliable businessperson and that the earnings from the venture have to be shared with the partner. Management of the joint venture could be a troubling issue, since one partner would have to trust the other to run it.

The least costly possibility for entering the Canadian market would be to *franchise* out the Mom & Pop's name, as well as some of the proprietary parts of the business, to a local firm. In this case, Mom & Pop's would allow the franchisee to use the restaurant name and would also help the franchisee set up and operate the facility. The full set of responsibilities (and sharing of revenues) would be determined in negotiations with the franchisee.

As a last possibility, the Westerfields could try some *combination* of the other strategies. For example, they could set up a joint venture and sell some of the proprietary food preparations to it on a fee basis. Or they could agree on a franchising operation but take some ownership position in that firm. The number of combinations is limited only by the imagination of the Westerfields (and, of course, by Canadian laws to some extent).

Without going into a detailed capital budgeting analysis, Pop believed it would be best to compare the good and bad points of each alternative and choose the one that seemed best on balance.

MOM & POP'S RESTAURANTS, INC.
Balance Sheet, Year-End 1993
(in $US 000)

Assets		Liabilities	
Cash	215	Notes payable	643
Marketable securities	68	Accounts payable	274
Accounts receivable	47	Taxes due	59
Inventory	180	Long-term debt	28
Fixed assets	1,302	Retained earnings	217
Total Assets	1,812	Shareholders' equity	591
		Total Liabilities	1,812

MOM & POP'S RESTAURANTS, INC.
Income Statement, 1993
(in $US 000)

Sales		3,152
Cost of goods sold		
Materials	1,051	
Labor	988	
Utilities	213	
Depreciation	130	
Gross profit		770
Selling expense	249	
Overhead	296	
Interest expense	67	
Net income before tax		158
Income taxes	47	
Net income after tax		111

PART

II

MANAGER IN THE WORLD ECONOMY

International Trade

This chapter discusses the economics of international trade. The main goals are to:

1. Demonstrate patterns of trade to indicate which countries and which products have been most important during the past half-century.

2. Explain why these patterns exist, based mainly on the theories of comparative cost advantage, the international product cycle, and imperfect competition.

3. Point out aspects of international trade that do not fit these theories very well and note some new concepts that attempt to deal with these aspects.

4. Describe criteria that company managers can use to make international business decisions involving trade; specifically, show how trade fits into the activities of the INC.

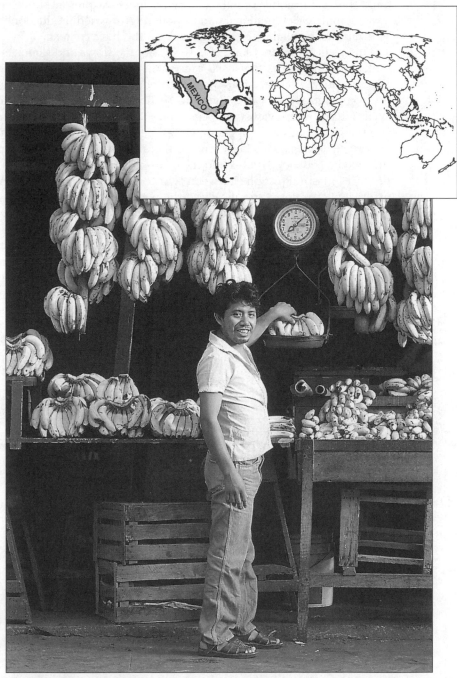

With increasingly open borders between countries and formal trade agreements coming to fruition, even local merchants like this man in Merida, Mexico, find themselves participating in international trade of raw and manufactured goods.

AllStock, Inc.

INTRODUCTION

The way in which international trade fits within the total range of international business activities has shifted dramatically in the post–World War II period. Early in this century, exports and imports, typically between unrelated firms, constituted the vast majority of intercountry business. At present, however, intra-MNE trade dominates international trade, and foreign-owned production is even larger. This chapter highlights the role of trade in the new context.

This section presents some measures of trade flows and sketches some of the underlying influences that have caused the flows to grow and shift as they do. The second section describes the most fundamental theory of international trade, the comparative cost view. The third section explains the international product cycle, a more recent view that focuses on the demand side, the technology factor, and the monopolistic competition view. The fourth section discusses some of the important discrepancies between the theories and actual trade patterns—issues such as the Leontief paradox and the cross-hauling of exports of the same type of product in both directions between two countries. The final section reviews the material and relates it specifically to the manager's concerns.

Let us begin with a look at some empirical evidence on trade patterns. Table 3–1a presents a number of comparisons between international trade flows earlier in the post–World War II period and those that have been occurring most recently. Ignoring the cost of insurance and freight, which causes the total figures for exports and imports to differ slightly, some definite trends can be seen. For instance, the industrialized countries maintained a fairly even balance in their aggregate trade flows up until the 1970s. By 1980, these countries showed an annual trade deficit (i.e., imports greater than exports) of about 10 percent with respect to the rest of the world, primarily the oil-exporting countries. This shift was reversed during the 1980s, so that now industrial country trade is fairly

TABLE 3–1a

World Trade Data (billions of US dollars)

	1950	1960	1970	1980	1990	1992
World						
Exports*	57.9	115.5	284.7	1,868.3	3,326.1	3,645.7
Imports†	59.3	121.0	298.4	1,923.4	3,429.5	3,763.5
Industrial countries						
Exports	36.4	83.9	220.3	1,239.4	2,453.6	2,646.3
Imports	39.8	85.5	227.2	1,369.6	2,572.2	2,703.5
Oil-exporting LDCs						
Exports	4.2	7.2	17.1	296.5	202.4	199.1‡
Imports	2.3	5.3	9.6	134.3	115.9	149.7‡
United States						
Exports	10.3	20.6	43.2	220.8	393.6	448.2
Imports	9.6	16.4	42.7	257.0	516.9	553.9
Nonoil LDCs						
Exports	17.6	24.7	46.5	312.0	687.3	808.9
Imports	17.3	30.1	60.5	399.7	741.6	904.9

*Export values are free on board (FOB).
†Import values include cost of insurance and freight (CIF).
‡1991 data.
Source: International Monetary Fund, *International Financial Statistics Yearbook,* 1993, and *Supplement on Trade Statistics,* 1988.

TABLE 3-1b World Exports and Imports, 1991 (millions of US dollars)

from to	US	Japan	EEC	Germany	UK	Indus. Countries	Oil-Exp. Countries	Nonoil LDCs	China	Total
US	—	53,634	112,197	25,897	24,375	268,910	21,442	149,944	8,003	444,422
Japan	95,010	—	65,706	23,895	11,913	188,914	18,697	126,555	10,079	336,873
EEC	89,433	31,971	838,445	202,947	108,501	1,114,832	52,027	186,584	8,500	1,375.5 (billions)
Germany	26,985	10,746	203,101	—	31,319	308,235	14,317	58,685	3,103	394,199
UK	19,051	5,029	95,984	25,790	—	139,787	10,434	29,775	947	180,828
Indus. countries	298,614	115,122	1,173,243	306,911	174,856	1,912.9 (billions)	103,685	518,558	31,544	2,569.7 (billions)
Oil-exp. countries	33,691	41,159	55,194	8,770	4,468	137,279	5,436	45,559	2,175	188,994
Nonoil LDCs	176,014	76,540	197,103	65,026	27,604	495,176	30,382	241,638	27,478	793,717
China	20,305	14,248	16,902	6,986	1,246	56,687	2,266	46,793	—	108,692
Total	509,300	236,633	1,456.4 (billions)	390,114	209,933	2,591.2 (billions)	140,912	845,575	63,957	3,577.7 (billions)

Note: Data include freight and insurance costs (c.i.f.).
Source: International Monetary Fund, *Direction of Trade Statistics Yearbook,* 1992.

balanced again. The United States in particular maintained a surplus of exports over imports until the recent period, but since 1970 has incurred a substantial deficit in its trade account. Oil-exporting less developed countries (LDCs) have consistently exported much greater value than they have imported, but of course the situation after the 1973 OPEC oil embargo and price hike is much more striking; in 1980, for example, exports were 121 percent greater than imports, and both were 15 times higher than in 1970. Then, with the drastic oil price decline in 1985, oil-exporting LDCs shifted back toward the historical situation, maintaining a 33 percent trade surplus in 1992.

Table 3–1b describes the trade flows by region for 1991. Note that the European Community is the largest trading group in the list. The United States is by far the largest single exporter and importer.

Table 3–2 presents another look at 20th-century international trade, this time comparing the volume of trade in various highly aggregated industrial sectors. Notice the huge shift in the composition of trade in the 1960s toward manufactured goods and in the 1970s toward minerals (especially oil) and away from other industries. Trade in minerals accounted for about 17 percent of the total in 1970, but for about 30 percent of the total in 1980, after the two major OPEC price hikes. Manufacturing, in comparison, fell from about 61 percent of total exports in 1970 to about 55 percent of the total in 1980. The original relationship was approximately reestablished in 1985, due to the oil price decline, and it continues today.

These tables point up an aspect of international trade that is usually de-emphasized in discussions of the reasons for trading and the distribution of benefits from trade: One fundamental basis for international trade is the **availability of natural resources** in each country. Any nation that possesses known and

TABLE 3–2   Development of World Exports between 1960 and 1992

	1960	1968	1970	1973	1975	1980	1985	1988	1989	1990	1991	1992
World Exports (billions of U.S. dollars, FOB)												
Total	129	240	313	575	875	1989	1936	2702	2891	3,261	3,313	3,508
Agricultural products	40	54	64	120	150	299	268	357	371	396	399	424
Minerals	22	41	52	96	207	569	425	388	405	465	442	433
Manufacturers	65	141	192	348	501	1095	1204	1909	2061	2,341	2,418	2,602
Other	2	4	5	11	17	26	39	48	54	59	55	49
Percentage of Total Trade												
Total	100	100	100	100	100	100	100	100	100	100	100	100
Agricultural products	31	23	20	21	17	15	14	13	13	12	12	12
Minerals	17	17	17	17	24	29	22	14	14	14	13	12
Manufacturers	50	59	61	61	57	55	62	71	71	72	73	74
Other	2	1	2	2	2	1	2	2	2	2	2	2

Source: General Agreement on Tariffs and Trade, 1987/88 (Geneva:1988); GATT Secretariat Press Release, March 22, 1990, and GATT, International Trade Statistics 1993 (Geneva: 1993).

accessible deposits of oil can export them, while other nations must either import oil or utilize substitute products (such as coal or other energy sources). The fact that a small number of nations possess most of the world's known and accessible oil deposits gives them a near-monopoly position as producers. In the 1970s, they used that position to raise prices and curtail output, leading to the large jump in LDC exports and mineral exports in Tables 3–1 and 3–2. In the 1980s, however, both prices and quantities of oil sold in world markets were declining, due to the demand curtailment and substitution effects encouraged by the increases in oil prices. Chapters 8 and the Appendix explore some additional aspects of the oil industry and its relations to international business; here we are mainly concerned with oil's surge to a substantial percentage of total world trade (about 16 percent in 1980). Thus, a very important basis for a country's export/import activities is resource availability.

In the next section, we continue to look at trade from a macroeconomic perspective, focusing on cost conditions that affect trade patterns. Then we present some additional rationales for trade and empirical examples before considering how the decision maker can utilize these perspectives in operating a firm.

THEORIES OF INTERNATIONAL TRADE: COMPARATIVE ADVANTAGE

Among the various views of the underlying *reasons* for trade, the cost-based theory has been developed extensively over more than two centuries, and a number of additional views have been offered to explain much of what it ignores. Anyone trying to understand the full set of reasons for the trade that takes place today should recognize at the outset that no single theory explains it all. Trade in different products occurs for different reasons. Trade in services differs in many ways from trade in tangible products. The theories collectively deal with all types of trade, and individually or together they can be used to construct policy, either for government regulators or for company managers.

The **comparative cost theory** of international trade, as developed by Ricardo and refined by Heckscher, Ohlin, and Samuelson,[1] states that *a country will gain from international trade if it specializes in the production and export of products that require relatively more input of its abundant production factors and if it imports products that require relatively more input of its scarce production factors.*

If we assume that prices in each country are proportional to costs and that costs are determined by the availability of production factors, the comparative advantage theory leads to these results.

Before proceeding with this very powerful concept, consider the simple bases that led to the above conclusions. The first step toward today's comparative cost theory was taken by Adam Smith in *The Wealth of Nations,* published in 1776. Smith reasoned that nations will gain from free trade as long as each partner has an **absolute** cost **advantage** in producing some product. For example, if England and France both produce machinery and wine, the production possibilities, assuming complete specialization in *either* machinery *or* wine, are:

	Machinery		Wine
England	100*	or	40
France	30	or	120

*These quantities are units of output, using the same quantity of factors of production in each country.

This means that each country has an absolute advantage, England in the production of machinery and France in the production of wine. If there are no barriers to trade between these countries, each can specialize in producing its advantageous product and trade with the other, thus obtaining more of both goods than before trade. (This result is explained in detail below for the case of comparative advantage.)

The second step toward today's comparative cost theory was taken by David Ricardo in *Principles of Political Economy and Taxation,* published in 1817. Ricardo showed that just as there are gains from trade under conditions of absolute advantage for each country, there are also gains from trade when one country has an absolute advantage in producing *both* products (as long as its *relative* superiority differs between products). His example involved England and Portugal producing cloth and wine, as shown in the table below. (The quantities are the outputs produced by the same amount of factor inputs for each product, assuming complete specialization in either cloth or wine.)*

	Wine		Cloth
England	80	or	90
Portugal	120	or	100

England can produce *either* 80 units of wine *or* 90 units of cloth.

Portugal has an *absolute* advantage in producing both products, but it has a relative or *comparative* advantage in producing wine. That is, Portugal's superiority in wine production is 120/80, or 1.5, while Portugal's superiority in cloth production is only 100/90, or 1.1. In the absence of trade barriers and as long as prices are proportional to costs, both England and Portugal can obtain more wine

*This presentation reverses Ricardo's original example, in which he discusses work-hours of inputs needed to produce a given level of output. To avoid confusion, we consistently discuss units of output produced by a given amount of factor inputs.

**ADDED
DIMENSION**

Companies and Comparative Advantage

Notice that the theory as presented so far relates to the benefits that a *country* would expect if it allowed international trade to take place. The company manager should view this information as a basis for choosing countries for production and export or countries for import sales. So, if it happens that lower costs of producing a product exist in country 1, the manager should look at possibilities for producing that product there and for exporting it to country 2, based on the theory of comparative advantage. Now let us see why this is true. ■

and cloth if Portugal specializes in producing (and exporting) wine and England does likewise with cloth.

Although 20th-century analysts have produced much more detailed assessments of the comparative cost theory, most of the newer work is still based on Ricardo's insight.[2]

Comparative Cost Theory

The easiest way to demonstrate the main implications of this theory is with an example involving two countries, two products, and two factors of production. Let us assume that each country's availability of factors of production has already led to a set of domestic costs for producing each product (before trade takes place) and proceed from there.

To emphasize that country size is not necessarily important in determining relative costs, consider the United States and Honduras. Let us work with a pair of standardized products that are clearly related to each country's relative endowment of production factors (e.g., agricultural land and physical capital).

For the sake of our discussion, the United States and Honduras are assumed to possess the characteristics depicted in Table 3–3 and Figure 3–1. In this situation, the United States is a substantially larger producer of both good A (*electrical appliances,* such as toasters, blenders, and hair dryers) and good B (*bananas*). Nonetheless, both the United States and Honduras may be able to consume more of each product under free trade than if they use only their domestic capabilities for production to satisfy their own consumption.

These two exhibits demonstrate the capabilities of each country to produce bananas and appliances, assuming that all available productive resources are

TABLE 3–3

Production and Consumption Possibilities for the United States and Honduras *(in thousands of bushels of bananas/month and thousands of appliances/month)*

United States		Honduras	
Appliances	Bananas	Appliances	Bananas
200	0	60	0
160	20	50	15
120*	40*	40*	30*
100	55	30	45
40	80	20	60
0	100	0	80

*Equals initial production and consumption points.

FIGURE 3-1

Production and
Consumption Possibilities
for the United States and
Honduras

utilized in these two industries. That is, if all of the people, machinery, and land
in Honduras were used to produce bananas, they could produce 80,000 bushels
of bananas per month. If all of these same productive resources were used to
produce appliances, they could make 60,000 appliances per month. Finally, if
some of the people, machinery, and land were used to produce each product, the
trade-offs would appear as points along the production possibilities curve (or as
pairs of output possibilities in Table 3–3). Notice that the P-P curves in Figure 3–1
have been drawn as straight lines, implying that no diminishing returns occur as
specialization increases. This also means that with trade, each country will be
induced to specialize completely in the production of one product. If diminishing
returns did occur, trade generally would lead to incomplete specialization in each
country.[3] The actual points on the production possibilities curves where consumers in each country choose to purchase appliances and bananas are determined
by their preferences, as reflected in indifference curves I_{Hon} and I_{US}.

Factors of Production

The theory of comparative advantage states that the production possibilities of each country arise from the productive capabilities of its factors of production. In our example, we can assume that banana production is more land intensive and that appliances production is more machinery intensive. Furthermore, we must assume that, in relative terms, Honduras possesses more fertile land relative to machinery and the United States possesses more machinery relative to fertile land (or that the **relative productivities** of land and labor give each country the advantage shown).* Stated in measurable terms,

$$\frac{\text{Quantity of fertile land}_{Hon}}{\text{Quantity of available machinery}_{Hon}} > \frac{\text{Quantity of fertile land}_{US}}{\text{Quantity of available machinery}_{US}}$$

If these conditions do hold, Table 3–1 is a reasonable representation of each country's possibilities. The United States, because of its larger endowments of all production factors, could produce more of either product than Honduras, but the United States is *relatively* more productive in appliances and Honduras in bananas.

From our initial production/consumption points for each country, we can reason that trade will be beneficial if it leads each country to a final consumption point at which more of either or both goods and less of neither good is consumed. So the final consumption of appliances and bananas must be at least as much as each entry in the table below. Remember that the choice of the initial consumption point is determined by consumers' tastes in each country, limited by the production possibilities. Gains from trade occur only if consumers in each country are able to consume on a higher indifference curve (or at least on the same curve) compared to pretrade conditions.[4]

Initial Consumption (and Production)

	A	B
United States	120	40
Honduras	40	30

Note: Appliances (A) are measured in thousands of appliances per month; bananas (B) are measured in thousands of bushels per month.

Now consider the relative efficiencies of each country in producing each good. If Honduras were to specialize completely in the production of bananas, it could produce 80,000 bushels per month (that is, 80 units of 1,000 bushels/month each and *no* appliances) compared to the United States' capability to specialize and produce 100,000 bushels per month (i.e., 100 units). Similarly, by specializing in appliance production, Honduras could produce 60,000 appliances per month (and no bananas) and the United States could produce 200,000 appliances per month. Clearly, the United States possesses an *absolute* advantage in the production of both products. However, we can also see that each country has a *relative* (or comparative) advantage in the production of one product.

Assuming complete specialization in the production of *appliances,* the United States has an advantage of $200/60 = 3.33$ over Honduras. If complete specialization

---

*Note that the United States can produce more of each good by specializing completely. This is *not* the same as absolute advantage, which occurs if the United States (or Honduras) can produce more of each good with the same amount of production inputs.

ADDED DIMENSION

Incomplete Specialization

Rather than talk about extremes in which each country uses all of its productive resources in these two industries, we can consider a given amount of resources (for example, 100 people, 100 acres of land, and 100 tons of machinery) in each country. Then, based on the productivity of these "production units," we can compare the relative efficiency of producing two products such as appliances and bananas in each country. In the case discussed here, the production unit in Honduras can produce either 60 appliances or 80 bushels of bananas during the month; that is, the same resources can produce only three-fourths as many appliances as bushels of bananas. In the United States, the production unit can produce either 200 appliances or 100 bushels of bananas; the same amount of resources can produce twice as many appliances as bushels of bananas. Clearly (we hope), the United States should trade an appliance that is worth only one-half of a banana in the domestic market to Honduras, where that appliance is worth four-thirds of a bushel of bananas. Analogously, Honduras could trade away a bushel of bananas, which is worth only three-fourths of an appliance in the domestic market, in exchange for two appliances in the United States. This discussion may complicate our presentation, but it paves the way for considering situations where countries do not specialize completely in producing just one product but specialize partially to favor the comparatively efficient product(s)—and they deal in many products rather than just two. ■

in *banana* production were carried out, the United States would maintain an advantage of $^{100}/_{80} = 1.20$ over Honduras. Thus, the United States has a *comparative advantage* in producing appliances.

On the other side, Honduras would operate at a disadvantage in producing either product. However, the disadvantage in producing bananas is only $^{80}/_{100} = 0.8$, while the disadvantage in producing appliances is $^{60}/_{200} = 0.3$. Honduras possesses a comparative advantage (i.e., less disadvantage) in producing bananas. In other words, Honduras possesses factors of production (i.e., land, labor, and machinery) that are relatively more efficient in producing bananas, and the United States possesses factors of production that are relatively more efficient in producing appliances.

The doctrine of comparative advantage states that when such relative production advantages exist and are reflected in prices, each country will be better off by specializing and trading rather than remaining economically independent. These results are more likely to occur (1) the fewer the restrictions placed on trade, (2) the lower the transactions costs involved, (3) the wider the gap in production advantages, and (4) the easier it is for productive resources to be shifted into the advantageous industry in each country.

With-trade Production Points

By considering with-trade production points, we can see numerically that trade may improve each country's consumption. If each country specializes where it has a comparative advantage, with-trade production will be as in the table below. Pretrade consumption of each product by *both* countries combined was 160 units per month of appliances and 70 units per month of bananas. Now total production exceeds each of these figures, so it remains only to price the products and distribute the output. Unquestionably, each country is *potentially* better off.

With-trade Production (units/month)

	A	B
United States	200	0
Honduras	0	80

The final consumption points will depend on consumers' preferences in each country, as reflected in the indifference curves for that country. We do know, however, that the United States will export *at most* 80 units of appliances per month and will demand *at least* 40 units per month of bananas in exchange to remain at least as well off as before trade. Similarly, Honduras will be willing to export *at most* 50 units per month of bananas in exchange for *at least* 40 units of appliances per month, so consumers there will be no worse off than before trade. Any trade of 40 to 80 units of appliances per month for 40 to 50 units of bananas per month will make each country better off than it was before.[5] We can assume that the final consumption points are as shown in the table below.

With-trade Consumption (units/month)

	A	B
United States	150	45
Honduras	50	35

(handwritten margin notes:)

US 80A ⟶ 40B $B = \frac{80}{40}A$

IA 50B ⟶ 40A $= 2A$

$B = \frac{40}{50}A$

$= 0.9A$

Implicitly, this means that the with-trade relative prices are 45 bushels of bananas/50 appliances = 0.9 bananas/appliances, or 1.11 appliances/bananas. That is, final consumption possibilities (if graphed on Figure 3–1) have a slope of more than the pretrade US trade-off and less than the Honduran one.

Next, let us consider *prices* explicitly to show that each country is better off in financial as well as real terms. The adjustment from pre- to with-trade prices can take place through changes in domestic prices in each country, through changes in the exchange rate, or both. To focus on "international prices," let us allow only the exchange rate to change while domestic prices in each country remain constant.

Assume that the domestic price of bananas in the United States before trade was 200 appliances per 100 bushels of bananas, or 2 to 1. If an appliance cost $10, one bushel (i.e., one unit) of bananas cost $20, according to Figure 3–1. In Honduras, the pretrade value of a bushel of bananas was three-fourths of an appliance. If we assume that an appliance costs 200 lempira, a bushel of bananas costs 150 lempira.

Pretrade Prices

	A	B
United States	$10	$20
Honduras	200 lempira	150 lempira

Once international trade is allowed, there must be some rate of exchange between lempira and dollars. Looking at the pretrade domestic prices, appliances were worth 200 lempira or $10, a ratio of 20 lempira/dollar, and bananas were worth 150 lempira or $20, a ratio of 7.5 lempira/dollar. As long as the exchange rate falls somewhere between these ratios, bilateral trade will make each country better off in financial terms. Let us assume, then, that the exchange rate becomes 15 lempira/dollar.

This exchange rate means that US consumers who want to buy Honduran appliances or bananas will face dollar prices of 200 lempira/15 lempira per dollar = $13.33 per appliance and 150 lempira/15 lempira per dollar = $10 per bushel of bananas. On the other hand, Honduran consumers looking at possible purchases of US appliances and bananas will see lempira prices of $10 × 15 lempira per dollar = 150 lempira per appliance and $20 × 15 lempira per dollar = 300 lempira per bushel of bananas. Clearly, US consumers will benefit from importing bananas and Honduran consumers will benefit from importing appliances. Since each country is large enough to satisfy total demand for the product it exports, complete specialization may occur in each (though not necessarily, due to various market imperfections—tariffs, factor immobility among industries, etc.).

With-Trade Prices *(at exchange rate of 15 lempira per US dollar)*

	A	B
United States	$10	$10 (on imports)
Honduras	150 lempira (on imports)	150 lempira

If the exchange rate changed to a level outside the range of 7.5 to 20 lempira/dollar, a disequilibrium would exist. At any exchange rate below 7.5 lempira/dollar, both countries would want to buy appliances and bananas from the United States. At any rate above 20 lempira/dollar, both countries would want to buy both products from Honduras. For example, if the rate is 5 lempira/dollar, Hondurans can import appliances for 50 lempira/appliance and bananas for 100 lempira/bushel and US consumers have to pay $40 for imported appliances and $30/bushel for imported bananas. In this case, both countries would buy both products from the United States until the exchange rate moved above 7.5 lempira/dollar or until US prices of appliances and bananas rose enough to accomplish the same result. (Alternatively, Honduran prices could fall to generate this result. The actual adjustment will depend on whether domestic prices or exchange rates are more flexible, but the result will be the same.)

This relatively simple framework demonstrates the potential real and financial gains available to any pair of countries that begin bilateral trade in two commodities. These results will generally be obtained for situations involving many countries and many products, as long as relative production efficiencies differ.[6] Some important problems that arise from market imperfections such as government controls and monopolistic company practices are ignored in this chapter, though they are critical factors for managerial decision making. Our only purpose here has been to present one underlying economic rationale for trade.

THE INTERNATIONAL PRODUCT CYCLE

The **international product cycle** is a concept developed by Raymond Vernon in the mid-1960s and based on the product life cycle in marketing analysis.[7] This concept is far more intuitively appealing than the comparative advantage theory as an explanation of post–World War II trade (and investment), especially

ADDED
DIMENSION   Comparative versus Competitive Advantage

Be careful to distinguish between these two concepts! *Comparative advantage* refers to the cost of producing some product or service in one country versus another. It is a concept based on relative cost of production between nations. *Competitive advantage* refers to a skill or capability a firm possesses that enables it to outcompete rivals in a given situation. It is used to compare two companies' abilities to compete in the same business. A firm may utilize comparative advantage to further its own strategy by obtaining inputs and products in locations where they are least expensive. That is, a firm may use imports to obtain low-cost factors of production, set up a sourcing investment in the low-cost country to produce the inputs for itself, or move its entire production process to a low-cost location. If the location is in another country, the firm is using *comparative advantage* to improve its competitiveness. Thus, the comparative advantage that exists in any country may be used by companies operating there to create a cost-based competitive advantage. ∎

regarding manufactured goods (in particular, differentiated products). The product cycle theory explicitly incorporates the multinational enterprise as an actor that undertakes international trade (and foreign direct investment). It focuses on market expansion and technological innovation, which are relatively deemphasized in the comparative advantage theory. Finally, it is a dynamic view, exploring the reasons trade flows shift over time. In all, it puts the phenomenon of international trade in a context that makes business sense in the world of changing technology and multiple markets that any firm faces.

The theory of the international product cycle has two fundamental tenets. First, technology is a critical factor in product creation and development, and the existence of proprietary technology gives some firms advantages over others. Second, market size and structure are critical factors in determining trade patterns.

The cycle itself consists of three stages: the new-product stage, the maturing-product stage, and the standardized-product stage. These stages are more or less analogous to the stages of the domestic product life cycle, though the decline and cessation of production of a product are ignored.

New-Product Stage

A *new product* is created by some firm or firms and does not exist prior to this. For example, pocket calculators, automobiles, specific drugs, and nuclear power plants were each created by one or a few firms whose scientists and engineers developed each product. When such an invention is sold in the market, it is called an **innovation,** or a **new product.** The first step toward a new product, then, is the process of scientific research, which leads to inventions.

The conditions under which an innovation will succeed depend greatly on the type of product and the type of market. If we consider manufactured products and national markets, we would expect a lot of innovations in nations where sufficient scientists and engineers are available and purchasers have sufficient incomes to buy the products. In his reasoning in the mid-1960s, Vernon explained that the largest percentage of new products would be introduced in the largest single national market with the highest per capita income—the United States. That is, he believed that innovations had the best chance for success in the United States at that time, because the United States then had more scientists and engineers and a higher per capita income than any other country.

Also important in the new-product stage is *flexibility* in production to suit the needs and desires of new purchasers.[8] Generally, when a new product is introduced, we would expect the demand for it to be relatively price inelastic. Purchasers who have no perfect substitutes available for the new product are likely to be more concerned (initially) with the product's useful characteristics than with its price. As the innovating firm receives feedback from purchasers about performance, reliability, and so on, it can alter the product to suit purchasers' preferences. Close contact with the market is therefore a very important factor in this stage. To achieve flexibility, then, the innovating firm will probably want to locate in or near a major potential market, where good communications are available. Once again, the United States is a very likely candidate for such a firm's location, though today, of course, Western European countries and Japan serve about equally well as appropriate markets for new products.

As the innovating firm discovers additional customers for sales of the new product, it may seek foreign demand, or demand may arise through requests for exports. If the innovating firm is a multinational, it may face the choice between exporting and setting up production in foreign markets. Smaller firms would generally look just at exporting, or perhaps contracting with a foreign firm to produce the product abroad. Thus, the initial entry of the new product into international business will probably occur through exports, and sooner or later that step may be followed by foreign production. Figure 3–2 presents an overview of the international product cycle, assuming that initial production occurs in the United States.

Notice that as the new-product stage progresses, exports provide a growing share of total sales. If sale of the new product is truly profitable, the innovating firm is likely to attract competitors both in the United States and abroad. Depending on the firm's success in retaining its proprietary ability to make the product, competition will arise sooner or later. Exports and the start-up of foreign production (the middle panel of Figure 3–2) may be carried out either by the innovating firm or by competing firms, depending on the ability of these firms to gain information about the product and access to foreign markets.

Two distinct shifts in the nature of the new business mark the transition from the new-product stage to the maturing-product stage. First, the likelihood that competitors will begin making the product, in the home country or abroad, means that *price* competition is likely to become more important. The innovating firm itself may establish facilities abroad to achieve lower-cost production as well as to serve foreign markets (especially in Europe, Canada, and Japan) with a product capable of being adapted to local market requirements. Second, the fact that competitors exist at all means that technology is diffusing, so that the original firm does not maintain its monopoly of the product.

Maturing-Product Stage   Each of these shifts leads to the **maturing-product** stage, which involves global diffusion of the product through exports and also through foreign production via foreign direct investment. This second stage is characterized by more price-elastic

FIGURE 3–2

The International Product
Cycle

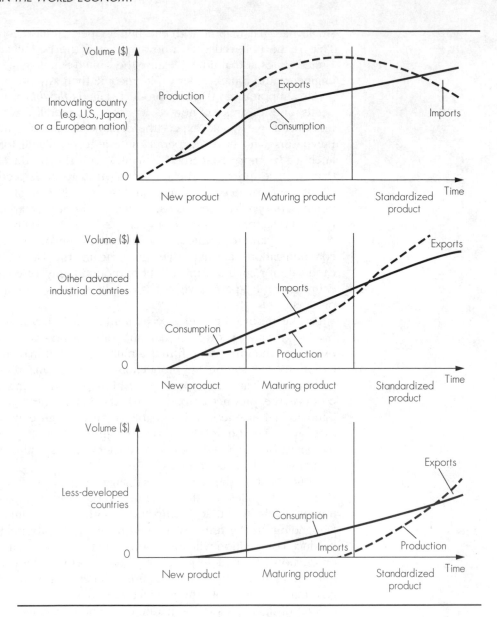

demand for the product, more standardization of the production process, and a
change in company strategy away from a focus on production (of this particular
product) and toward market protection. Both local and foreign competitors
typically challenge the innovating firm in its home market and abroad. In this
stage, product differentiation is common, and pursuit of new markets by competing firms becomes active.

Production in the home country typically levels off in this stage as market
growth slows. Lower-cost production methods and locations are often sought as
price competition increases. Toward the end of this stage, foreign production may
even be exported to the home country. Notice that both competition and
production tend to spread from the home country first to other industrial
countries and later to less developed countries.

Standardized-Product Stage

Finally, the **standardized-product** stage occurs when technology relevant to the product becomes widely available and price becomes the main basis for competition. In this stage, production of standardized products (or components) is often shifted to low-cost locations, including less developed countries. (see Figure 3–2, bottom panel). Also typical of the standardized-product stage is offshore assembly, in which parts of the product are still produced in the home country but assembly is done in cheap-labor countries, for final sale in many countries. Strategically, firms often try to avoid pure price competition in the standardized-product stage by differentiating their products.

Example: The Pocket Calculator

The standard pocket calculator offers a clear example of a product moving through the international product cycle. This "product" is defined here to be the battery-operated, hand-held computational instrument that adds, subtracts, multiplies, and divides electronically. Scientists at Sunlock Comptometer Corporation invented the product in 1961 and began marketing it soon afterward. At about $1,000 per calculator, the instrument was not cheap. But it performed functions formerly reserved for large computers and mechanical calculators, while offering the user a simple, portable, and independent computational capability. The alternative in terms of portability and independence from electrical outlets was the slide rule, which was far less accurate than the 6 to 10 digits usually available in a calculator.

Ignoring the refinements that allow pocket calculators to carry out complex calculations, store results, and even act as microcomputers, let us continue to look at the simple, four-function product. (The others can be defined as separate products to avoid confusion.) Within eight years of the introduction of pocket calculators, several additional firms (including a number of Japanese manufacturers) had entered the market with competing products, and the price had dropped to about $400 per calculator. Hewlett-Packard, Texas Instruments, Casio (a Japanese firm), and other electronics manufacturers developed similar models, which forced all manufacturers of pocket calculators to compete on price grounds in the United States and several foreign markets. Each of these developments indicated a move into the maturing-product stage. (The new-product stage lasted perhaps four to six years.)

In the early 1970s, more firms entered the market, several began to assemble their calculators in offshore locations such as Taiwan and Singapore, and price competition became truly fierce. In 1971, Bowmar Corporation, an American firm, introduced a four-function calculator that retailed for $240. By 1975, these calculators routinely sold for $10 to $15 and sometimes for even less. One could argue that pocket calculators had reached the standardized-product stage by 1975, with the production technology widely available, price competition (and hence costs) of utmost importance, and product differentiation widely used.

Thus, the international product cycle for simple calculators was completed in less than 15 years. The product itself remains in widespread demand, but producers now compete on the basis of price, other product characteristics, and distribution rather than on the basis of proprietary technology and new markets.

Example: The Polaroid Land Camera

Contrast the case of the pocket calculator with that of the Polaroid Land camera. In 1947, Edwin Land, the founder and manager of Polaroid Corporation, introduced a new photographic process. He had invented an instant-developing film that allowed a photographer to snap a picture and simply wait a few minutes for chemicals on the film to develop the final snapshot. First marketed in 1948, the Polaroid Land camera enjoyed a monopoly position for several *decades*.

Initially, the Polaroid Land camera took only black-and-white photographs, and the film processing was done inside the camera. In 1963, Polaroid introduced an improved version that processed the film outside the camera. (Each snapshot was removed from the camera immediately after the picture taking in a "sandwich" of developing chemicals, film negative, and print paper. Then the print was pulled away from the other materials, which were discarded.) Later, improved prints of both black-and-white and color pictures were offered. In 1972, Polaroid introduced another modification of the camera, which now ejects the final print directly from the camera after each picture. (The print develops in a few seconds, with no materials to be discarded.)

If the instant-developing camera is regarded as one product, ignoring its improvements over the years, we can conclude that the new-product stage lasted approximately 30 years. During that time, Polaroid had a monopoly on the market worldwide, expanding sales through both direct exports and foreign marketing and production affiliates. In 1992 47 percent of the firm's sales came from foreign operations located in 18 countries.

Only in 1976, when Kodak introduced an instant-developing camera using somewhat different technology, did competition for this product begin. Then, in 1984, Polaroid won a patent infringement case against Kodak, which forced Kodak out of the market for instant-developing cameras. In 1987, the instant-developing camera was still in the late new-product or early maturing-product stage—a huge contrast to the pocket calculator's cycle. Today Polaroid's proprietary technology continues to play a major role in competition for instant-developing cameras. Price competition has become more important, though not dominant, in Polaroid's effort to entice photographers away from single-lens reflex and Instamatic cameras. Thus, the international product cycle provides an appealing description of the sequence of events that takes place in the lives of many products. But, as we see with the instant-developing camera, it does *not* explain when the stages will begin or end.

While the theory of the international product cycle offers us a wealth of insights into international trade and the activities of multinational firms, it leaves some important questions unanswered. This theory does not tell us how long each stage will last, though it does illuminate key competitive aspects of each stage. Nor does it tell us explicitly how or when a firm should choose between exporting and setting up a local plant abroad, though it does mention costs as an important concern. It does not explain which country's firms are most likely to produce in any given market or which firms will move first. Finally, the theory is decidedly vague on the definition of a "product." Despite these limitations, when compared with other theories available today, this theory gives us substantial managerial insights into trade patterns in manufacturing.

An especially fortunate aspect of the theory of the international product cycle is its compatibility with the theory of comparative advantage. If we focus on trade that occurs primarily on the basis of comparative national cost conditions, the standardized-product stage of the international product cycle outlines broad aspects of such trade, and the comparative advantage view lays out a solid theoretical framework for analysis and decision making.

One additional theory of international trade that is based on demand-side considerations deserves comment at this point. Staffan Linder (1961) created a theory based on *similarity of demand patterns* to explain trade patterns in manufactured products. This theory was developed in the early 1960s, at about the same time the theory of the international product cycle was attempting to move emphasis in trade theory to the demand side. Linder reasoned that a major determinant of trade patterns is the level of a country's economic development. Countries at similar levels of development would have similar demand patterns and would be likely to trade among themselves. Intuitively, this idea is sensible, and we can think of the pharmaceuticals industry, the computer industry, and many others that display large trade volumes among developed countries and relatively few involving LDCs (with the exception of the offshore assembly done in LDCs for sale in developed countries). Linder's theory offers an underlying reason for expecting so much trade in manufactured goods among developed countries, even when many of their cost conditions are very similar.

EMPIRICAL CONTROVERSIES AND NEW THEORIES

While our discussions of comparative advantage and the international product cycle should offer insights into the patterns of international trade that take place today, quite a few phenomena defy explanation using these tools. The international product cycle itself was developed during a period of controversy about the comparative advantages possessed by the United States. Though this country appears to be quite capital rich relative to rival nations, Leontief and others found that US exports (compared to US imports) were relatively labor intensive rather than capital intensive. The reason for his paradoxical finding may be that the United States tends to specialize in more **technology-intensive** products, which utilize skilled labor in their production. (The Leontief paradox is discussed in Appendix 3–1.) This rationale is one of the bases Vernon used in his international product cycle theory.

US trade can be evaluated along these lines as shown in Figure 3–3. Note that the United States indeed has a surplus in exports of technology-intensive products relative to imports of the same products. The United States also has a trade surplus in services but a deficit in all of the other categories of products listed. The other industrial countries in the figure, except Canada, also have trade surpluses on high-tech products. These countries broadly show a net deficit in trade of standardized goods, implying that the rest of the world—particularly the newly industrializing countries (NICs) such as Korea, Taiwan, Hong Kong, and Singapore—are achieving an export surplus on those goods.

This phenomenon is consistent with the comparative advantage concept, since the NICs do indeed possess a *relative* abundance of low-cost labor relative to the industrial countries, and thus the NICs should export labor-intensive, standardized goods.

Intra-Industry Trade

Trade statistics abound with examples of two-way trade in apparently the same products between various trading partners. A simple reason for this unexpected phenomenon is that the statistics include many products in one aggregated category, so that what appears to be one product really turns out to be many. Indeed, much of the evidence is of exactly this type. Also, multistage production (including offshore assembly) leads to trade flows of one product both into and out of the same country where processing is done, while the actual items being moved are first inputs and then outputs of the product. However, after misclassified products have been excluded, there still turns out to be a substantial amount of cross-hauling in exactly the same products.

Two reasons for intra-industry trade have been proposed in recent years. First and more simply, the trade often takes place in *differentiated products*. That is,

FIGURE 3–3

Patterns of comparative advantage: Export/import (X/M) ratios in six leading countries, 1985

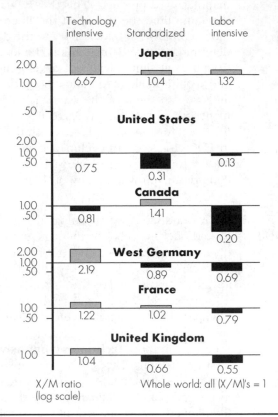

Technology-intensive manufactures—transport equipment (autos, planes, ships, motorbikes, etc.), machinery, chemicals, and professional goods.
Labor-intensive manufactures - textiles, apparel, footwear, and leather goods.
Standardized manufactures - all manufactures - technology-intensive and labor-intensive manufactures.
Source: Peter Lindert, *International Economics* (Homewood, Ill.: Richard D. Irwin, Inc., 1991).

products such as automobiles that are traded in both directions between the United States and Germany, or between Germany and Japan, are highly differentiated. German cars such as Mercedes and BMW are luxury autos that are sold in Japan and the United States, while those countries export Toyotas and Fords to Germany. This oversimplification of auto trade should not hide the fact that automobiles are highly differentiated, and thus even Toyotas, BMWs, and Fords can and do coexist simultaneously in the same market.

A second explanation of intra-industry trade focuses on *economies of scale*. Because such production scale economies limit the range of products that any country can produce (the cost of producing all products is clearly prohibitive for any one country), countries will specialize in a limited range of products. Then trading partners fill in each other's total product lines through exports. Countries choose which products to import based on their tastes and on the demands for different production inputs.

THE IMPERFECT COMPETITION THEORY OF TRADE

In recent years, trade theory has broadened to encompass the phenomenon of intra-industry exporting, concentration of manufacturing trade among advanced industrial countries, and market-related factors. This has occurred principally through development of an **imperfect competition theory** of international trade. This theory moves away from the traditional use of perfectly competitive markets, in which firms are price takers and produce similar products. It focuses on the differences between firms that permit better-endowed or better-positioned firms to obtain superior returns in international competition compared to their rivals. In fact, the theory has moved toward the idea of competitive advantages as presented in Chapter 2.

Under these conditions, a firm may realize economies of scale that permit it to achieve least-cost production when sales go beyond the local country's market. This means that to obtain such economies, the firm must export some of its output. Likewise, foreign competitors may find the same opportunity, and they too will use exports to expand sales and reduce their unit costs. Overall, the existence of important scale economies may explain both intra-industry trade and the pheomenon that some exports go against comparative advantage (because moving production to the low-cost location is more expensive than just exporting marginal production from the home country location.*

Additional understanding of trade patterns and dynamics comes from combining trade and direct investment theory, as first done by Vernon in the international product cycle. By looking at multiple competitive advantages such as economies of scale, proprietary technology, and preferential access to natural resources, we can begin to see how companies incorporate their overseas exporting and investing into their corporate strategy and thus contribute to international business activity overall. The next chapter pursues this idea in more detail.

CONCLUSIONS

Each of the trade theories discussed in this chapter can be recast in a microeconomic context, focusing on individual firms. The lesson to be learned from the comparative cost view, for example, is that when costs are very important in competition, it may be best for a firm to produce its products in low-cost countries rather than try to serve markets from its home country alone. Certainly, this lesson has been learned by the many US-based electronics firms that now manufacture in Singapore, South Korea, or Hong Kong to lower their production costs. Alternatively, a firm may find it best to import some products from low-cost suppliers rather than try to produce them itself. In fact, many export-import firms make their entire business from finding low-cost suppliers in various countries and sales in others, profiting from the use of comparative cost advantages in each product.

The theory of the international product cycle offers the manager advice about the dynamics of many industries as competition shifts from being based on proprietary technology to product differentiation to price (cost) minimizing. The high-tech firm may choose to leave the markets for its products when they enter the maturing or standardized stage to concentrate its efforts on developing new products and competing on the basis of its technology. The firm with a respected brand name may choose to focus its efforts on finding low-cost production sites and establishing an international distribution network to minimize delivery costs.

The other theories can also serve as guides for decision making. In every case, the firm needs to consider other alternatives besides exports (for example, foreign direct investment).

---

*This idea is presented in detail in Krugman and Obstfeld (1991), Chapter 6; a more sophisticated discussion appears in Helpman and Krugman (1989).

Looking specifically at individual countries, it appears that US companies are competing successfully in export markets with products that are relatively intensive in human capital. This may be restated in terms of companies' competitive advantages: US firms can succeed in export markets where their proprietary skills (such as technology and management know-how) are relatively important. Foreign firms can export to the United States products whose competitiveness depends more on other factors of production (e.g., low-wage labor, natural resources, different management skills), as well as in some segments of the high-tech markets. Firms may export in both directions when economies of scale favor such a strategy.

QUESTIONS

1. How can the manager of an international company use the comparative advantage theory in decision making? For example, suppose the company is Apple Computer and the manager is looking for a site to locate a new plant.

2. Explain the stages of the international product cycle. How can a manager use this theory in decision making? Use the case of the auto industry to illustrate your answer.

3. What are the main export products/services of the United States today? Why are US exporters able to compete successfully in these markets? (Figure 8–4 in Chapter 8 lists the main merchandise products, and Figure 8–3 shows several key service categories.)

4. Is the exchange rate important in the theory of comparative advantage? Why or why not?

5. Explain Leontief's paradox. Be sure to discuss several reasons the paradox may be more apparent than real.

6. What competitive advantage do the OPEC countries possess that allows them to compete in export markets? What theory of international trade applies to this example?

7. At what stage of the international product cycle are personal computers? Based on that view, what do you expect to happen in this market during the rest of the 1990s?

8. At what stage of the international product cycle is the automobile? What do you expect to happen in this market during the rest of the 1990s?

9. Given the information below, what should each country do? Why?

	Computers	Paper
United States	50	40
Canada	100	60

Note: Each cell represents the number of output units produced by one unit of inputs.

10. How does international trade relate to foreign direct investment?

REFERENCES

Baldwin, Robert. "Determinants of the Commodity Structure of U.S. Trade." *American Economic Review,* March 1971.

Buckley, Peter, and Robert D. Pearce. "Exports in the Strategy of Multinational Enterprises." *Journal of Business Research,* June 1984.

Ethier, Wilfred. *Modern International Economics.* 2nd ed. New York: W. W. Norton, 1983.

Giddy, Ian. "The Demise of the Product Cycle Model in International Business Theory." *Columbia Journal of World Business,* Spring 1978.

Greenaway, D., and C. R. Milner. *The Economics of Intra-Industry Trade*. Oxford: Basil Blackwell, 1986.

Grosse, Robert. "An Imperfect Competition Theory of the MNE." *Journal of International Business Studies,* Winter 1985. Gruber, W. H.; Dileep Mehta; and Raymond Vernon. "The R&D Factor in International Investment of U.S. Industries." *Journal of Political Economy,* February 1967.

Haberler, Gottfried. *The Theory of International Trade*. London: William Hodge, 1950.

Helpman, Elhanan, and Paul R. Krugman. *Trade Policy and Market Structure*. Cambridge, MA: MIT Press, 1989.

Hirsch, S. "An International Trade and Investment Theory of the Firm." *Oxford Economic Papers,* July 1976.

Hufbauer, Gary. *Synthetic Materials and the Theory of International Trade*. Cambridge, MA: Harvard University Press, 1966.

Krugman, Paul, and Maurice Obstfeld. *International Economics*, 2nd ed. New York: Harper Collins, 1991.

Linder, Staffan. *An Essay on Trade and Transformation*. New York: John Wiley & Sons, 1961.

Lindert, Peter. *International Economics,* 8th ed. Homewood, IL: Richard D. Irwin, 1993.

Ricardo, David. *Principles of Political Economy and Taxation*. Harmondsworth, Middlesex, England: Penguin Books, 1971. (Originally published in 1817.)

Tharakan, P., and Jacob, K.I. *Intra-industry Trade*. New York: St. Martin's Press, 1989.

Vernon, Raymond. "International Investment and International Trade in the Product Cycle." *Quarterly Journal of Economics,* May 1966.

Yoffic, David. *International Trade and Competition*. New York: W. W. Norton, 1994.

EXIM Company: Comparative Advantage in International Trade

Introduction

A very important factor in determining trade patterns between countries for many products is the cost of production. If this cost is lower in one country than the other, the first country will benefit from producing and exporting the product to the second. For example, if steel costs $300 per ton to make in Japan and $400 per ton to make in the United States, then (all other things being equal) US customers should buy (import) steel from Japanese companies. By the same reasoning, if airplanes cost $4 million to produce in the United States and $5 million in Japan, Japanese customers should buy (import) airplanes from the United States. In this example, the United States produces and exports airplanes, while Japan produces and exports steel. Each country has a *comparative advantage* in producing one product relative to the other country.

Obviously, countries do not export and import—*companies* do. For any company, the choice of products to export and import depends to some degree on the cost of production in the various countries where the company does business. The company should utilize comparative advantage to decide where (in which country) to produce its products and where to buy its inputs. In the case below, a US-based company sells many products in several national markets. The problem is to choose whether to obtain computer memory chips in the United States or Japan and perhaps to consider buying other components and peripheral equipment for resale as well.

The Case

EXIM Company is a Connecticut-based corporation that assembles computer circuit boards for use in personal computers manufactured by IBM, Apple, Compaq, NEC, and other original-equipment manufacturers. During its six-year history, the company has gone from a 2-person operation assembling memory expansion boards to a 30-person manufacturing business. It now makes a wide variety of multiple-function boards and other peripheral hardware used in the burgeoning personal computer market. The firm's annual sales grew by about 40 percent per year to just over $8 million in 1993.

EXIM was founded by an electrical engineer, Hans Klauser, and a recent MBA graduate of a local business school. These two entrepreneurs were able to

This case was written by Professor Robert Grosse as a basis for class discussion (revised 1994).

combine their basic knowledge of microcomputer hardware with an aggressive marketing strategy for the circuit boards. After borrowing $50,000 from a commercial bank and adding their life savings, EXIM's founders were able to generate enough sales to break even in the second year of operations and repay their entire loan by the end of the third year. Today EXIM uses 80 percent equity financing (earnings reinvested in the firm by the two owners, who continue to own all the stock shares) and 20 percent bank financing, mostly for working capital. The entire operation is housed in a rebuilt factory just outside West Haven, Connecticut.

Most of EXIM's sales go to the thousands of retail stores that sprang up in the United States during the 1980s and 90s to sell microcomputers and peripheral equipment to businesses, individuals, and other customers. In addition, similar stores in Canada and the United Kingdom have become important customers in the last two years. Export sales to individual customers have been fairly insignificant thus far, but an advertising campaign in two microcomputer magazines has led to sales in Mexico, Ireland, and even Pakistan.

Recently, competition from lower-priced boards, many of them imported from Asia, has begun to reduce EXIM's rate of growth in sales. Having read about the problems of the electronics industry and others in the United States due to their competition with Japanese and Korean firms, EXIM's general manager, Hans Klauser, was considering the idea of establishing an assembly operation somewhere in Asia. Klauser believed that his products were essentially "commodities," embodying technology that is readily available from several suppliers in the United States, Germany, and Japan. Therefore, his competitiveness would need to be based to some degree on the prices charged to customers. Superior quality and service could be used to improve sales somewhat, but the key factor would be price.

Klauser was particularly concerned about the cost conditions in each country, which were subject to substantial shifts due to differences in national inflation rates and exchange rate changes. The Japanese yen, for example, devalued by over 30 percent relative to the dollar in the early 1980s, then revalued by more than 20 percent in 1985 alone. Japanese inflation, in contrast, had paralleled US

TABLE 1 Yen/Dollar Exchange Rates and Inflation Rates

Date	U.S. Dollar/Japanese Yen Exchange Rates (in yen / $)	Japan	United States
1980	203.00	8.0	13.5
1981	219.90	4.9	10.4
1982	235.00	2.7	6.1
1983	232.20	1.8	3.2
1984	251.10	2.3	4.3
1985	200.50	2.1	3.5
1986	159.10	0.6	1.9
1987	123.50	0.1	3.7
1988	125.85	0.7	4.0
1989	143.45	2.3	4.8
1990	134.40	3.1	5.4
1991	125.20	3.3	4.3
1992	124.75	1.7	3.0
1993	111.85	1.2	3.0

TABLE 2   Production Costs of Computer Components in the United States, Japan, and Korea*

Component	Comparative Costs		
	United States	Japan	Korea
1 MB RAM chips (cost per chip)	$ 1.50	$ 1.10	$ 0.90
4 MB RAM chips (cost per chip)	7.80	6.60	Not available
Internal clock/calendar	9.75	9.70	10.50
Serial port and RS232 cable to attach peripheral equipment	24.00	24.50	23.50
Parallel port and RS232 cable to attach peripheral equipment	23.00	23.50	22.80
Software-in-a-chip to run ramdisk	25.00	35.00	Not available
Internal modem (2400 baud)	140.00	135.00	132.00
Internal modem (9600 baud)	255.00	260.00	270.00

*Data are listed in US dollars at the current exchange rate, December 1993.

inflation during most of the 1980s and early 1990s. Table 1 depicts the yen/dollar exchange rate during 1980–93 and the inflation rates of each country during the same period.

Labor costs favored the Asian locations, but not necessarily by enough to overcome a potential severe dollar devaluation. Total production costs of several relevant components in 1993 appear in Table 2.

Although the table presents only production costs of EXIM's potential suppliers, these are fairly close to the full delivered cost for almost all of the products, since transportation, insurance, and other costs are minimal for such small, lightweight, manufactured goods. Tariffs currently are less than 5 percent *ad valorem* on these electronic products coming into the United States.

The Leontief Paradox

Much of the international economic policy of governments worldwide is based on the concept of comparative advantage. That is, national governments tend to view the gains from trade as being quite real, and they try to obtain a larger share of the total gains for themselves. The United States has traditionally been the clearest and most consistent advocate and example of free-trade policy. Following the principle of comparative advantage, then, the United States should specialize in the production and export of products in which it has an advantage. Which ones are they?

We might expect that if we focus simply on capital-intensive versus labor-intensive goods, the United States would export the former and import the latter. Certainly, with its abundant capital resources, the United States would be expected to behave in this way. A study by subsequent Nobel prize–winning economist Wassily Leontief in 1953 showed that in fact, export goods from the United States are relatively more labor intensive and import-competing goods are relatively more capital intensive! What happened to the theory of comparative advantage?

A number of explanations have been given for what is now called the **Leontief paradox.** Some authors have attributed the findings to trade barriers that distort trade flows; others have looked at differences in natural resource availability across countries; still others have focused on differences in the characteristics of labor across countries.[9] Most analysts today agree that this last factor plays a large part in determining US trade flows (and also foreign direct investment flows). If we measure the "quality" of labor inputs (i.e., their productivity) rather than just labor-hours of work, it turns out that the United States tends to specialize in producing and exporting products that use relatively more "high-quality" labor (e.g., technology-intensive products that require more highly educated labor). Several analysts, including Hufbauer (1966) and Gruber, Mehta, and Vernon (1967), found empirical evidence supporting this point. This explanation is quite consistent with the international product cycle, which is based on the development of new technology and sees the United States as the country most likely to be the source of new products.

Both the international product cycle theory and the technology-based theory have had to be reevaluated since the early 1970s to recognize the comparable levels of development and market size in the European Community and Japan relative to the United States. Today it is possible to argue that both theories provide plausible reasons for trade to begin among the industrialized countries once an innovation has been introduced, but neither is able to explain where to look for innovations.[10] The imperfect competition theory offers the greatest explanatory power, incorporating both cost and market elements into a *firm-based* view of trade.

NOTES

[1]The current state of development of this theory is presented in Lindert (1993).

[2]Ricardo's analysis assumes constant opportunity costs in shifting production from one product to another in a given country. This point has been criticized by Haberler (1950) and others, and current economics texts use the increasing-cost approach. This text uses Ricardo's model because it allows more clarity in the exposition. See Lindert (1993), Chapters 2–4, for an excellent presentation of the pure theory.

[3]Normally, we would expect diminishing returns to occur as production is specialized more and more in the one product, hence using less and less efficient resources for producing it. And we would therefore expect *incomplete* specialization in each country. Our example simplifies the economics substantially, and any international trade text can be used to explore the added concerns of incomplete specialization. Graphically, the results of trade with incomplete specialization between two equal-size countries would be as follows:

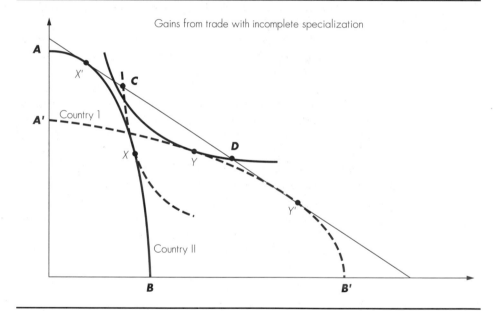

Gains from trade with incomplete specialization

Here country 1 produces and consumes initially at *Y,* and country 2 does so at *X.* With trade, each country partially specializes its production, at points *X'* and *Y',* and each can consume both goods at some point on segment *CD,* which is above the original indifference curves.

[4]In fact, consumers may choose a little less of one good and a lot more of the other after trade, as long as they end up consuming on a higher indifference curve. To

keep matters simple, we will assume that consumers choose more of both products when available.

[5]Thus, comparative advantage analysis tells us not only which country will specialize in production of which product but also what the limits will be on the real rate of exchange.

[6]See Lindert (1993) for a full treatment of these issues.

[7]Vernon's theory appeared in "International Investment and International Trade in the Product Cycle," *Quarterly Journal of Economics,* May 1966. The product life cycle in marketing appears, for example, in Chester Wasson, *Dynamic Competitive Strategy and Product Life Cycles* (St. Charles, Ill.: Challenge Books, 1974).

[8]Analogously, the firm may desire the flexibility to test the market using a limited capital commitment, before making expensive, highly illiquid investments in large-scale production runs.

[9]Much of the literature on the Leontief paradox is summarized in Baldwin (1971).

[10]Before the 1980s, several analysts demonstrated some patterns of innovation among industrial countries. For example, US firms tended to be labor saving in their innovations, European firms were relatively material and capital saving, and Japanese firms were relatively material and space saving.

4 Foreign Direct Investment

This chapter discusses the single phenomenon that most distinguishes the multinational enterprise from other types of firms, namely foreign direct investment (FDI). The main goals of the chapter are to:

1. Define foreign direct investment and show how it fits into the MNE's activities.

2. Explain why firms undertake FDI, especially in comparison with exporting or other kinds of international business ventures.

3. Show patterns of FDI that illustrate the relative size and importance of different countries, industries, and companies, with particular coverage of FDI in the United States.

4. Show how theories of international business, such as the international product cycle and competitive advantage, focus on FDI and discuss additional theories of FDI, such as Dunning's eclectic view.

5. Show how disinvestment fits into company strategy along with foreign direct investment.

South Africa's Nelson Mandela receives the keys to the city of Los Angeles in a public expression of the developing political, economic, and diplomatic relationships between Mandela's country and the United States.

©J.B. Diederich/Contact Press Images

INTRODUCTION

Foreign direct investment (FDI) has probably been the most heavily studied aspect of the activities of multinational enterprises during the last three decades. The causes and effects of FDI and the subsequent operations of foreign affiliates have been areas of extensive academic and public policy studies, which continue today. Similarly, the strategic fit of FDI and foreign affiliates within a company's global activities has become a central concern of more and more managers as increasing numbers of firms in many countries have looked abroad for markets and supplies. This chapter examines both of these aspects of FDI.

After defining key issues, the chapter focuses on the manager's view: Why should a firm consider FDI, and how does FDI fit into global strategy? Next, it discusses patterns of direct investment since World War II, with emphasis on the countries, industries, and companies most involved. Then it examines foreign direct investment coming into the United States, the largest single host country. Next, it offers explanations for the observed facts and draws some conclusions for company managers and government officials. Finally, the chapter covers *disinvestment,* the sale of an existing affiliate, which is the "final" stage in FDI, though most projects do not reach that stage. Detailed consideration of the operation of a foreign investment project is left for the chapters in Part III of this book.

What Is FDI?

Foreign direct investment (FDI) involves the ownership and control of a company in a foreign country. In exchange for the ownership, the investing company usually transfers some of its financial, managerial, technical, trademark, and other resources to the foreign country. The foreign company may be created as a new venture by the investor, or it may be acquired from an existing owner. Essentially, a company can view this kind of investment just as it views domestic investment, but in this case the project is located in another country. Just as a firm chooses among projects in capital budgeting domestically, it can add on foreign projects, which constitute FDI. Some investors bring in substantial funding with them, others borrow locally to finance their new affiliates, and yet others do both. Some investors transfer many people to work in the new affiliate, while others simply hire locally for staffing needs (or acquire an existing company that already has full staffing). The point is that although no particular type of resource needs to be transferred to carry out FDI, it is usually accompanied by some transfer of money and people.

The main concept behind FDI is the *control* of assets in another country. That is, foreign direct investment is generally undertaken by a firm that seeks to serve a new market for its products or services or seeks to obtain additional supplies for its existing markets. For example, Du Pont Chemical Corporation has used direct investment in 42 countries to market or produce its various products. Texaco, in contrast, has invested in oil exploration projects in dozens of countries, seeking additional petroleum supplies for its markets in the United States and abroad. In each case, the firm wants control over the foreign project to utilize its competitive advantages through the new facility.

Notice the contrast between this kind of investment and **portfolio investment,** in which the firm buys stocks, bonds, and other financial assets to hold in its portfolio. Du Pont holds a large and diversified portfolio of financial assets, including shares of other companies. However, its holdings of controlling interest in its own subsidiaries, and now of Conoco (an oil company), are *direct* investments that entail management of the activities involved. In balance sheet terms, portfolio investment relates mainly to the firm's holdings of marketable securities, while direct investment relates to the purchase and management of plant and equipment (plus other assets and liabilities of the direct investment project). The conceptual distinction between direct and portfolio investment is that the former requires control by the investor, whereas the latter is passive and requires no management effort by the investor.[1]

To reiterate: Foreign direct investment involves a controlling interest in a new or existing business enterprise in a foreign country. Such investment may be *financed* in many ways: The parent firm can transfer funds to the new affiliate and issue ownership shares to itself; it can borrow all of the required funds locally in the new country to pay for ownership; and it can use many combinations of these and other alternatives. The key point here is that *no* international transfer of funds is necessary; FDI requires only transfer of *ownership* to the investor, which may finance the transaction in innumerable ways.

Who Is Concerned about FDI?

Essentially the same business participants and regulators that appeared in Figure 2–1 as actors in the MNE's global dealings are the ones who are concerned about FDI. The MNE itself must view these actors as key parts of the environment in which it operates. Each home and host country *government* views the MNE and its direct investment projects as generators of income, employment, technology, and so on that must be regulated to obtain the best gains for the government (obviously a contradictory goal, since each actor cannot obtain all the benefits of the MNE's activities). *Competitors* in the host country worry about added competition, and competitors in the home country worry about the direct investor's strategic gains from the foreign operations. *Suppliers* and *customers* in each country generally view the direct investment as useful because it brings the MNE closer to host country customers and usually leads to an increased need for supplies. Finally, inside the MNE, *managers* and *workers* may have several perspectives on an FDI project, ranging from the expectation of new and interesting assignments to the anticipation of job losses due to the foreign project's replacement of domestic output.

Toyota Motor's investment in a joint venture with General Motors in Fremont, California, exemplifies these issues.[2] It is a direct investment because Toyota obtained 50 percent ownership and assumed approximately 50 percent managerial responsibility for the project. The US government views the foreign investment as *desirable* because it has created jobs in California but also as *questionable* because it has combined two of the largest auto manufacturers worldwide (which raises antitrust concerns). The Japanese government may view the investment as a necessary step to reduce US protectionist pressures against Japanese exports, but the investment could lead to fewer Toyota exports from Japan and to fewer jobs for Japanese workers, a negative result from Japan's viewpoint. Each company involved views the project as an opportunity to learn from its counterpart: GM is trying to transfer Japanese labor relations and productivity skills to its own people, and Toyota is learning much more about the US auto market and GM's operations. There may be fewer jobs for Toyota workers in Japan if the Fremont plant replaces them—or more jobs if more parts, components, and other Toyota products are sent to the United States as a result of the project. Finally, Toyota's suppliers in Japan may have to follow Toyota to the United States to maintain their sales, and Toyota's customers in the United States may experience a shorter delay before the delivery of new cars (though perhaps a higher price). Unfortunately, there is no simple way to evaluate beforehand all the implications of such a project.

As companies continue to seek better strategies for their businesses in different countries, and as governments change their views on foreign direct investment (through elections and other changes of power), the forces shaping FDI decisions will shift over time. Since companies are the central decision makers in FDI, their views of the investment process are considered first.[3]

THE STRATEGY OF FOREIGN DIRECT INVESTMENT

Why does a firm undertake foreign direct investment? A wealth of studies done during the 1960s and 1970s disclosed that the most important reason for entering a foreign market was to sell products that the firm already sold successfully in its home country.[4]* A reason that has grown in importance as international transportation costs have fallen substantially is to lower production costs by producing in a low-cost country for sales in other countries (often called *offshore assembly* or *foreign sourcing*). During the 1980s and 1990s the use of FDI to gain access to new technology has become a common phenomenon as well. These and other strategic concerns that may be bases for undertaking FDI appear in Table 4–1.

Notice that the reasons are grouped into supply-side and demand-side categories. While a company may focus on a particular reason as the basis for a given FDI decision, both kinds of factors should be considered when making the decision. Beginning with the supply side, we discuss each reason next.

The Supply Side

Lower Production Costs   On the basis of national comparative advantage, a company may discover that its product can be produced at lower cost in the foreign country than at home because of lower wages, cheaper real estate, or other differences in cost conditions. One strategy is to import the product from the country in which it can be produced more cheaply. Another strategy is to establish operations in the lower-cost country. Such a foreign direct investment may be used to produce and sell in the local, host country market or to export to the home country and elsewhere.

Lower Delivery Costs   The appropriate cost to use in choosing among production locations is **delivered cost**; thus, the cost of transporting products to the market should be considered along with the production cost. If the distance is long or tariffs are high between the home and host countries, local production in the host country may minimize the delivered cost, even if the production costs of the home and host countries are equal or somewhat favorable to the home country. Notice that delivery costs are defined to include *both* the cost of transportation and regulatory costs such as tariffs.

Acquisition of a Raw Material   If Japanese manufacturers want to obtain a secure source of oil for their plants, they must look offshore to suppliers, since no oil has been found domestically. Rather than contract with other companies for the purchase of oil, the Japanese firms may decide to invest in oil production abroad

---

*Since then, other motivations for FDI have been identified.

TABLE 4–1

Reasons for Foreign Direct Investment

Supply Side
1. To lower production costs
2. To lower delivery costs (costs of transportation, insurance, tariffs, etc.)
3. To acquire a necessary raw material
4. To do offshore assembly
5. To establish a "portfolio" of production sources (reducing risk)
6. To obtain technology and skills

Demand Side

1. To explore new markets
2. Because an export market was closed by a prohibitive tariff or quota
3. To establish a local presence with service and product availability
4. To meet "buy national" rules or preferences in the host country
5. To gain visibility as a "local" firm, employing local people, paying local taxes, etc.
6. To respond to rivals' threats.
7. To serve a "portfolio" of markets (reducing risk)

through direct investment. Similarly, US aluminum companies have invested in Jamaica and Brazil to mine bauxite for their manufacturing in the United States. Generally, a firm may look at foreign countries not only as targets for the sale of its products but also as potential sources of needed raw materials.

Offshore Assembly or Foreign Sourcing   This category is really a subcategory of the first one, focusing on production for sales outside the host country. Like FDI used to obtain raw materials, FDI used to do **offshore assembly** helps gain access to a factor of production, namely labor, that is cheaper or more productive than the home country supply. Many US electronics manufacturers utilize offshore assembly in Taiwan, Singapore, or Hong Kong to assemble their radios, TVs, stereos, calculators, and so on. They produce components in the United States, ship them to the Far East for assembly into final products, and then reexport the products to the United States for sale. Alternatively, a firm may choose to carry out its entire production process in the foreign country, using that site as a source from which to sell to the home country (and elsewhere)—hence the second category, **foreign sourcing.**

Portfolio of Production Sources   Firms that produce any kind of product or service may discover that it is advantageous to have multiple sources of supply. Having several sources of inputs lessens the danger of problems with any one supplier company or type of material. To reduce the risk of bottlenecks in production or distribution caused by problems that arise in any one country (e.g., strikes, civil unrest, poor quality), it also makes sense to have suppliers in different countries.

Access to Technology and Skills   When proprietary technology and/or management skills are key competitive advantages in an industry, firms may choose to establish operations in markets where those skills are readily available. Thus, direct investment can be expected to flow to locations where high-tech firms are concentrated and managerial skills are superior. This investment may be in the form of new subsidiaries set up by the foreign investors or joint ventures that tie foreign firms to local firms.

The Demand Side

New Markets   The most common reason for undertaking FDI is to use local production to establish new national markets for a product. The firm may choose among FDI, export from the home country, or some other strategy of serving the foreign market (e.g., licensing, franchising, a turnkey venture). If the foreign market appears large enough and local production seems feasible, FDI can be used to enter the market. Even if the firm already sells one product through exports in the host country, it may use direct investment and local production to sell additional products there.

Restriction of Exports   If a national market is closed by a prohibitive tariff or a quota, direct investment may provide an acceptable alternative. Because we are talking about a limitation on the *quantity* that can be sold in the foreign market, this is a demand-side constraint, not a price or cost constraint. Even if production in and export from the home country are less costly, a quota or total embargo will limit or eliminate sales through exports. In such situations, foreign direct investment and local production can fill the demand of the foreign market. This clearly was a major factor in attracting Japanese auto firms to set up production in the United States.

Local Presence   Often a local production presence will enable a firm to sell greater quantities of its products, because customers are confident that the firm is accessible for service and additional product supply. A firm that sells only through imports may not provide as good after-sale service or as great availability of additional products. Visibility as a local producer may convince buyers that the firm is seriously committed to the host country market and can be counted on to deliver contracted orders. Also, local production permits the firm to adapt products more closely to local demand conditions, a kind of flexibility that does not exist for firms that simply export.

"Buy National" Rules   Under certain conditions, most countries, including the United States, restrict purchases by government agencies to local, home country suppliers. The United States requires government agencies to buy from US suppliers if their product quality is acceptable and their prices are competitive with those of foreign bidders for the same contract.[5] Many other countries simply close contracts to foreign bidders, regardless of quality or availability. To avoid such restrictions, a firm may choose to establish a local production presence and thus become a local supplier in the eyes of government buyers.

A constraint similar to the "buy national" rules of governments may exist when local customers maintain a preference for buying from local suppliers, again effectively shutting out nonlocal producers from the market. (In the 1960s and early 1970s, many US-based multinationals changed their subsidiaries' names in Latin American countries to local-sounding names to avoid the negative connotation of being North American.) Japanese consumers have long demonstrated this preference; Lee Iacocca has tried to stir up similar nationalism in the United States.

Good Corporate Citizen   Another reason for establishing local manufacture or local provision of services is to gain respectability as a good corporate citizen in the host country by employing local people, paying local taxes, and otherwise participating in the host society. Such respectability may lead to more favorable perception by local buyers and even to more favorable treatment by the host government.[6] For this reason, sales may be higher through FDI and local production than through exports from the home country. The decisions by Toyota, Nissan, and other Japanese automobile manufacturers to set up plants in the United States in the late 1970s and early 1980s were substantially an effort to present themselves as good corporate citizens in this country (with positive effects, hopefully, on their car sales) and to avoid having penalizing quotas and other potential barriers placed on their exports from Japan.

Response to Rivals' Threats   If a rival firm enters some national market with local production, a firm may respond by similarly entering that market, to avoid being shut out through a tariff or other protection by the host government. A firm would also enter that market to avoid giving its rival an advantage from experience in producing locally. By entering the host market in this way, the firm precludes its rival from building a strong, monopolistic position there from which the rival could expand into other markets.

Each of these bases for deciding to undertake foreign direct investment may be used to justify such a decision, but it should not be the manager's sole justification; in every case, a full analysis is needed to compare direct investment with alternatives for accomplishing the same purpose. (The conditions that justify FDI relative to such alternatives as exporting or licensing are discussed in Chapter 3.) Before we return to the problem of deciding when to invest, we present some empirical evidence on FDI in the next section.

PATTERNS OF FOREIGN DIRECT INVESTMENT

Direct Investment by Country

The vast majority of foreign direct investment that has occurred historically has been made in the period since World War II. This is the result of the growth in national markets, coupled with the continued willingness of developed country governments to permit foreign ownership of local companies. In addition, such investment (and exports) has been facilitated by the tremendous decline in international transportation costs and improvement in transportation availability that have occurred in the postwar period.

Table 4–2 shows the distribution of worldwide FDI by country of origin, that is, based on the country from which multinational enterprises undertook foreign direct investment projects. Notice that the United States accounted for about half of the total investment over the whole period, though the US share declined fairly steadily, to less than 40 percent by 1983. Also notice that, after rebuilding their economies from war damage, both German and Japanese firms showed the most rapid growth in FDI during the postwar period. In fact, both of the traditional powers of the early 20th century, the United States and the United Kingdom, have seen a decline in their shares of global FDI, though firms from both countries continue to invest abroad and their FDI shares still lead those of other countries. (The recent trend has simply been for Japanese and German firms to invest abroad at a greater rate of growth.) FDI undertaken by all less developed countries combined accounted for less than 10 percent of the total reported in Table 4–2.

So far, we have examined only the source countries for FDI. Now consider the target or host countries. (An implicit point of the preceding paragraphs is that virtually all worldwide FDI comes from developed market economies. Very little comes from the less developed countries or the formerly communist countries.)

TABLE 4–2   Stock of FDI Abroad by Firms from Developed Market Countries (billions of US dollars)

Country of Origin	1967	1971	1975	1981	1985	1990	1991
United States	56.6	82.8	124.1	226.4	250.7	426.5	454.1
United Kingdom	17.5	23.7	30.4	65.5	104.7	244.8	232.3
Germany, Federal Republic	3.0	7.3	16.0	45.3	60.0	151.6	170.7
Japan	1.5	4.4	15.9	37.1	83.6	202.4	231.8
Switzerland	5.0	9.5	17.6	36.6	45.3	65.7	75.4
Netherlands	11.0	13.8	19.0	32.2	43.8	107.7	n.a.
France	6.0	7.3	11.1	24.6	21.6	110.1	n.a.
Canada	3.7	6.5	10.4	25.6	36.5	73.1	80.1
Sweden	1.7	2.4	4.4	n.a.	9.0	220.8	n.a.
Belgium–Luxembourg	2.0	2.4	3.6	n.a.	4.3	n.a.	n.a.
Italy	2.1	3.0	3.3	n.a.	12.4	57.1	65.0
Total above	110.1	163.1	255.8	493.3	671.9	1,659.8	1,309.4
All other[†]	4.0	5.0	7.2	52.3	41.6	59.8[‡]	66.9[‡]
Grand total	114.1	168.1	263.0	545.6	713.5	1,719.6	1,376.3

[†]Includes Austria, Denmark, Norway, Finland, Portugal, Spain, Australia, New Zealand, and South Africa.
[‡]All the above included except South Africa.
Source: *International Direct Investment Statistics Yearbook* (Paris: OECD, 1993).

Again, most of the direct investment flows occur between developed countries, and mostly toward Europe, though the United States has been the largest single target country for FDI in the whole period, and in the 1980s and early 1990s the balance of the flow shifted toward the United States. Table 4–3 shows these flows from 1967 to 1992.

Direct Investment by Company

Since ultimately we are concerned about the firms that engage in FDI, let us turn finally to a view of the companies most heavily involved in this activity. Studies carried out during the past two decades have regularly found that the most important direct investors are large, technology-intensive firms from the main industrial countries.[7]

The largest direct investors (in terms of dollar value) tend to be firms that carry out extractive ventures overseas (for example, oil exploration, copper and bauxite mining) and producers of capital-intensive goods (such as automobiles and chemicals). Also, the largest direct investors tend to be large exporters as well. They export machinery, parts, and components to their foreign facilities, as well as filling out product lines with domestically produced and exported products.

FOREIGN DIRECT INVESTMENT IN THE UNITED STATES

The Pattern by Industry

Looking specifically at foreign direct investment coming into the United States, we see a pattern similar to that in the rest of the industrial countries. That is, the dominant industries are petroleum, manufacturing, and services (mainly trade, real estate, banking, and insurance). The growth has been more rapid in services than in the other major sectors. These patterns can be seen in Figure 4–1, page 94, which traces FDI into the United States since the early 1970s. In the 1980s, and early 1990s not only had foreign direct investment grown faster than US FDI going abroad, but it had also grown faster than the US economy overall. That is, incoming FDI has provided a substantial boost to US national income (and also forced US firms to compete even harder in their own domestic market).

TABLE 4-3   Flows* of FDI into and out of Developed Countries, 1967-1992 (millions of US dollars)

Country and Country Group	1967-1972	1973-1978	1979-1984	1985-1988	1989-1992
Outflows of Domestic Capital (annual average)					
United States	6,412	11,641	7,510	22,160	31,402
Canada	269	967	3,113	3,852	5,515
Western Europe†	4,792	10,495	12,974	46,433	120,570
Austria	18	49	117	—	1,452
Belgium-Luxembourg	100	308	309	1,667	7,604
Denmark	42	68	98	—	1,909
Finland	35	36	205	785	2,115
France	376	1,051	2,342	6,137	27,293
Germany	836	2,137	3,023	7,070	21,255
Italy	251	262	1,170	2,489	5,780
Netherlands	463	877	543	4,095	13,707
Norway	12	123	253	889	1,254
Spain	25	81	251	516	2,324
Sweden	175	452	659	2,568	8,014
Switzerland‡	1,145	3,243	—	3,040	6,415
United Kingdom	1,314	3,438	5,422	17,177	21,098
Japan	331	1,809	3,587	14,760	35,048
Southern Hemisphere§	118	303	1,091	3,206	2,173
Australia	95	193	751	3,095	1,492
Total†	11,923	25,209	29,774	90,411	316,420
Inflows of Foreign Capital (annual average)					
United States	925	4,309	14,903	31,815	34,838
Canada	712	704	231	1,407	6,103
Western Europe†	4,419	8,241	9,690	25,309	89,933
Austria	62	114	212	—	476
Belgium-Luxembourg	319	959	1,032	1,817	8,891
Denmark	101	110	73	—	1,198
Finland	21	35	19	141	311
France	444	1,411	2,006	3,886	15,122
Germany	927	1,741	884	1,213	8,475
Italy	657	555	771	2,281	3,527
Netherlands	454	509	26	2,542	7,945
Norway	78	365	246	435	755
Spain	206	456	1,426	3,402	10,208
Sweden	103	59	131	473	2,385
Switzerland‡	252	517	—	1,284	3,000
United Kingdom	798	1,670	2,906	7,835	24,368
Japan	111	89	138	348	11,975
Southern Hemisphere§	1,052	1,112	1,683	2,362	7,063
Australia	813	860	1,589	2,677	6,097
Total†	7,218	14,455	26,694	61,241	242,670

*Includes reinvested earnings.
†Including countries not listed separately.
‡Derived from the year-to-year changes of estimated stock of direct investment assets and liabilities, respectively (estimates of the Union Bank of Switzerland).
§Includes Australia, New Zealand, and South Africa.
Source: International Monetary Fund, *Balance of Payments Yearbook* (Washington, DC: IMF, 1993).

The Pattern by Country of Origin

The main countries whose firms are undertaking this flow of FDI into the United States are, not surprisingly, the same countries that follow the United States in overall FDI worldwide: Great Britain, Japan, the Netherlands, Canada, Germany, Switzerland, and other European countries. Table 4-4 shows a disaggregation of the recent stock of FDI according to both industry and country of origin.

FIGURE 4–1

Foreign Direct Investment
into the United States

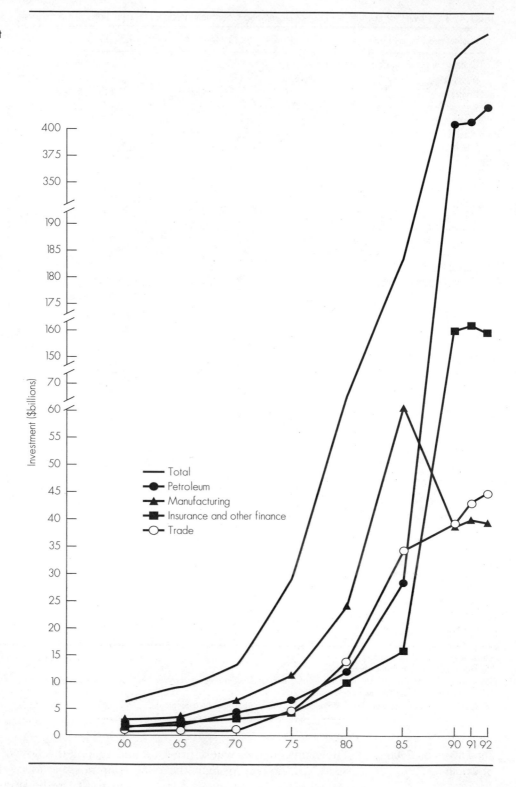

TABLE 4–4 Foregin Direct Investment Position in the United States by Industry and Country, 1991 (millions of US dollars)

Industry	UK	Japan	Netherlands	Canada	Germany	Switzerland	France
Petroleum	14,355	148	12,398	1,413	219	129	2,888
Manufacturing	42,259	18,545	18,267	16,066	15,466	10,927	15,053
Foods	8,699	892	2,368	n.a.	−69	2,445	1,362
Chemicals	−1	3,415	7,463	n.a.	8,543	3,390	4,481
Machinery	3,241	5,699	4,614	1,969	3,304	3,117	2,723
Wholesale/retail trade	7,517	30,564	7,089	-52	8,268	843	1,476
Banking	1,986	7,057	1,887	2,038	842	937	1,291
Real estate	3,824	15,259	4,537	10,530	1,156	133	119
Total	81,880	61,994	58,623	31,964	37,729	21,921	29,393

Source: US Department of Commerce, *Survey of Current Business*, July 1993.

That the British lead in overall FDI in the US market is not surprising, given Britain's number two position in worldwide FDI and its historical, political, cultural, and language ties to this country. Japanese FDI surged in the late 1980s to the second largest group, largely on the impressive strength of Japanese companies in global competition, particularly in the automobile industry. Dutch direct investment, especially in petroleum (Royal Dutch/Shell) and manufacturing (Philips and Unilever) surprisingly ranks third overall. Canada, with its proximity to this market, ranks among the leading source countries in virtually every category. While source country rankings give some idea of the nature of FDI in the United States, the real driving force behind successful entry into the US market is the companies that undertake that investment.[8] We focus on these firms next.

The Major Foreign Investors in the United States

The firms that have taken the leading FDI positions in the US economy tend to follow the largest firms in international business throughout the world. Table 4–5 lists the 25 largest foreign direct investors in the United States in 1992, along with some of their characteristics. Note that these firms compete in industries where US competitors are also strong. A fundamental reason for their ability to survive in the US marketplace is simply that demand is large enough to absorb multiple competitors. That is, the foreign firms do not have to outcompete American firms to survive. This is particularly true in the petroleum sector, where 4 of the 25 compete. The competitive advantages that the foreign firms do possess appear to stem largely from proprietary technology, goodwill based on high quality and performance, and lower costs—advantages very similar to those of successful US firms.

Current Trends

FDI in the United States grew tremendously during the 1980s and early 1990s. This phenomenon may be attributed to a variety of causes, including the recovery of the United States from the early-1980s recession before other industrial nations, the devaluation of the dollar relative to other widely traded currencies in the late 1980s and early 1990s, and the faster growth of non-US MNEs in the 1970s and 1980s as they caught up with US firms in size and geographic scope. In the late 1980s, the threat of increased protectionism in the United States encouraged many Japanese firms (such as the auto manufacturers) to set up operations in this country to avoid the possibility of harm due to greater import restrictions.

Because of the very large existing base of US FDI overseas, the *growth rate* of FDI in the United States is likely to exceed that of outgoing FDI throughout the

TABLE 4–5   The 25 Largest Foreign Investors in the United States, 1992

1992 Rank	Foreign Investor	Country	US Investment	% Owned	Industry	Revenue ($ mil)
1	Seagram Co. Ltd.*	Canada	EI du Pont de Nemours* JE Seagram	24 100	Chemicals, energy Beverages	37,208 3,799 41,007
2	Royal Dutch/Shell Group*	Netherlands/UK	Shell Oil	100	Energy, chemicals	21,160
3	British Petroleum Plc*	UK	BP America Standard Oil	100 100	Energy Energy	17,810
4	Grand Metropolitan Plc*	UK	Burger King Pillsbury Heublein Pearle Haagen-Dazs	100 100 100 100 100	Fast food Food processing Wines and spirits Eye care retailing Ice cream	6,350 3,447 1,633 635 590 12,655
5	Tengelmann Group	Germany	Great A&P Tea*	53	Supermarkets	10,499
6	Nestlé SA*	Switzerland	Nestle USA Alcon Laboratories	100 100	Food processing Pharmaceuticals	8,395
	L'Oréal	France	Cosmair	>50	Cosmetics	1,200 9,595
7	B.A.T Industries Plc*	UK	Brown & Williamson Tobacco Farmers Group	100 100	Tobacco Insurance	3,258 1,577
	Imasco Ltd.	Canada	Hardee's Food Systems	100	Fast food	4,757 9,592
8	Sony Corp.*	Japan	Sony Music Entertainment Sony Picute Entertainment Sony Electronics	100 100 100	Music entertainment Movies Consumer electronics	9,418
9	Unilever NV* Unilever Plc*	Netherlands UK	Unilever United States	100	Food processing, personal products	9,217
10	Petroleos de Venezuela, SA	Venezuela	Citgo Petroleum	100	Refining, marketing	9,173
11	Hanson Plc*	UK	Hanson Industries Smith Corona* Ground Round Restaurants* Marine Harvest Int'l*	100 48 33 44	Multicompany Office supplies Restaurant chain Food processing	8,026 372 226 90 8,714

*Publicly traded in the United States in shares or ADRs. Note: Some foreign investors on the list own US companies indirectly through the companies in italics.

E: Estimate.

Source: *Forbes*, July 10, 1993, pp 174–75.

1990s. Whether US or non-US firms will be more successful in foreign markets is quite another question, and one that US MNE managers will help resolve in the future. The perhaps even more important question—whether US firms will be able to survive competition *in the United States* from their foreign rivals—also remains to be answered. The grounds on which the competition will take place will almost certainly be the development of sustainable competitive advantages by the successful firms.

EXPLANATIONS OF THE FOREIGN DIRECT INVESTMENT PROCESS

How can the flows of FDI and the shifts in the company and country composition of FDI be explained? No single theory covers all the characteristics of the foreign direct investment process. Several views have been presented, however, that offer

TABLE 4–5   (concluded)

1992 Rank	Foreign Investor	Country	US Investment	% Owned	Industry	Revenue ($ mil)
12	Toyota Motor Corp.*	Japan	Toyota Motor Mfg.	100	Automotive	3,800E
			New Unitied Motor Mfg.	50	Automotive	2,600E
	*Nippondenso Co. Ltd.**	Japan	Nippondenso America	100	Auto parts	1,600
						8,000
13	Delhaize "Le Lion" SA	Belgium	Food Lion*	25	Supermarkets	7,196
14	Philips Electronics NV*	Netherlands	North American Philips	100	Electronics	6,138
			Whittle Communications LP	25	Publishing	213
	*PolyGram NV**	Netherlands	PolyGram Records	100	Music	816
						7,167
15	Hoechst AG*	Germany	Hoechst Celanese	100	Chemicals	7,044
16	Bayer AG*	Germany	Miles	100	Chemicals, health care	6,459
17	Ito-Yokado* Seven-Eleven Japan*	Japan Japan	Southland	64	Convenience stores	6,439
18	Ahold NV*	Netherlands	First National Supermarkets	100	Supermarkets	2,107
			BI-LO	100	Supermarkets	1,754
			Tops Markets	100	Supermarkets	1,477
			Giant Food Stores	100	Supermarkets	1,068
						6,406
19	Rhone-Poulenc SA*	France	Rhone-Poulenc Rorer*	68	Pharmaceuticals	4,096
			Rhone-Poulenc	100	Chemicals	2,300
						6,396
20	AXA	France	Equitable Cos*	49	Insurance	6,282
21	Siemens AG*	Germany	Siemens Corporation	100	Electronics	4,900
			Osram/Sylvania	100	Lighting	1,300
						6,200
22	Matsushita Electric Industrial*	Japan	MCA	100	Entertainment	4,000E
			Matsushita Elec Corp (Am)	100	Electronics	2,140
						6,140
23	Honda Motor Company Ltd.*	Japan	Honda of America Mfg	100	Automotive	6,100E
24	Frantz Haniel & Cie	Germany	Scrivner	100	Food distribution	6,000
			Gateway Foods	100	Food distribution	
25	Pechiney SA *Pechiney International*	France France	Pechiney Metals	100	Aluminum	378
			American National Can	100	Pachaging	4,537
			Howmet	100	Gas turbines	854
			Other companies	100	Metals distribution	73
						5,842

partial explanations of what is observed. The theory of the international product cycle, discussed in Chapter 3, clarifies several reasons for FDI. The theory of competitive advantage, presented in Chapter 2, sheds some light on company characteristics that often lead to FDI. The comparative cost view, presented in Chapter 3, adds some useful points regarding the choice of FDI versus other market-serving alternatives. Dunning's "eclectic view" (presented shortly) focuses on three types of variables that play important parts in explaining FDI. Finally, the concept of **internalization** can be used to tie together several of the other strands of thinking about FDI. This section reviews each of these theories as it relates to foreign direct investment.

International Product Cycle

The theory of the international product cycle hypothesizes that foreign direct investment (*or* host country production by local firms) will take place in countries that originally import a new product from the country where it is developed. That is, once a product has been introduced successfully into one country, subsequent export and foreign manufacture generally follow. If the innovating company chooses to produce overseas, its establishment of a foreign affiliate is FDI. By the time the product arrives at the standardized stage, cost considerations are foremost and low-cost production locations are sought, perhaps in low-wage areas of developed countries or in less developed countries. The international product cycle was discussed in some detail in Chapter 3; here an example may offer additional insights.

Radio Corporation of America (RCA), originally a division of General Electric Company, began producing television sets in the late 1920s. Television had been invented and reinvented in various forms during the previous 30 years by scientists in several countries, but RCA was one of two firms to introduce the product into the market successfully, in the early 1940s. (Du Mont Laboratories was the other firm; it began marketing televisions in 1939, along with RCA.) Initially, TV sets and programming were sold primarily in the United States, though sales occurred in Great Britain as well. The market for television remained very small until after World War II.

Domestic competition in television manufacture arose during the late 1940s, from General Electric itself (which had sold RCA) and from American Telephone & Telegraph. The market for televisions began to grow rapidly, with about 140,000 sets per month sold by 1948. RCA began exporting into the Canadian and European markets in the late 1940s.

Such US competitors as Westinghouse and Admiral entered the market during the 1950s. The Japanese producers Sony and Panasonic introduced competing products in the early 1960s, and by about 1965 television was in the maturing product stage. At that point (in 1964), RCA decided to use direct investment in Canada to serve that market with locally manufactured picture tubes. At about the same time, it established a manufacturing plant in England to serve the European market.

Ultimately, cost conditions became the overriding factor in TV competition, and RCA followed several firms into offshore assembly, choosing Taiwan (in 1970) and Ciudad Juárez in Mexico (in 1969) as its bases. Now the firm produces parts and components in more than a dozen countries, including the offshore assembly sites, and sells them in more than 50 countries. RCA has followed the international product cycle through all three stages, producing first in the United States, then in Canada and Western Europe, and now also in less developed countries.[9]

In an interesting turn of events, General Electric Company repurchased RCA in 1986, returning the firm to its original corporate parent. This merger of the two electronics giants has not altered RCA's direct investment strategy from the path just discussed.

Competitive Advantage

The theory of competitive advantage, presented in Chapter 2, explains foreign direct investment as one of the many ways a firm may capitalize on its proprietary assets. RCA was able to use FDI to take advantage of its new technology. Similarly, Texas Instruments and other calculator manufacturers have used FDI to assemble their products in low-cost countries. Of course, not all FDI is based on firms' taking advantage of proprietary technology. Relatively standardized products such as processed foods are produced and sold by foreign direct investors in many countries. Oil companies invest abroad not only to explore for oil but also to operate gas stations and produce and sell nonproprietary petrochemicals. Producers of farm machinery sell their tractors and other machines through exports to their own sales offices in many countries, and they also assemble many kinds of equipment abroad in direct investment projects.

Walt Disney Company provides a noteworthy example of the use of FDI to benefit from the firm's competitive advantages. After pursuing an essentially domestic strategy for many years, Disney opened a Disneyland theme park in Japan in 1984. The company was trying to profit from its major competitive strengths: the very widely accepted Disney characters, the firm's know-how based on experience in operating theme parks in California and Florida, and the uniqueness of its product.

At that time, Disney negotiated an agreement with local investors in which Disney receives royalties and fees from the park but does not own it. The overwhelming success of that venture—and Disney's failure to benefit from any ownership stake in it—convinced Disney's top managers that future ventures should be pursued with some equity interest.

Beginning at about the time of the opening of Tokyo Disneyland, the firm began negotiating to build a EuroDisneyland. This project was very carefully considered, beginning with 200 possible sites in Europe and ending with a choice between Barcelona (with better weather) and Paris (with a more central location in Europe). Disney ultimately invested in Paris and took a 49 percent share in the project, with the remaining shares sold to investors in Europe.[10] Thus, Disney chose to use direct investment to benefit from its competitive advantages, after discovering that a contracting agreement (in Japan) was suboptimal.

Comparative Cost

The comparative cost view of FDI follows on the theory of comparative advantage, discussed in Chapter 3. In this case, we look at an individual firm's choice of production locations based on *delivered* cost to its relevant markets. Just as the theory of comparative advantage shows the appropriate *country* to produce and export a given product based on production costs, the extension to FDI focuses on a *company's* use of this information. If it were really less costly to produce bananas in Honduras and appliances in the United States, United Fruit Corporation should look at Honduras as a site for FDI to produce bananas, which can then be exported to the US market. (Leave the appliances to another company!) Indeed, this is exactly what United Fruit (whose brand name for bananas is Chiquita) has done—not only in Honduras but also in El Salvador, Costa Rica, Ecuador, and other countries where banana production is very inexpensive due to favorable climatic conditions and inexpensive labor.

In the final analysis, what counts is *delivered* cost. So United Fruit or any other foreign investor must consider not only the production costs involved in the foreign country but also the transportation costs and tariffs or other restrictions that may apply to the product. This differs from traditional comparative advantage theory, which focuses only on *production* costs. Even if bananas could be produced more cheaply in Honduras than in Costa Rica and exported to Costa Rica, firms probably could not take advantage of this condition, because the government of Costa Rica places tariffs and other restrictions on imports. Similar problems also often arise from high transportation costs: Cement can be produced more cheaply in Colombia than in Venezuela, but the cost of delivering it to the Venezuelan market from a Colombian city such as Bogotá or Barranquilla is much higher than the production cost difference. So each country produces cement for domestic consumption and does not export it. The appropriate way for a company to take advantage of this situation would be to invest directly in each country to produce cement for the local market.

Dunning's Eclectic View

John Dunning (1977) has proposed a multifaceted "theory" of FDI that includes emphases on country-specific variables such as production costs and regulatory constraints, company-specific (ownership) variables such as proprietary skills and scale economies, and internalization variables related to the firm's choice to utilize its proprietary capabilities through its own affiliates or through dealings with other firms. Each of these three kinds of variables has been the focus of theories of international trade and investment. Dunning's view is "eclectic" in that it packages a number of competitive advantages together and uses the concept of internalization to provide decision-making rules.

Dunning's view is quite useful in forcing the decision maker to consider not only cost factors or demand forecasts but also other key issues. Thus, the size of the market may well justify entering it, but *location* factors may call for exports rather than FDI. Similarly, local production costs may favor direct investment, but if the company's resources (its *ownership* advantages) are too limited, FDI may be unfeasible and licensing a local firm (that is, not internalizing) may offer a viable alternative. By combining three distinct perspectives, Dunning's view enables the decision maker to avoid the trap of a narrow-minded focus on only a part of the full picture.

To reiterate, Dunning's **eclectic view** states that the FDI decision should be made on the grounds of these three factors:

1. *Ownership advantages:* the company's competitive advantages, such as proprietary technology, management skills, goodwill, and economies of scale.
2. *Location advantages:* the relevant cost, risk, and regulatory conditions in the countries under consideration. These include national production costs, tariffs, taxes, international transportation costs, and political risks.
3. *Internalization advantages:* the benefits that the firm would realize by itself operating in the host country versus the benefits of operating through a local distributor, licensee, or other contractee.[11] (See the next section.)

Internalization

Chapter 2 presented the idea that vertical or horizontal integration of a firm across national boundaries is a characteristic of the MNE. In fact, that integration is itself foreign direct investment: The firm that buys a metal mine or an oil well abroad is undertaking FDI, just as the firm that sets up a restaurant abroad that is similar to its domestic restaurants is undertaking FDI.

Internalization is a very useful concept because it focuses on the decision to internalize or not to internalize across national borders—that is, the decision to use or not to use FDI. The optimal decision should be based on the product's stage in the product cycle, the competitive advantages of the firm, and the costs of this alternative relative to others that are available. That is, internalization can be used as a broad label to encompass each of the more precisely focused views discussed above. The foreign investment decision then can be stated as follows: The firm should internalize foreign market and supply opportunities up to the point where the additional costs of internalizing outweigh the additional benefits of doing so.

Other Explanations for Foreign Direct Investment

A number of additional explanations for FDI have come from many different social science disciplines. Two of the more important ones are noted here.

Some political scientists writing about the global spread of capitalism have viewed the process of FDI as a natural tendency of capitalist firms, which need to find new markets for their products once existing markets have been saturated. The "exploitation" of foreign markets, then, enmeshes these markets in the international capitalist system.[12] This view of FDI emphasizes its negative aspects, namely control of part of the local economy by foreign owners and transfers of funds to the parent companies. The view is important because it is held by policymakers in some countries and because it always provides a rationale for penalizing foreign firms when a scapegoat is needed for economic or political problems.

Another view, presented by Jean Boddewyn (1983), looks at FDI in three steps: necessary conditions, motivations, and precipitating factors. This view regards virtually all of the reasons for FDI discussed above as *conditions* that may make FDI desirable. Boddewyn points out that all of these conditions are based on the premise or *motivation* that the firm is managed to maximize profits. Each condition offers a way for the firm to pursue its central goal of profit maximization—for example, reducing costs, enlarging market share, or creating new products. Finally, there must be some *precipitating factor* that induces the firm to take advantage of the conditions to seek its central goal. This last point is quite important. Firms have infinite possible strategies at their disposal, but for FDI to result, a clear definition of goals and acceptable alternatives and some precipitating event (such as a period of negative earnings or a change in leadership) are required.

In sum, each view of FDI presented above offers insights into the managerial and regulatory issues related to such investment. The company manager can benefit from utilizing the various views in considering the firm's choices for doing business in foreign countries, whether it be market-serving or supply-seeking business. The government policymaker can better understand the motivations of company managers by learning the key factors that affect company investment decisions.

DISINVESTMENT

This chapter has looked mainly at the process of entry into foreign direct investment, without considering in any detail the operation of the foreign affiliate once it has been established.* The termination of a foreign affiliate—that is, **disinvestment** (or divestment)—can be seen as almost a mirror image of the entry decision. Using Dunning's three-factor view of FDI, disinvestment can be rationalized when any of the conditions for FDI disappears. If a firm ceases to possess a competitive (or ownership) advantage relative to other firms in the host

---

*Operation of the foreign affiliate is the subject of much of Part III of this book.

country, the profitability of operating there may disappear. Or if political or economic changes in the host country make the local project no longer viable, the reason for being there (i.e., locational advantage) may disappear. Finally, the local affiliate may be unjustified if the firm no longer finds it useful to internalize the activity but may sell or rent it to another firm. In short, disinvestment may be justified once the conditions that originally justified FDI cease to exist.

In Boddewyn's terms, once changes in conditions make FDI unattractive relative to other alternatives and profitability would be better served by not operating the affiliate, all it takes is some precipitating factor to make the disinvestment decision. This precipitating factor may be the assignment of a new manager to supervise the company division in which the project is based; if the project shows poor results in its sales, profits, or costs, the new manager may look to disinvestment as a method to eliminate the problem. Another factor that may stimulate the firm to consider disinvesting is the threat of host government constraints ranging from expropriation, to higher taxes, to limits on financial transfers. In any of these cases, the decision to disinvest is usually made at the home office of the firm by a senior decision maker. This is in contrast to the FDI decision, which is often proposed by a middle-level manager or division and simply approved by the home office.[13]

The firm can utilize disinvestment strategically in the context of the international product cycle. A product in the innovation stage is generally produced in one country and sold domestically and through exports. As the product enters the maturing stage, market and cost conditions may justify FDI in host countries for local sales. As the product enters the standardized stage, cost conditions may justify closing high-cost production sites in favor of sites located in low-cost regions or countries. So, especially in the standardized-product stage, disinvestment may be part of a planned, strategic process of global production and sales in the MNE.

For example, Monsanto Corporation, a multinational chemical company, operated synthetic fiber plants in several Western European countries for many years. During the early 1970s, these operations became unprofitable due to price competition from firms that faced lower costs of production. After several years of losses, Monsanto decided to sell all of its synthetic fiber business in Europe, divesting the whole set of subsidiaries.[14] Rather than compete in the standardized stage of the product cycle for these products, Monsanto decided to place its resources into other products in earlier stages of the cycle.

CONCLUSIONS

FDI is a complex form of international business, necessarily involving the transfer of a company's ownership to foreign owners and typically involving transfers of funds, people, products, and other items. During the post–World War II period, the largest sector in which FDI has taken place has been manufacturing, though the single industry with the most foreign investment has been petroleum. The single largest source and target country for FDI is the United States, while German and Japanese FDI has been growing at the fastest rate during the past decade.

Firms undertake FDI to serve new markets, to obtain needed inputs for their domestic businesses, and generally for many of the same reasons that they undertake domestic capital investment. The reasons for going overseas also include international diversification, which allows firms to reduce the variability of their earnings. Foreign disinvestment may be a final step in a firm's strategy in a particular country, though it is by no means the logical end of FDI.

Foreign direct investment is *the* activity that makes a company multinational. However, it should be viewed as only one among several alternatives for serving host country markets (or for obtaining necessary factors of production). How can the manager decide when to utilize this alternative? Based on the above criteria, the manager needs to consider

1. Incremental cash flows from the project, as with any other capital investment
2. The costs of undertaking this alternative relative to the costs of other alternatives available to the firm, such as exports or some other contractual form
3. The strategic fit of the project within the firm's global activities, taking into account the firm's competitive advantages
4. Related to number 3, the issue of whether this type of internalization is preferable to other strategies, such as contracting with outside firms

Thus, armed with a pro forma capital budget and a statement of the firm's competitive advantages and strategy, the manager can decide whether or not FDI is the appropriate alternative to serve the company's goals in any given situation.

QUESTIONS

1. What do you think are the reasons Imperial Chemicals Industries (ICI) decided to invest in the US market? How would these reasons correspond to RCA's reasons for setting up manufacturing in Singapore?

2. In general, why would a company use FDI rather than exports to serve a foreign market?

3. Are direct investment and disinvestment simply mirror images of each other? What are the key differences between the decision process for direct investment and the decision process for disinvestment?

4. Compare competitive advantage, comparative advantage, and the international product cycle as explanations of FDI. How are the three theories related?

5. How does the concept of internalization relate to FDI?

6. Why did Japanese automobile manufacturers set up operations in the United States in the 1980s? How do your reasons fit with the theories discussed in this chapter?

7. Which countries are the main sources of foreign direct investment in other countries? Why? Which countries are the main recipients of FDI? Why?

8. Which companies were the main foreign direct investors in the 1980s and early 1990s? What enables these companies to compete in the various markets that they serve?

9. Observers note that the United States is becoming a service-based economy. Why has foreign direct investment by service firms not grown dramatically relative to FDI in other sectors?

10. What are the key differences between a domestic direct investment project and a foreign direct investment project? Should both types of project be evaluated similarly?

REFERENCES

Aharoni, Yair. *The Foreign Investment Decision Process.* Boston: Harvard Business School, 1966.

Boddewyn, Jean. "Foreign and Domestic Divestment and Investment Decisions." *Journal of International Business Studies,* December 1983.

Buckley, Peter, and Mark Casson. *The Future of Multinational Enterprise.* New York: Holmes & Meier, 1976.

Calvet, A. Luis. "A Synthesis of Foreign Direct Investment Theories and Theories of the Multinational Firm." *Journal of International Business Studies,* Spring–Summer 1981.

Casson, Mark. "The Theory of Foreign Direct Investment," in Peter Buckley and Mark Casson, *The Economic Theory of the Multinational Enterprise*. New York: St. Martin's Press, 1985.

Caves, Richard. *Multinational Enterprise and Economic Analysis*. Cambridge, England: Cambridge University Press, 1982.

Dunning, John. "Trade, Location of Economic Activity, and the MNE: A Search for an Eclectic Approach." In *The International Allocation of Economic Activity,* ed. Bertil Ohlin. New York: Holmes & Meier, 1977.

Dunning, John, and Robert Pearce. *The World's Largest Industrial Enterprises*. Westmead, England: Gower Publishing, 1981.

Froot, Kenneth. (ed.) *Foreign Direct Investment*. Cambridge, MA: National Bureau of Economic Research, 1993.

Grosse, Robert. *The Theory of Foreign Direct Investment*. University of South Carolina Essays in International Business, no. 3, December 1981.

Hymer, Stephen. *The International Operations of National Firms: A Study of Direct Foreign Investment*. Cambridge, MA: MIT Press, 1976. (Originally published in 1960.)

Itaki, Masahiku. "A Critical Assessment of the Eclectic Theory of the Multinational Enterprise." *Journal of International Business Studies* (Fall 1991).

Kindleberger, Charles. *American Business Abroad*. New Haven, CT: Yale University Press, 1969.

Penrose, Edith. "Foreign Investment and the Growth of the Firm." *Economic Journal,* June 1956.

Robinson, Richard (ed.). *Direct Foreign Investment*. New York: Praeger, 1987.

Vernon, Raymond. *Storm over the Multinationals*. Cambridge, MA: Harvard University Press, 1977.

NOTES

[1] This distinction is often difficult to draw when one firm buys partial ownership of another firm. Such an investment may be direct, even if only 5 to 10 percent ownership is purchased, if the investor is given management control. It may be a portfolio investment, even if 50 percent or more is purchased, if the investor does not exercise management control. For measurement of FDI, the US Department of Commerce arbitrarily defines ownership of 10 percent or more as direct investment.

[2] "GM–Toyota Accord to Produce Autos Gets Final Approval," *The Wall Street Journal,* April 12, 1984, p. 10.

[3] Governments may also be central decision makers in FDI, because many of the largest LDC multinational corporations are government owned, as are many multinational corporations in Europe (e.g., national oil companies, French banks, and British Steel).

[4] See, for example, Grosse (1981), which cites new evidence and several additional studies.

[5] United States Code, Section 10A ff.

[6] The "obsolescing bargain," discussed in Chapter 21, may wipe out expected profitability once the plant has been built. That is, once the firm has committed its funds and built the local facility, the host government gains a better bargaining position, since the physical investment is in place. The host government may then demand a greater share of the gains from the investment—through higher taxes, greater local management and ownership, and so on.

[7] See, for example, Caves (1982), Grosse (1981), and Robinson (1987).

[8] The country of origin *does* play an important role in determining FDI patterns to the extent that a strong currency affects all firms in a given source country. A strong currency makes it both less expensive to invest abroad and more compelling because exports are more expensive in the target country.

[9] "Television," *Encyclopaedia Britannica,* 1969; Stanley Kemper, *A History of Television* (Atlanta: Television Encyclopedia Press, 1965); and *RCA: An Historical Perspective* (New York: RCA, 1978).

[10] The EuroDisneyland project is described in Robert Wrubel, "Le Defi Mickey Mouse," *Financial World,* October 17, 1989, pp. 18–21.

[11]Dunning's view has been criticized by Itaki (1991), who shows that the firm's ownership advantage is not independent of location. Thus, his model may be collapsed logically to competitive advantages (including location) and the choice of whether to internalize or not.

[12]Theodore Moran, "Foreign Expansion as an Institutional Necessity for U.S. Corporate Capitalism," *World Politics,* April 1973.

[13]See Boddewyn (1983), and S. C. Gilmour, *The Divestment Decision Process* (Boston: Harvard Business School, 1973).

[14]See "Monsanto to Sell Acrylic Fiber Line in Europe," *The Wall Street Journal,* March 8, 1983.

International Food Corporation— France

Current Difficulties

The situation at International Food Corporation's (IFC) French subsidiary was driving the home office to distraction by the end of 1986. After 10 years of steady growth and profitability during the 1970s, IFC–France began to lose sales in 1980 and to actually lose money beginning in 1983. The problem was initially attributed to the unprecedented rise in the dollar's value relative to the franc during 1981–84, but the subsidiary's performance did not improve in 1985 or 1986, when the dollar dropped precipitously compared to the franc. (See Figure 1, which depicts the franc/dollar exchange rate during 1970–86, and Figure 2, which presents financial statements of IFC–France for 1986.)

The home office staff viewed this situation as a cause for real alarm, since the subsidiary had accumulated losses of over $US 160 million by the end of 1986. In

FIGURE 1

The Franc/Dollar Exchange Rate, 1970–1986

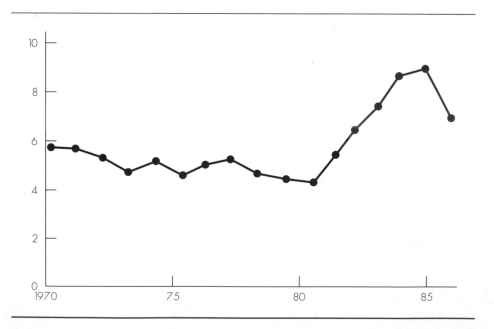

This case was written by Professor Robert Grosse in 1987 as a basis for class discussion.

FIGURE 2

Financial Statements of
IFC–France for 1986
(millions of US dollars)

Income Statement

Net sales and operating revenues	6,298
Operating expenses	5,974
Gross operating margin	324
Interest expense	345
Earnings before tax	(21)
Income taxes	0
Net income after tax	(21)

Balance Sheet

Assets		Liabilities	
Cash	163	Short-term debt	660
Short-term investments	411	Accounts payable	410
Accounts receivable	701	Accrued expenses	552
Inventories	709	Long-term debt	1,058
Net property, plant, and equipment	1,099	Deferred income taxes	187
		Stockholders' equity	216
Total assets	3,083	Total liabilities	3,083

contrast, the subsidiary's managers believed that a series of random events had combined to produce the red ink, but profitability would return even in 1987 and performance would be consistent with that of other IFC units within a few years.

In fact, Jean Bedouin, general manager of the French subsidiary, felt so positive that he sought permission to expand the local operation to manufacture a new line of frozen dessert products that had become very successful in the US market. He proposed that $US 15 million more be invested to build the new assembly line and cold-storage facilities needed for this purpose. Since Bedouin had exceeded company performance goals in the previous divisions that he had run, it was quite difficult for the home office to judge him harshly in this case.

Some Background on International Food Corporation

International Food Corporation was founded in 1949 through a merger of three medium-size US food-processing firms. Each firm had been facing severe competitive pressure from such market leaders as Kraft, Borden, and Standard Brands. The managers of the three companies chose a strategy of joining forces to reduce distribution costs and carve out a stronger market position in a greater variety of products than any of the companies had been able to achieve individually.

IFC's main product areas include dairy products such as cheeses, yogurt, and ice cream; canned fruits and vegetables and juices; frozen fruit pies and frozen vegetables; and such specialty products as mineral water, nonalcoholic coolers, and fruit-based diet sodas. Two of the founding companies had produced dairy products, and IFC still viewed dairy products as a core business. Frozen produce and specialty products, however, were the fastest-growing IFC businesses during the 1980s. The firm was committed to expansion in these two areas.

International Foods sells primarily to supermarkets and grocery stores in the United States. In fact, until the early 1960s, the firm's activities were confined almost entirely to North America. The United States and Canada accounted for 97 percent of its sales. The only sales elsewhere were exports on request to a handful of European wholesale customers and some cross-border sales from Texas and California into Mexico.

In 1963, IFC first entered the European market directly through a sales office and warehouse operation in Swindon, outside London. Based on the existing level of exports of canned produce to one English grocery chain, IFC's management believed that a local presence would enable the firm to sell to many more British customers. IFC began to process fruits and vegetables in the United Kingdom in 1965, when it became clear that lower costs could be achieved by manufacturing locally. IFC sales in the United Kingdom reached $US 30 million by 1968, and the stage was set for further European expansion.

The IFC French subsidiary was opened in 1969 by a senior manager of the British subsidiary. This was done expressly to diversify IFC's production base into Europe, since at the time Britain was not a member of the European Common Market. The French plant, near Lille, produced most of the same canned fruits and vegetables that the English plant produced. A few products were imported from England to fill out the line.

IFC operations in Italy and Germany were begun in 1975 and 1976, respectively. In each of these cases, IFC chose to license a local food-processing firm to manufacture and sell its brand-name frozen-food products. In return for the use of IFC's processing technology and its brand names, the local firm paid a royalty that amounted to 5 percent of sales. International Foods retained the right to establish quality control standards for these products, but in fact no serious problems arose with either licensee. The home office managers were not sure whether the current arrangements with the Italian and German licensees represented the best strategies for IFC, but since both regularly generated profits for the firm, they were left in place.

The Competitive Environment in France

During its entire life, the IFC subsidiary in France never attained a leading market share for any of its products. Although some of the specialty products were relatively novel in the French market when they were introduced, IFC was beaten out by Nestlé in several lines and by a local French producer in others. When price competition became severe at the end of the 1970s, the French subsidiary was unable to match the costs of three of its rivals and began losing market share. A major advertising campaign in 1981 succeeded in raising the subsidiary's market share in all of the canned-food lines, but recessionary conditions that lasted until 1984 led sales to stagnate all the same.

By the end of 1986, Jean Bedouin thought that the best strategy for escaping the weak market position of IFC–France was to move into local production of frozen fruits and vegetables. He had his corporate treasurer draw up a pro forma capital budget for the expansion needed to enter this segment in a major way. Based on a similar investment in the United Kingdom, he estimated that it would

FIGURE 3

Pro Forma Income
Statements for IFC–France
(millions of US dollars)*

	1987	1988	1989	1990	1991
Sales	379	517	575	652	748
Operating expenses	371	481	532	603	681
Gross operating margin	8	36	43	49	67
Interest expense	4	7	9	9	9
Pretax earnings	4	29	34	40	58
Income taxes	2	13	14	18	26
Net income after tax	2	16	20	22	32

*These data show the *marginal* impact of the frozen-food business.

cost $US 15 million to build a modern, highly efficient freezing plant and storage facility. This investment would be repaid within five years. The project would become profitable within two years, assuming no major reaction by rival firms to enter this market segment on a large scale. Bedouin's projections for IFC-France sales and profits, including the new project, appear in Figure 3.

Top Five Firms in 18 Industries (ranked by annual sales in millions of U.S. dollars, 1992)

	Sales 1992	Sales 1982	Growth of Sales (%)	Rank 1982
Aerospace				
Boeing (US)	30,414	9,035	336.6	2
United Technologies (US)	22,032	13,577	162.3	1
British Aerospace (UK)	17,839	3,592	496.6	4
McDonnell Douglas (US)	17,513	7,331	238.9	3
Allied-Signal (US)	12,089	—	—	—
Office Equipment				
IBM (US)	65,096	34,364	189.4	1
Toshiba (Japan)	37,472	10,153	369.1	2
Fujitsu (Japan)	27,911	3,519	793.2	4
Hewlett-Packard (US)	16,427	4,254	386.2	3
Canon (Japan)	15,349	2,331	658.5	5
Petroleum				
Exxon (US)	103,547	97,173	106.6	1
Royal Dutch/Shell (UK/Neth)	98,935	83,759	118.1	2
BP (UK)	59,216	51,322	115.4	4
Mobil (US)	57,389	59,946	95.7	3
ENI (Italy)	40,365	27,506	146.7	5
Electronics				
GE (US)	62,202	26,500	234.7	1
Hitachi (Japan)	61,465	16,262	378.0	3
Matushita Electric (Japan)	57,481	12,309	467.0	4
Siemens (Germany)	51,402	16,963	303.0	2
Samsung (S. Korea)	49,560	5,967	830.6	5
Chemicals				
E.I. Dupont (US)	37,386	33,331	112.2	1
Hoechst (Germany)	20,571	14,409	205.2	2
BASF (Germany)	28,494	12,960	220.0	4
Bayer (Germany)	26,625	14,346	185.6	3
Imperial Chem (UK)	21,549	12,873	167.4	5
Ind & Farm Equip				
Mitsubishi Heavy Ind (Japan)	23,011	13,220	174.1	1
INI (Spain)	21,654	—	—	—
Mannesmann (Germany)	18,235	6,783	268.8	3
BTR (UK)	15,726	1,268	1240.2	4
Fried. Krupp (Germany)	14,820	6,886	215.2	2

	Sales 1992	Sales 1982	Growth of Sales (%)	Rank 1982
Rubber				
Bridgestone (Japan)	13,860	2,860	484.6	4
Michelin (France)	12,623	5,567	226.7	2
Goodyear (US)	11,924	8,689	137.2	1
Pirelli (Italy)	6,691	4,210	158.9	3
Continental (Germany)	6,202	1,338	463.5	5
Motor Vehicles				
General Motors (US)	132,775	60,026	221.2	1
Ford (US)	100,786	37,067	271.9	2
Toyota Motor (Japan)	79,114	15,648	505.6	4
Daimler-Benz (Germany)	63,340	16,023	395.3	3
Volkswagen (Germany)	56,734	15,417	368.0	5
Metal Manufacture & Prod				
IRI (Italy)	67,547	24,815	272.2	1
Nippon Steel (Japan)	23,991	14,425	166.3	2
Thyssen (Germany)	22,731	12,947	175.6	3
Usinor-Sacilor (France)	16,419	—	—	—
Metallgesellschaft (Germany)	16,390	4,120	397.8	4
Building Materials				
Saint-Gobain (France)	14,297	7,805	183.2	1
Hanson (UK)	13,269	2,076	639.2	3
Lafarge Coppée (France)	5,868	2,499	234.8	2
Holderbank (Switzerland)	5,567	1,411	394.5	5
RMC Group (UK)	5,559	1,618	343.6	4
Tobacco				
RJR Nabisco (US)	15,734	10,906	144.3	1
American Brands (US)	8,840	4,026	219.6	2
Japan Tobacco (Japan)	8,794	—	—	—
Tabacalera (Spain)	4,388	2,087	210.3	4
Rothmans Intl (UK)	4,345	2,165	200.7	3
Beverages				
Pepsico (US)	22,084	7,499	294.5	1
Coca-Cola (US)	13,238	6,250	211.8	2
Anheuser-Busch (US)	11,401	4,577	249.1	3
Allied-Lyons (UK)	7,792	3,807	204.7	4
Kirin Brewery (Japan)	7,120	2,177	327.1	5
Food				
Philip Morris (US)	50,157	9,102	551.1	3
Unilever (UK/Neth)	43,963	23,120	190.2	1
Nestlé (Switzerland)	39,058	13,611	287.0	2
Conagra (US)	21,219	1,705	1245.0	4
Ferruzzi Finanziaria (Italy)	16,137	—	—	—
Paper & Wood Products				
International Paper (US)	13,600	4,015	338.7	3
Georgia-Pacific (US)	11,847	5,402	219.3	1
Weyerhaeuser (US)	9,260	4,186	221.2	2
Stora (Sweden)	8,223	—	—	—
Noranda (Canada)	7,139	2,264	315.3	4
Textiles, Apparel & Leather				
Toray Industries (Japan)	7,862	3,230	243.4	1
Hyosung (S. Korea)	6,335	2,061	307.4	4

	Sales 1992	Sales 1982	Growth of Sales (%)	Rank 1982
Haci Ömer Sabanci (Turkey)	6,083	2,510	242.4	2
Kanebo (Japan)	5,303	2,180	243.3	3
Teijin (Japan)	4,753	2,057	231.1	5
Publishing & Printing				
Matra-Hachette (France)	10,416	1,358	767.0	4
Bertelsmann (Germany)	9,741	2,567	379.5	1
Dai Nippon Printing (Japan)	9,605	2,470	388.9	2
Toppan Printing (Japan)	8,924	2,274	392.4	3
News Corp (Australia)	7,861	—	—	—
Leisure Time Industries				
Eastman Kodak (US)	20,577	10,815	190.3	1
Xerox (US)	18,089	8,456	213.9	2
Minnesota Mining (US)	13,883	6,601	210.3	3
Fuji Photo Film (Japan)	9,216	2,378	387.6	4
Baxter Intl (US)	8,471	1,671	506.9	5
Other Manufacturing				
Procter & Gamble (US)	29,890	11,994	249.2	1
Ruhrkohle (Germany)	15,712	7,246	216.8	2
Henkel (Germany)	9,025	1,709	528.1	3
L'oreal (France)	7,104	1,683	422.1	4
British Coal (UK)	7,082	—	—	—

Source: "The Fortune 500," *Fortune*, May 2, 1983; "The International 500," *Fortune*, August 22, 1983; "The Fortune 500," *Fortune*, April 19, 1993; "The International 500," *Fortune*, July 26, 1993.

5

Developing A Global Strategy

This chapter moves to the highest level of decision making in the firm—the selection of a global business strategy. The main goals of the chapter are to:

1. Define overall corporate objectives and clarify their relationship with strategy determination.

2. Show how to create strategic business units and use them to pursue corporate goals.

3. Explain four generic SBU strategies that have shown excellent results for companies during the past few decades.

4. Examine the means by which the firm can control its activities to ensure that corporate goals are achieved.

Disney chief executive officer Michael Eisner introduces a youngster to Mickey Mouse during the opening of Euro Disneyland in France.
Reuters/Bettmann

INTRODUCTION

How can the firm's decision makers choose whether or not to enter a new country market or to acquire a new business line? To this point in the discussion, the answer to these questions has been for the firm to carry out a thorough analysis of its competitive advantages and disadvantages relative to rival firms and to choose alternatives that take best advantage of its strengths and minimize the impact of its weaknesses. This analysis may lead to a decision to invest in overseas production to reduce costs, to undertake exports to serve untapped foreign markets, and so on. How can this reasoning be organized to create a global strategy?

In fact, the basic analysis is useful at each level of decision making in the firm. Competitive strategy is just as important a concern for the individual plant or office as it is for the entire corporation, which may have dozens of divisions and hundreds of plants and offices. What the firm must do as a whole is decide what kinds of businesses it wants to be in and what kinds of overall goals it has. Divisions and/or individual offices have more limited (typically *tactical*) choices, since they need to be consistent with the whole corporation's interests. Large corporations have even more levels of decision making, which need to be consistent to achieve the firm's objectives. In sum, while competitive strategy is a valuable concept to apply at each level of company decision making, these levels must be identified carefully and their strategies must be made consistent. This task can be organized into three stages that focus on three aspects of overall corporate strategy.

First, the firm must have a clear set of *overall objectives*. (For example, is the firm's goal to be in the transportation business, information services, or chemical production?) These overall objectives then lead to such choices as diversifying into a new industry or serving a major new set of customers (e.g., going out of making trains and into making autos; going into computers and telephones together instead of either business separately; or concentrating on consumer-oriented pharmaceuticals versus commodity chemicals). Should a multinational steel producer enter a very different industry such as oil (as US Steel did with its purchase of Marathon Oil in 1982)? Or should a consumer electronics firm expand into movie production and distribution (as Sony did with its acquisition of Columbia Pictures in 1992)? Such questions have no simple answers. The fundamental goals of the firm must be clearly established if it is to make decisions of this kind.

Second, the firm must select optimal *operating strategies* for its major business units. That is, it must choose among basic overall competitive strategies, such as Porter's four generic strategies: broad-line competition, global focus, national focus, and protected niche. Each of these strategies has proven to be sustainable in competition for major firms, while mixing them has often led to serious difficulties for the firm choosing that approach.

Third, the firm must *maintain control* over its widespread parts. Measurement and evaluation of financial decisions, production strategies, personnel relations, and other key operating activities are fundamental to a successful firm. Methods of achieving the necessary control and key areas that require clear control are discussed next.

Thus, global strategy encompasses overall objectives, specific operating strategies, and efforts to ensure acceptable performance of the firm's units. Figure 5–1 depicts the strategy cycle from the formulation of overall corporate goals, to the creation of operating strategies, to the measurement and evaluation of performance.[1]

We will look at these three levels of strategy sequentially in this chapter. But before examining each level in detail, some additional clarification may be useful.

FIGURE 5-1

Global Business Strategy in Perspective

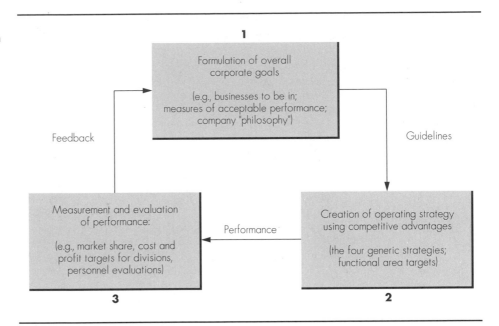

The formulation of overall corporate objectives requires some judgment as to the appropriate extent of the firm's activities. The question of optimal company size (in terms of sales volume, number of products, etc.) has not been resolved by either theoreticians or company managers.[2] Both diversification into new industries or countries and divestment of existing company activities may yield helpful or harmful results to the firm. (Note that, in terminology used before, this is the decision of whether or not to *internalize* a particular business activity.) Our approach is to point out major considerations that should be weighed in the expansion/contraction decision rather than to attempt to answer the question conclusively. In this light, we examine some of the major diversifications and divestments of the past few years.

Expansion/contraction decisions need to be made in the broad context of overall corporate policymaking. Although an almost infinite number of strategies have proven successful for firms over the years, in international business since World War II a handful of generic strategies have led to success in many industries and countries. These generic strategies enable firms to maximize the gains from their competitive advantages (such as possession of an international marketing network, proprietary technology, or government protection) and build defensible positions to ward off rival firms. Each strategy is appropriate not necessarily for an entire widely diversified firm but for each **strategic business unit (SBU)** in the firm. As a firm looks for new business opportunities or seeks to get out of existing businesses, it must carefully consider the fit of each activity into each SBU.

Finally, regardless of the strategy chosen and the operating policies established, top management at the home office needs some method to evaluate and control performance. Controls may be formulated in financial terms or in many other, often less quantifiable, ways. For example, one simple means of control is to place highly trusted personnel in charge of foreign (i.e., faraway) affiliates. To guarantee that these managers make decisions as the home office would like to

**IB
ILLUSTRATION:**

Strategic Business Units

Strategic business units, which are also discussed in Chapter 11, are groups of products, divisions, or other company activities that have sufficiently similar characteristics to justify their assignment to a single group for strategy development.* Each SBU is an operating unit with profit and loss responsibility for the activities within it. One criterion that may be used to create SBUs is to group product divisions that serve the same end users. Similarly, a second criterion could be products that utilize the same or similar technology, which then should be placed in the same SBU. For example, consumer products such as cosmetics should be assigned to a different SBU than bulk petrochemical products in a diversified chemical company. (The criterion in this case is consumer versus industrial products.)

Regardless of the number of industries or countries in which a firm does business, the fundamental strategic business units should be those that have sufficiently *dis*similar characteristics to justify the division of company activities into those units. For example, ITT unquestionably needs separate SBUs (and separate strategies) for its Hartford Life Insurance division and its Sheraton Hotel division. The production methods of these divisions are very different, their customers are quite divergent groups, and their competition differs greatly. Similarly, no matter how many internal applications General Motors can find for its Electronic Data Systems subsidiary, this computer company needs a separate strategy is to continue serving customers outside GM.

A recent organization chart of General Electric Company, the firm that initiated SBUs in the early 1970s, appears as Figure 5–2. Notice that the 30 business units are divided broadly along global product lines, with a handful of matrix-type units such as the international trading company and the corporate marketing division. These divisions have changed over the years as new businesses have been acquired (e.g., RCA Corporation in 1986) and as changes in the environment have called for different activities in different units.

The four generic strategies apply to strategic business units such as these and to entire firms that are less diversified (and constitute single SBUs by themselves). ■

*One useful discussion of the SBU concept appears in William K. Hall, ''SBUs—Hot, New Topic in the Management of Diversification,'' *Business Horizons,* February 1978. General Electric Company initiated the concept in 1971 and has been a leading proponent of SBUs since then.

have them made, a period of home office training might be used. Thus, one method of control might be to assign to foreign affiliates only managers with at least 2 (or 5 or 10) years of experience in the home office. Controls are needed to ensure that the MNE really does take advantage of its internationally transferable advantages, especially the sharing of *information*.

More common as a control mechanism in MNEs is the use of internal financial and operating reports. Most firms use frequent profit and loss reports, foreign exchange exposure statements, plant utilization data, and other information to monitor, evaluate, and direct foreign affiliates. These controls ensure that faraway and often relatively independent subsidiaries and branches are subjected to the same kinds of supervision as more easily accessible domestic affiliates.

The three broad areas of concern—overall objectives, generic strategies, and control—need to be examined in some detail. Let us begin with the formulation of overall corporate objectives.

FIGURE 5-2 General Electric Corporation

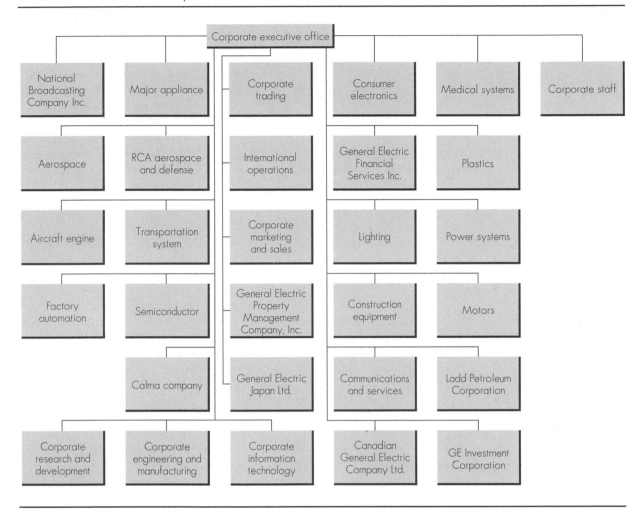

FORMULATION OF OVERALL CORPORATE OBJECTIVES

Major Considerations

At the highest level of strategy making, the firm must choose the businesses in which to compete and the vehicles through which to operate. In a small, relatively young firm, the strategy may be simple: try to cut costs and raise revenues so that profit is adequate for survival in the given market segment. In contrast, in a large, relatively long-lived MNE, strategy may require decisions to exit from persistently unprofitable businesses or countries and other decisions to enter new types of competition.[3] Whether the firm is large or small, new or old, high- or low-tech, a basic question needs to be addressed periodically: What is the fundamental goal of the firm?

From the theory of finance, we know that the firm's goal should be to maximize shareholders' wealth and, in firms with publicly traded shares, specifically to maximize the share price. The troublesome issue is that a manager must anticipate the reactions of rival firms to business strategies to make decisions that will help achieve the goal of maximizing shareholders' wealth. Such reactions are very difficult to forecast, and they create substantial uncertainty about financial plans.[4] Thus, while the goal is easy to define, business strategies to achieve it may be quite difficult to choose.

In nonfinancial terms, the goal of the firm may be to produce high-quality, low-cost products that offer real value to customers. (This type of goal often appears in the statements of company philosophy formulated by major Japanese firms.) While such a broad, imprecise goal does not lead directly to measurable performance criteria, it does focus attention on a central tenet of this chapter: that if the firm does not offer something of value to customers, its position will not be sustainable. A firm whose main product has been electric typewriters, transistor radios, or 45-rpm records can maintain its competitiveness only by moving into new products (e.g., electronic typewriters or personal computers, silicon chip–based radios, or compact disks). At the top level of decision makers, the firm must periodically evaluate its products, industries, and competitive advantages to see whether redeployment of company assets could yield better results.[5]

Example: ITT

ITT, originally International Telephone and Telegraph Corporation, provides an interesting example of asset redeployment under changing conditions. During the 1960s and early 1970s, the firm expanded as a conglomerate (under the leadership of Harold Geneen), with clear financial controls from the home office but a willingness to enter unrelated businesses that had good financial conditions and growth possibilities. At its peak diversification in 1970, ITT included such major divisions as the basic telecommunications service (which owned and operated telephone companies around the world), the telecommunications equipment division, Sheraton Hotels, Avis Rent-a-Car, Hartford Life Insurance Company, Continental Baking Company, Bobbs-Merrill (publishing), Levitt (home building), and Rayonier (forest products). The US stock market at that time reacted favorably to diversification (which was generally showing positive financial results), so ITT's shares were highly valued.

When the oil crisis struck and two major recessions followed during the 1970s, ITT entered a period of difficulty and transition. Interest rates rose substantially (making the financing of acquisitions much more expensive), the price of the company's stock fell, and the stock market shifted to a negative view toward conglomerates.

During the 1980s, ITT elected to regroup its business activities around three themes: (1) office and defense/space products; (2) insurance, financial, and hotel services; and (3) automotive products, electrical/electronic components, and fluid products. Gone are most of the unrelated divisions, while core, relatively high-tech manufacturing, plus hotels and financial services, remain. Even the original core telecommunications business was sold (in 1986) to the French firm CGE.[6] The company has also restructured internationally, with a strong focus on Europe and North America and a substantial retrenchment from the less developed countries. In a changing commercial and financial environment, this ability to reorient its global strategy is necessary for a successful MNE. The results of ITT's strategy for the 1980s were not exceptional, but the firm was continuously profitable. Results of chairman Rand Araskoug's consistently greater focus strategy will be seen as the firm moves through the 1990s.

Even if a firm has defined its business to be the production and marketing of some specific product (e.g., wood furniture), this fundamental basis of the firm's activity must still be reevaluated from time to time. In an annual plan, or in the context of a three-year or five-year plan, top management must consider the viability of the firm's production and marketing efforts. If competitors are undercutting prices and taking away market share, or if other materials are replacing wood for the firm's products, the firm must respond in some way to this change in the competition. It may elect to move production to a lower-cost location or to enter into the manufacture of plastic furniture. It may even choose to operate in a different country with different competitive circumstances. The important point is that top management should face the problem early on and set a strategy to deal with it before the firm finds itself in critical condition.

Figure 5–3 sketches the sequential process of definition and redefinition of the firm's businesses as competitive conditions change over time. It shows a hypothetical situation in which the firm discovers that a country SBU (Country 1 for Products A and B) and a product SBU (Product B for Countries 2 and 3) are more suitable to competitive conditions than the original structure. Also, a new product line, C, has been introduced and placed in a separate SBU (Product C, Worldwide). The firm's broad overall objective of providing high-quality, low-cost products, such as clothing or home electronics, may not have changed, but new technologies and shifting cost conditions alter the best way of achieving the objective.

Key International Aspects

Why does it make sense to create a global strategy rather than just a domestic strategy in each country of operation? Obviously, any firm must coordinate its divisions and the MNE must coordinate its affiliates in different countries. But substantial advantages are to be obtained from the multinationality of the firm itself. (These were discussed in earlier chapters.) First, each national market is

FIGURE 5–3   The Process of SBU Business Strategy Definition

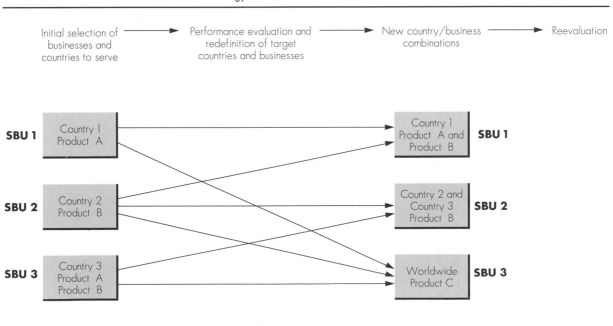

somewhat segmented from other national markets by legal restrictions, currency differences, language differences, and so on, so a successful strategy in one country can often be passed on to a "new" market in another country. Second, whatever the firm's products or services, some competitive gains arise from being multinational. If nothing more, there are potential benefits from the passage of information among affiliates in different countries in terms of low-cost suppliers, production methods, market conditions, and risks. Both of these points emphasize the added dimension of strategy making at the international level. The *process* is the same for domestic and international firms.

The central distinction of strategy making in international business is that its *alternatives* are far more numerous than those available to domestic firms. While the alternatives of the domestic firm (or the firm with domestic horizons) are limited to those available in the domestic market, the alternatives of the firm with a multinational horizon increase almost exponentially with the increase in the number of its markets. For example, any product that such a firm sells in the home country could conceivably be sold in over 100 other countries; any scale economies such a firm achieves in one business may become even greater if foreign operations are added; any diversification that such a firm undertakes in the domestic market could conceivably be extended overseas; and so on. Moreover, when competition in one country has reached the maturing or standardized stage of the international product cycle, competition in another country may still be in the new-product stage, thus allowing the firm different options there.

This international competitive advantage is nowhere more evident than in the chemical industry. Over the entire 20th century, the major chemical firms have produced some "commodities" such as polyethylene, analine dye, industrial resins, and other basic chemical building blocks that are standardized products in the life cycle and require large-scale production facilities to achieve low unit production costs. Because demand in any one country is often insufficient to use up the production of such large-scale facilities, the major chemical companies became multinational very early on (several before World War I).

Similarly, because the commodity chemicals do not provide large profit margins, the major competitors have expanded their horizons into production of high-tech specialty chemicals; into products that are related to basic chemicals, such as pharmaceuticals; and into various industry-specific products such as agricultural chemicals. Thus, the major firms tend to be quite diversified across both countries and product lines. The largest competitors include DuPont, BASF, Bayer, Hoescht, Dow, ICI, and the chemicals divisions of Exxon and Shell.

Bayer AG provides a good example of the global strategy of a successful competitor in this industry. This German company had operated in the United States since before World War I, but its US assets were expropriated as a result of the war. At that time Bayer lost the right to its well-known Bayer aspirin, which has belonged to Sterling Drug Company ever since. Bayer similarly lost foreign assets as a result of World War II. During the postwar period, Bayer has regained its position as one of the top two chemical companies in the world, along with BASF. (DuPont is larger because of its oil-company subsidiary, Conoco.) Only in 1970 did Bayer regain worldwide exclusive rights to its trademark, except in the United States and Canada. Sterling sold the trademark rights to Bayer for nonpharmaceutical products in North America in 1986.

Bayer's focus has historically been in industrial chemicals, but the firm's goal is to be a worldwide leader in chemical products more broadly. This objective has been served through expansion in agricultural chemicals, pharmaceuticals (Bayer owns Miles Laboratories in the United States), automotive chemicals, plastics, and photographic chemicals (Bayer owns Agfa-Gevaert), as well as general industrial chemicals. At the same time the firm has extended its network of affiliates around the world, with main concentrations in Europe and the United States and growing operations in Japan and Korea, as well as smaller ventures in Latin America, Africa, and Asia.

Bayer's strategy is truly global. In the mid-1980s, when the firm wanted to build a pharmaceuticals plant for worldwide sales of a blood-clotting agent, it chose a California location. At the same time, it chose to build a polycarbonate (industrial plastic) plant in Belgium for global sales of that product. In both cases, the economics of producing these products called for a central production facility to supply customers in many countries. The company had to operate multinationally to achieve competitive costs. Bayer is fairly typical of the other large chemical firms mentioned here in terms of its global approach to strategy.

Thus, setting a global strategy for an MNE opens up a huge array of opportunities that simply do not exist for domestic firms in any country and that offer the MNE competitive advantages ranging from cost reductions to added market availability to risk reduction.

The Question of Diversification

Given all we have said up to now, how can a firm decide on possibilities for *diversification?* The rule of thumb is certainly to enter only those businesses that generate net incremental value to the firm. But how can this be judged a priori? There is no simple answer, but some useful guidelines can be laid out. The following discussion concentrates on diversification possibilities for multinational firms in particular.

Perhaps the best way to evaluate possible new businesses for the firm, whether they be new countries to enter or new products to sell, is to examine the ways the firm's competitive advantages relate to the new business. If there are few or no **spillover benefits** from entering the new market, it is likely that other firms will be better able to compete there. This was what Chrysler experienced after its entry into European auto manufacture in 1964, accounting for its divestment in 1978. If the firm gains substantial cost savings by serving the new market from its existing facilities, competitiveness is possible.

If the firm is able to enter a business with risk characteristics very different from those of its existing businesses, its overall risk may be reduced. (For example, a new business whose sales patterns are countercyclical to the sales patterns of the existing business, over the year or over the business cycle, will stabilize the firm's sales and subsequent earnings over that period. This was clearly part of US Steel's expectation in acquiring Marathon Oil.) Since the firm's proprietary technology will not be reduced through using it in a new market, that advantage should help carve out a competitive position in any new market where the technology has an application. In short, every competitive advantage discussed in this book may offer the firm capabilities to enter new markets successfully.

Country diversification certainly has worked well for the major Japanese auto companies, which set up US manufacturing plants during the 1980s to preserve their sales in that market when the US government placed restrictions on their exports from Japan. Honda, Nissan, and Toyota all invested in local manufacturing of their automobiles in the United States, resulting in growing sales and market shares there. (See the discussion of the international auto industry in the Appendix.) While the decision to invest did not represent first-time entry into the market—that was already being served through exports from Japan—it did signify a major additional commitment to the market, and thus a key strategic decision. The Japanese firms as a group were able to reduce the *risk* of US government restrictions on their imported auto sales, while incurring the risk of losing their production-cost advantage in making the cars. Apparently, after more than a decade of experience, the Japanese firms have been able to transfer enough of their management techniques, quality control, and other skills to the US plants to maintain their competitive advantages over US rivals.[7]

Product diversification offers analogous benefits if the firm can really find synergies (spillover benefits) among the products involved. These synergies are very common in businesses such as food processing, where customers and technologies are similar among many food products. They also occur frequently in other consumer products businesses, such as home appliances, where brand advertising can cover multiple products and again customers and technologies are similar.

It appears even today that such benefits should be possible for firms that combine data processing (computer) businesses with telecommunications businesses. Since computer networks imply communication of information among computers, and since remote PCs are often used to communicate data through networks, the linkage seems obvious. Nevertheless, telecommunications companies such as AT&T have found the going quite rough when seeking to establish a presence in computers. A joint venture with Olivetti in the 1980s was scrapped; the acquisition of NCR still has not placed AT&T in a leading position in computers in the mid-1990s. NEC's vaunted "computers and communications" strategy of the 1980s has been revised drastically due to a failure to build the computer side of the business. On the other side of the same coin, IBM has not been able to establish a strong presence in telecommunications, despite its widely publicized acquisition of Rolm (a telecommunications switch manufacturer) in 1984; Rolm was divested in 1988. Apparently, the logic of diversifying across "related" product lines requires much more careful analysis of the competitive advantages and disadvantages of the situation than a cursory view might suggest.[8]

This point should not be overstated either. Diversification into related upstream or downstream businesses by oil, chemical, and food firms has often resulted in stronger, more stable competitive positions for those firms. Virtually all of the leading international oil firms are diversified into gasoline sales, petrochemicals, and other businesses besides crude oil production and refining. Similarly, major international chemical companies very often produce pharmaceuticals, agricultural chemicals, and industrial chemicals rather than just one narrow product line.

Timing

The establishment of overall corporate objectives is not a task that can be repeated usefully every month or year in the company's decision making. Unfortunately, no frequency for setting objectives will be appropriate for firms across industries, countries, and times. A task of senior management is to decide when such goal setting should be undertaken and to carry out the process with the participation of people throughout the firm. Generally, the more stable the businesses of the firm and the more stable the countries in which it operates, the less frequently its corporate objectives need to be reevaluated. On the other hand, this task must be done much more frequently when technology is changing rapidly, competition is growing quickly, or political instability or other severe country-specific risk exists in the countries in which the firm operates.

Having defined the firm's overall objectives, including product lines to sell and markets to enter, top management must select a broad strategic method for pursuing those objectives. Over time and across countries, different strategies will be successful. In current competition in North America, Europe, Japan, and the LDCs, several strategy alternatives have proven viable. Four of these strategies are presented next.

THE SBU FRAMEWORK: FOUR STRATEGIC ALTERNATIVES

The business strategy literature is replete with classifications of operating strategies for business units. The approach taken here follows Porter's (1980) analysis of global industries and is consistent with the competitive advantage view developed throughout the text. Based on his work with major MNEs, Porter defined the four generic strategies shown in Table 5–1. Each of these strategies provides a framework for both utilizing the firm's competitive advantages and choosing additional competitive tools to acquire. The four strategies are presented in increasing order of market focus and adaptation, that is, in decreasing order of product diversity. Broad-line global competition offers the widest variety of products/services to customers in many countries, while the protected niche is generally limited to a single country and a single product or product line.

Broad-Line Global Competition

This first strategic alternative is perhaps the most difficult to achieve. **Broad-line global competition** requires the production of a wide range of products or services in one or more industries. In computers, IBM competes in the segments for mainframes, minicomputers, personal computers, and software; most of its rivals focus on only one of these segments. (Unysis is primarily in mainframes, Digital Equipment Corporation in minis, Apple in micros, and Microsoft primarily in software.) In chemicals, Du Pont competes in raw materials (i.e., oil production), industrial chemicals, agricultural chemicals, and pharmaceuticals. Its rivals generally focus on only one or a couple of these major industry segments. (Texaco is primarily in oil, BASF in industrial chemicals, American Cyanamid in agricultural chemicals, and Merck in pharmaceuticals.) All in all, very few firms have the resources needed to maintain the strategy of broad-line competition because of the huge capital costs required and the susceptibility to competition from focused companies in individual industry segments. Nonetheless, benefits do accrue to the firms that can achieve this position, so the strategy can be sustainable.

Broad-line competition takes advantage of such major competitive strengths as physical and financial economies of scale and the possession of a multicountry production and selling network. That is, to compete successfully with more focused firms, the broad-line competitor must find spillover benefits (e.g., economics of scope) from its additional activities. Cost reductions from purchasing inputs that can be used for two or more products (i.e., those not available to single-product firms) are one such benefit. Another is the sales increases that arise from selling complementary products such as athletic shoes and socks or

TABLE 5–1

Strategic Alternatives in Global Industries

Broad-Line Global Competition	
Uses:	Large firms with substantial resources
	Product lines with sufficiently similar characteristics to enable the firm to benefit from cross-fertilization
Pros:	Allows low-cost production and product differentiation
	Enables spillover of experience curve benefits across product lines
Cons:	Requires large commitments of capital and management
	Subject to better-focused rivals in specific segments
Examples:	Exxon, IBM, Bayer, Nestlé, Philips
Global Focus	
Uses:	Firms that want to specialize in a market segment, based on either cost leadership or differentiation
	Products for which scale economies can be realized by producing or selling in more than one country
	Products that do not require adaptation to local conditions
Pros:	Allows low-cost production or differentiation worldwide
	Allows scale economies in promotion and production across countries
Cons:	Benefits lost if substantial adaptation to local markets in different countries is required
Examples:	Mercedes-Benz, Apple, Polaroid, McDonald's
National Focus	
Uses:	Countries in which adaptation to local demand is important
	Firms that have a competitive advantage in marketing
Pros:	Targets each national market to outcompete global firms
	May be more responsive to changing environments in each country
Cons:	Does not allow gains from global standardization
Examples:	Johnson & Johnson, Unilever, many consumer products firms
Protected Niche	
Uses:	Countries in which the host government is the customer or protector
	Firms that have a competitive advantage in government relations
Pros:	May provide sustainable advantage regardless of costs or rivals
	Once established often easy to maintain
Cons:	Entire advantage subject to shifts in host government policies
Examples:	State-owned enterprises, telecommunications services, defense contractors

Source: Concepts adapted from Michael Porter, *Competitive Strategy* (New York: Free Press, 1980), chap. 13.

toothpaste and toothbrushes (or even food/beverage service and hotel accommodations). Experience curve gains that accrue from the production and sale of one product may be transferable to other products. Finally, even within a product line, a firm that sells products ranging from low-cost to highly specialized items may be able to achieve greater sales and profits than a rival that aims at only one end or segment of the market.

The selection of a broad-line strategy depends, of course, on the benefits that the firm is able to obtain from this strategy in comparison with focused rivals and other broad-line competitors. The strategy should be maintained only as long as its benefits keep the firm ahead of rivals (or in whatever position the firm views as justifying continued participation in the particular business).

Historically, the financial performance of broad-line firms has been better in cases of vertical integration or diversification into related industries. Worse performance has been registered by conglomerated firms—firms that expand into nonrelated businesses and thus find fewer spillover benefits from their other units.

Global Focus

In contrast to broad-line competition, a **global focus** targets a particular industry segment for competition worldwide. This strategy fosters the achievement of scale economies by obtaining inputs, distributing inputs and final products, carrying out R&D, producing outputs, and promoting products worldwide. It also achieves cost savings through an experience curve advantage; by following the focus strategy, a firm should be able to gain a large market share and thus move rapidly along the experience curve. A strategy of global focus has been followed very successfully by McDonald's in fast-food restaurant service, by Black & Decker in power hand tools, and by Liggett & Myers in generic, unbranded cigarettes, to cite just a few examples.

Global focus is *not* limited to a low-cost strategy. Other focal points for competition include specialization in high-quality, expensive products or provision of the best after-sale service. Rolls-Royce, for example, follows a focus strategy in producing automobiles of very high quality, with high costs and high prices. Xerox is known for its rapid and excellent after-sale service of photocopying machines. Maytag is very well known for providing both high-quality electrical appliances and excellent after-sale service. In each case, the focus is on some aspect of competition that enables the firm to show superiority over rivals (i.e., to differentiate its product or service).

Other focus strategies may target any segment of a total market if the firm can successfully isolate that segment enough to outcompete competitors with broader lines. In the furniture business, for example, focus strategies have succeeded not only in the low-cost end of the market (e.g., Ashley, Dixie, and Singer), and in the high-quality, highly personalized end (e.g., Drexel Heritage, Baker, and Cheryl) but also in plastic furniture, metal furniture, wood crate furniture, and so on.

At the international level, the focus strategy implies worldwide concentration on one or a few products. While production may be standardized and economies of scale achieved in many activities, marketing may still differ across countries. In particular, successful low-cost producers in Europe, Japan, or the United States may find that their entry into lower-income LDCs places them at the top of the market for their products. Thus, a low-cost US-made power tool may compete at the expensive end of the power tool market in Latin American countries. Similarly, a low-cost European food processing firm may end up competing at the high-quality, high-price end of an African or Asian market even though it sells the same products both at home and abroad. In every instance, the firm that tries to follow a global focus strategy must evaluate the differences in competition from one market to the next before setting its focus in particular markets.

National Focus

National market characteristics may preclude the firm from pursuing the global focus strategy. If differences from country to country are too extreme, global competitors that standardize their complete strategies may encounter serious problems. For example, sales of the nylon jackets that a clothing firm produces for use in cold weather are likely to be quite low in tropical countries and also in

LDCs where nylon is very expensive compared to natural materials such as wool and leather. Thus, this firm may choose to specialize in outerwear ranging from heavy nylon jackets in most of the industrial countries, to nylon raincoats in tropical countries, to clothing made of natural fibers in LDCs (or high-cost nylon coats for the most expensive segment of the LDC markets). Chapter 13 discusses such issues in more detail.

When important market differences limit the global focus strategy, a **national focus** may be superior. By emphasizing its adaptability to local market conditions, a multinational firm may be able to outcompete its more standardized, less flexible rivals. In the 1990s, as more large MNEs from several countries arise in many industries, the ability to offer flexible, individualized products becomes increasingly important. The once common form of competition in fairly standardized products (the Model T Ford was said to be available "in any color you like, as long as it is black"[9]) was being replaced by more adaptive styling to serve different customer groups.

Protected Niche

The last generic strategy defined by Porter is establishment of a **protected niche.** This strategy aims specifically at obtaining government protection, either through support of the firm against competitors or through government purchase of the firm's product or service. Very often the protected niche is controlled by the government through ownership of the firm in question. For example, in most countries the national telephone company is state owned and is given a monopoly over the provision of domestic telephone service.* The protected niche strategy depends totally on the firm's ability to obtain government protection on a continuing basis.

The first form of protection, government support against competitors, may be obtained through bargaining with the government at the time of an initial investment. When a manufacturing MNE sets up a subsidiary in a country, the host government is often willing to negotiate some forms of incentives in exchange for a job-creating, revenue-producing investment. In this negotiation process, especially in LDCs, the MNE may be able to obtain tariff protection against imported goods that would compete with its local production. The MNE may also be able to negotiate a reduced tax burden, especially in industrial countries, which again places it in a preferred position relative to nonsubsidized competitors. These forms of government support need not be obtained at the time of the initial investment, but the firm's bargaining position is usually strongest at that time or at a time when it is deciding whether to close or relocate a facility.

The second form of protection, government purchase of the firm's product or service, may be obtained by negotiating a long-term purchase contract with a government. This gives the firm a guaranteed market, regardless of the activities of competitors during the life of the contract. Since government contracts are subject to nonprice determinants (that is, governments seek to serve goals other than minimizing costs: supporting local firms, rewarding firms that follow government policy prescriptions, etc.), the firm may find that once it has obtained an initial contract, subsequent contracts are highly likely to continue into the future.

---

*This situation is changing as privatization of state-owned companies becomes common. The national telephone company has been privatized in the UK, Mexico, Argentina, Chile, and several other countries in recent years.

Global Integration vs. Local Responsiveness

Another way to look at the choice of global strategies is to compare the industry characteristics that push the firm toward either greater standardization and integration or greater adaptation and responsiveness. The accompanying figure shows how any competitor's situation can be examined in this context; some industry examples appear in the diagram according to their broad characteristics.

While personal computers are fairly close to the point of greatest integration and least adaptation, restaurants (other than fast food) tend to fall at the opposite extreme, with great responsiveness to local tastes and little global integration. Industries in which government regulation is intensive, such as postal service or telecommunications, also tend to fall at the responsive end of the spectrum, whether or not important scale economies or other reasons for global integration exist.

This diagram is also useful for considering the firm's need to adapt or standardize its functional management (e.g., labor relations, marketing, production, R&D) and even within functions to adapt or integrate activities (e.g., within marketing, advertising, distribution, brands). In all, the idea is to consider explicitly the forces that pull the firm to either pursue a globally integrated, generally standardized strategy or respond to local pressures by adapting to those conditions. ∎

Governments often choose to create protected positions for firms that they themselves control—for example, through ownership. Thus, in many countries the most significant protected niches are held by state-owned firms that provide electric power, railroad transportation, postal service, and other utilities, as well as minerals and metals such as oil, copper, and bauxite. This limits the ability of a multinational firm to pursue a protected niche strategy in these areas. But plenty of other possibilities exist, and the MNE may even be able to supply products or services to the state-owned firms on a continuing basis.

Obtaining a protected market segment may be much easier than holding onto it. Often, when governments change, so does the status of favored industries and companies. Unless the firm pursues a policy of keeping the costs of the protected segment low or of carefully differentiating the products of the protected segment, its protected niche may lead to an inefficient position that will be eliminated once protection has been lost. The protected niche strategy is far more subject to political negotiating and positioning than the other three generic strategies, which depend to a greater extent on economic factors (such as cost minimization or tailoring output to satisfy specific market preferences).

CONTROL IN THE MULTINATIONAL ENTERPRISE

Once a firm has established its overall strategic objectives and chosen its plans for its business units, a final step is needed to ensure that these objectives and plans are implemented: The firm must create a **control** structure. The basic intent of controls is to have managers define goals clearly, observe whether those goals are being achieved, and reward behavior that works toward achieving the overall corporate objectives. Financial and managerial reporting, personnel evaluation, government relations, and dealing with rival firms are four important areas of management that require corporate-level control within the multinational firm. Highlights pertinent to our present focus are covered below; these areas are also discussed elsewhere in the text.

Financial and Managerial Reporting

Financial reporting is obviously an area that is both appropriate for control and easily measurable for evaluation purposes. Measures of corporate performance include sales, market share, profitability, and return on assets. Each firm may have different goals and capabilities in these areas, but no firm can operate indefinitely without earning positive profits and generating a positive return on assets.

At the international level, financial controls are needed for at least capital budgeting, operating performance evaluation, and exchange risk management. One commonly used form of financial control is the spending limit; foreign subsidiaries often are limited in making financial commitments at some specific dollar ceiling (e.g., $US100,000); expenditures greater than that limit require home office approval. Another common limitation requires the subsidiary to deal only in host country currency, except for items approved by the home office such as purchase of intracompany imports and payment of royalties and fees. This limitation avoids the expansion of companywide exchange risk beyond that generated by the activities of the subsidiary in local currency. These issues are also discussed in Chapter 15.

Managerial reporting refers to periodic information passing by the subsidiary to the home office on nonfinancial issues. These issues may range from inventory levels to political risk assessments to market analysis. Analysis of market trends in one country may alert the home office to possible shifts in other markets around the world. Analysis of government policies in one national context may also have application in other countries where the firm operates. This kind of information is just as important to the corporation in ensuring that the home office understands the activities of the foreign subsidiary and the environment it faces as the financial information is.

Personnel Evaluation

A second important control area is *personnel evaluation*. Managers must be judged not only on their achievement of financial targets but also on their ability to deal with people and pursue corporate nonfinancial goals. As noted earlier, one form of control over personnel is to assign managers to affiliates only after they have spent some time at the home office learning the details of the corporate strategy and being indoctrinated in the corporate culture. In addition, the performances of managers and support personnel must be evaluated for the purposes of compensation and career development. Thus, a system of information gathering must be established to obtain data on the administrative, technical, cooperative, and other skills of individuals in the firm.

Internationally, personnel must be chosen to be assigned to different countries and different kinds of operating affiliates. The skills necessary to perform well in foreign environments (e.g., patience, adaptability to cultural differences) add a key dimension to the other skills that require evaluation. As firms become more and more international over time, it is becoming increasingly important to employ managers who can function well with colleagues, superiors, and subordinates from different cultures.

Breaking the ethnocentric base of most firms that have their roots in one culture and one country is often extremely difficult. One area in which Japanese firms may encounter increasing problems is the integration of non-Japanese managers into higher-level corporate positions. Until now almost all general manager positions in Japanese firms' foreign affiliates have been filled by Japanese nationals. As these firms become more global in their activities, more pressure will arise to permit host country nationals to participate in management of these affiliates and to be integrated into top management in Japan as well. European and some American multinational firms have been much more successful in creating multicultural environments among senior management at home and in foreign affiliates.

Thus, personnel evaluation really is a strategic imperative in international firms as their horizons expand beyond ethnocentric, home country considerations. Control of this function is crucial to ensure that people with the proper skills are assigned to the appropriate positions in the home office and in affiliates around the world.

Government Relations

A third area that requires corporate-level control is *government relations*. In countries or situations in which the firm's activities are subject to a great deal of government intervention, there is undoubtedly a need for careful monitoring and evaluation of relations with the government. Even in relatively free markets, however, the importance of government policies such as taxes, subsidies, and limits on foreign competitors should not be underestimated.

At the international level, government relations become even more crucial to company success, since home and host governments often have different views as to the desirability of specific company activities—for example, foreign direct investment or even exports (imports to the other country). Careful and frequent reviews of government relations and an exploration of alternatives will help the firm avoid the hostage problem—the situation in which the firm is at the mercy of shifts in government policy in one country and has no options to lessen the impact of those shifts.

This concern has become a top priority during the past few years as the formerly communist countries of Eastern Europe open their economies to Western firms. Entering these markets requires a huge commitment of time and effort to build good government relations as the new governments of these countries decide how to build market-based economies.

Similarly, in the industrial countries of Western Europe, government relations became a high priority during the period of negotiations for Europe 1992, the push for creation of a single Europe in terms of business regulation and many other areas. US firms in particular had to evaluate their regulatory situations in the European countries in which they had operations, as well as study the possible impacts of changed regulations that could result from the Common Market's unification effort.

Dealing with Rivals

Finally, dealing with rivals requires corporate-level control. Although the firm cannot determine or control the strategies of its competitors, it can assess those strategies in terms of their impacts on its own activities. In addition, it can influence those strategies by its own actions. Monitoring the activities of competitors and attempting to estimate their reactions to the firm's own activities can enable the firm to develop a better strategy.

Caterpillar, Inc., for example, must assess the strategies of its rival Komatsu in different countries to plan its own global strategy of competing against Komatsu. And in recent years, the emergence of strategic alliances such as joint production or marketing agreements and joint R&D ventures requires an international firm to evaluate competitive conditions around the world to see in which cases and places such alliances make sense.

At the international level, the firm must consider rivals such as other multinational firms, local firms in each country of operation, and even firms in other countries that are potential competitors. While the complexity of analyzing international competition is much greater than that of analyzing domestic competition, the stakes are generally also greater. Much of the business strategy literature, and indeed this book, aims at developing sustainable strategies for firms involved in international competition.[10]

STRATEGIC VARIETY

International strategy must be constructed to fit the particular configuration of international activities that the firm possesses. The exporter with only one foreign affiliate that receives its products for sale in the host country will not need the same kind of strategy that is invaluable to a multinational firm such as Royal Dutch/Shell or Toyota. Also, a company that uses overseas subsidiaries for offshore production, which ultimately results in products that are sold in the home country, needs a different strategy than the firm that uses foreign production facilities to serve host country markets.

What really is needed more than any simplistic strategic model, which would not apply in all situations in any event, is a recognition that strategic *flexibility* should be the underlying basis for thinking. That is, the firm should follow careful analytical patterns such as those suggested above and then apply forward-looking thinking to anticipate future conditions and position itself to take advantage of them. While this point of view does not provide a convenient recipe for managers, it does alert them to the need for anticipating change rather than reacting to it. Kogut (1985) and Hamel and Prahalad (1989) offer some more concrete methods of employing this kind of thinking.

CONCLUSIONS

The development of a global strategy involves two levels of planning and the process of evaluation and control. First, the firm must establish overall corporate objectives—broad, long-term goals such as businesses to compete in and acceptable kinds of performance (e.g., in the risk/return framework). Second, the firm must develop for its strategic business units goals based on the four generic strategies: broad-line competition, global focus, national focus, and protected niche. Finally, the firm must establish clearly defined targets for performance, monitor that performance, and set up a feedback mechanism for realigning itself to meet targets more closely.

Overall corporate strategy must be to some extent ambiguous or open-ended, since the future business conditions under which the firm will operate cannot be known today and full contingency planning is impossible. However, the firm's top management can define broad corporate goals and acceptable means of pursuing them that will be able to survive changes in the environment. This level of planning needs to be fairly long term, since only over a period of years can the firm's performance and changes in the environment be observed adequately.

SBU strategy can be formulated and changed more frequently, since at this lower level more concrete, measurable goals can be established. Strategic business units can follow any one of the four generic strategies, from broad-line global competition to serving a protected niche, with the additional possibilities of focusing on a market segment worldwide or adapting to national market segments in different countries. Each SBU should be chosen to group activities of the firm that possess similar characteristics, such as technology, customers, location, and inputs.

Performance monitoring, evaluation according to some clear criteria, and reformulation of strategy are also necessary parts of strategy making. The MNE needs to develop methods for monitoring far-flung affiliates on financial conditions, personnel performance, government relations, and the activities of rival firms, as well as other key issues that may arise. More important than specific quantitative goals are targets designed to pursue the firm's main strategic objectives.

QUESTIONS

1. What is a strategic business unit? How should SBUs be selected from among a firm's divisions?
2. Using your knowledge of ITT from the chapter and any other sources, what would be the appropriate SBUs for that firm today? Why?
3. How can you distinguish among corporate strategy, business unit strategy, and operating strategy for a firm? What are the key characteristics of each?
4. Explain the four generic strategies for business units. How does each strategy apply in international business?
5. On what grounds can a business unit choose between a global focus and a national focus?
6. Why is control an important aspect of corporate strategy? How can control be achieved in a multinational enterprise?
7. How can a firm decide whether or not to diversify into a new industry in a country where it has not operated before? What criteria can it use to make this decision?
8. What is different about corporate and business unit strategies at the international level compared with the domestic level? That is, what is different about them for a multinational enterprise compared with a domestic one?
9. Explain how a firm could establish a protected niche strategy for its business unit in the telecommunications industry. What forms of business activity would be possible, and how could the firm use this strategy in more than one country?
10. Discuss some major spillover benefits from other business activities that could enhance the competitiveness of an MNE such as Dow Chemical in the pharmaceuti-

cals industry. That is, what advantages does Dow possess due to its diversified business units (in industrial chemicals, agricultural chemicals, specialty chemicals, cosmetics, consumer products, etc.) that purely pharmaceuticals firms do not have?

REFERENCES

Bartlett, Christopher, and Sumantra Ghoshal, *Transnational Management*. Homewood, Ill.: Richard D. Irwin, 1992.

Christensen, Roland; Kenneth Andrews; Joseph Bowers; Richard Hammermesh; and Michael Porter. *Business Policy*, 6th ed. Homewood, Ill.: Richard D. Irwin, 1987.

Donaldson, Gordon, and Jay Lorsch. *Decision Making at the Top*. New York: Basic Books, 1983.

Hall, W. K. "SBUs—Hot New Topic in the Management of Diversification." *Business Horizons*, February 1978.

Hamel, Gary, and C. K. Prahalad. "Strategic Intent," *Harvard Business Review*, May–June 1989.

Kogut, Bruce. "Designing Global Strategies: Profiting from Operational Flexibility," *Sloan Management Review*, Fall 1985.

Ohmae, Kenichi. *The Borderless World*. New York: Harper Business, 1990.

Porter, Michael. *Competitive Strategy*. New York: Free Press, 1980.

Porter, Michael (ed.). *Competition in Global Industries*. Boston: Harvard Business School Press, 1986.

Porter, Michael. "From Competitive Advantage to Corporate Strategy." *Harvard Business Review*, May–June 1987.

Prahalad, C.K., and Yves Doz, *The Multinational Mission*. New York: Free Press, 1987.

NOTES

[1] This scheme generally parallels that of Figure 12–1, with two exceptions. First, we do not cover the level of "implementing the operating plan" in the present chapter, which focuses instead on overall corporate strategy. Second, we do not consider organization structure in any detail in this chapter.

[2] See, for example, Edith Penrose's classic analysis of this issue in *The Theory of the Growth of the Firm* (Oxford: Oxford University Press, 1951); also see Anthony Sampson, *The Sovereign State of ITT* (New York: Viking Press, 1973), for the real-world case of ITT, a huge conglomerate in the 1960s and 1970s and a drastically reduced services firm today.

[3] Some people would argue that small firms are *more* likely to be flexible enough to leave unprofitable market segments, while large MNEs may be relatively inflexible and more likely to remain in weak market segments. This is an empirical question.

[4] This uncertainty cannot be eliminated, but the problem can be managed somewhat by specifying a range of potential rivals' responses and examining the firm's expected performance in each case. Such analysis has been facilitated dramatically by microcomputers and sophisticated financial planning programs.

[5] Gordon Donaldson and Jay Lorsch, *Decision Making at the Top* (New York: Basic Books, 1983), found, in a survey of 12 large, US-based MNEs, that their chief executive officers viewed *company survival* rather than maximizing shareholders' wealth as the primary objective of the firm. "They [the CEOs] are committed, first and foremost, to the enhancement of *corporate* wealth, which includes not only the firm's financial assets reflected on the balance sheet but also its important human assets and its competitive position in the various markets in which it competes" (p. 7).

[6] CGE purchased 63 percent of ITT's telecommunications division in 1986, naming the joint venture Alcatel. In 1990, ITT sold an additional 7 percent of the venture to CGE and in 1992 sold the remaining 30 percent.

[7] The success of the Japanese "transplant" auto factories was discussed widely during the 1980s. See, for example, Daniel Jones and Daniel Ross, *The Machine That Changed the World* (New York: Rawson Associates, 1990).

[8] Porter (1987) in fact shows that *most* of the diversification efforts of large US industrial firms during the past decade have led to worse performances by those companies

compared to their prediversification records. This is a strong argument in favor of "sticking to your knitting," that is, focusing on the businesses that utilize your firm's distinctive competencies.

[9]Henry Ford, *My Life and Work* (Garden City, N.Y.: Doubleday, 1922), p. 72.

[10]See, for example, Roland Christensen et al., *Business Policy*, 6th ed. (Homewood, Ill.: Richard D. Irwin, 1987).

HongKong & Shanghai Banking Corporation

Introduction

HongKong & Shanghai Banking Corporation (HSBC) was the world's 30th largest bank in 1980. Based in Hong Kong, the bank has carried out most of its business in Hong Kong dollars and US dollars, with substantial amounts of business in European currencies and Japanese yen as well. It has received deposits from local (Chinese) individuals and companies and has loaned the money to both local borrowers and international banks in the so-called eurocurrency market. HSBC has specialized in financing exports and imports, largely with firms in the countries of the British Commonwealth (Great Britain and its former colonies). The vast majority of the bank's business has been physically conducted in Hong Kong, though it had a large network of branches in Asia, a very large London branch office, and several US branches, plus a subsidiary bank in California and a representative office in New York in 1980. (The representative office was not allowed to do business directly; under US law, it had to refer all clients to the California subsidiary bank, the London branch, or the Hong Kong headquarters.)

In 1980, the bank was looking to expand in the US market. Its dealings in the eurocurrency market had led to large deposits of US dollars, British pounds, and other currencies, which the bank needed to lend to borrowers somewhere. Rather than continue to accept low profits from lending these funds to other banks, HSBC decided to seek new borrowers in the world's largest market, the United States. Although HSBC had over a century of experience in international banking, it had never considered a major move into the US domestic market. In the late 1970s, at a time when their British pounds, deutsche marks, and Japanese yen could buy far more dollars than in the 1950s and 1960s, many of the bank's clients were establishing offices, factories, and other investments in the United States.

The bank was also interested in moving into the US market as a hedge against the substantial risk of nationalization by the Chinese government. In 1997, the British colony of Hong Kong is scheduled to return to Chinese ownership, which will bring with it the possibility of major legal changes in rules for business. Because the People's Republic of China is a communist country, many observers expect Hong Kong to lose its free-market status. As the largest bank in the colony, HSBC very likely faces changes in its business activities. For this reason, the

---

This case was written by Professor Robert Grosse in 1986 as a basis for class discussion. Helpful information was provided by HSBC. Any errors of fact or interpretation are the responsibility of the author.

bank's managers and owners have been interested in establishing domestic activities in the United States, generally viewed as the least politically risky environment in the world.

In addition to having substantial deposits in several currencies and clients of several nationalities, the bank possessed another competitive strength: its large staff of experienced bankers who knew about both lending and borrowing opportunities in Asia that were little known to potential US clients. By operating directly in the US market, the bank would be able to take advantage of this expertise to earn additional profits.

HSBC has been operating in the United States since 1875, when it opened an agency in San Francisco. A second agency was opened in New York in 1880. The New York agency was converted into a branch in the 1970s, as a result of a change in New York's banking laws. In the 1960s HSBC acquired the Republic Bank of California, which had 11 branches in the state. The bank was renamed the HongKong Bank of California. Other branches were established in Chicago, Seattle, and Portland, and another subsidiary was set up in Houston. Under US banking rules in 1980, if HSBC wanted to open a full-service subsidiary in any other state, the California branch network and the Houston subsidiary would have to be divested.

The Case

Michael Sandberg, chairman of HSBC in Hong Kong, was considering the alternatives for expanding in the US market in 1980. The bank's top management wanted to diversify its assets and activities across the world, placing about one-third of the total in Hong Kong, Europe, and the United States. Sandberg believed it would be possible to set up an agency in New York, where over 90 percent of the international banking in the United States takes place. Similarly, it would be feasible to establish a branch bank, owned completely by HSBC and using a federal US charter, under the existing US laws. Additional representative offices could be placed in cities other than New York, but these facilities would be restricted to providing information to potential clients, who would still need to do business with HSBC in San Francisco, London, or elsewhere outside the United States. Finally, Sandberg considered forming a joint venture with an existing US bank, which would give HSBC immediate access to new clients and partial ownership and control of the venture. Each of these alternatives is discussed in more detail next.

Setting up an *agency* would allow HSBC to minimize the capital needed to enter the US market, since foreign bank agencies could use all of the capital of the parent bank as a base for their US lending. The agency would allow HSBC to lend to local clients as well as Chinese or other foreign borrowers. Deposits, on the other hand, were restricted to foreign depositors; US banking laws forbid agencies from taking local deposits. Many foreign banks enter the US market through an initial representative office, followed by expansion into an agency. While this alternative had no major financial costs, it would limit HSBC's business primarily to dealing with foreign clients.

The International Banking Act of 1978 allowed foreign banks to establish *Edge Act Corporations,* subsidiaries of banks that are allowed to engage only in

---

Note: The 50 largest US banks in 1980 are listed in Table 1 to show the size and other characteristics of relevant competitor banks and banks that could be considered for acquisition or joint venture partnership.

TABLE 1 The 50 Largest U.S. Banks in 1980

	Assets	Deposits				Loans		
	12/31/79 ($ mil.)	Total 12/31/79 ($ mil.)	Chg. From 1978 (%)	Time/ Demand (%)	For- eign (%)	Total OS 12/31/79 ($ mil.)	Chg. From 1978 (%)	Loan Loss Prov. 1979 ($ mil.)
1 BankAmerica (San Francisco)	108,389	84,985	12	75/25	50	58,772	16	226.2
2 Citicorp (New York)	106,371	70,291	13	87/13	75	65,712	21	233.4
3 Chase Manhattan (New York)	64,708	48,456	0	69/31	54	40,364	4	149.0
4 Manufacturers Hanover (New York)	47,675	38,156	18	63/37	46	25,639	14	105.9
5 Morgan (J.P.) (New York)	43,488	30,279	6	67/33	55	22,406	18	29.8
6 Chemical New York	39,375	28,987	16	67/33	43	20,719	14	60.0
7 Continental Illinois (Chicago)	35,790	24,007	13	78/22	48	23,182	26	70.0
8 Bankers Trust New York	30,953	22,437	20	63/37	48	16,228	18	47.5
9 First Chicago	30,182	21,106	21	84/16	57	15,737	14	84.0
10 Western Bancorp (Los Angeles)	29,687	23,631	12	63/37	9	17,353	14	97.3
11 Security Pacific (Los Angeles)	24,923	18,451	9	67/33	24	16,830	15	75.1
12 Wells Fargo (San Francisco)	20,593	15,831	7	73/27	15	15,193	18	62.9
13 Irving Bank (New York)	16,702	13,525	22	53/47	38	7,607(b)	7	34.5
14 Crocker National (San Francisco)	16,139	12,517	12	69/31	20	10,778	18	60.4
15 Marine Midland Banks (Buffalo)	15,728	12,509	11	73/27	39	9,268	12	45.2
16 First National Boston	13,760	8,965	15	74/26	53	7,183	27	49.0
17 Mellon National (Pittsburgh)	13,508	9,503	12	69/31	28	7,046	15	27.3
18 Northwest Bancorp (Minneapolis)	12,416	9,573	13	68/32	7	7,642	16	20.4
19 First Bank System (Minneapolis)	12,119	8,983	13	65/35	4	7,008	14	22.3
20 First International Bancaheres (Dallas)	11,504	8,921	15	67/33	28	6,041	15	24.9
21 Republic of Texas (Dallas)	10,798	7,647	13	68/32	32	5,510	20	16.5
22 National Detroit	9,506	6,896	-4	66/34	16	4,694	12	14.1
23 First City Bancorp of Texas (Houston)	9,505	7,597	16	61/39	12	4,633	18	22.7
24 Texas Commerce Bancaheres (Houston)	9,260	7,226	12	59/41	15	5,026	20	17.7
25 Bank of New York	8,994	6,870	16	67/33	32	4,376	22	24.8
26 First Pennsylvania (Philadelphia)	8,987	5,307	0	76/24	37	4,770	8	46.8
27 Seafirst (Seattle)	8,401	6,652	28	68/32	9	5,419	21	17.8
28 European-American Bancorp (New York)	7,776	6,370	7	55/45	37	4,456	18	19.9
29 Harris Bankcorp (Chicago)	7,108	4,929	9	66/34	24	3,311	22	7.0
30 NCNB (Charlotte, NC)	6,365	4,477	24	62/38	22	2,869	12	16.8
31 Philadelphia National	5,916	4,056	12	54/46	21	3,181	7	16.0
32 Pittsburgh National	5,563	3,912	18	69/31	3	2,958	25	11.0
33 AmeriTrust (Cleveland)	5,402	3,763	-6	69/31	5	3,265	13	11.4
34 Michigan National (Bloomfield Hills)	5,399	4,545	7	76/24	0	3,616	11	14.4
35 Northern Trust (Chicago)	5,358	3,912	7	64/36	24	2,405	17	5.0
36 Valley National Bank of Arizona (Phoenix)	5,199	4,331	18	66/35	1	3,386	18	19.0
37 First Wisconsin (Milwaukee)	5,107	3,673	7	56/44	12	2,812	16	5.0
38 Wachovia (Winston-Salem)	5,097	3,825	8	61/39	11	2,771	18	6.7
39 Detroitbank	5,067	3,527	2	73/27	2	2,666	21	5.5
40 Southeast Banking (Miami)	5,028	3,828	24	59/41	2	2,406	15	13.5
41 BancOhio (Columbus)	5,005	3,805	6	68/32	0	2,795	14	11.8
42 National City (Cleveland)	4,972	3,330	19	57/43	5	2,322	29	3.8
43 National Bank of North America (New York)	4,849	3,634	11	70/30	32	3,094	23	14.0
44 Mercantile Texas (Dallas)	4,709	3,332	13	57/43	4	2,678	24	10.5
45 Manufacturers National (Detroit)	4,526	3,608	4	70/30	4	2,808	9	8.0
46 Rainier Bancorp (Seattle)	4,496	3,457	9	67/33	16	3,191	15	13.4
47 US Bancorp (Portland)	4,431	3,512	10	65/35	3	2,963	12	8.0
48 Republic New York	4,408	3,287	36	85/15	41	2,168	32	18.5
49 Girard (Philadelphia)	4,360	3,247	5	57/43	21	2,461	8	11.6
50 Mercantile Bancorp (St. Louis)	4,327	2,941	7	61/39	9	2,177	11	12.2

TABLE 1 *Continued*

	Loans						Performance				
Change From 1978 %	Net Charge-offs as % of Loans	Fed. Funds Bor-rowed %	Net Oper. Income, 1979 ($ mil.)	Change From 1978 (%)	Return on Avg. Assets, 1979	Lever-age, 1979	Return on Com. Equity, 1979	Net Int-erest Income, 1979	Change From 1978 (%)	Oper. Income as % of Net Int. Income	5-Year Growth EPS (%)
28	0.3	4(d)	600.2	17	0.64	28.9	18.4	2,770	12	21.7	17.1
-18	0.3	9	544.2	13	0.58	27.9	16.1	2,587	10	21.0	10.8
-12	0.3	11	311.2	58	0.49	31.4	15.3	1,577	18	19.7	8.5
36	0.2(b)	7(b)	211.3	16	0.51	28.0	14.3	1,072	15	19.7	7.9
-11	0.0(b)	10(b)	288.3	8	0.72	21.8	15.6	847	14	34.1	9.0
-34	0.2	19	142.3	15	0.39	32.8	13.0	854	9	16.7	6.7
12	0.2(b)	34(b,d)	194.1	15	0.58	25.7	15.0	677	13	28.7	11.6
-41	0.2	17	114.5	39	0.37	36.8	13.5	608	16	18.8	6.0
-29	0.6	19	115.4	-12	0.45	22.1	10.0	464	-6	24.9	3.7
25	0.3	12(d)	214.9	28	0.77	23.8	18.3	1,184	19	18.1	22.0
2	0.3	11	164.5	24	0.78	24.1	16.8	874	17	18.8	23.3
32	0.3	10	130.2	12	0.68	24.4	16.5	737	16	17.8	20.1
72	0.3(b)	11(b)	69.0	25	0.46	31.1	14.3	399	22	17.3	10.1
22	0.4	5	89.4	19	0.56	28.2	15.8	637	16	14.0	21.2
-5	0.4	12	42.8	74	0.29	32.0	9.2	365	11	11.7	8.9
21	0.4	23	85.0	35	0.66	20.7	13.7	427	25	19.9	9.7
47	0.1	15	101.0	17	0.81	15.6	12.7	366	13	27.6	10.7
2	0.2	11	109.7	17	0.95	17.0	16.1	408	10	26.9	14.2
21	0.2	19	103.3	14	0.95	16.5	15.6	375	12	27.6	12.8
31	0.3	14	100.3	20	0.94	19.1	18.0	345	16	29.1	15.9
12	0.2	19	72.6	21	0.76	20.1	15.3	265	21	27.4	15.0
75	0.2	8	82.0	14	0.91	15.5	14.2	316	19	26.0	11.9
-2	0.3	8(d)	70.0	23	0.86	19.3	16.6	279	15	25.1	16.6
17	0.2	11	82.4	28	1.00	18.0	17.9	289	19	28.5	16.5
255	0.7	11	43.9	12	0.52	24.7	12.9	235	17	18.7	4.6
9	1.0	40	16.5	-47	0.17	28.0	4.7(g)	202	-6	8.2	-8.5
9	0.2	5	65.5	22	0.86	18.8	16.2	311	22	21.1	15.0
32	0.2	14	20.9	48	0.32	28.0	8.9	180	18	11.6	14.7
17	0.2	16(d)	35.5	10	0.55	20.4	11.2	150	11	23.7	0.8
11	0.6	12	44.5	25	0.80	19.8	15.9	193	19	23.0	20.1
3	0.5	7(d)	45.2	35	0.83	18.3	15.2	198	20	22.9	9.4
38	0.3	19	49.0	26	1.04	15.4	16.0	169	18	29.1	10.6
-14	0.2	21(d)	57.4	4	1.12	10.6	11.8	205	8	28.0	8.8
8	0.3	2	44.2	5	0.86	18.4	15.7	231	12	19.2	17.0
400	0.2	24	30.4	5	0.60	19.2	11.4	129	12	23.6	4.1
46	0.1	4	47.5	38	1.03	18.4	19.0	221	30	21.5	20.9
20	0.1	31	23.1	28	0.49	25.1	12.3	120	10	19.3	33.0
60	0.1	10	46.6	21	0.94	15.5	14.7	182	14	25.7	10.0
38	0.2	28	47.0	11	0.99	15.9	15.7	189	12	27.8	13.2
-16	0.6	4	36.9	41	0.86	18.1	15.6	191	18	19.4	14.1
37	0.4	19	32.2	5	0.70	16.1	11.2	183	11	17.6	8.2
21	0.2	29	53.6	10	1.28	12.9	16.5	183	11	32.9	11.7
-7	0.3	18	17.0	-8	0.38	15.6	6.3	143	7	11.9	-3.6
14	0.2	14	40.5	27	0.93	19.3	17.9	151	19	26.7	19.6
3	0.3	13	33.6	9	0.78	18.9	14.7	154	7	21.8	11.7
42	0.4	7	37.2	17	0.87	17.2	14.9	195	16	19.1	17.3
21	0.2	2	52.5	18	1.27	13.6	17.3	201	16	26.1	16.0
16	0.5	4	33.8	20	0.81	23.8	19.2	96	29	35.1	13.0
-9	0.3	22	31.6	32	0.77	19.7	15.3	137	15	23.1	17.2
30	0.4	15	32.7	21	0.88	17.5	15.1	123	14	26.5	7.7

(a) Year-end amounts; (b) Loans include direct lease financing; (c) Data are for banking operations only; (d) Includes other funds purchased and/or other funds sold; (e) Loans are net of unearned income; (f) Total interest income is not adjusted for tax equivalents; (g) Includes preferred stock.
Source: Standard & Poor's Compustat Services Inc.

141

international banking. Edge Act Corporations may not take deposits from local residents or make loans to them for domestic business, but they may take deposits from foreign residents and lend to anyone for international business. This alternative was even more restrictive than the use of an agency, so Sandberg quickly rejected it.

A *wholly owned subsidiary,* incorporated as a normal US bank, was another possibility. In this case, HSBC would need to invest enough funds in the subsidiary to start up its local lending business. Once established, the subsidiary could undertake any kind of activity allowed to domestically owned banks. This alternative would allow HSBC access to borrowing from the US central bank (the Federal Reserve). The full range of borrowing and lending possibilities would be open to the new subsidiary. To set up a subsidiary in New York, HSBC would need to sell the California and Houston banks, since US banking laws prohibited banks from owning full-service branches or subsidiaries in more than one state.

A subsidiary could be established by either creating a completely new bank, with new offices and new employees, or buying an existing bank with its established network of offices, people, and accounts. Clearly, the second choice would be preferable, but it would cost much more. Sandberg needed to examine the expected costs of opening new offices, perhaps in New York but also possibly in San Francisco, which is closer to Hong Kong and more closely tied to Asian business and where HSBC already had one subsidiary with several offices.

A *branch* could be established in a state in which the bank did not already have an existing affiliate. The branch would be a wholly owned affiliate of the parent bank, not incorporated separately. Establishing a new branch in 1980 would require selling the California and Houston operations, just as would opening a new subsidiary in a different state. The branch could (depending to some extent on differing state rules) take local deposits and make local loans, but it would be greatly restricted in participating in the rest of the US financial market, such as in Federal Reserve borrowing. Some states (such as Florida) do not allow foreign bank branches.

The use of additional *representative offices* was rejected immediately, since such offices would not allow HSBC direct participation in the US market. Sandberg did realize, however, that it might be desirable to have representatives in several cities, such as San Francisco, Chicago, Miami, and Los Angeles, to seek out additional business for the main office in New York. So representative offices were left as possibilities, to be considered only after the initial investment decision was made.

Finally, a *joint venture* with some other bank could be used. This strategy would enable HSBC to enter the US market with less capital investment than the other alternatives, but it would mean sharing the decision making and the profits of the venture. A joint venture would be formed as a normal US bank, similar to the subsidiary discussed above. The legal restrictions would be relatively unimportant; the key issue would be the management of the joint venture. Historically, very few joint ventures have lasted for more than a few years before the partners decided to stop the project and either operate alone or leave the market. Despite this drawback, Sandberg believed it would be worthwhile to seek a potential partner and compare the expected results of a joint venture with those of other alternatives.

The Foreign Exchange Market

The main goals of the chapter are to:

1. Explain how foreign exchange transactions take place.

2. Examine the main foreign exchange markets that operate in the United States.

3. Discuss the range of participants in foreign exchange markets and their motives for buying and selling.

4. Consider the various types of exchange arbitrage that take place in the interbank market and between different foreign exchange markets.

5. Explain the fundamental economic factors that determine the exchange rate in the absence of government intervention in the foreign exchange markets.

6. Show how firms can operate successfully in more than one currency without facing unacceptable levels of exchange risk.

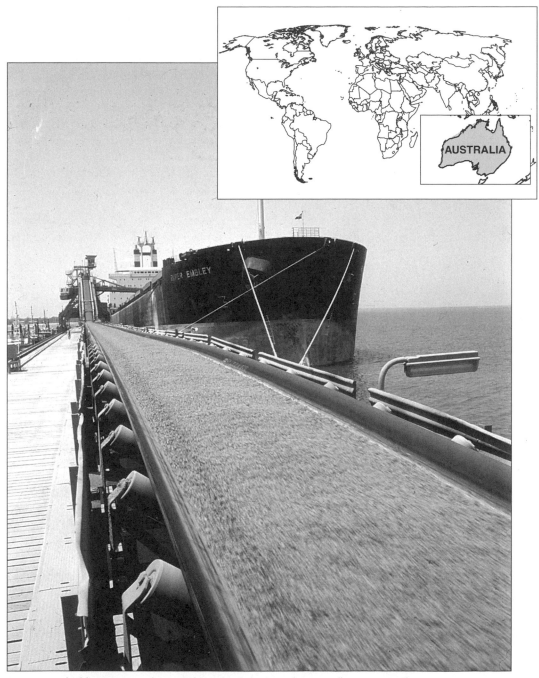

Bauxite, a valuable international commodity, is loaded onto a ship in Melbourne, Australia.
©Rick Altman/The Stock Market

INTRODUCTION   The truly fundamental differences between international and domestic business are that international business extends domestic concerns to include (1) different government-imposed rules and practices for doing business abroad or on a globally integrated scale and (2) the different national currencies used in different countries. The focus of this chapter is on these currencies and their interrelations.

This first section discusses the central concern in foreign exchange markets, the exchange rate. The next section examines the major institutions and activities that constitute the foreign exchange market in the United States today. The third section looks at the main categories of participants in foreign exchange markets worldwide. Since the exchange rate is the central variable of interest here, the fourth section looks at how it is determined. The final section considers the problem of exchange risk and methods for protecting the firm against such risk.

Currencies, like any other products, services, or claims, can be traded for one another. The **foreign exchange market** is simply a mechanism through which transactions can be made between one country's currency and another's. Or, more broadly, a foreign exchange market is a market for the exchange of financial instruments denominated in different currencies. The most common location for foreign exchange transactions is a commercial bank, which agrees to "make a market" for the purchase and sale of currencies other than the local one. In the United States, hundreds of banks offer foreign exchange markets in dozens of cities. However, over 40 percent of all foreign exchange business is done through the 10 largest banks in New York.[1]

Foreign exchange is not simply currency printed by a foreign country's central bank; rather, it includes such items as cash, checks (or drafts), wire transfers, telephone transfers, and even contracts to sell or buy currency in the future. Foreign exchange is really any financial instrument that carries out payment from one currency to another. The most common form of foreign exchange in transactions between companies is the draft (denominated in a foreign currency). The most common form of foreign exchange in transactions between banks is the telephone transfer, generally for transactions of $1 million or more. Far down the list of instruments, in terms of the value exchanged, is actual currency, which is often exchanged by tourists and other travelers.

Since no currency is necessarily fixed in value relative to others, there must be some means of determining an acceptable price, or **exchange rate.** How many British pounds (£) should one dollar buy? How many Brazilian cruzeiros should be paid to buy a dollar? Since 1973, most of the industrialized countries have allowed their currency values to fluctuate more or less freely (depending on the time and the country), so that simple economics of supply and demand largely determine exchange rates. In graphic form, Figure 6–1 shows that the intersection of the supply curve and the demand curve for German marks (DM) sets the price, or exchange rate, of marks in terms of dollars. Some of the participants in the foreign exchange market are listed below the graph; their specific activities are discussed in the following section.

Notice that the exchange rate of $0.5731 per DM is offered by one specific bank. This was the closing exchange rate quoted by Bankers Trust Company of New York for purchases of at least $1 million worth of deutsche marks on January 6, 1994. Another bank in New York may have quoted a slightly higher or slightly lower rate at the same time, and banks in San Francisco, London, or Tokyo probably quoted rates that differed even more. The rates quoted depend on each bank's interest in being involved in foreign exchange transactions and on

FIGURE 6-1

The Foreign Exchange
Market at Bankers Trust
Company of New York,
January 6, 1994

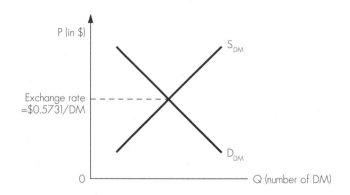

Suppliers of Marks	Demanders for Marks
US exporters	US importers paying in marks
German direct investors	US direct investors in Germany
US foreign investors remitting profits	German foreign investors in the United States remitting their profits
German portfolio investors	US portfolio investors in Germany
Bear speculators	Bull speculators

Arbitrageurs
Government "interveners"

the varying strategic positions and risks taken by the banks. Thus, the foreign exchange market among banks may be viewed as one large market or as many small markets with extensive (potential and actual) interrelations. Generally, the interbank market within any country is viewed as one market, and intercountry dealings are somewhat segmented by different rules and risks (though in the United States, the San Francisco market often offers quotations from various banks that differ noticeably from rate quotations in New York, due partly to the difference in time zones).

The differences in rate quotations may appear very small to an outsider. Deutsche marks may be quoted at $0.5734 at Citibank in New York and at $0.5747 at Bank of America in San Francisco. This difference seems small, but for every DM 1 million sold, the buyer of dollars in San Francisco receives an extra $1,600. Since the transactions are generally rapid and for values of $5 million to $10 million, such differences may add up to a substantial gain (or cost) to the participant in the foreign exchange market.

The various foreign exchange transactions just mentioned involve large commercial banks and large amounts of money. Most of the companies that do international business also utilize foreign exchange markets, but far less frequently than banks and for transactions that involve less money. Consequently, these companies' access to foreign currencies differs from that of the banks. (Specifically, banks make the market and companies pay for the use of this service.) The next section describes the various participants in the US foreign exchange market.

FOREIGN EXCHANGE MARKETS IN THE UNITED STATES

The Interbank Market

Figure 6–2 presents an overview of the foreign exchange markets operating today in the United States. This section discusses each of these markets in some detail.

Although the foreign exchange dealings of most managers involve a company buying from or selling to a bank, it is important for managers to understand the foreign exchange market among banks. This is because, as noted above, the vast majority of large-scale foreign exchange transactions are interbank, and these transactions tend to determine exchange rates, with which occasional market participants such as companies must deal.

Local and regional commercial banks may offer clients a foreign exchange service, which such banks provide on request by dealing through a larger bank,

FIGURE 6–2

US Foreign Exchange Markets

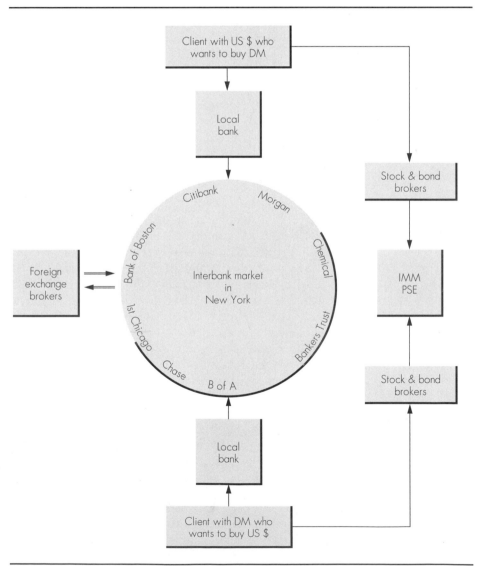

Source: Adapted from St. Louis Federal Reserve Bank *Review*, March 1984, p. 9.

typically in a large city (such as New York, Los Angeles, or Chicago). If a local bank receives a request to buy Swiss francs (SF) for an importer in New Jersey, it will call its correspondent bank in New York (say, Chemical Bank) and arrange to buy the SF for, say, $0.6753/SF. Then the local bank will add on its service charge so that the importer pays $0.6853/SF. Thus, the local bank earns $0.01 per SF, or about 1.5 percent on the transaction.

Chemical Bank, in turn, will either take the requested Swiss francs from its own holdings of that currency or enter the **interbank market** to buy them. Assuming that Chemical does *not* have the SF on hand, one of its foreign exchange traders will call several other major banks (or brokerage houses, which are discussed below) and contract to buy Swiss francs from the lowest bidder.

The interbank market generally operates with large transactions only—of about $1 million to $10 million exchanged for the equivalent foreign currency. On a typical day in 1992, the more than 100 members of the main association of commercial banks in foreign exchange dealings (called the Clearinghouse Interbank Payments System, or CHIPS) transacted roughly $192 billion of currency trades.[2]

The Brokers' Market

Another facet of large-scale foreign exchange dealing in the United States is the **brokers' market.** About half a dozen foreign exchange brokerage companies make markets for foreign currencies in New York (as well as in London and elsewhere), creating trading in many currencies similar to that in the interbank market. In this case, the key differences are that the brokers seek to match buyers and sellers on any given transaction, without taking a position themselves; they deal simultaneously with many banks (and other companies); and they offer both buy and sell positions to clients (where a bank may wish to operate on only one side of the market at any particular time).[3] Also, the brokers deal "blind," offering

TABLE 6-1

Aggregate Report on Total Foreign Exchange Daily Turnover as Reported by Financial Institutions in the US (Adjusted, $ millions)

Transaction Category	Total
I. Spot	
A. With other reporting dealers	
1. In the United States	27,508
2. Abroad	38,343
B. With Nonreporting counterparties	15,636
1. Financial institutions	13,218
2. All others	
II. Forwards	
A. With other reporting dealers	
1. In the United States	1,999
2. Abroad	3,582
B. With Nonreporting counterparties	4,077
1. Financial institutions	3,969
2. All others	
III. Swaps	
A. With other reporting dealers	
1. In the United States	15,840
2. Abroad	25,402
B. With Nonreporting counterparties	11,463
1. Financial institutions	5,908
2. All others	
IV. Options (Over-the-counter)	
A. With other reporting dealers	
1. In the United States	2,931
2. Abroad	7,051
B. With Nonreporting counterparties	3,178
1. Financial institutions	1,446
2. All others	
V. Exchange-Traded Derivatives*	
A. Currency futures contracts	5,988
B. Currency options contracts	4,762
Totals	192,301

*Not adjusted for double counting.
Source: Federal Reserve Bank of New York, US Foreign Exchange Market Turnover Survey, April 1992.

rate quotations without naming the potential seller/buyer until a deal has been negotiated. Brokers play a large role in the total market, arranging about 31 percent of total transactions, as shown in Table 6–1.

Before moving on to other foreign exchange markets, let us consider an example in which the spot market is used by a tourist planning a trip to Japan. This person wants to visit Tokyo to see a friend during Christmas vacation and to do some sightseeing. She is taking $1,000 with her and has already purchased the round-trip airline ticket. Since dollars cannot be used for most purchases in Japan, she needs to buy Japanese yen. How should she do it?

Looking at the currency trading listing in Table 6–2, she sees that Bankers Trust is offering to sell large quantities of yen at the rate of 112.7 yen per dollar. At the "retail" level—that is, for small transactions such as this one—she can expect to receive only about 105 yen per dollar. Indeed, when she called Bank of America and Wells Fargo Bank in San Francisco, they quoted rates of 106 yen per dollar. Instead of carrying the cash with her, she wants to get traveler's checks. Upon

TABLE 6-2

Foreign Currency Exchange Rates in the Interbank Market

CURRENCY TRADING

EXCHANGE RATES

Thursday, January 6, 1994

The New York foreign exchange selling rates below apply to trading among banks in amounts of $1 million and more, as quoted at 3 p.m. Eastern time by Bankers Trust Co.; Telerate and other sources. Retail transactions provide fewer units of foreign currency per dollar.

Country	U.S. $ equiv. Thurs.	U.S. $ equiv. Wed.	Currency per U.S. $ Thurs.	Currency per U.S. $ Wed.
Argentina (Peso)	1.01	1.01	.99	.99
Australia (Dollar)	.6856	.6870	1.4586	1.4556
Austria (Schilling)	.08154	.08185	12.26	12.22
Bahrain (Dinar)	2.6518	2.6518	.3771	.3771
Belgium (Franc)	.02764	.02767	36.17	36.14
Brazil (Cruzeiro real)	.0030163	.0030635	331.54	326.42
Britain (Pound)	1.4820	1.4880	.6748	.6720
30-Day Forward	1.4791	1.4849	.6761	.6734
90-Day Forward	1.4744	1.4804	.6782	.6755
180-Day Forward	1.4688	1.4748	.6808	.6781
Canada (Dollar)	.7568	.7576	1.3214	1.3199
30-Day Forward	.7564	.7572	1.3221	1.3207
90-Day Forward	.7557	.7566	1.3232	1.3217
180-Day Forward	.7548	.7557	1.3248	1.3232
Czech. Rep. (Koruna)				
Commercial rate	.0339559	.0339098	29.4500	29.4900
Chile (Peso)	.002388	.002391	418.73	418.15
China (Renminbi)	.115075	.115075	8.6900	8.6900
Colombia (Peso)	.001452	.001460	688.51	685.02
Denmark (Krone)	.1476	.1481	6.7767	6.7532
Ecuador (Sucre)				
Floating rate	.000503	.000503	1989.02	1989.02
Finland (Markka)	.17313	.17404	5.7760	5.7457
France (Franc)	.16876	.16951	5.9255	5.8995
30-Day Forward	.16826	.16901	5.9431	5.9168
90-Day Forward	.16751	.16827	5.9698	5.9428
180-Day Forward	.16668	.16744	5.9997	5.9723
Germany (Mark)	.5731	.5752	1.7450	1.7385
30-Day Forward	.5716	.5738	1.7494	1.7429
90-Day Forward	.5694	.5716	1.7562	1.7494
180-Day Forward	.5670	.5692	1.7637	1.7569
Greece (Drachma)	.003987	.004002	250.80	249.85
Hong Kong (Dollar)	.12949	.12947	7.7225	7.7235
Hungary (Forint)	.0100020	.0099800	99.9800	100.2000
India (Rupee)	.03212	.03212	31.13	31.13
Indonesia (Rupiah)	.0004734	.0004734	2112.51	2112.51
Ireland (Punt)	1.4225	1.4294	.7030	.6996
Israel (Shekel)	.3423	.3422	2.9210	2.9226
Italy (Lira)	.0005879	.0005918	1700.94	1689.85
Japan (Yen)	.008873	.008861	112.70	112.85

Country	U.S. $ equiv. Thu.	U.S. $ equiv. Wed.	Currency per U.S. $ Thu.	Currency per U.S. $ Wed.
30-Day Forward	.008879	.008867	112.63	112.78
90-Day Forward	.008900	.008887	112.37	112.53
180-Day Forward	.008944	.008930	111.81	111.99
Jordan (Dinar)	1.4495	1.4495	.6899	.6899
Kuwait (Dinar)	3.3501	3.3501	.2985	.2985
Lebanon (Pound)	.000584	.000584	1711.00	1711.00
Malaysia (Ringgit)	.3802	.3811	2.6300	2.6240
Malta (Lira)	2.5349	2.5349	.3945	.3945
Mexico (Peso)				
Floating rate	.3266479	.3266479	3.0614	3.0614
Netherland (Guilder)	.5124	.5143	1.9516	1.9444
New Zealand (Dollar)	.5564	.5624	1.7973	1.7781
Norway (Krone)	.1331	.1334	7.5140	7.4947
Pakistan (Rupee)	.0334	.0334	29.98	29.98
Peru (New Sol)	.4759	.4759	2.10	2.10
Philippines (Peso)	.03704	.03704	27.00	27.00
Poland (Zloty)	.00004874	.00004885	20517.00	20471.00
Portugal (Escudo)	.005638	.005665	177.38	176.51
Saudi Arabia (Riyal)	.26667	.26667	3.7499	3.7499
Singapore (Dollar)	.6281	.6245	1.5920	1.6012
Slovak Rep. (Koruna)	.0299850	.0299850	33.3500	33.3500
South Africa (Rand)				
Commercial rate	.2943	.2942	3.3983	3.3993
Financial rate	.2326	.2295	4.3000	4.3575
South Korea (Won)	.0012285	.0012361	814.00	809.00
Spain (Peseta)	.006890	.006916	145.13	144.59
Sweden (Krona)	.1217	.1221	8.2146	8.1927
Switzerland (Franc)	.6748	.6764	1.4820	1.4785
30-Day Forward	.6742	.6757	1.4833	1.4799
90-Day Forward	.6737	.6752	1.4844	1.4810
180-Day Forward	.6736	.6751	1.4846	1.4813
Taiwan (Dollar)	.038110	.038023	26.24	26.30
Thailand (Baht)	.03915	.03915	25.54	25.54
Turkey (Lira)	.0000676	.0000680	14800.00	14712.00
United Arab (Dirham)	.2723	.2723	3.6725	3.6725
Uruguay (New Peso)				
Financial	.223214	.223214	4.48	4.48
Venezuela (Bolivar)				
Floating rate	.00954	.00954	104.85	104.85
	— — —			
SDR	1.37014	1.37161	.72985	.72907
ECU	1.11270	1.11690	....	....

Special Drawing Rights (SDR) are based on exchange rates for the U.S., German, British, French and Japanese currencies. Source: International Monetary Fund.

European Currency Unit (ECU) is based on a basket of community currencies.

Source: *The Wall Street Journal,* January 7, 1994. p. C13.

calling the office of American Express in San Francisco, she found that yen-denominated traveler's checks were available but would cost her $1 for every 102 yen, plus a $5 service charge.

The tourist was willing to pay the extra cost to obtain the protection of traveler's checks, but one final problem arose. A friend who works in foreign exchange dealing at Wells Fargo Bank told her that the yen would probably decline in value relative to the dollar in the next few days. Since she would not leave for Tokyo for another week, she wondered whether it was worth waiting for the expected devaluation. The answer to this question is that no one knows! She can hope for a devaluation and delay purchase of the yen for a week, or ignore the potential gain—or loss!—and buy the yen today. In such a short time period, it is probably better to ignore the few days' variability in the exchange rate—since it could be favorable or unfavorable—and just buy the yen at the most convenient time before departing for Tokyo. (One more point to confuse the matter: She could buy traveler's checks in US dollars and exchange them for yen in Japan when needed. Again, no one can be sure what the yen's value will be during her vacation time in Tokyo!)

While this example does not offer a guaranteed way to make money from foreign exchange dealings, it does illustrate the kinds of problems that beset individuals and companies as they work with foreign currencies. Fortunately, there are some methods to help avoid the uncertainty involved in foreign exchange; they are discussed in the section below on "Methods of Protecting against Exchange Risk."

So far, our discussion has focused only on the *spot market,* that is, the market for immediate exchange of one currency for another. An additional, very large part of the US foreign exchange market is the set of instruments that allow contracting today for delivery of currency in the future. The main instruments of this type are forward contracts, foreign exchange futures contracts, and foreign currency options.

The Forward Foreign Exchange Market

The **forward foreign exchange market** at commercial banks in the United States offers banks, companies, and individuals the opportunity to contract *today* for a specific foreign exchange transaction in the *future,* at a fixed price (i.e., exchange rate). Forward contracts are negotiated between the offering bank and the client as to size, maturity, and price. Referring to Table 6–2, we see that Bankers Trust was offering to sell British pounds for $1.4688/£ in 180 days on January 6, 1994 (for quantities of at least $1 million).

The rationale for forward contracts in currencies is analogous to that for futures contracts in commodities; the firm can lock in a price today to eliminate uncertainty about the value of a future receipt or a payment of foreign currency. A firm may undertake such a transaction because it has made a previous contract, for example, to pay FF 1 million to a supplier in three months for some needed inputs to its operations. If the firm wants to eliminate the risk that its payment in three months will change in dollar terms (i.e., that the FF 1 million may cost more dollars then), it can contract with a bank to buy FF 1 million three months forward, at a price established today. (From Table 6–2, we see that that price was $0.16751/FF for a contract with Bankers Trust on January 6, 1994.) Thus, firms can use forward contracts to eliminate the risk of variability in future dollar costs or revenues due to exchange rate changes. This concept, called *hedging,* and other motives for using the forward market are discussed later.

Notice that in the above example, the forward contract used for hedging does *not* correspond directly to an insurance contract. The forward contract does fix a minimum "loss" for the firm by setting the guaranteed price of exchange in the future. Even if the dollar devalues to $0.18 per FF in three months, the forward contract holder is still able to buy 1 million FF for $0.16751/FF. However, if the French franc devalues over the next three months to, say, $0.15751/FF, the forward contract holder will have an **opportunity cost** of the difference between the forward rate and the (eventual) future spot rate (a difference of $0.01/FF, or 6.6 percent). Thus, the forward contract insures against potential losses *and* against potential gains in foreign currency value.

Forward markets exist in any currencies and for any maturities that banks are willing to offer. Most of the forward contracts used in the United States involve exchanges of US dollars for German marks, Japanese yen, British pounds, Swiss francs, Canadian dollars, and French francs. Maturities tend to be six months or less, though single-year and multiyear forward contracts are sometimes available.

ADDED DIMENSION

Rate Quotations

Exchange rate quotations come as two-digit numbers, bid/asked, with the preceding numbers assumed. A deutsche mark quote of 50/70 on January 6, 1994, meant an actual price of:

DM 1.7450 bid to buy one US dollar.

DM 1.7470 asked for selling one US dollar.

The bank is offering (bidding) to buy dollars for 1.745 marks per dollar and also offering (asking) to sell dollars for 1.747 marks per dollar. Of course, the actual transaction will involve $1 million or more, to be exchanged at those prices.

Rates are typically quoted on the **Continental basis,** as units of foreign exchange per dollar, everywhere. US banks have traditionally used the **American basis,** quoting $US per unit of foreign exchange. Clearly, whether the quote is DM 2.0 per dollar or $0.50/DM, the value is the same. *The Wall Street Journal* offers both types of quotations, as shown in Table 6–2.

Another means used to distinguish the two ways of presenting an exchange rate is to call a quotation of domestic currency/foreign exchange an **indirect quote.** Conversely, a quotation of units of foreign exchange/domestic currency is called a **direct quote.** This system has more general applicability to any pair of currencies, whereas the American/Continental system relates only to rates involving the US dollar. ■

The Futures Market in Currencies

A very similar type of instrument is available on several securities exchanges in the United States and abroad. The foreign exchange **futures contract** is an agreement to buy or sell a fixed amount of foreign currency for delivery at a fixed future date at a fixed dollar price. The main difference between futures and forward contracts in the United States is that futures contracts have fixed sizes (about $50,000 to $100,000, depending on the currency) and preestablished maturity dates. (All are 3-, 6-, or 12-month contracts maturing on the third Wednesday of January, March, April, June, July, September, October, or December.) Also, futures contracts are available for only a few currencies (Canadian dollars, German marks, French francs, Swiss francs, British pounds, Japanese yen, and Australian dollars) and only if a buyer and a seller can be found at the time. The futures market at the Chicago Mercantile Exchange is currently very thin (i.e., few contracts are traded) except for the three-month contracts denominated in Canadian dollars, German marks, Swiss francs, British pounds, and Japanese yen.

Futures contracts are more widely accessible to firms and individuals than forward contracts because of their smaller value and the margin requirements that enable brokers to obtain collateral from market participants. (However, the currently thin nature of this market does not allow participants the wide range of currencies and maturities that are available for large-scale transactions in the forward market.) The standard contracts available at the Chicago Mercantile Exchange are described in Table 6–3. Trading hours have been extended via the GLOBEX system, which permits worldwide access to CME contracts. In 1994 GLOBEX trading was available for about 19 hours per day around the world.

TABLE 6-3   Currency Futures Contract Specifications* at the Chicago Mercantile Exchange

	Australian Dollar (AD)	British Pound (BP)	Canadian Dollar (CD)	Deutsche Mark (DM)	French Franc (FR)	Japanese Yen (JY)	Swiss Franc (SF)
Trading unit	AD100,000	BP62,500	CD100,000	DM125,000	FR500,000	JY12,500,000	SF125,000
Quotations	US$ per A$	US$ per pound	US$ per C$	US$ per mark	US$ per franc	US$ per yen	US$ per franc
Minimum price change	.0001	.0002	.0001	.0001	.00002	.000001	.0001
Value of 1 point	$10.00	$6.25	$10.00	$12.50	$5.00	$12.50	$12.50
Price limits†	200 points	400 points	200 points	200 points	500 points	200 points	200 points
Months traded	January, March, April, June, July, September, October, December						
Trading hours‡ (Chicago time)	7:20AM–2:00PM	7:20AM–2:00PM	7:20AM–2:00PM	7:20AM–2:00PM	7:20AM–2:00PM	7:20AM–2:00PM	7:20AM–2:00PM
Last day hours	7:20AM–9:16AM	7:20AM–9:16AM	7:20AM–9:16AM	7:20AM–9:16AM	7:20AM–9:16AM	7:20AM–9:16AM	7:20AM–9:16AM
Last day of trading	Two business days before the third Wednesday of the delivery month						
Delivery date	Third Wednesday of the delivery month						

*Contract specifications are subject to change. All matters pertaining to rules and specifications herein are made subject to and are superseded by official Chicago Mercantile Exchange rules. Current Chicago Mercantile Exchange rules should be consulted in all cases concerning contract specifications. Check with your broker to confirm this information.
†Price limits are in effect from 7:20AM to 7:35AM each day, based on change of price from previous day's settlement.
‡Trading will end at 12:00 noon on the business day before a CME holiday and on any US bank holiday that the CME is open. 10/28/93 Trading from 6PM to 6AM is available through GLOBEX.
Source: Chicago Mercantile Exchange.

Foreign currency *options* are an additional instrument of the foreign exchange market in the United States; they are described in the box on page 156.

WHO USES FOREIGN EXCHANGE MARKETS?

Participants in the foreign exchange market range from multinational banks to travelers from Detroit to Windsor, Canada, from multinational companies to foreign central banks. Users of foreign exchange markets fall into five basic classes:

1. Traders/brokers
2. Speculators
3. Hedgers
4. Arbitrageurs
5. Governments (for intervention, that is, participation in the market to set an exchange rate)

Traders and Brokers

Foreign exchange traders work in commercial banks and may deal in spot market transactions or forward market transactions. Their goal in the market is to match up buyers and sellers of foreign exchange, charging an implicit fee (hidden within the exchange rate quotation itself) for providing this service. Such traders *may* buy or sell foreign exchange for the account of their own bank, thus creating foreign exchange risk for the bank. "Positions" of this kind are generally eliminated during the trading day so that the trader ends up finding a paired buyer/seller for each maturity and amount of foreign currency. (If the trader *does* accumulate one-sided transactions in one currency so that the bank finds itself with net foreign exchange due or owed, we call this *speculation*.) Among the buyers and sellers of foreign exchange that the traders serve are the millions of companies and individuals that export, import, or travel internationally and need foreign currency instruments to make their payments or cancel their receipts.

Foreign exchange brokers work in brokerage firms, which may also deal in spot or forward transactions. As noted earlier, such brokers attempt to match buyer and seller in a single transaction, with the margin between quoted rates plus a fixed fee as their commission. Brokerage firms typically deal only in foreign exchange transactions, not in any other financial instruments.

Both traders and brokers function primarily as *market makers,* profiting from their dealings through fees implicit in their rate quotations. In principle, they do not take one-sided positions in the market, though such speculation does occur and often leads to sizable gains (or losses) for banks and brokerage houses.

Speculators

Banks, companies, individuals, and governments may all function as speculators in the foreign exchange market at one time or another. A speculator is simply a participant in the foreign exchange market who takes an open position. That is, the speculator buys foreign currency without simultaneously contracting to sell it, or sells foreign exchange without possessing the currency to meet the obligation. Such short (net sale of foreign exchange) or long (net acquisition of foreign exchange) positions subject the speculator to the risk that the dollar value of the foreign currency will change before the position is eliminated.

For example, if you think the deutsche mark (DM) will go up in value relative to the dollar, you may buy 100,000 DM today and deposit them in some interest-earning instrument. You are long in DM. If you don't simultaneously sell 100,000 DM in the spot, forward, futures, or options market, you have an exposure in DM. If your guess is correct and DM do appreciate relative to dollars, your speculation will be rewarded with a profit when you finally sell the marks for dollars. If you are wrong, however, you will receive fewer dollars from your eventual sale of DM than you could have received otherwise.

Hedgers

Many companies and individuals take long or short positions in the foreign exchange market, not to speculate but to offset an existing foreign currency position in another market. That is, they engage in **foreign exchange hedging.** For example, a chemical company may agree to sell £500,000 of plastic to a buyer in London, payable in 180 days. This company has a de facto foreign exchange exposure, even though it has not entered the foreign exchange market. By contracting with a bank to sell £500,000 forward for dollars in 180 days, the company eliminates its foreign exchange exposure. Thus, one-sided participation in the foreign exchange market may *not* be speculation if the contract offsets an existing exposure of the company in some other transaction.

Hedging may be carried out in a variety of ways, many of which do not involve the foreign exchange market at all. The general issue of protecting against foreign exchange risk is discussed later in this chapter.

Arbitrageurs

Foreign exchange arbitrage involves simultaneous contracting in two or more foreign exchange markets to buy and sell foreign currency, profiting from exchange rate differences *without* incurring exchange rate risk. Foreign exchange arbitrage may be two-way, three-way, or intertemporal and is generally under-

ADDED DIMENSION

Foreign Currency Options

The most recently created type of foreign exchange market offers participants the *right* to buy or sell foreign currency in the future rather than the obligation to do so. Foreign currency options are similar to foreign currency futures in the United States in that the contracts are for fixed quantities of currency to be exchanged at a fixed price in the future. The key difference is that the option may be *exercised*, that is, presented for currency exchange, at *any* time between its issuance and the maturity date, *or* not at all.

A **foreign currency option** is a contract offering the holder the right to buy (namely, a **call option**) or sell (namely, a **put option**) a fixed amount of foreign currency for a fixed price during a fixed time period. The buyer of a call option on British pounds obtains the right to buy £31,500 at a fixed dollar price (i.e., the **exercise price**) at any time during the (typically) three-month life of the option. The seller of the same option faces a **contingent liability** in that the seller will have to deliver the British pounds at any time if the buyer chooses to exercise the option.

The market value (i.e., the price on "premium" that a buyer must pay to purchase the option) of an option depends on its exercise price, the remaining time to its expiration, the exchange rate in the spot market, and expectations about the future exchange rate. An option may sell for a price near zero, for thousands of dollars, or for anywhere in between. Notice that the buyer of a call option on British pounds may pay a small price to obtain the option but does *not* have to exercise the option if the actual exchange rate moves favorably. Thus, an option is superior to a forward contract having the same maturity and exercise price because it need *not* be used, and the cost is just its purchase price. However, the price of the option is generally higher than the expected cost of the forward contract, so the user of the option pays for the flexibility of the instrument.

Some recent currency option prices from the Philadelphia Stock Exchange are presented in Table 6–4. ■

taken by large commercial banks that can exchange large quantities of money to exploit small rate differentials.

Two-Way The simplest form of exchange arbitrage is **two-way arbitrage,** between any two currencies and between two places. Quotations for Swiss francs in the spot market on January 6, 1994, were

At Bankers Trust in New York: $0.6748/SF.
At Bank of America in San Francisco: $0.6753/SF.
At Lloyds Bank in London: $0.6784/SF.

An arbitrageur can buy SF in New York and simultaneously sell them in London, making a profit of $0.0036/SF, or 0.53 percent per transaction. While the percentage gain is small, it translates to $3,600 for every 1 million SF traded, and it involves no exchange risk. By repeatedly arbitraging this price (exchange rate) differential, the arbitrageur will make a profit until the exchange rate differential drops below the transactions cost (i.e., the telephone bill, plus the arbitrageur's salary, plus other relevant costs).

TABLE 6–4

Forex Options on the Philadelphia Exchange

OPTIONS — PHILADELPHIA EXCHANGE

Strike	Month	Calls Vol.	Calls Last	Puts Vol.	Puts Last
FFranc					**168.70**
250,000 French Franc EOM-European style.					
17	Jan	1000	0.94	...	....
17¼	Jan	1000	0.38	...	....
DMark					**57.28**
62,500 German Mark EOM-European style.					
55	Jan	...	...	50	0.05
62,500 German Marks EOM-cents per unit.					
55½	Jan	...	...	50	0.09
59½	Jan	100	0.05	...	....
Australian Dollar					**68.61**
50,000 Australian Dollars-cents per unit.					
68	Jan	...	...	50	0.20
69	Mar	1	0.80	...	....
British Pound					**148.07**
31,250 British Pounds-European Style.					
150	Jan	5	0.36	...	....
150	Mar	5	1.96	...	....
31,250 British Pounds-cents per unit.					
142½	Feb	3	5.55	...	....
145	Jan	...	...	21	0.10
147½	Jan	2	1.57	103	0.58
147½	Mar	...	...	62	2.49
150	Jan	112	0.24	...	....
150	Feb	100	1.25	...	....
152½	Feb	20	0.48	...	....
152½	Mar	100	1.30	...	....
British Pound-GMark					**258.40**
31,250 British Pound-German mark EOM.					
258	Jan	...	...	64	1.22
258	Mar	...	...	6	2.98
260	Jan	64	1.00	...	....
Canadian Dollar					**75.67**
50,000 Canadian Dollars-European Style.					
75½	Jan	8	0.41	...	....
50,000 Canadian Dollars-cents per unit.					
74	Mar	...	...	20	0.35
74½	Mar	71	1.50	...	....
75	Mar	2	0.75	300	0.09
75	Mar	21	1.13	...	....
75½	Jan	...	...	100	0.25
75½	Mar	61	0.84	...	....
76	Mar	143	0.75	...	....
76½	Jan	150	0.12	...	....
77½	Mar	170	0.27	...	....
ECU					**111.15**
62,500 European Currency Units-cents per unit.					
110	Jan	5	1.42	5	0.24
French Franc					**168.70**
250,000 French Francs-European Style.					
16¼	Jan	...	...	157	0.82
16¾	Jan	...	...	100	0.38
17¼	Jan	100	0.12	...	....
17¼	Feb	...	...	5000	4.70
GMark-JYen					**64.65**

Strike	Month	Calls Vol.	Calls Last	Puts Vol.	Puts Last
62,500 German Mark-Japanese Yen cross.					
64½	Jan	...	...	7	0.68
65	Mar	50	0.92	...	....
German Mark					**57.28**
62,500 German Marks EOM-cents per unit.					
56½	Jan	...	...	14	0.25
57	Jan	4	0.68	...	....
58	Jan	500	0.32	...	....
62,500 German Marks-European Style.					
56	Feb	...	...	100	0.27
57½	Jan	15	0.29	...	....
58	Jan	30	0.13	...	....
58	Mar	...	...	15	1.56
58½	Jan	15	0.05	...	....
59	Jan	...	...	15	1.63
59	Feb	100	0.24	...	....
62	Mar	9500	0.07	...	....
62,500 German Marks-cents per unit.					
55	Jan	48	2.30	...	....
55½	Feb	6	1.90	200	0.19
56	Jan	...	...	130	0.05
56	Feb	...	...	1	0.33
56	Mar	...	...	10	0.62
56½	Jan	...	...	19	0.10
56½	Feb	...	...	100	0.47
56½	Jan	5	1.51	...	....
57	Jan	12	0.56	155	0.16
57	Feb	2	0.89	212	0.61
57	Mar	...	...	29	1.08
57½	Jan	4	0.23	50	0.42
57½	Feb	210	0.61	203	0.83
57½	Mar	25	1.01	...	....
58	Jan	2437	0.10	483	0.84
58	Feb	12	0.50	6	1.12
58	Mar	1	0.81	74	1.54
58½	Jan	10	0.07	...	....
58½	Mar	200	0.29	...	....
58½	Mar	5	0.63	...	....
59	Jan	...	...	3	1.58
59	Feb	350	0.20	...	....
59	Mar	102	0.40	63	2.23
59½	Jan	...	...	6	2.11
59½	Feb	100	0.16	...	....
59½	Mar	10	0.29	5	2.52
60	Jan	196	0.01	3	2.60
60	Mar	10	0.21	63	3.04
63	Jan	...	...	3	5.59
63	Mar	6	0.05	10	5.76
Japanese Yen					**88.62**
6,250,000 Japanese Yen EOM-100ths of a cent per unit.					
90	Jan	15	0.47	...	....
6,250,000 Japanese Yen EOM.					

Strike	Month	Calls Vol.	Calls Last	Puts Vol.	Puts Last
90½	Jan	70	0.30	...	....
6,250,000 Japanese Yen-100ths of a cent per unit.					
86	Mar	...	...	20	0.54
87	Mar	...	...	4	0.86
87½	Jan	...	...	100	0.12
87½	Jan	...	...	10	1.03
88	Jan	...	...	135	0.21
88	Feb	...	...	15	0.79
88	Mar	...	...	61	1.17
88½	Jan	...	...	351	0.40
89	Jan	525	0.42	520	0.65
89½	Jan	500	0.24	100	0.91
90	Jan	10	0.16	...	....
90½	Jan	20	0.11	...	....
91	Mar	5	0.84	.	....
91½	Jan	30	0.04	...	....
92	Jan	...	...	2	3.15
93	Mar	5	0.40	3	4.29
94	Jan	20	0.01	...	....
95	Jan	20	0.01	...	....
95	Feb	40	0.06	...	....
95	Mar	60	0.20	...	....
96	Feb	10	0.05	...	....
97	Mar	...	...	47	8.25
104	Mar	...	...	10	15.22
6,250,000 Japanese Yen-European Style.					
88	Jan	...	...	20	0.20
95	Mar	...	...	1	6.18
Swiss Franc					**67.38**
62,500 Swiss Franc EOM-cents per unit.					
66	Jan	...	...	5	0.23
62,500 Swiss Francs-European Style.					
65	Mar	...	...	12	0.39
71	Feb	3	0.15	...	....
62,500 Swiss Francs-cents per unit.					
64	Feb	...	...	200	0.12
65	Feb	...	...	1300	0.20
65½	Mar	...	...	85	0.50
66	Feb	3	2.02	225	0.49
66	Mar	1	2.40	274	0.85
66½	Jan	5	1.02	1000	0.11
66½	Feb	...	...	650	0.55
67	Jan	6	0.87	...	....
67	Mar	...	...	27	1.04
67½	Jan	...	...	150	0.47
67½	Feb	32	1.20	...	....
68	Jan	1053	0.35	...	....
68	Mar	1	1.23	5	1.75
68½	Jan	...	...	4	0.86
68½	Mar	7	1.01	...	....
69	Mar	...	...	207	2.38
69½	Mar	75	0.76	...	....
71	Mar	20	0.45	...	....

Call Vol 39,947   Open Int ... 523,686
Put Vol 13,901   Open Int ... 442,261

Source: *The Wall Street Journal*, January 7, 1994, p. C13.

The same two-way arbitrage may also occur in the forward market or between forward and futures markets.[4] From the quotations here, we see that profitable arbitrage opportunities exist between the New York forward market and the Chicago futures market, as well as between the New York and San Francisco forward markets:

At Bankers Trust in New York: 111.8 yen/$ for delivery in 180 days.

At Bank of America in San Francisco: 109.9 yen/$ for delivery in 180 days.

At the Chicago Mercantile Exchange: 112.0 yen/$ for delivery on June 15, 1994.

An arbitrageur can buy yen in New York and sell them in San Francisco, both for exchange in 180 days, and earn 1.9 yen/dollar, or 1.7 percent per transaction. Similarly, an arbitrageur can buy yen in Chicago and sell them in San Francisco, to make 2.1 yen/dollar, or 1.9 percent per transaction. The difficulties with the latter transaction are that contracts may not be available for the desired amount or maturity date and transactions costs are higher for the intermarket exchanges. Nonetheless, both transactions may be feasible and profitable, even after costs are considered.

Three-Way   When the arbitrageur does not wish to operate directly in a two-way transaction because of restrictions on the market or for any other reason, profits may still be available through triangular or **three-way arbitrage.** In this case, the arbitrageur moves through three currencies, starting and ending with the same one and incurring no exchange-rate risk. Quotations from the London *Economist* and *The Wall Street Journal* in January 1994 showed the following two-way exchange rates:

$1.4820/£ at Bankers Trust in New York.

$0.1686/FF at Bank of America in San Francisco.

FF 9.00/£ at Lloyds Bank in London.

In this case, two-way exchanges are ignored and the transactions will be to (1) buy FF/sell dollars, (2) buy £/sell FF, and (3) buy $/sell £; *or* (1) buy £/sell dollars, (2) buy FF/sell £, and (3) buy $/sell FF.

The optimal transactions can be illuminated by creating **cross rates** from the quotations. For instance, if the arbitrageur wants to compare the London exchange rate with the other two, a pound/French franc rate can be created as

---

ADDED DIMENSION

Intertemporal (Interest) Arbitrage

Exchange arbitrage across maturities, or **intertemporal arbitrage,** is similar to the previous two forms in that it requires starting and ending with the same currency and incurring no exchange rate risk. In this case, profits are made by exploiting *interest rate differentials* as well as exchange rate differentials. Also, the intertemporal exchange arbitrageur (or interest arbitrageur) must utilize funds for the time period between contract maturities, whereas the two- and three-way arbitrageurs need funds only on the delivery date.*

Consider the following information:

At Bankers Trust in New York, the spot exchange rate is: SF 1.4820/$.

At Bankers Trust in New York, the 180-day forward is: SF 1.4846/$.

At Barclays Bank in London, the 6-month dollar (eurodollar) deposit rate is: 3.375 percent/year.

At Barclays Bank in London, the 6-month SF (eurofranc) deposit rate is: 3.8125 percent/year.

The interest arbitrageur who begins with U.S. dollars has two alternatives for using funds in intertemporal arbitrage. First, the funds may simply be invested in a dollar-denominated instrument, such as a eurodollar deposit at Barclays Bank. This investment pays 3.375 percent per year, or 1.6875 percent for the six-month investment. Alternatively, the arbitrageur may buy SF, invest in a franc-denominated instrument, and buy dollars forward. These three transactions create a dollar-denominated instrument, which pays 3.8125 percent/year, plus the percentage exchange-rate change. The forward premium on Swiss francs (i.e., the implicit exchange-rate change in percentage terms) is:

$$\frac{XRf - XRs}{XRs} = -0.175 \text{ percent/year } \text{6 month}$$

$$\frac{\$0.1686/FF}{\$1.4820/£} = £0.1138/FF \text{ in New York and San Francisco (or FF } 8.79/£)$$

Similarly, the pound/dollar cross rate is

$$\frac{£1/FF9.00}{\$0.1686/FF} = £0.6590/\$ \text{ in London and San Francisco (or } \$1.517/£)$$

The franc/dollar cross rate is

$$\frac{FF\ 9.00/£}{\$1.4820/£} = FF\ 6.0729/\$ \text{ in London and New York (or } \$0.1647/FF)$$

From these comparisons, the arbitrageur can see that the maximum profits from triangular arbitrage come from (1) buying FF for dollars in London, (2) selling FF for £ in San Francisco, and (3) buying \$ for £ in London; *or* (1) buying £ for dollars through the cross rate exchange, (2) selling the £ for FF through the cross rate exchange, and (3) buying \$ for FF through the cross rate exchange. Either of the two procedures will yield the same percentage profit, though it must be

where

 XR = Exchange rate ≡ \$US/foreign currency.

 f = Forward.

 s = Spot.

This means that the dollar value of the francs decreases by 0.175 percent/180 days between the purchase and sale of SF. Thus, the full return on this arbitrage is approximately: (3.8125 percent − 0.3500 percent) per year = 3.4625 percent per year, or 1.73 percent for six months. This is more than the return on a dollar instrument, so interest arbitrage should be undertaken here.[5]

The basic relation between interest arbitrage and domestic investment may be shown as

$$(1 + i\ \text{domestic}) \overset{e}{=} (1 + i\ \text{foreign}) \frac{XRf}{XRs}$$

where i = interest rate. This is called the **interest parity** equation. In equilibrium, both sides are equal. Most of the time, either domestic investment or interest arbitrage will be profitable, and such arbitrage tends to push interest and exchange rates to the point where the equation holds.

Because the interest parity relationship is generally close to equality, the percentage gains available to interest arbitrageurs are low. Large banks, which can commit large amounts of funds to foreign currency investments with low transactions costs (usually in the eurocurrency market), are the main participants in interest arbitrage. (Notice that earnings from interest arbitrage include both interest earnings, which are positive, and exchange rate earnings, which may be positive or negative.) ■

---

* The two foreign exchange contracts in intertemporal arbitrage, spot and forward, are a form of *swap* agreement. (That is, dollars are swapped for francs today and francs are swapped back for dollars in the future.) When the swapped foreign currency is invested in a money market instrument, the full set of three transactions constitutes *interest arbitrage*.

TABLE 6–5   Cross Rates in the New York Interbank Market

	Dollar	Pound	SFranc	Guilder	Peso	Yen	Lira	D-Mark	FFranc	CdnDlr
				Key Currency Cross Rates (late New York trading, January 6, 1994)					
Canada	1.3215	1.9578	.89140	.67741	.43167	.00792	.0008	.75752	.22302	....
France	5.9255	8.779	3.9970	3.0375	1.93555	.03551	.0035	3.3967	....	4.4839
Germany	1.7445	2.5845	1.1767	.89425	.56984	.01045	.0010	....	.29441	1.3201
Italy	1699.0	2517.1	1146.04	870.92	554.97	10.180	....	973.92	286.73	1285.7
Japan	112.65	166.89	75.987	57.746	36.797	....	.0663	64.574	19.011	85.24
Mexico	3.0614	4.5355	2.0650	1.5693	....	.0183	.0018	1.7549	.5166	2.3166
Netherlands	1.9508	2.8901	1.3159	....	.63722	.01169	.0011	1.1183	.32922	1.4762
Switzerland	1.4825	2.1963	....	.75994	.48426	.00888	.0009	.84981	.25019	1.1218
U.K.	.67499	....	.45531	.34601	.22048	.00404	.0004	.38693	.11391	.51078
U.S.	....	1.4815	.67454	.51261	.32665	.00599	.0004	.57323	.16876	.75672

Source: *The Wall Street Journal*, January 7, 1994, p. C13.

ascertained that the cross rates are in fact available as calculated. Cross rates available in the New York interbank market on January 6, 1994, are shown in Table 6–5.

Governments

Governments participate in the foreign exchange market as (1) buyers and sellers of foreign exchange and (2) the rulemakers. The reader should not become so engrossed in the economics of the foreign exchange market as to ignore the government's ability to change the exchange rate by fiat or to close trading in foreign exchange at any time. Since the major developed countries agreed to allow floating currency values in early 1973, most of those 10 to 15 countries have largely allowed the market to determine exchange rates. However, the other 170 countries of the world have fixed their currency values to the dollar, pound, or other currency, have used exchange controls to limit access to foreign exchange, and/or have not allowed a foreign exchange market to operate. In virtually all of these countries, no forward, futures, or options markets exist. (Mexico, in which a futures market and some forward contracts in pesos are available, is an exception.) The rationales of governments for intervening in the market are discussed below in the context of the balance of payments (also see Chapter 8). Here we need to recognize that government intervention is always a potential and often an actual concern.

As buyers and sellers of foreign exchange, governments act to influence the exchange rate and to reduce or augment holdings of various currencies in the central bank. If a country has been running a balance-of-trade deficit, it may be able to reduce the deficit by having the central bank buy foreign currency in the open market. Sufficient purchases will cause the local currency to devalue, making exports cheaper and imports more expensive to buyers. If export and import price elasticities are high enough, this may lead to an improvement in the balance of trade.[6]

DETERMINATION OF THE EXCHANGE RATE

Exchange rates are determined by the activities of the five types of actors described earlier. If one could calculate the supply and demand curves for each exchange market participant and anticipate government constraints on the exchange market, exchange rate determination would be fairly simple. The composite supply and demand for foreign exchange would be as depicted in Figure 6–1.

Lacking this information, the analyst can still rely on two fundamental economic relationships that underlie exchange rate determination. Note that this section considers only economic factors; government restrictions on the exchange market are ignored.

The two fundamental economic relationships are *purchasing power parity* and the *international Fisher effect*. The former posits that shifts in exchange rates will occur to offset different rates of inflation in pairs of countries, and the latter proposes that exchange rates will shift to offset interest rate differentials between countries.

Purchasing Power Parity (PPP)[7]

If a standard ton of polyurethane plastic costs $200 in the United States and DM 400 in Germany, **purchasing power parity (PPP)** requires an exchange rate of 2 DM/$. The same reasoning could be used for all products whose production processes are equivalent in two countries and that are traded between these countries. The exchange rate that comes closest to simultaneously satisfying all of these equilibrium conditions is the PPP rate—a rate that equates the internal purchasing power of the two currencies in both countries.

Assuming we begin from that exchange rate, what will happen if Germany's inflation is 5 percent and US inflation is 10 percent in the following year? Purchasing power parity requires that the exchange rate adjust to eliminate this differential. Specifically, it requires that

$$\frac{1 + \text{Infl}_{US}}{1 + \text{Infl}_{Ger}} = \frac{XR_{t+1}}{XR_t}$$

where:

Infl = Inflation rate.

t = Time period.

This means that inflation in the United States relative to inflation in Germany should be the same as the future exchange rate compared to the spot exchange rate. The relationship can also be written in a form similar to the interest parity equation by rearranging terms:

$$(1 + \text{Infl}_{US}) = (1 + \text{Infl}_{Ger})\frac{XR_{t+1}}{XR_t}$$

Purchasing power in each currency will be retained if

$$XR_{t+1} = \frac{1.10}{1.05}(\$0.50/DM) = \$0.524/DM, \text{ or DM } 1.909/\$$$

International Fisher Effect

The **international Fisher effect** translates Irving Fisher's reasoning about domestic interest rates to the transnational level. Fisher showed that inflation-adjusted (i.e., "real") interest rates tend to stay the same over time; as inflation rises or falls, so do *nominal* (unadjusted) interest rates, such that real interest rates remain unchanged. At the transnational level, nominal national interest rates are expected to differ only by the expected change in the national currency's price (i.e., the exchange rate). The international Fisher effect thus concludes that interest differentials between national markets will be eliminated by adjustments in the exchange rate. In terms similar to PPP, we see that

$$\frac{1 + i_{US}}{1 + i_{foreign}} = \frac{XR_{t+1}}{XR_t}, \text{ or } (1 + i_{US}) = (1 + i_{foreign})\frac{XR_{t+1}}{XR_t}$$

where i = the interest rate, usually on a eurocurrency deposit denominated in the given country's currency.

If the eurodollar deposit rate is 10 percent/year and the euro-French franc rate is 15 percent/year, the franc will be expected to devalue in the coming year by

$$\frac{1.10}{1.15} = 0.9565, \text{ or } 4.35 \text{ percent}$$

Notice that the international Fisher effect *will* operate in a free market, because investors will receive a higher return in French francs otherwise. As more and more US investors put their money in eurofrancs, the spot price of FF will rise. Similarly, as US investors return their franc earnings to dollars at the end of the period (year), this increased demand for dollars will cause the franc to devalue (in the future). Thus, dollar and franc earnings will tend to be equalized.

Combined Equilibrium Relationships

The future exchange rate, XR_{t+1}, will be partially determined by both of the above factors (PPP and international Fisher), which can be viewed in a general equilibrium context as shown in Figure 6–3. This figure also demonstrates the interest parity relationship, which provides another link between current and future currency values. Remember that these relationships are *equilibrium* economic conditions, which hold only approximately since substantial uncertainty exists about future conditions. Also, if a government intervenes to prohibit the market from determining exchange rates, the relationships may diverge substantially from the equilibrium conditions. Figure 6–3 shows the main economic influences that, along with government policies and other factors, combine to determine exchange rates.

A final caveat is in order. Despite the strong relationships among interest differentials, inflation differentials, and exchange rates, other important *economic* influences operate in international finance. Pure speculation can cause shifts in exchange rates, despite the fundamental economic conditions that have been described above. A country's balance-of-payments position (see Chapter 8) may affect the exchange rate, even though that position also affects interest and inflation rates as well. Since the abandonment of the Bretton Woods system of fixed exchange rates, exchange rate determination has been extremely uncertain—perhaps similar to the determination of future values of stock exchange indexes.

METHODS OF PROTECTING AGAINST EXCHANGE RISK

Exchange risk is a very real concern for financial managers, whether or not their firms are directly involved in international business. The fact that the prices of imported products and services often vary with the exchange rate means that a local firm's costs may depend on the exchange rate. Similarly, if any of the firm's sales are exported, its earnings may vary as foreign sales change due to exchange rate changes. Even a purely domestic firm faces these problems, since suppliers

FIGURE 6–3

Exchange Rate Determination

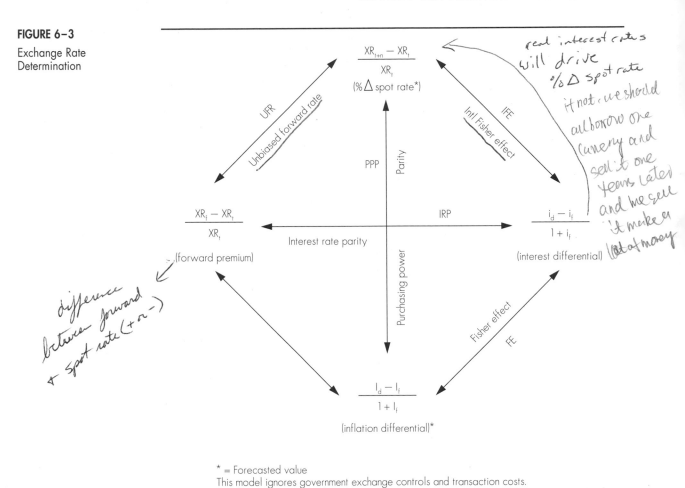

* = Forecasted value
This model ignores government exchange controls and transaction costs.
XR ≡ Domestic currency/foreign currency

and competitors that *are* doing international business will adjust to exchange rate changes, and this will affect the domestic firm.

From this perspective, exchange risk is *not* the risk that a local currency will decrease in value (devalue) relative to the dollar. *Exchange risk is the possibility that a firm will be unable to adjust its prices and costs to exactly offset exchange rate changes.* Thus, a US importer who faces 10 percent higher costs because of a dollar devaluation from DM 1.7/US$ to DM 1.53/US$ still has no exchange risk as long as the importer can raise his or her own prices by 10 percent without lowering total sales. (This result is the microeconomic version of purchasing power parity.) The problem may be viewed as one of "passing through" cost increases to the firm's customers via higher sales prices.

Similarly, the appropriate measure of exchange risk for financial instruments is the firm's possible loss or gain in purchasing power from exchange rate-adjusted interest rates. Investing in a US dollar account that pays 10 percent per year is better than investing in a French franc account that pays 20 percent per year if during the year the franc devalues by 12 percent.

Alternatives to Minimize Exchange Risk

Exchange risk exists whenever the firm's prices and costs cannot be exactly adjusted to offset changes in the exchange rate. Let us now consider a group of alternatives that will allow a firm to minimize (or at least reduce) its exchange risk. These alternatives fall into four categories:

1. Risk avoidance
2. Risk adaptation
3. Risk transfer
4. Diversification

Risk Avoidance   **Exchange risk avoidance** is the strategy of trying to avoid foreign currency transactions. A purely domestic firm can try to make all of its purchases from local suppliers of locally produced goods and make all of its sales to local buyers in competition only with other domestic firms. Obviously, this strategy is impractical, if only because all firms are affected by goods priced in foreign currency—automobiles, chemicals, steel, and so on. Also, there are very few industries that do not use imported materials, export some of their output, or compete with imported products.

Risk Adaptation   **Exchange risk adaptation** offers a more realistic alternative for protecting the firm against exchange risk. This strategy includes all methods of "hedging" against exchange rate changes. In the extreme, exchange risk calls for protecting all liabilities denominated in foreign currency with equal-value, equal-maturity assets denominated in that foreign currency. An illustration can best clarify this point.

Assume a French firm has contracted to buy $100,000 of machinery from a foreign supplier for use in its manufacturing operations. The purchase is payable in six months in US dollars. To eliminate foreign exchange risk completely, the firm may do two things. First, it may raise its own prices to customers once the six months pass to equate franc devaluation to price increase. (Note that this does *not* involve a foreign currency hedge.) If this option is not available, which is often the case, the firm may look to its other option: obtain some equal-value *dollar asset* maturing in 180 days. This may be as simple as depositing funds in a dollar-denominated bank account for six months or as arcane as arranging a swap of the dollar liability for some other firm's franc liability. Fairly standard methods of hedging an exposed dollar liability include

1. Obtaining a dollar-denominated financial asset (e.g., a time deposit or a CD) that matures when the liability comes due.
2. Finding a buyer for your firm's products and agreeing to receive payment in US dollars for the same value and time as the liability.
3. Finding a bank that will contract to buy francs from you and sell you dollars at a price fixed today for exchange when the liability comes due. (This is called a *forward contract.*)
4. Agreeing with another (e.g., North American) firm to exchange your dollar liability for that firm's (i.e., its French subsidiary's) franc liability.
5. Contracting for any other equal-value, equal-maturity dollar-denominated asset that will offset the exposed liability.

The firm's goal in choosing among these methods is to minimize the cost of protection against exchange rate risk.

Risk Transfer   The third strategy for reducing exchange risk is **exchange risk transfer.** This strategy involves the use of an insurance contract or guarantee that transfers the exchange risk to the insurer or guarantor. In many countries, the central bank offers exchange risk guarantees to importers and exporters of some products according to the bank's policies. Technically, though perhaps not realistically, any firm or government agency could issue a guarantee covering exchange rate changes to a local importer, at a price that would presumably reflect the risk.

Diversification   The final strategy for reducing exchange risk is **currency diversification.** Here a firm can reduce the risk of unexpected local currency devaluations by spreading its assets and liabilities across several currencies (e.g., deutsche marks, Swiss francs, and pounds in addition to US dollars). This strategy simply means, "Don't put all of your eggs in one basket." Domestically, a firm should deal with several suppliers and a variety of customers to reduce risk through diversification. Internationally, a firm should hold assets (and liabilities) in several currencies to reduce the impact of unexpected exchange rate changes.

The strategy that is probably most useful to the majority of firms is risk adaptation, or hedging. A key point of this section is to recognize that other alternatives may be used in many instances when hedging would be more expensive or otherwise less desirable. Nonetheless, the central problem in exchange risk management is hedging, and corporate treasurers should always be on the lookout for new instruments and techniques.

CONCLUSIONS

The foreign exchange market is a central part of international business. That market is really several distinct markets, including spot transactions as well as forward contracts, futures, options, and other instruments that vary from country to country.

The participants in the foreign exchange market include commercial banks—the most important participants in terms of the value of transactions undertaken—and many other actors in the private and public sectors, such as corporations, individuals, and governments. The main forces determining exchange rates tend to be the large banks that trade billions of dollars' worth of currencies daily.

Exchange rates are determined by government choice in each country. When, as in most industrialized countries today, the government allows the free market to operate, such economic factors as inflation differentials and interest rate differentials tend to determine exchange rates. Even so, forecasting exchange rates is a highly uncertain activity because of the wealth of factors that influence these rates.

Finally, protection against exchange rate variations is possible through many kinds of hedging strategies. Generally, companies, banks, and individuals want to find foreign currency liabilities to balance against their existing foreign currency assets, and vice versa. The ultimate decision to hedge or not hedge (i.e., speculate) is a matter of policy for the firm; there is no "right" answer.

QUESTIONS

1. Who are the main participants in the foreign exchange market in the United States? How does each participant affect the exchange rate?
2. Based on ~~Figure~~ *Table* 6-2 would you expect interest rates in Japan to be higher or lower than those in the United States? Why?

3. Given that France's inflation is about 6 percent per year at present, while US inflation is about 3 percent per year, what do you expect to happen to the franc/dollar exchange rate in the next few months? Why?

4. Explain the process of interest arbitrage. How can a bank profit from it?

5. What is the difference between the forward exchange rate and the future spot exchange rate?

6. How do foreign exchange brokers function in the US foreign exchange market?

7. Explain the influence of the US government in determining the exchange rate between the dollar and the Japanese yen. How does the Japanese government affect this rate?

8. Assume that the interest rate on 12-month US dollar deposits in London is currently 3.6875 percent per year and the rate on German mark deposits there is 5.1875 percent per year. The spot exchange rate is US $0.5757/DM. What do you expect the exchange rate to be in one year?

9. How would you hedge the value of your export sale of FF 10 million of computers to a French customer? You will be paid in 180 days in francs. On what basis would you choose among hedging methods?

10. Why do the exchange rates of the forward market and the futures market differ for similar maturities?

REFERENCES

Andrews, Michael. "Recent Trends in the U.S. Foreign Exchange Market." *Quarterly Review,* Federal Reserve Bank of New York, Summer 1984.

Dufey, Gunter. "Foreign Exchange Markets and Currency Risk," in Dennis Logue (ed.), *Handbook of Modern Finance,* 2nd ed., chap. 41. Boston: Warren Gorham and Lamont, 1990.

Giddy, Ian. "Foreign Exchange Options." *Journal of Futures Markets* 3, no. 2 (1983).

Kubarych, Roger. *Foreign Exchange Markets in the United States.* Federal Reserve Bank of New York, 1981.

Lindert, Peter. *International Economics,* 9th ed. Homewood, IL.: Richard D. Irwin, 1991.

Pauls, B. Diane. "U.S. Exchange Rate Policy: Bretton Woods to Present." *Federal Reserve Bulletin* (November 1990).

Shapiro, Alan. *Multinational Financial Management,* 3rd ed. Boston: Allyn & Bacon, 1989.

NOTES

[1] The clearing member banks of the New York Clearinghouse Association are Bank of New York, Bankers Trust, Chase Manhattan Bank, Chemical Bank, Citibank, European American Bank, Irving Trust, Manufacturers Hanover Trust, Marine Midland Bank, Morgan Guaranty, National Westminster Bank, and US Trust.

[2] "Summary of Results of US Foreign Exchange Market Turnover Survey Conducted in April 1992," Federal Reserve Bank of New York (xerox), 1993. p. 1.

[3] "Taking a position" means purchasing an asset (or a liability) denominated in a foreign currency without simultaneously matching it with a liability (asset) of the same value and maturity in the same currency. If a US bank buys Swiss francs, it takes a position in Swiss francs. When the bank sells those Swiss francs to a client, it eliminates the position.

[4] Ian Giddy has shown how similar arbitrage can be used between a forward market and an *options* market, since the combination of a put and a call option on the same currency is analogous to a forward contract. See Giddy (1983).

[5] Notice that analogous conditions face Swiss arbitrageurs, who *should not* buy dollars, invest in a eurodollar deposit, and buy SF forward under these conditions. (Check the results mathematically.) Thus, interest arbitrage *will* occur in the example, in this case by dollar-holding arbitrageurs.

[6]The Marshall-Lerner condition requires that the export elasticity of demand plus the import elasticity of demand be less than 1 for a devaluation to improve the balance of trade. See, for example, Lindert (1991), pp. I-4, I-5.

[7]This entire discussion refers to *relative* purchasing power parity (PPP). The stronger, absolute version refers to parity in the values of factor inputs used in the production of products whose prices reflect relative factor productivities. Relative PPP considers only *changes* in the relative price levels between countries, not the initial (absolute) levels.

Scholtes 6, 7
Rume

Fred's Furniture, Ltd.

Fred Fox walked out of his Piccadilly Circus store one afternoon in August 1994, shaking his head and wondering whether there was any solution to the foreign currency game. He had just contracted for the third time with his good friend Jean Marnier in Paris for an export shipment of FF 2,000,000 of tables, chairs, and sofas that would be sent in November and paid for in February 1995. The past two times Fox had dealt with Marnier on similar shipments, he later discovered that devaluations of the franc relative to the pound had left him with virtually no profit on the sales. This time he had been able to get Marnier to accept a 15 percent markup in the price quote (payable in francs) to offset the expected devaluation of the franc between now and next February. Unfortunately, he had been unable to persuade Marnier to pay in British pounds! The exchange rate risk still existed, and despite the price markup Fox was very unhappy about living with it.

A second, related problem compounded Fox's frustration. He had just agreed to buy a large supply of polyvinyl chloride (PVC) plastic, from which one of his local furniture suppliers would construct the ultramodern tables that currently made up about one-fourth of Fox's sales in England. He had already given a price quotation to his manufacturer, so there was no flexibility at that end. The supplier of this PVC was in Germany and demanded to be paid in German marks (in 120 days). Once again, Fox had tried to anticipate the possible impact of currency changes on this DM 200,000 transaction, but he had been unable to figure out a solution.

Fox sometimes thought that he was blessed with good fortune because he lived within the European Union, and the 12 member countries had eliminated almost all restrictions on exports of furniture among them. His export sales were growing very satisfactorily, except for the foreign currency problem. That problem, however, was a curse to his business, since Fox made no claim to be a "finance man," and he was truly baffled by the fluctuations among pounds, marks, francs, lire, and other currencies.

A trip to the local Barclays Bank office cleared up some of the issues for him. First, he discovered that he could contract for a forward sale or purchase of any of the currencies that he dealt with. By accepting a small premium or discount relative to the current exchange rate, Fox could guarantee a fixed exchange rate for his future purchases of marks (for pounds) and his future sales of francs (to buy pounds). The rate quotations relevant to the two transactions described above are listed in Table 1.

This case was written in 1986 by Professor Robert Grosse as a basis for class discussion (revised 1994).

TABLE 1

Interest Rate and Exchange
Rate Quotations Offered to
Fred Fox, August 1, 1994

Spot exchange rates: FF 8.73 per £
                    DM 2.57 per £

180-day forward rate: FF 8.76 per £   *offers this rate in 180 days*
120-day forward rate: DM 2.58 per £   "   " in 120 days

120-day or 180-day British pound deposit interest rate: 5.25% per year
180-day euro-French francs deposit interest rate: 6.00% per year
120-day euro-German mark deposit interest rate: 5.75% per year
Fred's Furniture would pay the deposit rate plus 2% per year for a loan.

Six-month put options on French francs at FF 8.75 per £ have a premium of £300 per contract; each contract
    is for FF 100,000.
Six-month call options on German marks at DM 2.59 per £ have a premium of £200 per contract; each
    contract is for DM 50,000.

Note: Each exchange rate can be used as a bid or offered rate as needed; ignore the difference.

    The Barclays banker also suggested that Fox consider financing his French franc receivable with a loan in francs rather than using British pound financing during the period from now until payment by Marnier's firm. This would enable Fox to balance out his furniture sale in francs with the loan repayment and also give him funds today that he could use in his ongoing business. Unfortunately for Fox, the banker also suggested that Fox consider taking out an option on future marks in the London International Financial Futures Exchange. Since Fox could not follow the banker's explanation of the way this instrument works, he determined to eliminate options as an alternative. All of the rate quotations given by Barclays to Fox are listed in Table 1.

    Beyond the short-term problem of dealing with the two transactions described above, Fox wants to establish some kind of system for handling future foreign currency business. He is highly risk averse when it comes to exchange rate risk, and his primary objective is to avoid large losses due to currency fluctuations.

Exchange Rate Arrangements as of December 31, 1992[1]

Pegged					
Single Currency				Currency Composite	
US Dollar		French Franc	Other	SDR	Other
Angola	Nicaragua[4]	Benin	Bhutan (Indian	Libya[6]	Algeria
Antigua and	Oman	Burkina Faso	rupee)	Rwanda	Austria
Barbuda	Panama	Cameroon	Kazakhstan	Seychelles	Bangladesh[4]
Argentina	St. Kitts and Nevis	Central African Rep.	Kiribati (Australian		Botswana
Aruba	St. Lucia	Chad	dollar)		Burundi
Bahamas, The[4]	St. Vincent	Comoros	Kyrgyzstan		Cape Verde
Barbados	Suriname	Congo	Lesotho[4] (South		Cyprus
Belize	Syrian Arab Rep.[4]	Côte d'Ivoire	African rand)		Czech Rep.
Djibouti	Yemen, Rep. of	Equatorial Guinea	Moldava		Fiji
Dominica		Gabon	Namibia		Hungary
El Salvador[4]		Mali	San Marino		Iceland[7]
Ethiopia		Niger	Swaziland (South		Jordan
Grenada		Senegal	African rand)		Kenya
Iraq		Togo	Turkmenistan		Kuwait
Liberia			Uzbekistan		Malawi
Marshall Isl.					Malta
Micronesia, Fed. States of					Mauritania
Mongolia					Mauritius
Netherlands					Morocco
Antilles					Myanmar
					Solomon Islands
					Tanzania
					Thailand
					Tonga
					Vanuatu
					Western Samoa
					Zimbabwe

[1]Current information relating to Democratic Kampuchea is unavailable.

[2]In all cases listed in this column, the US dollar was the currency against which exchange rates showed limited flexibility.

[3]This category consists of countries participating in the exchange rate mechansim of the European Monetary System. In each case, the exchange rate is maintained within a margin of 2.25 percent around the bilateral central rates against other participating currencies, with the exception of Italy, in which case the exchange rate is maintained within a margin of 6 percent.

[4]Member maintains multiple exchange arrangements involving more than one exchange rate. The arrangement shown is that maintained in the major market.

Flexibility Limited vis-à-vis a Single Currency or Group of Currencies		More Flexible			
Single Currency[2]	Cooperative Arrangements[3]	Adjusted According to a Set of Indicators	Other Managed Floating	Independently Floating	
Bahrain[5]	Belgium[4]	Brazil	Cambodia	Afganistan	Mozambique
Qatar[5]	Denmark	Chile[4]	China, People's Rep. of[4]	Albania	Nepal
Saudi Arabia[5]	France	Colombia	Ecuador	Australia	New Zealand
United Arab Emirates[5]	Germany	Lithuania	Egypt[4]	Bolivia	Nigeria
	Ireland	Madagascar	Greece	Brazil	Norway
	Luxembourg[4]		Guinea	Bulgaria	Paraguay
	Netherlands		Guinea-Bissau	Canada	Peru
	Portugal		Hong Kong	Costa Rica	Philippines
	Spain		Indonesia	Dominican Rep.	Romania
			Israel	El Salvador	Russian Fed.
			Korea	Finland	Sierra Leone
			Lao People's Dem. Rep.	Gambia, The	South Africa[4]
			Malaysia	Ghana[4]	Sudan
			Maldives	Guatemala	Sweden
			Mexico[4]	Guyana	Switzerland
			Pakistan	Haiti	Trinidad and
			Poland	Honduras	Tobago
			Sao Tome & Principe	India	Uganda
			Singapore	Iran	Ukraine
			Slovak Rep.	Italy	United Kingdom
			Slovenia	Jamaica	United States
			Somalia	Japan	Venezuela
			Sri Lanka	Latvia	Zaïre
			Tunisia	Lebanon	Zambia
			Turkey	Lithuania	
			Uruguay		
			Vietnam		

[5]Exchange rates are determined on the basis of a fixed relationship to the SDR, within margins of up to ±7.25 percent. However, because of the maintenance of a relatively stable relationship with the US dollar, these margins are not always observed.

[6]The exchange rate is maintained within margins of ±7.5 percent.

[7]The exchange rate is maintained within margins of ±2.25 percent.

Source: International Monetary Fund, "Exchange Arrangements, and Exchange Restrictions," Annual Report, 1993. Washington, DC: IMF, 1993.

Chapter 7

International Financial Markets And Institutions

This chapter considers foreign and international financial markets that allow firms to find sources of funds outside their home countries and to place available funds in portfolio-type investments outside the home country. The main goals of the chapter are to:

1. Review the basic characteristics of all the financial markets that may be available to a firm in international business.

2. Explain how the international monetary system functions and how it relates to both private sector firms and governments.

3. Give insights into domestic money and capital markets that exist around the world.

4. Describe the functioning of the euromarkets, both short term and long term.

5. Show how firms can take advantage of the opportunities available in all of these markets.

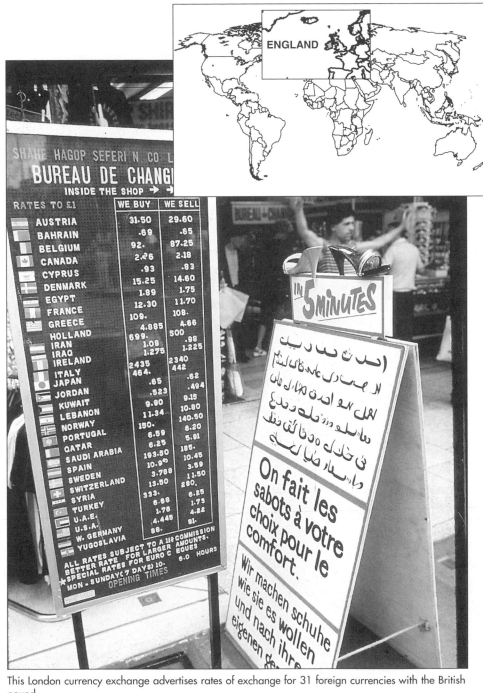

This London currency exchange advertises rates of exchange for 31 foreign currencies with the British pound.
©Eric Carle/Stock Boston

INTRODUCTION

Whether or not a company becomes directly involved in international business through exports, direct investment, and the like, there is still an important international market to consider, even for a domestic business: the market for borrowing and lending abroad. Often companies find that borrowing funds abroad is less expensive than borrowing domestically, in the United States or in any other home country. The relatively unrestricted "euromarkets" generally offer better terms to borrowers (*and* lenders) than do domestic financial markets in any country. Likewise, in the 1990s investors are discovering more and more opportunities to diversify their portfolios into holdings of foreign securities. This chapter explores the various foreign and international financial markets (except the foreign exchange market, which was discussed in Chapter 6) and examines ways to utilize them for domestic and international business.

Table 7–1 presents an overview of international financial markets. It should be emphasized that the final market to consider in conducting financial transactions in these markets is the market for real goods and services, or consumption. That is, the ultimate use of financial instruments in each of these markets is to claim goods and services, today or in the future.

International Financial Markets

The **international monetary system** is a market among the central banks of the countries that belong to the International Monetary Fund (IMF). This organization functions as a kind of central banking system for the national governments of its 151 members. Each member country deposits funds at the IMF, and in return each may borrow funds in the currency of any other member country. This system is *not* open to private sector participants, so it is not directly useful to company managers. However, agreements made between member countries and the IMF often lead to major changes in government policies toward companies and banks (such as exchange rate changes and controls and trade controls), so an understanding of the international monetary system may be quite important to managers. Regulation in this system comes through rules passed by the IMF's members. The major financial instruments used in the international

TABLE 7–1 International Financial Markets

Market	Instruments	Participants	Regulator
International monetary system	Special drawing rights; foreign exchange; position at the IMF	Central banks; International Monetary Fund	International Monetary Fund
Foreign exchange markets	Bank deposits; currency; futures and forward contracts	Commercial and central banks; firms; individuals	Central bank in each country
National money markets (short term)	Bank deposits and loans; short-term government securities; commercial paper	Banks; firms; individuals; government agencies	Central bank; other national government agencies
National capital markets (long term)	Bonds; long-term bank deposits and loans; stocks; long-term government securities	Banks; firms; individuals; government agencies	Central bank; other national government agencies
Eurocurrency market	Bank deposits; bank loans; eurocommercial paper	Commercial banks; firms; government agencies	Substantially unregulated
Eurobond market	Bonds; some equity issues	Banks; firms; individuals; government agencies	Substantially unregulated

monetary system are national currencies and a currency issued by the IMF itself, called the *SDR* (*special drawing right*). These points are defined more clearly, and the IMF system is discussed in detail, in the next section of this chapter.

A **foreign exchange market,** as we saw in the previous chapter, is a market in which financial instruments denominated in one currency can be exchanged for financial instruments denominated in another currency. Typically, most foreign exchange is sold through a country's commercial banking system in the form of bank deposits. Cash exchanges by traveling businesspeople and tourists are quite common, but nearly all of the vast quantities of money exchanged goes between banks, as account transfers, and in large amounts. Regulation of foreign exchange markets comes primarily from the national government of the country where the markets are located, through the central bank. The main instruments used in foreign exchange dealings include account transfers by telephone, wire, or otherwise; bank drafts; forward and futures contracts; and currencies.

National money markets and national capital markets are simply the national financial markets of countries other than the firm's home country. So, for a US-based company, the money and capital markets of France are international (actually foreign) financial markets. Access to such markets is often limited to "domestic" firms, which usually include locally incorporated subsidiaries of multinational enterprises. Thus, foreign money and capital markets are additional potential sources and users of funds for the MNE.

Short-term national financial markets, or **national money markets,** generally offer the MNE some opportunities to obtain or place funds. Typically, local bank deposits and short-term investments in Treasury securities give the firm an interest-earning opportunity for its locally available funds. A variety of additional instruments can also be found in many of the developed countries and a number of LDCs. Commercial paper, promissory notes, and short-term government obligations are just a few of these instruments. MNEs can often borrow from local banks or through the issue of some form of promissory notes, or sometimes directly from the government. For short-term funding and investing decisions, the MNE manager needs to be aware of the wide variety of money market instruments available in host countries.[1]

Similarly, long-term national financial markets, or **national capital markets,** offer additional opportunities to MNE financial managers. A number of countries have national securities markets in which the MNE can issue its own securities (stocks and bonds) or invest in the securities of other firms. In most countries, long-term bank loans provide a source of funds and national treasury issues provide investment possibilities. Regulation in both of these national financial markets comes from the national government through such agencies as the central bank, the treasury, and the securities exchange.

The fifth and sixth markets for financial instruments are the **euromarkets,** the short-term eurocurrency market and the long-term eurobond market. Each of these financial markets is characterized by the issuance of instruments (i.e., deposits or bonds) denominated in some currency other than that of the country where they are issued. The euromarkets are generally unrestricted by governments and establish their own pricing and other conditions.

The **eurocurrency market** is a largely short-term market for bank deposits and loans denominated in any currency except that of the country where the market is located. In London, for example, the eurocurrency market is a market for bank deposits (and loans) denominated in dollars, marks, yen, and any other currency except British pounds. In Paris, the eurocurrency market is a market for similar instruments denominated in dollars, marks, yen, pounds, and any other currency except French francs. Most transactions in this market involve maturities of less than one year, although some deposits and loans are long term. The main instruments used in the eurocurrency market are certificates of deposit, time deposits, and bank loans. During the past few years, euro-commercial paper has become a significant short-term instrument as well.

The **eurobond market** is a long-term market for bonds denominated in any currency except that of the country where the market is located. It is basically the long-term counterpart of the eurocurrency market (though there are also other important differences). The only instruments used in the eurobond market are bonds, denominated in various currencies and typically with a floating interest rate. Since regulation is minimal in the countries that permit eurobond issues, participants in this market depend for protection on the reputations of the other participants rather than on national securities laws.

The euromarkets offer investors and borrowers in one country the opportunity to deal with borrowers and investors from many other countries, purchasing and selling deposits, bonds, and loans denominated in many currencies. Euromarkets may be entered through affiliates of "eurobanks"—banks that participate in the euromarkets—in virtually any country. For instance, a eurodollar loan may be taken by a US company, dealing through the local office of a US bank that legally books the transaction in London. Similarly, a US investor may place a deposit in the eurodollar market simply by instructing a local US bank to create the deposit in its foreign branch in London, Panama, or any one of more than a dozen euromarket centers worldwide. Finally, eurobonds and euro-commercial paper may be issued by investment banking firms on behalf of company or government clients in several national markets simultaneously to many types of investors. In all, the euromarkets offer substantial opportunities to virtually any large or medium-size firm when it deals in financial markets for either borrowing or lending.

The last market of interest here is the **market for goods and services,** which is the ultimate destination of the financial instruments used in the other markets. Either at present or in the future, the various financial instruments will be utilized to purchase real goods or services from suppliers in one country or another. The key *social* benefits of the various international financial markets are that they facilitate the process of matching borrowers and lenders in all parts of the world and facilitate payments through widely accepted media of exchange. This chapter does not discuss the market for goods and services, since that is the ultimate target of all activities examined in the book.

Let us begin our consideration of international financial markets with a view of the intergovernmental system that provides a framework for the others: the international monetary system.

THE IMF SYSTEM

The first international financial market we will examine here may be viewed as either the most important of all or as one that is generally irrelevant to private business managers. The international monetary system is a financial market in which only central banks and the **International Monetary Fund (IMF, or the Fund)** operate, so private business plays no active role in it. On the other hand, rules for international financial dealings among countries are often set at the IMF, and substantial international loan decisions are made between governments and the IMF. Thus, the rules of the game in the other international financial markets are greatly influenced by IMF activities.

The international monetary system determines the exchange rate regime that prevails among the major developed countries, whose currencies are used for the vast majority of international payments. The IMF negotiates with governments of debtor nations for loans directly from the Fund and for loan conditions that are used subsequently as a basis for lending by private banks to these same borrowers. In addition, the IMF serves as an intermediary for emergency loans between member governments to cope with the capital flow or exchange rate crises that occur from time to time due to speculation in foreign exchange markets or other causes. All in all, the international monetary system plays a major role in determining the rules of the game for private companies and banks in international business, so managers need to understand its functioning.

Brief History

The International Monetary Fund was designed in 1944 at a conference of the Allied nations held at Bretton Woods, New Hampshire. Its general purpose was to provide a multilateral framework for avoiding international financial crises by establishing rules for national exchange rate policies and for adjustment to balance-of-payments disequilibria (discussed in the following chapter). It was specifically intended to avoid the disastrous financial contraction that occurred during the 1930s. As originally negotiated, and as implemented in 1946 when the Articles of Agreement were signed by the initial 46 member countries, the IMF system required *fixed* exchange rates among member countries, with gold as the basis for currency valuation. The US dollar was initially fixed at a value of $35 per ounce of gold, and all other currencies were fixed at values expressed in both dollars and gold.

Fixed exchange rates were a fundamental base of the Bretton Woods system. Under the Articles of Agreement, each country was obligated to maintain its currency value at the initially set value (the "par" value), with a band of ±1 percent of flexibility around the par value. If a foreign central bank demanded to sell a country's currency back to the issuer, that country was required to pay the equivalent amount of gold, US dollars, or some other acceptable currency.

To join the IMF, a country was required to make a deposit of gold (25 percent), plus its own currency (75 percent), such that each member country's total deposit relative to the total of IMF deposits was roughly in proportion with its share of world trade. Then each member country received the right to borrow up to 200 percent of its initial deposit at the Fund in any currency to help pay for imbalances such as the one mentioned above. If a country borrowed more than its original deposit, the IMF would stipulate economic policies that the borrower had to follow to receive more financial support. (This imposition of policy demands by the IMF is called *conditionality.*)

While the IMF sought to provide assistance for nations facing balance-of-payments problems, its only resources were the contributions of its member countries: quotas based on each country's part in world trade, which initially constituted about $9 billion. This relatively small amount of liquidity was not sufficient to support the post-World War II economic recovery, or specifically the payments imbalances, of even the European countries.[2] Ultimately, the US Marshall Plan injected the needed funding into the international financial system, and specifically into Europe, during 1948-52.

In fact, the IMF provided very little funding to its member countries in its early years. During the Suez crisis in 1956, it loaned $1.7 billion to Great Britain, France, and India. Later, during speculative runs on the British pound (i.e., periods when speculators sold large quantities of pounds for other currencies in expectation of a devaluation of the pound) in 1961 and 1964, it extended loans to Great Britain. By the end of the 1960s, the IMF was regularly providing credit to member countries, though still not at the levels that many analysts believed necessary to stabilize the system. (The alternative view is that the IMF should not provide credit to the member countries at all; rather, these countries should be forced to adjust their economies to escape balance-of-payments problems. Balance-of-payments adjustment is discussed in Chapter 8.)

At the end of the 1960s, the US dollar began to be the object of speculative pressure. The problem was severe, since the dollar constituted the base for the entire system of value (through its formal link to gold at $35 per ounce). The United States was unable to devalue to stop the speculation, and later it was unwilling to continue selling its gold holdings to foreign central banks that wanted to redeem their dollars. In August 1971, President Nixon announced that the United States would no longer sell gold to foreign central banks in exchange for dollars. In December 1971, he announced a devaluation of the dollar to $39 per ounce of gold.

These events essentially destroyed the Bretton Woods system of fixed exchange rates. Many initiatives to repair the system were presented during the following two years, but the United States would no longer accept the responsibility of providing the dollar as a fixed base for other currencies. In February 1973 the dollar was again devalued, this time to $42 per ounce of gold. In subsequent months, the IMF system was changed de facto to a floating exchange rate system that allowed each country to leave the value of its currency free to change with market forces or to fix that value to some other currency. Since that time, the United States has allowed the dollar to float in value relative to all other currencies, with occasional efforts by the Fed (the Federal Reserve System) to influence the dollar's relationship to particular currencies, such as the German mark and the Japanese yen.

The Current IMF System

Under the current IMF system, no limitations are set on each member country's decision to either fix its currency value relative to some other currency or allow it to fluctuate as supply and demand dictate. (Notice that it is impossible for one country to keep its currency fixed relative to all others if the others are not fixed relative to one another.) In 1976, an accord called the Jamaica Agreement altered the IMF charter to formally allow for floating exchange rates. Today, the exchange rate regimes used by each nation are substantially unrestricted, and government strategies to influence exchange rates are altered as desired.[3]

At about the same time that the link between the dollar and gold was broken, the IMF's members agreed to create a new currency that the Fund would issue when authorized to do so by a vote of the members. This currency, called the **special drawing right (SDR),** allows its holder to obtain (or draw) other currencies from the IMF (or from other members) when desired. SDRs have been created and issued on seven occasions to date. A total of SDR 21.4 billion existed in 1993; their total value was about $30 billion. In each instance, the SDRs were allocated to Fund members according to their quotas. This new "international money" has served to support a number of countries that encountered financial crises since 1971, allowing them to finance their imbalances, but it has not been a solution to imbalances in international financial flows. During the international debt crisis of the early 1980s, SDR use was wholly inadequate to deal with the more than $350 billion of dollar debt owed by Latin American countries to foreign lenders. Total IMF resources include member-country quotas, which totaled $205 billion at the end of 1993—so the Fund actually has quite substantial lending power.

Unresolved Problems with the IMF System

The IMF system today differs dramatically from the model established at Bretton Woods in 1944. Flexible exchange rates have been substituted for fixed ones; gold has been greatly reduced as an international monetary asset,[4] and its link to the dollar has been severed; a new reserve currency, the SDR, has been created to increase world liquidity; and, perhaps most important, the US dollar is no longer the single base for the IMF system of value. These major changes have come in response to problems and crises that have occurred during the past 45 years—yet the IMF system itself survives. While few people would argue that the IMF has led directly to greater international financial stability over its history, at least the system has been flexible enough to accommodate the various crises that have threatened it.

Several problems that remain in the system deserve note. First, there has always been an uncomfortable tension between the countries that want to utilize the IMF simply as a bank for reducing the negative impacts of balance-of-payments difficulties and the countries that want to utilize it to subsidize economic development. The "link" between the IMF and development finance was originally delegated to the World Bank (the IMF's sister institution). Traditionally, the IMF has loaned funds only for short-term uses, sometimes extending to two or three years. Many borrowing countries, especially the less developed ones, have repeatedly called for greater use of IMF resources to finance development projects. While there are often no clear differences between financing payments imbalances and financing development projects that may later reduce those imbalances, the IMF has not substantially widened its scope. In the 1980s, under the cloud of multiple international loan renegotiations by Latin American countries, the Fund began to extend longer-term loans and to reconsider its strategy. The ultimate result of this crisis still remains to be seen. It appears in the mid-1990s that the Fund will retain its basic form, and the resources of the World Bank will be expanded to assist more heavily in economic development.

A second problem that continues to plague the Fund is the issue of exchange rate regimes. Even as the flexible rate system moves through its third decade, there are repeated calls for a return to fixed, or more tightly constrained, currency values. The great instability of international financial dealings during the period since the initial OPEC oil crisis of 1973–74 has led some analysts to argue for a return to fixed rates. The evidence during the entire 20th century tends to suggest that no matter what exchange rate regime prevails, if international trade relations are unstable and payments imbalances are substantial, no exchange rate regime will be able to solve the problem. Thus, this problem most likely cannot be eliminated.

On the whole, the international monetary system plays an extremely important role in all international financial dealings by being the focal point for establishing

ADDED DIMENSION

Special Drawing Rights and the Private Sector

During the 1980s, SDRs became fairly widely used as a currency of denomination for private sector financial instruments such as bonds and long-term bank loans. Because the SDR has a value based on five currencies (see Figure 7–1), it is more stable as a borrowing or lending tool than any individual currency.

When the dollar devalues relative to other widely traded currencies, so does the SDR—but only 36 percent of the SDR's value is affected negatively. The other 64 percent of the SDR's value is based on marks, pounds, yen, and French francs, and these currencies may rise or fall relative to the dollar in such a situation. Overall, the changes must net out over all currencies, and an instrument such as the SDR changes relatively little in value compared to any single currency. The SDR is really a "basket" of currencies whose value is generally more stable than that of any one of its components.

Since the SDR is nothing more than an accounting convention, it cannot be used in final settlement of private sector accounts. That is, no such thing as an SDR bill or coin exists. However, since the SDR does have a value measurable in terms of any other currency, it can always be settled in dollars, marks, or any other currency (e.g., in so many "SDRs' worth of dollars"). Financial instruments can be purchased in SDRs' worth of different currencies and later paid out in SDRs' worth of the same or other currencies at maturity.

Just as the ECU (European Currency Unit) has gained wide acceptance as an instrument for denominating international financial transactions, so too the SDR promises to gain wide acceptance as a risk-reducing instrument. (The SDR has the advantage of including the US dollar in the group of currencies that determine its value, whereas the ECU is based only on European currencies.) At present, however, private sector investors and borrowers are using a much greater volume and value of ECU-denominated instruments than SDR-denominated instruments. ■

rules on exchange rates, exchange controls, intergovernmental loans, and other official transactions.

Since we have already examined foreign exchange markets in detail, we now turn to domestic money and capital markets in foreign countries.

FOREIGN MONEY AND CAPITAL MARKETS

In each country the MNE enters, it will be able to obtain some degree of access to local financial markets. The MNE will generally utilize such markets to perform necessary local financial transactions and often to hedge its local asset exposure through local borrowing (or its local liability exposure through local deposits or investments). But the MNE can also utilize local financial markets to obtain additional funding (or place additional funds) for its nonlocal activities. A Mexican firm, for example, may choose to borrow funds through its Houston affiliate to finance its local needs in Texas *and* finance some of its needs in Mexico.

Usually national financial markets are not fully accessible to foreign firms; they are largely reserved for domestic borrowers and lenders. In these cases, use of local financial markets must be supplemented by use of the financial markets in the country of the parent company or elsewhere. Typically, such problems arise in countries that impose exchange controls, which limit the MNE's ability to put needed funds in the affiliate. Selected information about national short- and

FIGURE 7–1

The Special Drawing Right
(on October, 11, 1993)

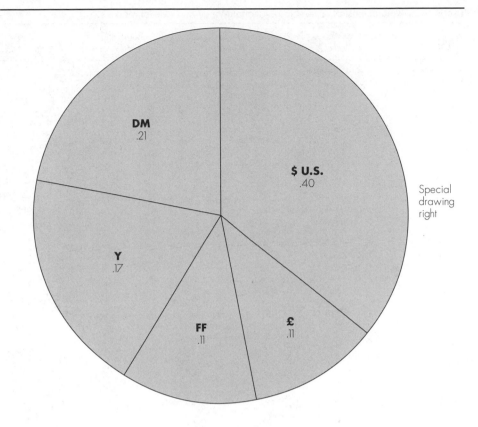

Distribution of value of the SDR,
the basic monetary unit of the International Monetary Fund

For example, in dollars: 1 SDR= $ ____ (.21) + $ ____ (.11) + $ ____ (.17) + $ ____ (.11) + _1_ (.40) = $1.42
                              DM   **FF**   **Y**   **£**   **$**

long-term financial markets in a number of countries is presented in Table 7–2. Notice that the developed countries in the table have far fewer restrictions on their money and capital markets and that the United States has the fewest of all. Exchange controls are the rule in LDCs and are fairly common in developed countries as well. During the late 1980s and early 1990s, there was a clear trend to reduce financial controls in developed, less developed, and formerly communist countries.

MNEs and National Money Markets

The advantages MNEs obtain from entering national money markets as *borrowers* of funds stem from the portfolio effect of holding liabilities in more than one (fluctuating) currency and from the local risk hedging that occurs as the MNE moves to balance local assets such as plant and equipment with local liabilities, such as local-currency borrowing. Additional benefits may occur if the local government subsidizes such loans through interest rate reduction, through tax breaks, or otherwise; a policy of this kind may be offered to attract the MNE's investment. This may lower the whole MNE's cost of capital if the subsidy does not disappear and if the interest rate remains below the comparable home currency rate during the borrowing period.

TABLE 7-2   Characteristics of Selected National Money and Capital Markets

Issue Country	Limits on Access to Market	Foreign Exchange Market	Borrowing Instruments Available	Size of Stock Market	Size of Bond Market
Argentina	Same treatment as local firms	Fixed exchange rate 1 austral = 1 dollar US; official and parallel markets; spot and forward markets	Short-term bank loans; overdrafts; commercial paper; discounted A/R*; factoring; medium-term and long-term bank loans	Buenos Aires bolsa lists 180 companies; 15 stocks account for 70% of trading	In 1992 $1.8 billion of corporate bonds were traded
Brazil	FDI limited in certain sectors: airlines, mining, petroleum, banking, media, power generation	Managed floating of cruzeiro; active parallel market; no forward market	Limited overdrafts; short-term bank loans; discounted A/R	São Paulo bolsa lists over 1,000 firms; fewer than 100 are traded regularly	Very thin market exists
Canada	Same treatment as local firms	Spot, forward, futures, options in Montreal and Toronto	Short-term bank loans; overdrafts; commercial paper;† B/A; long-term bank loans	Toronto exchange lists 1,154 firms	In 1992, C$ 17.9 billion issued; government issues in 1992 totaled C$ 78.9 billion
France	Same treatment as local firms	Spot, forward, and futures markets in Paris	Overdrafts; discounted A/R; commercial paper; factoring		In 1992, Ff 366 billion of total bonds issued, 53% by government borrowers
Germany	Same treatment as local firms	Spot and forward markets in Frankfurt	Short-term bank loans; discounted A/R; overdrafts; factoring		Very deep market for domestic DM and euro-DM
Hong Kong	Same treatment as local firms	Hong Kong dollar fixed to US dollar; spot, forward, and options markets	Overdrafts; short- term bank loans; discounted A/R; commercial paper	291 stocks listed; few foreign ones	None

*Accounts receivable.
†Banker's acceptances.

The advantages MNEs obtain from entering national money markets as *lenders* of funds stem from the portfolio effect of holding financial instruments in more than one currency. There may also be a gain from balancing local-currency assets and liabilities if an excess of local liabilities was held previously. In addition, local financial investments may be a necessary strategy when exchange controls or profit remittance limits exist; such investments offer the firm an outlet for retained earnings that yields interest. Sometimes an exchange control policy may make the local-currency interest rates higher than those available in other currencies (after adjusting for expected exchange rate changes). In these cases, higher than normal profits can be earned by investing funds in local instruments, although exchange controls may limit conversion of the profits into the home country currency, or a government-imposed exchange-rate change may wipe out the advantage.

MNEs and National Capital Markets

The advantages MNEs obtain from entering national capital markets as *borrowers* are similar to those obtained from entering national money markets. However, the opportunities are generally much more limited. Very few countries have substan-

TABLE 7–2   *Continued*

Issue Country	Limits on Access to Market	Foreign Exchange Market	Borrowing Instruments Available	Size of Stock Market	Size of Bond Market
India	Eight sectors are closed to foreign ownership	Rupee pegged to basket of currencies; licensed banks are only dealers; spot and limited forward markets	Overdrafts; short-term bank loans; discounted A/R	Over 4,700 companies listed on Indian stock exchanges	124.5 billion rupees of corporate bonds issued in 1992
Japan	Restricted not by law but by discrimination	Limited to registered banks and brokers; spot and forward markets	Overdrafts; short-term bank loans; discounted A/R; commercial paper; factoring	Tokyo exchange is the world's largest stock market	Very large
Korea	Restricted not by law but by discrimination	Managed floating of won; limited spot market	Overdrafts; short-term bank loans; discounted A/R; commercial paper; factoring	Korean Stock Exchange listed 502 companies in 1988	Strong market developing
Mexico	FDI not limited, except for financial, petroleum, media, and transportation sectors	Free market; spot and forward markets	Short-term bank loans; overdrafts; discounted A/R; commercial paper; factoring	255 firms listed on the Mexican bolsa; 45 are actively traded	In February 1993, $8.4 billion of corporate bonds outstanding
UK	Same treatment as local firms	Spot, forward, futures, and options markets in London	Short-term basic loans; overdrafts; discounted A/R; commercial paper; factoring	London Exchange lists 2,660 firms	Europound common; very large
USA	Same treatment as local firms	Spot, forward, futures, and options markets in New York and Chicago	Almost unlimited	New York Stock Exchange lists 1,822 firms	Very large and diverse

Sources: Business International Corporation, *Financing Foreign Operations* (1993 edition); various national sources.

tially developed stock markets, and those that do usually restrict the issuance of shares by foreigners. A few exceptions exist, such as the United States, the United Kingdom, Germany, and France, but even they serve only the largest and most creditworthy MNEs.[5] National bond markets, when they exist, are also very restrictive. Thus far, virtually all of the foreign bond issues have taken place in New York (called "Yankee bonds"), London, Switzerland, Germany, and Japan (called "Samurai bonds"). Table 7–3 gives some idea of the size of the foreign bond and eurobond markets. Note that the foreign bond market is simply the national bond market of any country as it relates to foreign institutions that seek to issue bonds in that market.

Notice that all of the foreign bond issues combined do not account for nearly as much funding as the eurobond market. Also notice that the eurobond market is dominated by US dollar issues, while the foreign bond market is far less concentrated in any one currency. (Swiss franc foreign bonds dominated such issues in the 1980s.) The amount of foreign bonds denominated in currencies

TABLE 7–3   Foreign Bond and Eurobond Market Characteristics (millions of US dollars)

	1981	1984	1985	1987	1990	1993
Eurobonds						
Total euro	31,616	79,458	136,731	140,535	199,584	406,694
US dollar	26,830	63,593	97,782	58,070	70,070	146,935
German mark	1,277	4,604	9,491	15,023	21,150	57,904
British pound	501	3,997	5,766	15,051	18,030	43,868
Japanese yen	368	1,212	6,539	22,563	33,065	46,805
European currency units	309	3,032	7,038	7,397	17,526	7,161
Other	1,697	3,020	10,114	22,431	12,561	104,021
Foreign Bonds						
Total foreign	21,369	27,953	31,025	40,253	30,385	76,806
US dollar	7,552	5,487	4,655	7,416	5,940	24,795
German mark	1,310	2,243	1,741	n.a.	n.a.	n.a.
British pound	746	1,292	958	n.a.	n.a.	n.a.
Swiss franc	8,285	12,626	14,954	24,301	13,741	27,394
Japanese yen	2,457	4,628	6,379	4,071	n.a.	14,770
Other	538	1,677	2,339	4,465	n.a.	9,847
Grand total	52,985	107,411	167,756	180,788	228,904	483,500

n.a. = not available.

Source: Morgan Guaranty Trust Company, *World Financial Markets,* various issues; Salomon Brothers, *Bond Market Research,* (various issues).

other than dollars is about 70 percent of the total. The eurobond market, which functions mostly outside the United States, is dominated by dollar issues, which constitute about 40 percent of that total. In all, dollar-denominated issues account for about 36 percent of the two types of international bonds.

Finally, the advantages MNEs obtain from entering national capital markets as *lenders* come mainly from diversification and from higher returns that may be protected by exchange controls, just as in the short-term market. Since the national capital markets are generally small, opportunities to use them are quite limited for foreign as well as domestic investors. Of course, since the main currencies of interest to MNEs and other international investors *are* those of the few large industrial countries, opportunities in those national capital markets do exist.

REGIONAL MONEY AND CAPITAL MARKETS

Until recently, the scope of financial markets and instruments was predominantly domestic or fully international, but not regional. In the past two decades, however, the European Union (formerly the European Community, which is discussed in Chapter 10) has designed both a regional monetary system (the **European Monetary System,** or **EMS**) and a regional currency unit (the **European Currency Unit,** or **ECU**) for intergovernmental financial transactions in the Union. While it seems unlikely that either of these institutions will achieve a position of serious rivalry with the private markets and instruments in the United States or the eurocurrency market, they have begun to establish a major presence in Europe. In 1984 a handful of banks began to offer deposits denominated in ECU, and a few years earlier some international lenders offered loans denominated in ECU.[6] Within two years, ECU-denominated eurobond issues became a multibillion-dollar market segment. (See the "tombstone" adver-

FIGURE 7–2

Tombstone of a Eurobond
Issue Denominated in ECU

Lavoro Bank Overseas N.V.

ECU 1,000,000,000
Euro Medium Term Note Programme

guaranteed by

Banca Nazionale del Lavoro S.p.A.

Series N° 1

Issue of a Series of US$ 34,000,000 in aggregate principal amount
of Floating Rate Notes due March 2000

In accordance with the terms of the Seriers N° 1 Notes (the Notes")
described in the Pricing Supplement dated as of March 26, 1993,
notice is hearby given that for the Interest Period from March 31,
1994 to September 30, 1994 the Notes will carry an Interest Rate
of 4.5625 % per annum.

The Interest Amount payable on the relevant Interest Payment
Date, September 30, 1994 will be US$ 23.19
per US$ 1,000 Note, US$ 115.96 per
US$ 5,000 Note and US$ 231.93   *The Calculation*
per US$ 10,000 Note   *Agent*

KBL **Kredietbank**
         Luxembourg

Source: *Europe,* The European Communities, December 1986, p. 22.

tisement of an ECU-denominated bond issue shown in Figure 7–2.) Undoubtedly,
this regional financial market will become even more influential in the years
ahead as a result of the emphasis on European monetary integration from the
Maastricht initiative. Indeed, the ECU may become the official currency in Europe
if monetary integration is achieved.

Historically, financial markets developed among the countries comprised by
the colonial empires of England and France. The **sterling area** refers to Great
Britain and a group of former British colonies that still deal among themselves in
British pounds. Similarly, the **franc area** refers to France and its former colonies,
which also continue to denominate a significant amount of business among
themselves in French francs. While substantial financial transactions are conducted within the sterling and franc areas, the eurocurrency market now
dominates the total volume of financial flows among the countries in these areas.

THE EUROCURRENCY MARKET

Definition

A eurodollar *is a dollar-denominated bank deposit located outside the United
States.* This simple statement defines the basic instrument called the eurodollar.
(Eurodollars are *not* dollars in the pockets of people who live in Europe! They are
deposit liabilities of banks.) The widely discussed eurocurrency market is simply

a set of bank deposits located outside the countries whose currencies are used in the deposits. Since over half of the deposits are denominated in US dollars, it is reasonably accurate to call this the **eurodollar market.** Notice that the eurodollar market is not limited to Europe; very large eurodollar markets exist in Tokyo, Hong Kong, Bahrain, Panama, and other cities throughout the world. For this reason, the eurodollar market is sometimes called the *international money market.*[7]

This financial market grew from its inception sometime in the late 1950s to a size of about $U.S. 5,784 billion at the end of 1992, as shown in Table 7–4.

Significance

What is the significance of the international money market? Since the eurocurrency market rivals domestic financial markets as a funding source for corporate borrowing, it plays a key role in the capital investment decisions of many firms. In addition, since this market also rivals domestic financial markets as a deposit alternative, it absorbs large amounts of savings from lenders (i.e., depositors) in many countries. In fact, the eurocurrency market complements the domestic financial markets, giving greater access to borrowing and lending to financial market participants in each country where it is permitted to function. Overall, the eurocurrency market is now the world's single most important market for international financial intermediation.

This market is completely a creation of the regulatory structures placed by national governments on banking or, more precisely, on financial intermediation. If national governments allowed banks to function without reserve requirements, interest rate restrictions, capital controls, and taxes, the eurocurrency market would involve only the transnational deposits and loans made in each country's banking system. Instead, national governments heavily regulate national financial markets in efforts to achieve various monetary policy goals. Thus, the eurocurrency market provides a very important outlet for funds flows that circumvent many of the limitations placed on domestic financial markets. Many national governments have found the impact of the eurocurrency market on their firms and banks to be favorable, so they have allowed this market to operate.[8]

Bases

Since the eurocurrency market is a creation of the regulatory structure, it may be helpful to think about the key underpinnings of the system that allow eurodollars. Essentially three conditions must be met for a eurocurrency market to exist. First, some national government must allow foreign currency deposits to be made so that, for example, depositors in London can obtain dollar-denominated time

TABLE 7–4

Eurocurrency Market Size and Growth (measured by foreign currency liabilities at end of period)*

	1971	1973	1975	1980	1985	1990	1992
Gross market size	150	310	480	1,524	2,846	5,996	5,784
Nonbanks	30	55	80	327	585	1,440	1,427
Official monetary institutions	15	40	70	150	112	175	156
Other banks	105	215	330	1,047	2,149	4,381	4,202
Eurodollars as a percentage of total	76	73	78	75	75	55	52

*In billions of US dollars.
Source: Morgan Guaranty Trust Company, *World Financial Markets*, various issues and Bank for International Settlements, *International Banking and Financial Market Developments*. Basle, 1993.

deposits there. Second, the country whose currency is being used—in this example, the United States—must allow foreign entities to own and exchange deposits in that currency. Third, there must be some reason, such as low cost or ease of use, that prompts people to use this market rather than other financial markets, such as the domestic ones. The eurocurrency market has met these conditions for the past three decades, and its phenomenal growth testifies that the demand for such a market has been very large.

A wide range of countries allow foreign-currency deposits to be held in their banking systems. Many of them impose restrictions (interest rate limits, capital controls, and so on) on these as well as on local-currency deposits, so that a free market does not exist. Other countries, including most of the developed countries and many of the newly industrializing countries, allow foreign-currency deposits that are not subject to the regulations placed on domestic deposits. In such countries, participants find more favorable interest rates, greater availability of funds, and greater ease of moving funds internationally. These countries tend to be the euromarket centers.

Only a few currencies have become popular as eurocurrencies. Generally, these are the ones used widely in international trade—the US dollar, the British pound, the French franc, the German mark, and a handful of others. The governments of all the nations whose currencies are being used have consented (or, more accurately, have not objected) to allowing foreign banks, companies, and individuals to hold and use deposits denominated in those currencies. This may appear to be a trivial point, but any limitation on nonresidents' use of dollar (or other eurocurrency) deposits would quickly eliminate that currency from the euromarket. The US government's temporary freeze on Iranian assets held in US banks in 1979 caused a tremendous crisis in the eurodollar market, because other participants saw the possibility of losing use of their eurodollars at the whim of the US government. The potential problem will continue to exist, but on the whole participants in the euromarket expect that full freedom to use the (dollar-denominated) deposits will continue indefinitely.

The third condition fundamental to the success of the euromarket is that it must possess advantages that will attract participants to the market. Those advantages include the ability to carry out dollar-denominated transactions outside the United States and the availability of favorable interest rates relative to rates in the domestic market. The first advantage clearly exists, because eurodollar account owners can sell their accounts to pay for other transactions, with no need to deal directly in the United States. The second advantage also exists, primarily because lack of regulation of the euromarket allows banks to reduce their costs and pass on the savings to clients in the form of lower loan rates and higher deposit rates. Figure 7–3 shows that the eurodollar deposit interest rate has a very small spread over the comparable domestic deposit rate. (The difference in lending rates to prime borrowers essentially disappeared during the 1980s.)

Eurocurrency Interest Rates

The base interest rate paid on deposits among banks in the eurocurrency market is called **LIBOR,** the **London interbank offered rate.** (Outside London, which is the center of the entire euromarket, the base rate on deposits is generally slightly higher.) LIBOR is determined by the supply and demand for funds in the euromarket for each currency. Because participating banks could default (and, infrequently, do default) on their obligations, the rate paid for eurodollar deposits

FIGURE 7–3　Interest Rates on Deposits, Domestic and Eurodollar

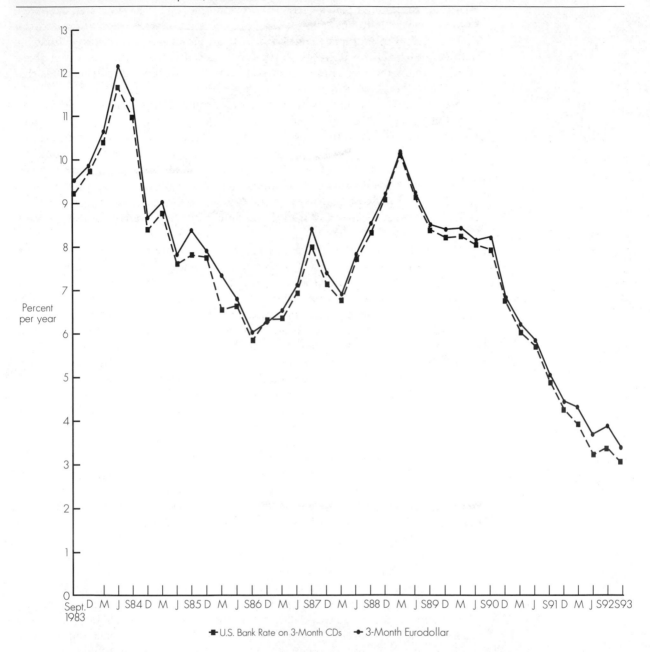

Percent per year

Sept. 1983

U.S. Bank Rate on 3-Month CDs　　3-Month Eurodollar

is always somewhat above the domestic Treasury bill rate. Also, because domestic banks must comply with Federal Reserve requirements, they offer slightly lower deposit rates than unregulated eurobanks, as shown in Figure 7–3.

The lending rate has no name comparable to the prime rate, but it is determined as LIBOR plus some margin, or spread, charged to the borrower. Banks generally do not require compensating balances or other implicit charges in addition to the spread over LIBOR in the euromarket. This also helps reduce the cost of using the euromarket for borrowers. The total cost of borrowing in the euromarket for a prime US corporation historically was marginally below the domestic US prime rate. Because of competition among lenders in both markets, prime borrowers have been able to obtain the same rate in both markets since the early 1980s.

Interest rates on other eurocurrencies generally follow the same pattern, though when capital controls exist in a particular country (e.g., France), borrowing rates may be higher in the euromarket (which is not restricted) than in the domestic market. Figure 7–4 traces three-month eurocurrency deposit rates during the past two decades. Notice that the countries whose currencies have tended to decline relative to other currencies during this period (such as France and Great Britain) show generally higher eurocurrency deposit rates than the "strong-currency" countries (such as Germany and Japan).

Other Market Characteristics

Transactions in the eurodollar market generally involve $US1 million or more, although in the past several years many deposits of $50,000 to $100,000 have been given at LIBOR, and loans of similar amounts have been offered at the analogous lending rates. The market is directly accessible to banks, which carry out about three-fourths of the total volume of transactions among themselves. Companies and individuals participate through their banks, generally at interest rates slightly less favorable than those offered among banks. (Investors may also participate in the euromarket indirectly by purchasing money market funds in the United States, when the funds themselves place large portions of their pooled investments in eurodollar accounts.)

Criticisms of the Euromarkets

Over the years, the eurodollar market has been criticized as contributing to worldwide inflation and creating major new risks in the international banking system. While neither claim has been proved (or disproved) conclusively, each is worth considering here.

Because the eurodollar market adds to the worldwide volume of dollar-denominated assets, it has been accused of increasing the global money supply beyond the control of the US authorities. This may be true to some extent, but a number of factors mitigate the total impact of eurodollars. First, eurodollars exist only as time deposits and certificates of deposit, never as demand deposits or cash. Hence, in the narrow definition of money that includes only cash and demand deposits, eurodollars do not even appear at all. Second, as already noted, about three-fourths of all eurodollars are interbank deposits rather than new credit to companies or individuals that may use it for capital investment and thus economic growth. The interbank transfers (sometimes called *pyramiding*) do not create any new credit, however measured. Finally, the eurodollar deposits used by companies and individuals for investment and consumption probably replace other (e.g., domestic) bank deposits that would have been used for the same purposes anyhow. That is, because the eurodollar deposits pay interest rates higher than domestic deposits, they often substitute for domestic deposits, and thus they are used for the same purposes that those deposits would have served. All in all, eurodollars probably add slightly to the total volume of economic activity worldwide because they provide a form of financial intermediation between depositors (savers) in many countries and borrowers (investors or

FIGURE 7–4

Three-Month Eurocurrency
Deposit Rates (year-end)

Source: Morgan Guaranty Trust Company, *World Financial Markets,* various issues.

spenders) in many countries that is more efficient than that of individual domestic
financial markets.

On the issue of increased risk, it has been argued that the eurocurrency market
has led to much greater extension of loans to troubled borrowers, such as the
governments of less developed countries that found it virtually impossible to
repay in the 1980s. Unquestionably, the eurodollar market provided the mechanism through which these governments borrowed most of the money loaned to

them in the 1970s. It is not clear, however, that any other financial markets would have fared any differently in the absence of eurodollars. Essentially, participation in the euromarket has opened one more type of business to international banks, and these banks must manage this business as prudently as they manage the other businesses in which they participate.

EUROBONDS AND EUROEQUITIES

Eurobonds are the long-term analogue of eurocurrencies. They are issued in countries of convenience and denominated in currencies other than the local one. With eurobonds, *taxation* of the interest income investors receive is a key concern, so most of them are issued in tax jurisdictions that do not impose taxes on such interest payments (e.g., Luxembourg). Eurobonds, like domestic US bonds, are issued by corporations and government agencies. They may be convertible into equity, and they may have fixed or floating interest rates.

Borrowers (i.e., issuers of eurobonds) utilize this market for three main reasons. First, no regulatory agency establishes rules for disclosure by issuers, so substantial red tape is avoided; however, this generally limits participation to blue-chip corporations and governments. Second, the interest rates can be marginally lower than those on domestic issues, because investors can usually avoid taxes on their interest income. Third, the issuer gains access to potential investors in many countries simultaneously because the investment banks that place the issue offer it internationally. From time to time, eurobond issue is stimulated by additional reasons, such as domestic bond market restrictions that lead issuers to seek overseas funding. In 1964, for example, the United States established capital controls that made foreign bonds less attractive to US investors (the interest equalization tax was effectively a tax on interest received by US citizens from foreign bond investments) and limited lending by US parent companies to their foreign subsidiaries. As a result, both US and foreign issuers that were trying to place dollar-denominated bonds turned to the fledgling eurobond market for their funding.

For the investor, the eurobond market offers these advantages: (1) all issues are structured to allow exemption from interest withholding tax on the income earned, and (2) the terms of eurobond issues are more varied than those of domestic bond issues. For example, eurobonds usually have shorter maturities than domestic bonds (five to eight years) and often have floating-rate interest payments.

During the 1970s and 1980s, the growth of the eurobond market was fairly similar to that of the eurocurrency market. In the 1980s, the vast majority of eurobonds were issued in US dollars, and the market continued to grow in both size and diversity (as shown in Table 7–3). By the early 1990s, issues in marks, pounds, and yen were rivaling those in US dollars.

Euroequities have emerged in the past decade in the London Stock Exchange as another long-term euromarket, analogous to domestic stock markets. As the name implies, euroequities are shares of publicly traded stocks traded on an exchange outside of the issuing firm's home country. They are bought and sold in shares denominated in the firm's home currency, so both company performance and exchange rate performance affect the returns on investments in euroequities.

In the United States, a market for such issues has operated for many years through an instrument called the **American Depositary Receipt (ADR)**, which is essentially a claim on a share of stock in the foreign stock exchange intermediated by a securities broker who issues the ADR. Euroequities rival ADRs and offer the flexibility of being direct share issues by the nonlocal firms. The market exists primarily in London, and thus it encompasses non-British company shares. In fact, even the ADRs of British companies are now traded on the London Stock Exchange, so full global trading is possible through the exchange.

The London Stock Exchange euroequity market grew rapidly in the late 1980s. By 1989, 52 brokerage firms were making a market for euroequities issued by 707 firms. The monthly turnover during January 1989 was 278 million shares. The growing demand for these instruments (based on the firms available for investment and the tax-avoiding structure of the issues), as well as the growing supply (by firms that are blue chip and want to gain access to investors from many countries through the London Stock Exchange), makes it likely that this market will increase in importance in global equities trading.

CONCLUSIONS

Whether or not a company or bank is involved in international trade, investment, or other international business, it is important that its managers understand some of the key aspects of international financial markets. The eurocurrency market may offer a low-cost borrowing opportunity, or the eurobond market may provide an outlet for selling new debt to a wider group of investors. The international monetary system establishes a framework within which governments set international financial policies that may affect many firms. The money and capital markets in foreign countries may offer opportunities to multinational firms that operate in those countries. The foreign exchange market determines the cost and availability of foreign currencies, used in business by many firms. Finally, all of these markets influence the functioning of the markets for real goods and services, the ultimate use for all financial claims.

QUESTIONS

1. How can a firm such as Ajax Steel in Peoria, Illinois, utilize the eurodollar market to minimize its financing costs? This firm is a medium-size manufacturer with no foreign sales.

2. How may the International Monetary Fund affect companies' activities in international business?

3. What is the difference between a eurobond and a domestic bond in the United States? Which one would you prefer to issue as a company manager? Which one would you prefer to buy as an investor? Why?

4. Does the eurodollar market add to world inflation? Explain why or why not using the material in this chapter and your knowledge of macroeconomics.

5. As a French resident, would you prefer to deposit your $1 million inheritance in a US bank or in the eurodollar market? Why?

6. If you were offered the opportunity to establish a deposit in London denominated in ECU, would you choose that rather than a deposit in British pounds or dollars? Why or why not?

7. What are the important differences between the Bretton Woods system and the current IMF system? How do these differences affect the MNE manager?

8. If your firm had a subsidiary in Japan and about 100 million yen in exposed assets (i.e., plant and equipment), how would you protect it against exchange risk?

9. If you managed the European operations of a large US-based MNE, in what market(s) would you seek long-term funding? Why?

10. What are the necessary conditions for the existence of a euromarket? Do you expect the eurodollar to exist 10 years from now? Why or why not?

REFERENCES

Business International Corporation. *Financing Foreign Operations*. New York: Business International Corporation, various issues.

Dufey, Gunter, and Ian Giddy. *The International Money Market,* 2nd ed. Englewood Cliffs, NJ: Prentice Hall, 1994.

Euromoney. London: Euromoney Publications, Ltd., various issues.

Grabbe, Orlin. *International Financial Markets* 2nd ed. New York: Elsevier, 1991.

Pozo, Susan. "The ECU as International Money." *Journal of International Money and Finance,* no. 6 (1987).

Tucker, Alan. *International Financial Markets*. St. Paul: West Publishing, 1991.

NOTES

[1] A very useful reference for examining the funding instruments in many developed and less developed countries is Business International Corporation's *Financing Foreign Operations*. This publication discusses short- and long-term financial instruments for about 60 countries, and it is updated annually.

[2] See the Economic Cooperation Act of 1948 (Public Law 472, 80th Congress), US Code Congressional Service, 1948.

[3] Exchange rate policies *are* constrained by the IMF if a country seeks to borrow more than its quota from the Fund. Also, a country does operate in violation of IMF rules if it imposes new exchange controls on current transactions without obtaining IMF approval; however sanctions are seldom applied unless the country seeks to borrow as above.

[4] Almost one-third of the world's monetary reserves were still being held in the form of gold at year-end 1991. See IMF *Survey,* November 8, 1993. p. 345.

[5] Some information about the rules on access to national stock markets by foreigners appears in Business International Corporation, *Investing, Licensing, and Trading Conditions* (New York: Business International Corporation, 1994).

[6] See *The ECU* (Luxembourg: European Communities, 1984). Also see "European Currency Units," *International Banking Report*, February 17, 1984, published by the London *Financial Times;* and "Edging Closer to a Common Currency," *Euromoney*, September 1985, pp. 19-28.

[7] See, for example, Dufey and Giddy (1994).

[8] Realistically, if any one government disallows the euromarkets, they can still function almost as effectively in other countries and currencies. At present, the US government has the most important role, since about 80 percent of eurodeposits are denominated in US dollars.

Bell South: Borrowing in International Financial Markets

Introduction

One of the major changes in the US business system in the 20th century occurred on January 1, 1984, when American Telephone & Telegraph (AT&T) was forced to sell its operating telephone subsidiaries. The US Department of Justice decided to deregulate long-distance telephone service by allowing other companies to compete with AT&T. To reduce AT&T's competitive advantage over other companies, the Justice Department required AT&T to sell all of its 22 regional telephone operating companies (i.e., the companies, such as Southern Bell, that actually provided telephone service in 22 regions of the United States). Now AT&T owns only a long-distance operating network of telephone service, its research division (Bell Labs), its manufacturing division (Western Electric), and a new data processing division (AT&T Information Systems).

The "breakup" of AT&T left the operating companies regrouped into seven corporations, with responsibility for providing local telephone service in seven areas of the United States. This change was truly dramatic. AT&T had been the largest private corporation in the world, and before 1984 each operating company had functioned only as a division of the national company and each division had made decisions only about telephone service in its area. Now each operating company had to make *all* decisions as an independent corporation, including decisions on financing, investing, and general business strategy.

The decision of interest in this case is the financing decision. How should a company finance its business activities? More specifically, how should it finance a major capital project? For any large corporation, and for many medium-size ones as well, the eurocurrency market offers very attractive financing opportunities. Bell South was chosen because its managers lack experience in dealing with the eurocurrency markets and because it definitely should take advantage of the opportunities available there. Additional financial markets available to corporations in the United States are noted for comparison.

The Case

In the aftermath of the decision by the US Department of Justice to dismantle (organizationally) the national telephone system in 1982, individual operating subsidiaries of AT&T were beginning to face major new decisions as soon-to-be-independent companies. Each operating company was very large by current industrial standards; Bell South alone had assets worth more than $21 billion and employed over 100,000 people. None of the operating companies had experience

This case was written by Professor Robert Grosse as a basis for class discussion. The specific borrowing situation is fictitious, and references to Bell South are based on publicly available information in 1986.

in large-scale financing, research and development in telecommunications, or the design of a marketing strategy, since all of these functions had previously been performed by AT&T (or Bell Labs) at the national level.

One of the first priorities established by Bell South's senior management in 1983 was to initiate a research program with a laboratory facility in either Raleigh, North Carolina, or Melbourne, Florida (near major concentrations of electronics companies). Since the company would not become independent until January 1, 1984, no actual investment could take place until then. Nonetheless, Bell South's managers wanted to be ready to go with their plans on "independence day."

Among the more difficult problems faced by David Green, treasury manager for Bell South, was the issue of financing the research lab, which was estimated to cost about $25 million. While this level of funding was not large compared to AT&T's total borrowing, it would present some difficulties for a newly independent Bell South (primarily because of this firm's inexperience in such negotiations). Green was discussing the problem with his recently hired assistant, who had just graduated from a prestigious school of business administration.

The assistant (i.e., you) was proposing to consider the idea of eurocurrency financing, for which lower interest rates were available and fewer restrictions existed on loans. Specifically, the assistant recommended the use of a eurodeutschemark loan, which could be obtained for close to one-half of the interest cost that had been offered for a domestic, dollar-denominated loan by NCNB (North Carolina National Bank). Other alternatives should also be considered, of course. Table 1 shows various borrowing options and their costs in August 1983.

The research facility has an expected life of 10 years. It will be financed separately each year, so every year the lowest-cost source of funds should be chosen. For the first year (effective on January 1, 1984), funding will be available at the interest rates shown in Table 1. Each type of lender also charges fees on the loan. The fees are paid one time—at the beginning of the loan period—and they are some percentage of the total loan value (as shown). Right now, the only task is to choose the funding source for the first year; subsequent borrowing decisions will be made at the end of each year.

In addition to a bank loan in the eurodollar market, Bell South can consider using a domestic bank loan. In either case, the company will pay the base interest

TABLE 1

Possible Sources of $25 Million, One-Year Borrowing for Bell South

Type of Funding	US$	C$	FF	DM	SF	Fees (paid up front)
Syndicated eurocurrency loan (LIBOR)	11.13	10.31	16.50	6.13	5.00	2.00 ⅝%
Eurobond issue	12.25	12.00	—	8.36	—	1.75
US domestic bank loan (prime rate)	11.50 +.25%					3.00
US domestic bond issue	12.65					2.25
US domestic equity issue (required rate of return)	18					2.25
Spot exchange rate (fx/$)	1 1.29		8.0	2.6	2.10	
One-year forward XR	1 1.23		8.4	2.3	1.95	

(Interest Cost* spanning US$, C$, FF, DM, SF columns)

*All interest costs are stated as annual percentage rates. Since one-year loans are being used, the rates must be renegotiated every year during the project. Bell South can be expected to pay a "spread" of ⅜ percent over LIBOR quotes and ¼ percent over prime, plus one-time, up-front fees, based on the value of the loan. Assume for simplicity that all interest is paid at the end of the full loan period.

rate, plus some additional margin to the bank lender. If the company issues new bonds, it will have to pay the interest rate shown, plus the up-front fee. If it issues new stock, investors will expect a return of about 18 percent per year, much higher than what the bank charges. Many other financing sources exist, but the choices shown are very commonly used in the US market.

LIBOR is the London interbank offered rate, the interest rate offered by banks in London for large deposits (eurocurrency deposits) from other banks. The lending rate does not have a name; it is just called "LIBOR plus the spread," and it varies depending on the creditworthiness of the borrower.

QUESTIONS

1. What is the cheapest way to finance the research facility without incurring exchange risk? [*Hint:* To do the calculations, assume interest rates remain constant during the life of the project.]

2. Should the company use long-term financing, such as a bond issue, so that it will not have to refinance every year?

Eurodollar Expansion and Contraction

Eurodollars are *not* money in the same way that checks and cash are. Eurodollars are time deposits or certificates of deposit, some of which have maturities of as little as one day. Hence, eurodollar deposits with very short terms are "quasi-money" and can be used by their holders in very much the same way as demand deposits. Other eurodollar deposits can be used in much the same way as domestic time deposits and CDs. This appendix explains the process of eurodollar creation, expansion, and contraction so that the reader can understand the basic mechanics of the market and of the not-so-arcane transactions that take place.

Let us begin with Metalworks, Inc., a company in Cleveland that produces small metal fittings for auto manufacturers. This company has an interest-earning checking account at Ohio Bank & Trust that regularly contains about $1 million more than the company uses for its operations. Rather than leave the money in a low-interest deposit, the financial manager of Metalworks decides to place the excess $1 million in an alternative, still very liquid, investment. The manager of Ohio B&T suggests a eurodollar negotiable certificate of deposit, placed at the bank's branch in London.

The eurodollar deposit would pay the interest rate, LIBOR, to Metalworks for three months, after which Metalworks could roll over the deposit at the new LIBOR or withdraw the funds and use them otherwise. Metalworks could hold the eurodollar CD for the entire three-month period or sell it at any time in the market for eurodollar CDs at whatever price buyers offer. Ohio B&T guarantees that it will buy back the CD at a small cost in reduced interest if Metalworks chooses to sell it during the three-month period. At this time, LIBOR is at 10.75 percent per year on three-month dollar deposits and Ohio B&T is paying 5½ percent per year on the checking account in Cleveland.

Having made the decision to go ahead, Metalworks deposits $1 million in the eurodollar deposit in London. That is, Ohio B&T has created an account on the books of its branch in London payable to Metalworks, even though all of the discussions took place in Cleveland. The three T-accounts below summarize this transaction, which constitutes the creation of 1 million eurodollars. (Note that DD means "demand deposit" and CD means "certificate of deposit.")

Metalworks, Inc.		Ohio B&T, Home Office		Ohio B&T, London Office	
A	L	A	L	A	L
−DD at Ohio B&T +CD at B&T London			−DD owed to Metalworks +DD owed to B&T London	+DD at home office	+CD owed to Metalworks

So far, no credit has been extended, even though 1 million eurodollars have been created. There was simply an exchange of one bank account for another. At this point, Metalworks is satisfied with its position. Ohio B&T, however, has accepted a new deposit that is costing it 10.75 percent per year, so it needs to find a use for the funds that will bring in more than that. Typically, the bank will look to other banks in the London market to purchase the funds. If Ohio B&T can find another bank that offers a slightly higher interest rate, it may lend the funds to that bank. Let us assume that Crédit Suisse needs funds for a loan that it wants to make in Switzerland, so its London branch offers Ohio B&T 10.90 percent per year for $1 million for three months. This second transaction appears as follows in the T-accounts of the participants:

Ohio B&T, Home Office		Ohio B&T, London Office		Crédit Suisse	
A	L	A	L	A	L
	−DD owed to B&T London +DD owed to Crédit Suisse	−DD at B&T home office +CD at Crédit Suisse		+DD at B&T home office	+CD owed to B&T London

In this step, Crédit Suisse has exchanged a CD payable to Ohio B&T, London, for a demand deposit at Ohio B&T, Cleveland, each for $1 million. Now Ohio B&T has solved its problem of finding a borrower for the funds, but Crédit Suisse has taken on the same problem.

Next, Crédit Suisse uses the funds to make a loan to Nestlé Corporation at an interest rate of 11.45 percent per year for the three-month period. Thus, Nestlé is paying a spread, or margin, over LIBOR of 0.75 percent per year. The final transaction in eurodollar expansion looks like this:

Ohio B&T, Home Office		Crédit Suisse		Nestlé	
A	L	A	L	A	L
	−DD owed to Crédit Suisse +DD owed to Nestlé	−DD at B&T home office +Loan to Nestlé		+DD at B&T home office	+Loan due to Crédit Suisse

Now $2 million of eurodollars exist (the CD of Ohio B&T's London office owed to Metalworks and the Crédit Suisse CD owed to B&T London), plus a eurodollar loan of $1 million. Assuming both deposits and the loan are held to maturity, these eurodollars will have a life of three months. All of the participants are in "equilibrium" in the sense that they are all earning a satisfactory return on their eurodollar dealings (assuming Nestlé has invested the money in some activity that pays more than 11.45 percent per year).

Eurodollar contraction occurs when the deposits mature and must be paid out. If each depositor simply redeposits the funds in another eurodollar deposit and Nestlé rolls over its loan, the accounts are rolled over and no change in the total number of eurodollars occurs. However, if any participant does not redeposit the funds in a eurodollar account, the number of eurodollars declines (though *not* the number of dollars in the B&T home office account).

Now assume Nestlé pays back the loan after three months and Metalworks shifts its deposit back to a demand deposit in Cleveland. In this case, Nestlé will pay Crédit Suisse $1 million plus interest ($28,625); Crédit Suisse will pay Ohio B&T, London, $1 million plus interest ($27,250); and Ohio B&T, London, will transfer $1 million plus interest ($26,875) to the account of Metalworks in Cleveland. At this point, no eurodollars remain and each euromarket participant is left with a profit (if Nestlé did indeed earn more than 11.45 percent per year on its use of the funds).

Because much business activity is refinanced repeatedly, the eurodollar market generally does not decline in volume. Also, because more and more firms and banks are entering the eurodollar market, the volume of eurodollars has tended to grow over the years.

The Balance of Payments

This chapter covers the measurement and interpretation of all international transactions between one country and the rest of the world: that is, the balance of payments. The main goals of the chapter are to:

1. Explain how the double-entry bookkeeping system of measuring balances of payments works.

2. Look at recent balances of payments for the United States and discuss their implications.

3. Show how balance-of-payments adjustment takes place.

4. Discuss the many implications of balance-of-payments problems from the perspective of private sector managers whose firms do business across national boundaries.

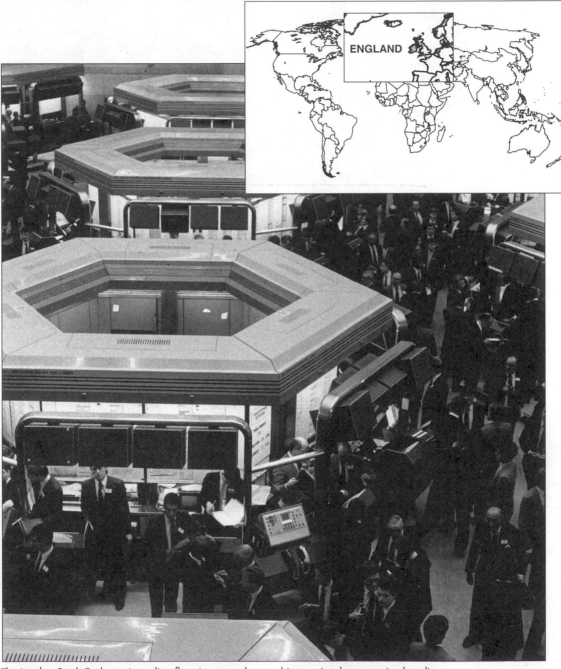

The London Stock Exchange's trading floor is centered around international computerized trading.
Reuters/Bettmann

INTRODUCTION

How well do we keep track of the millions of transactions that take place annually between exporters and importers, international banks and multinational companies? The bankers who tabulate the foreign exchange dealings of their own banks are only a part of the picture. How well can we account for the part of direct investment that occurs through overseas borrowing, yet affects the home country's international economic position? Even more simply, how well can we measure "international" transactions that are simply transfers of funds from the account of an importer to the account of a foreign exporter in the same bank?

The realistic answer to these questions is "not very well." National governments create elaborate accounts for the transactions between their residents and foreign residents, but it is often very difficult to obtain full and accurate information. Putting that problem aside for the moment, let us consider the methods that governments use to record each country's international transactions.

The most widely used measure of international economic transactions for any country is the balance-of-payments (BOP) statement. This record attempts to measure the full value of the transactions between residents of one country and residents of the rest of the world for some time period—say, one year.[1] The balance of payments is a *flow* concept in that it records flows of goods, services, and claims between countries over a period of time rather than a stock of accumulated funds or products. It is a *value* concept in that all the items recorded receive a monetary value, denominated in the given country's currency at the time of the transaction.[2] *The* **balance of payments (BOP),** then, *is a record of the value of all the economic transactions between residents of one country and residents of all other countries during a given time period.*

Why do we worry about measuring these transactions? We do so because if a country records a substantial imbalance between inflows and outflows of goods and services for an extended period of time, some means of financing or adjusting away the imbalance must be found. For example, when oil prices rose dramatically in 1973–74 and again in 1979, Brazil continued to import much the same quantity of oil but had to pay a much higher bill (total cost = price times quantity). Given no major change in Brazil's exports, the country ended up spending a lot more foreign currency on imports than it received from exports. This imbalance could have been financed if Brazil had borrowed funds from abroad, with the eventual obligation to repay the loans. The imbalance could also have been adjusted away if Brazilians had bought less of other imported goods or increased their own exports. Finally, Brazilians could have done nothing and just paid out more cruzeiros had OPEC countries been willing to accept this currency and hold onto it. (Technically, this would have been borrowing from OPEC, since OPEC would eventually spend the cruzeiros.) Anytime an imbalance occurs between a country's imports and exports of goods and services, it must be covered by an equal and opposite imbalance in flows of claims (e.g., money, bonds, official reserves).

Still, the manager may wonder why he or she should be concerned about this issue. So far the problem is macroeconomic, referring to a *country's* international transactions. The problem becomes much more important when we realize that national governments are likely to set their regulatory policies to reduce BOP imbalances. Thus, in the above example of Brazil, foreign *firms* may find themselves facing new tariffs or quotas; companies operating in Brazil may find that access to foreign exchange for imports or for profit remittance is limited, while subsidies are offered on exports; and foreign *bank* lenders may find new loan requests coming in from Brazil. All in all, the manager should recognize that the balance of payments is an *indicator* of subsequent government policy changes.

In another, equally important vein, the manager should be interested in national balances of payments because of their direct importance in determining exchange rates. Since the collapse of the fixed exchange rate system in 1971, most of the world's developed countries and many LDCs have been allowing the values of their currencies to fluctuate in the market (usually with some degree of government intervention). This means that, other things equal, when the supply of a country's currency in foreign exchange markets exceeds the demand, the currency will devalue. Such an excess supply could have occurred in the Brazilian example, unless some demand for cruzeiros arose for another purpose (e.g., for direct investment). Although it is the *total* demand and supply of the currency in foreign exchange markets that leads to exchange rate determination, many analysts believe a trade imbalance is likely to affect the rate, ignoring other sources of currency demand or supply. One must be careful to include all of these sources when attempting to judge exchange rate changes.

In the next section, we look at the full set of transactions that constitute the balance of payments and at the system of BOP accounting that is used to create the records used by governments. Then we examine the various account aggregates that are balances of payments. Next, we discuss the BOP of the United States in some detail. Because the balance of payments is a dynamic concept, changing daily as transactions occur, we then examine the adjustment mechanisms leading from surplus and deficit balances toward equilibrium points. Finally, we explore implications of the BOP for managers and how managers can use BOP information to make decisions.

BALANCE-OF-PAYMENTS ACCOUNTING

There is no such thing as *"the* balance of payments," since the accounts are organized in a double-entry bookkeeping system and for every debit entry there is a credit entry of equal value. There are seven or eight BOP measures; these group some international transactions together and leave others in a second, "everything else" category. In each case, the intent is to place the fundamental economic causes of transactions in the first group and the "payments" for them in the second group. Also, the former items are listed "above the line" and the latter are listed "below the line" in the actual accounts.

More specifically, consider the situation in which you (a US resident) go on vacation in Paris, buy some French wine for 35 francs, and bring it back to the United States. Ignoring everything except the wine purchase, we can classify that wine as a US import and list it in a simple balance-of-payments table as follows:

US BOP (Dollars)

	Inflows (−)	Outflows (+)
Products	7 of wine	
Money		7 spent

Note: Assume that the current exchange rate is $.20 = 1FF.

This simple table demonstrates many of the major principles of **balance-of-payments accounting.** First, all entries in the accounts must be in some currency value (e.g., dollars or dollars' worth, since the example is from a US perspective). Second, inflows of goods, services, and claims are segregated on one side of the ledger and outflows on the other. Third, a set of categories can be created in the vertical direction to separate kinds of flows—in the present example, to separate a product flow from a money flow. Fourth, inflows are recorded with a minus sign (−) and outflows with a plus sign (+). Fifth, if a horizontal line is drawn anywhere on the ledger, it is possible to add up the entries above the line and, separately, those below the line. (Obviously, a line drawn below all entries will yield a value of zero above the line, and no entries will be below the line. In this sense, there is no "total" balance of payments.) The summation of the entries above the line is called the balance of payments on the particular account (e.g., the trade balance), depending on where the line is drawn.

In our simple example above, if the line is drawn between products and money, we have an above-the-line total of −$7 in value and a below-the-line total of +$7 in value. If this wine is the only item exported or imported in the given time period, the country has a balance-of-**trade deficit** of $7. That is, the sum of all the entries above the line, where exports and imports are the *only* items in this category, is −$7, a deficit. The +$7 cash outflow appears below the line and is ignored in measuring the balance of trade; clearly, it *is* the other half of the same transaction.

Notice that this classification system is similar to a *company's* flow-of-funds statement, or its statement of net change in financial position, in which asset inflows are recorded as debits (−) and liability increases are recorded as credits (+). In the present example, the *country* has gained an asset, namely the bottle of wine, and the country has incurred a new liability, namely the dollars paid out to the wine seller. This analogy will be very useful in trying to understand the US BOP, as presented below. At this point, let us continue to develop the various accounts in simple form.

The basic balance-of-payments table is constructed to present, in descending vertical order, flows of goods, services, and gifts (i.e., current items); flows of long-term claims such as stocks and bonds; flows of short-term claims, including money; and, finally, flows of official international reserves. At whatever point "the line" is drawn, the items above the line may be viewed as being paid for by those remaining below the line. In our example, the balance of trade shows a bottle of imported French wine paid for by an outflow of $7 in money.

Table 8−1 presents a standard balance-of-payments table for the country Behrmania in 1994. We will look at each category (or account) individually.

Trade (or Merchandise Trade)

This account includes all inflows and outflows of products, whether consumer or industrial goods. It is possible that some of the entries are paid for with funds under heading E, while others are tied to foreign investment projects or gifts. If the oil import transaction takes place simply between a local firm and an OPEC exporter, it may involve only an outflow of cash or checks, with the total transaction appearing as:

	Debits − ($ Millions)	+ Credits ($ Millions)
A. Products	100 Oil imports	
E. Short-term capital flows		100 Cash or checks

TABLE 8–1

Balance of Payments for Behrmania, 1994 *(millions of US dollars)*

	Inflows (debits) –	+ Outflows (credits)
A. Merchandise trade	100 Oil imports 50 Chemical imports	80 Machinery exports 50 Grain exports
B. Trade in services	10 Value of services for foreign shipping	40 Licensing and management contractors
C. Gifts	15 Foreign aid value	5 Gifts from relatives abroad
D. Long-term capital flows	40 Foreign investment undertaken abroad	10 Bonds sold to foreigners 5 Long-term loans issued by foreigners
E. Short-term capital flows	20 Short-term securities bought from ROW	10 Short-term securities sold to foreigners 20 Outflow of funds to ROW
F. Official reserves flows		15 Paid in foreign currency by the central bank to ROW central banks
Total	235	235

Similarly, exports of grain to a less developed country may appear as a credit in row A and cash payment for the grain as a debit (i.e., an inflow) in row E. (The grain shipment appears explicitly in Table 8–1, while the payment has been lumped together with other cash inflows and outflows.)

If a Behrmanian company decided to set up a factory worth $40 million in Germany, it could send some machinery to Germany, along with some money. Ignoring the purchase of the factory (direct investment) initially, we would record $20 million of machinery exports and $20 million of funds outflow, both credit entries, as constituting half of the transaction. (The other half is foreign direct investment, a $40 million debit entry in row D, as discussed below.) This leaves $60 million more of machinery exports in Table 8–1, which we assume were made to unrelated foreign importers and paid for with checks.

Another Behrmanian company had previously built a plant in France (recorded in last year's BOP) that sells $50 million of chemicals back to the home office for domestic sale. Since the French affiliate is viewed as a foreign resident, this transaction appears as an import (as shown in Table 8-1), though payment for it may be made through an intracompany transfer of funds (i.e., a credit entry in line E) or perhaps through an exchange of technology or other service provided by the home office (i.e., a credit entry in line B). Assume that $10 million of the value was paid for in services and the rest in cash. The full set of entries related to the chemicals and machinery transactions is

	Debits – ($ Millions)		+ Credits ($ Millions)
A. Products	50 Chemicals		20 Machinery for FDI project 60 Machinery sold to unrelated importers
B. Services			10 Management services provided to subsidiary in return for chemicals
D. Long-term capital flows	40 Foreign investment in Germany		
E. Short-term capital flows	60 Checks received for machinery from importers		20 Funds for FDI project 40 Payment for chemicals

These two transactions alone begin to give us some idea of the enormous complexity of BOP accounts.

Services

How should we classify an airplane trip to the Bahamas in the BOP? While no physical product is exchanged, the service of airplane passage to Nassau is provided, at some price. We know that souvenirs purchased on this vacation are recorded as Behrmanian imports. In the same sense, the service of an airplane trip, "imported" from Bahamas Air, must be recorded as a debit. (Notice, however, that if Behrmanian Airlines flies to Nassau, tickets purchased by Behrmanians are *not* part of the BOP; they are simply a domestic service, which appears in national income accounts.)

A wide variety of services may be supplied—air, land, or sea passenger transport; similar merchandise transport; technology or management assistance; leasing or franchising; and so on. Behrmania has imported $10 million worth of transportation services for shipping merchandise abroad. Once again, this item appears in the BOP only if foreign shipping companies are used; a Behrmanian shipping company's services would not appear. This country has sold licensing and management services abroad, $10 million of which was supplied to the subsidiary in France and the rest to unaffiliated foreign firms. The total impact of service flows on the BOP is

	Debits – ($ Millions)	+ Credits ($ Millions)
A. Products	10 Part of chemicals sold to parent firm	
B. Services	10 Shipping	40 Licensing and management contracts
E. Short-term capital flows	30 Cash inflow	10 Cash outflow

Once again, the "payments" associated with service exports and imports need not be money; they may be service-related flows of goods or even other services.

Gifts or Unilateral Transfers

Probably the most difficult aspect of BOP accounting to grasp is the treatment of gifts. Put simply, the problem is that a gift creates no equal and opposite flow for the double-entry system. When Behrmanians receive checks totaling $5 million from relatives living abroad, what reverse flow occurs? There is none, so we create a fictitious entry called "unilateral transfers" in which to record the value of gifts given (as a debit) or received (as a credit). Perhaps the easiest way to understand this entry is to view it as a "thank-you note" for the gift. Thus, the Behrmanians record $5 million as a short-term capital inflow and $5 million as a unilateral transfer (or thank-you note) outflow. Behrmania receives the money, and the foreign relatives get only a fictitious thank-you note (plus substantial goodwill).

The government may be involved in making grants to foreign countries, or even in such things as paying pensions to Behrmanians living permanently abroad. Such official (government) gifts, like private gifts, appear as unilateral transfers. In the present year, the Behrmanian government made foreign aid disbursements totaling $15 million, all in the form of checks. Thus, the total gift-related entries are

	Debits − ($ Millions)	+ Credits ($ Millions)
C. Gifts E. Short-term capital flows	15 Foreign aid value 5 Funds from relatives	5 Value of gifts from relatives 15 Funds outflow

Long-Term Capital Flows

We already have seen how one long-term asset, namely a foreign direct investment project, was related to exports of capital goods and a short-term capital flow. Included along with FDI in this category of long-term claims are purchases and sales of stocks[3] and bonds, long-term bank loans, and long-term government claims. The division between long-term and short-term capital flows is the period of one year. That is, short-term claims mature in less than one year and long-term claims in a year or more. Each item is a "claim" in that it provides the owner with future purchasing power over goods and services in the currency of the claim. That is, long-term claims are presumably purchased by individuals or institutions that are willing to hold these stocks, bonds, or notes into the future, when they will be redeemed for cash that can be spent.

In the present year, two separate claims were issued in addition to the $40 million foreign investment project that Behrmanian investors undertook in Germany. Some local companies issued $10 million in bonds, which were purchased by foreign residents and paid for with checks, and Lloyds Bank in London loaned $5 million to a Behrmanian bank for a period of two years. The loan was disbursed through a wire transfer of funds from Lloyds. The results of these transactions appear in the balance of payments as

	Debits − ($ Millions)	+ Credits ($ Millions)

A. Products
D. Long-term
    capital flows
	40 FDI in Germany	20 Machinery for FDI project
		10 Bonds sold to foreign
		    residents
		5 Loan from Lloyds

E. Short-term capital flows	10 Payment for bonds 5 Funds from loan	20 Funds for FDI in Germany

Short-Term Capital Flows

The only remaining items in the balance of payments are short-term claims. These include public and private short-term flows and exchanges of official reserves among central banks. Short-term capital flows include exchanges involving all kinds of money market instruments, such as treasury bills, short-term certificates of deposit, commercial paper, banker's acceptances, and money itself (i.e., M1, currency plus demand deposits). These transactions may involve private firms, individuals, or governments. Much of the activity in this category relates to carrying out payments for exports, imports, and other items in categories A through D. However, a substantial amount of international investment occurs in short-term money market instruments, so this category cannot be viewed as just a set of payments.

In the current year for Behrmania, we have already seen short-term capital inflows worth $50 million and short-term capital outflows worth $85 million. In addition, foreign residents purchased $10 million of Behrmanian money market funds and Behrmanians purchased $20 million of foreign countries' treasury bills, in each case paying with checks. The net effect of these two last transactions is zero:

	Debits – ($ Millions)	+ Credits ($ Millions)
E. Short-term capital flows	20 T bills bought 10 Payment for money market funds	10 Money market funds sold to foreign residents 20 Payment for T bills

What remains is a net short-term capital outflow of $20 million, as shown in Table 8-1, and an unexplained outflow of $15 million more, which we will now see as a flow of official reserves.

Official Reserves Flows

Official reserves—assets held and traded by central banks and the International Monetary Fund—are the final category of entries in the BOP. Before discussing the types of official reserves available, it will be useful to conclude the Behrmania example.

The final $15 million outflow that remains unaccounted for is a buildup of Behrmanian currency in some exporting country's central bank. If we assume that the funds sent to France for FDI were deposited in a bank, we can also assume that this bank turned $15 million of Behrmanian currency over to the French central bank in exchange for francs. The French central bank then has the right to exchange the Behrmanian currency for French francs or other currency at the Behrmanian central bank. When this occurs, Behrmania's central bank gives up $15 million worth of its foreign exchange holdings. This transaction is entered as an outflow of official reserves. The total set of transactions appears in the BOP as

	Debits – ($ Millions)	+ Credits ($ Millions)
A. Products E. Short-term capital flows F. Official reserves flows	15* Part of chemicals value 15 Local currency returned by French government	15 Payment for part of chemicals shipment in Behrmanian currency 15 French francs given to French central bank by Behrmanian central bank

*The other $25 million value of chemicals imports is ignored here for simplicity.

Official reserves actually include much more than the foreign exchange held by the central bank of a country. In fact, four kinds of assets are regarded as official reserves:

1. Foreign exchange
2. Official gold
3. Special drawing rights (SDRs)
4. Position at the IMF

Although any country can hold official reserves, discussions of this subject generally refer only to member countries in the IMF, to which items 3 and 4 are available. We will continue on this basis too.

Official reserve assets are either held at the International Monetary Fund or held by a country's central monetary authority and recorded at the IMF. Such assets *must* be owned by the country's central monetary authority, for the simple technical reason that private sector institutions or individuals can hold gold and foreign currencies—and the intent of measuring official reserves is to look *only* at the government's position. Any net outflow of a country's official reserves in some time period means that fewer financial resources are available for the purchase of foreign goods and services (or, in another light, that fewer financial resources are available for intervention in the foreign exchange market to keep the currency from devaluing).

Special drawing rights (SDRs), discussed in Chapter 7, are the basic unit of account at the IMF. All national currencies and official gold holdings are valued in SDRs, which may be transferred among member countries' accounts when requested. SDRs themselves are created by decisions of the IMF, and they are distributed to member countries each time a new supply is created.

A country's position in the IMF is the amount of its net borrowing from the IMF during any period. For the most part, LDCs use such lending opportunities, while the developed countries and OPEC usually do not. When all of the transactions in accounts A through F are summed vertically, the debits and credits each total $235 million. Although this number gives some idea of the approximate size of international transactions, which can be compared across countries, it is used only as a check on the entries in each column. Much more important is the set of relationships among the accounts in the BOP.

BALANCES OF PAYMENTS

The Behrmanian BOP table can be redrawn in terms of the five most widely used balances, which correspond to the accounts in Table 8–1. Now, in Table 8–2, we need to sum up all of the entries "above the line" drawn below each balance to measure that particular balance of payments.

TABLE 8–2

Balances of Payments for Behrmania, 1994 *(in $ millions of US dollars)*

	Inflows (Debits) −	+ Outflows (Credits)	
A. Balance of (merchandise) trade	100 Oil imports 50 Chemicals imports	80 Machinery exports 50 Grain exports	20
B. Balance on goods and services	10 Value of services for foreign shipping	40 Licensing and management contracts	+10
C. Current account balance	15 Foreign aid value	5 Gifts from relatives abroad	0
D. Basic balance	40 Foreign investment undertaken abroad	10 Bonds sold to foreigners 5 Long-term loans issued to foreigners	−25
E. Official settlements balance*	20 Short-term securities bought from ROW	10 Short-term securities sold to foreigners 20 Outflow of funds to ROW	−15
F. Actual reserve flows		15 French francs sold to French central bank	+15

*Usually the official settlements balance is recorded as those items *below* the line, so in this case the balance should be +15. This means that an *outflow* of official reserves occurred, as shown in line F.

For example, the **trade balance** shows a *deficit* of $20 million, reflecting an excess of debits over credits *above the line* in this amount. This can be contrasted with the balance on goods and services, which shows such a net outflow of services that the balance is a *surplus* of $10 million. That is, merchandise trade plus services trade total a balance of +$10 million in value. Note that each balance includes the previous balance plus net flows in the next category. Thus, the **current account balance** includes the balance on goods and services plus unilateral transfers (and shows an even balance). Next, the **basic balance** includes the current account plus long-term capital flows and shows a deficit of $25 million. Finally, the **official settlements balance** shows a net outflow of official reserves, which can be viewed as a deficit on the basic balance plus short-term capital flows or as a surplus on official reserves. The latter terminology is generally used, and Behrmania's official settlements surplus means a loss of $15 million in official reserves.

   When reading a BOP statement, one should take care to interpret the official settlements balance properly. A value of +$15 million would normally be given for the Behrmanian example, referring to the net *outflow* of official reserves. All other balances are recorded and interpreted as previously discussed.

THE US BALANCE OF PAYMENTS

US Department of Commerce Accounts

Since 1976, the United States has used a format for presenting its balance of payments that appears very different from the tables shown earlier. Fortunately, entries in the new format can be interpreted according to the accounting rules already presented here, and indeed the conceptual format can be recreated from it. Table 8–3 presents the US balance-of-payments statements for selected years of the past decade as officially registered in the *Survey of Current Business* in the March issue each year.

While this single-column presentation of the US BOP looks substantially different from the format of Table 8-2, that format can be generated by placing negative entries in a debit (inflow) column and positive entries in a credit (outflow) column. In more specific terms, consider the trade balance. Merchandise imports in line 16 appear as a debit entry, while merchandise exports in line 2 appear as a credit entry. Their sum was −$96,138 million in 1992—a merchandise trade deficit (which also appears in the memoranda in line 64).

Actually, if lines 2 through 14 and 16 through 27 are placed side by side, the entire balance on goods and services has been reconstructed, with lines 1 and 14 as total exports and total imports (and line 65 as the balance itself). Notice that the balance on goods and services consistently shows a lower deficit value than the trade balance. This is because the United States continues to export more services than it imports, partially offsetting the large deficit in merchandise trade. At the beginning of the 1980s, income from US companies' direct investments abroad (line 12) was enough to offset the trade deficit by itself. As the United States ran a larger and larger trade deficit during that decade, the government was forced to borrow increasingly from abroad. By 1992, US government payments to foreign holders of Treasury bills and bonds and other securities (line 28) rose to almost $US41 billion, offsetting most of the income on US direct investment abroad. Some implications of this situation are discussed in the next section.

To understand the main factors contributing to the US trade flows, a disaggregation of the accounts would be useful. The same annual article in the *Survey of Current Business* presents trade flow data by broad industry categories and

TABLE 8-3 US Balance of Payments, 1980–1993, Selected Years (millions of US dollars)

	1980	1990	1991	1992	1993
1. Exports of goods, services, and income	340,887	652,936	704,914	730,460	753,898
2. Merchandise, adjusted, excluding military	221,781	389,550	415,962	440,138	456,756
3. Services	43,708	133,295	163,637	179,710	186,792
4. Transfers under US military agency sales contracts	7,470	9,899	10,691	11,015	11,259
5. Travel	9,985	40,579	48,757	53,861	58,601
6. Passenger fares	2,582	12,251	15,627	17,353	17,849
7. Other transportation	11,041	22,407	23,625	22,773	23,508
8. Royalties and license fees	6,993	15,291	17,799	20,238	20,414
9. Other private services	4,645	32,173	46,444	53,801	56,434
10. US government miscellaneous services	362	695	693	869	827
11. Income receipts on US assets abroad	76,029	130,091	125,315	110,612	110,339
12. Direct investment receipts	37,068	54,444	49,221	49,888	55,815
13. Other private receipts	36,436	65,702	67,990	53,687	49,527
14. US government receipts	2,525	9,945	8,104	7,038	4,997
15. Imports of goods, services, and income	−333,810	−722,730	−716,624	−763,965	−830,631
16. Merchandise, adjusted, excluding military	−249,135	−497,665	−489,398	−536,276	−589,244
17. Services	−41,181	−106,919	−118,341	−123,299	−131,114
18. Direct defense expenditures	−10,779	−17,119	−16,215	−13,766	−12,286
19. Travel	−10,384	−38,671	−36,958	−39,872	−42,329
20. Passenger fares	−3,533	−8,963	−10,636	−10,943	−11,256
21. Other transportation	−10,981	−23,463	−23,297	−23,454	−24,511
22. Royalties and license fees	−757	−2,644	−3,980	−4,986	−4,748
23. Other private services	−2,980	−13,819	−25,154	−27,988	−33,595
24. US government miscellaneous services	−1,767	−2,240	−2,097	−2,290	−2,388
25. Income payments on foreign assets in the United States	−43,494	−118,146	−108,886	−104,391	−110,273
26. Direct investment payments	−8,853	−1,782	3,675	−1,630	−9,837
27. Other private payments	−22,140	−78,494	−73,575	−61,582	−58,545
28. US government payments	−12,501	−37,870	−38,986	−41,179	−41,891
29. Unilateral transfers, net	−6,959	−22,329	8,028	−32,895	−32,509
30. US government grants	−4,506	−17,486	24,487	−14,688	−14,438
31. US government pensions and other transfers	−1,287	−2,947	−3,462	−3,735	−3,948
32. Private remittances and other transfers	−1,165	−1,896	−12,996	−14,473	−14,126
33. US assets abroad, net (increase/capital outflow [−])	−84,502	−57,506	−62,220	−50,961	−143,872
34. US official reserve assets, net	−8,155	−2,158	5,763	3,901	−1,379
35. Gold	—	—	—	—	—
36. Special drawing rights	−16	−192	−177	2,316	−537
37. Reserve position in the International Monetary Fund	−1,667	731	−367	−2,692	−44
38. Foreign currencies	−6,472	−2,697	6,307	4,277	−797
39. US government assets other than official reserve assets, net	−5,111	2,976	3,397	−1,609	−106
40. US credits and other long-term assets	−9,697	−7,319	−12,123	−7,147	−5,642
41. Repayments on US credits and other long-term assets	4,308	10,327	16,522	5,596	8,891
42. US foreign currency holdings and US short-term assets, net	278	−32	−1,002	−65	−355
43. US private assets, net	−71,236	−58,524	−71,379	−53,253	−142,388
44. Direct investment	−20,592	−33,437	−27,135	−34,791	−50,244
45. Foreign securities	−3,188	−28,476	−45,017	−47,961	−125,377
46. US claims on unaffiliated foreigners reported by US nonbanking concerns	n.a.	−1,944	5,526	4,551	n.a.
47. US claims reported by US banks, not included elsewhere	46,608	5,333	−4,753	24,948	34,582
48. Foreign assets in the United States, net (increase/ capital inflow [+])	47,626	86,303	66,980	129,579	226,380
49. Foreign official assets in the United States, net	16,179	32,425	18,407	40,684	71,225
50. US government securities	11,827	29,310	17,116	22,403	52,791
51. US Treasury securities	9,640	28,643	15,815	18,454	48,700
52. Other	2,147	667	1,301	3,949	4,091
53. Other US government liabilities	1,375	1,703	1,600	2,542	1,890

TABLE 8–3   *Continued*

	1980	1990	1991	1992	1993
54. US liabilities reported by US banks, not included elsewhere	–84	2,998	–1,668	16,427	13,959
55. Other foreign official assets	3,061	–1,586	1,359	–688	2,585
56. Other foreign assets in the United States, net	31,466	53,879	48,573	88,895	155,154
57. Direct investment	8,204	37,213	11,497	2,378	31,519
58. US Treasury securities	2,693	1,131	16,241	36,893	24,320
59. US securities other than US Treasury securities	7,443	1,781	34,918	30,274	79,612
60. US liabilities to unaffiliated foreigners reported by US nonbanking concerns	n.a.	3,779	–405	741	n.a.
61. US liabilities reported by U.S. banks, not included elsewhere	1,687	9,975	–13,678	18,609	12,208
62. Allocations of special drawing rights	1,152	—	—	—	—
63. Statistical discrepancy (sum of above items with sign reversed)	35,605	63,526	–1,078	–12,218	26,735
Memoranda					
64. Balance on merchandise trade	–27,354	–108,115	–73,436	–96,138	–132,478
65. Balance on goods, services, and income	7,077	–69,794	–11,710	–33,505	–76,733
66. Balance on current account	118	–92,123	–3,682	–66,400	–109,242

Source: *Survey of Current Business,* various issues.

regions of the world. Looking at the 1992 balance of trade as shown in Table 8–4, it appears that the main sectors contributing to US merchandise exports were capital goods other than autos ($105 billion), industrial supplies and materials ($69 billion), agricultural products ($26 billion), food products ($21 billion), and automobiles ($25 billion). Before drawing conclusions about the US comparative advantage, we must consider imports too. The second half of the table shows that the largest categories of imports in 1992 were industrial supplies and materials ($71 billion), capital goods other than autos ($74 billion), nonfood consumer goods ($116 billion), autos ($25 billion), and petroleum ($41 billion).

Clearly there is a large overlap of categories that register both imports and exports. To some extent, this is attributable to differences in the countries involved. The United States ships lots of autos and parts to Canada, but imports a much greater value in autos from Western Europe and Japan. (Trade in autos is approximately balanced with Canada under the U.S.–Canada Automotive Agreement.) Similarly, the United States exports capital goods throughout the world, but registered a large deficit in this trade with Japan.

While a careful examination of the underlying reasons for the various flows and a more detailed look at specific product categories are beyond the scope of this chapter, we can see that the United States is clearly a net exporter of agricultural products as well as capital goods (such as electrical and nonelectrical machinery and aircraft). This is so for two reasons. First, the United States simply produces a surplus quantity of agricultural products that other countries need. Second, the US agricultural industry is technology and capital intensive relative to that of the rest of the world. It is likewise clear that the United States is a huge oil importer because of insufficient domestic supply, as well as a net importer of autos and industrial supplies and materials. Notice that the United States has a large trade deficit in each year shown in Table 8–3, and that oil, auto, and consumer goods imports have contributed the largest portion of this deficit.

Returning to the summary BOP (Table 8–3) and moving down the column, we find unilateral transfers (gifts) in lines 29 through 32. In this case, all entries are *net* values—credits minus debits. Since only one column is being used, the total addition to or subtraction from each type of claim is recorded, netting total flows during the given year. Line 29 sums all nonmilitary gifts into and out of the United States for the year, showing a net debit value of $32,895 million for 1992. For most advanced industrial countries, in fact, unilateral transfers are a persistent net debit entry because of foreign aid and private gifts going abroad. Conversely, in many LDCs, with the exception of the OPEC countries, unilateral transfers persistently add up to a net credit entry. The "thank-you notes" pile up in the industrial countries, while the aid itself goes to LDCs. When unilateral transfers are added to trade in goods and services, we obtain the current account balance, which appears in line 66.

The US capital accounts are extremely different from our conceptual presentation. In the official presentation, assets in foreign countries that are bought or sold by US residents are recorded in lines 39 through 47. This aggregation of all claims in the US BOP emphasizes the individuals and institutions that generate these flows, but it obscures the long-term/short-term dichotomy of the conceptual view. Foreigners' assets in the United States appear in lines 49 through 61 and are summed up in line 48.

It is fairly easy to separate official reserves flows from the other capital accounts. Lines 35 through 38 list the categories of official reserves, and line 34 shows the net change in reserves. These entries can be placed at the bottom of the table after eliminating them from the summary line 33. Thus, in 1992, US asset flows abroad were $50,961 million (i.e., an outflow of funds), and they were $54,862 million when official reserves are segregated out. The official reserves loss (outflow) was $3,901 million.

Because the data collection process is so difficult, with literally billions of transactions among millions of entities to record each year, the US BOP (or the BOP of any other country) unquestionably lacks complete coverage. Some international transactions simply do not get recorded, and thus the total volume of transactions is understated. Also, because banks, exporters, foreign investors, and so on report to different agencies and on different forms, the entities that *are* recorded may not balance overall. Thus, "statistical discrepancy," a special category to account for errors and omissions, is placed in line 63. As the ability to record more and more of the transactions that occur improves, the size of this entry should decline. Considering just the few most recent years, however, the discrepancy is often huge—$12,218 million in 1992, for example.

For additional discussion of the US balance-of-payments format and specific entries, see *Survey of Current Business,* June 1978, part 2, and Maldonado (1980).

Implications of the US Balance of Payments for International Firms

What do all of these transactions mean to business managers operating in the United States? First, the persistent balance-of-trade deficits during the 1990s portend increasing government policy restrictions on US imports. These restrictions have included implicit quotas on Japanese auto imports (see Chapter 9 for details) and ever-increasing calls for protectionism to help reduce imports in general. Second, one would expect a tendency for the dollar to devalue relative to the currencies of the major trading partners with which the United States has bilateral deficits, such as Canada, Britain, Japan, and Germany. While protectionism grew somewhat during the 1980s, the value of the dollar shifted wildly from revaluation of about 40 percent in the early 1980s to devaluation of a similar

TABLE 8–4 US Merchandise Trade by Major End-Use Category for Selected Areas and Countries (balance-of-payments basis, millions of dollars)

	Canada			Western Europe		
	1990	1991	1992*	1990	1991	1992*
Exports	**82,866**	**85,006**	**90,423**	**111,383**	**116,802**	**114,391**
Agricultural products	4,866	5,288	5,574	7,809	7,797	8,373
Nonagricultural products	78,000	79,718	84,849	103,574	109,005	106,018
Foods, feeds, and beverages	4,740	5,209	5,456	5,956	6,085	6,693
Industrial supplies and materials	19,433	19,139	20,009	29,153	29,044	28,306
Capital goods, except automotive	26,012	26,121	27,740	53,162	57,566	55,066
Automotive vehicles, parts, and engines	21,760	22,499	23,449	3,907	4,301	5,092
Consumer goods (nonfood), except automotive	7,543	8,760	9,754	14,576	14,918	15,309
Exports, n.e.c.	3,378	3,278	4,015	4,629	4,888	3,925
Imports	**93,099**	**93,008**	**100,724**	**109,161**	**101,884**	**111,429**
Petroleum products	7,440	7,469	7,239	5,784	3,843	4,673
Nonpetroleum products	85,659	85,539	93,485	103,377	98,041	106,756
Foods, feeds, and beverages	4,351	4,561	5,171	5,995	5,824	6,191
Industrial supplies and materials	35,781	35,311	38,016	28,041	24,663	27,393
Capital goods, except automotive	13,237	13,903	14,051	33,914	34,261	37,156
Automotive vehicles, parts, and engines	29,861	28,782	31,752	14,071	11,210	12,463
Consumer goods (nonfood), except automotive	3,733	3,833	4,623	21,673	20,855	22,736
Imports, n.e.c., and US goods returned	6,136	6,618	7,111	5,467	5,071	5,490

	Latin America and Other Western Hemisphere			Mexico		
	1990	1991	1992*	1990	1991	1992*
Exports	**54,286**	**63,233**	**75,335**	**28,109**	**33,140**	**40,469**
Agricultural products	5,141	5,755	6,757	2,574	3,021	3,813
Nonagricultural products	49,145	57,478	68,578	25,535	30,119	36,656
Foods, feeds, and beverages	4,492	5,015	5,970	2,211	2,586	3,326
Industrial supplies and materials	16,031	18,380	20,280	7,694	8,934	10,761
Capital goods, except automotive	19,399	22,469	26,810	9,457	11,294	13,586
Automotive vehicles, parts, and engines	5,615	6,914	9,362	4,516	5,372	6,726
Consumer goods (nonfood), except automotive	6,168	7,586	9,871	2,889	3,429	4,410
Exports, n.e.c.	2,581	2,869	3,042	1,342	1,525	1,660
Imports	**64,354**	**62,971**	**69,160**	**30,508**	**31,495**	**35,588**
Petroleum and products	18,410	15,673	15,840	5,279	4,678	4,747
Nonpetroleum products	45,944	47,298	53,320	25,229	26,817	30,841
Foods, feeds, and beverages	9,391	8,908	8,824	2,926	2,801	2,665
Industrial supplies and materials	27,114	24,171	24,826	8,539	7,748	8,031
Capital goods, except automotive	7,359	7,460	8,422	5,869	6,124	6,921
Automotive vehicles, parts, and engines	7,944	8,710	10,297	6,984	7,871	9,519
Consumer goods (nonfood), except automotive	10,477	11,590	14,160	4,659	5,345	6,700
Imports, n.e.c., and US goods returned	2,069	2,132	2,631	1,531	1,606	1,752

*Preliminary.

Source: *Survey of Current Business*, March 1993.

magnitude by early 1987, then to general revaluation (except relative to the yen) in the early 1990s. This is only part of the story, however; capital flows must be considered along with trade flows to get a full understanding of the pressures on the exchange rate.

TABLE 8–4 *Continued*

	Germany			Japan			Australia		
	1990	1991	1992*	1990	1991	1992*	1990	1991	1992*
	18,299	**20,759**	**20,348**	**47,807**	**47,213**	**46,856**	**8,303**	**8,255**	**8,731**
	1,136	1,084	1,177	8,087	7,777	8,489	226	281	271
	17,163	19,675	19,171	39,720	39,436	38,367	8,077	7,974	8,460
	746	743	780	8,580	8,619	9,683	219	272	268
	3,879	3,789	3,961	15,236	14,857	13,452	1,836	1,940	1,907
	9,966	11,625	10,898	14,432	15,140	15,075	4,530	4,248	4,665
	1,180	1,557	1,923	1,759	1,485	1,826	438	321	400
	1,803	2,177	2,269	6,902	6,143	5,868	813	875	995
	725	868	517	898	969	952	467	599	496
	27,999	**26,025**	**28,750**	**89,594**	**91,502**	**96,858**	**4,409**	**3,970**	**3,666**
	68	71	163	42	33	60	456	147	119
	27,931	25,954	28,587	89,552	91,469	96,798	3,953	3,823	3,547
	531	547	612	327	336	349	1,177	1,148	1,132
	5,273	5,128	5,506	8,470	8,477	9,311	2,304	1,819	1,577
	10,249	10,021	10,605	34,361	36,031	39,285	327	326	327
	8,033	6,599	7,813	32,207	32,829	33,251	239	276	228
	2,734	2,725	3,086	12,891	12,477	13,053	186	195	203
	1,179	1,005	1,128	1,338	1,352	1,609	176	206	199

	OPEC (non–Latin America)			Asia (non-OPEC)			Hong Kong, Republic of Korea, Singapore, Taiwan		
	1990	1991	1992*	1990	1991	1992*	1990	1991	1992*
	9,668	**12,899**	**14,414**	**62,837**	**69,988**	**75,698**	**39,881**	**44,386**	**46,882**
	1,780	1,482	1,524	8,118	7,596	8,186	5,191	4,979	5,239
	7,888	11,417	12,890	54,719	62,392	67,512	34,690	39,407	41,643
	1,443	1,111	1,180	5,788	5,564	6,322	3,497	3,587	3,876
	1,981	2,358	2,394	19,918	22,135	21,399	13,505	14,818	14,387
	3,430	4,927	5,930	28,272	32,058	36,843	16,833	19,314	21,412
	1,144	2,361	2,856	1,664	1,870	3,322	1,275	1,411	2,541
	1,175	1,458	1,578	4,915	5,216	5,728	3,424	3,524	3,774
	495	684	476	2,280	3,145	2,084	1,347	1,732	892
	27,359	**23,566**	**24,014**	**100,716**	**104,532**	**120,723**	**60,353**	**59,219**	**62,372**
	24,382	19,886	18,841	2,365	1,387	1,141	228	127	248
	2,977	3,680	5,173	98,351	103,145	119,582	60,125	59,092	62,124
	373	468	542	4,223	4,438	4,953	747	732	705
	25,609	21,454	20,774	11,028	10,438	11,414	5,415	5,548	6,013
	37	102	201	26,546	28,411	34,655	20,032	20,656	24,053
	6	6	15	3,265	3,030	3,131	2,794	2,490	2,342
	1,212	1,444	2,383	54,096	56,607	64,638	30,341	28,738	28,141
	122	92	99	1,558	1,608	1,932	1,024	1,055	1,118

Initially, the US merchandise trade deficit was financed largely by income on US assets abroad, such as remittances from foreign subsidiaries and interest on foreign loans. By 1983 even these flows had become inadequate to balance the excess of imports over exports, and by 1985 the negative balance on goods and services had jumped to over $100 billion per year. This situation would have presented a major crisis for any other country. The United States benefited from the fact that the US dollar was (and is) the base currency for international business transactions and is viewed as a relatively stable store of value. Thus, the huge deficits have been financed by massive capital inflows—investments by foreign nationals who want to hold US securities or invest in US businesses. As a result, by 1986 the United States had become a major net capital importer for the first time since the last century, and this situation continues today.

These circumstances have created major concern among US policymakers, who realize that any important shift in investors' confidence away from the United States could trigger even greater dollar devaluation and serious economic recession. If incoming foreign direct and portfolio investments do not finance the trade deficit, either official reserves must be used to make payment (i.e., to buy back dollars from foreign central banks) or expenditures on imports must be constrained (and/or exports must be subsidized) by policy to move closer to a balance. Continuing dollar devaluation is expected to improve the trade balance automatically, as exports become cheaper to foreign buyers and imports more expensive to US buyers, but as of 1994 this adjustment has been wholly inadequate to equilibrate exports and imports. Let us consider the adjustment process in more detail.

THE ADJUSTMENT PROCESS

Balance-of-payments adjustment may occur through any sequence of events that leads from a situation of net positive or negative official reserve flows to a balance in which no official reserves flow. Such adjustment takes a country from an initial deficit (or surplus) to equilibrium. The means for achieving BOP adjustment are numerous, ranging from trade and capital controls for restricting each of these accounts, to interest rate policy aimed at influencing capital flows, to exchange rate change, which affects all accounts. Tracing the intricacies of each policy or event and its impact on a country's internal and external balance is far beyond the scope of this text.[4] Therefore, let us consider the simple adjustment process in the real world of flexible exchange rates.

The **automatic adjustment mechanism** for a country that allows the value of its currency to fluctuate in the foreign exchange market is based on the exchange rate itself. When a country runs a balance-of-trade deficit, importing more than it exports, its currency will begin to accumulate in the hands of foreign exporters (or their banks). At some point, those foreign firms and banks will view their holdings of this currency as an excess and will begin to sell it off and bid its price down. As in any market under conditions of excess supply, the price of the product (namely, the currency) will fall to eliminate the excess. (This is exactly the same mechanism we discussed in Chapter 6 as the adjustment process for the foreign exchange market.) When the price of the home currency falls, exports become cheaper to foreign purchasers and imports become more expensive to domestic consumers, leading to a tendency toward trade equilibrium as exports increase and imports decline.[5]

The automatic adjustment mechanism also responds to imbalances in the capital accounts; however, such interactions are substantially more complex. In the 1990s the capital accounts have greatly overshadowed the value of trade flows among the industrial countries, so it is all the more important to examine adjustment of capital flows to BOP imbalances. As noted earlier, interest arbitrageurs will operate to equate interest differentials and forward premiums (or discounts) among major convertible currencies. Since the forward exchange rate is a good estimator for the future spot rate between any two countries' currencies, we can see that any change in either country's interest rate or the spot exchange rate will have an impact on the forward rate (and hence the future spot rate). Now if for some reason our domestic interest rates rise, foreign arbitrageurs and investors will purchase our assets now and sign forward contracts to convert back to their own currencies in the future. The net result will be that the initial outflow of claims (i.e., ownership of home country assets) causes the spot exchange rate to revalue (home currency/foreign currency $\downarrow$) and the forward rate to devalue (home currency/foreign currency $\uparrow$). Foreign interest rates may also rise as other countries try to lure back investors. In addition, the initial inflow of investment may cause home country interest rates to fall as demand for home country assets rises. Initially, the home country will export additional financial claims, pushing the official reserves BOP toward surplus; once the exchange rate changes (and interest rates adjust), a reverse flow of claims will occur.

A clearer and no less important phenomenon relates to the long-term capital account. If home country investors and banks invest/lend more abroad than foreigners lend to the home country, we will face a deficit on long-term capital. Other things equal, this will lead to a devaluation of the home currency, because there will be an excess demand for foreign exchange to buy foreign long-term assets. The devaluation will make foreign assets more expensive, thus enticing both foreign and home country investors to buy home country assets. The final tendency is toward equilibrium in capital flows, with the final exchange rate being an equilibrium rate.

The above description of the adjustment process is intended to demonstrate the *automatic* steps that would occur without government intervention. Once a deficit or a surplus occurs, the government may impose controls on various BOP accounts, or it may "finance" the deficit by borrowing from foreign banks and other foreign lenders. For example, when copper prices fall and Chile faces a BOP deficit on the current account, Chile's government may borrow from the IMF or from private banks. By borrowing foreign currency in exchange for a loan commitment, Chile obtains an inflow of official reserves (the foreign exchange) that may exactly offset the outflow needed to pay for the trade deficit. Chile's BOP returns to equilibrium, with the commitment to repay the loan eventually (and lose official reserves in the future).

Chile could avoid the need for future repayment of the loan by aiming instead to control specific balance-of-payments accounts. For example, Chile could place restrictions on imports and offer incentives to exports, thus pushing the trade balance in a favorable direction. Similarly, Chile could offer incentives to foreign direct investment, in this case improving the long-term capital account and leading toward a basic balance surplus. A country can use these policies separately or together to avoid letting the automatic adjustment mechanism function, with the problem that ending the policies may lead to the automatic adjustment anyway. At any given time, however, a country may prefer to utilize these policies rather than accept a currency devaluation or a need to borrow more from international lenders.

Even from this brief view, we can see that BOP adjustment may be a very complex process, though one that has important implications for a company or bank dealing with any given country. The main concern of this chapter has been to sketch the components and determinants of the BOP itself, not to investigate the adjustment process in detail. The conclusions, then, relate to the *pressures* on a country to adjust—which may be alleviated by automatic adjustment, by government policies on foreign exchange, trade, and investment, or by both.

Table 8-5   The UK Balance-of-Payments Position, 1978–1992

	1978	1979	1980	1981	1982	1983	1984	1985
Millions of Pounds								
	35,380	40,637	47,357	50,998	55,558	60,684	70,488	78,392
	39,533	46,925	49,773	51,169	56,978	66,101	78,967	85,027
	36,573	43,814	45,792	47,416	53,421	62,237	75,601	81,336
1985=100								
	80.0	82.7	83.7	82.6	85.3	87.2	94.5	100.0
	76.5	82.8	78.9	75.8	80.3	87.2	96.5	100.0
	55.5	61.4	70.0	76.2	81.4	88.0	94.9	100.0
	59.4	63.3	69.3	74.8	80.7	88.0	95.5	100.0
Minus Sign Indicates Debit								
	2,163	−783	6,862	14,127	7,897	5,470	2,058	3,920
	67,121	86,018	109,620	102,158	96,658	91,963	93,487	100,862
	−70,185	−92,991	−106,267	−95,198	−93,492	−94,340	−100,601	−104,817
	−3,064	−6,973	3,353	6,960	3,166	−2,377	−7,114	−3,955
	23,116	29,746	35,317	32,849	29,781	28,717	28,115	30,838
	−16,174	−21,680	−27,008	−25,406	−24,742	−22,966	−22,435	−22,583
	22,356	38,241	56,200	76,044	78,582	65,426	69,570	68,321
	−20,627	−35,440	−56,408	−73,244	−75,871	−60,900	−63,695	−64,737
	−244	−413	−473	115	82	510	493	405
	−3,200	−4,263	−4,118	−3,191	−3,100	−2,940	−2,875	−4,369
	−3,028	−6,070	−1,106	−6,274	−1,750	−3,005	−8,316	−5,081
	−2,404	271	−6,795	−9,251	−12,842	−9,017	−11,318	−11,313
	−2,556	−13,935	−1,582	18	15,548	3,089	−3,737	6,912
	−245	−55	154	−132	350	−1,591	−1,199	−1,027
	−2,725	−11,531	2,929	4,121	15,844	4,772	221	10,750
	415	−2,350	−4,665	−3,970	−646	−93	−2,759	−2,811
	3,432	1,872	1,936	1,787	−3,700	1,347	8,974	251
	−2,392	−18,644	−685	407	5,153	−2,117	−12,339	−5,312
	2,392	18,644	685	−407	−5,153	2,117	12,339	5,312
	4,319	−1,743	−229	5,028	2,420	910	1,302	−551
	−1,962	−1,271	−326	−298	−290	−57	—	—
	−198	20,770	1,989	−4,002	−7,803	353	9,429	3,676
	233	888	−749	−1,135	521	910	1,608	2,186
	3,961	−2,358	−1,319	5,325	2,852	1,056	1,893	−3,419
	−358	−615	−1,090	297	432	146	590	−2,869
Billions of Pounds								
	47.48	54.90	62.62	67.43	72.69	80.06	91.85	102.21
	33.41	38.83	48.94	55.37	60.36	65.79	69.76	73.81
	31.06	36.93	41.56	41.30	44.82	48.62	54.97	60.35
	1.80	2.16	−2.57	−2.77	−1.19	1.47	1.30	.82
	101.24	119.99	139.61	155.41	170.65	187.03	200.26	218.95
	−45.37	−54.35	−57.61	−60.39	−67.76	−77.53	−92.67	−98.87
	168.52	198.21	231.77	254.85	278.89	304.31	325.80	357.27
	.81	1.21	−.18	−.18	1.25	1.46	2.83	2.65
	169.32	199.41	231.59	256.10	280.35	307.15	330.15	359.91
	321.40	333.50	323.42	319.19	324.62	336.50	344.35	357.27
	52.4	60.0	71.7	79.8	85.9	90.4	94.6	100.0
Mid-Year Estimates								
	55.84	55.88	56.33	56.35	56.31	56.35	56.46	56.62
End of Period								
	1.6616	1.6883	1.8700	1.6392	1.4636	1.3855	1.1798	1.3151
End of Period (ag) Period average (rh)								
	2.0345	2.2240	2.3850	1.9080	1.6145	1.4506	1.1565	1.4445
	1.9195	2.1216	2.3263	2.0279	1.7505	1.5170	1.3363	1.2963
	226.00	512.00	589.50	397.50	456.90	381.50	308.30	327.00
End of Period (ec) Period Average (ed)								
	....	1.5445	1.8062	1.7652	1.6659	1.7525	1.6398	1.6251
	....	....	....	1.8136	1.7846	1.7072	1.6932	1.6989

Source: International Monetary Fund, *International Financial Statistics Yearbook* 1993.

Table 8-5 *Continued*

1986	1987	1988	1989	1990	1991	1992	
							International Transactions
72,988	79,849	81,655	93,771	103,692	104,818	108,290	Exports 70
86,176	94,026	106,571	121,699	126,086	118,786	125,844	Imports, cif 71
82,186	90,735	101,826	116,837	120,527	113,703	120,546	Imports, fob (on a BOP basis) 71.v
104.0	109.8	112.5	117.3	125.1	126.9	130.7	Volume of exports 72
107.2	114.8	130.5	140.8	142.7	138.6	147.4	Volume of imports 73
90.2	93.8	94.1	101.6	107.0	107.3	108.7	Unit Value of exports 74
95.4	97.7	97.0	104.0	107.9	108.4	108.5	Unit Value of imports 75
							Balance of Payments
−26	−7,559	−28,789	−35,587	−29,390	−11,549	−21,460	Current account, nie 77a.d
106,422	129,847	143,078	150,696	181,729	182,582	187,439	Merchandise: exports fob 77aad
−120,483	−148,866	−181,237	−191,239	−214,471	−200,868	−212,060	Merchandise: imports fob 77abd
−14,061	−19,019	−38,160	−40,544	−32,742	−18,286	−24,621	Trade balance 77acd
36,469	43,839	46,402	46,556	54,174	52,516	53,047	Services: credit 77ahd
−26,778	−32,923	−38,606	−39,996	−45,990	−44,557	−47,447	Services: debit 77aid
71,157	80,409	102,782	123,310	144,487	140,239	121,528	Income: credit 77ajd
−63,640	−74,320	−94,869	−117,459	−140,576	−139,068	−114,917	Income: debit 77akd
112	−205	−480	−491	−535	−531	−485	Private unrequited transfers 77afd
−3,284	−5,340	−5,857	−6,964	−8,208	−1,863	−8,565	Official unrequited trans.,nie 77agd
−8,490	−15,789	−16,014	−4,951	14,900	3,638	4,393	Direct investment, nie 77bad
−16,916	38,883	6,470	−32,115	−19,380	−25,964	−19,809	Portfolio investment, nie 77bbd
24,350	−22,954	24,723	54,830	22,013	49,135	18,299	Other capital, nie 77g.d
−731	−676	254	3	−319	−3,890	1,387	Resident official sector 77gad
25,829	−19,991	19,429	23,533	15,268	27,357	−10	Deposit money banks 77gbd
−748	−2,287	5,040	31,293	7,064	25,668	16,922	Other sectors 77gcd
4,555	597	12,077	3,455	9,814	−851	17,222	Net errors and omissions 77e.d
3,472	−6,823	−1,532	−14,369	−2,044	14,409	−1,355	Overall balance . . . . 78..d
−3,472	6,823	1,532	14,369	2,044	−14,409	1,355	Reserves and related items . . . . . . 79..d
−1,430	−20,187	−4,885	8,805	−121	−4,970	2,290	Reserve assets 79dad
—	—	—	—	—	—	—	Use of fund credit and loans . . . 79dbd
−4,802	25,857	6,560	7,499	2,076	−9,393	−745	Liab.const.fgn auth.reserves 79b.d
2,760	1,153	−143	−1,935	89	−45	−189	Exceptional financing 79a.d
							Memorandum items
−5,555	−23,293	−2,385	9,342	−1,068	−6,021	5,347	Total change in reserve assets 79e.d
−4,125	−3,107	2,500	538	−947	−1,051	3,057	of which: Revaluations 79f.d
							National Accounts
98.32	107.03	107.71	122.05	133.50	134.92	138.74	Exports of goods and services 90c.c
79.38	85.35	91.73	99.03	109.88	121.92	129.81	Government consumption 91f.c
64.51	74.08	89.86	103.26	106.03	95.66	91.96	Gross fixed capital formation 93e.c
.72	1.39	4.78	3.14	−1.46	−5.17	−2.11	Increase/Decrease (−) in stocks . . . 93i.c
243.03	267.52	302.06	330.53	350.41	367.53	386.61	Private consumption 96f.c
−101.07	−111.87	−124.79	−142.69	−147.73	−140.46	−148.78	Imports of goods and services 98c.c
384.89	423.50	471.34	515.32	550.35	573.34	595.21	Gross domestic product 99b.c
5.10	4.08	5.05	4.09	2.47	.50	3.20	Net factor inc/pmts (−) abroad . . . 98n.c
389.99	427.58	476.39	519.41	552.82	573.84	598.41	Gross nat'l. expenditure = GNP . . . 99a.c
372.04	389.95	407.13	415.73	417.91	408.56	406.02	Gross dom. prod., 1985 prices . . . 99b.r
103.5	108.6	115.8	124.0	131.7	140.3	146.6	GDP deflator (1985=100) 99bir
56.76	56.93	57.07	57.24	57.41	57.65	....	**Population** 99z
							Exchange Rates
1.2055	1.3192	1.3447	1.2217	1.3552	1.3078	1.0996	Market Rate . . . . .ac
1.4745	1.8715	1.8095	1.6055	1.9280	1.8707	1.5120	Market Rate US $ per £ . . . . .ag
1.4670	1.6389	1.7814	1.6397	1.7847	1.7694	1.7655	Market Rate US $ per £ . . . . .rh
390.90	484.10	410.25	401.00	385.00	353.60	333.25	London Gold Price (US $ per ounce) . . . c
1.3794	1.4351	1.5419	1.3463	1.4126	1.3964	1.2528	ECU Rate . . . . ec
1.4948	1.4138	1.5057	1.4872	1.4011	1.4265	1.3607	ECU Rate . . . . ed

EVALUATING THE BALANCE OF PAYMENTS

How can one interpret a deficit (or a surplus) on any given balance of payments? That is, what should one expect, in terms of exchange rate changes or government policies, when a particular balance of payments is not balanced?

Consider the situation of the United Kingdom during the past two decades as presented in Table 8–5. The United Kingdom ran a fairly persistent trade deficit during this time (line 77acd), with surpluses only during the global recession of 1980–82. This deficit was frequently compensated for by exports of services (such as interest on foreign loans), which resulted in current account surpluses until the late 1980s.

As a result of the current account balance of payments, a fairly stable or revaluing British pound would be expected until 1987, then devaluation until the present. Line ag in the table shows that the dollar/pound exchange rate increased (the pound revalued) steadily after the discovery of large North Sea oil deposits in UK territory in 1976, until the global recession beginning in 1980. During the 1980s, the pound generally devalued for the first half of the decade and revalued during the second half, finishing at $US1.93 per pound at year-end 1990. The pound has devalued since then, ending 1993 at $US1.48 per pound. There appears to be a rather weak relationship between trade flows and the exchange rate in this situation, which has been true for the largest industrial countries for most of the period since the change from fixed to floating exchange rates in 1971–73.

Looking further down in the balance of payments, capital flows can be seen to play an important role in the overall picture. Since only net flows are shown here, it is not obvious that the inflows and outflows of both short-term and long-term investments are much greater than the value of export and import trade. Given that the euromarkets are centered in London, the huge value of euromarket activity discussed in Chapter 7 indicates this point more clearly. The capital flow picture itself is fairly mixed over the period, with generally large net long-term capital inflows (increased ownership of British direct and portfolio investment abroad) and mostly short-term outflows. In fact, the official reserves balance is needed to draw some conclusions.

Even the official reserves BOP demonstrates a weak link to the exchange rate changes. Line 79.d lists official reserve inflows (with a − sign) and outflows (+). In periods in which official reserves increase, the pound tends to increase in value. In many years in which official reserves decline, the pound declines as well. This outcome is broadly in line with balance-of-payments economics as outlined earlier in the chapter; however the relationship is quite weak.

It should be recognized that the industrial (OECD) countries tend to be the ones whose economic conditions are reflected in the BOP most directly, since these countries impose few barriers to trade and investment. The United Kingdom, for example, despite the swings in trade and investment flows, only proceeded to open its economy even further during the past two decades, regardless of "problems" in the BOP.

Less developed countries, with typically much smaller amounts of capital flows relative to trade flows, tend to have a greater correspondence between the trade balance and the exchange rate, but their governments also intervene much more heavily in the foreign exchange market and in import and export trade. In Latin America, for example, most countries have intervened to push their exchange rates (relative to the US dollar) toward maintaining purchasing power parity between domestic and US goods. The balance of payments indicates pressures for exchange rate change and for government policy intervention, but many additional factors determine whether or not the anticipated changes actually take place.

CONCLUSIONS

The balance of payments is a very complex subject for nonspecialists. Managers should understand BOP accounting so that they can use BOP data in company strategy formulation. Generally speaking, BOP data for several years are needed to draw useful conclusions. Because automatic adjustment to BOP imbalances is limited by governments, no simple management decision rules can be derived from BOP data alone. Also, because governments intervene in different ways and at different times to alter exchange rates and exchange policies, BOP analysis can enable a company manager to understand only the key influences involved; the timing of government policies remains fairly unpredictable. Understanding these influences can help the manager create a business plan that minimizes the risks associated with likely BOP conditions in a given country.

Balance-of-payments accounting is similar to financial accounting for a company, especially to the financial statement called *statement of net change in financial position*. It is a flow concept, measured over a period of time. It includes all transactions between residents of a country and residents of all foreign countries during a given period.

There is no such thing as *the* balance of payments. The debits and credits in the total set of entries in a BOP account must add up to the same amount. If only certain entries are included, the BOP may not balance—for example, if the BOP is confined to exports and imports of merchandise, the trade balance. The official reserves balance is the final balance in a BOP account, and even it may not provide a clear picture of a country's position. Borrowing of official reserves that must be paid back later adds to the official reserves balance surplus, and the country may use such a loan to try to hide its BOP problems.

BALANCE-OF-PAYMENTS PROBLEMS

Instructions:

1. Make the proper entries for the following transactions on the accompanying worksheet.
2. Calculate the current account balance-of-payments surplus or deficit.
   ROW = Rest of the world. You may assume that all values are in thousands of US dollars, if you wish.

   a. Residents of the United States exported $5,000 of merchandise to residents of ROW, who paid by drawing on their accounts with the Chase Manhattan Bank.

   b. US tourists spent $120 for goods and services while traveling in ROW. They paid in ROW currency, which they obtained by cashing American Express traveler's checks at ROW banks.

   c. Diplomatic missions of foreign governments spent $150 in the United States, drawing on their deposits in US banks.

   d. The US government made cash grants of $1,000 in economic aid to less developed countries. The governments of these countries used $300 of the grants to buy machinery in the United States. They held the remainder on deposit in a US bank.

   e. Residents of the United States imported $7,200 of merchandise from ROW residents, of which $4,000 was paid by drafts drawn on deposits of US banks in ROW banks and $3,200 was paid through an increase in the deposits of ROW banks in US banks.

f. The ROW central bank bought $200 of gold from the US government, paying for it with a check drawn on its deposit with the Federal Reserve Bank of New York.

g. US ships carried goods for ROW merchants. The shipping charges of $300 were paid through a draft drawn on the ROW merchants. (ROW merchants paid their bank, the ROW bank increased the deposits of US banks, and US banks paid the shipping companies.)

h. Private citizens in the United States received merchandise gifts from foreigners valued at $60.

i. US residents bought $400 of bonds issued by a Japanese utility and paid for the bonds with checks drawn on their accounts in US banks. The Japanese utility held the proceeds in US banks.

j. US residents sent $250 of US currency through the mail as gifts to persons in ROW.

k. The US government donated $1,000 of surplus wheat to needy countries in ROW.

l. A US multinational firm set up a factory in ROW, sending $5,000 in cash and $10,000 in machinery to the ROW location.

m. Bank of America made a $7,500 loan, payable in one year, to an ROW businessman (who had a deposit of $2,500 at Bank of America).

n. The US Fed floated a $100,000 bond, denominated in SDRs and payable in two years. The bond was purchased by the ROW central bank and paid for in SDRs.

Worksheet

	Debit	Credit
A. Goods and services		
1. Merchandise		
2. Transportation		
3. Travel		
4. Miscellaneous, government		
B. Unilateral transfers		
1. Private		
2. Government		
C. Long-term capital		
1. Foreign direct investment		
2. Private portfolio investment		
3. Government investment		
D. Short-term capital		
1. Private		
2. Government		
E. Official reserves		
1. SDRs		
2. Foreign exchange		
3. Position in the IMF		
4. Gold		

QUESTIONS

1. What exactly is measured in a balance of payments? In a double-entry BOP accounting system, how can the accounts fail to balance?

2. Explain how the trade account in a country's BOP may be related to the short-term capital account.

3. Of what importance is the BOP of a host country (such as the United Kingdom in the text example) to the MNE manager? Of what importance is the home country's BOP?

4. How can a country's balance of trade be in a deficit while its current account is in a surplus?

5. Explain why the balance of payments is organized into trade, gifts, long-term capital, short-term capital, and official reserve accounts. Why is it useful to draw these distinctions?

6. As a company manager in Great Britain in 1994, when oil prices have fallen 25 percent compared to 1990 prices, what would you expect the trade balance to show? What government policies would you expect? What automatic adjustment would you expect to occur, other things equal?

7. If interest rates are higher in the United States than in Japan, what would you expect the capital accounts to show? (*Note:* What if the interest rates in both countries have not changed from last year?) Does the exchange rate make any difference?

8. What impact does the IMF have on balances of payments when it creates new SDRs and distributes them to member countries? (The Chapter 7 discussion of SDRs may help you in answering this question. SDRs are the liabilities of the IMF itself, and they are reserve assets to the countries that receive them.)

9. Looking at the US BOP in Tables 8–3 and 8–4, what automatic adjustments and policy changes do you anticipate for the next year?

10. How can a country such as Brazil finance its foreign debt, which was about $100 billion in 1994? Specifically, use balance-of-payments categories to show what kinds of transactions would generate foreign currency for Brazil.

REFERENCES

International Monetary Fund. *Balance of Payments Manual,* 4th ed. Washington, DC: IMF, 1977.

Maldonado, Rita. "Recording and Classifying Transactions in the Balance of Payments." *International Journal of Accounting,* Fall 1979, pp 105–33.

Stern, Robert. *The Balance of Payments.* Chicago: Aldine Publishing, 1973.

"U.S. International Transactions." *Survey of Current Business,* various issues.

NOTES

[1] For balance-of-payments purposes, a *resident* is generally defined as an entity or person residing in the country for one year or more.

[2] This valuation scheme, then, leads to a summary BOP that includes home-currency values of transactions from different dates, when exchange rates may have differed. Because the BOP is a flow measure, no end-of-period adjustment is made for asset/liability valuation changes.

[3] The distinction between stock ownership as portfolio investment and stock ownership as direct investment is not easy to draw. The US Department of Commerce defines FDI as 10 percent or more ownership of a firm (see Chapter 4) for most purposes. Other governments often use 25 percent ownership as the dividing line.

[4] The various views of BOP adjustment are presented very clearly in Stern (1973).

[5] This result will occur only if the devaluation causes export quantity to rise enough so that export *value* (price × quantity) increases, and vice versa for imports. The mathematical condition that underlies this reasoning is the Marshall-Lerner condition. The Marshall-Lerner condition appears on p. 641 in Peter Lindert's *International Economics,* 9th ed., 1991.

The Debt/Equity Swap: American Express Bank in Mexico

Introduction

During the entire decade of the 1980s, borrowers in Latin American countries faced a continuing crisis of debt servicing to foreign creditors. Conversely, the foreign lenders saw their Latin American loans shift from fairly ordinary risks to nonperforming, rescheduled, and otherwise impaired assets. The Latin American countries encountered major difficulties in obtaining sufficient foreign currency (mainly US dollars) to meet their needs for interest and principal payments to foreign banks and other lenders, in addition to suffering through the global recession of 1981–83. While the problem originated with government sector borrowers, by 1982 it had nonetheless spread to creditworthy private sector borrowers as well, since they were unable to obtain foreign exchange except at staggering cost and often with substantial delay.[1]

The fundamental reason for the crisis throughout Latin America is the period of overborrowing from foreign lenders during the 1970s, immediately after both oil shocks (1973–74 and 1979–80). The OPEC cartel's successful effort to raise oil prices caused a massive transfer of purchasing power to the oil-exporting countries. They, in turn, spent some of their new income on increased imports and invested most of the rest in the international banking system. The commercial banks were left with huge amounts of new deposits (although most of the money was simply taken from accounts of industrial country depositors and moved to accounts of OPEC depositors), but, more important, a need to lend them out. Because the oil crisis caused large transfers of purchasing power from industrial, oil-importing countries, those nations experienced economic down-turns in the aftermath. The recessionary conditions (especially in 1975–76 and 1981–82) left the banks facing a reduced demand for borrowing among their traditional clients and a need to seek out new ones. In addition to new clients in the industrial world and in the communist countries, the banks extended much more credit to less developed country borrowers, especially in Latin America. International indebtedness increased by over 20 percent per year in all four of the largest countries in the region (Argentina, Brazil, Mexico, and Venezuela) during 1973–82, while national income and exports grew by less than half that rate.

This case was written by Professor Robert Grosse as a basis for group discussion. The detailed information provided by American Express Bank, Ltd., is gratefully acknowledged. Any errors of fact or interpretation are the responsibility of the author. The continued help of Mr. José Muzaurieta is gratefully acknowledged. Revised April 1989.

During the time since the Latin American debt crisis "officially" began with the declaration by Mexico's government on August 20, 1982, that it could not meet foreign debt payments, dozens of government policies and corporate strategies have been suggested and tried as solutions to the problem. One of the most successful of these ideas is the debt/equity swap, that is, the exchange of an existing, typically value-impaired bank loan for an equity investment in the borrower country. This case explores the structure and functioning of such a swap in Mexico that involves the central participation of American Express Bank.

A Debt/Equity Swap

The basic concept of a debt/equity swap is to transform a problem loan into another form of credit to the borrowing country, namely, an equity investment. Typically, the loan is a problem because the debtor fails to make the interest and principal payments on time, often because of unavailability of the foreign currency in which payment must be made. This situation, in turn, occurs due to balance-of-payments problems in the given country.[2] The debt/equity swap then calls for exchange of foreign loans for equity investments in local businesses. This type of transaction bolsters capital investment in the local economy and does not lead directly to severe pressures to exchange the local currency for dollars.

The debt/equity swap involves at least four key parties in the total group of transactions. First, there is a foreign bank that wants to dispose of a loan to the government or a private sector borrower in the country in question. Second, there is another foreign firm that wants to invest in a capital project in the same country. Third, there is the monetary authority (and perhaps other government agencies) of the given country, which must agree to permit exchange of the loan contract for local currency that will be used in the investment. Finally, there is an investment banking intermediary that looks for buyers and sellers of the loans and negotiates with the monetary authorities for any permissions that are required. A simple debt/equity swap is depicted in Figure 1, which also shows the specific process involved in the American Express project.

Since the loan is nonperforming or otherwise impaired in its servicing, the originating bank may be willing to sell it at a discount just to dispose of it. As Table 1 shows, the discounts at which foreign commercial banks have been willing to sell their Latin American loans have grown to over 50 percent for most countries in the region. Typically, the potential loan seller is contacted by an intermediary, such as an investment banking firm, that is seeking sources of funds for clients who want to invest in Latin American countries, and vice versa. The most active brokers in these swaps have been NMB Bank (of the Netherlands), Morgan Guaranty, Shearson Lehman Hutton, Bankers Trust, and Merrill Lynch. These intermediaries seek out both loan sellers and buyers, trying to profit by putting them together and arranging the deals.

Once a loan seller and buyer have been found, the intermediary must negotiate with the Latin American government involved to obtain whatever permissions may be necessary to redeem the dollar loan for some value in local currency. The value the loan buyer receives is typically some percentage below the direct face value of the loan translated from dollars into local currency. This amount is still substantially higher than the dollar value that the buyer paid to obtain the loan. Once permissions have been arranged, the loan buyer takes the local currency (e.g., pesos), and invests it in a capital project that was proposed in the permission request to the government in that country.

FIGURE 1

A Swap of Sovereign Debt for Equity in a New Capital Project

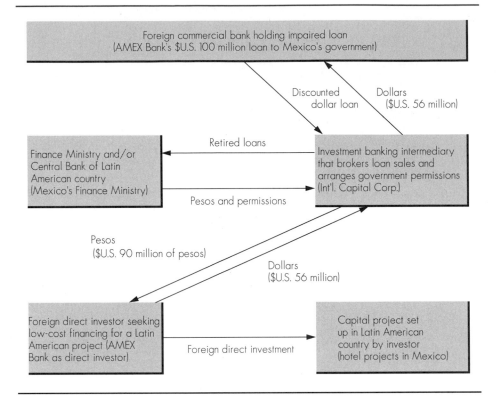

TABLE 1

Prices of Latin American Loans

| Country | Loan Sale Price Relative to Face Value (in percent) | | | | |
	July 1985	July 1986	July 1987	July 1988	May 1989
Argentina	60–65	63–57	46–49	24–26	15–16
Brazil	75–81	73–76	58–61	51–52	36–37
Chile	65–69	64–67	68–70	60–61	58–60
Colombia	81–83	80–82	81–83	65–67	55–58
Ecuador	65–70	63–66	45–47	25–27	10–12
Mexico	80–82	56–59	55–57	51–52	41–42
Peru	45–50	18–23	10–12	05–06	04–06
Venezuela	81–83	75–78	70–72	54–55	37–38

Source: Shearson Lehman Brothers International, Inc.

This transaction is viewed favorably by each participant. First, the original lending bank is able to sell its problem loan, taking the discount as a real loss in value of the original loan as the price of this sale. (The bank usually is able to lower its tax liability as a result of the loan loss, so not all of the discount is really "lost".) The new investor is able to obtain local currency at a substantial discount relative to ordinary financing costs. The host government is able to eliminate some of its foreign dollar debt and related servicing problems by replacing it with new direct investment. Finally, the investment bank earns fees by bringing the various parties together.

The debt/equity swap should still be seen as an imperfect solution by the original lender and the borrowing country. The original lender takes a real loss on its loan rather than continuing to hope for improved loan servicing in the future. The borrowing country eliminates a foreign debt that was not being serviced as contracted, but it replaces this obligation with an increase in foreign equity investment, which itself implies costs (e.g., dividend remittances and other funds flows from subsidiary to parent).

The Mexican Government's View of $US100 Billion of Foreign Debt

The Mexican government participated actively in the exorbitant expansion of foreign indebtedness during the 1970s. Although not an OPEC member, Mexico nonetheless is a major oil exporter. When extensive new petroleum reserves were discovered in 1976, foreign lenders flocked to Mexico City to extend new credit to the government and other borrowers. (The national oil company, PEMEX, controls all petroleum producing and refining in the country. PEMEX is one of the most important international borrowers in Mexico.) Table 2 shows Mexico's foreign debt skyrocketed to over $U.S.100 billion by 1986, growing at an annual rate of about 29 percent during the 1973–81 period.

Most of the growth in foreign credit to Mexican borrowers during this period went to the government sector, and much of it was invested in projects that did not lead to generation of dollars for repayment. The foreign lenders lacked a full grasp of the extent of credit being extended, since no formal information channels existed for aggregating total dollar loans to public or private Mexican borrowers. By 1982 the Mexican government found that it could not meet interest obligations on its part of the total foreign debt, since insufficient dollars were available at the Central Bank. The first step taken, in August of that year, was to declare a moratorium on debt servicing. Subsequently, the government has repeatedly renegotiated maturities, interest rates, fees, and other loan conditions with its foreign creditors. No single solution has appeared to limit the process of renegotiations, but the Mexican government made a number of suggestions.

One proposal was to convert some of the loans into long-term obligations such as bonds. As a result of negotiations with the US Treasury and Morgan Guaranty Bank, in 1988 Mexico was able to issue about $1.1 billion of 20-year, zero-coupon bonds backed by the US Treasury in exchange for $3.7 billion of existing (discounted) loans.[3] Another proposal was to reduce debt-servicing payments and/or the debt itself via renegotiations of the loan terms. This proposal was used in the Brady Plan begun by the US government in 1989, and it has led to both loan principal reductions and lower interest rates on the outstanding debt. A third proposal was to convert some of the debt into capital investment in Mexico. This proposal has resulted in a formal program of debt/equity conversion, which was used in the present case.

The program began haltingly in 1986 with a small number of transactions, including the American Express agreement discussed later. Despite the uncertainties involved, over $US2 billion of swaps were authorized in the first two years of the program.

The government's view of debt/equity swaps is decidedly ambivalent.[4] Foreign debt reduction is carried out by allowing greater foreign direct investment (i.e., greater foreign ownership in the economy) and printing new pesos to finance it. This technique has inflationary implications, though not excessive ones if the amount of debt swapped is small relative to the domestic money

TABLE 2   Indicators of Mexico's International Financial Position

1970	1971	1972	1973	1974	1975	1976	1977	1978	1979	1980
Pesos per SDR: End of Period (aa) Period Average (rb)										
12.5	13.6	13.6	15.1	15.3	14.6	23.2	27.6	29.6	30.0	29.7
12.5	12.5	13.6	14.9	15.0	15.2	17.8	26.4	28.5	29.5	29.9
Pesos per US Dollar: End of Period (ae) Period Average (af and rf)										
12.5	12.5	12.5	12.5	12.5	12.5	20.0	22.7	22.7	22.8	23.3
12.5	12.5	12.5	12.5	12.5	12.5	15.4	22.6	22.8	22.8	23.0
12.5	12.5	12.5	12.5	12.5	12.5	15.4	22.6	22.8	22.8	23.0
Billions of Pesos										
17.5	18.8	21.2	28.3	37.3	36.3	53.5	102.0	135.6	204.9	357.5
.5	.4	.3	.3	1.5	5.8	8.4	23.2	41.4	89.3	225.7
—	—	—	—	.5	5.4	8.4	22.3	40.7	86.4	214.4
1.1	1.0	1.1	2.0	1.9	2.3	5.2	10.3	8.8	12.4	10.2
—	—	—	—	—	—	2.5	4.2	3.4	8.2	8.0
30.8	30.1	34.0	47.7	75.7	82.1	90.9	133.0	184.2	275.6	447.0
29.3	28.7	32.4	45.4	72.1	78.3	86.4	117.8	175.5	262.5	425.7
Millions of US Dollars: Minus Sign Indicates Debit										
−1,068	−835	−916	−1,415	−2,876	−4,042	−3,409	−1,854	−3,171	−5,459	−10,750
1,348	1,409	1,717	2,141	2,999	3,007	3,475	4,604	6,246	9,301	15,511
−2,236	−2,158	−2,610	−3,656	−5,791	−6,278	−5,771	−5,625	−7,992	−12,131	−18,896
−888	−749	−894	−1,515	−2,791	−3,272	−2,295	−1,021	−1,745	−2,830	−3,385
1,587	1,762	2,100	2,699	3,369	3,352	3,728	3,608	5,178	6,702	6,483
−1,822	−1,906	−2,187	−2,673	−3,574	−4,263	−4,996	−4,610	−6,797	−9,556	−14,132
25	26	25	41	57	59	73	88	104	131	245
30	31	39	33	65	81	83	82	88	94	39
323	307	301	457	678	609	628	556	824	1,332	2,156
−19	23	50	64	−82	156	430	1,345	737	−393	42
322	436	477	1,298	2,450	3,902	3,936	2,710	3,560	4,239	8,332
−442	−69	−89	404	171	625	1,585	2,757	1,949	−281	−220
219	125	13	185	381	782	551	−2,138	−1,420	−58	1,042
252	74	254	−431	−479	−1,203	−2,996	3	−143	654	−4
29	130	178	157	74	204	−860	622	386	315	818
8	7	−11	−13	−41	—	−87	7	6	3	195
45	40	43	—	—	—	—	—	—	72	73
—	15	2	27	4	−58	−3	—	17	6	−8
83	192	212	171	37	146	−950	629	409	396	1,079
—	—	—	—	—	—	—	—	—	—	—
—	—	—	—	—	—	300	−300	—	—	—
−83	−192	−212	−171	−37	−146	649	−328	−409	−396	−1,079
		8.6	12.8	16.9	21.8	27.1	33.6	40.8	53.8	

Sources: IMF, *International Financial Statistics Yearbook, 1989,* Washington, DC: IMF, 1989; World Bank, *World Debt Tables, 1989–90.* Washington, DC: World Bank, 1990.

supply. Also, the borrowing country may find that new investment is not generated by the swap program; rather, investors who would have invested anyway simply use the swap mechanism to reduce their financing costs. (This possibility apparently has not been borne out in Mexico, where swap-financed investments led to a doubling of foreign investment from 1986 to 1987 and then a large decline in 1988, when the swap program was suspended.)

Furthermore, for the borrowing country, the swap may be viewed as a subsidy for foreign investors to the detriment of domestic investors. This eventuality has

Table 2 *Continued*

1981	1982	1983	1984	1985	1986	1987	1988	
								Exchange Rates: **Preference indicated**
30.5	106.4	150.7	188.7	408.3	1,129.6	3,134.8	3,069.5	Market rate/par or central rate .... aa
28.9	62.3	128.4	172.0	260.8	717.7	1,782.1	3,054.9	Par rate/market rate .... rb
26.2	96.5	143.9	192.6	371.7	923.5	2,209.7	2,281.0	Market rate/par or central rate .... ae
24.5	56.4	120.1	167.8	256.9	611.8	1,378.2	2,273.1	Market rate/par or central rate .... af
24.5	56.4	120.1	167.8	256.9	611.8	1,378.2	2,273.1	Par rate/market rate .... rf
								International Transactions
480.9	1,231.8	2,632.0	4,082.4	5,705.1	10,083.5	28,939.2	47,208.0	Exports 70
338.3	941.9	1,822.0	2,754.3	3,799.9	3,896.2	11,788.7	15,075.0	Petroleum 70a
325.5	912.5	1,780.5	2,507.7	3,438.2	3,426.2	10,751.3	13,215.0	Crude Petroleum 70aa
8.2	19.0	61.6	79.5	139.6	519.0	680.6	1,082.4	Coffee 70e
5.5	27.4	46.8	68.1	92.0	98.5	658.6	832.3	Shrimp 70bl
590.1	774.7	972.4	2,010.8	3,597.5	7,229.7	17,951.0	44,577.5	Imports, cif 71
563.7	742.8	923.4	1,920.2	3,456.0	6,905.2	17,145.1	42,573.0	Imports, fob 71.v
								Balance of Payments
−16,061	−6,307	5,403	4,194	1,130	−1,673	3,968	−2,905	Current account, nie 77a.d
20,102	21,230	22,312	24,196	21,663	16,031	20,655	20,657	Merchandise: exports fob 77aad
−23,948	−14,435	−8,550	−11,255	−13,212	−11,432	−12,222	−18,905	Merchandise: imports fob 77abd
−3,846	6,795	13,762	12,941	8,451	4,599	8,433	1,752	Trade bal., 77aad + 77abd 77acd
7,535	6,290	6,266	8,182	7,881	7,653	9,244	·11,172	Other goods,serv.,&income: cre. 77add
−20,053	−19,695	−14,927	−17,339	−16,202	−14,389	−14,357	−16,444	Other goods,serv.,&income: deb. 77aed
246	232	255	325	327	345	384	452	Private unrequited transfers 77afd
57	71	47	85	673	119	264	163	Official unrequited trans., nie 77agd
2,835	1,655	461	390	491	1,523	3,246	2,594	Direct investment 77bad
1,160	921	−653	−756	−984	−816	−397	−627	Portfolio investment, nie 77bbd
14,943	5,773	−67	42	−796	−274	1,195	−2,464	Other long-term capital, nie 77bcd
2,877	2,042	5,144	3,870	−159	−1,240	8,012	−3,402	Total, 77a.d + 77bad—77bcd 77c.d
7,414	−6,886	−8,527	−3,574	1,782	694	−5,047	−2,770	Other short-term capital,nie 77d.d
−9,016	−6,791	−925	−973	−1,765	458	2,605	−467	Net errors and omissions 77e.d
1,275	−11,635	−4,308	−677	−3,706	−88	5,570	−6,639	Total, lines 77c.d—77e.d 77f.d
19	42	120	65	72	46	74	21	C'part to mon./demon. of gold 78a.d
69	—	—	—	—	—	—	—	Counterpart to SDR allocation 78b.d
−30	−12	30	139	−313	−190	39	−171	C'part to valuation changes 78c.d
1,333	−11,605	−4,158	−472	−3,947	−232	5,684	−6,789	Total, lines 77f.d—78c.d 78d.d
—	6,846	7,558	2,827	975	—	—	—	Exceptional financing 79a.d
—	1,217	−1,217	—	—	—	—	—	Liab.const.fgn author. reserves 79b.d
−1,333	3,542	−2,183	−2,355	2,972	232	−5,684	6,789	Total change in reserves 79c.d
67.0	82.0	89.3	97.5	98.1	103.9	104.8	—	Total foreign debt outstanding = (in billions of US dollars at year-end)

been seen by the Chilean government (and others) as a reason to open the swap program to *domestic* as well as foreign investors who seek to undertake capital projects. Finally, the borrowing government needs to recognize that the swap does not eliminate foreign indebtedness; it just alters the form. Direct investment projects generate dividends, royalties, and often other income to the foreign investors. These flows replace the interest payments on foreign debt. Although the net effect on funds flows is difficult to measure a priori, it can be argued that, whereas the principal of a foreign loan is ultimately repaid along with the periodic interest payments, foreign direct investment projects are generally not divested, so the initial capital infusion is not usually returned to the foreign firm.

The AMEX Bank Swap

In 1985, American Express Bank (hereafter AMEX Bank or the Bank) had loans outstanding to Mexican borrowers worth about $US650 million. About 80 percent of these loans were to official Mexican government agencies such as the Central Bank and the Ministry of Economy. The Bank was looking for methods to restructure its Mexican portfolio such that the total amount of funds committed could be reduced and/or the loans could be shifted onto some basis that would permit debt servicing to resume more or less normally. One option that had surfaced in the previous year was the idea of swapping dollar loans for pesos that would then be invested in Mexican businesses. Since American Express Company has a clear, long-term commitment to operating in Mexico, the idea of buying into a Mexican company or financial institution instead of continuing the interminable struggle for servicing the dollar loans was appealing. While the Bank was prohibited from entering into commercial, nonbanking ventures in the United States, this restriction did not apply to overseas activities.[5] Accordingly, AMEX Bank began to investigate possible investments in the Mexican market.

The Bank considered the purchase of an existing Mexican banking company or a new investment in a financial services company, but these choices were eliminated because Mexico forbids foreign purchases of financial institutions. Given American Express Company's overall goals of providing travel-related services as well as regular commercial and investment banking services, the Bank also considered possible investments in the tourism industry. After substantial internal discussions within American Express and talks with Mexican government officials, it was agreed that the first step into debt/equity ventures would be the purchase of pesos to invest in a series of new hotels to be constructed in various sites in Mexico.

Discussions with the Mexican government began with the Ministry of Finance, the agency responsible for representing the government in negotiations with participants in debt/equity swaps. Simultaneously, the firm undertook discussions with officials in the Ministry of Tourism, which is also centrally involved in the industry affected by the project. Senior officers of the Bank traveled to Mexico to meet with the finance minister and other officials who needed to give approvals for redeeming the initial loans, disbursing the pesos, incorporating the hotels, and various other key aspects of the total arrangement. These discussions took place over a period of about six months, and a basic agreement was reached to permit American Express Bank to sell approximately $US100 million of its own sovereign loans (i.e., AMEX Bank's loans to the Mexican government and its agencies). When the final agreement was reached, the chairman of American Express Company, James Robinson, flew to Mexico, where he and Mexican President Miguel de la Madrid signed the contract.

It was agreed that the sale of the loans would be paid in pesos at the current market exchange rate, with disbursement over time as the funds would be used in hotel construction and operation. At the time of this deal, when the Mexican government was just beginning its swap program, the discount offered to AMEX Bank was about 10 percent below the face value of the loans translated into pesos. In 1988, this discount was about 20 percent. (Note that this percentage is *not* the swap discount rate for sale of dollar loans. It is the final discount for acquisition of pesos that the foreign investor receives. Since American Express Bank sold its own loans, it did not enter into the dollar swap with another intermediary.) That meant that the Bank received $US90 million worth of Mexican pesos. Subsequently, these pesos were disbursed to pay bills incurred in the hotel business, when invoices were presented by AMEX Bank to the Ministry of Finance. Thus, the swap itself involved immediate cancellation of the original bank debt, but only periodic disbursement of pesos for specific expenses (e.g., *not* for working capital or for imported products) incurred in creation of the hotel businesses. The key transactions involved in the entire swap process are sketched in Figure 1.

The original agreement called for construction of five hotels in three cities around the country, namely, Cancun, Acapulco, and Puerto Vallarta. Each hotel project had to receive approval when the specific details of construction, additional financing, partnerships with Mexican investors, and so on were decided. That is, the original swap agreement called for using the pesos to finance construction and operation of five hotels, but each detailed hotel project required subsequent specific approval before funds would be authorized.

The disbursements of funds are *not* made to AMEX Bank; rather, they go directly to the suppliers and contractors involved in the hotel projects. Since the payout is not immediate, the funds in the swap account earn interest, in this case at a rate in dollars that is slightly above the original loan interest rate.[6] Payout is in pesos, but they are drawn out of the dollar-denominated swap account at the market exchange rate prevailing at the time of the disbursement.

AMEX Bank has entered into joint ventures with Mexican partners in all seven of the hotels constructed under the agreement, retaining majority ownership in three of them. While Mexico's Foreign Investment Law of 1973 requires at least 51 percent Mexican ownership of new ventures established after that date, exceptions are made when the government deems the projects to be important to national development interests. Apparently, the hotel investments do meet these criteria, and AMEX Bank has decided to remain majority owner in three of the projects. In addition, AMEX Bank has a strong minority position in the other hotels. The partners are all large Mexican construction firms that the Bank brought into the discussions early on and are doing the hotel construction in each location.

As far as actual management of the hotels is concerned, the Bank does not possess the expertise needed in such ventures. Thus, contracts with Sheraton (three cases), Radisson, Hilton, Club Med, and Marriott have been concluded in each hotel project for one of those firms to operate and manage the facilities. The fees paid by AMEX Bank for this service are similar to those paid by other hotel owners who obtain franchises from the major hotel chains.

Since the original swap agreement was signed in 1986, the number of hotels permitted has been extended from five to seven. Four of them were operating in mid-1989, and the other three are under construction. Additional projects are possible.

For a variety of reasons, not the least of which is the distinctly different nature of the swap business compared to traditional commercial banking, American Express decided to create a new division for dealing in these activities. Accordingly, AMEX Bank formed a wholly owned subsidiary called International Capital Corporation as its own intermediary in the Latin American debt swap business. The managers of this subsidiary were responsible for negotiating with the Mexican government, the various contractors and subcontractors in Mexico, and with any other participants in the swap process just described. The subsidiary also seeks other opportunities for AMEX Bank to swap its Latin American debts elsewhere in the region and opportunities to serve as intermediary for other banks and investors who can use its expertise in debt/equity swaps.

CASE APPENDIX: BACKGROUND ON AMERICAN EXPRESS COMPANY

American Express Company (AMEX) was one of the three or four leading financial institutions in the United States in 1986. Its major competitors include Citicorp, Merrill Lynch, and credit card associations such as VISA and MasterCard that are controlled by banks, as well as other major firms in the various market segments served by AMEX subsidiaries.

American Express began as a credit card and tourist service firm in the early 1900s. By the time of this case, AMEX had grown into a gigantic provider of financial services, with annual sales of over $US10 billion. Even so, the basic business of providing credit and access to funds for business and pleasure travelers continued to play a major role in the company's activities. The Travel Related Services division accounted for about 42 percent of the entire firm's sales in 1986.

The strategic goals of American Express include positioning the firm as one of the top three providers of financial services in the United States. Similar positions are sought in other countries in those segments of the financial markets that are open to foreign competitors. Since US banking laws still prohibit full-scale national commercial banking, as well as direct participation by AMEX in commercial banking due to its other activities, the firm has positioned itself in the 'nonbank' area through acquisitions of Shearson Lehman Brothers (a major investment banking firm), Investors Diversified Services (a large investment advisory service), and expansion into the insurance business.

In the United States, American Express does *not* function as a commercial bank, due to the banking laws that prohibit deposit taking and some other functions from companies that are involved in investment banking, insurance, or any commercial or industrial activity. However, due to a historical quirk, AMEX Bank Ltd. operates in New York as a provider of international banking services such as trade financing, eurocurrency transactions, syndicated lending, and other generally wholesale-type services to domestic and foreign clients. The bank also has branches throughout the world, including Latin America, where it provides a broad range of banking services.

American Express views Latin America as a highly desirable market for its various services and has been expanding there for the past decade. Most of the firm's business is in the larger countries such as Brazil, Mexico, Venezuela, and Argentina. Due to its proximity to the United States and its many tourist attractions, Mexico has always been the leading Latin American market for AMEX. Brazil ranks second among AMEX's Latin markets, followed by Argentina and Venezuela.

CASE NOTES

[1] Most private sector debt was and still is in the form of short-term trade financing and working capital loans. The medium-term portion of private foreign borrowing in many cases has been assumed by Latin American governments, which then collect local currency from the private sector borrowers and "consolidate" the foreign-currency liabilities with their other official foreign debt.

[2] The logic can be taken further. The balance-of-payments crisis is often due to reduced demand for (or prices of) exports and/or government policies that stimulate excessive domestic demand.

[3] Mexico's government "auctioned" the bonds to interested banks, accepting 55 percent of the offers from 139 banks from 18 countries. The resultant bond sales were discounted at an average of 70 percent of the loans' face values, reducing Mexican official debt by $2.6 billion. The bonds mature in the year 2008, pay LIBOR + 1 5/8 percent interest, and are collater-

alized by US Treasury zero coupon bonds. See Morgan Guaranty Bank, *Press Release,* March 1988.

[4]In fact, the formal debt/equity swap program outlined here has been held in abeyance since the end of 1987, pending the Salinas government's decision on whether or not to restart it.

[5]See, for example, *The Wall Street Journal,* August 13, 1987, p. 3, for a discussion of the Federal Reserve ruling that permits US banks to be exempted from Regulation K limits for the purpose of acquiring nonfinancial companies in Latin America and other heavily indebted less developed countries.

[6]This was viewed as a major positive feature of the agreement by AMEX Bank. In 1988, the Mexican government chose to fix the exchange rate (during the period before national elections, such that Mexicans' purchasing power rose as local prices rose). Thus, the dollar interest gain of somewhere around 7 percent was swamped by Mexican inflation of about 60 percent during the year, making the funds in the swap account lose approximately half of their value during 1988.

Chapter

9

Barriers to International Trade and Investment

This chapter begins the direct consideration of government policies that affect international business activities. The main goals of the chapter are to:

1. Examine six major types of trade and investment barriers and note why they exist.

2. Explain the reasons that governments use barriers to imports and to capital outflows.

3. Show the economic impacts of three specific trade barriers: tariffs, subsidies, and quotas.

4. Discuss current US trade policies.

5. Note some of the current government policies that limit international capital flows.

6. Suggest some strategies for company managers to deal with barriers to trade and investment.

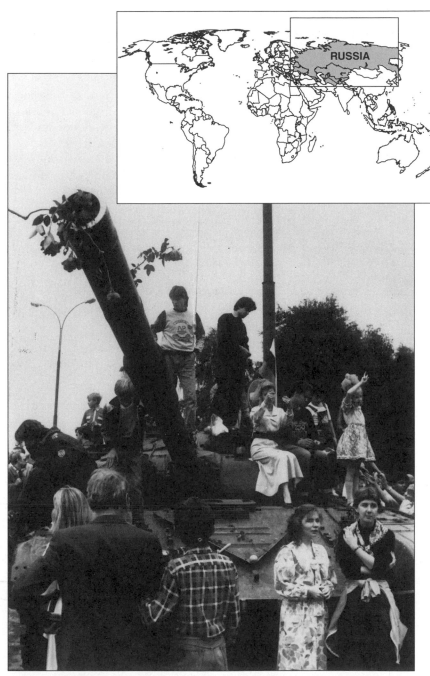

Amidst the collapse of the Soviet Union, several divisions of the Soviet army took the side of Russian Parliament defenders, as shown in this Moscow photo.
The Bettmann Archive

INTRODUCTION

Thus far, we have focused primarily on the activities of companies and on the functioning of the markets in which they compete. Little emphasis has been placed on the regulatory restrictions companies face. We have seen direct investment (plus local production) and exports as substitutes when barriers disallow or restrict one or the other but have not discussed the barriers themselves in any detail. In this chapter we cover some of the major types of restrictions on company exports (on *imports,* from the view of the receiving country's policymakers) and international capital flows.

In the next section, we discuss and analyze some of the most common forms of restrictions. Then we consider the host government's point of view on trade and investment policies. Next, we examine the economic impacts of three major types of trade barriers. With these basics in place, we discuss actual policies, looking specifically at US commercial policy. Then we discuss home and host country *investment* controls. Finally, we look at suggestions for corporate strategy in light of the barriers.

COMMON FORMS OF BARRIERS

Barriers to international flows of goods and services can be grouped into six broad categories for convenience of discussion:

1. Price-based constraints (e.g., tariffs, subsidies).
2. Quantity limits (e.g., quotas, embargoes).
3. Buyers' or sellers' cartels (e.g., OPEC, the International Sugar Agreement, the Multifibre Arrangement).
4. Other *NTBs* (nontariff barriers) on trade.
5. Financial limits (e.g., exchange controls, profit remittance limits).
6. Limits on FDI entry and operations.

Each of these categories is described in this section and discussed in more detail in subsequent sections.

Tariffs and Subsidies

All countries use price-based constraints, that is, **tariffs,** on their imports. In fact, tariffs are a form of tax, paid on goods shipped internationally. Tariffs are generally charged on imports as a tax that raises the cost of importing goods. They are usually charged as a percentage of the value of the goods shipped, that is, on an *ad valorem* basis. The United States, for example, has a long list of tariff rates charged on imports, ranging from zero to 211 percent (on tobacco), with an average of about 3.3 percent *ad valorem*.[1] Clearly tariffs are intended to raise the cost of importing into a country. This accomplishes three goals: (1) It makes local production more competitive, (2) it generates revenue for the government, and (3) it reduces the quantity of imports. Tariffs present a cost to consumers, who must pay a higher price for protected goods than they would pay if there were no tariffs.

Following similar reasoning, most countries also offer **subsidies** to some domestic companies so that their products can better compete with imports. In this case, domestic producers are aided directly, typically through low-cost loans or tax breaks that lower their cost of doing business, while imports are not aided and may still face additional tariffs. The federal government of the United States offers little of this type of support, though some individual states and local governments offer incentives that constitute subsidies for local producers.[2] The main cost of a subsidy is that someone must pay for it—generally the taxpayers of the subsidizing country.

A second form of subsidy is the export subsidy, which a government may offer to stimulate the exports of domestic firms. In this case, the government provides financial aid to exporting firms through, for example, tax breaks or low-interest loans. In turn, these firms export more and stimulate national income. This form of protectionism also has a cost: The country receiving the exports will face unfair competition from the subsidized firms.

Quotas and Embargoes

Quantity limits, such as **quotas,** are also used to restrict international trade. Here the limitation is on the number of units of a product that may be imported or on the market share allowed to imports. Quotas are sometimes imposed on exports as well. For example, a "voluntary" quota on Japanese auto exports to the United States allowed the Japanese automobile producers to export 1.65 million cars to the United States from April 1994 through March 1995, leaving the rest of the market to domestic producers, including Japanese transplants (*and* to imports from other countries). Under a slightly different policy, Canada allows foreign banks to hold a total of not more than 12 percent of bank deposits in the country—a limit on market share rather than a limit on the amount of deposits. A quota can be established at any level of import quantity. The particular type of quota that sets the limit at zero imports is called an **embargo.** Often an embargo is placed on imports for clearly political reasons (e.g., to penalize an adversary during a war) rather than to stimulate domestic production or serve any strictly economic goal. For example, the United States has had an embargo on imports from Cuba since 1961. The main economic costs of quotas are that they limit access by consumers to otherwise available products and tend to raise the prices of the protected products.

Cartels

Cartels operate in international trade to fix prices or quantities sold in various markets. The restrictions function in much the same ways as the controls of individual governments noted above; however, they are imposed not by individual governments but by a group of producers or consumers of a particular product. Virtually all of the cartels in operation today are associations of countries, because most countries have outlawed company cartels through their antitrust policies. The OPEC cartel is a group of oil-producing countries that restrict both the quantity and the price of the oil its members sell. (See the appendix to this book for a detailed look at the international oil industry.) The International Sugar Agreement establishes a base price for exports of sugar and market shares for the exporting countries that participate in the agreement. Cartels constrain the market for international trade in individual products in many of the same ways as the controls imposed by individual governments.

Nontariff Barriers

Other **nontariff barriers (NTBs)** to international trade appear in national regulations and practices. These include a wide variety of barriers, ranging from bureaucratic delays in processing requests for import permits, to quality standards that preclude foreign-produced goods, to buy-national programs that require governments to purchase from domestic suppliers. In each case, the NTBs raise the cost of importing and thus tend to reduce the country's total imports.

Consumers in the protected country generally find that NTBs lead to lower availability and higher prices of protected products.

A second set of restrictions related to the trade controls discussed above are capital controls. These government policies are used to limit flows of funds or other financial instruments across national borders. Capital controls can also restrict trade by limiting exporters' and importers' access to foreign exchange.

Exchange Controls

Financial limits such as **exchange controls** are generally used to restrict outflows of foreign exchange. A country may choose this policy to avoid devaluation of its currency, which would otherwise take place through the free market for exchange rate determination because of an excess supply of the currency in the foreign exchange market. A country may also limit access to foreign exchange to curb importers' ability to pay their suppliers, thus restricting imports. Another purpose of exchange controls is to stimulate exports by simply offering exporters a more favorable rate of exchange (so that they can sell their foreign-currency receipts for more local currency). For example, some Latin American countries have allowed exporters to exchange their dollars at the unrestricted exchange rate, which gives more local currency for each dollar sold. Brazil, among other

---

**ADDED
DIMENSION**

The Multifibre Arrangement: An Attempt to Manage Textile Trade

The **Multifibre Arrangement (MFA)** is an especially interesting commodity cartel, which groups 42 producing and consuming countries. It is an umbrella agreement that establishes basic principles for negotiating bilateral textile trade arrangements between participating countries. This market-sharing agreement was originally begun in 1957 as a temporary restriction of Japanese cotton textile exports to the United States. In 1961, this was expanded to cover several cotton-exporting countries. Subsequently the agreement was reformulated in 1974 into the first Multifibre Arrangement, covering multiple producer and consumer nations. This arrangement was renewed for the fourth time in 1986 and subsequently renewed annually until being incorporated into the Uruguay Round of GATT in 1994.

The MFA basically permits consuming countries to establish import quotas for their trading partners. It is diametrically opposed to the GATT principles, and it was implemented and has been renewed due primarily to the strong US textile lobby of several southeastern states, whose production competes with these imports. The MFA is particularly thorny for the United States in its dealings with Latin American and Caribbean countries, because it limits those countries' key textile exports at the same time that the United States is demanding that those countries open up their economies to US exports. The United States currently operates bilateral quotas with 41 countries (many LDCs plus Japan) on cotton; wool; synthetics; and silk, linen, and ramie textiles. The estimated cost to US consumers of this protectionism was about $US52,000 per job saved in the US industry in 1986 (Cline, 1987, chap. 8).

As a result of the Uruguay Round of GATT negotiations, textiles and apparel *were* included in the general GATT rules. Over a period of 10 years, MFA restrictions must be progressively dismantled. At the beginning of the year 2004, the MFA will cease to exist and GATT rules will apply fully (GATT, 1994). ∎

countries, formerly restricted importers' access to dollars by requiring a large deposit of funds several months before an import shipment was received—a very costly process. Brazil and other countries have also frequently limited the number of dollars domestic travelers are allowed to purchase for trips abroad. Brazil dropped these restrictions in the early 1990s.

Exchange controls may be used specifically to regulate capital markets rather than aiming at exports or imports. Often a country has discovered that speculators have begun to push down the value of its currency; to stop this activity, the country may limit access to foreign exchange or otherwise restrict financial transactions that tend to devalue the currency. Such controls undoubtedly have an impact on exports and imports as well.

The main forms of exchange controls in use today include fixed exchange rates, with limited access to foreign exchange; different exchange rates for different categories of market participants; and bureaucratic controls, such as "red tape," that require the expenditure of substantial time and effort to get access to foreign exchange. Each of these forms of exchange controls can be used to both restrict imports and control capital flows. The main costs of exchange controls are the loss of trade and investment that would have taken place in their absence.

Foreign Investment Controls

Foreign investment controls range from the rejection of all foreign direct investment, as formerly existed in several communist countries, to limits on the activities of foreign-owned firms, such as limits on profit remittances and other financial transfers. Controls of this kind include both price-based policies, such as taxes or price controls, and quantity restrictions, such as limits on the entry of foreign investment. India, for example, requires that foreign investors sell 60 percent ownership to local investors when an investment is made; it taxes profit remittances to parent firms and restricts various other activities of foreign investors. Until the end of 1984, Canada limited the quantity of foreign direct investment through a screening of potential investors carried out by the Foreign Investment Review Agency.[3]

Foreign investment controls generally create competitive conditions that favor local firms competing with foreign-owned firms within the country. The costs of foreign investment controls are the lost FDI they deter; these costs are difficult to measure, though they are clearly positive.

Altogether, barriers to international trade and investment impose tremendous limitations on the ability of market participants to determine the prices and quantities of products sold in international business. The purpose of this chapter is not to criticize the barriers but to understand them and see how to deal with them. Let us look next at governments' reasons for utilizing the various barriers.

REASONS FOR BARRIERS: THE HOST GOVERNMENT'S VIEW

Tariff, subsidy, quota, and other policy constraints on trade vary, literally from month to month, not only among countries but also within individual countries as economic and political conditions and even governments change. While there is no single main reason for imposing these barriers, it is possible to construct an overview of the government concerns that lead to them. Table 9–1 presents the reasons that underlie much of the trade and investment policy in use today.

The principal goals of controls on trade or direct investment flows are to promote national economic growth and to forgo balance-of-payments adjustment. These goals can be approached in many ways. For example, the classic strategy

TABLE 9-1

Reasons for Trade and
Investment Controls

1. To protect import-competing domestic firms (includes saving jobs).
2. To promote import substitution.
3. To reduce reliance on foreign suppliers.
4. To encourage local and foreign direct investment.
5. To reduce balance-of-payments problems.
6. To promote export-based growth.
7. To promote infant industries.
8. To achieve health and safety standards.
9. To restrain foreign firms from dumping.
10. To serve political goals.

of CEPAL (the United Nations Economic Commission for Latin America) during the 1960s and 1970s was to replace imports with local production; this called for raising tariffs to cut imports. In contrast, the strategy of Japan and ASEAN (the Association of South East Asian Nations) has been not so much to restrict imports but to subsidize exports and thus help them compete in world markets. Altogether, the reasons for imposing trade controls that appear in Table 9–1 can be traced to the goals of stimulating or preserving national economic output and improving the balance of payments. (An additional goal to note is protection to achieve political ends, such as penalizing unfriendly countries.)

Improving the balance of payments may mean eliminating a deficit or reducing a surplus. For the most part, countries facing a balance-of-trade surplus simply acquire financial claims on deficit countries, without encountering any pressure to "improve" the situation toward a balance. Countries with a trade deficit, on the other hand, spend their available foreign exchange to pay for imports, and ultimately they must either eliminate the deficit or run out of foreign currency with which to finance it (unless recurring loans can be used to finance the deficit indefinitely). Thus, for balance-of-payments purposes, governments most often use trade controls in efforts to eliminate trade deficits. Consider separately each reason for controls listed in Table 9–1.

Protecting Import-Competing Domestic Firms

This rationale is used virtually everywhere. The United States imposes tariffs on imported steel, uses "voluntary" quotas on imported autos, and subsidizes domestic exporters to improve their ability to compete with foreign producers. Such measures are widely used because, among other reasons, the companies and people hurt by the foreign competition make strenuous efforts to convince the government that restrictions would benefit them. For example, the United Auto Workers and the Big Three auto manufacturers (GM, Ford, and Chrysler) in the United States are highly visible groups that can lobby relatively effectively for protection against foreign competition. Similar conditions exist in every country for some industries, and various forms of protection exist everywhere to protect import-competing firms.

Promoting Import Substitution

Using this justification, many less developed countries have established very high tariffs on selected products. In this way, they hope to encourage local or foreign investors to undertake local production of formerly imported products. This would both reduce a trade balance deficit and provide additional jobs for local workers. Import substitution policy has not proven effective for any country trying to achieve an "economic miracle," such as occurred in Japan in the 1950s and 1960s and Singapore and Hong Kong in the 1970s, but it can be part of a development strategy aimed at fostering new capital investment in specific industries. In this sense, the import substitution argument can be compared to the infant industry argument presented shortly.

Reducing Reliance on Foreign Suppliers

Most national governments prefer to obtain domestically whatever goods and services they may need for protection against a foreign political or military power. With few exceptions, most countries supply their own armed forces, their own defense systems (though equipment may be imported), and their own supplies of many critical materials such as food. The types of controls usually imposed to achieve this objective are not tariffs but government contracting agreements under which the government buys the required products or services only from domestic suppliers or produces them through government agencies. The US government, for example, must buy its supplies from domestic suppliers, unless foreign competitors offer substantially lower prices and acceptable quality.[4] It purchases some products, especially defense-related ones, *only* from domestic suppliers.

Encouraging Local and Foreign Direct Investment

Tariffs and NTBs are sometimes used to encourage the replacement of imported goods with locally produced goods. Often Latin American governments have raised tariffs on specific goods that they wanted to see produced locally as part of a development strategy. Many governments raise barriers on imports of specific products to foster local production of those products, regardless of the nationalities of the companies that produce them. In an often cited case, the Mexican government negotiated with John Deere Company and several other tractor manufacturers to allow four of them to produce their products locally, while denying other tractor manufacturers access to the Mexican market.[5]

Reducing Balance-of-Payments Problems

All of the points made up to now have related directly or indirectly to the attempts of governments to increase domestic economic activity. These attempts also affect the balance of payments. Some restrictions on trade and investment, however, are imposed specifically to improve the BOP. These restrictions are generally not product or industry specific; rather, they limit broad classes of imports or all imports, or they support exports or local production generally. Moreover, restrictions aimed at improving the BOP may be placed on capital flows as well as on imports and exports. This type of government policy generally is imposed during balance-of-payments crises, when official reserves are flowing out of the country.

Promoting Export-Based Growth

The strategy of export-led growth rests on a combination of the two basic economic reasons for trade and investment barriers. By encouraging exports through some type of subsidy, a government can foster greater production (and employment) at the same time that it reduces a balance-of-payments deficit *without* limiting other countries' access to the national market. Since World War II, this strategy has vied for acceptability among less developed countries with the CEPAL strategy of import substitution (though there is no conceptual reason why both strategies cannot be followed simultaneously).[6] Unquestionably, export-led growth is the preferred strategy worldwide in the 1990s.

Promoting Infant Industries

Virtually every developed country raised tariffs and NTBs during its period of development to enable new industries to start up without being overwhelmed by competition from established firms abroad. A policy of imposing a tariff or other barriers for a limited period of time to enable an infant industry to begin operation has received wide acceptance. Unfortunately, there is no clear measure of the appropriate time period for infant industry protection; thus, such policies often tend to continue indefinitely. The infant industry argument for protection rests completely on the premise that the protection will be eliminated when the new industry has achieved competitive status, which is often difficult to define.

Achieving Health and Safety Standards

National health and safety requirements for products and services are generally applied to both imports and locally made goods or services. The process of verifying that imported items meet these standards may be used as a barrier to entry. Imports may be discouraged by simple red tape that forces the potential importer to spend much time and money to obtain proof of qualification. Or rules may be set that require expensive alterations of foreign-made goods to meet domestic product norms. The US requirement that imported cars be modified from their home country configurations to meet the pollution control standards of the Environmental Protection Agency is a barrier that substantially raises the prices of those cars. Similarly, the US Food and Drug Administration uses a lengthy and expensive process of testing pharmaceutical products before allowing them to be sold in the domestic market. The result of these standards may be simply to ensure the safety of consumers, or it may in fact be to keep out competition.

Restraining Foreign Firms from Dumping

A monopolistic practice often seen in business is the attempt by one firm to cut prices temporarily to take sales away from competing firms. When the competing firms leave the market or go bankrupt, that firm controls the market and is free to raise its prices. In international trade, the practice of selling into a foreign market at a price below the firm's cost is called **dumping.** Because dumping tends to harm local firms and strengthen foreign competitors, it is restricted in most countries. While dumping is widely agreed to be "unfair" trade, it is quite difficult to measure a firm's actual costs or arrive at some "fair" market price. Very little consensus exists on any measure of dumping that would be appropriate for use as a standard for limiting the practice. Also, dumping claims are often used unjustifiably to criticize the practices of foreign low-cost producers that enter a home market. (The steel imports case in this chapter provides a useful example of the problems in defining and coping with dumping.)

Serving Political Goals

This last rationale may in fact be part of the basis for many protective policies ostensibly pursued for other reasons, but here we focus on restraints that are imposed for specifically political reasons. For example, the motives for the US embargo on exports to Iraq after the invasion of Kuwait were essentially political. Similarly, political motives have given rise to the various limitations on trade the US government has imposed on communist countries and on South Africa from time to time. The policies adopted to pursue a noneconomic goal may actually cause some degree of economic hardship.

Evaluation of Barriers

The reasons for restricting international trade that are presented here generally are not justifiable on economic grounds. That is, the functioning of comparative advantage is typically hindered by the barriers, and thus these barriers reduce world welfare. (The next section of the chapter shows how the costs arise from these restrictions. The following section presents measures of the economic impact of US trade barriers, which consistently demonstrate a significant cost to US consumers due to the tariffs, quotas, etc.)

When a country imposes tariffs or nontariff barriers to limit imports, the resulting decline in imports raises consumers' costs and/or reduces availability of the products relative to free-trade conditions. If the foreign country retaliates against the initiator of such restrictions, the initiator may lose exports as well. Overall, consumers will suffer because of the barriers, total jobs may actually decline in the country (though jobs in the protected industry may not fall), and the country may even fail to improve the trade balance due to retaliation by the foreign country. This fundamental problem serves to reject the first six reasons for trade barriers listed in Table 9–1.

Not all trade barriers can be rejected so easily. For example, the infant industry argument is a *dynamic* rationale for temporary support of industries that will become freely competitive after a period of protected incubation. Similarly, the argument for encouraging local investment can be a rationale for *temporary* protection to support creation of an infant industry.

The use of trade barriers to preclude dumping by foreign competitors is certainly appropriate on economic grounds, since it eliminates a monopolistic practice by the foreign firms. Also, the imposition of health and safety standards that apply to *all* firms, domestic and foreign, can restrict imports, but such standards presumably serve the public interest by protecting consumers from unwanted health and safety risks. Other logical, economically defensible rationales for trade barriers that protect the public interest may be found as well. The fundamentally flawed rationales are mainly those that invoke barriers for the sake of protecting domestic jobs or improving the balance of trade.

Finally, it should be recognized that trade policy, like other government policy, is not driven solely by economic reasoning. Political, social, and other types of concerns may justify barriers to imports or funds flows even though economic costs arise. It may well be in the US interest to disallow trade with Cuba and North Korea for political reasons, despite the (fairly minor) economic costs involved. Similarly, it may be rational for Israel to restrict trade with Arab countries and vice versa, for religious and cultural rather than economic reasons. These noneconomic criteria should not be ignored.

The foregoing discussion has simply explained some of the reasoning behind trade and investment barriers. Next, let us consider some of the economic problems raised by the use of three trade barriers.

AN ECONOMIC COMPARISON OF THREE TRADE BARRIERS

A Simple Graphic Analysis

Typically, when a government seeks to protect a domestic industry, it implements a tariff on imports, a quota on imports, or a subsidy of domestic producers. Let us consider the economic implications of each of these policies in a hypothetical situation. Figure 9–1 compares the three policy choices for Bhagwatia, a country that wants to protect its steel industry.

DS_s and DD_s are the domestic supply and demand for steel, respectively. WS_s is the production of steel available from all other countries combined—the world supply of steel. If the home country's supply of and demand for this product are relatively small compared to the world supply, the world price is essentially a "given" to Bhagwatia and the world supply curve is perfectly elastic, a horizontal

FIGURE 9–1

The Bhagwatia Steel
Industry

line across the figure. The price charged by foreign suppliers is WP_s, the world price
of steel. Under conditions of free trade, producers in the home country will supply
OA of steel and importers will sell AB of steel so that total sales equal OB of steel.
Notice that the figure is drawn so that domestic consumers would gain by importing,
because they could consume more steel at a lower price than they could if the
country simply produced all steel locally (and consumed at point X in the figure).

If the government wants to raise domestic output of steel of OA', it can use a
tariff of size CE (which is an *ad valorem* percentage of $CE/A'E$), as shown in panel
1 of Figure 9–1. This raises the import price for domestic consumers to OT.
Domestic producers of steel will sell OA' of output at the new, higher price, while
foreign suppliers will sell only $A'B'$. The initial effects of this policy are

1. Increased domestic production and employment, assuming no retaliation by
   foreign governments (domestic producers sell AA' more *and* charge CE more).
2. Decreased domestic consumption of steel at the new, higher price (from OB
   to OB').
3. Improved balance of trade because of reduced imports (from AB to $A'B'$).
4. Increased government revenue from the tariff receipts (CE times $A'B'$).
5. Loss of Bhagwatia welfare (equal to the two shaded areas in panel 1).

The tariff alters consumers' marginal allocations of income, since it raises the
price of steel relative to the prices of other goods and services sold in the country.
If the country began in free-market equilibrium, this result represents a misallo-
cation of income. A tariff may be easy to impose politically, since it appears to
penalize "foreigners" relative to domestic producers, and the true costs are not
readily apparent.

If the government wants to raise domestic output to OA' using a *subsidy*, the
subsidy must push domestic supply out to A' at price WP_s. This is shown by the
new supply curve, $DS_s + SUB$, in panel 2. In this case, the domestic price stays at
WP_s, and imports are reduced by only AA'. (To cut imports by as much as the
tariff did, the government would need a subsidy large enough to shift out the
supply curve by $AA' + BB'$.) The subsidy shown in the graph has the following
initial effects:

1. Increased domestic production and employment, assuming no retaliation
   (from OA to OA').
2. No change in total domestic consumption of this product; no change in
   price.

3. Improved balance of trade because of reduced imports (from *AB* to *A'B'*).

4. New government revenue needed to pay for the subsidy (value equal to *HI* times *OA'*).

Subsidies do not alter consumers' marginal allocations of income, because they leave prices unchanged. When a government chooses a revenue-generating policy (such as raising taxes) to pay for a subsidy, taxpayers can clearly see the impact of the policy; thus, a subsidy is more visible than a tariff to consumers and taxpayers. In conceptual terms, a subsidy is generally preferable to a tariff, because although both have economic costs, the subsidy does not affect relative prices. In pragmatic political terms, and in the United States in particular, subsidies are viewed as "handouts" not to be distributed freely to companies without clear and substantial justification; thus, tariffs tend to be more readily accepted.

If the government of Bhagwatia wants to raise domestic output to *OA'* using a *quota,* the quota must be set such that domestic output is pushed up to *OA'* from panel 1, as shown in panel 3. The quota will delegate *OQ* to imports, leaving the rest of the market at any given price to domestic producers. Essentially, this can be viewed as a case with a supply curve shaped as shown in the heavy lines in panel 3. The imports take *A'B'* at price *P**, and domestic producers sell *OA* plus *AA'*. This quota has the following initial effects:

1. Increased domestic production and employment, assuming no retaliation (from *OA* to *OA'*).

2. Decreased domestic consumption of steel at the new, higher price.

3. Improved balance of trade because of reduced imports.

4. No change in government revenues or expenditures.

5. Loss of consumer welfare because consumption is reduced by *BB'*.

The initial impact of a quota is as obvious as that of a tariff. Like a tariff, a quota misallocates income by altering the relative price of the product being protected. A quota does not generate revenue for the government, as a tariff does, or require government expenditure to pay for it.

All of these results will differ somewhat if domestic demand is very price elastic, if domestic supply is very price elastic, or if the world price is not perfectly price elastic. The results will also differ if the country began in an already biased position, that is, with some trade barriers already in place. In that case, the value of the new barrier must be compared with the situation under the previous conditions—a kind of second-best problem.

Empirical Estimates of the Costs of Protectionism

A number of estimates have been made of the impact of trade restrictions on the US economy in recent years. Table 9–2 summarizes findings from a recent study concerning the economic impact of US tariffs and quotas on US consumers. Each of these estimates is intended to measure the net cost to consumers in terms of higher prices, reduced availability of imports, and spillovers into other parts of the economy. The measures are shown as net *gains* to the United States if the protection is eliminated. Notice that virtually every protectionist policy is associated with a very large cost. For instance, quotas on textile imports under the Multifibre Arrangement cost US consumers over $200,000 per job per year; tariffs on imported orange juice cost US consumers over $460,000 per job per year.

TABLE 9-2 Estimated Direct Employment Effects of Liberalization, 1990

Product Category	Decrease in Domestic Production (millions of dollars)*	Decrease in Employment Opportunities (number of workers)†	Consumer Gain per Job Lost (dollars)	Net National Gain per Job Lost (dollars)
Protected by high tariffs				
Ball bearings	13	146	438,356	6,849
Benzenoid chemicals	230	216	>1,000,000	46,296
Canned tuna	33	390	187,179	25,641
Ceramic articles	38	418	244,019	4,785
Ceramic tiles	28	347	400,576	5,764
Costume jewelry	115	1,067	96,532	4,686
Frozen concentrated orange juice	101	609	461,412	57,471
Glassware	165	1,477	180,095	6,093
Luggage	25	226	933,628	115,044
Polyethylene resins	192	298	590,604	67,114
Rubber footwear	116	1,701	122,281	7,055
Softwood lumber	86	605	758,678	19,835
Women's footwear, except athletic	218	3,702	101,567	2,971
Women's handbags	32	773	191,462	16,818
Protected by import quotas				
Agriculture				
Dairy products	513	2,378‡	497,897	43,734
Peanuts	18	397	136,020	55,416
Sugar	548	2,261‡	600,177	256,966
Maritime	1,434	4,411	415,325	126,049
Protected by "voluntary" export restraints				
Apparel	10,851	152,583	138,666	50,543
Textiles	1,773	16,203	202,061	55,175
Machine tools	169	1,556	348,329	247,429
Total	16,697	191,764	168,520§	54,348§

*This column represents the volume effect of liberalization calculated using base-year prices.
†The number of direct jobs affected is assumed to be proportional to the volume change in domestic production. For example, for ball bearings the volume of domestic production is expected to decrease from 416 million units to 412 million units. Employment in this industry is thus projected to decrease by [1 − (412/416)*100 = 0.96 percent, or from 15,000 to 14,854 production workers.
‡Workers in processing plants only.
§Weighted average.
Source: Gary Hufbauer and Kimberly Elliott, *Measuring the Costs of Protection in the United States* (Washington, DC: Institute for International Economics, 1994), pp. 12–13.

Elimination of the protectionist policies would save US consumers more than $50,000 per year for each job lost, after accounting for unemployment compensation and retraining expenses for laid-off workers.

US COMMERCIAL POLICY

The basic tariff structure of the United States remains as outlined by the Smoot-Hawley Act (the Tariff Act of 1930) and amended from time to time. In 1934, for example, the Reciprocal Trade Agreements Acts amended Smoot-Hawley, allowing the president to negotiate tariff changes. More recently, the Trade Reform Act of 1974 spelled out detailed provisions for aiding US industries harmed by imports, ranging from additional protection to financial assistance for the injured firms and employees.

The attempts to lower trade barriers since World War II have been largely *multilateral* rather than bilateral. That is, the objective has often been to set tariff treatment that applies to many trading partners rather than only two. In 1946, the General Agreement on Tariffs and Trade (GATT) was formed by 22 countries as a forum for negotiating multilateral tariff reductions. (GATT is discussed in more detail in Chapter 10.) The United States has participated in eight rounds of negotiations since that time, with the result that US tariffs today average only about 3 percent *ad valorem* to most countries of the world.

Additional US commercial policy has taken a wide variety of forms in recent years, such as

1. Dumping charges under the Trade Act of 1974, Sections 201 and 301.
2. An orderly marketing agreement for color TV imports.
3. A "voluntary" quota on imports of Japanese automobiles.
4. The Caribbean Basin Initiative, which eliminates tariffs on a wide variety of goods imported from Caribbean countries.
5. The Trading-with-the Enemy Act, which forbids trade with a small number of communist countries (e.g., Cuba and North Korea).
6. The Export Sales Company Act, which subsidizes US exports.
7. "Buy American" requirements for some government purchases.
8. Trade adjustment assistance, which compensates firms and workers whose income has been harmed by imports.

Each of these policies serves to "distort" the free-market process of international trade. However, since the initial situation was *not* one of free trade, each policy should be evaluated as a second-best alternative compared to other choices.

Probably the most visible US trade restriction in the past several years has been the imposition of retaliatory tariffs against products that are "dumped" in the US market. Whether the goods are dumped at prices below cost (or below domestic market price) and prosecuted under Section 301 of the 1974 Trade Act or unfairly subsidized by the home government and thus prosecuted under Section 201, the penalties apply. These two instruments have been used extensively during the past several years by US firms competing against imports in an effort to combat their foreign competitors. In both cases, once an accusation has been made formally, the importing firm must post a bond with the US Department of Commerce, which will be held until the case is resolved. This policy obviously imposes a cost on the importer, even if the firm is eventually found innocent of dumping; about half of the cases brought in the past five years have resulted in an affirmation of dumping and payment of penalties.

The **orderly marketing agreement** for color TV imports followed reasoning similar to that of the trigger-price mechanism. In 1977, the US government negotiated an orderly marketing agreement with the government of Japan that established a quota on TV imports from Japanese companies and an additional quota on imported unassembled TVs from Japanese companies. Much of the TV imports then began to come for Korea and Taiwan. Thus, in 1980s, the orderly marketing agreement with Japan was extended to TV imports from those two countries as well. By the end of 1981, color TV imports had leveled off and US domestic production had increased substantially, though much of the additional

US production was merely assembly of unfinished TVs from the restricted countries.[8] This program was discontinued in the mid-1980s.

The **voluntary quota** on Japanese auto imports can be viewed as a form of orderly marketing agreement. It established annual limits on total Japanese auto exports to the United States. If these "voluntary" limits are not followed, the US government is expected to impose mandatory constraints on auto imports. Thus, the implication is that the limits are actually mandatory. As of 1994, a maximum of 1.65 million cars per year were permitted to be imported from Japan.[9]

The **Caribbean Basin Initiative** simply eliminated tariffs on most imports from countries in the Caribbean region (including Central America). This policy was proposed in 1982 to improve the economic conditions of US allies in the region and thus help ensure their support for US political policies. The tariff part of the initiative was implemented in January 1984. While some major exports from the region are excepted (e.g., sugar, coffee, tin, textiles), thousands of manufactured products and other goods are covered. Obviously, this is a free-trade policy, not a restriction on trade.[10] Another major free-trade initiative is the North American Free Trade Agreement, discussed in the next chapter.

The **Trading-with-the-Enemy Act** disallows exports to and imports from countries that have been determined to be enemies of the United States by the US government. North Korea has been included among such countries since 1950, Cuba since 1961, and Vietnam since 1975. Depending on the particular year and circumstances, other communist countries have also been included. Immediately after the Soviet invasion of Afghanistan in 1979, for example, US-Soviet trade was severely limited. Most of the restrictions imposed at that time were terminated in 1980.[11]

In 1984, the US policy of encouraging exports through income tax deferral (the DISC legislation) was replaced by the **Foreign Sales Corporation Act.** This act allows US exporters to establish overseas affiliates to manage their export sales, and these affiliates are legally exempt from current US taxation on the income from such sales until the earnings have been remitted to the parent firm in the United States.[12] This policy offers a direct subsidy to US exports by reducing the taxes paid by exporters.

For some purchases, when bids from domestic suppliers are competitive with bids from foreign suppliers, the federal government of the United States is required to **buy American.** This policy has not been clearly implemented, and individual government agencies appear to be following it in a relatively uncoordinated way.[13] As previously noted, however, purchases of defense-related materials by the US government are carefully restricted to reliable, US-based suppliers.

Finally, **trade adjustment assistance (TAA)** is offered to aid US firms and individuals that have been harmed by competition from imports. This assistance takes such forms as loans to help companies retool so that they can compete with imports; direct unemployment compensation to individuals, who are expected to seek new jobs in other industries during the period of compensation; and counseling to help individuals find alternative employment.[14]

In 1988 the US Congress passed the Omnibus Trade and Competitiveness Act, which reaffirmed the country's position in favor of free trade but established new means for dealing with unfair trade practices by foreign exporters. This legislation gave the US trade representative authority to impose penalties on foreign exporters when they can be shown to be dumping products in the US market or when their products are subsidized by a foreign government. It also called for new penalties in the area of intellectual property rights, disallowing imports when the foreign firm(s) are shown to infringe on patents of US firms. More broadly, the act allowed the US government to impose penalties on imports from countries that restrict US exports through nontariff barriers in an effort to generate more "fair" trade.

The 1988 act also expanded the coverage of trade adjustment assistance, adding more benefits (namely unemployment compensation and retraining subsidies) for employees laid off due to competition from imports and offering incentives to firms hurt by imports if they either retool to become more competitive or shift their activities to other kinds of business. In addition, a 12-member Competitiveness Policy Board was established to examine the ability of US firms to compete in domestic and foreign markets and recommend policy to assist firms toward that end.

In sum, US commercial policy is a patchwork of regulations, most of which are intended to promote free trade and economic growth, but a small number of which are highly visible programs to aid specific (politically powerful) industry sectors. The trade adjustment assistance program is intended to help companies and workers shift to more competitive activities, thus allowing comparative advantage to work, yet not ignoring the burden of adjustment felt by the less competitive sectors of the economy.

EXCHANGE CONTROLS AND CAPITAL CONTROLS

Though often less clearly linked to international trade than trade barriers, *exchange and capital controls* play a part in restricting trade flows. In this case, the controls are placed on the movement of money or other financial instruments among countries. A simple control such as limited access to foreign exchange can cut imports just as effectively as a tariff if it disallows importers from obtaining the means of payment they need for their purchases. Such **exchange controls** are used throughout the world, though in recent years the industrial countries have largely eliminated them.

In addition, **capital controls** generally intend to improve a country's balance-of-payments deficit by limiting capital outflows. This policy goes beyond improving the trade balance and includes the possibility of improving the basic balance (which includes direct investment and long-term loans) or even the official reserves balance (which includes short-term capital flows). Capital controls focus on limiting investment activity, whereas exchange controls generally focus on limiting trade flows.

For example, from 1982 to 1989, Venezuela used a system of multiple exchange rates to both reduce imports and encourage capital inflows. Importers, in most cases, were required to buy foreign exchange at the market rate, which in mid-1988 was about 30 bolivars per US dollar. Most new and existing loans from abroad, on the other hand, could be repaid at a rate of 15 bolivars per dollar, a much more manageable cost for the local borrowers. (Exporters could sell their foreign exchange receipts at the market rate, thus receiving more bolivars for their domestic needs than what the official rate would give.) In early 1989, Venezuela's government unified the exchange rate and now allows the market to determine the rate.

The United States has not used exchange controls, though it has imposed some financial controls. The most widely discussed US controls were the capital controls imposed on US-based multinational firms in the mid-1960s. Initially (in 1965), these controls were voluntary, requesting that MNEs finance their foreign subsidiaries through foreign borrowing rather than through financial transfers from the United States. In 1968 the controls were made mandatory, requiring that affiliates in Europe and a few non-European countries not receive additional financing from the US parent firms, while allowing limited funds transfers to affiliates in less developed countries. The MNEs found so many ways to circumvent the controls (not the least of which was a tremendous expansion of borrowing in the eurodollar market) that the ultimate effect on the US balance of payments was probably minimal. The controls were dismantled in 1974.

Investment controls may be defined to include limits on foreign *direct* investment. This type of control is the rule rather than the exception today. Almost every country restricts some kinds of foreign direct investors from doing business in the domestic market. The limits range from nearly total disallowance (in Cuba and Albania, for example) to selective permission of investors (in many less developed countries and formerly communist countries). Direct investment controls generally do *not* seek to improve the balance of payments; their purpose is to maintain domestic ownership and control over key segments of the economy. These controls are discussed in detail for selected countries in Chapters 20 and 21.

COMPANY STRATEGIES FOR DEALING WITH THE BARRIERS

The fundamental strategy for coping with trade and investment barriers is to utilize the firm's competitive advantages to best function under them. Since methods for using trade and investment to overcome constraints on these activities were presented in Chapter 2, we need not discuss them again here. However, a few specific strategies that may be appropriate when additional barriers to imports are imposed are worth considering.

Each time the cost of importing a product rises, the relative advantage of producing it locally increases. This points to the alternatives of direct investment, licensing of a local firm, use of a turnkey venture, or some other organizational strategy that employs local production. The multiproduct firm may consider negotiation with the government to produce or only assemble a small number of products locally in return for permission to import other products without prohibitive tariff barriers. The increase in import cost due to the new barrier may force the firm to consider the other alternatives for the first time, and it may actually have been less costly (i.e., more profitable) to produce locally even before the new barrier was in place.

Another strategy the firm should consider is to establish production in more than one country to remove the "hostage" problem, in which the firm is dependent on supply from one national source for sales in perhaps several countries. By using a portfolio of production sources, the firm can reduce the bargaining power of any one national government over its multicountry operations. Even though costs would probably be minimized by producing in just one country, the risk of regulatory change or other problems may make using a portfolio of production sources a better solution. The trade barriers discussed in this chapter should remind the manager that each national operation of the firm is subject to the national rules of that country—rules that can be altered at any time.

Many countries allow relatively unrestricted importation of intermediate goods (e.g., unassembled TVs or autos) but impose substantial tariffs and NTBs on final products. Such a regulatory environment may favor local assembly of a product, while the vast majority of the product's value is produced elsewhere. This strategy has been widely used in Latin America, where most countries want to encourage the growth of domestic manufacturing and reduce their dependence on imports. Pharmaceutical firms, auto companies, and other manufacturers have found that local assembly (formulation in the case of drugs) enables them to avoid very high tariffs and NTBs without committing a large capital investment to a small or politically unstable country.

The major Japanese producers of cars and trucks have already chosen to set up local production in the United States to reduce the expected impact of increasingly restrictive US policy on auto imports. Nissan manufactures both cars and trucks in Tennessee. In 1984, in a joint venture with General Motors, Toyota began producing a compact car in California; Toyota also manufactures cars in Kentucky; Honda produces cars and motorcycles in Ohio and lawn mowers in South Carolina; Mazda makes cars in Michigan; Mitsubishi produces cars in a joint venture with Chrysler in Illinois; and Subaru and Isuzu produce cars in a joint venture in Indiana. This strategy is clearly political, since the costs of delivering a car to the US market have been lower for Japanese producers than for U.S. producers. (See the auto industry analysis in the Appendix.)

The appropriate strategy in any situation, of course, will depend on the specific conditions involved. However, it is possible to conclude that, as suggested in Chapter 2, the best approach to thinking about alternative strategies is to evaluate the firm's competitive advantages and compare the ownership strategies on that basis.

CONCLUSIONS

This chapter covered a wide range of aspects of barriers to international trade and investment. We defined the most common forms of barriers first and then looked at the reasons governments utilize them. Economic analysis of the barriers showed that they generally harm an economy more than they help it, but strong conclusions in any case depend on the situation the country faces. An economic loss may well be justified in the face of political gain. Most of the evidence regarding US barriers appears to show that they have not benefited the US economy as a whole, though they may have helped firms protected by them. The policy of trade adjustment assistance attempts to reduce the burden of adjustment borne by workers and companies that become noncompetitive as a result of imported products.

Company strategies for dealing with protectionist policies follow the same criteria noted previously. Firms can shift between alternatives such as foreign direct investment and imports when barriers make one alternative preferable to the other. They can diversify their international operations to avoid the hostage problem that occurs when they are dependent on one national market or supply source and thus one national government has sovereignty over their activities. And, of course, they can try to pass on the costs of trade and investment controls to their customers.

QUESTIONS

1. How can a French clothing manufacturer cope with a recent increase in the tariff on its shipments of garments to the United States, its biggest export market? Present your answer in terms of cost conditions, competitive market conditions, and strategic goals.
2. What are the basic principles of US trade policy today? How do specific policies follow these principles?

3. What is the difference between a tariff, a quota, and a subsidy in terms of their economic impact? (Assume all three limit imports to achieve a given increase in domestic production and sales.)

4. Assume South Korea's government offers low-cost loans to exporters to stimulate the economy. How would you, as a manager of a US firm competing with Korean firms, react in your activities? That is, how would you alter your present business, which is 100 percent domestic production and sales? Also, would you try to influence the U.S. government or to utilize its programs in this situation? If so, how and why?

5. What is a solution to the steel imports problem in the United States, viewed from the perspective of a US steel company? (Use the case at the end of this chapter for additional information.)

6. What should the US government do to deal with the current problems of the steel industry? Why?

7. What is the probable impact of direct investment controls on the flow of FDI into a country? Does the United States use any such controls? Which countries do?

8. Is there any industry in which the United States could justify using an infant industry tariff? What justifications are used for US tariff policy?

9. Explain the idea of dumping. What is an appropriate policy that a national government might adopt to deal with the dumping of foreign products?

10. As manager of Toyota Motors Company in Japan, what would you do when faced with a "voluntary" limit on the number of cars you can export to the United States? Give details.

REFERENCES

Bhagwati, Jagdish, *Protectionism.* Cambridge, MA: MIT Press, 1988.

Canto, V, and A Laffer. "The Effectiveness of Orderly Marketing Agreements: The Color TV Case," *Business Economics,* January 1983.

Cline, William. *The Future of World Trade in Textiles and Apparel.* Washington, DC: Institute for International Economics, 1987.

Coughlin, Cletus, and Geoffrey Wood. "An Introduction to Non-tariff Barriers to Trade." Federal Reserve Bank of St. Louis *Review,* January–February 1989.

Hufbauer, Gary, and Kimberly Elliot. *Measuring the Costs of Protection in the U.S.* Washington: Institute for International Economics, 1994.

Khanna, Ram. "Market Sharing under the Multifibre Arrangement: Consequences of Non-tariff Barriers in the Textile Trade." *Journal of World Trade Law,* 1990.

Lindert, P. *International Economics.* 9th ed. Homewood, IL: Richard D. Irwin, 1992.

Mathieson, Donald, and Libiana Rojas Suarez. "Liberalization of the Capital Account: Experiences and Issues", *Occasional Papers no. 103.* Washington: IMF, March 1993.

NOTES

[1] According to the US International Trade Commission, US tariffs in 1993 averaged 6 percent on *dutiable* items. Many items enter the United States with no tariff at all, including thousands of goods imported from less developed countries under the generalized system of preferences (GSP). Overall, the average US tariff in 1993 was about 3 percent *ad valorem*.

[2] The program of trade adjustment assistance (TAA) does support US firms hurt by import competition, but this support is paid mainly as unemployment compensation to laid-off workers. See *United States Code Annotated*, Title 19, Custom Duties, Sections 2271–2298. The compensation arrangement lapsed in December 1985 and was passed into the general federal program of unemployment compensation. In March 1986, the compensation arrangement was reinstated for six years, retroactive to December 1985.

[3] In 1984, Canada switched from a policy of using the Foreign Investment Review

Agency to limit FDI coming into the country to a policy of promoting inward FDI to stimulate economic growth and changed the agency's name to Investment Canada.

[4]The requirements for US government purchases from domestic suppliers appear in the *United States Code Annotated,* Title 41, Public Contracts, Sections 10a–10d.

[5]John Deere de Mexico, SA de C.V., Harvard Business School case 9-313-239.

[6]Of course, promotion of exports is a means of subsidizing one country's products at the expense of import-competing products in other countries. The OECD (industrial) countries generally disallow export subsidies by their trading partners, since these subsidies offer unfair competitive advantage to the recipient firms. On the other hand, less developed countries are usually permitted to use such subsidies to increase their firms' abilities to compete internationally. (That is, the industrial countries usually do not retaliate against such subsidies by LDCs.)

[7]It should be recognized that the reasoning presented here compares free trade with restricted trade using the stated barriers. If the country begins with some existing situation of trade restrictions, one cannot simply conclude that reducing one trade barrier will unequivocably improve the country's welfare.

The argument in favor of reducing reliance on foreign suppliers *may* have ajustifiable political/strategic basis. That is, if the foreign country at some time chooses to restrict its supply of the product due to a political decision, the importing country may indeed suffer a loss of critical goods. On economic grounds, this problem should be factored into the calculus as a risk of buying from the foreign supplier, which may or may not be cause for replacing the imports.

[8]Canto and Laffer (1983).

[9]*Automotive News,* February 16, 1986, and March 10, 1986.

[10]The Caribbean Basin Initiative was passed into law in 1983. In January 1985, the tariff provisions of the initiative were finally enacted.

[11]The Trading-with-the-Enemy legislation appears in the *United States Code Annotated,* Title 50, War and National Defense Appendix, Emergency and Postwar Legislation, sections 1–43.

[12]The Foreign Sales Corporation was established as part of the Trade and Tariff Act of 1984.

[13]See note 4.

[14]See note 2.

The Steel Imports Problem

Competitive Conditions in the Industry

"The U.S. steel industry was hard hit by the deep recession of 1974–75 and the sluggish recovery of world steel demand that followed. . . . Current capacity utilization rates in the industry are near 80 percent compared to a peak of 97 percent in 1973. Profit rates are less than half of 1974 peak levels." In addition, "the U.S. balance of trade in steel has shifted. In 1955, the U.S. exported more steel than it imported; today, imports are supplying nearly 18 percent of domestic requirements, and our exports of steel are negligible." (1977)[1]

"The large U.S. steel producers are running out of time. . . . If we have no desire as a government to have a viable, strong steel industry . . . then we will not have one. . . . From 1978 to 1981 the real cash flow of six major U.S. steelmakers fell to minus $7.4 billion. . . . Last year (1982) when only 48 percent of the nation's steel capacity was operating, imports accounted for 22 percent of the U.S. market. If current trends continue, they could grow to 40 percent within the next decade." (1983)[2]

"U.S. major mills' pretax losses were $15 per metric ton in 1993 versus losses of $33 per ton in 1992. The recent peak profit was about $60 per ton in mid-1989. After a 3 percent rise in the first quarter of 1994, we expect spot prices to fall back to the 1993 fourth quarter level; however, profits will be improved because the mills are expected to secure a 4 percent rise in their contract prices. . . . The world steel market remains depressed. The composite Antwerp spot export price has fallen 31 percent from a peak of $575 per ton in early 1989 to $394 per ton currently. The entrance of the Eastern European and CIS steelmakers into the world export market and the abrupt halt in Chinese steel purchases in June 1993 shocked export market prices." (1994)[3]

All of the above statements reflect the continuing problems of the US steel industry in the 1990s. Many of the major firms have gone into bankruptcy or been acquired by remaining firms in the industry; in 1994, only half a dozen major steelmakers remain. Average return on equity in the industry was negative during the 1980s. Even the leading firm, U.S. Steel, has diversified such that about half of its business is now in the oil industry (from the acquisition of Marathon Oil Company). This case presents a perspective of the industry that focuses on the possible strategies domestic steelmakers and the US government can use to deal with the crisis.

The difficulties US steel producers encountered in the 1970s arose because of (1) increases in the cost of producing steel products and (2) increases in steel

---

This case was written as a teaching note by Professor Robert Grosse, October 1978 (revised 1994).

imports, especially from Japan. The cost increases from 1972 to 1977 occurred mainly because (1) coal prices rose 138 percent, (2) iron ore prices rose 76 percent, and (3) steel scrap prices rose 133 percent. In addition, from 1973 to 1977, hourly employment costs rose 66 percent while productivity rose at only 1.9 percent per year.[4] Profitability in the steel industry was 3.5 percent in 1976, well below the average for all manufacturing.

The difficulties that continue into the 1990s include relatively high wage costs; relatively low productivity; a strong dollar until 1985, which led to higher U.S. prices relative to major trading partners such as Japan and Germany; increasing competition from newly industrializing countries such as Brazil and South Korea; and worldwide overcapacity in the industry, which is leading to widespread losses and government subsidies to local steel industries in many countries. Profitability for the US industry has been negative in almost every year during the past decade. Table 1 compares some of the industry conditions in the United States with three major trading partners: Japan, Germany, and the United Kingdom.

The Perspective of the US Government

The US government's policies will reflect basic views of international economics. Since World War II, the United States had been the champion of free trade. This position has clear theoretical implications: that free trade leads to increased world output and employment and increased economic interdependence. Empirical studies tend to support the view that output, employment, and interdependence all increase with freer trade. Free trade, however, requires free competition in the markets for production factors in each country and adoption of a laissez-faire policy by each national government to satisfy the theoretical assumptions and generate the expected benefits. If a government subsidizes exports, retaliation by the government of the importing country may be justified, since such subsidies interfere with free-market operations, thus altering the distribution of benefits from trade. The facts of the present case need to be clarified on three counts:

1. What are the costs of production in each country?
2. What subsidies do Japanese and European governments offer?
3. What existing US policies are available?

See Table 1 on the first point. Since we lack the time and resources to conduct further analysis, let us accept the US government conclusions on the second point: "Recent evidence suggests that the value of the various subsidies offered by governments to their steel producers does not represent a significant share of total production costs. Unpublished FTC figures place the value of these subsidies at less than 1 percent of total cost for Japan, West Germany, and Italy." With respect to the third point, the US government has used tariffs, voluntary restraints, trigger prices and subsequent fines, and trade adjustment assistance to remedy the problems created by imports.

If we wish to pursue the free-trade ideal and disallow "cheating" that may occur through government subsidies, we need to evaluate the Japanese steel prices versus Japanese steel production costs, adjusted to exclude subsidies. Graphically, we need to see whether the Japanese price is lower than the average total cost (of production *plus* delivery).

As long as the Japanese sell steel in Japan at prices high enough to pay for total fixed costs plus variable costs, they can sell any excess abroad at prices that cover

TABLE 1 Steel Industry Operating Conditions in Four Industrial Countries, 1976, 1986, 1990, and 1993 (*US$/metric ton*)

	United States	Japan	West Germany	United Kingdom
1976				
Labor costs				
Manhours per ton shipped	11.12	9.47	9.53	18.27
Employment cost per hour	12.18	5.62	8.17	4.44
Employment cost per ton	135.37	53.09	77.90	81.03
Material costs				
Iron ore per ton	48.78	32.77	38.29	38.30
Coal cost per ton	44.54	57.39	62.18	58.95
Total materials cost	190.26	159.42	203.21	188.91
Total cost per ton*	350.61	262.50	308.22	306.38
Total revenue per ton	352.52	280.59	333.97	301.67
1986				
Labor costs				
Manhours per ton shipped	6.41	6.05	7.21	6.49
Employment cost per hour	24.14	14.16	15.96	12.12
Employment cost per ton	154.64	85.73	115.06	78.69
Materials costs				
Iron ore per ton	69.35	42.18	61.98	60.24
Coal cost per ton	51.63	64.79	73.31	60.22
Total materials cost	289.82	251.14	269.48	264.75
Total cost per ton*	481.71	426.47	428.97	366.67
Total revenue per ton	603.89	553.55	508.38	470.74
1990				
Labor costs				
Manhours per ton shipped	5.4	4.6	5.7	5.7
Employment cost per hour	26.5	24	31	22
Employment cost per ton	144	100	178	109
Materials costs				
Iron ore per ton	64	69	64	74
Coal cost per ton	39	48	49	44
Total materials cost	312	282	306	314
Total cost per ton*	459	382	463	423
Total revenue per ton	517	594	592	614
1993				
Labor costs				
Manhours per ton shipped	5.05	4.02	5.06	5.00
Employment cost per hour	32.1	31.1	34.2	19.6
Employment cost per ton	162	125	173	98
Materials costs				
Iron ore per ton	74	63	62	60
Coal cost per ton	40	47	53	42
Total materials cost	323	305	294	275
Total cost per ton*	485	430	467	373
Total revenue per ton	617	699	598	525

*Does not include financing costs.

Source: Paine Webber, Inc., *World Steel Dynamics,* "Cost Monitor #9," 1987; "Cost Monitor #13," 1991; "Cost Monitor #16," 1994 (New York: Paine Webber, Inc.).

only the variable costs and still remain profitable. As far as our data are concerned, it does *not* appear that the Japanese are dumping the steel products shown.

The "trigger price" system, which allowed the United States to penalize Japanese (or other) importers for dumping, offered a highly visible means of protection for US steel producers. Unfortunately, this system did not improve the efficiency of these manufacturers.

Any real solution to this problem will require the US steel producers to become cost competitive. Perhaps this competitiveness could occur if US producers specialized in some steel products and left others to be sold by importers. Trade adjustment assistance, which is consistent with the goal of free trade, will allow workers to be retrained and factories retooled so that US employment is not seriously harmed. Consumers, of course, will benefit from the lower prices of steel imports.

This brief commentary certainly does not "solve" the steel imports problem. However, it does provide some factual information necessary for taking an informed position and carrying out an analysis of many of the major issues involved in the controversy. There are two key questions: (1) What are the potential strategies for US steelmakers, and (2) what is an optimal policy for the US government?

CASE NOTES

[1] Taken from the Council on Wage and Price Stability (COWPS) report to President Carter, October 5, 1977.

[2] Taken from "Time Runs out for Steel," *Business Week,* June 13, 1983.

[3] Peter Marcus and Karlis Kirsis, *World Steel Dynamics* (New York: Paine Webber, February 1994), p. 3.

[4] All data are from the report to the president from the Council on Wage and Price Stability.

10 Economic Integration and International Business

This chapter continues the discussion of government policies that affect international business, focusing on multilateral agreements among governments to reduce business barriers among member countries. The main goals of the chapter are to:

1. Note the basic costs and benefits of economic integration (such as trade creation and trade diversion).

2. Explain the structure and functioning of the General Agreement on Tariffs and Trade (GATT).

3. Explore the types of economic integration and discuss country groups that illustrate each type.

4. Explain the structure and functioning of the European Union.

5. Describe the structure and functioning of the North American Free Trade Agreement (NAFTA).

6. Explore company strategies for dealing with integration rules.

Peter Sutherland, director general of General Agreement on Tariffs and Trade (GATT), speaks at a meeting in Montevideo during the Uruguay round of talks.
Reuters/Bettmann

INTRODUCTION   Economic integration involves the establishment of transnational rules on economic activity that lead to greater trade and economic cooperation among countries. That is, a group of nations can (often painstakingly) negotiate a set of commonly accepted rules on intragroup trade and other economic relations that lead to increased (more beneficial) commercial dealings among them. By creating a multicountry market, the group encourages larger-scale (lower-cost) production and greater competition among firms in the group, promoting efficiency in each national economy involved. Generally, economic integration efforts have been made at the regional level, encompassing 5 to 10 countries in close geographic proximity. One of the most important transnational agreements is the General Agreement on Tariffs and Trade (GATT), which now involves 118 nations throughout the world.

At present, the most visible result of regional economic integration is the European Union. This group was formed after World War II to pool resources to promote reconstruction and generate rapid economic growth after the destruction caused by the war. The European Union (often called the Common Market) is discussed later in some detail, as are the North American Free Trade Agreement (NAFTA), the Andean Pact (among five Latin American countries), ASEAN (among five Asian countries), and Caricom (among more than a dozen Caribbean islands).

Economic integration efforts among less developed countries (LDCs) tend to pursue the goals of increased economic ties and growth, plus increased political power in dealing with the developed countries. Countries within Latin America, the Caribbean, Africa, and Asia have joined together in almost a dozen regional integration agreements. Each of these agreements has sought to raise the level of economic development of the member countries and to create a better bargaining position with the developed countries. Thus far, the accomplishments of the LDC integration efforts have been small, but the goals remain important, and such efforts are likely to continue.

Economic integration involves sharing the costs and benefits that result from reducing barriers to commerce and financial dealings among member countries. Each member of an integration group must agree to give up some national policy prerogatives to a transnational (regional) authority, typically on such issues as tariffs and movements of labor and capital among the countries in the group. Each country expects this policy to generate gains from increased trade and other business activity, such as foreign direct investment, that will exceed the costs of adjusting to the new rules.

The groups that have implemented regional economic integration affect company activities in a number of ways, but primarily by altering the rules on exports and imports among members of the group. Additional effects include changes in tax rates and policies, removal of restrictions on movements of money and people among member countries, and other regulatory changes. These effects are discussed later in the context of specific economic integration efforts.

The basic economics of regional integration concern the shifts in business activity that occur as a result of the integration process. Two fundamental principles relate to the trade effects of integration. First, if the integration group causes member countries to alter their production toward greater efficiency (i.e., toward their comparative advantages) and to trade more extensively with one another, trade creation occurs. **Trade creation** is the result of reducing trade barriers among member countries, whose firms subsequently compete more freely with one another. More efficient, lower-cost producers in member countries will gain markets from less efficient producers, thus creating more exports among the countries in the group.

FIGURE 10-1

Trade Creation in Product X between Countries 1 and 2

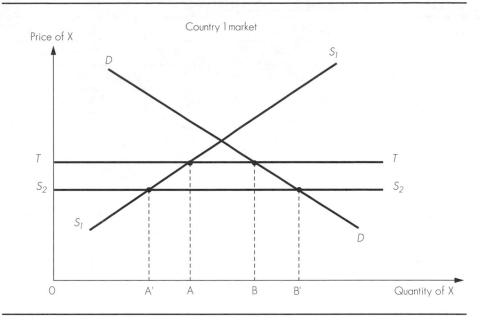

The creation of new trade is demonstrated in Figure 10–1. S_1S_1 and DD are the country 1 supply and demand curves, respectively, for any good that may be traded between countries 1 and 2. The graph assumes country 2 is the more efficient producer of the product, as shown by its supply curve, S_2S_2. The trade barriers before economic integration are depicted by the vertical distance between country 2's supply curve and the supply-plus-tariff curve labeled TT. When countries 1 and 2 agree to eliminate tariffs between themselves, country 1's consumption of the product increases from B to B'. Consequently, country 1's firms supply only OA' (instead of OA) amount of the product, and the rest, $A'B'$, is imported from country 2. This trade creation benefits country 1 by lowering the price of the product to consumers and forcing productive resources to be shifted to other, more efficient uses.

Second, if the integration group causes member countries to decrease their trade with nonmember countries, **trade diversion** occurs. Trade diversion would occur in the above example if the tariff reduction caused imports from country 2 to replace other imports from the rest of the world, which is more efficient but still faces the unreduced tariff of country 1. Thus, trade diversion is the loss of production and exports from more efficient nonmember countries to less efficient member countries that are protected by tariffs or other barriers against nonmembers.

Empirical studies of these effects in regional integration groups have tended to demonstrate substantial trade creation and little trade diversion within developed-country groups but less impressive results among less developed countries. Table 10-1 presents measures of the trade creation effects of regional economic integration in both industrial and developing-country groups. Notice that among the LDC blocs, only the Central American Common Market demonstrated a large percentage of intragroup trade (over 20% of total trade), and that group virtually ceased to operate after the fall of the Somoza regime in Nicaragua in 1979. The European Union countries have moved from about one-third intragroup trade to over 50 percent, though membership has increased substantially as well.

TABLE 10–1   Trade Creation Effects of Regional Integration

A. Intratrade of Developed Countries by Region

Economic Groupings (regions)	Value of Intratrade[a] (US $ billions)					Share of Intratrade in: World Exports (%)					Total Group Exports (%)				
	1960	1970	1975	1980	1982	1960	1970	1975	1980	1982	1960	1970	1975	1980	1982
EEC (6)	10.3	43.4				8.0	13.9				34.6	48.9			
EFTA[b]	2.9	9.4				2.3	3.0				15.7	21.8			
EEC (expanded)[c]			145.9	347.0	303.0			16.7	17.3	16.4			49.4	52.8	51.9
Trade in manufacturers between ex-panded EEC and residual EFTA member countries			45.1	105.9	85.1			5.2	5.3	4.6			12.9	13.7	12.4
Intratrade in manufacturers of residual EFTA member countries			8.5	14.8	12.4			1.0	0.7	0.7			16.1	12.8	12.0
USA–CANADA[d] (preferential)	—	5.1	11.1	15.7	19.6	—	1.6	1.3	0.8	1.1	—	8.7	8.0	5.7	7.2
CMEA[e]	8.1	18.4	44.4	79.0	82.3	6.3	5.9	5.1	4.0	4.5	62.3	59.4	57.4	51.0	49.8
Total	21.2	76.1	225.0	562.4	502.4	16.6	24.4	29.2	28.1	27.2	34.6	34.5	45.2	46.7	44.7

[a]Based on exports (f.o.b.) data.
[b]Excluding goods shown in annex D of the Stockholm Convention.
[c]The expanded nine-country EEC.
[d]Trade under the US–Canada Automotive Products Agreement negotiated in 1965.
[e]Council for Mutual Economic Assistance.
Source: UNCTAD (1984), p. 38.

From a conceptual point of view, the total economic gains generated by the formation of an integration group tend to be larger when (1) the member countries initially have very high trade barriers among themselves so that more trade creation occurs, (2) the member countries possess relatively similar comparative advantages so that less trade diversion occurs, (3) the number of member countries is larger so that more comparative advantages can be exploited, and (4) the tariffs imposed on nonmember countries are lower so that less trade diversion occurs.[1]

Before turning to *regional* integration examples, we discuss the most important *global* agreement on the reduction of trade barriers: the General Agreement on Tariffs and Trade (GATT).

THE GENERAL AGREEMENT ON TARIFFS AND TRADE (GATT)

The **General Agreement on Tariffs and Trade (GATT)** is an institutional structure the industrialized countries established just after World War II to promote expanded trade among its members and avoid the protectionism practiced during the prewar depression years. Initially, in 1948, GATT had 23 member countries. In 1994 there were 118 members, including industrialized, less developed, and formerly communist nations. Clearly GATT is more than a regional effort to share trade benefits among a small group of countries; it is a global effort at economic integration to enhance the gains generated by trade.

GATT maintains a permanent secretariat of about 300 people located in Geneva, Switzerland. The main functions of the secretariat are to collect information and carry out studies of trade issues that are relevant to the governmental negotiations held under GATT's auspices. Decision making is reserved for the representatives of the member countries, who approve exceptions to the basic rules that favor global free trade (e.g., permission for the European Union to extend tariff reductions only to its members).

GATT has served as a forum for negotiating multilateral reductions in trade barriers. Since 1948, eight "rounds" of negotiations have occurred, ending with the Uruguay Round, which was concluded in 1994. In each round, tariff levels among GATT's members have been reduced and other trade-liberalizing steps have been taken. The Tokyo Round in the 1970s was the first to focus specifically on reducing nontariff barriers, namely customs valuation (which can be used to overassess imports), government procurement, import licensing, subsidies, antidumping measures, and technical barriers to trade. By the end of the Tokyo Round, tariffs among GATT member countries averaged less than 10 percent *ad valorem* on all products, though greater tariffs and other restrictions still exist in some countries and on agricultural products more than on manufactured goods.

GATT was formed as a multilateral institution for improving trade relations among its members. It specifically sought to avoid bilateralism, in which pairs of countries negotiate trade agreements that exclude other countries. A fundamental concept in GATT negotiations is the **most-favored-nation (MFN)** principle, which requires that any tariff reduction negotiated between any two members of GATT be extended to all members. Thus, if the United States and Japan agree to reduce tariffs on their trade in electrical appliances, the same reduction must be passed on to the other members of GATT. Most-favored-nation treatment has ensured the continued multilateralism of a large part of international trade negotiations since World War II.

Many exceptions have been made to GATT's basic rules. Since sovereignty ultimately rests with national governments, any transnational agreements such as GATT are, of course, subject to the continued willingness of countries to participate and accept the rules. The main exceptions to adherence to GATT's rules have been allowed to countries facing a balance-of-payments crisis. Such countries are generally permitted to erect temporary restrictions on imports until the balance-of-payments crisis ends. In addition, countries that form a regional bloc for economic integration are allowed to create trade policies that are more favorable to members of the bloc than to outsiders, as long as the bloc does not raise new trade barriers against other members of GATT. Each regional bloc discussed next has tried to eliminate trade barriers among its members and to leave in place barriers to the imports of other countries.

In 1986, a conference was held in Punta del Este, Uruguay, to discuss the formal opening of a new round of GATT. The Uruguay Round began in 1987 but did not conclude until the end of 1993. This eighth round of negotiations focused on a number of nontariff issues, along with general pursuit of lower tariff barriers among the member countries. The final level of tariff reductions exceeded the originally stated goal of one-third reductions across the board. For US firms, this meant substantial reductions in barriers to their exports of scientific equipment, semiconductors, and computers, among other products.

GATT's range of trade barrier reductions was extended in the Uruguay Round to include trade in services such as financial services, telecommunications services, and distribution. The rules were also expanded to cover trade-related investment measures (TRIMs) that hinder foreign direct investment and trade-related intellectual property rights (TRIPs), which protect companies' proprietary technology.

REGIONAL ECONOMIC INTEGRATION: THE BASIC TYPOLOGY

Economic integration in its broadest sense signifies the expansion of commercial and financial ties among the nations of the world. This process has been going on for centuries, making rapid advances as transportation and communication among nations become easier and less costly. Various political empires of the past pursued economic integration as a policy for economic development, seeking in this way to realize gains from trade and specialization. Since World War II, economic integration has been pursued by small groups of countries that wanted to expand their national markets, increase their economic and political power, and realize the economic gains of greater intragroup trade. Half a dozen regional blocs were established in the 1950s, and many more have been established since then. To understand the rationales behind these blocs and see their impacts on business activities, it will be useful to present a typology of integration forms.

Though no regional bloc fits perfectly into any of the following categories, each can be placed reasonably accurately in one or another, and the categories are quite distinct. Five increasing levels of **regional economic integration** can be distinguished:

1. Free-trade area
2. Customs union
3. Common market
4. Economic union
5. Political union

Each succeeding level of integration involves greater cooperation among the bloc's member countries, and at the ultimate level the bloc members become unified into a single political entity, a new country. Most regional blocs remain at some level of integration without seeking to attain closer ties. Some analysts argue, however, that the greatest integration yields the greatest gains from integration; thus, underlying pressures toward greater ties may exist.[2] These pressures were certainly evident as Great Britain debated entry into the European Common Market from its inception and eventually joined that regional group in 1973. Pressures to dissolve or limit political union while retaining economic integration have become quite visible in Canada (with the Quebec separatist movement) and in the Commonwealth of Independent States (CIS) among the members of the former Soviet Union.

Free-Trade Area

The first level of economic integration, the **free-trade area,** involves the elimination of tariffs on trade among the countries in the regional group. Most of the integration efforts in the post–World War II period have begun from this base. Following the reasoning of Chapter 3 concerning the benefits of free trade, each participant in the free-trade area expects to gain by specializing in the production of goods and services in which it possesses comparative advantages and by importing from other countries in the group products and services in which it faces comparative disadvantages. Thus, trade should be *created* among member countries, giving them less expensive access to more goods. (Note that this trade may take place between unrelated firms or within MNEs that operate in more than one member country.)

A cost of free-trade areas to member countries is trade diversion from outside countries. Since tariffs on imports from nonmember countries remain, some trade may be diverted from the most efficient producers outside the area to less efficient producers inside the area, which are still protected by tariffs. In the extreme, if every country belonged to one free-trade area, the gains to all would be maximized. Given the numerous and complex reasons for trade barriers that exist today, regional blocs have formed free-trade areas to obtain a kind of second-best gain, since full free trade appears unattainable.

Among the free-trade areas is the European Free Trade Area (EFTA), formed at about the same time as the Common Market (in 1960) and composed of those Western European countries that did not become Common Market members. Today the members of the EFTA are Austria, Norway, Sweden, and Switzerland. (The United Kingdom and Denmark left EFTA to join the Common Market in 1973, as did Portugal in 1985.) The Latin American Free Trade Association (LAFTA), originally composed of the Spanish-speaking countries in South America plus Brazil and Mexico, has evolved into a group called ALADI (Asociación Latino Americana de Integración), which includes the same countries. Even after 30 years of existence, this group has *not* been able to eliminate tariffs or other trade barriers among its members. It has, however, led to some reduction of trade barriers and an increase in economic cooperation.[3]

A final free-trade area that was negotiated recently illustrates a possible trend in international economic agreements for the 1990s. The North American Free Trade Agreement, signed in 1993, effectively created a free-trade area in North America. Mexico's entry into free trade with the United States and Canada marks the first linking of industrial and less developed countries in a free-trade area. This movement parallels the highly publicized effort of the European Union countries to expand their integration and the various efforts in Asia to create a regional trading bloc there. NAFTA provides for elimination of tariffs and NTBs to virtually all trade among the countries (with exceptions such as auto trade, which is restricted by a previous US-Canada agreement).

Customs Union

The second level of regional economic integration, the **customs union,** involves the elimination of tariffs among member countries plus the establishment of a common external tariff structure toward nonmember countries. As with each succeeding form of integration, member countries are required to give up control over more economic policies to the group than they gave up at the previous level, in this case the regulation of imports from outside countries. The additional benefit from this policy is intended to be the avoidance of bias in attracting imports to the group; if external tariffs differ from country to country, outsiders will favor importing into the lowest-tariff member country to sell in the whole group. In this way, the lowest-tariff member of the group would benefit at the expense of the other members. The common external tariff eliminates that possibility.

None of the regional integration groups in existence today have been formed specifically to achieve a customs union. Most of these groups aim for even greater economic ties among their members, that is, a common market or even economic union. In fact, because of slow progress in attaining further levels of integration, several of the regional integration groups can be categorized as customs unions. The Caribbean Common Market is one such group, and the Andean Pact is another. The former group includes 12 of the English-speaking islands of the Caribbean (all former British colonies); the latter includes Bolivia, Colombia, Ecuador, Peru, and Venezuela. In both of these groups, efforts to reduce trade barriers and increase intragroup business are under way, but thus far neither has achieved the regulatory harmonization of a common market.

Common Market

The third level of economic integration, the **common market,** is characterized by the same tariff policy as the customs union plus freedom of movement for factors of production (i.e., labor and capital) among member countries. A common market is perhaps the ultimate feasible step in multicountry associations for permitting individuals and firms to carry out their transnational business activities in member countries without facing barriers to movements of products, people, or money. This level of integration avoids the intercountry regulatory bias on trade and direct investment, both of which are thus left to determination by market factors.

The best example of a regional group that constitutes a common market is the European Common Market, also known as the European Union. This bloc of 12 countries includes Belgium, Denmark, France, Germany, Greece, Ireland, Italy, Luxembourg, the Netherlands, Portugal, Spain, and the United Kingdom. It is discussed in some detail next.

Economic Union

An **economic union** is characterized by harmonization of economic policy beyond that of a common market. Specifically, an economic union seeks to unify monetary and fiscal policy among its member countries. A common currency, or a permanently fixed exchange rate, is one aspect of an economic union. Harmonized tax rates and tax rate structures are other aspects. To a large degree, national governments participating in an economic union relinquish control over much of national economic policy to the group.

As one might expect, due to these major policy constraints, few economic unions exist. At present, only the Belgium–Luxembourg Economic Union (BLEU) fits into this category. Belgium and Luxembourg maintain a fixed exchange rate (1 Belgian franc = 1 Luxembourg franc) and a highly coordinated set of monetary policies. Their tax rates and structures are virtually identical. They reach their other political decisions on a largely separate basis, and each maintains a distinct political existence. These two countries are the smallest in the Common Market and have allied themselves with each other primarily to gain a larger voice in European affairs.

The European Union, via its "Europe 1992" initiative, defined its objectives broadly to achieve the status of an economic union. That is, the group seeks to establish a monetary harmonization (under the Maastricht Treaty) that will lead to a common currency, plus much greater harmonization of fiscal policies. These goals are accompanied by a long list of additional steps that are leading to reduced restrictions on business and on individuals as they move among member countries of the EU. As the European countries continue to pursue competitiveness with North America and Japan, it is conceivable that the EU may indeed achieve most of the characteristics of an economic union during the 1990s.

Political Union

The highest level of regional economic integration is **political union,** under which all economic policies are unified. Countries that unite under a common government lose their national identities and become parts of a single state. Important examples of political unions are Canada and the United States, each of which combined independent states into a single country. In fact, since the members of a political union cease to be separate countries, perhaps political union should not be considered a part of economic integration at all. However, political union does form the logical end point of increased economic cooperation among a group of nations.

The issue of political union has become especially significant in the 1990s, as the members of the Commonwealth of Independent States, formerly the Soviet Union, grapple with their opening up to a pluralistic political system and, simultaneously, the acceptance of a market economy. This overwhelming shift in direction has led some of the states to seek membership in the EU and others to seek new political linkages and redefine economic interdependence. East Germany joined West Germany to form a political union, that is, a single country. Several other former Soviet allies, such as Poland and Hungary, are pursuing membership in the European Union, which may imply economic (though not political) union. It remains to be seen just how much economic union can be achieved without a single political power.

The fall of the Berlin Wall and the opening of the Eastern bloc is by far the most significant international political and economic event of the second half of this century. Nonetheless, major changes in direction are occurring in other parts of the world. Political union in Canada, for example, has been challenged once again by the Province of Quebec, which seeks to protect its unique French-based culture and society through greater independence. It appears that this independence will occur through greater political freedom within the sovereign state, but the results may very well include an increased ability of the provincial government to tax its residents and spend revenues according to its own decisions. Other Canadian provinces are examining their own options in light of the Quebec strategy, so we may see a much weaker federation of provinces in Canada by the end of the decade.

One conclusion to be drawn from this discussion is that the forms of economic integration themselves are evolving during the 1990s. Most countries view freer trade as desirable and are promoting this goal through membership in GATT and through development of regional economic blocs. Historically, full fiscal and monetary unification have been achieved only within nation states. The events of recent years show that some regional blocs are pursuing greater unification at the same time that some nations are permitting states or provinces greater autonomy in their fiscal and monetary affairs. The definitions of political and economic union may need to be reworked by the year 2000.

In sum, the five levels of economic integration do not necessarily represent a sequence of steps toward political and economic union. But they do present strategic alternatives for groups of countries that seek to increase their international (intragroup) trade and thus benefit from the larger market created by the integration group. Table 10–2 lists examples of integration groups.

TABLE 10-2

Levels of Economic
Integration

Level	Examples	Members
1. Free-trade area	North American Free Trade Agreement (NAFTA)	United States, Canada, Mexico
	European Free Trade Area	Austria, Norway, Sweden, Switzerland
	Latin American Free Trade Area (ALADI)	Argentina, Bolivia, Brazil, Chile, Colombia, Costa Rica, Ecuador, El Salvador, Guatemala, Honduras, Mexico, Panama, Paraguay, Uruguay, Venezuela
	Mercosur	Argentina, Brazil, Uruguay, Paraguay
2. Customs union	Andean Pact	Bolivia, Colombia, Ecuador, Peru, Venezuela
	Caricom	Antigua and Barbuda, Bahamas, Barbados, Belize, Dominica, Grenada, Guyana, Jamaica, Montserrat, St. Kitts–Nevis, St. Lucia, St. Vincent, Trinidad and Tobago
3. Common market	European Union	Belgium, Denmark, France, Germany, Greece, Ireland, Italy, Luxembourg, Netherlands, Portugal, Spain, United Kingdom
4. Economic union	Belgium–Luxembourg Economic Union	Belgium, Luxembourg
5. Political union	United States, Canada	

THE EUROPEAN UNION

History

Soon after the end of World War II, various policymakers and analysts began promoting the idea of some sort of Western European union.[4] One goal of the union was to ensure the cooperation of the countries in the region and thus avoid another cataclysmic war. A second goal was to create another economic and political force to deal with the Soviet Union and the United States, which arose from World War II as the leading world powers. US policy has broadly supported these goals from the beginning, and through the Marshall Plan it provided substantial funding (about $200 billion) for European reconstruction from 1948 to 1952. Several regional organizations were formed in the early postwar years, including the Organization of European Economic Cooperation (OEEC), in 1948, which later became the Organization for Economic Cooperation and Development (OECD), and the Council of Europe, in 1949, which focused more on political than on economic issues.

The European Coal and Steel Community, a cooperative venture among Belgium, France, Germany, Italy, Luxembourg, and the Netherlands, began operating in 1952. This organization removed barriers on intragroup shipments of coal, iron, steel, and scrap. In 1957, the same six countries established Euratom to regulate and monitor the production of nuclear energy. Finally, also in 1957, they formed the European Economic Community (EEC). The combination of these three integration efforts became known as the **European Community (EC),** and more recently as the **European Union (EU).**

The Treaty of Rome, which established the European Economic Community, laid out a schedule for the elimination of intragroup tariffs, the creation of a common external tariff, and guidelines for additional harmonization of such economic policies as tax structures, exchange rates and controls, immigration among member countries, and agricultural support programs. Although the objectives of the integration process were not achieved exactly as scheduled, all of them have been realized, even with the expansion of the EU to include Denmark, Ireland, and the United Kingdom in 1973. (Greece entered the EU in 1981; Portugal and Spain joined in 1985.) Thus, the European Union is truly a common market, and its members continue to pursue harmonized and joint economic policies that could lead to a further level of economic union by the end of the 1990s. Figure 10–2 shows the geographic and economic scope of the EU.

The most recent major step in European integration was the Maastricht Treaty, which formally created the **European Union (EU)** in 1993. The treaty takes the 12 member countries closer to economic union, with a specific goal to create an economic and monetary union (EMU) by 1999. This agreement calls for creation of a European central bank and a common currency. The Maastricht Treaty also creates a Common Foreign and Security Policy (CFSP) that establishes a structure of intergovernmental cooperation in this area.

Institutions

The European Union operates through four main institutions:

1. The Council of Ministers, which has one plenipotentiary representative from each member country.
2. The Commission, which has 17 members chosen by the member governments. (The five largest countries each choose two commissioners.)
3. The European Parliament, which has 518 members who are elected directly by the voters in each member country.
4. The Court of Justice, which has one judge from each member country, plus one additional judge chosen from France, Germany, Italy, or the United Kingdom on a rotating basis.

The *Council of Ministers* is the ultimate decision-making body of the European Union. Its 12 members are the foreign ministers of each country, though other representatives are often used when specific issues are under discussion, for example, the agriculture ministers when agricultural policy is being debated. With the exception of the budget, which is handled primarily by the Commission and the Parliament, the Council makes all the final decisions of the EU. It meets and has staff in Brussels, Belgium.

The Council of Ministers makes decisions only on proposals presented to it by the Commission. The main technical analysis and consensus building take place in the Commission, which is generally viewed as being relatively Europe-oriented and not biased toward the national interests of any individual country.

The *Commission* functions mainly as the executive branch of the European Union, drafting legislation for proposal to the Council, overseeing the implementation of Union policies, and carrying out studies of key policy issues. Although the council retains the ultimate authority to adopt Union legislation and policies, the Commission prepares the decisions and regulations and does most of the technical work. The approximately 10,000 members of its staff form the main body of EU employees. The Commission's staff, like that of the Council, is located in Brussels.

FIGURE 10-2   The European Union: A Union with No Internal Frontiers

FIGURE 10-2 *Continued*

The *European Parliament,* consisting of 518 members who are elected directly by voters in the 12 member countries, has been developing its range of functions over the past decade. Although established by the Treaty of Rome in 1957, the Parliament did not become a directly elected body until 1979. At present, the Parliament serves mainly as the watchdog on EU expenditures, though it also evaluates other decisions of the Council. It meets in Strasbourg, France, but its secretariat of over 2,000 people is located in Luxembourg.

Finally, the *Court of Justice* serves as the official interpreter of European Union law. Most of its cases have related to interpretation or application of the Treaty of Rome, based on actions by member countries, individuals, and companies. As EU rules have become more closely interwoven with national laws in the member countries, the court has increasingly been serving as a court of appeals for national courts when EU issues are involved. The court's 460 staff members and 11 judges have offices in Luxembourg.

Impact on Business

The European Union's impact on business activity in and among the member countries has been widely debated over the years. Most of the empirical studies on that impact have shown that on balance, the EU has created much more trade than it has diverted from the rest of the world. Table 10–3 summarizes a number of such studies that appeared in the 1960s and 1970s. Similar conclusions have been drawn concerning the effects of the accession of Denmark, Great Britain, and Ireland to the EU.

As far as foreign direct investment is concerned, the conclusions differ somewhat. Studies have shown that the EU played an insignificant role in the growth of FDI in its region; what mattered most appears to be the size of the individual national markets (Scaperlanda and Mauer, 1969). A 1986 study of both trade and direct investment impacts on national incomes in each EU member country showed across-the-board favorable effects. Denmark was the only country to show a negative net impact of integration during 1974–81, mainly because of very little trade creation (Marques Mendez, 1986).

TABLE 10–3   Estimates of Trade Creation and Diversion in the EU

Author	Period Studied	Trade Created				Trade Diverted[†]			
		All Goods ($ billions)	(%)*	Manufactures ($ billions)	(%)*	All Goods ($ billions)	(%)*	Manufactures ($ billions)	(%)*
Prewo	1970	19.8	23	18.0	34	−2.5	6	−3.1	15
Truman	1968								
Unadjusted		—	—	9.2	26	—	—	−1.0	7
Adjusted		—	—	2.5	7	—	—	0.5	4
Balassa	1970	11.3	13	11.4	21	0.3	1	0.1	0
Kreinin (unweighted average of three estimates)	1969–70	—	—	8.4	—	—	—	1.1	—
Williamson and Bottrill	1969	—	—	11.2[‡]	25	—	—	0	0
Aitken	1967	9.2	14	—	—	0.6	2	—	—

*Percentages relate to total and extra-area imports of all goods and manufactured products.
[†]Numbers with negative signs represent external trade creation.
[‡]Unweighted average of alternative estimates.
Source: Robson (1980), p. 177.

The effects of the EU on other business activities have not been studied in as much detail as its impact on trade and direct investment. Most likely, some additional transnational business activity in Europe has resulted from the establishment of the European Union, given the group's focus on creating a regional market. For example, efforts to create regional MNEs to compete with US-based firms have led to the formation of Airbus Industrie, which currently competes actively with such firms as McDonnell Douglas and Boeing. An intra-EU effort to create a globally competitive semiconductor and electronics consortium recently led to a pooling of resources by several European electronics companies (although IBM is seeking to be included in the group). The regional MNEs are expected to gain economies of scale and access to additional technology (and perhaps other competitive advantages) that would not be available to any one firm. Overall, EU-wide initiatives to stimulate additional business activities appear to have generated more than just trade and direct investment in the region.

These initiatives have included efforts to facilitate the movement of working people among member countries. As a result, in the late 1960s, the labor markets of each member country were opened up to the residents of other member countries, but additional policies were needed to harmonize health and pension benefits for workers who moved among member nations (and also to harmonize licensing requirements for various professions, which differ somewhat in each member country). Another initiative is the European Monetary System (discussed in Chapter 7), which is part of the EU's attempt to facilitate capital movement among its members. Although this system has not eliminated the problems of exchange rate fluctuations and speculative capital flows, it has improved the ability of EU member countries to deal with intraregional financial problems.

EU 1992

The Commission of the European Union issued a white paper, called *Completing the Internal Market,* in 1985. This paper outlined the steps needed for the EU to achieve a single market for products, services, people, and financial dealings by year-end 1992. It essentially called for the EU to finish the process of becoming a full common market, with free movement of labor, capital, and goods, by the end of 1992.

This process was formally reinforced by the Single European Act, which was ratified by the governments of all 12 members of the Union and went into effect in 1987. The act committed each member country to eliminating restrictions on trade and financial flows by the end of 1992. A list of 300 key barriers to a single market was compiled, for systematic elimination during the period up to December 1992. (By early 1994, agreement had been reached to eliminate virtually all of these barriers.)

The impact of the policy changes for foreign businesses are quite significant. For large, multinational firms that already have extensive operations in European countries, the creation of a single market enables them to rationalize their production and distribution systems, as barriers to cross-national shipments have been fully dropped. In fact, these firms are being pressured to become truly European, as their competitors feel the same pressures and move to achieve economies of scale in both production and distribution. Companies such as Nestlé and Philips, along with Ford of Europe and IBM, are challenging their rivals to become equally European and to achieve the same low costs and high efficiency that these leaders in regional integration are attaining.

Airbus Industrie

One major consequence of forming a single European market is that European firms have been able to achieve scale economies large enough to make them competitive on a global scale with US-based and Japanese firms. One interesting partnership was founded as a consortium of European aircraft manufacturers to produce commercial aircraft. In 1966, four European firms formed a joint venture called Airbus Industrie to begin design and production of a passenger aircraft capable of competing with Boeing, Lockheed, and McDonnell Douglas in the international market. The four European firms—Aerospatialle (France), Messerschmitt (Germany), British Aerospace, and Construcciones Aeronauticas (Spain)—individually lacked the capital base needed to design, test, produce, and sell large passenger aircraft in competition with the US giants.

By pooling the partners' financial and technological resources, as well as obtaining guaranteed orders from government-owned airlines in Europe, Airbus Industrie was able to begin selling wide-bodied jets in the early 1970s. Although the consortium has not yet reached profitability (losses were estimated at more than $US10 billion through 1990), by 1989 the firm had taken almost one-third of the wide-bodied segment of the market with its A300, A310, and A320 planes. Because the Airbus planes served a market segment that the large US manufacturers had not reached at the time (viz., wide-bodied planes for 250 to 300 passengers on short and medium hauls), the firm carved out a short-term competitive advantage. The advantage has been eroded with the development of the Boeing 767, but Airbus had captured several major sales commitments of more than $US1 billion in the early 1990s. Thus, it appears that the consortium may become a viable competitor against the US producers.

The governments of each European partner in Airbus Industrie have judged that the technological, political, and other benefits of a locally owned and managed aircraft manufacturer outweigh the continued financial burden the firm has placed on them since the early 1970s. Each has been satisfied to have a *piece* of the total, since each realized that its own economy was not large enough to sustain commercial aircraft production.[5] ∎

For non-European firms that do not have active operations in the region, EU reality now provides the challenge to enter the world's largest single market. Obviously, the EU's policy changes do not eliminate cultural differences that lead to different tastes and preferences, most important for consumer goods. It will still be necessary to advertise in different languages across the Union and to provide different clothing styles, food tastes, and so on where preferences differ. However, for industrial-goods producers, the unified Europe is truly attractive with its market of over 340 million people whose incomes rival those of US consumers and its geographic concentration.

As the reductions in barriers are realized, more and more companies will create European strategies and presences. Their size will encourage such firms to pursue additional industrial-country markets, such as those in Japan and North America. For this additional reason, companies from North America and Japan need to consider the EU as a challenge, since future competitors in their home markets are increasingly likely to come from Europe.

One fear of non-European firms is that the EU may create a "Fortress Europe" that is hostile to business from nonmember countries. This concern is probably overstated, since any outside firm still can establish a subsidiary within the EU. One serious concern, however, is the Union's position of requiring "reciprocity" in the home country for EU firms if companies from that country want access to the EU. If a country such as Brazil restricts foreign microcomputer firms operating there, or Canada (and many other countries) restrict foreign banks in opening operations there, firms in those industries from those countries will very likely encounter restrictions in the EU. This is a potential problem for US firms in industries such as textiles (where the United States has quotas on foreign textile imports), banking (where the United States does not permit full nationwide banking), and agriculture (where the United States has quotas and other restrictions on various products such as sugar and coffee).

To balance the optimistic tenor of the preceding discussion, it should be noted that many difficulties continue to hinder the EU's functioning. Primary among these difficulties is the Common Agricultural Policy, a system of subsidies and other support for EU farmers, which currently uses up over half of the EU budget. As new members join the EU, the problems imposed by agricultural policy will become even greater.

EU Expansion

In March 1994, the EU received finalized applications from Sweden, Finland, Austria, and Norway to join the Union. These applications need subsequent approval by the European Parliament and by national referenda before each of the four potential new members can officially join the group. The implications of this EU expansion depend on how quickly the four new members achieve compliance with group rules and policies; once this occurs the EU market will offer even greater opportunities to firms.

North American Free Trade Agreement (NAFTA)

This regional agreement among the three countries of North America essentially brings Mexico into the previously negotiated US-Canada Free Trade Area. In 1993, NAFTA was approved by the three countries' governments after a complicated process of negotiations among the countries as well as within the legislative bodies in each country.

The agreement calls for immediate elimination of tariffs on most goods among the three member countries. Tariffs and other barriers on textiles are to be eliminated over a period of 5 to 10 years. Automobiles and parts are subject to "balanced" trade under the US-Canada Auto Agreement. The addition of Mexico has mainly led to reductions in limits on imports of auto parts, an industry in which Mexican firms were previously highly protected. Under the agreement, most tariffs on automobile parts are scheduled to be eliminated at 20 percent per year, resulting in total elimination within five years.

Beyond the traditional area of free trade in goods, NAFTA covers a number of additional issues. Investment in financial services, for example, has been opened up across the three countries through a gradual phaseout of limitations on ownership of local banks by other member country banks over a period of 10 years. Environmental protection is made a special topic in the agreement, with rules prohibiting companies from seeking "pollution havens" in one member country to sell in the others. Likewise, intellectual property rights protection is included in the agreement to ensure that Mexican rules and enforcement on patents, copyrights, and trademarks are made consistent with similar rules in Canada and the United States. In fact, specific "side agreements" were included in the NAFTA accord to protect labor (to improve working conditions and living standards) and the environment (to cooperate on conservation and environmental protection and enforce domestic environmental laws).

Overall, NAFTA has created a free-trade group that rivals the European Union in size, while becoming the first such group to include both industrial and less developed countries.

OTHER INTEGRATION EFFORTS

The Andean Pact

Among the various integration processes undertaken by less developed countries, one particularly focused effort to obtain maximum benefits from foreign multinational firms is the Andean Pact. This group was formed in 1969 among Bolivia, Chile, Colombia, Ecuador, and Peru, with Venezuela joining four years later (and Chile withdrawing in 1976).

In 1971, the Andean Pact countries established a foreign investment code (*Decision 24*) precluding foreign direct investment in some sectors, such as banking and telecommunications, and requiring all foreign investors to sell down to minority ownership positions within 15 years. At about the same time, the group enacted a series of sectoral programs that assigned key industry sectors to specific members of the group such that they would receive preferential access to one another's markets for the assigned products. Both of these ambitious projects were imperfectly implemented, highly criticized, and ultimately dropped since they failed to produce the desired results.

In the early 1990s, the Andean Pact countries renewed their commitment to achieve a full free-trade area and, beginning on January 1, 1995, eliminated tariffs among the members. The establishment of a common external tariff appears likely in the near future. Even more important, a free-trade agreement with the United States has been discussed, though the preference of the US government thus far has been to negotiate with individual national governments, first in Mexico, then in Chile.

Caricom

Since the mid-1960s, the British colonies in the Caribbean have moved through several regional alliances, beginning with the West Indies Federation, passing through the Caribbean Free Trade Area, and ending with the current **Caribbean Common Market (Caricom).** Since its establishment in 1973, Caricom has created a common external tariff (which completed the customs union) and pursued several additional steps toward becoming a full common market. A regional market standards council now attempts to unify product standards, thus avoiding that nontariff barrier; a Caribbean Enterprise form of incorporation allows regional companies to move money and people freely among the member countries; a regional air transport policy ensures full air service to the member countries on a regionally owned airline (LIAT); and several financial agreements have been made, including the creation of a regional development bank and a balance-of-payments stabilization fund. Mainly because of the small size of the entire market, the fact that the countries are not industrialized, and the difficulties of transportation among members, Caricom has not become a major economic policy tool.

ASEAN

The **Association of Southeast Asian Nations (ASEAN),** founded in 1967, includes six less developed countries of Asia: Brunei, Indonesia, Malaysia, the Philippines, Singapore, and Thailand. These countries are characterized by an abundance of natural resources (except Singapore), very large international trade sectors, and an emphasis on liberal (free-market) economic development. Singapore is already the site of substantial offshore assembly of manufactured goods, while the others still rely heavily on exports of raw materials. ASEAN has reduced intragroup tariffs and eliminated some nontariff barriers to trade. It has undertaken industry sectoral programming somewhat similar to that of the Andean Pact, and thus far with similarly unspectacular results. Overall, the ASEAN group differs from other LDC blocs in its favoring of private enterprise, although, as with other LDC blocs, its efforts to promote intragroup trade and investment have been only somewhat successful. The most noted impact of ASEAN has resulted from its strategy of bargaining collectively with the European Union, Japan, and international organizations to obtain better market access for ASEAN exports.[6] As a combined market of more than 330 million people and with the world's fastest economic growth rate over the past decade, ASEAN is becoming an increasingly attractive location for international firms.

STRATEGIES FOR DEALING WITH ECONOMIC BLOCS

There are as many strategies for dealing with integration groups as there are groups, since each set of countries offers different opportunities and risks to firms. Because a central aim of every economic bloc is to create a multicountry market with few restrictions on business among member countries, international firms should consider establishing operations within each bloc as the market there justifies. For example, if the combined market of Caricom countries is large enough to justify local production, such production should be considered. If the bloc has not achieved free trade internally, or if barriers to the outside firm are not too difficult to overcome, local operations may not be justified. In the case of Caricom, most foreign firms set up operations in the country or countries that offer adequate market size or access to some desired raw material (e.g., Jamaica or Trinidad) and regard other members of the bloc as marginal additional markets. Because few of Caricom's policies affect foreign firms significantly, Caricom as a bloc is unimportant in most company decisions. Similar conclusions generally apply to the other LDC groups, since all of them have either failed to carry out their intended integration policies or established rules that do not play a key role in company decisions.

The European Union is a different story. This bloc of developed countries offers the foreign investor an opportunity to set up a facility in one or more of the 12 countries to serve, tariff free, a combined market of over 320 million people with very high average per capita incomes. Many companies have set up one or a few facilities to serve the 12 countries. Several major US pharmaceuticals manufacturers have set up plants in Ireland (which offered key tax incentives) to produce basic chemical entities for use throughout the EU. Ford has plants in France, Germany, Belgium, and England that supply autos for sale throughout the EU. The list of US firms that use a regional strategy in the EU is very long indeed. In this case, low barriers to international business and a very large regional market have attracted firms that view the EU as one market, just as the EU members intended. The Europe 1992 initiative served only to focus more attention on this already attractive market.

Regardless of the size of the integration group or the level of development of its member countries, the firm that designs a regional strategy still faces some risk. This risk arises from the fact that the member countries remain separate political entities, free to undo group policies or to raise new barriers to intraregional business. Thus, an investment in one member country that has been set up to serve the entire integration group may be greatly affected by a shift in that country's willingness to continue participating in the integration group on the same basis. At this time, such risk appears to be fairly small in the EU and in NAFTA, whose member countries are committed enough to justify regional companies' strategies. However, in virtually every other example of free-trade areas, customs unions, or common markets (especially among LDCs), the regional market shows signs of breaking down or failing completely.

CONCLUSIONS

Economic integration efforts play an important role in international business, primarily because they signal groups of countries that are trying to create regional markets, which may be attractive to firms. Probably the most important integration project in existence today is GATT, which is not regional at all. GATT has led to reductions in tariff barriers to trade among 118 countries such that firms operating in any one of these countries usually face relatively low tariff costs when they ship internationally. Other integration schemes have also created new opportunities for firms to take advantage of low intragroup barriers to trade and other business activities. The European Union is clearly the most important of the regional blocs, because its large market and high degree of success in eliminating barriers offer substantial gains to firms that pursue a regional strategy. NAFTA is becoming another key bloc, which may extend further through the Americas.

The competitive advantages that firms may realize from participation in a regional integration scheme generally relate to the economies of scale—particularly in production and distribution—made possible from operating in a larger (regional) market in comparison with a smaller (national) one. For most regional blocs thus far, the multicountry market has *not* become a full reality, so firms have been unable to benefit as much as expected. The EU, on the other hand, has stimulated a large amount of regional business, since markets of its member countries have become sufficiently linked for firms to operate relatively freely throughout the region.[7]

Economic integration has not proven to be a solution to the problems of economic development, which are far more difficult than a simple tariff-reducing or investment-stimulating program could resolve. However, it may have demonstrated that specific regional cooperation efforts can lead to successful projects such as regional development banks, technical cooperation, and political power, not to mention increased intraregional trade. Also, the regional blocs have helped propel member countries toward broader, global free trade via expansion of the blocs and via new rounds of GATT liberalizations.

QUESTIONS

1. What are the main benefits to a *country* from joining an economic integration group?
2. What are the main benefits to a *company* from entering an economic integration group (through foreign direct investment)?
3. How does GATT affect the pattern and trends of international business?
4. How would you expect a GATT on foreign direct investment to affect international business? (Assume it would try to accomplish goals analogous to those pursued by the existing GATT on international trade.)

5. Define the five levels of regional economic integration. Where do the European Union, NAFTA, and the Andean Pact fall within this range?

6. How does NAFTA affect business in the United States, Canada, and Mexico? Which country receives the benefits, and which pays the costs?

7. What are the major differences in approach between ASEAN and other LDC integration schemes? Do you expect ASEAN to succeed over the next five or six years? Why or why not?

8. Compare the institutions and policies of the European Union with those of the Andean Pact. Will the Andean Pact approach the EU in importance as its member countries continue to develop?

9. What kind of strategy could a firm follow to operate in NAFTA?

10. Explain how a company such as RJR-Nabisco could establish a strategy for operating in the European Union. How would a strategy for Lockheed Aircraft need to differ from one for RJR-Nabisco.

REFERENCES

Arndt, H W, and Ross Garnaut. "ASEAN and the Industrialization of East Asia." *Journal of Common Market Studies,* March 1979.

Behrman, Jack N. "The Halting March to International Economic Integration." *Business in the Contemporary World,* Autumn 1989.

Chernick, Sidney. *The Commonwealth Caribbean.* Baltimore: Johns Hopkins Press, 1978.

Grosse, Robert. *Foreign Investment Codes and the Location of Direct Investment.* New York: Praeger Publishers, 1980.

Magee, John. "1992: Moves Americans Must Make." *Harvard Business Review,* May–June 1989.

Marques Mendez, AJ "The Contribution of the European Community to Economic Growth." *Journal of Common Market Studies,* June 1986.

Morawetz, David. *The Andean Group.* Cambridge, MA: MIT Press, 1974.

Robson, Peter. *The Economics of International Integration.* London: Allen & Unwin, 1980.

Scaperlanda, Anthony, and Laurence Mauer. "The Determinants of U.S. Direct Investment in the E.E.C." *American Economic Review,* September 1969.

Swann, Dennis. *The Economics of the Common Market.* 5th ed. Harmondsworth, Middlesex, UK: Penguin Books, 1984.

Tsoulakis, Loukas. *The New European Economy.* Oxford: Oxford University Press, 1993.

United Nations Conference on Trade and Development. *Handbook of International Trade and Development Statistics.* Geneva: UNCTAD, 1984.

NOTES

[1] See Jacob Viner, *The Customs Union Issue* (New York: Carnegie Endowment for International Peace, 1950).

[2] See, for example, Peter Robson, *The Economics of International Integration* (London: Allen & Unwin, 1980), chaps. 1, 2.

[3] See, for example, "A Long Road Ahead for ALADI," *Latin American Weekly Report,* September 24, 1982, p. 9.

[4] See, for example, Carl Friedrich, *Europe: An Emergent Nation?* (New York: Harper & Row, 1969), chap. 1.

[5] See Badiul Majumdar, "Upstart or Flying Start? The Rise of Airbus Industrie," *The World Economy,* September 1987.

[6] See H W Arndt and Ross Garnaut, "ASEAN and the Industrialization of East Asia," *Journal of Common Market Studies,* March 1979.

[7] Many limits to intra-European business, even in manufactured goods, still exist. An interesting example of problems encountered by Philips, the Dutch electrical equipment firm, appears in *The Wall Street Journal,* August 7, 1985, pp. 1 ff.

PART

III

MANAGING THE MNE

11

Effects of Culture and Ethics

Culture and ethics are important to the international businessperson. MNEs deal in a variety of cultures and must do so effectively. Culture affects both strategic and operating decisions, and managers approach different problems and opportunities wearing their own cultural masks. This chapter looks at how culture affects MNEs' competitive advantages and everyday management decision making. It also looks closely at business ethics in the international arena. In some situations, the ethics are clear and ethical behavior is easy to accomplish. In others, what is ethical is not so evident. The main goals of the chapter are to:

1. Examine how cultural variables affect the competitive advantages of MNEs.

2. Learn about the practical and cross-cultural schools of thought regarding the universality of management practices.

3. Note how different cultural variables affect management decision making.

4. Learn how to use the self-reference criterion to one's advantage when making cross-cultural decisions.

5. Examine business ethics in international business, with special reference to the international applicability of ethics concepts.

6. Become sensitive to the situational factors affecting management behavior and how these factors may be interpreted in the ethics sense.

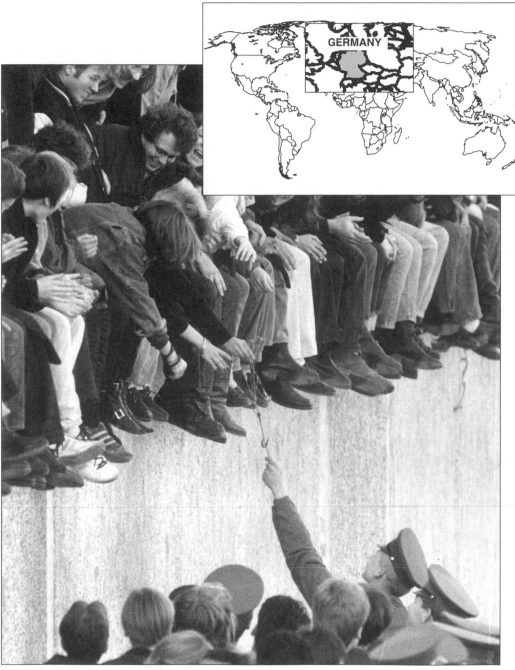

An East Berlin border guard hands a flower back to West Berlin citizens sitting atop the Berlin Wall by the Brandenburg gate.

Reuters/Bettmann

INTRODUCTION

What is culture? Why is it important in international business? These questions have become increasingly important over the past few years. They deal with the implementation of strategy, or how firms accomplish their business objectives. "Culture" can either facilitate or hinder business effectiveness. It does this by affecting which business decisions are made, how they are made, and how they are implemented. As expected, culture also affects management communications, an especially important matter for the MNE that operates across various cultures with culturally diversified management and technical staff.

Consistent with the unifying theme of this book, this chapter begins with a discussion of cultural influences on the competitive advantages of MNEs. Managing in multicultural environments is then discussed and cultural differences that affect managerial effectiveness are illustrated. The analysis of culture concludes with a close look at a prescription for cross-cultural management decision making.

Next, the chapter turns to the issue of business ethics, which is becoming increasingly important both domestically and internationally. It is also closely related to culture. This discussion centers on an extended case analysis involving Eastern Air Lines and drug smuggling from South America into the United States. It illustrates that ethics can be difficult to define, that at times it may be unclear which of several parties is responsible for resolving ethical problems, and that, at the margin, realistic trade-offs between ethics and economics may well have to be addressed.

CULTURE AND THE COMPETITIVE ADVANTAGES OF MNES

Chapter 2 gave considerable attention to the concept of competitive advantages. Fourteen such advantages were listed (in Table 2–4) and discussed. The chapter examined how to "take advantage" of these competitive advantages and analyzed alternative methods for exploiting competitive advantages through alternative forms of foreign involvement. Let's return to some of these topics and put them into a cultural perspective. But first, we need a working definition of *culture*.

Anthropologists might well define **culture** as consisting of behavioral patterns, values or beliefs, art forms, institutions, and so on that are characteristic of a "community of social expression." E T Hall, for years a prominent researcher on culture and management, identifies several key features of culture. Culture is acquired, or learned; various aspects of culture, such as values and behaviors, are interrelated; and culture pertains to groups of people and defines the boundaries among different groups.[1] For our present purposes, we should note that culture includes values and behavior patterns, is a product of conditioning, involves groups of people, and distinguishes one group from others. Culture affects what people see in a situation, what these observations may mean in terms of imputed intentions or motives, and the responses deemed appropriate.

Because the press and other media usually focus on politically defined areas called "countries," we often equate cultural boundaries with national boundaries. But culturally distinctive groups are not necessarily always countries. Also, individuals may belong to several different culturally defined groups simultaneously, with any single cultural influence varying depending on the time, the issue, and so forth. For example, one may be German, Christian, and young. Being identified with each of these groups may likely result in differing values and behaviors regarding different issues and times. For example, younger Italians and younger Austrians may be more similar in certain consumption patterns or work attitudes than are younger Austrians compared to older Austrians.

Keeping in mind these different considerations regarding culture, let's look again at some of the competitive advantages outlined in Chapter 2.

Proprietary Technology

The competitive advantage of **proprietary technology** relates to culture in several ways. The cultural characteristics of a particular society affect product design itself, for example, by determining use conditions and expectations regarding product longevity (i.e., useful life). Witness the trend toward "low maintenance" products in the United States. Note how Germans in general have a more evident "lifetime of value" standard, especially for big-ticket items, than do Americans. Culture affects process technology too. For example, India's Mahatma Gandhi's outlook on the use of machinery was negative. Gandhi believed labor-saving machines often put workers "on the streets to die of starvation."[2] One could argue that the incidence of innovation in product and process technologies is also affected by culture. In the United States, the market-oriented entrepreneur is intrinsic to the decentralized, capitalistic economic system. Historically, the US environment has been the most prolific spawning ground of new products that the world has known. In contrast, Japan has traditionally purchased advanced technologies and then worked to perfect them in terms of product quality and cost minimization via process technology enhancements.

Cultural risk is certainly important to both the development and the transfer of product and process technologies. Some products can succeed in one foreign market and not another, or substantial product adaptation may be required to make them successful. Process technology may have to be adjusted to reflect a cultural nuance such as the long midday lunch break in the traditional Latin American firm and the effect it would have on the operation of a printing company or any other business in which extensive setup time is required prior to a production run. Firms that overlook the need to adapt to the local culture do so at considerable risk to their competitive potential. Successful adaptation may also be difficult to accomplish in firms whose corporate culture is monolithic or ostensibly risk averse.

Goodwill

Regarding **goodwill,** cultural risk is probably most evident in the potential for misreading the extent and durability of the franchise allegedly developed via time and experience in the home market as that franchise is commercially exploited in the foreign market. Mistakes can be made in market segmentation strategy, pricing strategy, and so on. The franchise may or may not be transferable. Products bearing labels of the European fashion houses, such as Pierre Cardin and Gino Pompeii, sell in upscale market segments around the globe. Chrysler, on the other hand, eventually withdrew from direct participation in European markets. Why couldn't Chrysler transfer its US franchise successfully? The answer lies, in part, in the production cost increases associated with Chrysler's need to move quickly in upgrading process technologies at its (former) European subsidiaries. For example, in the United Kingdom, Chrysler (i.e., its subsidiary Rootes) "bought out" the old piece rate practice by paying workers time-measured wages well in excess of industry norms. Also, the Chrysler brand name had no special appeal for Europeans.

Scale Economies in Operations and Finance

Scale economies in production, purchasing, distribution, and financing were listed in Chapter 2 as potential sources for competitive advantages. The first of these is probably the most vulnerable to cultural risk. Large-scale production operations may be bound by product market limitations, such as extensive segmentation reflecting, for example, cultural diversities within the customer base that affect product use, or resource market limitations, such as the lack of an industrial plant-oriented culture among the workers. On the latter point, there is a famous case involving a Colombia-based textile manufacturer that established a modern plant in a rural area near Medellin. This firm encountered excessive absenteeism and other problems involving personnel behavior, including widespread instances of fathers beating daughters who were employed at the plant because the daughters brought home more money than the fathers did. People living in rural or peasant communities had difficulty adjusting to an industrial setting, and the company had difficulty adjusting to the rural or peasant setting. The period of transition was very costly. (Think, for a moment, how you as a manager would deal with such a situation.)

Purchasing and distribution also encounter some exposure to cultural risk. Lot sizes may be affected by changes in process technology. The availability, price, and quality of raw materials and vendor-supplied components may be influenced by culture. The propensity of dockworkers or perhaps miners to go on strike may be relevant here, as may be the work ethic or the industrial culture. Local shopping habits often affect distribution. For example, people living in the smaller towns and villages of Europe and in Japan prefer to shop almost daily. This leads to a more atomized distribution channel structure and possible losses of scale economies.

The scale economy that is probably least vulnerable to cultural risk is financing. Money is generally fungible internationally. Some funds-sourcing strategies relate to impersonal international capital and money markets and are thus generally not exposed to cultural nuances. Others, however, involve a wide range of types of funding sources, such as "building societies" in Great Britain and the *financieras* prevalent in Latin America. Such financing can vary considerably country by country, reflecting local values and practices. The use of debt can also reflect local values and practices. In Japan, for instance, a 4-to-1 debt to equity ratio, unheard of in the West, is not at all unusual.

Government Protection

Perhaps surprisingly, **government protection** can be substantially culture bound. Witness the free-market philosophy so predominant in the United States and the difficulties some industries and unions have had in convincing the US government to protect domestic markets through import restrictions. The idea of protectionism is foreign to the cultures of numerous American citizens. On the other hand, developing countries historically had often agreed to erect import restrictions to protect growing domestic industries. Multinationals setting up plants in such countries could often expect this kind of support for local production. Those investing abroad might also expect to find varying degrees of hostility among host country personnel, including government officials. For US MNEs, the "ugly American" syndrome can be very real—and nearly impossible to overcome. Some host government reactions here are to protect the home culture from foreign influences based on different values.

Human Resource Management

Because it deals directly with people, **human resource management** is significantly culture bound. For example, personnel practices and policies concerned with promotion, compensation, layoffs, and unionization vary considerably across (and even within) countries. In Japan, promotions are often based on age and seniority. In the United States, they are based on seniority and equivalent capability (if the company is unionized) or merit (if the company is not unionized). Compensation is likewise based on age and seniority in Japan and on seniority or merit in the United States. As a form of employee compensation, profit sharing is common and substantial in Japan but hardly evident in the United States and Europe. Layoffs of workers fly in the face of management's commitments and self-esteem in Japan, but are commonplace in the United States. Unions are often company specific in Japan, industry specific in the United States, trade specific in the United Kingdom, and politically specific in France. Thus, it is nearly impossible for the MNE to generalize cross-culturally regarding human resource management. However, there has been some movement recently toward similarities in practices as markets have become increasingly competitive in the open, global economy.

The challenge for MNEs is to learn not only how to accommodate differences in practices within the technological, financial, marketing, and managerial constraints facing them but also how to transfer practices that have been found to be especially productive in one locale to other locales, a difficult but potentially rewarding initiative.

Scale Economies in Advertising

Technology (e.g., the media available), government regulation, and culture all influence **scale economies in advertising.** Such economies rely on the repetition of standardized advertising appeals. The amount, content, and delivery of advertising messages may well have to accommodate cultural nuances, however. Advertising is much less prevalent in Iran today, for example, than it was in the days of the shah. Some messages may be irrelevant or even offensive, depending on the cultural setting. The "Coke adds life" theme, which is designed to promote consumption by showing how Coke fits in nearly everywhere, would probably be ineffective in Buddhist settings, which typically value the suppression of desires.

Message delivery involves the use of media. Some media are culturally inappropriate for promoting certain types of products. For example, feminine hygiene products are advertised on television in the United States but not in Latin America. In some countries, the use of particular media may have important political implications. Terpstra reports, for example, that the two leading newspapers in Colombia, *El Tiempo* and *Espectador,* support different political groups and that the smart promoter might do well to advertise in both.[3] The bottom line here is that purchase decisions are made by people, and therefore the motivation to buy may well reflect people-specific characteristics. Such characteristics sometimes manifest a transnational homogeneity—when they reflect income level, for instance. Often, however, cultural influences are dominant in defining them. Only when the former situation exists can scale economies in advertising be realized.

Multinational Sourcing and Marketing Capabilities

Culture also affects multinational sourcing and marketing capabilities, two competitive advantages that are distinctive to MNEs. The **multinational sourcing** advantage implements a set of intermediate production, purchasing, and/or logistic relationships. The establishment of these relationships (e.g., purchase contracts) incorporates management's appraisals of the performance risks it has identified. As time unfolds, events with a low probability of occurrence may indeed take place. A civil war might erupt, for example, or US dockworkers might refuse to unload cargo from Iraqi ships. Similarly, unanticipated events may occur that change the basic premises underlying the production, sourcing, or marketing patterns originally defined (e.g., US consumers may again prefer big [or small] cars), thus precluding the benefits expected from those patterns. Such events could result from cultural change or from management's misreading of the cultural environment. Similar comments might be made regarding **multinational marketing** networks.

The key point is that sourcing and marketing capabilities relate to both resource and sales markets and how these markets are linked through the MNE. These capabilities allow the MNE to locate the most profitable resource and sales (product) markets and to link them systematically. Culture is a concern relevant to the ongoing, efficient operation of these linkages.

Managerial Experience

Managerial experience in several countries, another competitive advantage distinctive to MNEs, is both dependent on and constrained by cultural variations. The abilities to understand different cultures and conduct effective cross-cultural operations are competitive requirements unique to MNEs. The cultural differences evidenced internationally can provide the very basis for an MNE's ability to generate a competitive position. The learning curve effect, which energizes the MNE system and provides the competitive edge, is itself predicated on the successful transfer of management know-how between parent and subsidiaries. Cultural heterogeneity, however, complicates the transfer of such know-how and adds a special risk dimension to the transfer process. Some firms avoid this risk by not transferring management know-how to certain areas. For example, Kujawa reports that not all Japanese firms operating in the United States bring in Japanese systems of people management because they often have less risky alternatives (e.g., unique process technologies) for achieving the competitive success of their US-based subsidiaries. On the other hand, some Japanese firms were successful in the US market because of their ability to take advantage of the management expertise developed at home. For these firms, the cultural disparity between the United States and Japan relevant to industrial relations provided the very opportunity they needed for competitive success.[4]

International Diversification

International diversification is essentially a portfolio concept used to reduce risk and cost. It is pertinent to the global, MNE level; that is, it is the corporate headquarters that manages the "portfolio." The strategy is not culturally neutral, however. Its success ultimately turns on the profitable operation of the units contained in the portfolio. This situation returns us to the whole host of considerations regarding culture and competitiveness that we have already discussed.

MANAGING IN THE MULTICULTURAL ENVIRONMENT

There are two schools of thought regarding managing multiculturally. One, the practical school of thought, contends that good managers function the same regardless of the cultural environment; cultural differences don't really matter. The other, the cross-cultural school, argues that management behavior and effectiveness are affected by the culture in which managers operate.[5] The preceding discussion on culture and competitive advantages supports the cross-cultural school perspective. Let's explore both schools of thought more deeply.

The Practical School

According to Black and Porter, the "practical" school of thought is so named because practicing managers (in the United States) are most often selected for overseas assignments with little or no regard for their cultural awareness and sensitivities. The key criteria are whether or not the manager was successful in

ADDED DIMENSION

La Casa del Whopper

Consider Burger King's experience in adjusting to Venezuelan tastes and preferences at its restaurants in Caracas. The hamburger buns don't come with sesame seeds on them anymore; the Venezuelans kept brushing them off. Catsup is sweeter, and milk shakes are sweeter and creamier. The menu includes soft ice cream, which is everyone's favorite dessert in Latin America. Latins are late diners, so the Caracas Burger Kings stay open as late as 1:30 A.M. Everything else, however, is standard Burger King. For example, frozen french fries (which are imported, since Venezuela doesn't grow the "right kind" of potatoes) are prepared according to parent company specifications.

Burger King has learned that cultural adaptation must relate to business enhancement and that simply adapting to local cultures may be counterproductive. For example, Burger King originally served wine in its French restaurants, but customers tended to linger and visit over their glasses of wine. This affected table turnover and revenues. You can't buy wine at a French Burger King anymore! ∎

Sources: Mimi Whitefield, "La Casa del Whopper Goes South," *Miami Herald,* November 29, 1982, p. 5; information provided by Burger King Corporation, Miami, Florida, May 7, 1991.

the domestic operation, and, of course, whether he or she is willing to accept the foreign assignment. The practical school contends good management practices are effective everywhere.[6]

Miller was the first to provide evidence (in 1973) that MNEs actually possessed the practical school orientation.[7] Later studies by Tung and Black showed that approximately 70 percent of Americans appointed to foreign management assignments had no special preparation and training.[8] This behavior would be rational only where decision makers believed no training was necessary, that is, where success in a prior assignment was sufficient to ensure success in a foreign assignment. This is the practical school in action. Several comparative management scholars, such as Negandhi and Prasad,[9] have also long contended that culture does not play a major role in managerial effectiveness.

A major research finding reported by Black and Porter in 1991 raised serious doubts about the efficacy of the practical school approach. Black and Porter conducted a statistical analysis of American and local managers' behaviors and the relationship of these behaviors to job performance in the United States and in the foreign country. They found US managers behaved essentially the same in the United States and in the foreign country, but there was no positive correlation between these behaviors and successful job performance in the foreign country (as there was in the United States).[10] This finding is contrary to practical school thinking.

The Cross-Cultural School

The roots of the cross-cultural school also date back many years. Farmer and Richman, in their 1965 classic *Comparative Management and Economic Progress,* presented and defended the view that the effectiveness of managers' performances vary in accordance with the cultural context in which the managers' behaviors occur.[11] In other words, culture matters.

Ouchi's 1982 popular report of his research on the correlation between corporations' profitability and their "Z-ness", or presence of Japanese management–like practices, and on the competitive superiority of Japanese management practices further supports the cross-cultural school.[12] More recently, others have identified links among culture, management behavior, and corporate competitiveness. Abbeglen and Stalk, for example, identify elements in the Japanese work ethic, group orientation, and so on as constituting what some contend is a "benign conspiracy" underpinning Japanese firms' competitiveness.[13]

Reconciling the Two Schools of Thought

For our purposes, it seems safe to say that culture matters. But there are also commonalities pertaining to managerial effectiveness that are independent of culture. These commonalities are embedded in the identity of the management performance necessary for success. For example, studies conducted by management scholars in both the 1970s and 1980s found that successful managers at home and abroad shared high, common values regarding productivity and ability and that certain skills, such as effective interpersonal and communication skills, and certain behaviors, such as flexibility, respect, and sensitivity, were common to successful managers regardless of the cultural context.[14]

All this suggests that some elements of the management process (e.g., listening and communicating) and some management attitudes and behaviors that are process related (e.g., valuing ability and training) seem to be universal. But management behavior and decision making often have to be conditioned to accommodate cultural differences if they are to succeed. To illustrate, *Nation's Business* reported that (inexperienced) American tractor exporters, in negotiating with potential Japanese buyers, lowered their export price on three occasions in the face of silence by the Japanese, who were not rejecting any proposal by their silence but were merely "thinking over" the proposal, a reportedly typical Japanese "motivating" practice.[15] Surveys, such as those reported on by Ricks, Fu, and Arpan in their classic *International Business Blunders,* are replete with other examples of management mistakes based on managers' insensitivities to cultural differences.[16]

This all suggests, then, that management must (1) be aware that cultural differences matter, (2) be generally knowledgeable about the types of cultural differences that can affect management effectiveness when operating cross-culturally, and (3) be able to make decisions incorporating necessary and relevant cultural factors. The first of these three points was addressed in the preceding discussion. We now turn to the latter two.

Cultural Differences Affecting Managerial Effectiveness

There are many ways to categorize culturally related behavior. Hofstede has identified four dimensions of national culture that have important management implications. These are *power distance* (the extent to which a society accepts an unequal distribution of power among people within an organization), *uncertainty avoidance* (a society's tolerance for uncertainty and the extent to which it will diminish uncertainty by supporting career stability, eliminating or reducing deviant ideas and actions, etc.), *individualism/collectivism* (social Darwinism—discussed later—versus group identification and responsibility), and *masculinity/femininity* (the extent to which a society espouses "male" values, such as assertiveness and the acquisition of material goods, over "female" values, such as caring for others and the quality of life).[17]

Hofstede goes on to relate differences among societies on these four dimensions to their implications for supervisor/subordinate relationships (for example, the larger the power distance, the greater subordinates' dependence needs), the role of laws and rules as they apply to different classes of people within a society, the use of status symbols, the need for consensus (where uncertainty avoidance is strong), and so on.[18]

Hofstede's work encouraged managers to look at national cultures in ways that differed from those of the past, and this was an important contribution. But let's look too at some of these more traditional perspectives, which typically include (among others) communication and education, achievement motivation, attitudes toward work, group identification, concepts of time, and hierarchical relationships.

Communication and Education

Gift giving, which is a form of communication, can be quite culture bound, as are other forms of communication. Westerners, for example, express cordiality and friendliness via the handshake. Respect and social position are dominant in the greetings of Japanese businesspeople, who bow before each other. Indeed, the angle of the bow will vary by the amount of respect due. The point to remember, according to Ronen, is that language (either spoken or silent) conveys social reality as well as providing for communication.[19] This is clearly evident in the dialogue presented in Table 11–1. (Note the role of "power distance.")

Formal education is also typically viewed as culture bound. It is not valued in some societies, possibly little valued in certain subgroups within societies, and highly valued in others. Educational systems and vehicles also vary widely across countries and cultures. Business schools, for example, are less prevalent outside the United States and Canada. They are a fairly recent addendum to the educational systems in other countries. Literacy levels and social/technical competencies usually correlate positively with the value placed on education.

Achievement Motivation

McClelland's benchmark study *The Achieving Society* provided a host of basic insights into **achievement motivation.**[20] McClelland reported that behavior

TABLE 11–1

Communication Perceptions—Beware!

Behavior	Perception
American: How long will it take you to finish this report?	*American:* I asked him to participate. *Greek:* His behavior makes no sense. He is the boss. Why doesn't he tell me?
Greek: I don't know. How long should it take?	*American:* He refuses to take responsibility. *Greek:* I asked him for an order.
American: You are in the best position to analyze time requirements.	*American:* I press him to take responsibility for his actions. *Greek:* What nonsense: I'd better give him an answer.
Greek: Ten days.	*American:* He lacks the ability to estimate time; this time estimate is totally inadequate.
American: Take 15. Is it agreed? You will do it in 15 days?	*American:* I offer a contract. *Greek:* These are my orders: 15 days.

Source: From *Interpersonal Behavior* by H. C. Triandis. Copyright © 1977 by Wadsworth Publishing Company, Inc. Reprinted by permission of Brooks/Cole Publishing Company, Pacific Grove, California 93950.

patterns follow thought patterns; that is, people behave according to how they think. If people think about achievement, they have a desire or need for achievement and will seek to be achievers. McClelland noted that achievers universally exhibit three distinguishing characteristics: taking personal responsibility for solving problems, setting moderate achievement goals and taking moderate risks, and needing performance feedback. These characteristics, according to McClelland, position achievers as likely business executives.

The competitive, entrepreneurial business environment provides achievers with opportunities to "take command" by setting a strategy and implementing it, to be aggressive and take chances in the marketplace, and to value profits—which are, in fact, market-generated feedback on the appropriateness of the achiever's actions. Taking a broader perspective, a society whose business function responds to the needs of achievers will attract achievers to the enterprise sector and will thus be an achieving society. Moreover, a society that responds to achievers in this way creates an environment conducive to the economically effective application and growth of achievement motivation in general. The whole system feeds on and favors itself. Some observers would contend that Argentina and Chile in the early and mid-1990s illustrate the kind of (re)orientation McClelland is talking about.

In support of his conclusions, McClelland observed and recorded the incidence of achievement orientation in different societies and found a strong, positive correlation between a high need for achievement and high economic growth. He found such a correlation when analyzing a society through time and when comparing different societies at a given point in time. For a business manager in an MNE context, achievement orientation is very important. It correlates with economic growth and expanding profit opportunities and with societal interests in economic achievement. It identifies foreign markets that are likely to be more accommodating to business success and, conversely, less antagonistic toward business in general.

Attitudes toward Work

Attitudes toward work are closely related to achievement motivation. The ideas are slightly different, however. Attitudes toward work include the "work ethic," the allocation of different types of work among different groups within the society, and even the relationship between labor and capital.

The **Protestant work ethic** is often cited as one of the driving forces in the development of the US economy. This contention rests on the fact that in its early days, the United States was populated via a large influx of immigrants from the United Kingdom, Holland, and other European countries. Many of these immigrants reflected a sociocultural heritage based on Puritan, Calvinist, or Lutheran doctrines that differed from Catholicism in several important relevant respects. In a classic essay written near the end of the large-scale European immigration into the United States, Fullerton noted that in Protestantism the person-God relationship is direct and individualism is emphasized in the struggle for salvation. The idea of work in this view pertains to discipline, that is, the fortification of the individual against temptation. Work is commanded by God and is an end in itself. Fullerton contrasted this perspective with the situation he saw in Catholicism, where the church mediates, as it were, between a person and God (e.g., via the sacrament of penance) and is itself populated by religious clerics who establish standards for the laity. The result was, in the Protestant view, that the daily living of Catholics was too casual and that the work of Catholics did not directly equate with prayer.[21]

Given these differences, one might expect that the commitment to work will differ considerably between societies embracing the Protestant view of work and those embracing the Catholic view. Management in a US MNE operating in a Latin country may be well advised to temper its expectations and structure its operations to accommodate the different concept of work likely to be held by its Latin employees.

To be sure, attitudes toward work are also influenced by factors other than religion. Geography and climate, for example, are important influences. Temperature extremes, whether hot or cold, affect living patterns, including work-related activities. Attitudes toward work may also differ between private sector and public sector employment and may vary with the size of the enterprise. For example, Harris and Moran report that in France there is little incentive to be productive in the government bureaucracy and in public concerns, but French workers in the private sector

have the reputation of being productive. Part of the explanation . . . may lie in the French tradition of craftsmanship. A large proportion of the French work force has been traditionally employed in small, independent businesses where there is widespread respect for a job well done. Many Frenchmen take pride in work that is done well because traditionally they have not been employed in huge, impersonal industrial concerns.[22]

Further evidence of the productivity differences between privately owned and publicly owned enterprises is seen in "privatization" trends, especially in the United Kingdom and some of the continental European and Latin American countries, where some public enterprises that had become noncompetitive and required government subsidies have been sold to private interests.

Attitudes toward work reflect the distribution of different kinds of work among different segments within a society. Social class distinctions may well determine who does manual labor—indeed, they may even bestow a "right" over such work by a specific class. In England, for example, class consciousness has greatly influenced labor-management relations. Historically, the factory-level work group was quite independent. It had its own leadership and its own allocation of effort and income, and it contracted with management on piece payment rates and production schedules.

Attitudes toward work are readily seen, then, as affecting a variety of management decisions, such as staffing, production scheduling, equipment utilization, and process technology, as management seeks to work efficiently and competitively within whatever constraints society imposes.

Group Identification

Group identification, a hallmark of the "Japanese management style," which both fascinated and perplexed European and US managers in the 1970s and 1980s, is generally credited with delivering substantial productivity gains. Japanese workers are seen as intensely loyal to their work groups and committed to group success. Individual interests and values give way to those espoused by the group. Harmony and hard work characterize the workplace. Labor-management relations are essentially nonadversarial in this model. New equipment and work methods are introduced without making workers fear for their jobs. Some roots of the model, including the development of communities and the difficulties of living off the land, can be found in the social structure of imperial Japan. Other roots are more recent, such as the paternalism that developed among the business class in response to the emigration of farmers into industrial centers.

In contrast, **social Darwinism** and the **rugged individualist** are often used to typify the keys to economic growth in the United States. Concepts of opportunity and entrepreneurship go hand in hand with "survival of the fittest." The Protestant ethic, the "frontier," and an abundance of natural resources (including fertile land) all favored the growth of individualism. It's not difficult to see why Americans have a hard time understanding Japanese business.

Other dimensions of group identification are also important to the international manager. For example, different ethnic groups, or subcultures, often exist within a society (e.g., the Flemish and Walloons in Belgium), and relations among these groups may not be harmonious. Staffing problems may result from the existence of such groups, as may difficulties in crossing market segments.

Concepts of Time

Cultures vary considerably in how they view time. In the United States, punctuality is valued. Typically time is of the essence (as are those favoring strong uncertainty avoidance in Hofstede's model). Executives are often "time driven." Their day is defined in terms of a series of time slots through which they are programmed. Some executives even take courses in "time management." Other societies hold quite different views of time. In some African cultures, for example, time is not a constraint. Lateness is considered acceptable behavior. Time bends to accommodate behavior. People who are pressed by time are not trusted. Latins are famous for their "tomorrow" attitude. The stereotype is one of laziness, but in fact the origin of the attitude is an uncertain future. Why stress a timely behavior when the circumstances of tomorrow may well require a different behavior?

ADDED DIMENSION

Is It Cultural Imperialism or Economic Imperialism?

France's biggest film star, Gerard Depardieu, says, "European cinema is in danger of dying." *Le Monde,* the popular French newspaper, recently wrote, "It is a question of the survival of certain forms of culture of the Old Continent." French director Roger Planchon writes in *Le Figaro,* "History will remember that at the end of this century, America committed a great genocide of national languages and culture which, taken together, constituted the spiritual wealth of the planet Earth."

These concerns, interestingly enough, were being expressed just as the issue of whether or not cinema should be included in international trade negotiations was being debated. Are the French, as characterized by an executive of the Motion Picture Export Association, "using the cultural argument as a fig leaf?"

There is no question that the French have been trying to protect their film industry. French law mandates that 40 percent of prime-time television programming be French products and that a percentage of all movie receipts in France go to finance new French films. Yet French filmmakers seem to be losing the battle. In 1992, 57 percent of the films shown in France were American, up from 31 percent in 1979. In 1992, America exported $3.7 billion worth of TV programming to Europe, compared to $288 million exported from Europe to the United States.

What do you think? Is it cultural imperialism? Is it economic imperialism? Or is it just possible that cultural and national boundaries are becoming less and less relevant to consumers today? ∎

Source: Sharon Waxman, "French Version of Hollywood Fears GATT Will Hurt Troubled Industry," *The Miami Herald,* October 3, 1993, p. 4K.

Time orientation is important in understanding people and how they behave, as Table 11–2 illustrates. Many Americans, for example, are future oriented. Peasant-dominated societies are more concerned with the here and now. The Chinese and other Oriental cultures are very concerned with the past. Different views of time affect interpersonal relationships, the pace with which business can be conducted, and even product definition. Where time is valued, you'll probably see timesaving products. Household appliances generally originate in the United States, where family members, not household servants, perform the routine cleaning and cooking chores and the demands on these people are typically seen as endless. "Time" influences business decisions in a variety of ways.

Hierarchical Relationships

Culture also affects **hierarchical relationships.** Vertical organization structures of six or more layers are often evident in the United States, and decision-making and authority levels are allocated by hierarchical standing. In Japan, functional organizations are typically flatter and communication is more horizontal. Participation in decision making is less a function of responsibility than of knowledge. In the Latin cultures, people and personalities dominate. Key people, the chiefs (*jefes*) control decision making. The worker's task is to perform routine jobs and call on the *jefe* for decisions. This leads to an inordinate amount of paper shuffling and a lack of initiative among employees at the lower skill levels. It also leads to economic and social dependencies of workers on their *jefes* and therefore to paternalism.

Hierarchical relationships are thus seen to affect reporting and control, communication, documentation, attitudes toward paternalism, the locus of initiative, and so on. Interestingly, workers at a Spanish subsidiary of a US multinational, in a dispute with management, refused to eat the lunch provided by the company and to use company-provided transportation to get home. These actions, which the workers took at some cost, registered the workers' denial of their *jefes'* paternalism. They were a slap in the face of the Spanish management. Managers in the US parent had a hard time understanding their significance.

The preceding example illustrates that cultural characteristics vary considerably across societies and that the potential of these characteristics for affecting business decisions and success is significant.

TABLE 11–2

Time and Conflict (a continuation of the dialogue in Table 11–1)

Behavior	Attribution
In fact, the report needed 30 days of regular work. So the Greek worked day and night, but at the end of the 15th day he still needed to do one more day's work.	
American: Where is the report?	*American:* I am making sure he fulfills his contract. *Greek:* He is asking for the report.
Greek: It will be ready tomorrow.	[Both make the attribution that the report is not ready.]
American: But we had agreed it would be ready today.	*American:* I must teach him to fulfill a contract. *Greek:* The stupid, incompetent boss! Not only does he give me the wrong orders, but he doesn't even appreciate that I did a 30-day job in 16 days.
[The Greek hands in his resignation.]	[The American is surprised.] *Greek:* I can't work for such a man.

Source: From *Interpersonal Behavior* by H. C. Triandis. Copyright © 1977 by Wadsworth Publishing Company, Inc. Reprinted by permission of Brooks/Cole Publishing Company, Pacific Grove, California 93950.

Making Decisions

If we accept that cultural differences exist and that management needs to take these differences into consideration when making decisions, the question then arises as to how this might be most effectively accomplished. This issue is addressed to some extent in Chapter 17 on personnel management and training. The chapter confirms the emergence of the truly international manager. If the modern international manager is of necessity cosmopolitan, and if key (international) decisions are made by or with important inputs from various managers and technical specialists from around the globe, these decisions will likely be sensitive to cross-cultural elements. This says simply that decision making must be **culturally adaptive;** that is, decisions must accommodate the cultural environment. Local customs can affect everything from product design to marketing to production technology. They have to be addressed so that both strategy and operations will reflect their impact.

Decision makers must also be culturally adaptive; they can't just rely on "practical school" behavior that is based on a **self-reference criterion (SRC).** We use an SRC when we impose our own standards or expectations when observing or being affected by others' behaviors. For example, many US companies have a hard time setting up marketing organizations in Japan. They often blame the Japanese government and the Ministry of International Trade and Industry (MITI) for holding back on the required approvals. They think the US government should negotiate with the Japanese government to eliminate or streamline this approval process, thus ensuring their successful entry into the Japanese market. There is likely more to it than this, however. Given the demographics of the country, distribution is highly fragmented in Japan. Moreover, distributors, from wholesalers to retailers, are often already associated with Japanese firms that will be the American firm's competitors. Japanese companies just don't walk away from these relationships. They are fiercely loyal to suppliers and/or distributors. Success in getting into the Japanese market entails much more than getting beyond government barriers. This simple example illustrates that the SRC is really a "blinder" hindering cultural adaptation.

In a classic on dealing with the SRC, Lee outlines a four-step procedure for isolating and eliminating the SRC in business decision making:

1. Define the business problem or goal from the home country perspective.
2. Define the same problem or goal from the local perspective.
3. Compare the two definitions and note the differences, that is, the SRC influence.
4. Eliminate the SRC difference, redefine the problem or goal, and proceed toward some optimal solution.[23]

To illustrate this procedure, Jain uses the example of designing an automobile for the Pakistani market. The US perspective identifies an auto as a necessity item, designed for high speed, performance, and comfort. In Pakistan, the auto is hardly affordable, and then by but a few. Moreover, it must be durable, efficient, and not ostentatious (since materialistic living is frowned on). Comparing the US and Pakistani perspectives brings out important differences regarding the role and function of an automobile. In Pakistan, the auto should be inexpensive, easily maintained, highly fuel efficient, and simple in design.[24]

It is important to note here that the SRC is a beneficial starting point when making decisions across cultures. It provides decisionmakers with comfortable "benchmarks" against which to identify and hopefully better understand the impact of cultural traits on managerial decisions.

BUSINESS ETHICS

When considering business ethics in the international business arena, the issue of bribery usually comes to mind first. Bribery is important in international business for several reasons. First, it is often culturally defined. *La Mordida* (the "bite") is an accepted custom in several Latin societies. It is a payment to someone to secure a sale, an approval by some government agency, or whatever. In most industrially advanced societies, such *mordidas* don't exist. Second, when excessive and when used for inappropriate purposes, bribes are seen by all as illegal and unethical. The Recruit scandal in Japan in the late 1980s, in which a company bought political favors by paying large sums of money to selected legislators and government officials, was so pervasive and mind boggling that it brought down the Takeshita government. Similar bribery allegations helped tumble the Hosokawa government in Japan in 1994.[25] Third, home country rules prohibiting bribes can seriously affect the competitiveness of some MNEs in societies where bribes are necessary to the conduct of business. All too often, executives of US MNEs are hindered because local firms and other MNEs are able to secure local government favor by paying off certain local officials. Differential tax treatments regarding such expenditures are another problem. For example, for US MNEs, bribes are not a deductible business expense anywhere; for Japanese MNEs, they are deductible everywhere; for German MNEs, they are not deductible if the bribes were domestic, but they are if foreign.

Chapter 14, "Accounting and Taxation," discusses the US Foreign Corrupt Practices Act and US MNEs' obligations under the act. It should be noted here, though, that the act makes bribes illegal but allows for "grease" payments to low-level officials to cut through bureaucratic delays and obstructions to doing business in a timely fashion. For example, a firm can give a special inducement to a port authority to move product from a warehouse to a truck within some desired time period.

Business Ethics: The Broader International Context

The issue of bribery is important, but it is only one of several that are significant in international business. The issues multiply when one considers that countries' legal systems themselves reflect those countries' ethical standards, that differences in laws and standards exist, and that MNEs operate in different countries with different laws and ethical standards.

Consider, for example, the firm that sells children's sleepwear in foreign countries that does not meet safety (fire hazard) standards in its own country. Consider the firm that transfers high-pollution (toxic-producing) production to developing countries where environmental legislation and controls are not in place. Consider the firm that locates production in societies where the working classes are politically oppressed and economically disadvantaged.

Your thoughts on each of these examples may vary depending on your own sense of ethics. But surely most of you would be opposed to selling unsafe sleepwear anywhere. Many would be opposed to foreign direct investments made to avoid local environmental controls. Probably some of you would be opposed to locating production in areas where wages reflect workers' economically disadvantaged status. Many Americans, for example, believed that Occidental Petroleum's activities in the Soviet Union during the Stalin era were ethically questionable, and many also questioned the ethics of American firms' participation in South Africa during the time of apartheid. Regarding the latter instance, others may well believe that the best thing MNEs could do for politically oppressed and economically disadvantaged workers would be to give these workers jobs! The issues here are not legal issues. Firms were operating in all instances within the legal confines of the different societies involved. But the ethics can be questionable.

Let's look at a real-life case and see where we think the ethical issues lie and how we feel about them.

The Eastern Air Lines Drug-Smuggling Case[26]

Smuggling drugs from Latin America into the United States via Eastern Air Lines became all too common in the latter 1980s. Cocaine was packed into an airplane's wheel wells, bathroom panels, legitimate cargo, and the flooring of shipping containers.[27] The Eastern baggage handlers and ramp supervisors involved in the smuggling ring waited until the regular baggage cleared customs, then removed the coke-filled baggage from its hiding places and mixed it with luggage in the domestic arrival area to be collected by accomplices for further distribution.[28]

The huge profits available from drug trafficking obviously provided a basis for the corruption of the Eastern Air Lines staff involved. But there was more to it than just money. Staff were threatened. At times, new hires in Miami were greeted with a "bullet in the palm" by smuggling ringleaders. In Colombia, employees were coerced by death threats to "look the other way" as drugs were put onto aircraft. Eastern employees actually received death threats. Several Colombia-based officials and employees at Eastern and other airlines flying similar routes were murdered; others found minicoffins outside their homes. They all resigned.[29]

Some observers would contend that Eastern's labor-management difficulties at this time likely complicated the drug-smuggling problem. Employees who were distrustful of management and likely contentious regarding management initiatives directed toward employees on the drug-smuggling issue would probably not have cooperated to help end the problem.

Eastern, of course, paid dearly for these problems. In 1985, Eastern was fined $1.2 million. By 1989, the (proposed) figure for current infractions had grown to $13 million. In addition, the airline contended it lost some $7 million annually due to passenger losses stemming from the aircraft delays and cancellations caused by US Customs' searches and seizures of aircraft.[30]

One could well contend that both Eastern Air Lines and its employees were big losers in the drug war.

The Management Involvement and Response

Eastern's management knew as far back as 1984 that flights were being used to smuggle drugs into the United States. In 1985, some 22 drug busts were made aboard Eastern's planes, and an Eastern aircraft was eventually impounded. Some observers believed it was the seizure of the aircraft that really brought management's attention to the drug-trafficking problem. Later that year, US Drug Enforcement Agency (DEA) officials busted cocaine traffickers using Eastern on two occasions. Eastern security agents then began cooperating with DEA officials, and a large number of Eastern employees were indicted in early 1986.[31]

Management's initial attitude toward drug smuggling was consistent with that of other carriers: Drug smuggling was simply not Eastern's problem; rather, it was a police problem. However, Eastern eventually responded by installing a special security system costing $3 million per year. The system included training a 17-person security force, installing surveillance cameras at selected airports, and establishing special baggage-handling procedures for passengers. In addition, Eastern temporarily suspended flights to Barranquilla, Colombia, while it implemented improved security procedures, attempted to drugproof planes by removing plastic panels secured with screws with metal panels that were riveted in place, installed a drug "hotline" for employees to call in tips, and fired and otherwise disciplined employees involved in drug smuggling or infractions of security procedures.[32]

But the drug-smuggling problems still persisted. In 1988, for example, eight Eastern Air Lines planes carrying over 1,000 pounds of cocaine were seized at Miami International Airport.[33]

The US Government's Role For years, the US government has focused on the supply side of the drug problem. Lacking sufficient funding, however, interdiction originally was not successful. In the early 1980s, stepped-up funding and interdiction efforts successfully curtailed the activities of drug runners using small planes and fast boats. This led drug smugglers to use commercial aircraft to transport ingeniously hidden drugs along with regular cargo and passengers' baggage. This led to Eastern's problems.

The Anti-Drug Act of 1986 identified commercial carriers as an integral part of the drug transshipment problem and provided for substantial financial penalties, even for carriers who were unwitting collaborators in transporting drugs. This, of course, got the attention of all commercial shippers and justified their increased costs in developing responses to be in compliance with the act.[34]

Evaluating the Eastern Air Lines Case This case raises a lot of interesting questions pertinent to the ethics issue. Did Eastern "ask" for drug smugglers to use its flights? Why did drug smugglers turn to using its flights? Was Eastern responsible for this? Was management's original attitude inappropriate in the face of the growing drug-smuggling problem? Why did management change its attitude? Who paid for Eastern's enhanced security procedures? Can a firm afford to be proactive on problems such as this? Should it be proactive? Since the drug problem is so pervasive, should the US government have funded commercial carriers' responses to reduce the trafficking? What were the responsibilities of governments and government agencies in other countries where drug trafficking begins or transshipments are accomplished? Answers to these questions will likely vary depending on one's knowledge and values.

CONCLUSIONS

This chapter explored what culture is and why culture is important in international business. Culture was defined as consisting of distinctive groups of people with acquired, interrelated values and behaviors.

All of the MNE's 14 potential competitive advantages are affected to varying degrees by diversity in cultural environments. Culture can influence *proprietary technology*, for example, as related to product design by affecting product use conditions. Process technology may need adaptation as it is transferred from one country to another. Different cultural environments were identified as giving rise to competitive advantages; the United States, for example, has traditionally been very receptive to product innovations. Americans, according to the stereotype, are typically willing to try new things. It was noted that the transferability of *goodwill* is dubious and depends on homogeneous strands of cross-cultural similarities between markets.

Of the five advantages related to scale economies, the advantages in production and advertising are probably the most susceptible to cultural risk. To the extent that culture affects market size and segmentation or the behavior of in-plant personnel, it has an impact on *scale economies in production.* The amount, content, and delivery of advertising messages, and hence *scale economies in advertising,* are affected by cultural nuances. Culture may also affect the availability, price, and quality of raw materials or vendor-supplied components and thus *scale economies in purchasing and distribution. Scale economies in financing,* when related to the international money and capital markets, are not generally vulnerable to cultural risk. Financial institutions, however, can vary substantially country by country and often reflect cultural attitudes toward saving and lending. The use of debt itself may be regarded as highly desirable in some cultures and as socially unacceptable in others.

Government protection, which is a public policy statement and should reflect public interests and values, is typically influenced by culture. The United States, for example, has eschewed trade protectionism for at least the past 50 years.

Human resource management, which deals directly with people and their behavior in the workplace, is obviously affected by culture. If, for example, a group of production managers were transferred from either Italy or Germany to a factory in Japan or Canada, the adjustments required of all parties would be fairly extensive.

Multinational sourcing and marketing capabilities lead into the establishment by the MNE of transnational purchasing, intermediate production, and/or logistic relationships and marketing patterns that themselves depend on the given set of existing or anticipated conditions. Many of these conditions can be influenced by people and hence are culture bound.

The competitive edge provided by *managerial experience in several countries* is rooted in cultural differences. If all environments were totally homogeneous, the ability of MNE management to bring in superior (e.g., more productive) practices would give it no advantage over local management. It is the differences in experiences internationally and the capacity to learn from one situation to be more effective in another that can give the MNE an advantage over purely local firms. Similarly, *international diversification,* to be an effective strategy, requires success in simultaneously operating in different political, economic, and cultural environments.

Two approaches to managing in a multicultural environment were discussed: the practical school, which says that good management practices are effective everywhere, and the cross-cultural school, which says that managers' performances vary with the cultural context within which managers function. The two schools come together if we acknowledge that managers everywhere share common values and certain skills, but adjust the management process and some managerial behaviors to accommodate cultural differences across operating environments.

The chapter then discussed some important cultural differences affecting managerial effectiveness. These included Hofstede's power distance, uncertainty avoidance, individualism/collectivism, and masculinity/femininity characterizations regarding different societies and their effects on management. They also included commentary on the more commonly identified cultural factors affecting management decision making, such as communications, education, achievement motivation, attitudes toward work, group identification, concepts of time, and hierarchical relationships.

The section on culture closed with a normative discussion on the need to be aware of the self-reference criterion (SRC) when making cross-cultural decisions. The SRC was identified as an important tool in analyzing cross-cultural problems and opportunities.

Next, the chapter turned to the issue of business ethics. Business ethics were discussed initially in terms of the bribery issue so typical of international businesspeople's concerns. Bribes are generally considered wrong in all societies, but nonetheless exist in some. "Grease payments," which are endemic to almost all developing countries, were differentiated from bribes. The need to avoid bribes puts MNEs in some countries at a competitive disadvantage, since local firms and other MNEs may well participate in making bribes.

Business ethics in the broader international context are concerned with the issues arising from doing business in two or more countries, each with its own laws and codes of ethics. Some of these issues appear straightforward, and there is considerable agreement by parties in all societies as to appropriate business behavior. Others may well reflect differences in values across different societies. The Eastern Air Lines drug-smuggling case illustrated the difficulties inherent in identifying and criticizing behavior believed to be either ethical or unethical.

QUESTIONS

1. Define the term *culture*. How can culture be ubiquitous and yet distinguishing?
2. Give an example of a business practice that you think reflects cultural origins.
3. Give an example of a cultural difference between two environments and show how it affects business.
4. After initially transferring its operating policies from the United States to France, Burger King (*a*) adjusted them to suit its own needs in light of the local cultural environment or (*b*) adjusted them to accommodate the local environment. With which of these two explanations do you agree? Could you agree with both?
5. How does culture relate to competitive advantage? Give an example of cultural differences destroying an MNE's competitive advantage. Give an example of cultural differences enhancing an MNE's competitive advantage.
6. Contrast the position of the practical school with that of the cross-cultural school as to the universality of effective management practices. Give some examples of practices that appear to be consistent with each school.
7. What is an SRC? Have you ever used an SRC when examining the behavior of others? How can international businesspeople put the SRC to work for them?
8. Distinguish between bribes and "grease payments." Why are bribes almost universally seen as unethical, whereas grease payments are acceptable as a necessary way of doing business? Can a grease payment ever become a bribe?
9. Are ethical standards transferable internationally?
10. Eastern Air Lines had some real problems in dealing with drug smugglers, as did the US government. What ethical issues were involved for Eastern? For the US government?

REFERENCES

Adler, Nancy J *International Dimensions of Organizational Behavior.* Boston: PWS-Kent Publishing Company, 1991.

Adler, Nancy J, and John L Graham. "Cross-Cultural Interaction: The International Comparison Fallacy." *Journal of International Business Studies,* Fall 1989, pp. 515–37.

Bartlett, Christopher A, and Sumantra Ghoshal. *Transnational Management.* Homewood, IL: Richard D Irwin, 1992. See especially Chapters 2 and 7.

Graham, J L, and D Andrews. "A Holistic Analysis of Cross-Cultural Business Negotiations." *Journal of Business Communications,* Fall 1985, pp. 63–77.

Jamieson, I. "The Concept of Culture and Its Relevance for an Analysis of Business Enterprise in Different Societies." *International Studies of Management and Organization* 12, no. 4 (1982–83), pp. 75–105.

Moller, J. Orstrom. *Technology and Culture in a European Context.* Copenhagen: Copenhagen Business School, Institute of International Economics and Management, 1991.

Paine, Lynn Sharp. "Managing for Organizational Integrity." *Harvard Business Review,* March–April 1994, pp. 106–17.

Ronen, Simcha. *Comparative and Multinational Management.* New York: John Wiley & Sons, 1986.

Shibagaki, Kazuo; Malcom Trevor; and Tetsuo Abo (eds.). *Japanese and European Management: Their International Adaptability.* Tokyo: University of Tokyo Press, 1989.

Studemann, Frederick. " 'Green' Bank Puts Principles First." *International Management,* October 1993, pp. 32–35.

NOTES

[1] E T Hall, *Beyond Culture* (Garden City, NY: Doubleday, 1977), p. 16.

[2] D P Mukerji, "Mahatma Gandhi's Views on Machines and Technology," in *Culture and Management,* ed. Ross A. Weber (Homewood, IL: Richard D. Irwin, 1969), p. 113. Reprinted from *International Social Science Bulletin 6,* no. 3 (Paris: UNESCO, 1954), pp. 411–23.

[3] Vern Terpstra, *International Dimensions of Marketing* (Boston: Kent Publishing, 1982), p. 162.

[4] Duane Kujawa, "Technology Strategy and Industrial Relations: Case Studies of Japanese Multinationals in the United States," *Journal of International Business Studies,* Winter 1983, pp. 9–22; Duane Kujawa, "Flexible Production Systems and Japanese Multinationals' Experiences in the U.S. Automotive Industry: Strategic Imperatives and Strategic Dividends" (Miami: International Business & Banking Institute, University of Miami, Discussion Paper Series, 1990).

[5] J. Stewart Black and Lyman W. Porter, "Managerial Behaviors and Job Performance: A Successful Manager in Los Angeles May Not Succeed in Hong Kong," *Journal of International Business Studies,* First Quarter 1991, pp. 99–113.

[6] Ibid., pp. 101–2.

[7] Edward L Miller, "The Selection Decision for an International Assignment: A Study of the Decision Maker's Behavior," *Journal of International Business Studies,* Spring 1973, pp. 49–65.

[8] Rosalie Tung, "Selection and Training of Personnel for Overseas Assignments," *Columbia Journal of World Business* 16 (1981), pp. 68–78; J Stewart Black, "Work-role Transition: A Study of American Expatriate Managers in Japan," *Journal of International Business Studies,* Summer 1988, pp. 274–91.

[9] Anant R Negandhi and S B Prasad, *Comparative Management* (New York: Appleton-Century-Crofts, 1971).

[10] Black and Porter, "Managerial Behaviors."

[11] Richard N Farmer and Barry M Richman, *Comparative Management and Economic Progress* (Homewood, IL: Richard D. Irwin, 1965).

[12] William G Ouchi, *Theory Z: How American Business Can Meet the Japanese Challenge* (New York: Avon Books, 1982).

[13] James C Abbeglen and George Stalk, Jr., *Kaisha: The Japanese Corporation* (New York: Basic Books, 1985).

[14] See, for example, George W England and R Lee, "The Relationship between Managerial Values and Managerial Success in the United States, Japan, India, and Australia," *Journal of Applied Psychology* 59 (1974), pp. 411–19; Bernard M Bass and Phillip C Berger, *Assessment of Managers: An International Comparison* (New York: Free Press, 1979); Frank Hawes and Daniel Kealey, "An Empirical Study of Canadian Technical Assistance," *International Journal of Intercultural Relations* 5 (1981), pp. 239–58; Brent Ruben and Daniel Kealey, "Behavioral Assessment of

Communication Competency and the Prediction of Cross-Cultural Adaptation," *International Journal of Intercultural Relations* 3 (1979), pp. 15–47.

[15]"Blunders Abroad," *Nation's Business,* March 1989, p. 54.

[16]David Ricks, Marilyn Y C Fu, and Jeffrey S Arpan, *International Business Blunders* (Columbus, OH: Grid, 1974).

[17]Geert Hofstede, "Managing Differences in the Multicultural Organization," in *Organizational Psychology,* ed. David Kolb et al. (Englewood Cliffs, NJ: Prentice Hall, 1984), pp. 309–31. (Note: This a reprint of Hofstede's original article by the same name, which appeared in *Organizational Dynamics,* Summer 1980.)

[18]Ibid.

[19]Simcha Ronen, *Comparative and Multinational Management* (New York: John Wiley & Sons, 1986), p. 97.

[20]David C McClelland, *The Achieving Society* (Princeton, NJ: D. Van Nostrand, 1961).

[21]Kemper Fullerton, "Calvinism and Capitalism," *Harvard Theological Review* 21 (1928), pp. 163–91. Reprinted in Ross A Weber, ed., *Culture and Management* (Homewood, IL: Richard D Irwin, 1969), pp. 91–111.

[22]Philip R Harris and Robert T Moran, *Managing Cultural Differences* (Houston: Gulf Publishing, 1979), p. 223.

[23]James A Lee, "Cultural Analysis in Overseas Operations," *Harvard Business Review,* March–April 1966, p. 110. For an extended discussion of Lee's model and the SRC, see Subash C Jain, *International Marketing Management* (Boston: Kent Publishing, 1984), pp. 208–11.

[24]Jain, *Marketing,* pp. 209–11.

[25]"Kumamoto, Arkansas," *The Economist,* April 9, 1994, p. 36.

[26]This case benefits from research conducted by Don L. Major, a doctoral student at the University of Miami's Graduate School of International Studies.

[27]"Drug War Drains Airline, Ships," *The Miami Herald,* January 16, 1989, p. 6.

[28]"The Eastern Connection; Coke Was a Frequent Flier," *Newsweek,* February 24, 1986, p. 8.

[29]"Drug War" and "Old Foes Are New Allies in Drug War," *The Miami Herald,* January 23, 1989, "Business Monday" sec., p. 8.

[30]"Drug War."

[31]Ibid.

[32]"Drug War"; "Firm Turns to Army-Style Surveillance," *The Miami Herald,* January 16, 1989, p. 6.

[33]"Drug War."

[34]Ibid.

NUMMI

New United Motor Manufacturing, Inc. (NUMMI), is a 50–50 joint venture between Toyota Motor Corporation and General Motors Corporation, respectively the third largest and largest automobile companies in the world. NUMMI, which began production in late 1984, assembles smaller-size cars designed by Toyota. It is located in Fremont, California, and employs about 2,500 people. The plant receives components and parts from Toyota plants and suppliers in Japan and from suppliers in the United States. The cars it assembles are sold to marketing organizations belonging to each of its parent companies.

Why a "NUMMI"?

NUMMI was conceived during the early 1980s, an admittedly tumultuous time for the auto industry in America. High energy prices and changing consumer preferences had resulted in an expanding demand for smaller, high-quality, more fuel-efficient cars. Japanese auto producers, Toyota among them, were operating under a program of Japanese export quotas on cars shipped to the United States, a program intended to (1) give US-based producers "breathing time" to adjust their production to meet market needs and federal standards on increased fuel efficiency and (2) encourage Japanese auto companies to establish production in the United States.

One could speculate at length about the factors that motivated Toyota and General Motors (GM) to join together to form NUMMI. At the time, however, articles in the press focused on two important considerations.

Toyota found the idea of producing in the United States attractive for short-term reasons, such as the quota, and for long-term reasons, such as its own business philosophy and the global competitive environment the auto industry faced. At the same time, it was interested in lowering the risks associated with beginning US production by bringing in a partner knowledgeable about US marketing and labor-management practices and by learning how to manage successfully in the United States. General Motors, on the other hand, was comparatively inexperienced in small-car production, and in the worker-management and vendor-supplier relationships needed to make such production cost competitive. It saw the joint venture with Toyota as an opportunity to

This case was written by Professor Duane Kujawa. Information on NUMMI's operations was obtained by the author during onsite research in September 1986. The research was part of a larger research project directed by Professor Tetsuo Abo at the University of Tokyo's Institute of Social Science and funded by the Toyota Foundation in Japan. The support from Professor Abo and the Toyota Foundation is gratefully acknowledged, as is the cooperation of New United Motor Manufacturing, Inc.

participate, in a substantial way, with one of the world's foremost cost-competitive producers of high-quality, small cars and to learn from the experience and transfer what it learned to other GM operations. From this perspective, General Motors' participation in NUMMI would serve to enhance GM's potential for future success in small-car production.

Thus, there were sound business reasons for creating NUMMI. Lowering the risks associated with possible future financial and operating commitments of impressive magnitudes motivated both Toyota and GM to come together in NUMMI.

But NUMMI involved other risks, risks that were intrinsic to its very nature. Could Toyota's Japan-based management system be implemented successfully in the United States? NUMMI would be breaking new ground and creating a distinctive, hybrid corporate culture reflecting both Japanese and American culturally based traits and culturally influenced institutions. At the beginning, neither GM nor Toyota was really sure that an experiment like NUMMI could succeed.

The GM-Toyota Contractual Relationship and Toyota's Responsibility for Running the Plant

The joint-venture agreement between GM and Toyota gave Toyota responsibility for operating the plant and established an eight-person board of directors consisting of four Toyota representatives and four GM representatives. Although the board is the ultimate decision-making body, it cannot by itself change the joint-venture contract. Toyota runs the plant, and this situation can be changed only if both Toyota and GM agree.

In implementing its responsibility for running the plant, Toyota has drawn on its experience with its production system in its Japanese plants, an experience that reflects substantial and compelling Toyota-specific and "Japanese" influences and characteristics. Those influences and characteristics determine the entire NUMMI system, a system that differs noticeably from that found in "traditional" US auto plants. To enable us to place differences in perspective, let us note first some of the fundamental features of the traditional US system as seen in auto and other types of plants over the years.[1]

The "Traditional" US System

The automobile assembly-line concept was built around the idea of engineering the production job down to a series of discrete worker tasks. The simpler these tasks, the better, since that made it possible to use less expensive workers. Production engineering made these workers more productive by providing them with specific operating methods and tools, many of special design. Production engineering also determined output standards and time standards against which to measure worker "efficiency." The quality control department checked to see whether the product produced was within a perceived tolerable quality range. Training was limited to what was necessary to make the worker more effective at his or her present job.

The traditional US auto plant was a unionized plant, and its work practices reflected a variety of influences regarding workers' and unions' interests in job control and income protection. For example, there were typically a large number of job classifications and wage levels reflecting the various tasks that workers performed. An employee usually worked strictly within his or her job classification. Critics of the traditional system believed it was "dehumanizing" and permitted no personal identification between the worker and the job, the product, or the company.

Relationships with suppliers were typically subject to periodic review and "rebidding." This meant vendors would prepare proposals, which might or might not be accepted, to supply certain components, made to the buyer's specifications and design configuration, for a particular model year. The relationship was tenuous and often temporary. If a new vendor came in with a lower price and was deemed reliable, a new supply relationship was created. Critics saw this behavior as denying the benefits of experience and promoting an orientation toward short-term profit on the part of vendors. Both of these effects were seen as impairing product quality. Vendors shipped on a periodic basis, and buyers routinely performed receiving inspection and testing before putting these shipments into their inventory.

Before leaving our discussion of the US system, it is important to note that many of its practices have distinctively American roots. Scientific management principles have long been part of the US industrial culture. They pertain to the procedures for engineering a job down to its simplest tasks. Social Darwinism (the "survival of the fittest") comes into play when workers' and vendors' interests are constantly subjected to competitive and impersonal market tests. "Extended hierarchical relationships" come into play when workers are merely "hands" that need to be managed and supported from above. The distribution of power reflects these relationships.

Toyota's Plant Management Approach at NUMMI

Visualize an automobile assembly line such as that used at NUMMI. As the line moves along, teams of employees work together on the car, installing, for example, the battery and battery cables or certain dashboard components.

Each team is responsible for its increment of work on each car. Quite important, each team is also responsible for assigning specific tasks among its members, and these assignments may rotate hourly, daily, weekly, or whatever as the team wishes. Each team sets its own task sequence and is responsible for the quality of its work.

If a team is having difficulty with the number of tasks it has to complete during the time it has the car, the allocation of tasks within the team or among teams may be changed. The key is to have each team working productively on each car during its allotted time.

The members of each NUMMI team generally get together about 10 or 15 minutes before the starting time to exercise as a group and to socialize. These activities take place at a "team room," which is right on the shop floor. The team room also serves as a meeting place when work-related issues need attention. Each team uses a structured, systematic technique for identifying and resolving any scheduling and quality problems that arise.

As expected, training is important and varied at NUMMI. Workers must be able to do all the jobs within their team's jurisdiction. They are also encouraged to work occasionally on other teams and to learn the jobs of those teams too. There is only one pay grade, or job classification, for production workers at NUMMI. All production workers are paid the same wage after 18 months of service. There are also three higher pay classifications, one for maintenance technicians, the others for tool and die and tool and die tryout personnel.

NUMMI utilizes the "just-in-time" inventory system that Toyota developed in Japan. All components, parts, and subassemblies flow together in a continuous process paced by the main assembly line. Suppliers deliver their products to the

NUMMI plant on a nearly continuous basis, in some cases every few hours or so. There is minimal receiving inventory and little receiving testing or inspection of supplier-provided parts.

NUMMI works with qualified suppliers on a long-term basis. The team approach is again key here. Suppliers work on the design and quality of their products, with substantial assistance from NUMMI when required. Purchase relationships are of indefinite duration. Suppliers know what is expected of them in terms of product schedule and quality. They also know that NUMMI will help them solve problems.

Some Cultural Dimensions of NUMMI's Approach

Ringi is the Japanese participatory approach to decision making. Communication with the objective of understanding is a hallmark of *Ringi*. This approach underlies NUMMI's team system. A corollary of the Japanese participatory approach is that problems are identified and solved at the bottom levels in the hierarchy, which possess a detailed knowledge of whatever the situation demands. Management does not impose solutions; workers don't pass problems up.

Kaizen is the Japanese concept of constant improvement. The plant is a "living" institution. It is constantly learning and changing. Work teams always focus on how to improve what they are doing. Job rotation and cross-training, which give workers a more complete perspective on the production process, are relevant here.

The concept of "purity of intent" is rooted in Japanese culture.[2] Individuals are seen as being meant to think for themselves and to take action, sometimes significant action, if that is deemed to be needed. For example, any NUMMI worker can stop the assembly line if he or she believes this is necessary for safety, quality, or other important purposes. And management would recognize the action as acceptable even if it turned out to be the wrong thing to do, since the worker's intent was correct. From the management perspective, however, the support of management and the other team members ensures that the action would never turn out to be the wrong thing to do.

How Has NUMMI Been Doing?

Before assessing NUMMI's performance, it is important to note that there are really four partners in this joint venture, not just Toyota and GM. The United Automobile Workers (UAW) and the employees themselves are also very important partners. The UAW has been especially accommodative in developing "new" ways of doing things. For example, it has accepted wage systems and pay classifications that depart considerably from the traditional ones. The work environment at NUMMI is much less adversarial than that of its predecessor. The evidence is solid on this: At any given time, five or six grievances (i.e., workers' complaints against management that allege a violation of the labor agreement) are usually outstanding at NUMMI. Yet a few years back, when the same plant was run by a US auto company (and eventually shut down), the outstanding grievances typically totaled at least 1,000. Absenteeism at NUMMI is about 5 to 6 percent; it was 20 percent or more under the prior operator. Interestingly, about 80 percent of the workers now covered by the labor agreement at NUMMI also worked at the plant under the prior operator.

How has NUMMI been doing? Quite well, apparently, in terms of its union-management and employee relations. Moreover, the Toyota production system and methods of work force organization have been implemented at NUMMI and are operating well.

Compared to Toyota plants in Japan, NUMMI is also doing quite well. Product quality at NUMMI is as high as that at Toyota's plants in Japan. Worker efficiency is close to that of Toyota's plants in Japan and higher than was originally expected. Because employee turnover rates are higher in California than in Japan and because NUMMI's work force has less experience with the Toyota system than has Toyota's work force in Japan, management believes worker efficiency at NUMMI is about as high as possible.

NOTES

[1]The author stresses that the discussion of conditions in US plants is indeed about "traditional" conditions. We should note here that in contrast to "traditional" conditions, many cooperative innovations, developed by both the union and management, have been finding their way into US auto plants.

[2]S Prakash Sethi, Nobuaki Namiki, and Carl L. Swanson, *The False Promise of the Japanese Miracle* (Marshfield, MA: Pitman Publishers, 1984), p. 15.

12

Strategy and Organization Structure

Strategy involves goal setting and the planning needed to attain goals. Organization structure involves grouping activities and allocating management decision-making authority among different operating units, or among levels of management within units. This chapter looks at both of these interrelated subjects. The main goals of the chapter are to:

1. Define *organization structure* and note its relationship to both strategy and the business environment.

2. Review briefly the essence of strategic management and planning in the MNE.

3. Determine the rationales for and the key organizational features of ethnocentric, polycentric, and geocentric structures.

4. Examine the different organization forms that characterized MNEs as MNEs evolved and the rationales behind those structures.

5. Investigate the impact of today's highly competitive global environment on MNEs' operating structures and organizational relationships.

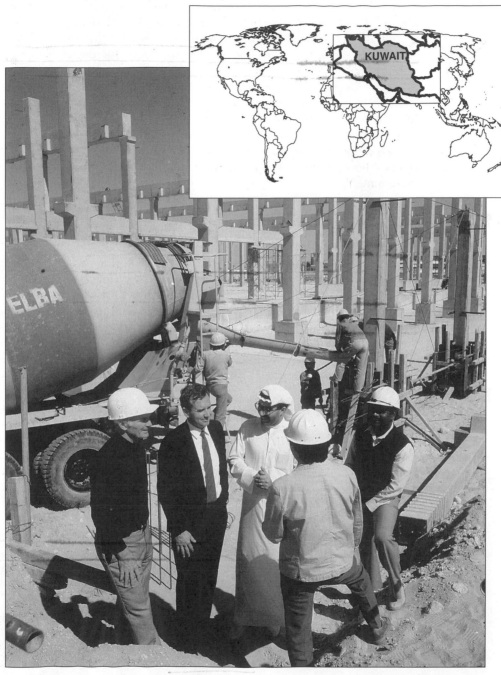

Kuwaiti businessmen, in both native and Western dress, talk with construction workers on a building site.
©James Willis/Tony Stone Images

INTRODUCTION

Chapter 5, "Developing a Global Strategy," discussed the importance of strategy and control to competitive advantage, the assignment of strategy to strategic business units (SBUs), and multinational firms' four basic, generic strategies: broad-line competition, global focus, national focus, and protected niche. This chapter builds on the content of that chapter and deals with strategy and organization structure—that is, the manner in which firms, at both the MNE and SBU levels, group activities and allocate authority for decision making among different operating units or among levels of management within units.

Topics discussed in this chapter include strategy, the basic nature of the strategic management process, the kinds of decisions typically taken at the MNE level that significantly affect organization structure, the generic types of strategy and structure combinations employed by firms involved in international business, the evolution of organizational structure within the MNE, and some important organizational issues confronting MNEs in an increasingly competitive operating environment.

STRATEGY DEFINED

Strategy

Strategy involves goal setting and the planning needed to attain goals.[1] It also involves translating plans into programs and monitoring programs to ensure that they remain goal directed. Strategy is pertinent to two levels within the enterprise: the corporate level and the strategic business unit (SBU) level.

At the corporate level, two primary considerations in setting strategy are synergy and balance. The different SBUs in the corporate "portfolio" must realize some operational benefit, or **synergy,** derived from their common corporate parentage. For example, automatic welding technology (including the use of robots) developed for use in Nissan's plants in Japan is also used at the Nissan plant in Tennessee.

Alternatively, or in addition, different SBUs may complement, or **balance,** one another in terms of cash needs or cash flows. For example, stable and profitable cigarette sales produce substantial revenues for the tobacco operations at RJR Nabisco that provide the financial resources needed to implement the firm's current global product diversification strategy. In this sense, tobacco sales in the United States can be seen as enabling the food products group to expand in Europe or Latin America.

For the corporate level to serve some competitively meaningful role, either synergy or balance must be present. If synergy or balance were not present, the SBU would bear the burden of sustaining the corporate level without receiving any benefit in return. In such circumstances, the corporate structure, serving no economic or commercial purpose, would be forced by a competitive marketplace to disintegrate.

Strategy at the SBU level is operations driven. It is concerned with competition, technology, production, logistics, marketing, taxes, and so on. Scale economies, learning curve effects, and similar phenomena are especially pertinent. Managers at the SBU levels are more market driven, are more concerned with the typical management functions, and are typically responsible for the "bottom line." Consider the Burger King franchisee in Venezuela. Management there is on the "firing line" day in and day out, but it relies heavily on Burger King US, the franchisor, for direction on product quality control, production techniques, new products, and so on.

STRATEGIC MANAGEMENT AND PLANNING IN THE MNE

Chapter 5, "Developing a Global Strategy," deals with strategy alternatives, but it doesn't cover the strategic management process as experienced in multinational firms. This topic is addressed here. We look first at the strategic management and planning process and then at strategic issues pertinent to MNEs. The process, we admit, is not so distinctive when comparing MNEs to purely domestic firms. In contrast, however, the issues are indeed distinctive.

Strategic Management: The Basics[2]

Strategic management is a process that can be conceptualized in terms of six fundamental steps, as shown in Figure 12–1.

① Formulating the mission statement defines why the organization exists. Business organizations exist to make profits, but typically their mission statements go beyond this purpose and indicate how the firm will pursue profits compared to how other firms might do so. For example, "Flying the friendly skies of United" suggests that United Air Lines wants to compete on the basis of high-quality service. The **mission statement** thus begins to define the firm.

Determining strategic objectives and formulating the master strategy answer three basic questions: Where are we? Where do we want to be? How do we get there?[3] These answers, in turn, build on a detailed analysis of the firm's internal strengths and weaknesses and of the external opportunities and threats that confront it. (The literature refers to this as the **SWOT analysis.**) Consistent with the mission statement and in light of the SWOT analysis, the firm then sets its ② **strategic objectives** and its ③ **master strategy,** the basic blueprint on how to accomplish the strategic objectives.

④ Setting the organization and implementing the operating plan constitute the implementation phase of the strategic management process. Setting the organization involves organizational structuring. It allocates the tasks that must be done to implement the master strategy, and it defines responsibilities and allocates power within the organization. Implementing the ⑤ **operating plan** involves short-term planning, setting operating targets, determining budgets, and so on.

⑥ **Control,** the final step in the strategic management process, consists of monitoring strategy implementation, measuring performance against preestablished standards, and taking corrective action when necessary. (Various approaches to strategic control are discussed in Chapter 5.)

FIGURE 12–1

The Strategic Management Process

ADDED DIMENSION

Matsushita's Mission and the Beginning of Strategy Implementation

Mission statements and master strategies can be vague concepts at first. To clarify the concepts a bit, let's look at what Matsushita, the maker of Panasonic and Quasar products, is and what it says about its mission.

Today Matsushita is "home" to 250,000 employees worldwide. It produces and sells over 14,000 products in more than 130 countries. Its global sales total over $58 billion. Traditionally Matsushita manufactured consumer electronics products, but as a result of its pursuit of new products and technologies, it now serves industrial, office, and communications markets as well.

Matsushita's basic mission statement is its creed:
Through our industrial activities, we strive to foster progress, to promote the general welfare of society, and to devote ourselves to furthering the development of world culture.

Matsushita's more specific mission is to focus on "key areas of technological growth which will have a tremendous impact on society in the near future." These are communications and information-processing technologies, semiconductor components and materials technologies, advanced video and audio technologies, and production engineering technologies such as robotics and factory automation.

Visualize Matsushita as the high-tech, R&D-oriented company that it is, and, from a global perspective, try to identify broadly the strengths and weaknesses such a company might have in addressing issues such as new-product development and the understanding of specific market segments. ∎

Source: Information abstracted from *Matsushita Electric Corporation of America,* an undated brochure provided by company officials; *Fortune* "International 500", July 26, 1993.

Strategic Issues in the MNE

Strategic issues are those that have long-term implications. Therefore, they most often involve risk assessment and risk taking. What are these issues from the MNE perspective? The more important issues are identified in the discussion that follows.

MNEs must decide which countries and regions are most appropriate for business expansion. Then they must ask: How should this expansion be implemented—that is, which product(s) should be marketed and/or produced in the country? What is the best entry form—exporting, local production via a wholly owned subsidiary, joint venture (with a foreign or domestic partner), or a licensing relationship?

MNEs must also decide on a product strategy:

What are its global products?

What is the extent of product adaptation required by local markets?

How can the MNE network best respond to the production synergies evident from product standardization while responding to the distinctive consumer characteristics that local markets may well dictate?

Where should MNEs do their financial sourcing? New York, London, Tokyo . . . ?

How should it handle risks, such as exchange risks and political risks?

When and under what circumstances should the MNE pull out of a country?

Returning to entry strategy and form, when are strategic alliances appropriate, and should such alliances ever be made with government-owned companies?

What should the executive development programs consist of at both the corporate and subsidiary levels?

Several other questions are certainly pertinent:

How distinctive (or universal) are the market determinants of product, promotion, distribution, and other policies?

What products, product cores, and component parts can be produced most economically on an internationally integrated basis? On a country or regional basis?

If scale economies in production and marketing are optimal for relatively small markets, what opportunities for product differentiation and competitiveness exist?

How can the product and the production and marketing functions be disaggregated to allow for an effective blending of scale economies and learning curve effects and the differentiation necessary for the MNE to respond to market peculiarities?

These questions, most of which are decided at the corporate level, cover a variety of fundamental issues. Some of these issues are pertinent to the MNE because they involve crossing country, market, or cultural boundaries; others apply because they involve dealing in international markets (e.g., foreign exchange or capital markets). One thing is certain: These issues surely present the MNE with a more complex business environment. But they also provide the MNE with business opportunities from which it alone is strategically poised to benefit.

THREE CLASSIC STRATEGIES/ STRUCTURES: ETHNOCENTRIC, POLYCENTRIC, AND GEOCENTRIC

Rutenberg sees the "two economic reasons that sustain most international diversification" as *experience curves* (synergy) and *risk spreading* (balance).[4] Experience curves, in the extreme, would lead to globally centralized power, or ethnocentric organization. Risk spreading, on the other hand, requires a portfolio of reasonably unrelated, globally distributed subsidiaries—a polycentric organization.[5] Why do these two strategies lead to these particular structures, and what do the strategies mean operationally? A description of Perlmutter's classic MNE structures helps to answer this question. Figure 12–2 diagrams the three structures.

The Ethnocentric Organization

The Rationale for Ethnocentrism Experience curve effects result in declining costs of operations (e.g., production, marketing, and distribution). These effects require standardization, which allows learning through repetition, which results in increased efficiency. In the aerospace industry, an 80 percent experience curve seems to be the historical standard in manufacturing. This means that every time cumulative production doubles, costs of production decline to 80 percent of the previous level. The **experience curve effect** is thus readily seen as an important competitive weapon. Standardized production lowers costs of production and

FIGURE 12–2

The Three Classic MNE
Strategies/Structures

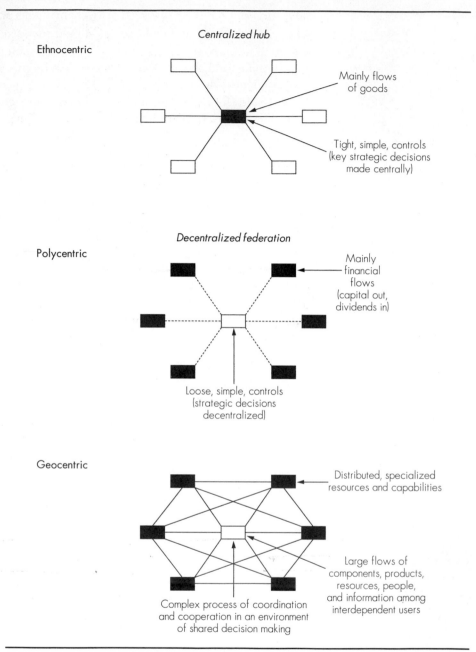

Ethnocentric

Centralized hub

Mainly flows
of goods

Tight, simple, controls
(key strategic decisions
made centrally)

Polycentric

Decentralized federation

Mainly
financial
flows
(capital out,
dividends in)

Loose, simple, controls
(strategic decisions
decentralized)

Geocentric

Distributed, specialized
resources and capabilities

Large flows of
components, products,
resources, people,
and information among
interdependent users

Complex process of coordination
and cooperation in an environment
of shared decision making

Source: Adapted from Christopher A Bartlett and Sumantra Ghoshal, *Transnational Management* (Homewood, IL:
Richard D Irwin, 1992), chap. 5.

enhances profit margins and competitiveness. For the MNE, competitive success
entails effectively transferring what was learned in one location to other locations.
Doing this positions the MNE further down the experience curve and gives it a
competitive advantage over firms operating only in local markets. In Chapter 2,
this effect was labeled "managerial experience in several countries."

Ethnocentrism in Operation   The strategy/structure implications here are fairly straight-forward. The multinational enterprise operates on global product mandates and is typically organized at the top on a product division basis. This is a niche strategy made viable by the presence of a globally identifiable market segment that permits, for example, standardization in production and, for the MNE able to transfer experience internationally, the delivery of a competitive edge.

Ethnocentrism, as a management core strategy, carries with it distinctive organizational and operational characteristics.[6] As already noted, the organization is divisionalized at the top on a product basis. The divisions manage their own inventories and logistic flows internationally. Products are designed for the home (parent company) market and manufactured in large factories located where costs are lowest. These factories serve both domestic and export markets. In this environment, products are not likely to be adapted, in any substantial way, to reflect foreign market differences. Both internal and external pressures exist for uniform, global product pricing. The finance function is typically controlled at the MNE level, and profits remitted to the parent company are the bottom line in evaluating foreign investment opportunities.

Ethnocentrism, like any strategy, has the potential to create certain kinds of problems as it is being implemented. In its eagerness to take advantage of experience effects, management may overlook market niches that are best served by products adapted to satisfy localized preferences. Moreover, these overlooked niches may be where future market growth is concentrated, to the potential detriment of the firm's predominant position in its well-established market. That experience curve benefits are proportionately larger in the earlier stages of production (i.e., with newer products) magnifies the significance of this problem.

Another difficulty may arise when customers in a particular area or country see representatives of the various company product groups operating under different policies. Ethnocentrism can result in customers' perceptions of a disorganized company presence and, more important, in their disaffection with one company division because its policies appear less beneficial to the customer than the policies of another company division.

Yet a third problem of ethnocentrism is that it can lead to management self-assuredness that is overly insular. This, in turn, can lead to difficulties in certain social and operating areas, such as government relations and industrial relations.[7]

The Polycentric Organization

The Rationale for Polycentrism   In contrast to the ethnocentric MNE, the **polycentric organization** finds that marketing or production considerations favor geographic diversification. Nuances of local markets mandate a unique product strategy for each market. Alternatively, the production technology may be such that optimal scale economies are realized with small production runs, especially with regard to total market size, or that scale economies are insufficient to offset the freight and other costs that exporting to the market would entail. Hence, in the extreme case, the polycentric MNE consists of a set of freestanding SBUs that have very little, if anything, to offer one another operationally.

Polycentrism in Operation   What, then, are the benefits to these SBUs of their common affiliation with the parent company? Actually, the benefits can be significant, but they must be appraised at the MNE level. They arise from portfolio effects on the one hand and from profit maximization on a global basis on the other hand. This latter point relates to the ability of the SBUs in a polycentric organization to price more aggressively in different, geographically segmented markets.

How do portfolio effects operate to the benefit of the MNE? In marketing, for example, demand conditions may well vary from country to country. A slump in France may be offset by a boom in England. This results in less variation in total MNE sales and earnings and a lower cost of capital. Demand for certain products may develop and mature in different countries at different times. This allows MNEs to extend product life cycles. In manufacturing, the production structure of the polycentric MNE is more dispersed than that of the ethnocentric MNE. Thus, risks are diversified in the polycentric structure and, because of portfolio effects, are lower than they would be otherwise at the MNE level. For example, a strike has less of an effect on overall production in the polycentric MNE than in the ethnocentric MNE. This difference would also hold true for the demise of an important supplier or a shift to a more contentious political environment.

The key point with regard to profit maximization in the polycentric structure is that maximum profits result from the freedom to price according to what individual markets will bear. (Picture a market in which you could price your product according to its "value" to each customer. You would vary your price by customer and would thus be enriched. In fact, your supply curve would exactly coincide with the market demand curve. Happiness!) This strategy is viable, of course, only where geographically defined markets are indeed separable and distinctive.

The polycentric organization has its drawbacks, too. Since the SBUs are separated, and perhaps jealously so, there tends to be little communication among them and little opportunity for them to learn from one another. Potential synergies are never realized. Moreover, if one accepts the notion that product markets are becoming increasingly internationalized, the geographically segmented customer base essential for polycentrism could be seen as a generally vanishing phenomenon. Where does this leave the polycentric organization? In the forefront of a difficult but necessary adjustment process!

The Geocentric Organization

The Rationale for Geocentrism   An alternative to the ethnocentric and polycentric organizations is the **geocentric organization.** It has a global perspective, and it seeks to maximize total global returns to the MNE. It is especially relevant to the global matrix structure, to be discussed later, and to the multiproduct firm with a niche strategy based on the firm's ability to deal successfully with distinctive markets that require unique products—all of this balanced against the firm's multiproduct capabilities and its desire to benefit from scale economies.

Geocentrism in Operation   The geocentric organization is typically a matrix organization. The markets of the MNE are distinctive enough to require a distinctive product response across countries or regions. This denies the MNE the opportunity to benefit from ethnocentrism. On the other hand, enough commonalities exist—for example, in the customer base or in component parts or product cores—to permit scale economies and experience curve effects. This precludes the opportunity to benefit from polycentrism. Geocentrism, then, is a global concept attuned to local market needs. (It calls for the firm to "think global, but act local.")

The geocentric organization is often defined as a hybrid that includes elements of geographic and product structures. Its objective is to blend these two elements into a competitive, profitable market presence. Hence the matrix structure—and a critical need for internal communication and for a corporatewide perspective on what constitutes success. These are difficult needs to address, especially if the MNE has traditionally been ethnocentric (centralized power) or polycentric (dispersed power). Often the need for geocentrism evolves as product markets mature. Market trends are, in a sense, forcing that evolution. The transition from ethnocentrism or polycentrism to geocentrism is thus typically a real phenomenon addressed by many MNEs, but a totally geocentric firm may be hard to find. The transition is certainly not a simple one.

The preceding commentary on ethnocentrism, polycentrism, and geocentrism in MNEs is highlighted in Table 12–1.

Having identified some of the environmental pressures (both internal and external to the MNE) that influence organization structure in the generic categories of ethnocentric, polycentric, and geocentric, we now turn to a more detailed description of alternative organization structures.

STRUCTURAL CHANGE AND THE EVOLUTION OF THE MNE

Much of the growth of multinational enterprises in the manufacturing and service sectors has taken place over the past four decades. The pattern of that growth was traced to some extent in the earlier chapters, especially Chapters 3 and 4, in the discussions of the international product cycle relative to international trade and foreign direct investment. Further consideration of the product life cycle (PLC) model as it illustrates organizational change and key strategy points would certainly be useful in the present context. Let's turn back the clock to the mid-1950s or so and examine the roots and growth process of what has become the modern MNE. (To facilitate discussion, the following focuses only on firms in the manufacturing sector.)

ADDED DIMENSION

Ford Motor Company: From Poly to Geo and Beyond!

Prior to the 1970s, Ford–US, Ford–UK, and Ford–Germany were really separate and distinctive operating units. They all designed and built cars for their local, or close-by, markets. Then, as the 1970s unfolded, Ford realized scale economies in design and production were becoming available as production technologies were being developed that meant larger production runs at lower total production costs, and consumers' tastes were converging, especially regarding the European Community and, to a lesser extent, Europe and the United States in the small-car segment of the US market.

During the 1980s, the commonalities in consumers' preferences solidified substantially within Europe, forcing additional integration between Ford's German and British operations and among other Ford plants established in France, Belgium, and Spain to supply components and assemblies to Ford–UK and Ford–Germany. In reality, the polycentric structure of pre-1970 times is gone. Today Ford of Europe is the effective organizational entity! ■

TABLE 12-1

The Three Classic MNE Strategies/Structures Compared

	Basic Rationale	Key Features/Implications
1. The Ethnocentric MNE	Cost cutting via learning curve effects transmitted by parent to subsidiaries	Company strives for globally standardized products and production processes Company targets market niches that are similar internationally Strong headquarters involvement at all levels Company too often overlooks new markets; extensive communication needed (that is hard to provide cross-culturally and over long distances)
2. The Polycentric MNE	Cost/risk reduction via portfolio effects at the parent level; agility to respond to local market conditions	Company (including subsidiaries) thrives on product and market distinctiveness in different countries Company enjoys maximum freedom in product pricing (because markets are separate and distinctive internationally) Internal communication not important; few internal transfers of knowledge internationally Long-term prognosis for the polycentric MNE is negative; product markets becoming increasingly similar internationally
3. The Geocentric MNE	Ethnocentric and polycentric pressures balanced in favor of optimizing the MNE system	Company is typically organized on a matrix basis—product and geographic divisions Best structure for handling changing market preferences and new products Internal communication critical Key personnel developed over the long term and on the basis of global experience

Setting the Stage

Following World War II and into the 1950s, income levels advanced substantially in the United States, giving rise to significant and expanding levels of discretionary spending by US citizens. Producers increasingly responded by offering products designed to satisfy new and expanding market segments with distinctive tastes and preferences. This, in turn, led to product differentiation as a basis for competitive strategy and to market segments in which income levels were important determinants of demand characteristics. These market segments, almost by definition, were not highly competitive initially. For these and other reasons, oligopolistic market structures were spawned; a small number of producers served (shared) the market and enjoyed above-average returns.

At this point, there was nothing international about the firm. It was busy learning about and responding to domestic market opportunities. Organizations were often structured on a product or functional basis, with power centers likely to be located in engineering and manufacturing or perhaps even marketing. Organization charts were typically like those to be presented here. The **functional structure,** shown in Figure 12–3, was usually the first one to be implemented.

There was a single product or narrow product line, and management power clearly ascended the pyramidal organization structure. The functional structure facilitated internal technical and marketing coordination. As more numerous and more distinctive market niches developed, so did product lines and the need for the firm to move to a **product structure** (see Figure 12–4). This organizational

FIGURE 12–3

Functional Structure

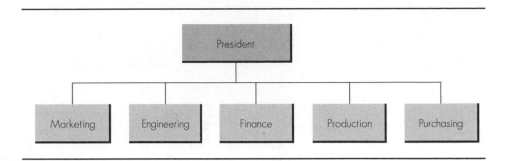

form allowed the firm to segment internal operations to match them with product and market differences. It continued to facilitate internal coordination. As in the functional structure, power in the product structure was hierarchically defined.

Fortuitous Exports

At this time, products that were successful in the US market were also found to be in demand in foreign markets such as in Canada and Western Europe, where income levels and income-related tastes and preferences were similar to those in the United States. Research showed that exports to these markets were often unsolicited. This implied that intermediaries, typically either foreign or domestic firms that were specialists in exporting, with knowledge of what US producers were bringing to markets and what would sell overseas (mainly in advanced industrial societies), were creating export markets by requesting products from US suppliers.[8]

Firms did not systematically exploit export markets during this period. Exports were handled by the domestic divisions and frequently were viewed simply as orders placed by yet another customer—that happened to be located in New York, London, or some other port city—who was handling the shipping of products to customers in foreign markets. At this point, there was still nothing international about the firm from the organizational perspective. But from the operational and financial perspectives, the firm began to depend on exports.

FIGURE 12–4

Product Structure

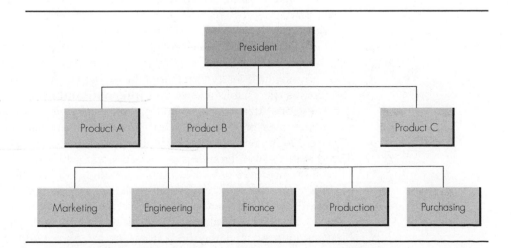

FIGURE 12–5

The Export Department:
Exports Worthwhile but
Not Significant

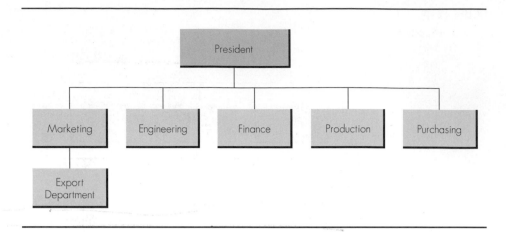

Deliberate Exports

As **accidental exports** attracted the attention of management, firms became involved in direct exporting. Exports had become important, accounting for a goodly share of production and profits. Company sales representatives began calling on overseas customers, but product modifications to secure foreign sales were minimal, and sales contracts were typically denominated in dollars. In these earlier times, exports by US pharmaceutical companies, for example, typically involved products packaged for the US market and were priced in dollars.

By now the firm had established an **export department,** often within marketing, which was initially concerned with logistics–packaging, shipping, letters of credit, insurance, and so on (see Figure 12–5). The customers of this department were often viewed as less familiar and less reliable than those of the domestic divisions, so to some extent the department had to negotiate with the domestic divisions to secure product for export sales. Thus, foreign sales were given a lower priority than domestic sales. In fact, during periods of robust home demand when production was pushing capacity limits, it was not unusual to cut exports so that domestic customers could be satisfied. A modern-day illustration of this greater emphasis on the domestic market is provided by the steel minimills in the United States, which often export excess supply rather than selling off inventory at depressed prices at home—a practice that would spoil their domestic market.

But with the continued expansion of foreign sales, often accompanied by intensifying home front competition as other domestic producers cut into the firm's innovative lead, corporate attitudes began to change. In some cases, the result was the establishment of an **international division** (still concerned only with exports) that operated on a par with the domestic divisions and had some influence over product design, availability, and price in the export markets (see Figure 12–6). Gradually, as its volume grew the international division accumulated some power. From being a product and schedule "taker," this division now had influence over production schedules and product allocation and was able to justify minor product modifications necessary for export success. Singer Company and its famous sewing machine operations grew this way.

We can draw several conclusions at this point. Perhaps the most important is that exports are affecting the bottom line in a measurable way. Organizationally,

FIGURE 12-6

The International
Department: Exports a
Substantial Part of
Company Sales

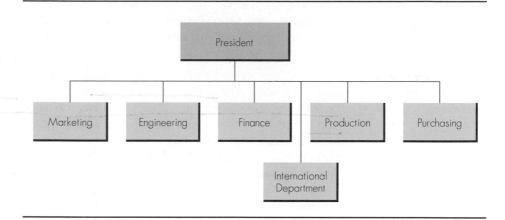

the international division has credibility. Now the firm's strategy is to serve both domestic and foreign markets with domestically based production. Both domestic and export markets are valued for their profit contributions. This means more funds are available for R&D, for capital investment, and for dividends. These funds strengthen the firm regardless of where it operates. Thus, success in the export market is seen as important for success in the domestic market. Serving both domestic and foreign markets rather than just domestic markets often results in scale economies in production or research and engineering and thus lower product unit costs. Export market success enhances domestic market success in this regard too.

Expanded Competition and the Competitive Response

Competition continued to build in the domestic market as other firms imitated the success formulas of the original firms. For the same reason, competition developed in the export markets too. Domestically, the innovative firms had responded by defining market segments more precisely and bringing more varied products to the marketplace. The result was that product lines grew, enabling these firms to enjoy some level of above-average profits over a now extended period of time. In this earlier period, the vulnerability of the MNE in the foreign markets was exposed because far-flung logistic and management networks were costly and products sold overseas were not fully adapted to the consumer preferences of the foreign market. Competitors producing in Western Europe and Canada, for example, were able to imitate the competitive essence of a product and yet package the product to meet distinctive preferences of consumers there. They produced and marketed within their local markets (which were export markets to the MNE). The US MNEs were at a product disadvantage—and possibly a cost disadvantage too, since they faced tariffs, international shipping costs, and other charges not imposed on the foreign competition. They responded by opening plants in their export markets.

These foreign direct investments were significant in many ways. They allowed the US MNEs to get inside tariff barriers, and they eliminated transcontinental shipping and insurance costs. Perhaps more important, they facilitated significant product adaptation, a fine-tuning of product design in response to distinctive use conditions in foreign markets. Also important, as these overseas subsidiaries gained experience, the "new" products developed to meet increasingly competitive domestic markets were channeled into overseas markets. This gave the subsidiaries competitive strengths that reflected the positive synergistic effects associated with a multinational enterprise.

Structural Implications of Foreign Direct Investment

Putting plants overseas affected the "mindset" of MNE management in several important ways. The balance sheet exposure of having assets placed in foreign countries required that top management pay closer attention to foreign operations. The transfer (export) of product and/or process technologies, required initially to get the foreign plant on line, and the ongoing transfer of component parts between the parent and the **foreign subsidiary** meant, in some cases, substantial attention to foreign operations by lower-level management and technical staff. The firm's marketing activities, which began with exporting, were now adapting to new logistics patterns and enhanced sales potential. The production and distribution pipeline was shorter now, and the firm was able to be more price competitive. The subsidiary's sales revenues were definitely denominated in local currency, as were many of the costs of its operations. Parent company nationals were typically on assignment at the subsidiary. Local management now had considerable control over production, marketing, and other functions and had more flexibility to respond effectively to competitive opportunities in the marketplace. The firm's strategic objectives at this time were to establish a solid market presence by building on the technical, financial, and managerial expertise provided by the parent and to eventually expand market share.

Organizationally, these early days of foreign direct investment saw a group of geographically defined subsidiaries reporting to the parent through an international division (see Figure 12–7). Often this international division was organizationally parallel to the product or functional divisions. The structure was a hybrid, with responsibilities allocated between domestic and international via a set of nondistinctive categories. It was a logical structure, though, in terms of historical evolution. The international division was already in place before the subsidiaries were established. Its roots went back to the days of deliberate exports. Figure 12–7 typifies the international division within a general product division structure with manufacturing subsidiaries in several countries.

FIGURE 12–7

Foreign Direct Investment: The Early Days

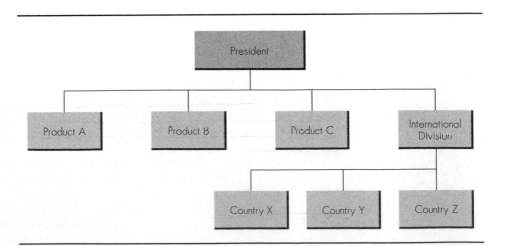

FIGURE 12–8

The Global Structure:
Narrow Product Line

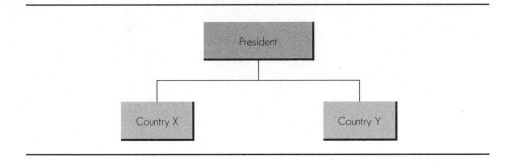

The Drive to Structural Maturity

As scale economies in production grew and markets were developed outside the traditional geographic domain of each subsidiary, the business effectiveness of the geographically defined subsidiary declined. In some MNEs, subsidiaries in different countries could even be found competing with one another in some third markets. If product lines were fairly narrow, product groups with both domestic and foreign jurisdictions were typically formed (see Figure 12–8). If broad product lines were the rule, the **matrix structure** was the answer. In this case, country- or subcountry-level managers reported to both area and product managers (see Figure 12–9). It was their job to balance global or regional rationalization needs against local market needs or nuances. They were "company specialists" rather than just market or technical specialists. The organization charts in Figures 12–8 and 12–9 illustrate these two structures.

It should be noted that some companies do not prefer the matrix-type structure, and rightly so. Single-product companies and companies with a dominant, distinctive product (such as Coca-Cola) need not evolve into the matrix structure. Product proliferation, on the other hand, almost invariably leads to a matrix organization. The strategy implications here are fairly straightforward. The subsidiary is an extension of the parent, and it benefits from the parent's market dominance in a single or narrow product line. The multiproduct firm, on the other hand, must find the niche that requires product uniqueness but still allows it to gain from positive linkages among its products and markets. Success here involves fine-tuning and considerable knowledge of both company capabilities and market opportunities. The matrix structure makes possible the "team" response required for success in situations where no one person has all the knowledge or all the information needed.

The Driving Force of the Market: The Rationale of Change

The preceding discussion on the evolution of the MNE and the accompanying structural changes may appear to imply that management is consistently reactive, that it merely adapts to changes in its competitive environments, at times even begrudgingly. This conclusion would be fairly accurate for the emergent MNE. It does not mean, however, that change is made without intelligence or that management's behavior is without a rationale. The marketplace conveys a lot of information!

By participating in and paying attention to the market, management receives important feedback on the commercial propriety of its behavior. Accidental exports, for example, give the firm important information not only on the marketability of the product overseas but also on market potential, pricing

FIGURE 12–9

The Global Matrix
Structure

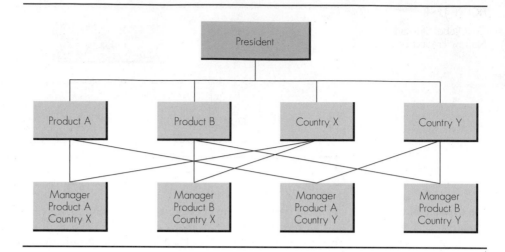

strategy, characteristics of customers (including their motivations for buying), locations of customers, distribution channels, and so on. Also, quite important, most business organizations are justifiably cautious. They just don't throw funding into projects unless they have a reasonable expectation of success. Success in an initially limited market justifies (and helps fund) expansion. It gives the project and the project team credibility. It allows management to compete intelligently with other potential users of the firm's limited funds. Put somewhat differently, it would be fair to say structure does not change without reason.

Changes in the marketplace provide a rationale for changing structure. The successful (lasting) firm responds properly to those changes.

No One Universally Best Organization Structure

Some may interpret the preceding discussion to suggest that the matrix organization structure, ostensibly compatible with the geocentric approach, is superior to the others. One cannot draw this conclusion. The best structure will be a function of firm size, extent of foreign operations, product nature, product line, availability of financial and/or human resources, market conditions, and so on.

For example, the small firm—a new entrant to the market—would likely reflect the early stages of organizational development for international operations. The simple product or functional structure would most likely be appropriate. In this case, the size of the export market would determine whether the firm had an export department. Large firms develop new products too, and depending on such strategy determinants as the scale economies in production and the willingness of the firm to take risks (as the new product is introduced globally), an ethnocentric, global product structure may well be the best organization structure for bringing these new products to market successfully.

IMPACT OF INCREASED GLOBAL COMPETITION ON STRATEGY AND ORGANIZATION STRUCTURE

During the past decade or so, the global marketplace has become increasingly competitive. Multinational enterprises have emerged from Europe, Asia, Latin America, and elsewhere to challenge the market supremacy of the traditional leaders. The business world today is substantially characterized by global competition, shorter than ever product life cycles, powerful MNEs with significant financial and R&D capabilities and globally distributed production and marketing organizations, generally favorable national economic policies increasingly supportive of market mechanisms, and high-tech information networks that result in efficient, nearly instantaneous communications.

The MNE strategy implications of these environmental factors are several. One is that the lead time required for bringing new products to (global) markets must be as short as possible, as must the response time the MNE needs to answer competitors' initiatives in new-product introductions, other marketing innovations, production and logistics cost-cutting efforts, and so on. Another implication is that MNEs must compete in markets that are increasingly risky. This section looks at two of the more important ways in which MNEs have responded organizationally to these strategic considerations: internally via enhanced organizational flexibility and externally via the forming of joint ventures and other strategic alliances.

Enhanced Organizational Flexibility

The geocentric, matrix organization structure just discussed is an important organizational concept and form. But today there must be more to an organization than simple functional and product overlaps as competitive pressures call on the firm for increasingly timely, effective competitive responses and initiatives. The MNE's need to coordinate internally is more important than ever, and it must do so in the face of increasingly globally diffused activities and capabilities.

Martinez and Jarillo recently examined empirical studies on MNEs regarding the evolution of MNEs' organizations and internal coordination mechanisms as product markets have become increasingly competitive and resource markets increasingly geographically diversified.[9] Their findings show that coordination mechanisms other than formal organization structure and the allocation of decision making within a hierarchial structure (that is, the centralization/decentralization issue) have evolved in more recent times. These other coordination mechanisms include formalized and standardized policies, rules, and job descriptions and the implementation of strategic planning and control procedures. They also include the more subtle forms of mechanisms such as the development of international task forces, teams, and committees; extensive informal personnel contacts, such as via meetings, conferences, management transfers, and so on; and enhanced socialization via the building of an organizational culture characterized by shared objectives and values.

Martinez and Jarillo examined a total of 85 research articles. Figure 12–10 displays a frequency distribution showing their findings on the use of these different coordination mechanisms during various time periods. Their study clearly shows that MNEs are increasingly using other, more flexible and informal coordination mechanisms in the more recent, highly competitive times.

Joint Ventures

MNEs form joint ventures with either other MNEs or local firms typically for strategic reasons. They seek to access important technology, for instance, or to enter certain markets, or to enter markets more quickly than would be possible otherwise. Dow Chemical and Eli Lilly formed an international joint venture, Dow-Elanco, to expand their product base in agricultural chemicals and obtain a market share large enough to justify future R&D expenditures.

Geringer defines a joint venture as a legal entity jointly owned by two or more legally distinct organizations that share in the joint venture's decision-making

FIGURE 12–10

Evolution of the Studies on Mechanisms of Coordination as Used by MNEs

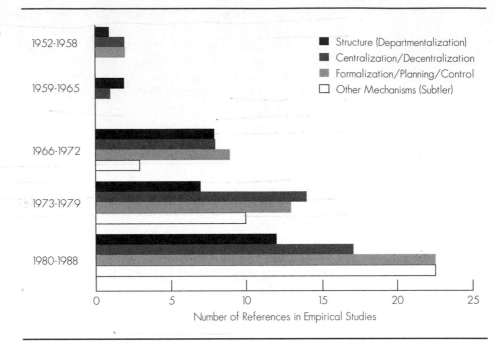

Legend:
- ■ Structure (Departmentalization)
- ■ Centralization/Decentralization
- ▩ Formalization/Planning/Control
- ☐ Other Mechanisms (Subtler)

Number of References in Empirical Studies

Source: Jon I Martinez and J Carlos Jarillo, "The Evolution of Research on Coordination Mechanisms in Multinational Corporations," *Journal of International Business Studies,* Fall 1989, p. 496.

activities.[10] The joint venture (JV) is a separate organization from those of its owners. However, linkages certainly exist between the JV and the owners (firms). The ownership linkage is evidenced by the composition of the JV board of directors. Management contracts and licenses between the JV and its owners are also likely to exist. These contracts define the relationships among the different parties, including the allocation of control and the nature of any coordination mechanisms.

The challenge to those firms involved in international JVs, according to Geringer and Hebert, is to have coordination and control (via contractual and/or more subtle coordination mechanisms as identified above) vis-à-vis the joint venture without burdening the JV with an administrative or organizational hierarchy whose costs (including inefficiencies introduced into the JV) outweigh the gains from the successful implementation of the JV's strategy.[11] Firms involved in JVs today are becoming increasingly aware of this challenge.

CONCLUSIONS

Strategy consists of two main parts: formulation and implementation. Formulation is based on SWOT analysis. Implementation requires people, money, organization, and so on—the structure through which strategy operates. Strategy involves setting goals and doing the planning necessary to attain them. It operates at the corporate and SBU levels. At the former level, the main concerns are synergy and balance; at the latter level, operating effectiveness and efficiency are paramount. Structure, at its best, is the institutional embodiment of strategy implementation.

The strategic management process was defined as consisting of six components: formulating the mission statement, determining strategic objectives, formulating the master strategy, setting the organization, implementing the operating plan, and applying a control system. Various strategic issues pertinent to the MNE were identified. Some of these issues, such as market selection, entry strategy, and ownership strategy, arose because the MNE crossed country, market, and cultural boundaries. Others arose because the MNE was operating through international markets with characteristics peculiar to themselves, such as the foreign exchange and capital markets. The complexity of operating multinationally presents the MNE with both a challenge and an opportunity. It makes success difficult, but it also makes successful strategies defensible (at least over some intermediate period).

Three classic strategies/structures were discussed. The ethnocentric organization relies on scale economies and learning curve effects to develop and sustain a low-cost competitive strategy. The polycentric organization, on the other hand, has fewer opportunities for scale economies and learning curve effects because it has to deal with diverse and distinctive geographically defined markets. This often results in multiple power centers within the MNE and, as time and technology unfold, in resistance to changes that are necessary to meet competitive threats. The geocentric organization is an alternative to both ethnocentrism and polycentrism. It balances market needs favoring distinctive approaches against the firm's multiproduct capabilities and its desire to benefit from scale economies and learning curves. The geocentric organization is typically a matrix organization.

The evolution of the MNE provides an illustrative and relevant example of the interplay between strategy and structure. Highlights of this evolutionary process included fortuitous exports and the development of an operating and financial dependence on foreign markets. Deliberate exporting followed, which meant that foreign sales had become an objective in their own right. By this time, an export department had probably been established to facilitate logistics matters. Afterward, in many cases, exporting became more important and product modifications, special pricing strategies, and the like were developed to enhance foreign sales. The export department then gave way to the international division, a more internally influential unit. Exports were now affecting the bottom line in a substantial way.

As competition expanded in both domestic and foreign markets, firms implemented several defensive strategies, including product line expansion at home (and later abroad) and direct investment in foreign markets. The latter strategy enabled the MNE to produce within tariff walls and eliminate heavy shipping costs. Very important, it allowed product modification, the fine-tuning of product specifications to the incomes, tastes, and use conditions peculiar to the foreign market. Drastic organizational change accompanied foreign direct investment. Within the MNE, not only were marketing and logistics changed, but production, engineering, personnel, accounting, finance, and so on were redefined to include multinational operations. Initially, the geographic definition of operations gave rise to geographically defined organizational structures.

As the mature multinational evolved, as product lines expanded overseas (in the same way they expanded domestically), and as competitive conditions became increasingly difficult, many firms moved to the global matrix structure, a team-based approach to blending company capabilities with market opportunities.

The chapter concluded with a review of the evidence showing MNEs are developing more complex, informal internal control and coordination mechanisms in the face of increasing competition and other factors. It also noted that joint ventures are typically formed for strategic reasons and offer distinct challenges to the owners in terms of organizational fit and coordination.

QUESTIONS

1. How are synergy and balance relevant to strategy? Give some examples of synergy in MNEs. Give some examples of balance. If neither synergy nor balance were present in a particular MNE, could the corporate level be justified? Could it be sustained?

2. What are the six components of the strategic management process? How do these components relate to Matsushita and to the text discussion of Matsushita? Why are they important?

3. What is the driving force behind the ethnocentric organization? Give three examples of companies that behave ethnocentrically.

4. What is the driving force behind the polycentric organization? Give the theoretical argument behind the statement that global profit maximization is most likely to occur in the polycentric organization.

5. How does geocentrism differ from ethnocentrism and polycentrism? Is geocentrism the strategy/structure of the future?

6. What were the internal, organizational effects of fortuitous exports? Of deliberate exports?

7. Why would the international department have more power than the export department? What is "power" in this context? What does power mean in terms of the firm's future direction?

8. Why does foreign direct investment affect the organization structure so significantly? How does it affect the organization structure?

9. What kind of organization structure do you think would be best for an oil company? For a diversified food company?

10. In terms of organization structure, how are MNEs responding to today's highly competitive environment?

REFERENCES

Abegglen, James C, and George Stalk, Jr. *Kaisha: The Japanese Corporation*. New York: Basic Books, 1985.

Bartlett, Christopher A, and Sumantra Ghoshal. *Managing Across Borders: The Transnational Solution*. Boston: Harvard Business School Press, 1989.

Bartlett, Christopher A; Yves L Doz; and Gunnar Hedlund. *Managing the Global Firm*. New York: Routledge, Chapman & Hall, 1990.

Contractor, Farok J, and Peter Lorange (eds.). *Cooperative Strategies in International Business*. Lexington, MA: Lexington Books, 1988.

Garland, John; Richard Farmer, and Marilyn Taylor. *International Dimensions of Business Policy and Strategy*. Boston: Kent Publishing, 1990.

Gates, Stephen R, and William G Egelhoff. "Centralization in Headquarters-Subsidiary Relationships." *Journal of International Business Studies,* Summer 1986, pp. 71–92.

Kiggundu, Moses N. *Managing Organizations in Developing Countries: An Operational and Strategic Approach*. West Hartford, CT: Kumarian Press, 1989.

Kujawa, Duane. *Japanese Multinationals in the United States: Case Studies*. New York: Praeger Publishers, 1986.

Mascarenhas, Briance. "International Strategies of Non-Dominant Firms." *Journal of International Business Studies,* Spring 1986, pp. 1–26.

NOTES

[1] For an extensive report on strategic management, especially as it pertains to the MNE, see William H Davidson, *Global Strategic Management* (New York: John Wiley & Sons, 1982).

[2] This account of the strategic management process was adapted from James M Higgins, *Organizational Policy and Strategic Management,* 2nd ed. (Hinsdale, IL: Dryden Press, 1983).

[3] Ibid., p. 65.

[4] David P Rutenberg, *Multinational Management* (Boston: Little, Brown, 1982), p. 12.

[5] For the original presentation on ethnocentric, polycentric, and geocentric MNE structures and strategies, see Howard V Perlmutter, "L'Entreprise internationale—trois conceptions," *Revue Economique et Sociale,* May 1965. (A translation appears in *Quarterly Journal of AISEC International,* August 1967.)

[6] See, for example, Rutenberg, *Multinational Management,* pp. 16–18.

[7] See, for example, International Labour Office, *Social and Labour Practices of Some U.S.-Based Multinationals in the Metal Trades* (Geneva: ILO, 1977), and Rutenberg, *Multinational Management.*

[8] Claude L Simpson, Jr., and Duane Kujawa, "The Export Decision Process: An Empirical Inquiry," *Journal of International Business Studies,* Spring 1974, pp. 107–17.

[9] Jon I Martinez and J Carlos Jarillo, "The Evolution of Research on Coordination Mechanisms in Multinational Corporations," *Journal of International Business Studies,* Fall 1989, pp. 489–514.

[10] J M Geringer, *Joint Venture Partner Selection: Strategies for Developed Countries* (Westport, CT: Quorum Books, 1988).

[11] J Michael Geringer and Louis Hebert, "Control and Performance of International Joint Ventures," *Journal of International Business Studies,* Summer 1989, p. 248.

Windmere Corporation

Windmere Corporation manufactures and markets a diversified line of consumer electrical products. Sales in 1993 totaled $171 million, nearly three-and-one-half times the 1980 figure of $50 million.

In 1993, Windmere's product line consisted of several models of hair (blower) dryers, hair curlers, curling irons, lighted makeup mirrors, shavers and related personal beauty products, electronic air cleaners, oscillating fans, nail dryers, and wand-type massagers. These products are marketed under a variety of brand names, including Signature, Pro, Windmere, Boss, Solid Gold, Prelude, Mirror-Go-Lightly, Fabergé, Brut, and Ronson.

Time and Change

In 1973, Windmere marketed only two products: "permanent lash clusters" and the 1,000-watt Pro hairstyling dryer. From 1973 to 1993, its product line expanded enormously and its sales (of consumer products) grew 600-fold, from $306,000 in 1973 to the $171 million of 1993. Indeed, during this period Windmere grew at a rate nearly 10 times that of the consumer electrical products industry in general. This was an impressive accomplishment.

The Hong Kong Connection

From the very beginning, Windmere sourced its electrical personal care products in Hong Kong. Indeed, from the early 1970s on, the company purchased products from different factories and trading companies in the old British crown colony.

Windmere's founder and current board chairperson, Belvin Friedson, personally developed this strategy and personally established the commercial contacts in Hong Kong. The idea was really quite simple. Consumer hair care products were fairly standardized and could be produced quite cheaply in Hong Kong, with its comparatively low labor costs. In fact, many producers there were capable of making such products. They sold directly to buyers and also through Hong Kong–based trading companies.

The arm's-length buying arrangement was a learning experience for Windmere. It soon became evident to Friedson that quality control, scheduling, and other considerations, including Windmere's growing satisfaction with sourcing in Hong Kong and its desire to expand its activities there, required that it secure a longer-term relationship with its suppliers. Accordingly, Durable Electrical Metal

This case was written by Professors Duane Kujawa and Harold Strauss, School of Business Administration, University of Miami, Coral Gables, Florida. The authors gratefully acknowledge the cooperation and assistance of Windmere Corporation, and especially Windmere's president, David Friedson, in providing company-specific information. Revised 1994.

Factory, Ltd., a Hong Kong–based, independent manufacturer that had emerged as one of Windmere's more important suppliers, joined Windmere in establishing several joint ventures. Durable-Belson, for example, was set up in 1975 as a manufacturing joint venture. In 1977, two other joint ventures were established: Dubel Industrial, Ltd., an injection molding operation, and Kamwon Electrical Factory, Ltd., an electrical products manufacturer. Subsequently, Windmere acquired 50 percent ownership of Durable itself.

Similarly, K C Lau & Co., Ltd., a trading company with which Windmere had developed a good working relationship, was acquired in 1978. This too was done for control reasons, but there were also reasons that went beyond scheduling, documentation, and financial considerations.

Windmere had learned that operating without the aid of a Hong Kong–based trading company resulted in higher prices and poorer-quality goods and services. It worked with several trading companies, but was displeased with nearly all of them. This was because Windmere was dissatisfied with certain Hong Kong "business practices," such as paying trading companies or their key personnel "face money" or kickbacks that were over and above the normal commissions earned. The company believed that operating through a controlled trading company would ensure a more honest, dependable relationship. It also believed that a controlled trading company could help expand Kamwon's and Durable's businesses more effectively. Subsequently, K C Lau & Co. was merged into PPC Industries, Ltd., another trading company and a wholly owned subsidiary of Windmere.

By 1980, Windmere had thus put into place the basic operating structure that it deemed was necessary to be competitive and to grow as a provider of low-cost, high-quality consumer electrical products to markets in the United States.

Establishing Production in the People's Republic of China

As Windmere's marketing success and its sourcing needs expanded, the company began to look beyond Hong Kong, where labor was becoming increasingly expensive and seasonally scarce. Lai Kin, the managing director of its Durable joint venture, set up an assembly operation in Canton in the People's Republic of China (PRC) in 1980. Labor rates were much lower there, but so were productivity and product quality. David Friedson, Windmere's president, put it this way:

At this time, the modernization of China had begun, but it was in a rudimentary form. The authorities in Canton could not understand our needs, and the workers had no concept of what [factory] work meant. Productivity was extremely low; the defect rate of products was extremely high; and the experiment was doomed to failure. At the insistence of Mr. Lai we allowed the experiment to continue because we thought we would lose face with the Chinese if we withdrew.[1]

Lai's persistence led to a second attempt to establish operations in the PRC. Man Fung Village, which is in the Shenzhen Special Economic Zone and lies about 35 miles north of Hong Kong, was the scene of a special challenge in 1981. Durable transferred a production line, complete with workers and equipment, from Hong Kong to an old theater in Man Fung Village to demonstrate what the Hong Kong Chinese could do in terms of efficiency and productivity. The mayor and people of Man Fung Village were impressed with this demonstration. They committed themselves to duplicating what they saw in that old theater. Early the next year, the village put up some facilities and about 100 workers signed up to work there. Durable provided equipment, middle management, supervision, and training.

The rest is history!

Within a few years, the operation employed 2,700 workers and was the largest employer in the Shenzhen Zone. Moreover, Durable's workers were making about double the standard wage for government jobs in China. They were able to build large, two-story villas that were beyond the reach of the average Chinese worker. Compensation typically totaled over $65 a month, including bonuses, which, even with transportation costs factored in, resulted in a cost savings of about 50 percent compared to Hong Kong–based production.[2] Interestingly, with the success of the Man Fung operation, Durable believed it could close its Canton plant without "losing face."

Windmere's president, David Friedson, states that in the company's opinion,

China provides us with the best value in labor for producing the kinds of products that we produce. This is based on the actual cost of labor as well as other benefits, such as free land and buildings the Government provides and the close proximity to our Hong Kong facilities.[3]

By 1988, nearly 75 percent of Durable's output was produced in China. It was capped at that level, however, since Windmere didn't want to "become wholly dependent on a single source."[4] In January 1989, Windmere expanded its ownership interest in Durable to 80 percent. In May 1994, Windmere expanded its ownership interest to 100 percent. An organization chart depicting the relationships among Windmere's major affiliates and divisions is presented in Figure 1.

FIGURE 1

Windmere Corporation Organization Structure

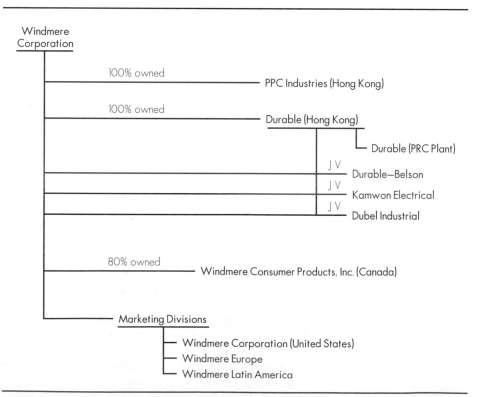

Note: The structure depicted here pertains to the material presented in the case and is useful in understanding the relationships discussed in the case. It is not an "official" organization chart provided by the company.

Recent Developments

Over the last decade, Windmere added several products to take advantage of its low-cost production in Hong Kong and the PRC. In 1986, for example, Windmere acquired the Mirror-Go-Lightly line from Jerdon Industries. In early 1987, Windmere introduced the Clothes Shaver (a device to remove lint and fuzz from wools and linens), which was an immediate, robust success. The Crimper, a heated styling element introduced in late 1986, was also very successful (especially because of Bo Derek's crimped hair style in the hit movie "10"). Plac Trac, a new approach to home plaque removal and dental care, was added in 1989, as was the Guardian line of electric shock protection personal care products. "Scent Island" was added in the early 1990s.

As 1993 came to a close, Windmere was positioning itself as a newly emergent low-cost, world-class manufacturer of small consumer appliances. It had expanded distribution in the United States and was establishing the "Windmere" brand name worldwide.[5] Windmere Europe and Windmere Latin America, two new marketing divisions, had been established. Moreover, Durable was now manufacturing for "third parties," such as Rival, Sunbeam, and Hamilton Beach. Sales to such third parties were $46 million in 1993.

NOTES

[1]Letter from David M Friedson to Dr. Harold Strauss, dated August 13, 1984.

[2]Michael Browning, "Dade Capitalist Brings Holiday Joy to Chinese," *Miami Herald,* January 30, 1984, pp. 1A, 11A.

[3]Letter from Friedson to Strauss.

[4]"Strong Rebound: Windmere Back in the Black after Heated Court Battle," *Barron's/ Investment News & Views,* February 9, 1987, p. 45.

[5]Shearson Lehman Hutton, "Report on Windmere," April 28, 1989; and *1993 Annual Report,* Windmere Corporation.

13

Marketing Management

The main goals of the chapter are to:

1. Develop an appreciation for the complexity of marketing management in the MNE, especially with regard to the effects of environmental nuances on the MNE's internal operations and competitive strengths.

2. Review the evolution of marketing management within the MNE.

3. Examine how the international marketing environment provides opportunities for MNEs, specifically in connection with
   a. Product influences and pressures for product adaptation or standardization.
   b. Pricing concerns and the basis for setting an optimal pricing strategy.
   c. The transferability of experiences among markets and the importance of place.
   d. Promotion influences and promotion as an MNE competitive advantage.

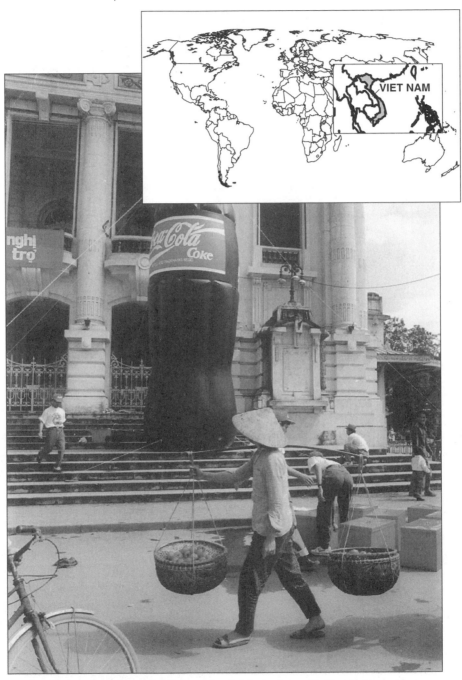

A Vietnamese vendor looks at the 30-foot inflated Coke bottle outside Hanoi's Opera House during the launching of the American soft drink.

Reuters/Bettmann

INTRODUCTION

As some earlier chapters suggested, marketing in the multinational enterprise can be especially challenging and complex.

The Extractive Industries

For MNEs in the extractive industries that deal with commodities that follow global pricing trends, marketing will probably involve long-term contracts with provisions stipulating consistency in product quality, timely delivery, and periodic price adjustments based on changes in some price index. For example, Intercor, the coal mining joint venture of Exxon and the Colombian government, sells premium-quality bituminous coal, mainly to electric utility companies in Europe. Sales contracts, which specify quality standards, quantities, and delivery dates, are typically for five or more years. Prices are keyed to spot market prices, which vary during the term of the contract.

The Service Industries

In services, the product is "produced" at the time of sale or consumption. The buyer-seller relationship is personalized and therefore substantially influenced by environmental, including cultural, factors. Thus, an advertising agency such as J Walter Thompson would approach potential clients in Japan with considerable deference to age and seniority and an appreciation for the participative, consensus-style decision making typically found in larger Japanese firms. This would require an extensive and patient selling effort.

The Manufacturing Industries

In manufacturing, the MNE is also often quite marketing intensive. On the one hand, it may seek to maintain competitiveness by extending product life cycles through advertising, packaging, branding, distribution, and the like. On the other hand, it monitors changing market needs and may respond to them by introducing new products. Heinz catsup, for example, has been around for nearly a century, but its plastic, squeezable bottle is less than 10 years old. The new sales generated by this ostensibly simple packaging innovation have helped Heinz capture over 50 percent of the US catsup market. Over a third of the company's revenues now come from products new to Heinz in the past decade, such as Weight Watchers frozen dinners and desserts. Heinz has capitalized on recent trends toward nutritious dieting and natural foods. It is benefiting from its experiences with these trends in the United States as they expand in Europe.

Complexity of Marketing Management in MNEs

Marketing management is typically seen as involving functional expertise that is especially pertinent at the SBU level. But there is more to this in an MNE context. At the international level, the MNE/SBU tries to identify and implement marketing strategies and programs that benefit in one area from experiences gained in other areas or that can effect positive scale economies by allocating fixed costs (for example, in R&D related to product development) over two or more markets. At this level, marketing management can be dealing with both a number of products that are in various life cycle stages in a single market area and single products that are in various life cycle stages, depending on the market area. This means that strategies, staffing, and other functions are more complicated and demanding both within individual markets and internationally.

Keegan identifies three basic approaches to global marketing management. The first is the "standardized" approach, in which products, distribution channels, promotional activities, and so on are standardized to the greatest extent possible, thus contributing to low-cost operations. A second is the "decentralized" approach, in which local, market-specific factors need to be addressed in product planning and promotion or else sales and profits will suffer inordinately. The third is the "integrative" approach, which draws on the advantages offered by both standardization and decentralization; that is, it requires adaptation to meet local market needs, but also looks to standardize products, promotions, and so on to minimize costs. Finding this "balance" at the point of maximizing long-term profits is naturally a difficult challenge.[1]

The key points here are that marketing management is more complex in the MNE than in the non-MNE and that MNE/SBUs with global marketing responsibilities must respond to two major issues: one dealing with the environmental variations and similarities that affect marketing strategies and programs and the other focusing on the internal operations that can give rise to competitive strengths unique to the MNE (see Figure 13–1). Responding to these issues effectively is international marketing management's challenge.

This chapter considers both issues. The environmental analysis is especially important to the MNE in dealing with the unification or fragmentation influences[2] that affect product, place, price, or promotion, the traditional four Ps of marketing. The internal analysis is important in implementing marketing programs that successfully utilize opportunities to benefit from scale economies in production, R&D, and so on, as well as opportunities to benefit from experiences in one market that make the firm more effective (profitable) in other markets. First, we discuss marketing management and the growing importance of environmental and internal analyses as the MNE evolves from emergent to mature. Then we examine the four Ps fairly extensively in the context of the international marketing environment.

FIGURE 13–1

Marketing Management in the MNE

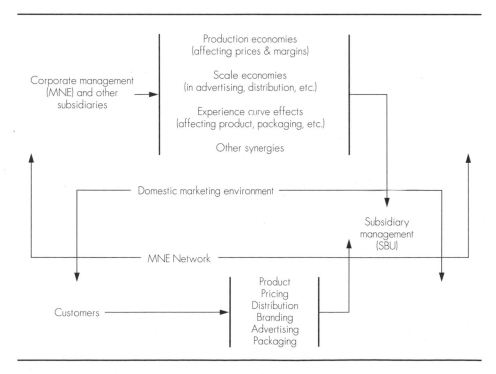

MARKETING MANAGEMENT AND THE EVOLUTION OF THE MNE

Accidental Exporting

As noted in Chapter 12, "Strategy and Organization Structure," many of today's large MNEs began their international involvement via accidental or fortuitous exporting in the 1950s and early 1960s. In those days, export marketing management was fairly simple. The product was determined to suit the domestic market, as was the price. There was no deliberate promotional program aimed at foreign markets, and often distribution was either the buyer's responsibility or simply involved shipment to the domestically based exporter that was buying the product. The same packaging and warranty policies that were used in domestic sales were used in foreign sales.

Deliberate Exporting

As foreign sales grew, deliberate exports displaced accidental exports and the producer's participation in international marketing began to expand. Sales representatives were assigned to foreign markets, and producer-developed distribution channels were now used. Logistics received increasing management attention. Product pricing strategies became more market based, but this presented some special problems. One problem concerned the cost add-ons associated with exporting, such as shipping, insurance, tariffs, and packaging; another concerned the currency required. (In these times, exports were nearly always denominated in dollars. This put currency risk on the foreign customer.) Operating margins were required to cover the cost add-ons. Prices had to be high enough to do this while still leaving room for profits. What product adaptation existed at this time generally centered on technical modifications to meet foreign use conditions. Foreign marketing research was embryonic. Follow-up service was just being developed, and its absence presented a real barrier to more successful market penetration, a situation not unlike the one faced by many of the US firms that sought to export to Japan in the 1980s and early 1990s.

When a firm established an international department, marketing management grew in importance. Extensive foreign sales offices were set up, as were warehouses and repair centers. Exports were now a substantial portion of total sales, and there was increasing integration between domestic and foreign marketing groups on product planning, production scheduling, and so on. Foreign marketing research expanded, and the firm was beginning to look for synergies in product design and promotional appeal between the domestic and foreign markets.

Producing in Foreign Markets

With the onset of foreign direct investment, marketing activities and the importance of marketing management increased dramatically. (For many firms, this took place in the late 1960s.) The defensive nature of this initial investment (recall the discussion on this subject in Chapter 12) meant that foreign markets were becoming very competitive for firms that were merely exporting to them. Producing overseas gave rise to new products that were designed to closely fit foreign market needs. Marketing research for foreign markets blossomed. Distribution channels were shortened and redefined. Given the heightened competition, promotional activities (including advertising) expanded. Competitive pricing strategies became commonplace, as did pricing in local currencies. Margins were tighter. Firms began looking for competitive advantages through scale economies in marketing via product R&D, distribution, advertising, and so on.

Marketing and the Mature MNE

Over time, management's response to these kinds of competitive pressures culminated in what by the mid-1970s had come to be called the **mature MNE.** In this organizational form, effective international marketing management is crucial. Such management involves coordinating, among the parent and its subsidiaries, product development and new-product introduction strategies, taking advantage of experiences in one market to improve positions in other markets, benefiting from scale economies in production and marketing, and so on, while paying close attention to the distinctiveness of some markets and what this implies with regard to decentralized, market-specific strategies and operations. It may also involve the MNE entering strategic alliances of various forms to enhance competitive advantages by reducing the lead times from product definition, to production, to marketing.

This discussion of marketing and the MNE underscores the effect of the environment on the MNE's marketing strategies and decisions. The changing environment the MNE faces results in both structural and operational changes within the MNE. Understanding international marketing management requires a more detailed knowledge of these varied environmental influences—our next subject.

THE INTERNATIONAL MARKETING ENVIRONMENT AND ITS CHALLENGES TO MNES

The world is indeed complex, and a review of each market, nuance by nuance, would be impossible to accomplish in a text such as this. The decision-oriented nature of management suggests that a more appropriate approach to the environment would be to focus on decision topics and to center on concepts. Marketing's **four Ps**—product, price, place, and promotion—require management decisions and make up the **marketing mix,** a term that identifies marketing both strategically and operationally. Our discussion of the environment centers on the four Ps.

Product

Producers view products as having a distinctive configuration that is definable and reproducible. The **product** can be anything from an American Express card, which is governed by a set of policies determining its use while limiting the company's exposure and risk, to a Mazda Miata sports car, which is produced by means of a deliberate and controlled process to guarantee product quality and minimize costs. Consumers, however, view products as satisfying needs. To many, the American Express card provides global liquidity and connotes a sense of personal financial maturity, and the Miata reinforces a self-image of youthfulness and excitement. Marketing management's first task is to identify consumer needs and define their product impact (e.g., how these needs influence product design).

Research indicates that consumer needs are usually determined by economic (e.g., income) and sociocultural (e.g., legal, religious, cultural) factors. The American Express card and the Miata, for example, are popular with high-income consumers and have a sort of "universal," cross-country appeal. Within country markets, consumers and nonconsumers of these products would correlate well with high and low income levels, respectively. In contrast, some products—foods, clothing, housing, and the like—are often more culture based. To illustrate, beer can vary considerably depending on culturally accepted variations in consumers' tastes and preferences. Dutch and Canadian consumers, for example, like heavier beers; German consumers strongly prefer regional or local beer brands; Japanese consumers lately prefer "dry" beers; and Irish consumers, of course, like a heavy, dark, sweet "stout."

To some extent, **culture-based products** tend to be "necessities" (Wouldn't most college students consider beer a necessity?) and **income-based products** tend to be "discretionary" purchases. Given these market-based characteristics of consumer buying behavior, rising or high income levels facilitate a product policy that transcends country or cultural barriers. Cultural characteristics, on the other hand, make for a variety of discrete markets, which in turn leads to a fragmented product policy, that is, the design of different products to serve different markets.

Actually, a variety of factors—some compelling, others not—exert fragmentation, or decentralization, influences on product design and packaging. For discussion purposes, let us begin with the idea that a product can be the same (i.e., standardized) in the foreign market as it is in the home market and put the burden of justifying **product modification** on foreign market factors. What could justify product modification?

Technical Factors   All products must be technically consistent with their environments. A classic example is the voltage of electric current, which may vary (e.g., from 110 volts in the United States to 220 volts in Europe). Another is the use of different measurements by different countries, such as feet and pounds instead of meters and kilograms. Production technology may differ from one country to another. The availability of capital equipment or highly skilled workers may also vary country by country. These differences, in turn, may affect product design or quality. Certain raw materials may be unavailable locally. Import restrictions or economic factors may force products and production processes to be altered so that available raw materials can be utilized.

Use Conditions   Products may be used in drastically different conditions from one market to another. Western Europe's long history of urban development, with villages and cities having narrow roads to accommodate the horses and buggies of days gone by, has certainly influenced automobile size. The bumpy brick roads often found in older towns and the often poorly maintained roads in rural areas mean that more durable autos and tires have to be built. Climatic conditions, transportation capabilities, and storage facilities all influence product configuration.

**IB
ILLUSTRATION**

Cultural Change and the Youth of Today

Japanese youth like to munch on Big Macs. Russian youth love blue jeans. American youth jog along with their Sony Walkmans. They all idolize the same rock stars and drool over the same "hot" cars. The youth of today seem to have a lot in common, no matter where they live.

Not so with the older folk! They value "tradition" more. In fact, in some societies the young and the old even see themselves as belonging to different cultures. The young are always seen as a problem. There is genuine concern over what the future holds for them and with how the different generations "get along."

Two conditions come to mind. First, young people are not yet settled in their ways. They are just establishing their own identities and are therefore generally quite open to change. Second, income has been advancing in almost every society, so many of today's youth are concerned only with discretionary spending; they get the necessities at home. These two conditions favor both homogeneous, cross-cultural behavior and products that are truly multinational. Do you agree? Why or why not? ■

Legal Environment The variations in laws from country to country affect products in numerous ways. Many countries have safety and pollution control standards. Products must be modified to meet these standards—for example, automobiles imported into the United States since the mid-1960s, when special safety regulations went into effect. (It might be noted that British Leyland Motor Corporation's Austin-Healey sports car was withdrawn from the US market at that time because management decided not to adjust its classic design to meet the new safety requirements.) Foods and drugs are also usually heavily regulated areas, as is noise abatement. Terpstra reports, for example, that British lawn mowers are kept off the German market because they do not meet Germany's stringent noise control laws and that countries differ considerably in the amount of sugar, fruit, and juice they allow in jam, the amount of water they allow in canned fruit and vegetables, and the preservatives they allow in cereals.[3] (For the 12 countries comprising the European Union, many of the legal barriers causing segmented markets were eliminated in 1992.) Developing countries frequently limit the number of models of a product and the prices at which products may be sold. Any of these legally imposed constraints obviously affects product design.

Use conditions and the technical and legal environments leave a firm that wants to serve a particular market little room for discretion. Other factors, both economic and sociocultural, allow firms varying degrees of discretion with regard to product adaptation. These factors include income levels and income dispersion, educational levels, and consumer tastes and preferences.

Income What people earn determines what they can afford. Regardless of overall income level, many countries are similar in that they all have a high-income stratum that has the discretionary income to afford the big-ticket item. Certain items, then, such as French perfumes, are used in all of these countries by people with high incomes. Key variables here, aside from income levels and income structure, include the size of the various income groups and their effective purchasing power. Country markets may, in some cases, be dominated by higher- or lower-income classes. In such cases, the kinds of products or product variations that will sell in the high-income countries differ considerably from the kinds that will sell in the low-income countries.

It is not unusual, for instance, for stripped-down versions of products sold in high-income areas to be marketed in low-income areas. For example, Singer sells a line of sewing machines in parts of Africa that are often simple and handpowered; in Europe, it sells a line of electrical machines with insertable cams to automate complicated patterns. Income levels and the dispersion of income help define market size, which in turn influences the selection of process technology and product configuration.

Education The general level of education affects product decisions both directly and indirectly. A highly literate market, for example, would typically demand more complex products. Product sophistication should match consumer sophistication. Computers and other electronic apparatus find limited markets where illiteracy prevails, as do products with complicated maintenance requirements, such as chain saws.

Consumer Tastes and Preferences What consumers desire is often related to culture, as discussed in Chapter 11, "Culture and Ethics." Toyota learned this the hard way in 1956, when it designed a small car for the Japanese market that it thought would be adaptable to the US market.[4] The home market version had a 20-horsepower engine and a top speed of 62 miles per hour. It weighed nearly three quarters of a ton, and it was not fuel efficient compared to other small cars being sold in the United States. The lack of fuel efficiency turned off small-car lovers, the smallness was unappealing to consumers who wanted style, and the performance characteristics were not attractive. The car, which was marketed under the name Toyopet (a self-deprecating name at best), presented a confusing message to American consumers, and flopped. No firm can afford to ignore consumer tastes and preferences.

The history of the MNE, brief as it is, contains numerous examples of firms that have misread local market preferences for products of certain sizes, configurations, colors, and so on.[5] For example, Campbell Soup, an American company, had difficulty adjusting its products to suit the tastes of its European consumers. Knorr Soup, a European company, found it difficult to break into the US market with its dehydrated soups due to US consumers' preference for soup in liquid form.

MNEs' Responses   Firms must decide whether or how they want to respond to the aforementioned economic and sociocultural factors. What would Campbell sell in Europe had it not sweetened its tomato soup? Marginal analysis would be the appropriate method to employ here. What would be the sales revenues and costs if the product were not adapted to accommodate local influences? What would they be if it were? What alternative approaches might be taken? Which alternative would be the most profitable? Interestingly, one could argue that the MNE's product analysis should always seek to favor standardization, since it is in standardization that the MNE has competitive strengths vis-à-vis other firms. In this sense, MNEs can be seen as market leaders in market segments where tastes and preferences are converging internationally and where products (or product cores) are thus being standardized internationally.

Price

Setting a product **price** is a difficult task at best. Ideally, the firm prefers as few constraints as possible on its product pricing. The only constraint that most firms want to accept is that imposed by competition, but even then the typical corporate strategy is to reduce or eliminate the effect of competition on pricing, for example, through the implementation of a strategy involving product differentiation. Firms want to set prices so that they can maximize profits under the given market conditions. Multinationals have more than this to deal with, however. Price strategy for a global market must accommodate considerations that would not exist otherwise, or at least would be less pressing. These considerations include price escalation when exporting, transfer pricing, dumping, price controls, and price differentials among segmented markets. Each of these considerations is explained next.

Price Escalation When Exporting   **Price escalation when exporting** refers to the percentage add-ons to the ex-factory price of a product by the intermediaries that make up the distribution network and by tariffs as the product goes from domestic producer to foreign customer. The ex-factory price is amplified by the combined amount of these add-ons, multiplied by one another. Distribution

IB ILLUSTRATION

**The Standardization versus Adaptation Debate
Kentucky Fried Chicken in Japan**

Since the opening of the European Common Market in the 1950s, debate has raged about the feasibility and desirability of standardizing marketing strategy across countries versus adapting it to local conditions. The opposing arguments are largely that standardizing allows the firm to cut costs by realizing economies of scale, while adapting allows the firm to expand sales by better meeting local consumer preferences.

Kentucky Fried Chicken (KFC) entered the Japanese market in the early 1980s with an initial strategy of transferring its full restaurant concept, from the menu items to the location and construction of the stores, to Japan from the United States. Consumer products, particularly food and clothing, are often seen to be especially sensitive to cultural differences and thus are good candidates for adaptation to local conditions in different countries. Nevertheless, following Levitt's (1983) reasoning that markets around the world are becoming more homogeneous and that multinational firms need to standardize whenever possible, KFC launched its Japanese strategy of standardized marketing.

Initial results were quite poor. Japanese consumers preferred smaller quantities of food than the US-sized packages sold by KFC (e.g., 20 pieces of chicken in a bucket), and they also had somewhat different tastes (e.g., preferring less salty French fries and sweeter cole slaw). Also, the stand-alone stores that KFC used in the United States were extremely expensive to obtain and operate in Japan, where land is scarce and real estate costs are exorbitant.

KFC's local manager eventually convinced the home office to permit the Japanese stores to offer a menu of smaller portions, sweeter cole slaw, less salty French fries, and fried fish as an additional item, all of which produced an immediate surge in sales in Japan. KFC also switched to stores located in malls and in existing strips of stores, which cut real estate expenses dramatically, although it entailed a significant investment in downsizing the restaurant kitchens and eating areas to fit into the smaller available space. KFC Japan kept the red-and-white stripe pattern of store design, sold primarily fried chicken, and even put Colonel Sanders mannequins in front of the stores, thus maintaining key features of the MNE's global strategy. By 1990, KFC operated over 300 stores in Japan and contributed importantly to the firm's global sales and profits.

This experience demonstrates the difficult decisions MNEs encounter in choosing between standardization and adaptation in international marketing. The "right" answer depends on the product, the market, the competition, and many other factors. Managers need to carefully consider the costs and benefits to the global firm in making decisions such as these. ∎

Source: This discussion is based largely on the case "KFC-Japan" in Christopher A. Bartlett and Sumantra Ghoshal, *Transnational Management* (Homewood, IL: Richard D. Irwin, 1992) and on the TV documentary on the same subject shown on the program "60 Minutes."

channels are typically longer when exporting than when selling domestically. For the MNE exporting an end product, price escalation cuts into sales and profits by biasing the product's final price upward. For the MNE exporting component parts or subassemblies, on the other hand, although price escalation still exists, it is not as big a problem. There is less price escalation for components and subassemblies than for end products, and the effect is thus smaller than otherwise. The value added by the foreign-based production is not exposed to price escalation. Also, the MNE typically handles the international distribution of components and subassemblies in-house (via commercial shippers), where costs are not subject to percentage add-ons.

Transfer Pricing   What a subsidiary is charged by another subsidiary or the parent company for the intracompany sale of a product or part is termed the **transfer price.** For the exporting unit, the transfer price affects sales revenues; for the importing unit, it affects costs. The transfer price also affects the amount of money that flows between the exporting and importing units (the goods transferred have to be paid for), the amount of the tariffs paid on the transferred items, and the amount of the profits (or losses) realized at each unit (since transferred goods are part of the cost of goods sold at the importing unit and part of the total income received at the exporting unit). If firms were totally free to set transfer prices as they wished and were not concerned about where funds were accumulated in the MNE network, they would probably do the following for parts or products sent to subsidiaries:

1. Set prices high in countries where income taxes are high.
2. Set prices low where imports come in at high tariffs.
3. Set prices high where the parent company has a problem getting profits out of the country where a subsidiary is located.
4. Set prices low if income taxes in the parent country are high.

In reality, the MNE is not free to set transfer prices in whatever manner it wishes, because governments are generally concerned about the amounts of income taxes and tariffs collected. At best, the price the company sets is justifiable, reasonable, and acceptable to the government. Typically, an arm's-length price, one that would be set between two unrelated firms in a competitive marketplace, is deemed acceptable. Alternatively, the price may be negotiable between the company and the government agency involved and be pegged at a justifiable and reasonable level. At worst, from the company's perspective, the government sets the price at whatever level it wants to and collects taxes and tariffs accordingly. Deliberate attempts by MNEs to present their records in a fraudulent manner to evade taxes or tariffs are, of course, illegal, criminal acts. For internal accounting and control purposes, however, a company can use whatever transfer prices it wishes.

Dumping   Another major concern that affects the pricing strategies of MNEs is **dumping.** The General Agreement on Tariffs and Trade (GATT) forbids selling products in export markets at less than the prices for which they are sold in the home market. This restriction is meant to preclude the introduction of disruptive, predatory pricing practices whereby, for example, an exporter could establish a monopoly in a foreign market by pricing deceptively low to drive competitors out of that market and then increase its prices at will. Under GATT, a country can erect a retaliatory tariff to offset dumping. (Chapter 9 discussed some of these issues.)

Price Controls   Governments, especially governments of developing countries, have been known to set product prices. But from time to time, **price controls** also appear even in developed countries—in the United States, for example, in the early 1970s. Price controls can present some real problems. Some MNEs have

IB ILLUSTRATION

As an International Trade Commissioner, How Would You Vote?

The International Trade Commission (ITC) voted two to one that imported sweaters from Hong Kong, Korea, and Taiwan are being sold in the United States at less than "fair value." Thus, the US Customs Service is to collect antidumping duties (i.e., duties assessed as a percentage of the merchandise cost above the normal tariff) ranging from 5.86 percent on imports of manmade fiber sweaters from Hong Kong to 115.5 percent on imports from a specific firm in Hong Kong—Prosperity Clothing, Ltd./Eastern Enterprises, Ltd.—because the firm did not cooperate with the ITC antidumping investigation.

The US National Knitwear and Sportswear Association praised the ITC's decision, since it would "provide a welcome boost for the beleaguered domestic sweater industry." On the other hand, the American Association of Exporters and Importers objected and noted that the ". . . sweater business has changed dramatically . . . from a basics business to a fast-changing, fashion-forward business." A spokesperson for the association recently noted, "Imports have filled a void for high-quality and novelty sweaters; they have not damaged a domestic industry." With special duties affecting imports from Hong Kong, Korea, and Taiwan, consumers will be injured. The sweaters they want just won't be available at attractive prices. ∎

Source: *Women's Wear Daily,* September 6, 1990, p. 23.

abandoned foreign markets because of their inability to price products at profitable levels. Price controls are typically evident in markets where there are inflationary pressures, and they are usually applied in both product and resource markets. As a result of local political pressures, wages are sometimes allowed to advance, while the firm is not allowed to pass this cost increase along in the form of a higher product price. Profits become squeezed. In such situations, the firm's short-run options are quite limited. It can continue to press the government to approve a product price increase, or it can downgrade the cost (and quality) of the product, a risky strategy in a competitive market. Being the low-cost producer in the market, a long-term strategy, provides the best hedge, but even that may not be sufficient in an especially difficult situation.

The Pricing Strategies of MNEs Unless a firm deals in commodities that sell in world markets at world prices (e.g., oil, copper, or coal), it wants to maintain separate prices that correspond to the specific cost and competitive conditions of its various markets. Apart from the aforementioned situations that interfere with the firm's ability to implement this pricing strategy, competitive market forces themselves may compromise the firm's ability to maintain price differentials among (otherwise) segmented markets. Markets that were heretofore effectively separated may now have greater elements of commonality, such as those that might result when tariffs between countries are lowered or eliminated, when shipping costs between markets decline, when consumer tastes change and become similar between markets, or when the customer is itself a multinational enterprise that buys from the firm in several geographic markets. As MNEs grew during the 1970s, for example, Citicorp found that its geographically indepen-

**IB
ILLUSTRATION**

Who Is Protecting Whom?

The US International Trade Commission (ITC) recently voted that the US "high content flat panel display industry" was materially injured by Japanese imports.

An interesting twist to the case is that America's most successful computermakers are lined up in support of the Japanese firms. These include IBM, Apple, Compaq, and Tandy. They buy flat panel displays from the Japanese, who they say are the only ones capable of supplying them with the volume and quality needed. If antidumping duties were applied, the US computer firms would either have to discontinue models that use the panels or shift production of laptop computers offshore.

If duties are applied, who is the winner? Certainly not the Japanese producers. Is it the American computer manufacturer? Or the American consumer? How about the American firms producing flat panel displays? ■

Source: *Electronic News,* August 13, 1990, p. 1, and September 3, 1990, p. 1.

dent, nation-based subsidiaries were ill equipped to serve the needs of MNEs effectively. A basic problem was that each Citicorp subsidiary was charging clients according to local market norms. As a result, subsidiaries of MNEs were being charged more than the parent company was paying in the home country. The MNEs pushed for (and succeeded in getting) homogeneous, company-specific pricing on a global basis.[6]

As we have seen, pricing can be very complex. At best, the firm wants to remain unconstrained so that it can price to meet its objectives and the requirements of individual markets. Nonmarket elements, such as governments, that constrain the firm's pricing behavior detract from the desirability of serving the markets where they exist. Changes in market-based elements, such as consumer tastes and the emergence of MNEs as customers, may well force the firm to change its pricing strategy, perhaps by segmenting a market on the basis of something other than geography. Examples of such segmentation include product differentiation according to consumers' incomes or tastes; quantity discounts for large-volume buyers; and variations in branding, packaging, or distribution. Barcardi rum, for example, sells Anejo (premium), Bacardi (standard), and Castillo (low grade), with some variations, in the United States and many other countries, both rich and poor. In each market, the sales and profit margins associated with each grade of rum will vary depending on income distribution, tastes and preferences, the extent of competition in each segment, and so on.

Place

The concept of **place** is considerably more complicated for a firm that functions on a multinational basis than for a firm that functions purely domestically. Place is both strategically and operationally important to the MNE. In the strategic sense, the importance of place arises because for some products there are global markets that typically follow a lead (single-country) market. In the operational sense, place encompasses both global logistic networks and in-country distribution management.

The Strategy Perspective Place is traditionally viewed as the location of the market served by the firm. For the international firm, place issues invariably focused on foreign marketing research and the difficulties of doing such research. These matters are still important to the MNE. Forecasting foreign market potential, for example, is necessary for a host of important decisions, especially the decision to serve the market in the first place. Data must be collected and interpreted country by country, an extremely difficult task. Consider, though, the advantage that the experienced MNE, with experienced staff on location in the foreign market, has over the new entrant to that market.

As a strategy variable at the MNE level, place pertains to the location of the new-product introduction, or the **lead market,** and to the interrelationships among markets that allow the MNE to benefit from experiences in one market that can make it more competitive in other markets. To an MNE, lead markets are typically the higher-income markets, where, as previously discussed, market size and market segments, with distinctive buying patterns influenced by income levels, tastes, and preferences, encourage innovation (i.e., bringing new products to market) and reward successful innovation (e.g., with substantial profits).

In the 1950s and 1960s, the United States was the most important lead market and the home country of most of the multinationals in manufacturing industries. In those years of the emergent MNEs, there was even concern that domination of foreign economies by American MNEs would lead to global US hegemony.[7] Then income levels expanded in Japan, Western Europe, and Canada, and MNEs based in these countries established themselves in foreign markets. By the 1990s, their successes in product innovation resulted in competitive advantages both at home and in other countries (including the United States).

Today the mature multinational views the concept of the lead market somewhat differently. The ethnocentric MNE probably still views the home market as

ADDED DIMENSION

Kodak's Successful Instamatic Camera Failure

In 1963, Kodak introduced its then revolutionary Instamatic camera simultaneously in 28 country markets. Sales were immediately fantastic. During the first two years after the Instamatic was introduced, almost 5 million units were sold outside the United States, the first time in the company's history that the international sales of a new product exceeded sales in the home market.

But Kodak had its problems too. Sales had been seriously underestimated. Production lagged demand significantly in the first few years. Kodak *lost* a lot of business! Moreover, its competitors benefited from seeing Kodak's market success with the Instamatic and had time to respond by bringing out competitive products. To prevent this, of course, Kodak could have built up huge inventories of Instamatics prior to the global launch. But this would have been a costly strategy and, prior to the launch, a risky one. Alternatively, Kodak could have introduced the product on a sequential basis in each of its markets. But this strategy too would have had its own set of benefits and risks. ∎

Source: Based on David P Rutenberg, *Multinational Management* (Boston: Little, Brown, 1982), pp. 260–61.

the lead market. The home market is its experience base and is seen as essential to the firm's long-run success. For the polycentric MNE, however, there are several distinctive, comparatively isolated important markets. Such an MNE is, by definition, fragmented. Each market has its own decision center and a rather provincial perspective.

The lead market concept is most meaningful to the geocentric MNE. It has distinctive characteristics that provide the geocentric firm with opportunities to excel internationally. The lead market is the one that can give the geocentric firm the greatest overall, global competitive advantage. Thus, the lead market is typically the one that offers the firm the greatest opportunity for quick market penetration and large-scale operations. The potential positive learning curve effects or scale economies would be most fully realized in such situations to the benefit of subsidiaries in **follow-on markets,** which can learn from the lead market experience, and to the benefit of the total MNE, which has now established a durable, competitive presence in a major market capable of giving financial and technical support to activities in other markets. Thus, a third criterion addressed in the selection of a lead market is the extent to which experience in that market is relevant to potential experiences in other markets. If such a relationship exists, the lead market has special value pertinent to the MNE's competitive success.

Figures 13–2 and 13–3 graphically depict the lead market/follow-on market concept. Two products, color TVs and VCRs, are depicted in terms of their market

FIGURE 13–2

Market Absorption Curves:
Color TVs

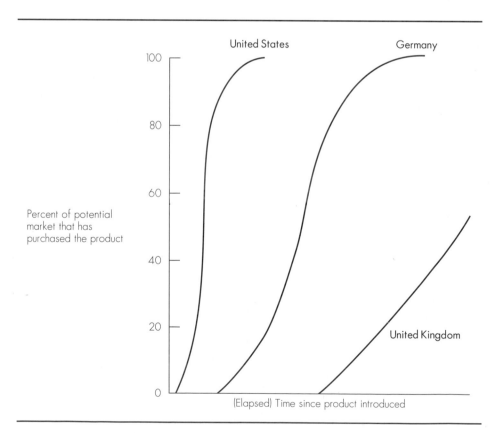

FIGURE 13–3

Market Absorption Curves: Videocassette Recorders (VCRs)

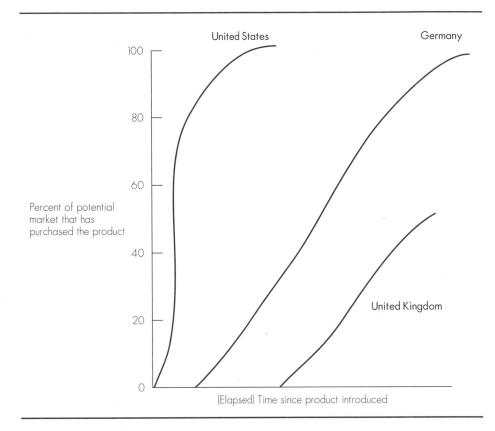

absorption patterns (i.e., the patterns of each product's sales through time) in several national markets. Figure 13–2 shows the patterns for color TVs in the US, German, and British markets. The figure depicts the US market as the lead market (where the product was initially introduced, at time 0). As time passed, an increasing percentage of the US market purchased color TVs until finally a market saturation point was reached. Sales of color TVs are shown as beginning in the German and British markets later than time 0. Eventually, sales in these markets also reached their saturation points. A similar set of **market absorption curves** is presented in Figure 13–3 for videocassette recorders (VCRs).

Let's look at the value of the information shown in Figures 13–2 and 13–3 to the firm that is experienced in consumer electronic products and is planning to introduce a new product, say, a compact video camera. (Recall that the curves reflect actual experiences with the other two products.) The slopes of the curves reflect the rates of sales growth in each market and assist the firm in planning production capacity and production rates. The proximity of the different country curves gives the firm solid expectations for global market growth, including the rate and country-by-country distribution of that growth. Depending on the specific data represented by the curves, as well as the relevant scale economies, shipping costs, tariffs, and so on, and the expected competitive reactions, the firm may decide, for example, to export from the United States to the German market during the latter stages of US market penetration and the earlier stages of German market development. Similarly, it may want to use German production to satisfy the initial

British demand. If the economics of production and distribution required it, parallel production facilities would eventually be operating in all three countries.

The data are useful to the firm for even more than decisions on capacity planning, market entry, and production allocation. For example, the slope of each curve can be influenced by industry and company practices regarding pricing, advertising, and so on. The distances between the country-specific curves can be reduced, depending on the firm's market entry and timing strategies. MNEs have options regarding pricing, promotion, markets, and so on that can alter the patterns and locations of the curves to fit their profit and strategy objectives more precisely.

General Electric was a pioneer in the use of market absorption curves. Today many companies use them, including Westinghouse, Sony, Panasonic, Siemens, and Philips.

The Operations Perspective   As an operations variable, place pertains to the MNE's establishment and management of global logistic networks and to its management of distribution within a country market.

The logistic problems confronting emergent MNEs initially centered on exporting—moving the product from the domestically located factory to a foreign market. As foreign direct investment occurred, "captive" exports of parts and subassemblies, from parent to subsidiary, grew in volume. In the mature MNE, the logistics function is much more complex. To be competitive, the firm must source wherever costs are lowest to support globally distributed production centers serving both domestic and export markets.

Figure 13–4 presents the **global logistic network** of the Helicopter Division of France's Société Nationale Industrielle Aerospatiale. The fairly extensive network involves the shipment of components (rotors) and subassemblies (airframes) between plants in France and plants in the United States and Brazil. Fully assembled helicopters are shipped from Brazil to markets in South America and from the United States to customers in Mexico, Canada, and the Caribbean Basin. The US subsidiary, Aerospatiale Helicopter Corporation (AHC), also maintains spares and maintenance bases in Mexico and Canada, where parts from both the parent and AHC are inventoried. The US subsidiary purchases engines and avionics from US suppliers (Lycoming and Collins, respectively) and manufactures and installs its own interiors. A similar sourcing pattern exists at the Brazilian subsidiary. The French parent markets fully assembled helicopters throughout Western Europe and parts of Asia. Sales in Eastern Europe are accomplished through licensees in Rumania and Yugoslavia and in parts of Asia through licensees in India and Indonesia. These licensees import components and subassemblies, including engines and avionics, from France and provide locally manufactured interiors.

We could present more complicated patterns of logistics networks, but the conclusions would remain the same: (1) Intracorporate product transfers combined with local sourcing can be intricate and costly to establish and maintain, and (2) their efficient management is essential to the competitiveness of the firm. Viewed slightly differently, one could conceptualize that geographically distributed production facilities provide the MNE with cost efficiencies that enhance competitiveness and profitability but that the movement of parts and products among these facilities results in distribution costs that diminish the cost savings resulting from these location advantages. The value of effective, internal communication pertains to both the establishment and the operation of geographically

FIGURE 13–4

Global Logistic Network: Société Nationale Industrielle Aerospatiale, Helicopter Division

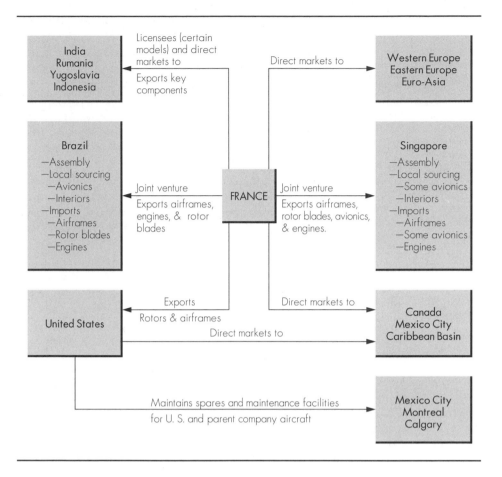

distributed facilities. The whole "problem" is best resolved through linear programming, with the optimal solution considering not only direct shipping and packaging costs but also inventory charges and the scale economies realized in production when a single production site serves multiple markets.

On this last point, an interesting illustration was provided by Ford Motor Company's international sourcing patterns on four-cylinder engines. Early in the 1970s, Ford-Britain put a new four-cylinder engine plant on-stream to serve both the British and US markets. As demand in the UK grew, production for the US market was shifted to a new Ford-Brazil plant. Eventually, as both Brazilian and US demand grew, production was shifted to a new Ford-US plant.[8]

Decisions regarding distribution systems within countries must consider a set of variables totally different than those related to global logistic networks, where costs and timing are the key concerns. With **in-country distribution,** cost and timing are again important, but local conditions, institutions, and cultural influences are also significant.

One approach to in-country distribution is to secure the services of distributors outside the firm, which in turn are responsible for selling the product in their respective countries or local markets. In this instance, the MNE is accessing the foreign market through indirect exporting. It is effectively buying local expertise, but it can no longer determine distribution costs, ensure product quality, and maintain timely delivery schedules. (The classic case of the French wine producer that exported to the United States through local agents comes to mind here. The US importing company let thousands of bottles sit in a New York warehouse during a winter freeze. The wine was ruined, but the importer sold it anyway—at depressed prices. It took the French vintner several decades to overcome the bad product image caused by this importer's indiscretion.)

Indirect exporting may be the only sensible approach, however, for smaller MNEs or for MNEs serving smaller markets. Moreover, the loss of control will vary depending on precisely which form of indirect exporting is selected. The loss is greatest when ownership of the product is transferred to a buyer that in turn exports the product to the foreign market. Examples here include **export commission agents,** which buy on behalf of foreign clients; **export merchants,** which buy for their own account and then sell to foreign customers; and **international trading companies,** which, like export merchants, buy for their own account but then often sell in the foreign market through their parent companies. The Japanese *sogo sosha,* such firms as Mitsui and C Itoh, are classic examples of international trading companies. More recently, however, such firms as General Electric and Kmart have established international trading companies. In the United States, the Export Trading Company Act, passed in 1982, enables small and medium-size US firms—companies that are often too small to go after foreign markets—to combine export operations in a separate **export trading company,** exempt from antitrust law as long as this does not adversely affect their competitive practices in the domestic market. Bank holding companies are permitted to hold stock in export trading companies, a privilege that is designed to make financial services more readily available to potential customers.

Indirect exporting may also involve using agents that export on behalf of a supplier without taking title to the exported goods. Such agents include **manufacturer's export agents** and **export management companies,** firms that represent several noncompeting manufacturers overseas and often even provide shipping and promotional services. (It should be mentioned that international trading companies and export management companies, may buy and sell for their own account and may operate on a commission basis.)

Most MNEs serve their major foreign markets through direct exporting or foreign-based production. During direct exporting, these firms may or may not procure logistics support, such as that offered by freight forwarders, customs brokers, and distributors. Similarly, foreign-based production to serve foreign markets would probably involve local distributors, wholesalers, and retailers. Whether or not to use such intermediaries is essentially a "make-or-buy" decision that turns on comparative costs, operating margins, or other expectations related to sales or profits. In turn, these factors are likely to be influenced by local conditions, institutions, and culture.

For example, in some countries, like Japan, distribution systems are multitiered and complex, while in developing countries, they are often "lean," that is, with few specialized intermediaries except in the larger cities.[9] Both wholesaling and retailing are generally more atomized outside the United States than within it. This may require the MNE to work with several parallel channels within a country market and to stand prepared to provide channel participants with inventory and technical support on a timely basis. If the firm is a US MNE, this will represent a different way of doing business than it was accustomed to at home.

Promotion

When a firm is dealing with the four Ps of marketing, **promotion** is probably the one in which the environmental influence is greatest. Promotion seeks to activate the motivation to purchase by conveying the message that the firm needs to get across the desirability of its product. Promotion typically deals with advertising, personal selling, and sales promotion, which usually involves brochures, displays, exhibitions, samples, and so on. However, promotion does not exist alone. Place and price, for example, are often closely related to promotion, as are product design features and product quality. How often have we heard that a product "sells itself" or that there is a 20 percent price discount during a special promotional period? Promotion, as noted, more often relates to advertising, personal selling, and sales promotion. Promotion is normally place specific and therefore very culture bound.

Promotion Practices Vary Internationally In many countries, legislation or industry practices significantly affect advertising. In the United States, for example, such products as liquor and cigarettes cannot be advertised on television, and advertising messages, regardless of media, are subject to "truth in advertising" standards. In Sweden and Great Britain, among other countries, advertising is subject to a "purchase" tax just like that paid on a product purchased in a store. In some countries, governments must preapprove advertisements for certain kinds of products. In yet others, certain media, such as television, may not be available for advertising. Restrictions of these kinds often lead to what the MNE may consider creative forms of advertising, such as billboard advertising at local soccer fields.

Global surveys on advertising show considerable differences among countries in both media selection and per capita advertising outlays.[10] In the United States, for example, 32 percent of all advertising outlays are spent on print media; in Japan, 35 percent; and in Australia, 49 percent. In the United States, 22 percent of all advertising outlays are spent on the TV media; in Australia, 34 percent; and in Canada, 17 percent. In Venezuela, advertising expenditures absorb about 1.0 percent of GNP (gross national product), which is about 40 percent of advertising's share of GNP in the United States. Among the factors affecting these distributions are living standards, infrastructural development, and regulation.

Because of language, ethnic, and religious differences among customers, **personal selling,** by its very nature, is largely country or subcountry bound. This is especially true for consumer goods firms, whose personal selling is concentrated mainly among the wholesalers and retailers with which the firm deals. For firms dealing with intermediate goods, economic factors typically become more important in the purchase decision. Such firms often put together selling teams so that all the relevant expertise—marketing, technical, financial, and so on—can be brought to bear on the purchase decision. One could also argue that mature intermediate products involve personal selling that is more culture or country bound than the selling of innovative products, whose producers have more control or influence over the purchase decision.

The Promotion Strategies of MNEs For the multinational enterprise seeking to obtain and implement competitive advantages, the question of the global standardization of promotional strategies and campaigns is quite important. To some extent, scale economies do exist, for example, in advertising—that is, in advertising research, copy preparation, and so on. The big plus, however, is the experience effect. A successful promotional campaign in one market may indeed bode well for similar successes in other markets. As mentioned earlier, income-related influences on consumers' tastes and preferences often override cultural and country-related influences in the product-specific areas that are more likely dominated by MNEs. Cross-cultural and cross-country similarities that correspond to similarities in income levels provide a rationale for similarities in promotional campaigns. To the extent that an MNE can transform a promotional program in one country into a competitively superior or more timely program in another country, it will benefit from an experience effect. The business world is replete with examples of this process. Marketing-intensive firms such as Coca-Cola, Heinz, Ford Motor, and Exxon have successfully developed and implemented international promotion programs.

CONCLUSIONS

International marketing management varies considerably based on the product and the market. For the global MNE, the challenge is to create and sustain a competitive edge based on experiences elsewhere or on scale economies that are unavailable to other firms.

International marketing management has changed considerably within the MNE as the MNE has grown and matured. In the early years, product and price were set by domestic demand conditions, and exports were mainly fortuitous. Later firms became more deliberate regarding exports. Technical adaptation to foreign product markets began, as did more direct involvement in the logistics function. As export markets grew, international departments, foreign marketing activities, and production integration between foreign and domestic markets evolved. Direct foreign investment, itself occasioned by the need for enhanced competitiveness in foreign markets, expanded the nature of the marketing function dramatically. New products were introduced. Pricing strategies became more market specific, and promotion and distribution were subjected to closer local control. In today's mature MNE, the keys to success are parent-subsidiary coordination on production and marketing issues and close attention to the distinctive characteristics of local markets. This contention was examined more closely in the discussion of each of the major decision-making areas of marketing management, categorized in terms of marketing's traditional four Ps.

Product is defined by the nature of consumers' needs and is substantially influenced by both culture and income levels. Culture and the local economic and institutional settings make for the fragmentation of products; higher and rising income levels generally lead to the unification of products. More specifically, technical factors often result in product modifications to meet local market needs. Use conditions, climate, transportation capabilities, and storage facilities, which may differ from market to market, also lead to product adaptations, as do legal, income, educational, and consumer influences and maintenance requirements.

Most firms, including MNEs, want as much freedom as possible with regard to *price* so that they can price according to market conditions and, hopefully, maximize revenues and profits. The MNE's product pricing must accommodate a broader set of considerations than that faced by the exclusively domestic firm. Price escalation when exporting, the result of the percentage add-ons of channel participants and tariffs, multiplies ex-factory price increases. Transfer pricing on items that move among units within the MNE can affect overall revenues, the direction of revenue flows, and the taxes and duties paid in different countries. Transfer prices are generally closely scrutinized by governments. Dumping, which involves selling at unfairly low prices in foreign markets, is prohibited by GATT. Price controls are another concern of the MNE. At one time or another, many countries set product and resource prices, leaving the MNE with few short-run options. Finally, the problem of maintaining price differentials among markets that are otherwise segmented is also germane to the MNE. While markets maintain a geographic separation, certain segments across geographic boundaries may be developing into homogeneous markets. This presents the MNE with a pricing problem as it seeks to maintain price differentials among location-specific and product-specific markets.

Place is important to the MNE as both a strategy variable and an operations concern. In the strategic context, MNEs have the capability to identify lead markets that provide them with internationally transferable experiences and integrated production practices that result in competitive advantages. As an operations concern, global logistics networks can be very complex in mature MNEs, and their efficient and timely operation can contribute to the MNE's competitive advantages. In-country distribution systems are similarly important, but they are influenced to a greater extent by local conditions, institutions, and cultures. Firms may engage in indirect exporting, thus buying local expertise at the cost of losing control. They may export directly and may produce and distribute within the foreign market, thus requiring flexibility and adaptation as operational hallmarks and management characteristics.

Promotion is probably the most environmentally influenced of the four Ps. It can take on many forms, and it can follow from decisions made regarding product, price, and place. However, promotion generally pertains to advertising and personal selling, both of which are substantially influenced by market-specific factors. Personal selling, by its very nature, is fairly culture bound. For the MNE, the challenge is to find promotional strategies and programs that are transferable internationally. Cost savings are one incentive here, but the experience effect as related to the potential effectiveness of programs is considerably more important.

QUESTIONS

1. What are the two major issues confronting marketing managers in the MNE? How does marketing management in the MNE differ from marketing management in a purely domestic firm (if at all)?

2. How have the emergence and maturation of the multinational enterprise influenced the development of the international marketing management function? The domestic marketing management function?

3. Rising personal income generally expands discretionary purchasing power. How does this fact benefit the global marketing presence of the MNE?

4. Identify the main factors influencing product design among MNEs, especially the factors that exert fragmentation pressures. What should the MNE be doing in the face of such pressure?

5. Identify the main factors influencing the pricing strategy of MNEs. Is the maintenance of price differentials among segmented markets unique to MNEs? What similarities and differences might exist between a domestic firm that is trying to maintain a market segmentation strategy via product differentiation and an MNE that is trying to maintain a market segmentation strategy across geographically segmented markets for a single product?

6. How does the GATT influence MNEs' pricing strategies? What are some of the inherent problems associated with any country's attempt to control dumping?

7. What are the major features of the lead market concept as a tool for strategic marketing planning?

8. How does the operations variable *place* affect the competitive strategy of MNEs? Characterize the importance of logistics in MNEs' competitive strategy as the MNE has evolved from emergent to mature.

9. What are the main points regarding in-country distribution that an MNE must consider? What trade-offs with regard to in-country distribution strategy must the MNE evaluate?

10. Why is the question of the globally standardized advertising campaign relevant to an MNE?

REFERENCES

Al-Eryani, Mohammad F; Pervaiz Alam; and Syed H Akhter. "Transfer Pricing Determinants of U.S. Multinationals." *Journal of International Business Studies,* Third Quarter 1990, pp. 409–26.

Boddewyn, Jean J. "Comparative Marketing: The First 25 Years." *Journal of International Business Studies,* Spring–Summer 1981, pp. 61–80.

Cateora, Philip. *International Marketing.* Homewood, IL: Richard D Irwin, 1990.

Douglas, Susan P, and Dong Kee Rhee. "Examining Generic Competitive Strategy Types in U.S. and European Markets." *Journal of International Business Studies,* Fall 1989, pp. 411–36.

Doyle, Peter; John Saunders; and Veronica Wong. "A Comparative Study of Japanese Marketing Strategies in the British Market." *Journal of International Business Studies,* Spring 1986, pp. 27–46.

Gillespie, Kate, and Dana Alden. "Consumer Product Export Opportunities to Liberalizing LDCs: A Life-Cycle Approach." *Journal of International Business Studies,* Spring 1989, pp. 93–112.

Kashani, Kamran, and John A Quelch. "Can Sales Promotion Go Global?" *Business Horizons,* May–June 1990, pp. 37–43.

Levitt, Theodore. "The Globalization of Markets." *Harvard Business Review,* May–June 1983, pp. 92–102.

Norburn, David; Sue Birley; Mark Dunn; and Adrian Payne. "A Four Nation Study of the Relationship Between Marketing Effectiveness, Corporate Culture, Corporate Values, and Market Orientation." *Journal of International Business Studies,* Third Quarter 1990, pp. 451–68.

NOTES

[1] Warren Keegan, *Global Marketing Management* (Englewood Cliffs, NJ: Prentice Hall, 1990), pp. 489–93.

[2] *Unification and fragmentation influences* refer to concepts initially identified by John Fayerweather. A unification influence facilitates the global strategy and competitive distinctiveness of MNEs. A fragmentation influence requires a location-specific response from the firm. See John Fayerweather, *International Business Strategy and Administration* (Cambridge, MA: Ballinger Publishing, 1982), pp. 300–27.

[3] Vern Terpstra, *International Dimensions of Marketing* (Boston: PWS-Kent Publishing, 1988), p. 87. Some of the other examples in this section are also noted in this reference.

[4] "Toyota Concern to Build Car to Sell for $1,250," *The New York Times,* February 9, 1956, p. 2.

[5] For numerous examples, see David Ricks, *Big Business Blunders* (Homewood, IL: Richard D Irwin, 1983).

[6] David P Rutenberg, *Multinational Management* (Boston: Little, Brown, 1982), chap. 1, "Organizational Structures and Tensions" (First National City Bank case), pp. 1–9.

[7] This concern was first expressed in Jean-Jacques Servan-Schreiber, *The American Challenge* (New York: Atheneum Publishers, 1968).

[8] Information obtained during interviews with Ford Motor Company's world head-

quarters staff, Dearborn, Michigan, in 1971 and 1972. See also "Cleveland Plant to Manufacture Pinto Engine Castings," *Iron News,* November 1971, p. 4, and "Ford to Build Mavericks in Brazil; Plans $150 Million Investment," *The Wall Street Journal,* March 3, 1972, p. 3.

[9]Philip R Cateora, *International Marketing* (Homewood, IL: Richard D Irwin, 1990), pp. 570–71.

[10]Keegan, *Global Marketing Management,* pp. 489–95. (Some of the percentages were calculated from data presented in Keegan.)

Case

Monster Chomp Cookies in Brazil

Beatrice Companies, Inc. is a highly diversified producer of processed foods, beverages, consumer products, chemicals, and other products in 30 countries, with sales offices and licensees in over 120 more. In 1984, Beatrice's sales were about $12 billion worldwide, with U.S. sales accounting for about three quarters of that amount. In that year, less than 5 percent of Beatrice's sales were made in Latin America, although the company was then a market leader in most of the products it sold in the region.

Beatrice Enters Brazil

Beatrice entered the Brazilian market in 1983, through its acquisition of 80 percent ownership in an existing local firm, Ailiram, S. A. Ailiram was a local manufacturer of cookies and candies in the São Paulo state, selling mainly to retail stores outside the city of São Paulo. Ailiram's cookies were very similar to those sold by dozens of other Brazilian firms—plain, fairly undifferentiated, round cookies and biscuits made of wheat flour and sugar. The company was formed in 1945, and by 1983 it had grown to include two manufacturing plants and 1,000 employees. Beatrice intended to use Ailiram as a base for entering the national Brazilian market, first by pursuing sales to supermarkets—a fast-growing segment for food product distribution—in the city of São Paulo, then by expanding product lines and distribution throughout the whole country.

Soon after the acquisition, managers of the subsidiary were planning a strategy to break into the highly competitive market for sales of cookies to supermarkets. A survey showed that about a dozen other companies already sold similar products to leading supermarkets and that Ailiram would have very little chance to displace any of them unless it produced a new type of cookie.

The Creation of Monster Chomp

On a trip to the United States, one Ailiram executive noticed the highly successful Monster Chomp cookies that were sold there. She felt that this product would have good sales potential in Brazil since cookies of this kind were not being sold in that country. Ailiram's attempt to sell to supermarkets would be greatly enhanced by the appealing packaging of Monstrinho Creck cookies. These would sell at the top end of the cookie market, where only a few other brands were competing. By successfully selling Monstrinho Creck cookies, Ailiram would

This case is reprinted from *Case Studies in International Business for ESL,* by Christine Grosse and Robert Grosse, Prentice Hall, 1988. Reprinted by permission of Prentice Hall. Eleven additional cases on international business are available in this same source.

establish an image of high-quality, innovative products and demonstrate to supermarkets that it knew how to mass-market cookies. Both of these goals had been set by Beatrice, which wanted to compete nationally throughout Brazil in both cookie and candy markets.

The Monster Chomps sold in the United States were much thicker and softer than the cookies normally sold in Brazil. Ailiram's managers felt that cookies had to be hard and flat in order to meet Brazilian children's tastes—but that their shape could be unusual. Thus, they decided to produce a hard, flat cookie that looked as if a monster had taken a bite out of it. The flavors initially chosen were chocolate, vanilla, and coconut.

A completely new package design was chosen to appeal to children between the ages of 5 and 12. (A survey showed that children up to the age of 10 accounted for almost 50 percent of Brazilian cookie consumption.) The package, shown in the accompanying illustrations, depicts a friendly monster with a chomp out of a cookie on its front. On the back of the package, some child's game is shown and a lesson about safety or some other constructive message is presented. Thus, the package provides both an appealing, funny advertisement and an educational lesson.

The advertising campaign to introduce Monstrinho Creck in the São Paulo area was quite expensive. Initial estimates were for a total marketing cost of about U.S.$500,000. As shown in Tables 1 and 2, this expense would virtually eliminate any profit for the first year of sales. Subsequently, prospects appeared very good for a growing profit margin and greater sales. The expected return on sales of 13–15 percent is similar to that of other Beatrice products, but this expected return does not take into account the high risk of doing business in Brazil at present (i.e., during the debt crisis of the 1980s).

TABLE 1

Monstrinho Creck Cookies—Eight-Month Forecast, 1984

	May	June	July	Aug.	Sept.	Oct.	Nov.	Dec.
Price index	100							166
Retail price (200 grams)	600							
Ailiram sales price (net, 200 grams, Cr$)	400	423	456	484	512	545	578	615
Ailiram sales price (net, 1 kilogram, Cr$)	2,000	2,115	2,280	2,420	2,560	2,725	2,890	3,075
Ailiram sales (tons)	120	350	280	300	330	350	330	300
Net trade sales (Cr$ millions)	240	740	638	726	845	954	954	923

TABLE 2 Monstrinho Creck Cookies—Three-Year Forecast

	1984 (8 mos.)	1985	1986
Price index	100	180	260
Exchange rate (average, Cr$)	1,600/U.S.$	2,880/U.S.$	4,160/U.S.$
Avg. Ailiram sales price (net, 1 kilogram, Cr$)	2,551	4,592	6,631
Ailiram sales (tons)	2,360	6,065	7,670

	1984 (8 mos.)		1985		1986	
	Cr$ mil.	Percent	Cr$ mil.	Percent	Cr$ mil.	Percent
Net trade sales	6,020	100.0	27,850	100.0	50,860	100.0
Cost	3,492	58.0	15,875	57.0	28,990	57.0
Gross margin	2,528	42.0	11,975	43.0	21,870	43.0
Advertising	491	8.2	1,453	5.2	2,107	4.1
Sales promotion, trade	122	2.0	29	0.1	—	—
Sales promotion, consumer	50	0.8	111	0.4	51	0.1
Sales promotion, merchandising	71	1.2	278	1.0	334	0.7
Market research	49	0.8	79	0.3	51	0.1
Total marketing expenses	783	13.0	1,950	7.0	2,543	5.0
Gross contribution	1,745	29.0	10,025	36.0	19,327	38.0
Sales expense	1,264	21.0	5,292	19.0	9,663	19.0
Administrative expense	289	4.8	1,114	4.0	2,034	4.0
Total sales and administrative expense	1,553	25.8	6,406	23.0	11,697	23.0
Profit contribution	192	3.2	3,619	13.0	7,630	15.0

Chapter

14

Accounting and Taxation

Accounting systems vary considerably country by country. This fact presents problems for MNEs that have to report operations on a consolidated basis in the system of the parent company's country. Moreover, parent companies must account for foreign purchases and sales and report foreign operations on their own books. Tax systems differ country by country, and MNEs want to avoid being "double-taxed" on profits that subsidiaries earn and send home. This chapter covers such issues. The main goals of the chapter are to:

1. Explain how and why accounting and taxation differ between MNEs and domestic companies.

2. Explore why countries differ with respect to accounting systems.

3. Describe how MNEs account for foreign purchases and sales and report foreign operations on the parent's books.

4. Describe how MNEs report foreign and domestic operations on a consolidated basis, including
   a. The definition and handling of conversion and translation gains and losses.
   b. US financial standards on consolidations and disclosures.

5. Examine how income deferral and foreign tax credits work to the benefit of the MNE.

6. Examine accounting/management information systems in MNEs.

7. Explain how MNEs achieve compliance with the US Foreign Corrupt Practices Act.

In Ottawa, Canadian Prime Minister Jean Chretien acknowledges his supporters after winning the country's federal election.
Reuters/Bettmann

INTRODUCTION

Accounting and tax matters are typically seen as administrative concerns. Financial reporting requires adherence to a set of prescribed procedures and standards. Tax laws mandate a certain type of recordkeeping and reporting and the payment of taxes to the appropriate authorities. For the purely domestic firm, accounting and tax matters do not usually result in competitive advantages, although every manager certainly wants to keep as much profit as possible by minimizing taxes.

Accounting Differences of MNEs

For the MNE, the situation differs somewhat. Accounting and tax matters are obviously more complex, and they can have a direct effect on the MNE's profitability and competitiveness. For example, astute handling of taxes can result in legitimate tax avoidance and increased profits or deferred taxes. Why locate profits in France, which has a 33.3 percent tax rate, instead of Taiwan, where the rate is 25 percent? Also, timely and accurate MNE systemwide financial reporting can lead to more informed management (and better management decisions) and more informed investors (which, hopefully, makes the firm a more attractive investment). Enhanced profits and more effective management should make the firm more competitive. Relationships among competitiveness, multinational operations, international accounting, and taxation will be visited at various points in this chapter.

Financial accounting systems differ country by country, and managers in multinational firms must be aware of these differences to know what information their accounting records really convey. For similar reasons, managers must be aware of the special circumstances and rules affecting the handling of international transactions and the parent company's consolidated statements reporting on the MNE's global situation. Financial accounting at the subsidiary and parent levels reflects not only traditional accounting practices but also laws and regulations regarding disclosure (with publicly held companies) and taxation. Variations in accounting practices and in exchange rates, which alter the unit of measurement, complicate the financial accounting systems of MNEs.

In addition to financial accounting systems, most firms utilize managerial accounting systems or managerial information systems that in some cases reflect slight modifications to financial accounting data already generated and, in other cases collect additional data useful for managerial control purposes. This chapter deals with managerial accounting for the firm that operates cross-nationally and cross-culturally. (Management control systems in general are discussed in Chapter 15 in the section on control.)

Tax Differences of MNEs

Tax laws also differ country by country. Moreover, tax laws must address the location of income and define the territorial extent of the jurisdiction of the taxing authorities. Taxation at just the domestic level can be quite complex and can be even more complicated at the international level. This chapter highlights taxation in the MNE and the MNE's strategies for avoiding or reducing taxes. It discusses key tax topics relating to multinational operations, such as (for US MNEs) deferral, Subpart F income, and foreign tax credits. It also discusses the tax advantages of using a foreign sales corporation. Finally, it looks at management responsibilities under the US Foreign Corrupt Practices Act.

ACCOUNTING

Because accounting systems deal with numbers, they are perceived as being precise. In the sense that they report specific numerical measurements, they *are* precise. But the purpose of an accounting system is to convey information, and measurement of activity in monetary terms is simply the mechanism used to achieve this purpose. What is to be measured, how it is to be measured, and how often it is to be measured are important questions that an accounting system must address. Answering them involves people and judgments. An **accounting system** is thus a contrived system. Its objectives, rules, and methods are established by people who have needs that they hope the system will fulfill. In brief, it is place specific.

Cross-Country Differences in Accounting Systems

Consistent with this perspective, Zeff's classic *Forging Accounting Principles in Five Countries* demonstrated that such influences as theory, practice, and social, political, and economic conditions come together to determine an accounting system.[1] Early on, Choi and Mueller identified 15 such conditions, some of which follow.[2]

1. *Type of economy involved.* Inventory methods, audit functions, and cost accounting techniques are affected by whether the economy involved is agrarian, extractive, or industrialized.
2. *Legal system.* Code law countries favor codification of accounting principles and procedures; common law countries are typified by private, professional organizations that establish accounting policies.
3. *Social climate.* Concepts of public disclosure and social responsibility have had considerable influence on accounting practices in the United States. In Switzerland, which requires substantially less public disclosure than the United States, the influence of such concepts is far smaller. In some Latin countries, accounting is equated with bookkeeping and seen as socially unimportant.
4. *General levels of education and facilitating processes.* People need to know mathematics to use the quantitative information in an accounting system effectively. Computerization requires the presence of electronic data-processing installations.

As expected, accounting practices are found to vary country by country. For example, disclosure of the cost of sales is a reporting requirement in Brazil and the United States, a minority practice in the United Kingdom, seldom found in Sweden, and not permitted in Germany.[3] (Periodic reports published by major accounting firms and available in most university libraries present highlights of accounting practices in selected countries.)

Accounting for International Transactions

Firms active in international business often deal in foreign currencies. Exports and imports, for example, may well be denominated in foreign currency and entail trade credit of 30, 60, or 90 days or longer. Dividends paid by a foreign subsidiary are denominated in the home currency of that subsidiary and are usually declared weeks prior to actual payment. Debt denominated in foreign currency entails scheduled servicing requirements that involve purchasing foreign currency for delivery at some known future date. Such **international transactions** have to be reflected in the company's accounting records.

FIGURE 14–1

Accounting for Foreign Currency Transactions: The Three Alternative Situations—Export Sale Illustration

U.S. Exporter   Importer

1. Foreign currency received at time of sale and sold for dollars

1,600 DM's

2. Trade credit extended to importer — no hedge

Account Receivable
1,600 DM's

Account Payable
1,600 DM's

3. Trade credit extended to importer — hedged

Account Receivable
1,600 DM's

Account Payable
1,600 DM's

Forward Exchange Contract
Sell 1,600 DM's at 1.7 DM per $ when received in the future

Three alternative situations may apply in accounting for transactions denominated in foreign currency. To understand these alternatives, consider the export sale illustrated in Figure 14–1.

Alternative 1: Immediate Payment The exporting firm does not hold the foreign currency beyond the date of its receipt, which is also the date the sale is made. Financial accounting standards in the United States require that assets, liabilities, sales, and expenses initially denominated in foreign currency be reflected in the accounts in the dollar equivalent on the date they arise. In the present case, the foreign currency would be converted into dollars in the exporter's accounts on the date the sale is made. The exporter's accounts would also reflect the net dollars received when the foreign exchange is sold.

To illustrate, consider an export sale to a German buyer for 1,600 deutsche marks (DMs). On the date of sale, the DM is trading at 1.6 DM per dollar. Ignoring bank charges for selling the DMs, the sale generates $1,000 in revenues for the exporter. Excluding the credit to finished goods inventory and the debit to cost of goods sold, the debit and credit entries are simply as follows:

```
Dr: Cash . . . . . . . . . . . . . . . . . . . . . . . . . . . . . . . . .   $1,000
Cr: Sales Revenues . . . . . . . . . . . . . . . . . . . . . . . . . . . .              $1,000
```

Alternative 2: Trade Credit   In this case, the exporter is willing to accept payment for the goods in foreign currency at some future date *and* does not cover this exposure with a forward market transaction. The accounting principle identified in alternative 1 would still hold as far as initial entries are concerned. Thus, the entries on the date of sale are as follows:

```
Dr: Account Receivable  . . . . . . . . . . . . . . . . . . . . . . . . . .   $1,000
Cr: Sales Revenues . . . . . . . . . . . . . . . . . . . . . . . . . . . .              $1,000
```

(Note that the account debited is Account Receivable and not Cash. This reflects the fact that the sale was made on trade credit.)

During the period of time for which the trade credit was extended, the DM depreciates to 1.8 DM per dollar. This lowers the dollar value of the sale of the export to $889 at the time the receivable is collected. (Don't forget that the sale, by contract, is for precisely 1,600 DMs.) Settlement of the account thus involves a **conversion loss** (that is, a loss incurred when an account is settled), which is reflected on the exporter's books in this way:

```
Dr: Cash . . . . . . . . . . . . . . . . . . . . . . . . . . . . . . . .   $889
Dr: Foreign Exchange Transactions. . . . . . . . . . . . . . . . . . . . .   $111
Cr: Account Receivable. . . . . . . . . . . . . . . . . . . . . . . . . . .              $1,000
```

The Foreign Exchange Transactions account is debited for foreign exchange losses and credited for foreign exchange gains. It is an income statement account that is closed out to profit and loss at the end of the accounting period.

To complicate matters a bit, consider the same case but with the exporter's accounting period ending during the time period in which the trade credit is extended and after the DM depreciation. To reflect conditions as factually as possible, the foreign exchange loss is reflected in the end-of-period reports as follows:

```
Dr: Foreign Exchange Transactions. . . . . . . . . . . . . . . . . . . . .   $111
Cr: Account Receivable. . . . . . . . . . . . . . . . . . . . . . . . . . .              $111
```

The foreign exchange loss in this case is termed a **translation loss** (that is, a loss on a transaction that has yet to be settled). Later, when the export is paid for, the following accounting entries are made:

```
Dr: Cash . . . . . . . . . . . . . . . . . . . . . . . . . . . . . . . .   $889
Cr: Account Receivable. . . . . . . . . . . . . . . . . . . . . . . . . . .              $889
```

Alternative 3: Trade Credit—Hedged   This alternative is like alternative 2, except that the exposure of the foreign exchange receivable due to the export is exactly offset by a forward exchange contract requiring the sale of 1,600 DMs. The initial

IB ILLUSTRATION

Can You Figure This One Out?

On December 15, 1994, Keebler Company, a wholly owned US subsidiary of the British firm United Biscuits (Holdings), Ltd., declared a dividend of $2 per share, payable on January 15, 1995. The British parent holds 1 million shares. (All of these figures are hypothetical.) Assuming the applicable accounting rules are like those described for the US exporter in the text, United Biscuits closed its fiscal year on December 31, from December 16 to December 28, 1994, the British pound went from $1.92 to $1.94, and there was no forward market hedge on the dividend receivable, what accounting entries would United Biscuits show on its books on December 15, 1994, December 31, 1994, and January 15, 1995? What entries would Keebler Company show on these same dates? ■

entries related to the sale of the goods and the account receivable would remain precisely as shown above. However, subsequent entries will reflect the forward market transaction. No accounting entries are made to record the forward contract at the time the contract is made (i.e., at the time of the sale). Assuming the forward contract rate is 1.7 DM per dollar, the dollars collected by the exporter (when the DMs are received per the export sale and paid out to complete the forward contract) total $941. The accounting principle is that forward contracts offsetting specific foreign currency receivables or payables are included in the dollar basis of the original foreign currency transaction. Hence, the subsequent accounting entries are as follows:

Dr: Cash $941	
Dr: Foreign Exchange Transactions. $59	
Cr: Account Receivable.	$1,000

In this instance, the foreign exchange loss (debit) has been reduced to $59 because of the forward exchange contract. If the contract had been written at a rate of 1.6 DM per dollar, there would be no foreign exchange transactions loss at all.

In their 1979 international survey of accounting practices, Fitzgerald, Stickler, and Watts reported that the US accounting practices described in connection with alternatives 1, 2, and 3 are consistent with the accounting practices followed in most other advanced industrial societies.[4] In 1988, Kubin confirmed this was still the situation.[5]

Consolidations

A **consolidated statement** is a single balance sheet or income statement that combines the financial accounts of the parent and its subsidiaries. All MNEs, US or otherwise, prepare consolidated statements so that managers, lenders, investors, and others can understand the overall financial situation of the firm. **Consolidation** is required of publicly held US firms. It is a tedious process requiring adherence to specific procedures and is performed at the parent company level. Before we discuss consolidation in more detail, we need to understand some basic definitions and concepts. (Recall that we are concerned mainly with the situation pertinent to the *US* MNE. The situation would be different for other parent-company nationalities.)

A consolidated statement pertains only to a parent and its subsidiaries. For accounting purposes, a **subsidiary** is a foreign corporation more than 50 percent of whose common stock is owned by the parent (implying parental control). Technically, if the parent owns 50 percent or less of the foreign entity's common stock, that entity is an **affiliate,** not a subsidiary. The foreign entity is considered a **branch** if it is not incorporated in the foreign country but exists as an office or extension of the parent and is legally constituted as a branch. If affiliates and branches are not consolidated per se, how are they handled at the MNE level? This question is important, and answering it necessitates a brief digression from our discussion of consolidation.

The parent company's books (nonconsolidated) carry any foreign entity (subsidiary, affiliate, or branch) as an investment reflected on the asset side of the balance sheet. For example, a branch is reflected in the plant and equipment accounts depending on what buildings, furniture, and so on are physically in place at the foreign entity. An affiliate or a subsidiary is shown in a specific investment account, such as Investments in Foreign Companies.

Income from a foreign branch is considered the same as income to the parent since the branch is simply an extension of the parent. Income from an affiliate can be handled by either the cost method or the equity method, depending on the level of parent company ownership. If parent ownership is below 20 percent, the **cost method** must be used; that is, the affiliate's income is recognized on the parent's books only when the parent receives it in the form of dividends. When such income is received, income is credited and cash is debited. If parent ownership is 20 percent or more (meaning the foreign entity can be an affiliate or a subsidiary and is not just a financial investment), the **equity method** is used. Here the parent's investment account is increased by the income that the foreign entity earns, in proportion to the parent's ownership share, whether or not that income is paid out in dividends. In this case, income at the affiliate, as allocated to the parent, is credited and the investment account is debited. When a dividend is paid out of the earnings, the investment account is credited and cash is debited. Figure 14–2 illustrates these alternative methods for handling income.

Preparing a Consolidated Report

A **consolidated report** involves the line-by-line summary of the balance sheet and income statement accounts of both the parent and its subsidiaries. The first step in this process is to restate subsidiaries' accounts, if necessary, to reflect the generally accepted accounting principles used by the parent company. In preparing a consolidated report, accounts denominated in foreign currencies at subsidiaries have to be translated into the currency of the parent company's country, and the question of which exchange rate should be used to do this must be resolved. For the United States, the rule is to use the exchange rate applicable to dividend payments by the subsidiary. In some cases, this rate is a market rate used for all foreign exchange transactions; in others, where exchange restrictions or multiple rates exist, the dividend rate is applied.

Another question arises when the exchange rate used varies through time, that is, when there has been a devaluation or a revaluation between the currency of the subsidiary country and the currency of the parent country. Two kinds of accounting-related management problems are generated by exchange rate changes. One has to do with conversion gains and losses and the other with translation gains and losses.

FIGURE 14-2

Accounting for Income:
Parent Company's Books

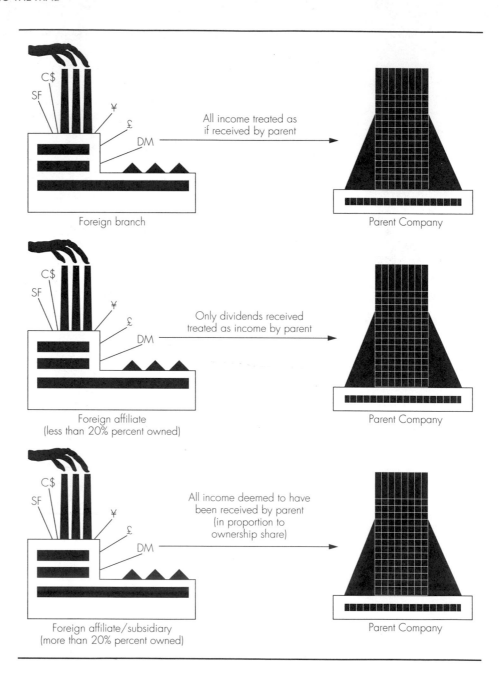

All income treated as
if received by parent

Foreign branch

Parent Company

Only dividends received
treated as income by parent

Foreign affiliate
(less than 20% percent owned)

Parent Company

All income deemed to have
been received by parent
(in proportion to
ownership share)

Foreign affiliate/subsidiary
(more than 20% percent owned)

Parent Company

Conversion Gains/Losses   When the subsidiary has assets or liabilities that require payment or receipt in a foreign currency and the value of that currency changes relative to the currency of the subsidiary's home country, conversion gains or losses are generated. The values of accounts so affected change in terms of the subsidiary's currency, and these changes alter real future cash flows at the subsidiary level. The situation discussed here is illustrated below in the case of Sympático, SA, a Mexican subsidiary of New York–based Friendly Industries, Inc. Half of Sympático's accounts receivable are due from customers in the United States and are dollar based, as is the parent company loan. The remainder of

Sympático's accounts receivable are based in Mexican pesos. In our illustration, the peso has devalued from 3.000 to 3.750 pesos per dollar during the 1995 fiscal year. To keep it simple, let's assume Sympático's performance in FY1995 was "flat." Indeed, had it not been for the devaluation, Sympático's books at the close of FY1995 and FY1994 would be identical.

3.000 Pesos/$ ⇒ 3.750 Pesos/$

SYMPÁTICO, SA
Balance Sheet
(pesos)

	End of Fiscal Year	
	1994	1995
Assets		
Cash	45,000	45,000
Accounts receivable		
Peso-denominated	60,000	60,000
Dollar-denominated	60,000	75,000
Plant and equipment	180,000	180,000
Liabilities		
Accounts payable	90,000	90,000
Bank loan	75,000	75,000
Parent company loan	45,000	56,250
Net worth	135,000	138,750

At the close of FY1995, Sympático had to adjust the peso value of its accounts receivable to reflect the 15,000 additional pesos it would receive when it converted the $20,000 account receivable as it was collected. Likewise, the $15,000 loan from Friendly remains at $15,000 regardless of the peso/dollar value. Sympático will now need 56,250 pesos to pay it off, not the 45,000 pesos reflected in the 1994 statement. The net effect of these two adjustments is shown in a 3,750 peso increase in net worth (in this case).

Once the parent has adjusted the subsidiaries' accounts to reflect potential conversion gains or losses, the preparation of the consolidated statements can proceed. The basic rules for US MNEs are fairly simple: Assets and liabilities, balance sheet items, are translated at the rate of exchange in effect on the date of the consolidated statement; revenues and expenses, income statement items, are translated at the average rate of exchange in effect during the reporting period.

To illustrate, let's return to our example of Sympático, SA, and Friendly Industries, Inc., but let's show Sympático as having made some profits during FY1995.

SYMPÁTICO, SA
Income Statement
January 1, 1995 through December 31, 1995
(pesos)

Revenues		675,000
Expenses		
Cost of goods sold	405,000	
Selling and administrative costs	135,000	
Interest on debt	33,750	
Depreciation—buildings	16,875	
General management costs	16,875	
Total expenses		607,500
Operating income		67,500
Income taxes		33,750
Net income		33,750

If the deterioration in the dollar value of the peso occurred at an even rate during 1995, the average rate of exchange would be the midpoint between the January 1, 1995, rate of 3.000 pesos/dollar and the December 31, 1995, rate of 3.750 pesos/dollar, or 3.375 pesos/dollar. This 3.375 pesos/dollar rate would be the one used to translate Sympático's income statement accounts. Note that this rate is applied to all accounts, even those whose values reflected on the income statement are based on historical costs—"depreciation" and perhaps "cost of goods sold." To illustrate, two income statements for Friendly Industries follow, one for the parent alone and the other for the parent and the subsidiary on a consolidated basis.

FRIENDLY INDUSTRIES, INC.
Income Statement
January 1, 1995 through December 31, 1995
(thousands of dollars)

	Parent Company	Consolidated
Revenues	$36,000	$36,200
Expenses		
Cost of goods sold	$18,000	$18,120
Selling and administrative		
costs.	5,000	5,040
Interest.	2,000	2,010
Depreciation	3,000	3,005
General management.	1,000	1,005
Total expenses	29,000	29,180
Operating income.	7,000	7,020
Income taxes.	3,000	3,010
Net income	$ 4,000	$ 4,010

(handwritten margin note: $ 200,000 comes from this state...)

It should be noted that the adjusted balance sheet items, accounts receivable and the parent company loan, do not directly affect the income statements of either the parent or the subsidiary. The exchange rate change will increase the interest in pesos that Sympático pays to service its debt to the parent company. This interest is included in the interest expense indicated on the income statements.

Translation Gains/Losses   Balance sheet consolidation is a bit more complicated than income statement consolidation, although mid-1980s changes approved by the US Financial Accounting Standards Board have substantially simplified the consolidation procedures of MNEs. The exchange rate used is the rate in effect on the date of the consolidated balance sheet. Prior to consolidation, as noted above, the books at the subsidiary level must be adjusted to reflect changes in assets or liabilities due to an exchange rate change. Thus, Sympático had to change its accounts receivable and parent company loan accounts to show their changed peso values when the peso went from 3.000 to 3.750 per dollar. These changes resulted in a 3,750 peso credit adjustment to Sympático's net worth. They will have an identical impact on the company's consolidated net worth. Indeed, since exchange rate changes alter the values of asset and liability accounts reported on a consolidated basis and companies typically show a positive net worth where assets exceed liabilities in value, adjustments will have to be made to the consolidated net worth accounts.

These adjustments offset the net effect or residual resulting from the inequality between assets and liabilities and from the fact that all of the subsidiary's asset and liability accounts are translated to the consolidated balance sheet at the same rate of exchange. These are translation gains/losses resulting from consolidation. There are thus two sources of adjustments to consolidated net worth: (1) those resulting from *conversion gains/losses* as the subsidiary adjusts its own books to reflect changes in the subsidiary's own local-currency value of assets and liabilities based on currencies other than its own and (2) those resulting from *translation gains/losses* as the structure of accounts (i.e., assets exceed liabilities) and the translation rules regarding the use of a single exchange rate result in residuals that have to be recorded in the consolidated statement.

Consolidation Illustrated

Let's proceed by illustrating these principles with Friendly Industries. As a first step, Sympático's balance sheet, changed to show the situation where Sympático actually earned 33,750 pesos profit during FY1995, follows. (For simplicity, the 33,750 peso increase in net worth is balanced by a similar increase in cash.)

SYMPÁTICO, SA
Balance Sheet
December 31, 1995
(pesos)

Assets

Cash	78,750
Accounts receivable (total)	135,000
Plant and equipment	180,000

Liabilities

Accounts payable	90,000
Bank loan	75,000
Parent company loan	56,250
Net worth	172,500

Before consolidation, any intracompany transactions are netted out. For example, Sympático's parent company loan, a liability, is offset by an asset on the parent's (nonconsolidated) books reflecting the loan due from Sympático. Similarly, Friendly's investment account showing its ownership of Sympático is netted out against Sympático's net worth account balance reflecting Friendly's ownership position. Assuming Friendly, the parent, had a flat year in 1995, the consolidated balance sheets for FY1994 and FY1995 might thus look as follows:

FRIENDLY INDUSTRIES, INC.
Consolidated Balance Sheet
(thousands of dollars)

	End of Fiscal Year	
	1994	**1995**
Assets		
Cash	$ 815	$ 821
Accounts receivable	3,040	3,036
Plant and equipment	16,060	16,048
Liabilities		
Accounts payable	630	624
Bank loans	825	820
Long-term debt	10,000	10,000
Net worth		
Common stock	3,600	3,600
Earned surplus	4,860	4,860
Cumulative translation adjustment	0	1

The net result of the consolidation is a one-time $1,000 credit to the net worth account Cumulative Translation Adjustment. The $1,000 credit can be explained by looking at the changes in the dollar basis of each individual account at the end of FY1994 and FY1995. Recall that such changes can be caused by exchange rate changes resulting in (1) conversion gains or losses, (2) translation gains or losses, and (3) changes in the subsidiary's accounts owing to operations during the period (the 33,750 peso increase in cash in the present example). The changes in Friendly's accounts can be explained as follows:

Account	Change	Comment
Cash	$ 6,000 dr	Gain of 33,750 pesos during fiscal year yields a dollar gain of $9,000. Translation loss on 45,000 pesos is $3,000.
Accounts Receivable	4,000 cr	Conversion gain of $4,000 on 15,000 peso write-up on dollar-based receivables. Translation loss on 120,000 pesos is $8,000.
Plant and Equipment	12,000 cr	Translation loss on 180,000 pesos is $12,000.
Accounts Payable	6,000 dr	Translation gain on 90,000 pesos is $6,000.
Bank Loan	5,000 dr	Translation gain on 75,000 pesos is $5,000.
Cumulative Translation Adjustment	1,000 cr	Entry to balance out net effect of conversion and translation gains/losses.

Note that the sum of the debit changes equals the sum of the credit changes, so that the net effect of the changes is zero. This follows since the entry to Cumulative Translation Adjustment is a balancing entry. This is always the way residual gains or losses derived during consolidation are handled.

US Financial Accounting Standards on Consolidation and Disclosures

The accounting procedures regarding consolidations just discussed are those required of US MNEs by Financial Accounting Standard 52. Specifically, FAS 52 requires that

1. A subsidiary's books be kept in the **functional currency** of the subsidiary, that is, its home currency (pesos in Sympático's case).
2. Changes in a subsidiary's foreign-currency assets and liabilities be reflected in changes in its functional currency records.
3. The exchange rate on the balance sheet date be used to translate assets and liabilities from the subsidiary's functional currency accounts into the parent's **reporting currency** accounts (dollars in Friendly's case).
4. A **weighted-average exchange rate** be used to translate income statement accounts from the functional currency into the reporting currency.
5. Net gains or losses arising from consolidation be reported directly as charges or credits to a special account in stockholders' equity (that is, to Cumulative Translation Adjustment in the Friendly case).

An exception to these rules occurs, however, when the subsidiary operates in a hyperinflationary environment or when its operations, financing, and cash flow are highly dependent on the parent. The parent's currency then serves as both the functional currency and the reporting currency. In such a situation, assets carried at historical costs—fixed assets and, in some instances, inventories—are

TABLE 14-1

The H J Heinz Company's FY1994 Performance by Geographic Profit Centers (in millions of US dollars)

	Identifiable Assets	Sales	Operating Income
North America	$3,993	$4,380	$ 588
Europe	1,551	1,685	372
Asia/Pacific	729	817	89
Other	108	164	20
Total H J Heinz Company and subsidiaries	$6,381	$7,046	$1,069

Source: The H J Heinz Company, *1994 Annual Report*, p. 38.

translated at historical rates of exchange. Other balance sheet items continue to be translated at current rates.

Income statement accounts similarly differentiate between accounts that are carried at historical costs and those that are not. In the former instance, such accounts use historical costs and the historical exchange rates that were in effect when the purchases were made. In the latter, such accounts continue to use the average exchange rate for the period. Translation gains or losses are taken as periodic charges or credits to income. They are not taken directly to equity.

The importance of understanding FAS 52 is underscored by Choi's observation that the current-rate translation basis (notwithstanding the exceptions noted) required by FAS 52 in the United States is also the method used most frequently in Japan and Europe.[6]

Financial accounting disclosure, including disclosure of foreign operations, is accomplished by means of the consolidated statements reporting just discussed. Reporting solely on foreign operations is another matter. For US firms, FAS 14 is the controlling policy statement. FAS 14 requires financial reporting by business segments, including geographic segments. To illustrate, Table 14–1 presents a financial report pertaining to the H J Heinz Company's global operations.

Accounting practices and standards could be treated in considerably greater depth. Here, however, we have confined ourselves to presenting some important concepts that should help managers better understand some of the fundamental accounting implications of multinational operations.

Managerial Accounting/Information Systems

Accounting information systems pertaining to management decision making can be varied and complex. Such systems are conditioned by many influences, including the nature of the financial reports; the records needed to prepare the financial reports and the usefulness of such records (or the ease with which they can be modified) for decision-making purposes; product configuration; process technology; local financial practices; the legal, cultural, and social environments; and so on.

The key issue regarding an appropriate **management information system (MIS)** is essentially similar to the issue discussed on product configuration and advertising in Chapter 13. That issue is to determine the appropriate balance between a **universal MIS**—uniform, easily understood at all management levels, and efficient to produce—and an MIS that is substantially adapted in each instance to fit the nuances of discrete, local environments.

For the ethnocentric MNE, the universal MIS is the ideal. Decisions at the parent level dominate the MNE network, and the parent generally imposes operating standards that determine operations everywhere. Parent company managers insist on information flows that are easily understood and consistent in their measurement of activities at all subsidiaries. Note that this is not a bad MIS policy for the ethnocentric MNE. It is in agreement with the firm's corporate strategies and functional policies. The fact that the firm dominates a global market and that the parent is the source of this dominance allows it to disregard local influences on operations. Production, marketing, and other functions are carried on in the same way at both the parent and subsidiary levels. For example, IBM's personal computer plant in Mexico operates under production standards and an MIS similar to those in place in its US personal computer plants.

For the polycentric MNE, a universal MIS makes little sense. Operations decisions and key managerial decisions are made at the subsidiary level. There is little need to accumulate information for use at the parent level. For example, Ford-Germany's cars have differed substantially from Ford's US cars, and Ford's US and German markets have been geographically segmented. Installing a global MIS would be of questionable value to Ford—and in fact the parent and its European subsidiaries were fairly autonomous, with infrequent information exchanges below the board of directors level, until some product integration policies came on line in the early 1970s.

For the geocentric MNE, the need is to find the balance between an MIS that consistently portrays operations at all subsidiaries and one that accommodates local nuances giving real meaning to the data and information transmitted. For example, H J Heinz has manufactured powdered baby food in Italy that was packaged in the United States and sold in the People's Republic of China (PRC). (This was an interim arrangement pending completion of a baby food processing and packaging plant in the PRC.) In this case, Heinz had to transmit a lot of information internationally and also had to develop the information base it needed to successfully market a product in China. For the geocentric MNE, such as Heinz, finding the appropriate balance between global information needs and local market information needs is a compelling necessity.

The theory of the MNE discussed in Chapter 2 revealed that MNEs have several competitive advantages over purely local firms. The effective transmission and implementation of these advantages within the parent-subsidiary MNE network gives the MNE units their competitiveness. This means management at all levels must have some fundamental, universal understanding regarding technology, operations, and so on. This, in turn, requires information feedback, effective management communication, and the like. The MIS must contain some measurements that are common to all locales. Where local nuances obviate this possibility, extra care must be taken to train managers in what their MIS is really telling them.

TAXATION AND THE MNE

The issue of taxation is especially important to the MNE, since the MNE operates in multiple taxing jurisdictions (i.e., countries) and has options for avoiding or deferring taxation in certain countries. Income, which is typically taxed at the source, has more than a single source when generated at the subsidiary level. The country in which the subsidiary is located views the subsidiary as a source; the country in which the parent is located views the MNE structure as a source. In some cases, US MNEs can defer US income taxes by retaining profits at the subsidiary level; in other cases, they cannot. Through foreign sales corporations, US firms can defer taxes. In all cases, however, the US Internal Revenue Service (IRS) has the final word on how much a firm's taxes are. This section discusses these and related topics.

TABLE 14-2

Alternative Methods for Recognizing Taxes Paid at the Subsidiary by the Parent Company's Home Country

Item	Double Taxation	Income Deduction	Tax Credit
Operating income	$100,000	$100,000	$100,000
Subsidiary's taxes	30,000	30,000	30,000
After-tax income	70,000	70,000	70,000
Parent's taxes	50,000	35,000	20,000
Net after-tax income to parent	$ 20,000	$ 35,000	$ 50,000

Note: The applicable income tax rate at the subsidiary is 30 percent; at the parent, it is 50 percent.

Income Taxes: The General Case

The after-tax income to the parent generated by profits at the subsidiary can vary considerably, depending on the handling of foreign taxes in the country of the parent company. The payment of the foreign tax by the subsidiary can be ignored (resulting, effectively, in double taxation), acknowledged as an income deduction (as it is in the United States for income taxes paid to state governments), or recognized as a dollar-for-dollar tax credit. Table 14–2 illustrates the use of these alternative approaches and their bottom-line results.

The example in Table 14–2 gives quite different results, depending on how the taxes paid by the subsidiary are handled by the tax authorities at the parent company level. The net, after-tax income to the parent ranges from $20,000 to $50,000! Fortunately for business executives who want to minimize taxes, bilateral tax treaties between the United States and a large number of other countries (including Germany, France, the United Kingdom, and other countries where large amounts of US direct investment are in place) allow for a US tax credit for foreign income taxes paid by subsidiaries. It seems reasonable too that if the parent company's country is to allow tax credits for taxes paid by subsidiaries in other countries, the books of those subsidiaries should be "reconstructed" to conform to the depreciation and other tax-related rules of that country. Most tax authorities, including the US Internal Revenue Service, reserve the final word on taxes, and Section 482 of the US Tax Code allows the IRS to reconstruct a company's records, if necessary, and assess the tax due. This assessment, of course, can be appealed to the US Tax Court. Assuming the tax accounting rules have already been accommodated, let's look at a concrete example to see how tax credits work.

Taxation Illustrated

Magna Corporation's wholly owned French subsidiary, Monser, SA, has closed its fiscal year with pretax profits of 8 million francs. Monser's dividend payout ratio is 50 percent, and the (assumed) French income tax rate is 25 percent. Magna's US federal income tax rate is 35 percent, and the rate of exchange is FF 5 per dollar. To complicate matters a little, let's also assume there is a 10 percent French tax on dividend remittances to foreigners. The actual funds received by Magna can be determined in this way:

		5 FF/$	
Monser's pretax profit	US$ 1,600,000	FF 8,000,000
French income taxes	400,000	2,000,000
Monser's after-tax profit	1200,000	6,000,000
Dividends declared (50 percent)	600,000	3,000,000 ×10%
Less: Dividend remittance tax	60,000	300,000
Dividends received by Magna		
In French francs	540,000	2,700,000
In US dollars		540,000

Since Magna prepares its own income statement, dividends received from a subsidiary represent taxable income, and since there is a tax treaty between the United States and France that allows for a tax credit on foreign taxes paid, the taxes that Magna was reported to have paid in France on its portion of Monser's income can be deducted from Magna's US tax bill. (Recall that in the absence of a tax treaty, there would be no tax credit for foreign taxes paid.) This may sound more complicated than it really is. Let's return to our example.

Magna received a net-of-all-taxes dividend of $540,000 from Monser. The taxes that this $540,000 bore were the $60,000 (FF 300,000) that Monser paid in dividend remittance taxes *plus* the French income taxes of $200,000 (FF 1,000,000) that Monser paid on the FF 4 million that it had to generate in pretax income in France to fund payment of the dividend. These taxes are important, since if local taxing authorities give a credit for foreign taxes paid, the dividend at the parent's level must be "grossed up" to include these taxes. The **grossed-up dividend** thus represents the total taxable income imprinted to have been received by the parent. The system has to work this way if the foreign taxes are subsequently credited against US taxes due. Let's return again to our example:

easy way

Net dividends received by Magna	$540,000
Plus: Dividend remittance tax	60,000
Plus: French taxes paid by Monser on dividend received by Magna	200,000
Grossed-up dividend to Magna	800,000
US income tax on grossed-up dividend.	280,000
Less: Foreign tax credit	260,000
US taxes payable—preliminary determination	$ 20,000

The last line, US taxes payable, is a preliminary determination in that this amount can still be offset by unused foreign tax credits on income from Magna's subsidiaries in other countries or by unused foreign tax credits generated from foreign operations in the past seven years. In no instance, however, can unused foreign tax credits be used to reduce taxes on domestically produced income. The rationale for grossing up the dividend to include the foreign taxes paid on it is that if one tax is to be a credit against the other, both have to be applied to the same income base. If this were not the case in our example, Magna's initial tax determination would be 35 percent of $540,000, or $189,000. A US tax of $189,000 would be wholly offset by French income taxes of $200,000. The idea that all US taxes could be eliminated in the face of a foreign income tax rate lower than the US rate (i.e., 25 percent/35 percent) is irrational.

Income Taxes: A Special Case

Income tax rates for businesses vary considerably country by country, as Table 14–3 illustrates. In fact, some countries don't tax business income at all, and other countries don't tax income from foreign sources. The former include Bermuda and the Cayman Islands; the latter include Panama and Liberia. Wouldn't the astute MNE set up a holding company in one of these countries to receive the dividends of its subsidiaries, which it could then divert (as investments) to other subsidiaries? (If such a holding company never paid a dividend to the US parent, the parent company could defer US income taxes forever.) Many US MNEs pursued this practice prior to the passage of the Revenue Act of 1962. President Kennedy was outspoken in his opposition to the practice, which, although legal, effectively exempted multinationals from paying US income taxes on foreign earnings (for the time being). The provisions of the Revenue Act of 1962 that eliminated the practice were the policy response to his initiatives.

TABLE 14-3

Corporate Income Tax Rates in Selected Countries as a Percentage of Taxable Income*

Country	Tax Rate	Country	Tax Rate
Australia	39%	Philippines	35%
France	33.3	United Kingdom	33
Turkey	46	United States	35
Mexico	35	Japan	37.5
Singapore	30	Taiwan	25
Brazil	25	Hong Kong	17.5

*Tax and tax rates may vary with definitions of *taxable income,* which may differ according to sources and deductibles allowed, with levels of earnings, and with uses of earnings, for example, distributed as dividends or undistributed. Rates shown are maximums.

Source: Data were collected from various sections in Price Waterhouse's *Corporate Taxes: A Worldwide Summary,* 1993 Edition (except for the US tax rate, which is current as of the end of 1994).

The act specifically defined a **controlled foreign corporation (CFC)** and Subpart F income to isolate and tax holding company earnings. A CFC is a foreign corporation that is 50 percent or more owned by US "shareholders," defined as US citizens (including corporations) holding 10 percent or more of the common stock. (Thus, a US citizen that owned less than 10 percent did not qualify as a US "shareholder" for the purposes of this act.)

Subpart F income is defined as the income received by a foreign-base company. A **foreign-base company** is a CFC that derives income from investments, sales, services, or shipping. Subpart F income is deemed to have been received by the US parent of the CFC. It is not deferred, unlike the operating income that a subsidiary derives from the actual conduct of a business and does not pay to the parent as dividends, as with Monser and Magna. There is one exception, however: the **10/70 rule.** This rule recognizes that subsidiaries may have income from numerous sources—production and sales, investments, and so on. The 10/70 rule stipulates that if less than 10 percent of a CFC's income is Subpart F income, full deferral applies. If more than 70 percent of a CFC's income is Subpart F income, none of it is deferred. (If Subpart F income constitutes between 10 and 70 percent of the CFC's income, the CFC's income is allocated between deferred and not deferred in the same ratio as its origin.)

If Monser were a holding company, and if its 8 million franc income were from dividends, management fees, and royalties, those 8 million francs, equal to $1.6 million, would immediately be taxable income to Magna, whether or not Monser declared any dividend. The initial US tax would be $560,000, but $400,000 of this would be offset by income taxes paid in France by Monser. (Note that there would be no US tax credit for dividend remittance taxes, since in this instance Monser paid no dividend to Magna.)

The Foreign Sales Corporation

Several countries have established schemes for subsidizing exports by "relieving" export profits or revenues of taxes. In many European countries, for instance, firms that export are rebated by governments for the taxes their export products carried. A major business tax in Europe is the **value-added tax (VAT).** This tax is applied to the value added by each producer/processor/distributor as a product progresses through the stages of production and distribution. It is applied to both intermediate products and final products. The total value-added taxes paid on a product are returned by the government to the exporter, thus making exports more price competitive in world markets than they would be otherwise. In the United States, channeling exports through a **foreign sales corporation (FSC)** can, like the VAT, result in tax advantages.

A US company can establish an FSC to handle its exports and accumulate profits on its export sales. Approximately 65 percent of the profits of the FSC will be tax exempt. Certain procedures and restrictions apply, however. For example, the FSC must be physically located outside the United States or in a US possession other than Puerto Rico, and it must actually participate in the conduct of export business. It cannot be a mere "shell." It must maintain an office, keep records, participate in sales solicitations and negotiations, and handle order processing, billings, and collections. The parent and its FSC are free to establish transfer prices on export goods as they see fit; however, profits at the FSC are limited to the larger of 1.83 percent of the total revenues generated by exports and 23 percent of the total income of the FSC and its parent.[7]

Dividends remitted by the FSC to its parent corporation are totally tax free at the parent level. At most, therefore, 65 percent of the profits at the FSC (which equals 65 percent of 23 percent of the combined, total corporate profits, or 15 percent of the total corporate profits) are tax exempt. Since countries in which an FSC is located can also tax the FSC's profits, the preferred location for FSCs is the US Virgin Islands, where US tax laws prevail.

There are other special situations where tax laws authorize tax benefits and advantages, for example, the FSC for small businesses, which does not require an offshore location. Inquiries on these and other tax-related issues should always be directed to a competent authority such as a tax accountant.

Taxation: The Management Impact

How do the tax matters just discussed relate to management? In many ways, tax considerations are one of several important inputs into management decision making. They are certainly relevant to the strategic management function at the corporate, MNE level, especially with regard to decisions on ownership structures, plant location, production allocation, target market selection, and financing. The astute manager will incorporate tax effects on cash flow projections when building the database appropriate to the planning function.

At the SBU level, tax concerns need to be addressed (perhaps jointly, in some cases, by both SBU-level and corporate-level managers) in decisions on intracorporate product transfers and transfer prices, personnel assignments, cash management and short-term financing arrangements, dividend policy, export strategy, profit planning, and accounting systems.

The foregoing illustrates that many factors affect an MNE's tax strategy. Frequently the ethnocentric manager will be concerned with individual "strategies" that aim at tax reduction as a primary objective, such as transfer pricing to locate profits in low-tax jurisdictions, delaying dividends to delay paying income taxes at the parent, or loading high-tax areas with MNE-benefiting operations and expenses (such as R&D expenses). In the polycentric structure, management is concerned with tax avoidance only at the subsidiary level. The geocentric manager sees taxes as only one of a variety of factors affecting MNE decision making. For example, moving funds from subsidiary to parent would be influenced by funding needs at both levels, the movement of such funds on the cost of capital, tax effects, and so on. In the geocentric MNE, moving funds may well be determined via a linear programming approach in which tax minimization is but one of several objective functions.

ADDED DIMENSION

Is the VAT a Good Tax for America?

For several years, Americans have been debating whether or not to have a value-added tax. There are pros and cons.

Those favoring the tax contend it would eliminate the competitive advantages enjoyed by firms exporting from countries in which the VAT is now in effect. They also note that since the VAT would replace the income tax, it would encourage savings. This is because paying income taxes cuts into both consumption and savings, and the income from savings is taxed again later as those savings generate more income. Doesn't America need more savings?

Those opposing the tax contend the VAT would be inflationary, regressive, complex, costly to administer (e.g., collect), and discriminatory (as the level of the VAT varied by industry).

How do you feel about the VAT? Is it a good tax for America? Would Europeans answer these questions differently than Americans? ▪

MANAGEMENT RESPONSIBILITIES UNDER THE FOREIGN CORRUPT PRACTICES ACT

During the 1970s, there was considerable public concern in the United States (and elsewhere) over unethical business practices—bribes to secure sales contracts, falsification of corporate records, and so on. Many of these practices, engaged in outside the United States, involved dealings between representatives of US corporations and officials of foreign governments. In response, legislation was enacted in 1977 to mandate corporate control over firms' activities in this regard.

The **Foreign Corrupt Practices Act** forbids bribes and similar questionable conduct, requires that funds not be made available for the payment of bribes and other dubious financial activities, and mandates that companies develop and apply internal accounting and control procedures to support the requirements of the act. A compelling feature of the act is that its penalties for noncompliance include not only fines for both companies and company officials but also *imprisonment of company officials*.

The Omnibus Trade and Competitiveness Act of 1988 amended the Foreign Corrupt Practices Act of 1977. It defined more specifically the type of business acts that are not permissible under the law (thus clearing up considerable ambiguity) and provided for substantially increased fines for violations. To illustrate, payments to foreign agents must now be to agents who are knowingly engaged in illegal conduct (such as bribery), and fines can reach as much as $2 million per company per violation.

Although the internal accounting and control procedures mandated by the act are costly, they may save money by reducing the potential for fraudulent activities. When the act was first passed, many observers believed its antibribery provisions would put US firms at a competitive disadvantage overseas. A 1984 study, however, suggests that this has not been the case. The act has caused no loss of foreign sales by US firms.[8]

CONCLUSIONS

Accounting and tax matters are especially challenging to MNE management. Both are complex and rewarding. When properly approached and implemented, accounting systems and tax strategies, especially those that pertain to the transfer and evaluation of management expertise and the minimization of cash outflows stemming from taxes, can support the competitive presence of MNEs both at home and abroad.

Accounting systems reflect environmental influences, such as the legal climate and levels of education, and vary somewhat country by country. The chapter discussed accounting for international transactions and consolidation accounting. The rules germane to each of these activities are fairly complex, and the recordkeeping is tedious. Management's responsibility is to learn the rules and ensure that they are followed.

The taxation of MNEs varies depending on the answers to a host of questions. Is there a tax treaty between the home and host countries? If so, what are its provisions? Is the foreign entity an operating company or simply a holding company? What are the levels of taxes abroad and of the dividends remitted to the parent? What is the overall foreign tax credit limitation? Can export income be channeled through a foreign sales corporation? The questions can go on and on.

In the United States, management has special responsibilities under the Foreign Corrupt Practices Act. The most difficult one to address is the requirement for internal accounting and managerial controls to ensure compliance with the act. Managers who fail to comply face a jail sentence.

QUESTIONS

1. Explain how accounting and tax matters can affect the competitiveness of an MNE.
2. Distinguish between financial accounting and managerial accounting/information systems. Distinguish between accounting for international transactions and accounting for consolidations.
3. Identify three environmental factors that have influenced the development of indigenous financial accounting systems. Describe specific results of these influences.
4. Explain the differences between the "trade credit" and the "trade credit—hedged" cases when accounting for international transactions.
5. Distinguish between a parent company's financial statements and the consolidated statements. Where does an investment in a subsidiary appear on the parent's books? On the consolidated statements?
6. What is FAS 52? What are its major provisions?
7. Distinguish between a conversion gain/loss and a translation gain/loss. Of what significance is the difference between the two?
8. In the Magna Corporation example, change the French income tax rate to 30 percent. What will Magna's US taxes then be?
9. Distinguish between Subpart F income and ordinary income. Why is this distinction necessary?
10. Identify some management problems that must be resolved when a foreign sales corporation is established. Of what benefit is a foreign sales corporation?

REFERENCES

AlHashim, Dhia D, and Jeffrey S Arpan. *International Dimensions of Accounting.* Boston: PWS-Kent Publishing, 1988.

Bavishi, Vinod B. *International Accounting and Auditing Trends.* Vols. 1 and 2. Princeton, NJ: Center for International Financial Analysis and Research, Inc. 1989.

Beresford, Dennis R. "What's the FASB Doing about International Accounting Standards?" *Financial Executive,* May–June 1990, pp. 17–23.

Corporate Taxes: A Worldwide Summary. New York: Price Waterhouse, 1993.

Kostin, Edward B, ed. *International Tax Summaries 1990: A Guide for Planning and Decisions.* Coopers & Lybrand International Tax Network. Somerset, NJ: John Wiley & Sons, 1990.

Militzer, Ken, and Ilona Ontscherenki. "The Value Added Tax: Its Impact on Saving." *Business Economics,* April 1990, pp. 32–37.

Morehead, Jere W, and Sandra G Gustavson II. "Complying with the Amended Foreign Corrupt Practices Act." *Risk Management,* April 1990, pp. 76–82.

Reinstein, Alan, and Albert D Spalding. "Accounting and Auditing Implications of Complying with the United States' Foreign Corrupt Practices Act Amendments of 1988." *International Journal of Accounting* 26 (1991), pp. 18–26.

Rubin, Ken, and Bryan Lundstrom. "Foreign Sales Corporations for Manufacturers." *Management Accounting,* October 1992, pp. 57–60.

United Nations. *International Accounting and Reporting Issues.* New York: UN, 1990.

Walter, Ingo. *Secret Money: The Shadowy World of Tax Evasion, Capital Flight, and Fraud.* Lexington, MA: Lexington Books, 1985.

NOTES

[1] Steven A Zeff, *Forging Accounting Principles in Five Countries: A History and an Analysis of Trends* (Champaign, IL: Stipes Publishing, 1972).

[2] Frederick D S Choi and Gerhard G Mueller, *An Introduction to Multinational Accounting* (Englewood Cliffs, NJ: Prentice Hall, 1978), pp. 24–28.

[3] Konrad W Kubin, "Comparative Accounting Systems," in *Handbook of International Management,* ed. Ingo Walter (New York: John Wiley & Sons, 1988), chap. 23, pp. 23–24.

[4] R D Fitzgerald; A D Stickler; and T R Watts, *International Survey of Accounting Principles and Reporting Practices* (New York: Price Waterhouse International, 1979).

[5] Kubin, "Comparative Accounting Systems," p. 23–25.

[6] Frederick D S Choi, "Accounting for Multinational Operations," in *Handbook of International Management,* ed. Ingo Walter (New York: John Wiley & Sons, 1988), chap. 22.

[7] Detailed information on foreign sales corporations can be found in analyses of the Tax Reform Act of 1984 prepared by most major accounting firms and by Commerce Clearing House.

[8] J L Graham, "The Foreign Corrupt Practices Act: A New Perspective," *Journal of International Business Studies,* Winter 1984, pp. 107–23.

Hurricane Canoe Corporation

Hurricane Canoe Corporation (HCC) is a major US canoe manufacturer located in Orlando, Florida. The firm is not large by overall US industrial standards, but it is the second largest canoe builder in the world. With annual sales of about $200 million and assets of nearly $100 million in North America and Europe, HCC is clearly beyond the small-business stage. Its sales growth has exceeded 20 percent per year since 1988, and its prospects for continued success appear good.

Most of HCC's growth has come through expansion of its distribution network. The firm's main products have remained basically the same over the years: canoes, paddles, safety and camping gear, and some specialty clothing. Its diversification has been primarily geographic (rather than through new products), though some of its sales outlets have added other firms' canoes and canoe rentals to their product lines. HCC's US operations reported sales of $72.7 million and profits before taxes of $11.4 million in 1994 (exclusive of management fees and royalties from foreign operations).

Hurricane Canoe began its foreign operations in the late 1970s by establishing a sales office in Montreal, Quebec. Canadian canoeists rank among the most avid in the world, and HCC had great expectations for Canadian sales of its high-performance Kevlar and ABS boats. These expectations were borne out by sales of hundreds, then thousands, of boats in the first eight years of the Canadian operation. Subsequently, HCC established a wholly owned assembly operation in Windsor, Ontario, which currently produces one-third of HCC's North American output. At present, 75 percent of the Windsor operation's output is sold in Canada, and the balance is exported to the United States at a price to HCC-owned distributors of cost plus 10 percent. Pretax profits in Canada last year (1994) were $5.8 million on sales of $45 million.

After several years of small-volume exports to European purchasers, Hurricane Canoe established a regional sales office in Frankfurt, Germany, to serve the Common Market. This wholly owned subsidiary established ties with unaffiliated distributors throughout Europe. Selling canoes and peripheral equipment manufactured in both the United States and Canada, the Frankfurt office showed a 1994 pretax profit of $16.8 million on sales of $48.8 million. During the past five years, sales of the Frankfurt office have been growing phenomenally at 25 percent per year.

In 1988, HCC formed a joint venture with Kirk and Steuergard, SA (K&S), of Denmark, the world's leading manufacturer of Olympic-style canoes. In return for

---

This case was written by Professor Robert Grosse. Revised 1994.

a 49 percent contribution of capital, technology, and management, HCC received 49 percent ownership and exclusive distribution rights for K&S boats in North America. This $5 million investment in Copenhagen was a sizable commitment of funds, but the investment was paid back within three years and profits continue to grow rapidly. The joint venture's sales and pretax profits were $25 million and $6.9 million, respectively, in 1994. Currently this affiliate is capitalized at $9.7 million.

Hurricane Canoe's most recent foreign venture is a 100-percent-owned assembly plant near Barcelona, Spain. HCC saw low-cost assembly, plus tariff-free access to the European Union, as adequate justification for the investment. HCC spent $4.5 million during the start-up phase of operations, and at year-end 1994 it had assets worth $2.9 million in the Barcelona plant. During 1994, sales of this plant were a modest $6.5 million, and initial operating problems led to a loss of $1.2 million.

Hurricane Canoe's policies require that each subsidiary remit 50 percent of its after-tax earnings to the parent company. Each affiliate—that is, the Danish joint venture—pays out 50 percent of pretax earnings in dividends. A management fee totaling 2 percent of sales is charged to all wholly owned subsidiaries. A royalty totaling 5 percent of sales is charged to all manufacturing affiliates.

Tax rate data for the countries within which Hurricane Canoe operates are presented in Table 1. Using these data as necessary, complete Table 2 to figure Hurricane Canoe's US income taxes last year. From a total tax perspective, what costs is HCC bearing to maintain its ethnocentric 50 percent dividend payout ratio from overseas operations in the face of rapid growth and high cash needs in its European operations? (As a basis for comparison, assume no dividends are paid out by the operations in Germany and Denmark and that the Canadian subsidiary requires that two-thirds of its after-tax profits be reinvested in Windsor.)

TABLE 1

Tax Rates (percent)

	United States	Canada	Germany	Denmark	Spain
Corporate income tax	35	43.5	45/30*	34	35
Dividend withholding tax	0	25	25	30	25
Royalties and fees withholding tax	0	25	25	0	25

*In Germany, the corporate income tax rate is 45 percent on undistributed profits and 30 percent on distributed profits (i.e., dividends paid out).

TABLE 2

US Income Tax
Calculations (in millions of
US dollars)

	United States	Canada	Germany	Denmark	Spain
Country Level					
Sales	72.7	45.0	48.8	25/12.3	6.5
Pretax profit	11.4	5.8	16.8	6.9/3.4	−1.2
Income tax	_____	_____	_____	_____	_____
After-tax profit	_____	_____	_____	_____	_____
Dividends		_____	_____	_____	_____
Parent Level (consolidated, except as noted)					
Gross dividends		_____	_____	_____	_____
Less: Dividend withholding tax		_____	_____	_____	_____
Net dividends	_____	_____	_____	_____	_____
Management fees		_____	_____	_____	_____
Royalties		_____	_____	_____	_____
Total fees and royalties		_____	_____	_____	_____
Less: Fee/royalty withholding tax		_____	_____	_____	_____
Net fees and royalties	_____	_____	_____	_____	_____
Grossed-up income		_____	_____	_____	_____
US tax—initial		_____	_____	_____	_____
Less: Foreign tax credit		_____	_____	_____	_____
US tax due (by country)	_____	_____	_____	_____	_____
Total US tax due	_____				

15

Financial Management and Control in the International Firm

This chapter discusses the opportunities and problems that face multinational firms because they operate in a multicurrency, segmented-market world. The main goals of the chapter are to:

1. Discuss how capital budgeting analysis for an MNE differs from that for a domestic firm.

2. Explain the concept of country risk and discuss methods for dealing with it.

3. Show how the MNE can make financial structure decisions based both on its total capitalization and on market conditions in the countries where it operates.

4. Describe how working capital management for an MNE differs from that for a domestic firm.

5. Define *transaction, translation,* and *economic exchange risk* and discuss methods for dealing with each.

6. Describe how the MNE can establish financial controls.

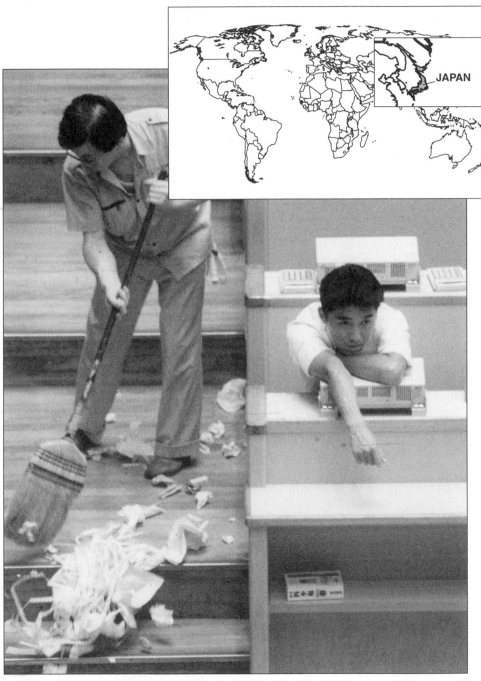

JAPAN

A Tokyo stock broker slouches over his desk as a janitor sweeps off trashed documents and paper at the end of a trading day.
Reuters/Bettmann

INTRODUCTION

Any firm with affiliates in at least two countries (even with a simple sales office abroad) needs to deal with differences in the financial environments of those countries—differences in their tax systems, their currency systems, and numerous other areas. Can you imagine trying to keep the books of a company such as Johnson & Johnson, which is required to maintain financial records according to the different accounting standards in the dozens of countries where it operates, plus records for use in internal control? Beyond the chores of recordkeeping, the firm operating at this level obtains opportunities to transfer funds (and products) between countries, utilize financial markets in each country to serve its global needs, and diversify its risks internationally. Increasing numbers of MNEs, such as Chrysler and General Electric, are building internal financial institutions so that they can take advantage of these opportunities around the world. This chapter explores the opportunities and problems of firms in such an environment.

The issue of measuring an MNE's tax liabilities was covered in the previous chapter; this chapter focuses on the firm's ability to arbitrage tax jurisdictions (that is, reduce global taxes paid by incurring expenses in high-tax countries and showing higher profits in lower-tax countries) and in general to deal with taxation in each country of operation. Similarly, national financial markets and the euromarkets were discussed in Chapter 7; here the emphasis is on using these markets to optimize the financial position of the multinational firm. The issue of exchange risk was treated in Chapter 6; this chapter considers such risk in the context of a firm that does repeated international business and maintains long-term assets abroad. Finally, we consider the full set of financial issues in a firm whose subsidiaries in different countries compete for use of the available financial resources. This chapter treats the topic of multinational financial management as a whole.

The chapter is structured to cover major issues in corporate finance as they apply to the international context. Basic financial management can be divided into two broad headings: (1) choice and management of *sources* of funds and (2) choice and management of *uses* of funds. At the international level, exchange risk management must be added. Figure 15–1 depicts the topics that constitute the substance of the chapter. Overall financial management requires *control* over each type of decision depicted in the figure, especially since financial managers in each affiliate may make decisions that affect the total corporation's financial position.

In the next three sections, we explore aspects of long-term asset and liability management. Then we cover working capital management. Next, we consider a more extensive presentation of exchange risk management than that given in Chapter 6. Finally, we discuss the problem of financial control.

The main uses of funds in a business can be divided into long-term capital projects and such short-term assets as cash, securities, accounts receivable, and inventories. Long-term overseas projects are our first subject for discussion.

CAPITAL BUDGETING IN THE MULTINATIONAL ENTERPRISE

Capital project evaluation follows many of the same principles in an international firm as in a domestic firm, though additional variables and risks must be considered. Specifically, foreign projects must be evaluated for exchange risk, country risk, different financing costs, and any problems associated with the transfer of products, services, or funds due to government controls in any of the relevant countries. To see how these factors appear in the analysis, consider the following example of a food-processing plant to be constructed by a US-based company in Shapironia.

FIGURE 15-1

Financial Management in
the MNE

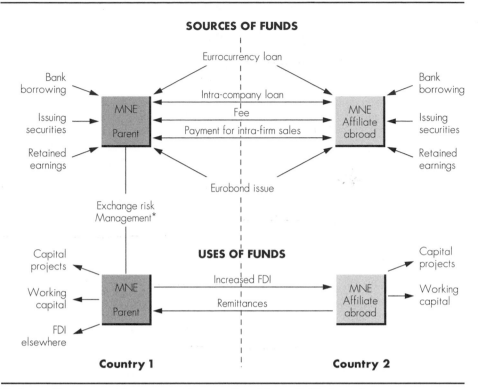

*Exchange risk management is a companywide concern that relates to all of the issues shown above.

The company has developed the following pro forma income statement for the proposed investment project:

Proposed Shapironia Processing Plant
Pro Forma Income Statement, Typical Year
(in local currency)

Sales	10,000,000
Cost of goods sold	
Local materials	1,000,000
Imported materials	2,000,000
Labor	3,000,000
Overhead expenses	600,000
Interest on loan from parent firm	400,000
Net income before tax	3,000,000
Local tax—50%	1,500,000
Net income after tax	1,500,000

Assuming the investment made by the parent firm is 4 million in local currency, the project appears to have a simple return on capital of about 38 percent per year (1,500,000/4,000,000). As long as the firm's cost of capital is less than 38 percent, the project is worth undertaking.[1] The normal, domestic concerns apply to this project evaluation; that is, the estimate is only as good as the forecasts of costs and sales. In addition, this foreign project faces potentially important considerations such as exchange risk, currency inconvertibility and other country risks, and preferential local borrowing opportunities.

Exchange risk will affect the US dollar value of the profits earned, potentially raising or lowering them substantially. For example, if the local-currency value rises by 10 percent in relation to the dollar, net income after tax will rise (in dollar terms) by 10 percent, other things equal. However, if imported materials come from the United States, that cost (in local currency) will fall. Similarly, if the loan is made in dollars, interest cost (in local-currency terms) will fall. Sales, if any are exported from Shapironia, may decrease due to the exchange rate change.[2] In sum, a rise in the value of the local currency relative to the US dollar will tend to cause an increase in dollar profits from the affiliate, and such profits will tend to fall if the local currency devalues relative to the dollar.

Country risk (defined shortly) is another concern in the attempt to evaluate this project properly. If the host government decides to restrict profit remittances, then, no matter how profitable the project, the MNE will not be able to utilize its earnings elsewhere in the firm or to distribute them to shareholders. This problem is known as **currency inconvertibility,** regardless of whether the cause is a political decision or simply an economic reality. If discontent with the Shapironia government leads to strikes or violent confrontation between the government and opposition groups, the plant may be damaged or its production curtailed. Not all country risk is negative; if the government chooses to reduce corporate taxes to stimulate greater investment, the project may generate greater profitability than that shown above. In sum, country risks need to be considered when the full set of the project's financial implications is being judged.

Borrowing costs may differ in Shapironia and the United States. Thus, if the firm uses its **weighted-average cost of capital*** in capital budgeting decisions, this project should be adjusted to account for any locally subsidized borrowing opportunity that exists. Many countries (and states or provinces within countries) offer low-interest loans to corporate investors to attract production facilities and jobs. If this is true in Shapironia and if the firm chooses to borrow some funds locally, the subsidized capital cost should be reflected in the capital budget.[3] The project as shown uses an intracompany loan whose interest may be charged at the parent's actual cost of funds or marked up (or down) to achieve greater (or lesser) transfer of funds to the parent.

Finally, recall that the capital budget measures the project's *incremental impact on the whole firm.* Thus, if there are export sales from the parent to this new affiliate, those new sales must be counted in the evaluation. If the project replaces sales that were formerly exported to Shapironia, those lost sales must be counted. Any other intracompany impacts should also be measured in the project evaluation. This means the project should be judged in comparison with other alternatives available to the firm serving the Shapironia market. If exports from the United States offer a greater incremental profitability than the proposed plant, exports should be chosen. In summary, the incremental gains to the firm from the proposed project should be compared with the potential gains from other international business alternatives that may be available.

---

*The weighted-average cost of capital (WACC) is the firm's cost of obtaining funds from the various sources available. Each source of funds is weighted (multiplied) by the percentage of total capital it provides. Thus, the WACC is W_1 (cost of using retained earnings) + W_2 (cost of bank borrowing) + W_3 (cost of other source of funds), where each cost is stated as an annual percentage rate and each W is the percentage of total capital from that source.

COUNTRY RISK MANAGEMENT

Definition

Country risk is the decrease or increase in a firm's value that may result from unexpected changes in the external, political or economic environment.

Country risk generally refers to a full range of environmental factors that may affect the firm's performance in a particular country. Normal business risks are excluded from this category, but most of the other factors that are outside the firm's control are included. Thus, country risk includes the risk that a government will alter its policies toward the firm or its products (e.g., through price controls), thus lowering or raising profitability or asset values. It also includes the risk of civil war, foreign war, riots, strikes, and other violent social acts that disrupt business. Efforts to harm foreign firms or the particular firm through kidnappings, assassinations, sabotage, or other means fall into this category. Although expropriation of the firm's assets by the host government occurs very infrequently, it constitutes a major country risk. Remember that not all country risks are negative. For example, when a government changes its policies to the firm's advantage (e.g., by lowering taxes or providing some kind of subsidy), this positive outcome also constitutes country risk. Since most decision makers are concerned with "what could go wrong?", country risk discussions usually focus on the negative side.

All of these factors are considered country risks because all can lead to losses (or gains) for the firm for reasons it cannot foresee or control and because all constitute discontinuities in the firm's external environment. In other words, country risks must involve *changes* in the environment that can affect the firm. Therefore, an *existing* government policy that disallows profit remittances is not a country risk; it is a business condition in the particular country. The possibility of expropriation can be considered a virtual nonrisk for most manufacturing investments in most countries; almost all expropriations since World War II have taken place in extractive industries (e.g., oil, copper, bauxite) and in a handful of less developed countries (primarily in Latin America and the Middle East).

Country risks may be macrorisks or microrisks. A **macrorisk** applies to all foreign firms doing business in a particular country. For example, the changes in taxation or profit remittance rules that often occur in LDCs generally apply to all the foreign firms in those countries. A **microrisk,** on the other hand, applies to one firm or one group of firms. For example, Saudi Arabia's decision to nationalize its oil industry in 1974 constituted a risk for foreign oil companies there, but that risk did not carry over into the manufacturing sector. Even more firm specific was the campaign by several public interest groups against Nestlé during the 1980s, when Nestlé was accused of promoting its infant formula in poor LDCs in a manner that overstated the benefits and understated the risks. Similarly, ITT's reported involvement in attempts to overthrow the Allende government in Chile in the early 1970s led to substantial government reprisals in Chile and a continuing wariness on the part of Latin American governments with respect to ITT activities.[4] This country risk is company specific.

What exactly is at risk? The answer clearly depends on the type of firm and its activity in the country. A manufacturing plant typically exposes physical facilities, people, and money to country risk. A sales office may leave only a small number of people and a small amount of equipment at risk. An international bank loan may expose only money to country risk. The correct measure of exposure is that part of the firm's worldwide business that could be affected by unexpected economic or political events or policies in the given country. To determine an appropriate strategy for dealing with this risk, the firm must establish the importance of the risk to its overall operations.

The full scope of the issues involved in country risk is so broad that it cannot be presented in detail here. Kobrin (1982) encompasses the range of "potentially significant managerial contingencies generated by political events and processes" in his definition of country risk. Miller (1992) considers country risk to include "general environmental uncertainties [such as] political instability, government policy instability, macroeconomic uncertainties, social uncertainties, and national uncertainties." Every definition of country risk focuses on the potential impact of political or economic factors on company performance.

Measures of Country Risk

A number of very large firms and banks go to great lengths to measure country risks in their businesses. Texaco and Royal Dutch Shell, for example, maintain corporate staff groups of political risk analysts who keep up with political conditions in countries where the firms do business and try to anticipate important changes in those conditions. Similarly, Bankers Trust Corporation and a handful of other multinational banks operate country risk staffs that track political and economic conditions abroad and try to assess their implications for the banks' loan portfolios. Instead of accumulating very detailed knowledge about a large number of countries, many firms create country ranking systems, which they use to compare country risk internationally (and presumably to avoid very risky nations).

Several independent services create country risk ratings. A typical service is *Euromoney* magazine's annual Country Risk Rating, which is based on a measure of different countries' access to international credit. Figure 15–2 presents the ratings for 1993.

Unfortunately, it is not possible to know the future, so country risk forecasters are doomed to failure as crystal ball analysts. However, some value can be gained from their efforts if these are viewed as an attempt to keep in touch with conditions in the various countries so that signals of policy changes are not overlooked. The fall of the shah of Iran and the overthrow of the Somoza regime in Nicaragua led to widespread focus on country risk analysis in MNEs during the past two decades. The demise of the Soviet Union, the reunification of Germany, and the continued major changes in former Soviet bloc countries have renewed this issue during the 1990s. It is not possible to predict the next major upheaval of this kind. However, it may be possible to anticipate that a country will increase taxes or be unable to make payment on its foreign debt. The opening of the former Soviet bloc countries now provides a huge set of potential opportunities for international firms. Country risk assessment is vitally needed to enable firms to decide on their resource commitments to Russia, Poland, the Czech Republic, and other such nations. If country risk analysts pursue such more modest but more realistic goals, they may indeed offer useful inputs into corporate decision making.

Currently analysts measure country risks with methods ranging from estimates of the probability that governments will be overthrown to nonquantitative commentaries on the styles of decision making employed by national leaders. Most country risk analysis done today evaluates macrorisk, since the available models do not readily handle highly idiosyncratic, company-specific factors. Each firm must then assess the bearing of the macrorisk evaluations on its own specific circumstances.

Country Risk and Financial Decision Making

How can country risks be incorporated into a firm's decision making? At the level of capital budgeting, either cash flows or a discount factor can be adjusted to account for such risks. Models have been developed to do exactly that.[5] While no model can incorporate such an imprecise factor with complete accuracy, at least there can be no argument that country risk should be taken into account.

FIGURE 15-2 Euromoney Country Risk Ratings, 1993

Rank		Country	Rating (0-100)	
1993	1992		1993	1990
1	6	United States	97.4	85.7
2	1	Japan	97.2	91.9
3	18	Luxembourg	96.9	91.1
4	3	Switzerland	96.6	87.6
5	5	France	95.7	89.9
6	8	Canada	95.6	85.8
7	2	Netherlands	95.2	89.9
8	7	Austria	95.1	89.9
9	12	Denmark	95.0	85.7
10	9	United Kingdom	94.7	83.5
11	11	Norway	93.9	84.9
12	14	Singapore	93.7	84.8
13	4	Germany	93.2	82.7
14	10	Belgium	92.8	85.4
15	20	Taiwan	91.9	79.2
16	15	Australia	90.9	74.4
17	19	New Zealand	90.2	73.5
18	17	Spain	89.1	81.9
19	13	Sweden	88.7	87.4
20	21	Ireland	87.9	85.7
21	16	Finland	87.5	86.2
22	25	Hong Kong	85.2	71.2
23	22	Italy	85.2	83.6
24	24	Iceland	84.7	69.0
25	23	Portugal	84.5	79.2
26	29	Korea (Repub)	81.6	82.0
27	27	United Arab Emirates	80.6	56.0
28	31	Malaysia	78.5	75.8
29	32	Israel	78.1	49.9
30	26	Saudi Arabia	78.0	60.0
31	30	Bahrain	75.8	60.0
32	36	Thailand	75.2	72.2
33	34	Brunei	75.1	72.1
34	33	Kuwait	74.0	27.9
35	28	Greece	73.8	64.7
36	42	Oman	72.6	59.0
37	38	Qatar	72.5	44.8
38	43	China	71.5	65.1
39	39	Malta	70.1	73.9
40	41	Cyprus	69.7	70.0
41	35	Chile	68.8	54.4
42	40	Indonesia	68.4	65.7
43	49	Czech Republic	64.5	61.7
44	37	Turkey	64.1	54.0
45	44	Bahamas	62.9	—
46	46	Hungary	61.6	60.8
47	48	Colombia	60.7	45.0
48	45	Mexico	60.4	58.6
49	47	South Africa	60.0	55.0
50	50	Tunisia	58.1	50.0
51	53	Botswana	57.3	60.3
52	52	Uruguay	54.1	60.1
53	57	India	54.3	58.7
54	61	Barbados	53.3	55.3

FIGURE 15–2   *(Continued)*

Rank		Country	Rating (0–100)	
1993	1992		1993	1990
55	54	Argentina	50.5	33.3
56	56	Morocco	50.2	42.5
57	55	Papua New Guinea	50.0	48.5
58	64	Belize	49.9	38.0
59	51	Venezuela	49.0	46.1
60	60	Fiji	47.7	57.0
61	74	Slovenia	47.6	—
62	77	Phillipines	47.3	41.4
63	58	Slovakia	47.2	—
64	62	Trinidad & Tobago	46.9	47.6
65	90	Jordan	46.0	31.0
66	99	Iran	45.8	33.8
67	63	Mauritus	45.7	66.5
68	65	Pakistan	45.0	52.7
69	59	Zimbabwe	45.0	46.0
70	69	Ghana	45.0	33.9
71	73	Costa Rica	44.7	35.0
72	71	Poland	44.6	43.0
73	86	Egypt	43.8	39.6
74	87	Paraguay	43.6	53.0
75	72	Romania	43.2	43.3
76	76	Sri Lanka	43.2	42.4
77	70	Brazil	42.6	45.0
78	79	Vanuatu	42.2	45.0
79	66	Algeria	40.9	47.0
80	75	Syria	40.8	22.3
81	68	Kenya	40.4	43.2
82	83	Seychelles	39.5	—
83	113	St. Lucia	39.1	—
84	95	El Salvador	38.9	25.7
85	85	Bolivia	38.6	28.3
86	67	Gabon	38.4	35.8
87	119	Guatemala	38.1	26.0
88	80	Lesotho	37.9	36.0
89	106	Dominican Rep.	37.6	28.0
90	100	Jamaica	37.5	39.0
91	89	Bangladesh	37.0	39.3
92	94	Ecuador	36.8	30.0
93	78	St. Vincent & Grenadines	36.8	—
94	88	Gambia	36.2	28.9
95	97	Libya	35.5	28.7
96	93	Panama	34.8	50.8
97	109	Honduras	34.4	26.0
98	103	Djibouti	34.3	25.2
99	98	Namibia	34.3	18.9
100	84	Senegal	34.0	37.8
101	96	Nigeria	33.6	33.0
102	135	Bhutan	33.0	—
103	128	Vietnam	32.8	—
104	82	Nepal	32.8	—
105	—	Malawi	32.6	40.0
106	111	Mali	32.1	36.8
107	81	Cameroon	31.6	37.0
108	102	Guinea	31.4	—

FIGURE 15-2 *(Continued)*

Rank			Rating (0-100)	
1993	1992	Country	1993	1990
109	115	Yemen	31.3	—
110	110	Burkina Faso	31.3	—
111	120	Grenada	31.3	—
112	92	Niger	31.0	28.6
113	101	Croatia	30.9	—
114	155	Benin	30.9	—
115	108	Macedonia	30.1	—
116	141	Lebanon	30.1	19.6
117	139	Peru	29.9	28.9
118	121	Central African Rep.	29.6	—
119	114	Antigua & Barbuda	29.3	—
120	116	Madagascar	29.2	25.4
121	105	Burundi	29.0	—
122	117	Estonia	29.0	—
123	107	Rwanda	28.9	36.9
124	124	Cote d'Ivoire	28.7	25.2
125	91	Bulgaria	28.5	34.7
126	133	Chad	28.4	27.2
127	145	Cape Verde	27.9	—
128	112	Togo	27.8	—
129	134	Kazakhstan	26.6	—
130	118	Lithuania	26.5	—
131	130	Haiti	26.3	23.2
132	123	Latvia	26.0	—
133	157	Myanmar	25.9	25.0
134	138	Guinea-Bissau	25.7	—
135	137	Tanzania	25.2	33.7
136	147	Zambia	24.9	23.0
137	129	Russia	24.7	—
138	125	Yugoslavia (Serbia)	24.7	42.2
139	132	Belarus	24.6	—
140	127	Uganda	24.2	19.4
141	126	Ethiopia	23.8	19.3
142	142	Albania	23.8	27.0
143	104	Angola	23.7	25.6
144	146	Kyrghystan	23.5	—
145	140	Mauritania	22.9	22.8
146	122	Ukraine	22.6	—
147	149	Mongolia	22.5	—
148	143	Turkmenistan	22.2	—
149	131	Bosnia-Herzegovina	21.9	—
150	150	Sao Tome & Principe	21.9	—
151	148	Georgia	21.2	—
152	159	Sierra Leone	21.1	28.9
153	144	Uzbekistan	21.0	—
154	151	Congo	20.5	27.4
155	167	North Korea	19.4	—
156	160	Guyana	19.1	19.4
157	136	Zaire	18.9	21.5
158	164	Mozambique	18.9	13.6
159	154	Armenia	18.6	—
160	156	Moldova	17.7	—
161	158	Afghanistan	17.1	—
162	169	Cambodia	16.2	—

FIGURE 15-2   (Concluded)

Rank		Country	Rating (0–100)	
1993	1992		1993	1990
163	152	Tajikistan	15.8	—
164	168	Iraq	15.7	18.4
165	153	Azerbaijan	15.7	—
166	162	Liberia	14.8	17.3
167	161	Nicaragua	12.0	14.5
168	163	Sudan	11.0	14.5
169	166	Somalia	10.6	—
170	165	Cuba	9.4	25.4

The Euromoney country risk method: The *Euromoney* country risk assessment uses nine categories which encompass three broad categories (analytical indicators, debt indicators, and access to international finance). *Euromoney*'s September 1993 ranking incorporates a change in our weighting system, giving greater weight to the economic performance and political risk categories, and less weight to categories rating access to international borrowing.

The different scores for each category (detailed below) are calculated into the weighted scores as follows: the highest figure in each category receives the full mark for the weighting. The lowest receives zero. The score for other figures is calculated proportionately according to the formula: final score=(weighting/(maximum figure − minimum figure)) × (figure − minimum figure). The ranking table shows only the final scores after the calculation for weightings.

The categories are:

Economic data (25% weighting). Taken from the *Euromoney* global economic projections 1993–94 (see following page). The score is calculated from the sum of the overall economic performance evaluations for 1993 and 1994.

Political risk (25%). *Euromoney* polled risk analysts, risk insurance brokers and bank credit officers. They were asked to give each country a score from 0 to 10. A score of 10 indicates nil risk of non-payment, a score of 0 indicates that there is no chance of payments being made. Countries were scored in comparison both with each other and with previous years. Country risk was defined as the risk of non-payment or nonservicing of payment for goods or services, loans, trade-related finance and dividends and the non-repatriation of capital. This category does not take into account the creditworthiness of individual counterparties in each country.

Debt indicators (10%) Scores are calculated from the following ratios taken from the World Bank World Debt Tables 1992–93: debt service-to-export ratio (TDS/XGS); current account balance-to-GNP ratio (CAB/GNP); external debt-to-GNP ratio (EDT/GNP). Figures are the latest available, mostly for 1991. Scoring is calculated on the basis of (EDT/GNP) + (TDS/XGS × 2)–(CAB/GNP × 10), with the lower the score the better.

Because of the lack of consistent economic data for OECD and rich oil-producing countries, they all automatically score full points. Developing countries which do not report debt data to the World Bank, score zero. Successor states of countries which have split take the former country's figures.

Debt in default or rescheduled (10%). A score from 0 to 10 based on the amount of debt in default or which had to be rescheduled over the last three years. 0=no non-payments; 10=all in default. Scores based on World Bank World Debt Tables 1992–93.

Credit ratings (10%). Average of sovereign ratings from Moody's and Standard & Poor's. Countries without credit ratings or with less than BB-score 0. Countries with only a short-term rating score the equivalent of BBB.

Access to bank finance (5%). Calculated from disbursements of long-term private non-guaranteed debt in 1991 as a percentage of GNP, OECD countries automatically score 10. Source: World Bank World Debt tables 1992–93.

Access to short-term finance (5%). Score is calculated according to which OECD consensus group the country belongs to: score 10 for Group I, 5 for Group II, 0 for Group III. Coverage from US Exim Bank and NCM: score from 10 to 0 depending on level of coverage available. A slightly different scoring method may mean that some countries for which coverage has not changed since September 1992 may have a different score.

Access to international bond and syndicated loan markets (5%). Analysis by *Euromoney* of syndicated loan and international bond issues since January 1989 and a judgment of how easy it would be for that country to tap the market now. 10=no problem whatsoever; 8=no problem on 95% of occasions; 6=usually no problem; 4=possible dependent on conditions; 2=just possible in some circumstances; 0=impossible.

Access to and discount on forfaiting (5%). Scored from a combination of the maximum tenor available (up to seven years) and the forfaiting spread over riskless countries such as the United States. Score=maximum tenor minus spread. Countries for which forfaiting is not available score zero. Data supplied by Morgan Grenfell Trade Finance Limited.

Source: *Euromoney*, September 1993, p. 363–66.

Consider how country risk is generally used in decision making in large firms today. Surveys of both industrial corporations and banks (e.g., Kobrin, 1982; Grosse and Stack, 1984; Mascarenhas and Sand, 1985), have found that some individual or group within the firm assesses political and economic risks and that this assessment is then used in corporate investment or lending decisions. The sequence of events pictured in Figure 15–3 illustrates the basic method of

FIGURE 15-3

Country Risk in the
Investment/Lending Process

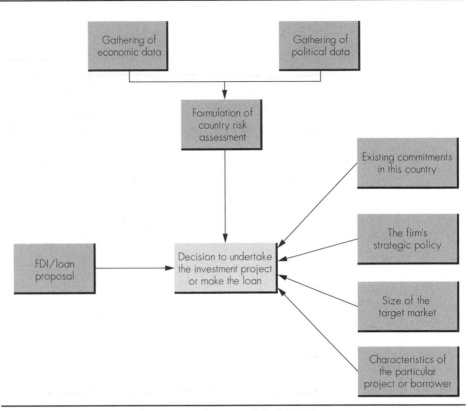

Source: Based on statements in Kobrin (1982) and Grosse and Stack (1984).

incorporating country risk into the decision-making process. Notice that political factors are combined with economic factors to create an evaluation of the overall environment in the host country. The actual lending or investment decision is also influenced by several other key factors, and indeed country risk may be viewed as relatively unimportant in many cases.

Methods for Dealing with Country Risk

Given that there is no way to forecast country risk with certainty, what can a firm do to cope with it? The methods for dealing with country risk are very similar to the methods for dealing with exchange risk discussed in Chapter 6. These methods are (1) avoidance, (2) transfer, (3) adaptation, and (4) diversification.

Avoidance The firm can *avoid* country risk by minimizing activities in or with countries that are perceived to be highly risky and by using a higher discount factor (that is, a higher required rate of return, which reflects a higher cost of capital) for projects in riskier countries. This strategy may not be feasible unless the firm develops some measure of risk that it can apply to projects in the various countries of interest to it. Such a measure may fail to achieve its purpose if some unexpected risk arises. For example, the United States, generally viewed as the least politically risky country in the world, created a huge political risk for its grain exporters by restricting their shipments to the Soviet Union during the Afghanistan crisis of 1979–80. Similarly, US manufacturers of oil pipelines and electronic equipment repeatedly faced unpredictable US government policies with regard to their sales to Eastern bloc purchasers. In sum, a firm may follow the strategy of risk avoidance, yet still be harmed by country risks.

Risk Transfer   Most developed countries offer country risk insurance to their exporters and often to their direct investors. This is a form of risk *transfer*. In the United States, the Eximbank offers policies to exporters that cover such risks as war, civil unrest, and currency inconvertibility.[6] In addition, the Overseas Private Investment Corporation (OPIC) offers insurance policies to US foreign investors to cover such risks as expropriation, civil or foreign war damages, and currency inconvertibility.[7] In Great Britain, similar policies are offered by the Export Credit Guarantee Department (EGDC), in Germany by an agency called Hermes, and in Canada by the Export Development Council (EDC). At the multilateral level, the World Bank operates the Multilateral Investment Guarantee Agency, which offers insurance policies analogous to those of OPIC. In each case, some or all of the country risks a firm encounters may be transferred to the government agency in exchange for the payment of insurance premia.

Adaptation   A third method for dealing with country risk is to *adapt* the firm's activities to reduce such risk. Just as assets in a currency that is exposed to exchange risk can be hedged by incurring liabilities in the same currency, so can assets exposed in a given country be hedged with liabilities in the same country. A factory in Egypt can be hedged against country risk by financing its operation through local borrowing or by incurring local accounts payable. Notice that country risk must be hedged through liabilities (or assets, depending on the exposure) *located in* the host country, whereas exchange risk may be hedged in the eurocurrency markets regardless of the country of location.

Many other means of adapting the firm's business to reduce country risk can be devised. One possibility is to support social and charitable activities in the host country to demonstrate the firm's good corporate citizenship. Another is to support political parties and politicians (particularly the ones in power) to gain their favor. The fundamental goal of this strategy is to alter the firm's activities in a manner that reduces the probability of negative government actions.

Diversification   The fourth method for dealing with country risk is to *diversify* across national borders so that problems in one country do not debilitate the firm. Then, if a strike, war, or natural disaster causes the firm to cease operations in one country, facilities in other countries will allow it to remain in business. With such possibilities in mind, firms that assemble clothing or electronic products in less developed countries often set up plants in two or more countries. Similarly, if taxes rise in one country, production or funds may be moved to another country to avoid the extra cost. Diversification does not reduce the country risk in any given country; it merely allows the firm to survive risky events by operating in other countries and reduces the overall risk.

As with exchange risk, the four strategies for protecting against country risk are not mutually exclusive. They may be used separately or in combination, depending on the availability and cost of each strategy in a particular country.

DEBT/EQUITY CONSIDERATIONS

Financial structure in a multinational enterprise is complicated by the fact that the "normal" **debt/equity ratio** differs from industry to industry and from country to country. For example, the average debt/equity ratio in large Japanese companies is about 2.75 to 1. In the United States, this ratio is generally far less than 1, averaging about 0.6 for nonfinancial industries as a whole. As a rule, the total financial structure of an MNE follows the standards of the home country financial market, since shares are usually traded there. On the other hand, a US company's affiliate in Japan may be able to operate successfully with far higher leverage than that of the parent, given local conditions in Japan. Thus, the financial structures of foreign affiliates may differ from that of the overall firm or that of the parent in particular. The only limitation is that the financial structure of the affiliate must not cause the financial structure of the entire firm to deviate from acceptable standards in the home country.

The funding sources available to a foreign affiliate of an MNE include debt and equity from the parent and local financing in the host country. Figure 15–4 presents a view of these sources that expands on the view presented in Figure 15–1. The sources of credit to the MNE are divided between short- and long-term loans and between direct and intermediated provision of funds through a bank or some other financial institution.

The entire MNE may choose to meet its external financing needs by borrowing through an affiliate in a low-interest country if such funding is available and if exchange rate protection still leaves financing costs lower than those in other currencies. As already noted, since the MNE is evaluated by investors in the home country, its overall debt/equity structure must satisfy the financial community in that country. However, if the firm sells shares of an affiliate in the host country's financial market, the debt/equity position of the affiliate is an important issue.

For a wholly owned foreign subsidiary that does not sell shares in the host country, the debt/equity ratio should be determined by overall corporate needs. If funding is available at low cost (adjusted for expected exchange rate changes), local borrowing is appropriate. If a substantial amount of assets is exposed locally,

FIGURE 15–4   International Sources of Credit (including markets and intrafirm transfers)

Borrowing	Domestic inside the Firm	Domestic Market	Foreign inside the Firm	Foreign Market	Euromarket
Direct, short-term	Intrafirm loans, transfer pricing, royalties, fees, service charges	Commercial paper	International intrafirm loans, international transfer pricing, dividends, royalties, fees		Eurocommercial paper
Intermediated, short-term		Short-term bank loans, discounted receivables	International back-to-back loans	Short-term bank loans, discounted receivables	Euro short-term loans
Direct, long-term	Intrafirm loans, invested in affiliates	Stock issue Bond issue	International intrafirm long-term loans, FDI	Stock issue Bond issue ADR issue	Eurobonds, Euroequity
Intermediated, long-term		Long-term bank loans	International back-to-back loans	Long-term bank loans	Euro long-term loans

Direct means borrowing from owners of wealth (e.g., investors); *intermediated* means borrowing from a financial intermediary (e.g., a bank).

local borrowing provides a hedge to both exchange and country risks. If the local currency is expected to devalue substantially, then, even if local interest rates are high, it may make sense to borrow locally, assuming the expected postdevaluation interest costs would be lower than the home country costs.

Local equity financing may be forced on the firm if the host government demands partial local ownership of foreign enterprises. This situation exists today in many less developed countries and in most of the formerly communist countries. In this case, the affiliate's debt/equity ratio may be skewed toward equity, especially if the parent seeks to avoid sending funds into that country. That is, financing for the affiliate would come from the local partner's equity investment plus retained earnings, and other funding would be sought only after these sources were used up.

In countries with restrictions on funds transfers, such as profit and royalty remittances, equity financing would again be sensible—using those funds that cannot be taken out of the country. That is, if funds are blocked from transfer abroad, the MNE must reinvest them locally; investing the funds in the existing operation (i.e., profit reinvestment) may offer a greater benefit than placing them in local financial instruments such as bank deposits or government securities. This strategy is widely used by multinationals, though most would prefer the freedom to take their funds out of the host country.

Finally, notice that *if* the MNE is able to lower its total borrowing costs by utilizing foreign sources of funds, it has gained an advantage relative to domestic firms that limit themselves to domestic financial markets in any country. If the MNE has a lower weighted-average cost of capital for any given capital budget, it will undertake more projects than the purely domestic firm (or will be more profitable in the same projects).

WORKING CAPITAL MANAGEMENT

The MNE can use working capital decisions to reduce currency and political exposures, cut down on its total liabilities, maximize returns on available funds, and minimize the cost of obtaining financing. Each of the main categories of working capital—cash, accounts receivable and payable, short-term loans, and inventories—can be used to pursue these goals.

Cash

Consider a multinational firm such as Nestlé (based in Switzerland) whose network of affiliates extends around the world. Each affiliate has its own customers and suppliers, as well as financial ties to the rest of the company. Viewing the company as a single unit for purposes of cash management can yield far better results than would be obtained if each affiliate managed its cash independently. For example, much less foreign exchange protection is generally needed if all of the affiliates are evaluated together than if each affiliate hedges its own position. The French subsidiary may have a large amount of accounts payable in francs that can be hedged simply by placing the German affiliate's excess cash into French franc assets, such as eurofranc deposits. Similarly, the Canadian subsidiary may possess a large amount of Canadian dollar assets that can be hedged by having the US company contract some liabilities (e.g., by purchasing equipment) denominated in Canadian dollars. The whole company may coordinate its borrowing efforts through the British subsidiary, which uses the London eurocurrency market.

Centralized cash management offers five kinds of potential gains to the MNE:

1. By pooling the cash holdings of affiliates where possible, the MNE can hold a smaller total amount of cash, thus reducing its financing needs.
2. By centralizing cash management, it can have one group of people specialize in the performance of this task, thus achieving better decisions and economies of scale.
3. By reducing the amount of cash in any one affiliate, it can reduce country risks as well as financial costs.
4. It can net out intracompany accounts when there are multiple payables and receivables among affiliates, thus reducing the amount of money actually transferred among affiliates.
5. Its central cash management group can ensure that cash management decisions aim at corporate goals rather than the goals of individual affiliates when these might conflict.

The first kind of gain results simply from better use of the cash held by the firm. If each affiliate holds enough cash to meet its transactions needs, precautionary needs, and speculative needs (following the Keynesian categories of money demand), far more cash is likely to be held than is needed *companywide*. A domestic company centralizes the cash management function at one location (usually the home office), and an MNE can do the same. The key difference between the two is that the MNE is often restricted in its ability to shift funds among affiliates internationally; thus, less centralization is possible at the MNE level. Any reduction in cash holdings, however, enables the firm to reduce its financing needs, thus lowering costs.

The second kind of gain relates to the development of management skills. By centralizing the cash management function, even if funds are left in the affiliates for the most part, the firm can utilize the skills of a specialized group of cash managers. Gains from this group's decision making should include economies of scale in borrowing, since the group can borrow to meet the entire company's needs and then distribute funds to affiliates as required. Also, the group should develop detailed knowledge of financial opportunities worldwide, thus enabling the firm to borrow at lower cost or lower risk than firms lacking such expertise.

If the MNE reduces its total assets through centralized cash management, it also reduces both its exchange risk and its country risk in that fewer assets are at risk worldwide. The country risk does not change, but the exposure of the company to that risk decreases. Country risk may also be hedged or transferred by the decision makers in the cash management group, who have greater access to protection tools than do managers in any one affiliate.

Whether or not actual cash is placed in a central location, such a location can be used to keep track of financial flows within the MNE. When accounts among affiliates lead to partially or totally offsetting transfers, the cash management center can *net* the transfers and move only the final sum required. For example, if Nestlé France sells $1 million of products to Nestlé US, it will incur an account receivable in, say, 180 days. Simultaneously, the home office in Switzerland may borrow $1 million from Nestlé US. If Nestlé Switzerland sells some products to the French affiliate, the bill could be denominated in dollars to partially or completely offset the other two liabilities. Thus, this fourth kind of gain from international

FIGURE 15-5

Some Methods of Moving
Funds in the MNE

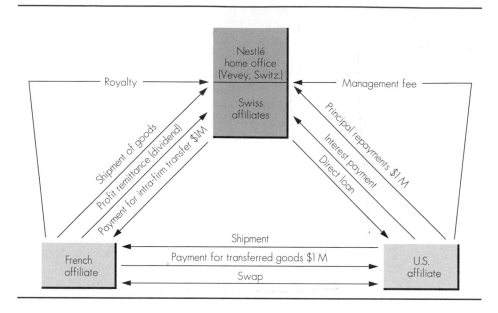

cash management involves (and is called) **multilateral netting of accounts.** Figure 15-5 shows these three transactions, as well as other methods of shifting funds among affiliates in the MNE. Notice that the funds transfer methods depicted may be used not only to carry out the transactions discussed above but also to transfer funds to a desirable location to minimize taxes or avoid exchange and country risk in any country. If Nestlé wants to shift more funds to the United States to expand its operations there, it can lend or invest more from the home office, swap assets between affiliates (e.g., accounts receivable from the United States for cash from France), remit less from the US affiliate, and even use New York as a cash management center, shifting available cash from other affiliates to that central location for redistribution as needed.

The fifth kind of gain from centralized cash management relates to business strategy. Placing the cash management function in one location, either at the home office or at a location closely monitored by the home office, makes better control possible. In this way, the firm can ensure that cash management decisions are made to meet global corporate needs rather than to improve an affiliate's position, possibly at the expense of the rest of the company. This is especially true with respect to hedging, which should be decided at the corporate level, since virtually every affiliate is likely to have assets or liabilities in another currency that are partially or totally hedged by balance sheet items of other subsidiaries.

While centralized cash management offers obvious and potentially very large benefits, it also presents some problems. Most important, if freedom to manage cash is taken away from the affiliate manager, some of the affiliate's ability to improve its performance is also removed. The evaluation of each affiliate must recognize this point. (This idea is discussed further in the section on controls.)

Another problem with internationally centralized cash management arises when national rules restrict financial transfers into or out of some countries. Virtually all less developed countries and many developed ones limit funds outflows through exchange controls or taxation. Some countries specifically disallow international netting of payments. Because of such restrictions, international cash management today requires a great deal of knowledge about national financial constraints and often requires a decentralized strategy of funds transfers due to these constraints.

Accounts Receivable

Accounts receivable (A/R) management may be divided according to the type of customer: A/R due from outside customers and A/R due from other affiliates of the firm. Receivables due from outside customers are the typical source of exchange risk, which can be handled as discussed in Chapter 6. Receivables due from other affiliates can be priced and timed to maximize the gains for the MNE if a central policy is devised.

To deal with the exchange risk created by contracts with outside customers, the MNE can use any number of hedging strategies. In addition, it can substantially reduce the expected cost by setting appropriate credit terms (to discourage late payments or penalize for them to account for expected devaluation of the receivable) and by pricing to account for expected exchange rate changes. The key to managing foreign-currency accounts receivable is to plan the currency and price *before* contracting, that is, before creating the receivable. One way to eliminate exposed accounts receivable is to discount them by creating banker's acceptances, factoring, or forfaiting. (These three discounting methods are discussed in Chapter 18.)

Intracompany accounts receivable can be managed to serve a variety of company goals. Assume, for example, that the firm wants to move as much money as possible from a foreign affiliate to the home office. One way to do this is to have the foreign affiliate prepay any intrafirm purchases and, conversely, have the parent delay any payments due to the affiliate. Another is to price the intrafirm shipment such that the home office shows greater profit. (Some legal limitations on the use of these transfer strategies exist in most countries; for example, prepayments are limited to at most 90 days in many countries.)[8]

To move funds from a foreign affiliate to the parent firm, the parent can charge a high transfer price for sales to the affiliate. The **transfer price** is simply the price the affiliate pays for an intrafirm sale of some product or service. If the product is a computer that costs the firm $1,000 to manufacture, the transfer price might be $1,000, in which case the manufacturing affiliate earns no profit. If the foreign affiliate is simply a sales office, it might sell the computer to an outside customer for $3,000. Figure 15–6 depicts the transactions involved. Now, ignoring transportation costs and taxes, the foreign affiliate shows a profit of $2,000 on the sale. The firm could just as easily have charged $3,000 to the foreign sales office for the computer, leaving the entire $2,000 profit in the manufacturing affiliate. Or the firm could have charged a transfer price of between $1,000 and $3,000 to share the profits between affiliates. The "optimal" transfer price would move the funds wherever the firm desires, subject to government constraints and the costs of carrying out the transfer. Important criteria for choosing transfer prices are the tax rates in each country, government-imposed price restrictions, and the risks of holding funds in a given currency and country. This simplified example is intended to offer a view of the basic issue in transfer pricing rather than to say that either of the two extreme prices is "optimal" or even legally possible.

FIGURE 15–6

Transfer Pricing in the MNE

All in all, the management of accounts receivable is an area of great opportunity for the MNE and one in which the purely domestic firm lacks the same options.

Inventories

Inventory management in an MNE parallels inventory management in a domestic firm. In addition, its concerns include physical risk reduction through diversification of location (if inventories are held in more than one country) and exchange risk increase due to denominating inventories in different currencies. Like centralized cash management, centralized inventory management offers cost-reducing opportunities to the MNE. If the firm produces the same product in more than one country, it can reduce the levels of the inventories it needs globally by shipping products from locations where extra inventory exists to locations where inventory is drawn down.

Diversification of inventories across countries cannot be overemphasized as a potential advantage of the MNE. If for any reason its production or shipment in one country is curtailed, the MNE with multiple production sites can serve various markets from other sources. Financially, the firm's cost would be lowest at one particular site at any given time. Strategically, its ability to ship from several sites reduces its risk of sales losses due to strikes, other production problems, and adverse political developments that arise in any one country.

Accounts and Notes Payable

To some extent, accounts and notes payable can be managed in the same way as accounts receivable. That is, for accounts and notes payable from one affiliate of the firm to another, the firm can use the timing and pricing of transfers to move funds where and when desired. Payables to outside suppliers and lenders are a key source of foreign exchange risk, which can be managed as discussed previously. Except for dealing with exchange risk, the MNE can manage foreign payables as the domestic firm does, with the aim of minimizing the cost of making necessary payments.

EXCHANGE RISK MANAGEMENT

We have discussed exchange risk primarily in relation to *transactions* denominated in foreign currency. In addition, exchange risk exists in the translation of financial statements and, in principle, for future, so-far unspecified activities of the firm. Three kinds of exchange risk should be differentiated: (1) transaction risk, (2) translation risk, and (3) economic risk. Each kind of risk is important to the MNE, and each leads to somewhat different conclusions for hedging strategies.

Transaction Risk

When a specific contracted asset or liability is denominated in a foreign currency, it is subject to **transaction risk,** or the risk of an unexpected change in its home-currency value during the time to maturity. Accounts payable and receivable, loans, and bank deposits denominated in foreign currencies are examples of items that are subject to such exchange risk. Each foreign-currency transaction can be hedged (or not) with some offsetting transaction in the same currency and with the same maturity.

Translation Risk

Translation risk is the risk of value changes in foreign-currency assets and liabilities on the balance sheet, whether or not the transactions occur during the accounting period. For example, the plant and equipment of foreign subsidiaries is subject to valuation change even if no purchase or sale of such items takes place during the accounting period. Because balance sheet information is reported to US securities regulators and in financial statements published in the United States, valuation changes in the foreign operations of US firms become public knowledge. Loss in the value of foreign-currency assets, regardless of its impact on company earnings, may negatively affect investors' perceptions of a firm. To avoid the appearance of weakness due to the devaluation of foreign assets, firms often try to hedge their balance sheets through financial contracts (such as forward contracts or money market hedges). This issue was discussed in Chapter 14; conclusions as to the desirability of **balance sheet hedging** are ambiguous. On the one hand, since investor decisions may be based on valuation changes in foreign-currency assets, the firm should hedge to avoid investor preoccupation with such changes. On the other hand, since the valuation of foreign-currency assets may not affect the economic viability of the project, it would be a waste of effort for the firm to deal with such changes.

Economic Risk

Economic risk is the risk of unexpected changes in future cash flows from foreign operations (and from activities denominated in foreign currencies, wherever they occur). Such risk is most important to the firm, since future cash flows are the basis for the firm's value. Unfortunately for the manager, it is not possible to know with certainty the full set of future cash flows that will occur. Thus, a hedging strategy cannot be perfectly matched with such cash flows. To deal with economic risk, the firm may choose to follow a generalized strategy of hedging transactions when they are contracted and trying to balance foreign-currency assets and liabilities as they appear on the balance sheet. Or the firm may choose not to hedge at all, on the assumption that future currency fluctuation will be approximately offset by price changes in each country (i.e., that purchasing power parity will approximately hold). Despite the inherent difficulty of predicting future foreign exchange exposures, ultimately the firm should be concerned about economic (foreign exchange) risk as the key variable in exchange risk management.

In fact, all three kinds of foreign exchange risk play important parts in the management of an international firm. No single hedging strategy can cover them all, so the MNE manager must devise plans for dealing with each. Fortunately, both transaction and economic risk deal with future cash flows; thus, the management of these two kinds of risk can be combined fairly readily. For example, the firm can hedge all occasional exports denominated in foreign currencies and seek local-currency financing for the entire production of its foreign affiliates. Then, if it does not employ balance sheet hedging (as suggested earlier), it can follow a consistent and simple hedging strategy. Judging from the immense volume of material dealing with corporate foreign exchange management strategies, it is safe to say that MNEs generally do *not* follow such simple strategies. Instead, they combine some hedging with some speculation in an effort to maximize their results from foreign exchange dealings.[9]

An Example of Exchange Risk Management

Consider the situation faced by a US-based firm such as American Express Company (AMEX) when its subsidiary in the United Kingdom reports the purchase of £5 million of office equipment (mainly furniture and computer terminals) for the subsidiary's tourist service offices throughout that country. This equipment is to be paid for in 180 days in British pounds. The strategies for dealing with exchange risk in this transaction depend on the whole firm's position in British pounds. The problem can be analyzed as follows.

First, if American Express already has an existing asset exposure in Great Britain due to its subsidiary's ongoing activities, that position may partially or wholly cover the new transaction. In other words, if American Express–UK has a balance sheet that shows net sterling (pound) assets, typically because foreign subsidiaries have some dollar liabilities, the new account payable may partially offset that asset exposure.

Second, the same results may occur even if the British subsidiary has been operated to cover ongoing exchange risk in the United Kingdom. In the event that American Express has placed funds in euro-British pound deposits in one of its other subsidiaries (e.g., in France or Germany), the new account payable may offset the existing exposure. *Note that the exposure is still not covered unless the maturity of the existing asset matches the six-month maturity of the new liability.*

Third, American Express can look for some financial hedging technique to avoid the exchange risk. For example, some new asset such as a bank deposit or short-term security could be purchased with a maturity of 180 days and a value of £5 million. Or a forward contract could be arranged with a bank to sell dollars and buy pounds in 180 days. Through the London International Financial Futures Exchange (LIFFE) or through one of the US futures exchanges, American Express could arrange a futures contract or option contract to hedge the account payable. The alternatives are numerous, but the basic goal is to find some British pound asset that matures in 180 days, worth £5 million, to hedge the new liability that calls for a cash outflow of £5 million in 180 days.

The following table lists relevant financial information if American Express were making this hedging decision on May 16, 1994:

Spot exchange rate	$US 1.5020 / £1
180-day forward exchange rate	$US 1.4809 / £1
180-day LIBOR in pounds	5.75% / year
180-day LIBOR in dollars	4.56% / year
6-month sterling call option strike price	
The options cost $US 875 per contract at the CME, with £31,250 per contract.	$US 1.50 / £1
6-month sterling futures contract rate	
The futures contracts have £62,500 per contract.	$US 1.47 / £1

American Express can use this information to evaluate various financial hedges for the sterling account payable.

First, the firm can use a simple forward contract to hedge the exposure. A forward contract to buy British pounds would cost about $US 7.4 million in six months, as follows:

$$£5,000,000 \times \text{\$US } 1.4809/£ = \text{\$US } 7,404,500.$$

This forward contract completely hedges the account payable, because it will result in receipt from the bank of £5 million in 180 days, which will be used to pay the supplier of office equipment.

A second alternative is to place funds now into a pound-denominated investment that matures in six months. The choice shown above is a eurosterling account that pays 5.75 percent per year for the six-month period. The dollar value of pounds for AMEX to buy today can be calculated by discounting the future pounds that are needed to a present value of pounds that must be deposited today to achieve that sum in six months. The calculations are as follows:

$$£5,000,000 / (1.02875) = £4,860,267.$$

This first step shows that the interest earned in the eurosterling deposit for 180 days will be 2.875 percent and that £4,860,267 must be deposited today to reach the value needed to pay the account payable. Next, the dollars that must be used today to buy these pounds is

$$£4,860,267 \times \text{\$US } 1.5020/£ = \text{\$US } 7,300,121.$$

It should not be surprising that the hedging cost is lower for this alternative, since the funds must be paid *now* rather than in 180 days. To compare the two choices, they must be placed in the same time period. This requires discounting the forward contract value using the relevant discount rate, which would be

$$\text{\$US } 7,404,500 / (1.0228) = \text{\$US } 7,239,441,$$

the implicit return to depositing funds in a eurodollar account (comparable to the europound deposit), namely 4.56 percent per year. This results in a lower cost of hedging in the forward market.

A third alternative is to use a futures contract hedge in the LIFFE or the Chicago Mercantile Exchange (CME). Using the CME's quotes, we see that American

Exchange Risk Hedging Techniques

To Hedge an Exposed Liability	To Hedge an Exposed Asset
Buy fx in the forward market	Sell fx in the forward market
Buy fx in the futures market	Sell fx in the futures market
Buy fx call options	Buy fx put options
Invest/deposit in a fx instrument	Borrow in a fx instrument
Incur accounts receivable in fx	Incur accounts payable in fx
Swap liabilities with another firm	Swap assets with another firm
Obtain any other fx asset	Obtain any other fx liability

In each instance, the hedge must produce an equal-value asset (liability) in the same currency with equal maturity to offset the exposed liability (asset). ■

Express could buy future pounds for $US 1.49 per pound in contracts worth £62,500 per contract. Multiple contracts could be bought, so that with 80 contracts the company could obtain the needed £5 million. However, since the exchange rate is *worse* than the forward rate (i.e., it costs more dollars to buy the pounds), AMEX will not consider a futures hedge.*

Each of these financial hedges can protect American Express against foreign exchange risk. The company will want to choose the least costly hedge in this case, namely the forward market hedge. In other situations, one or another of these three alternatives will be the most beneficial to the firm. Beyond these choices, American Express should consider the possibility of structuring its business such that it could use British pound assets (e.g., accounts receivable, investments, etc.) to hedge liabilities such as this purchase of equipment. A broad range of hedging techniques are shown in the accompanying "Added Dimension" box.

CONTROL: IDENTIFYING OBJECTIVES, EVALUATING AFFILIATE PERFORMANCE, AND MAKING PERFORMANCE CONSISTENT WITH GOALS

Control is the fundamental function of management that involves developing profit plans for the firm and its divisions and then deciding what to do when actual operating results differ from those planned. For a foreign investment project, the financial control process generally begins with putting together a set of pro forma financial statements (income statement, balance sheet, cash flow report), such as the income statement shown at the beginning of this chapter. Then detailed budgets are developed for individual divisions, allocating the full capital budget to the specific purposes for which it will be used. During the time period after the creation of these plans, the firm's management observes the

---

*The *option* contract can also be used to hedge this transaction. American Express could buy 160 call options as listed in the example, for a total premium of $US 140,000. For this price, American Express would receive the right to buy pounds at the strike price of $US 1.50 per pound, a much worse price than the forward and futures contracts. (Actually, options for lower strike prices are available at much higher premia.) The option does not look attractive unless American Express wants to speculate that the pound will go down in value even below the forward contract price. If this happens, by *not* exercising the options, AMEX could simply buy pounds in the spot market in 180 days and benefit from the lower price. The option is generally useful if the firm wants to speculate *or* if the original commercial contract may not be fulfilled so that the pounds may not be needed after all.

results and notes any deviations from the budgets. Usually, of course, actual results differ from budgeted ones. Finally, the firm develops and implements a management plan for dealing with the deviations. The process is cyclical—as each planning period ends, another begins—and new budgets and managerial contingencies may be developed.

In the multinational firm, the potential for substantial home office control over affiliates exists because major capital budgeting usually requires more resources than those available in an affiliate, and home office assistance is needed to carry out capital projects. In addition, financial reporting to the parent company provides an informational basis for controls, which may or may not be exercised, depending on the extent of the firm's decentralization. Finally, because the people assigned to manage foreign affiliates are usually well known to the home office managers, an informal, personal contact ties affiliates to the home office. All of this means that the home office has the potential to impose heavy controls on the activities of foreign affiliates.

The process described so far is substantially equivalent to the one used to evaluate and control domestic divisions in a firm. But foreign affiliates face a wide range of additional factors that may affect their performance, and these factors should be considered when setting the goals and judging the performance of affiliates. How should the managers of foreign affiliates be evaluated for their financial performance? If they are evaluated in local-currency terms, the home office must worry about hedging foreign-currency exposures and about remitting or reinvesting profits. If they are evaluated in home-currency terms, managers must deal with exchange risk and remittance policy. If they are limited in their financial dealings due to centralized cash and foreign exchange management policies but are evaluated in home-currency terms, it must be recognized that their options are limited. On another issue, if transfer prices are set to move funds to the home office, foreign profitability will look lower than it would if these prices were set to keep more funds in the affiliates. Correct evaluation of the performance of affiliate managers must take into account the constraints imposed on the affiliates.

Most managers and outside analysts agree that foreign affiliates must be evaluated in home-currency terms, since home-currency investors judge the firm as a whole. Therefore, the firm must create an evaluation scheme that produces home-currency performance measures, adjusted to account for the limitations placed on the affiliate by the home office.

CONCLUSIONS

Financial management in a multinational firm involves far more expanded concerns and opportunities than those involved in financial management in a domestic firm. Foremost among these concerns and opportunities is foreign exchange risk management, which is considered in several chapters of this book. Ultimately, foreign exchange risk management seeks to maximize the present value of future cash flows into the firm, just as most other aspects of financial management attempt to do.

The issue of country risk arises when the firm operates in more than one national legal jurisdiction. The MNE is able to avoid total dependence on national authorities for its ability to operate; when the national government in one country places limitations on the MNE, the MNE can turn to other countries for sales, production, and so on. We will see this asymmetry in bargaining power again when we explore the government-business relationship in Chapters 20 and 21.

The MNE cannot avoid country risks completely, but it can reduce them through hedging, insuring, and diversifying strategies.

The capital structure of a multinational firm is limited primarily by the existing norms in the firm's home country, but that does not stop the firm from using different structures in host countries as local conditions dictate. Extensive borrowing may be used in high-risk countries to reduce political and economic exposures of assets. It may also be used in low-interest countries whose currencies are not free to adjust to eliminate interest differentials. This strategy may create highly leveraged affiliates, but it can be used to finance many other parts of the MNE more cheaply than local borrowing elsewhere. Also, locally subsidized financing often presents opportunities for borrowing that may lower the MNE's average cost of capital.

Working capital management presents a wealth of opportunities for minimizing financing costs and maximizing returns on available funds through the use of foreign markets and euromarkets. From centralized cash management, to multilateral netting of accounts payable, to pooling inventories, the MNE has far more flexibility than purely domestic firms. Because of its ability to move funds internationally, the MNE can arbitrage tax and other regulatory jurisdictions to minimize taxes and other costs of operation.

All in all, international finance is one of the most exciting, dynamic areas of corporate management at the international level, but it is also one of the most complex.

QUESTIONS

1. What are the main benefits and drawbacks related to the centralization of cash management in a multinational enterprise?

2. Define country risk. How may it affect a multinational firm?

3. Explain the difference between transaction and translation risk in foreign exchange risk management.

4. What competitive advantages does an MNE possess relative to local firms in terms of international financing opportunities?

5. How can a firm such as United Technologies, which has subsidiaries in Mexico and Argentina, protect these affiliates against both country and foreign exchange risk?

6. How can an MNE utilize intracompany accounts (such as loans, fees, and product shipments) to deal with exchange risk?

7. What is a transfer price? In dealing with its American affiliates, what transfer pricing policy should Nissan use to keep more funds in its Japanese affiliates?

8. What does it mean to say that the cost of capital is lower in Japan than in the United States? If this is true, how can US-based MNEs that have affiliates in Japan take advantage of the situation?

9. Explain why economic risk rather than translation or transaction risk is the measure of foreign exchange risk that should concern the MNE manager.

10. Should the managers of an MNE's foreign affiliates bear the responsibility for exchange risk management, or should this task be centralized? Explain your choice carefully.

REFERENCES

Brewer, Thomas, ed. *Political Risks in International Business*. New York: Praeger Publishers, 1985.

Economist Intelligence Unit. *Financing Foreign Operations*. New York: Economist Intelligence Unit, current edition.

De la Torre, José, and David Neckar. "Forecasting Political Risks for International Operations." *International Journal of Forecasting*, 4, 1988.

Eiteman, David, and Arthur Stonehill. *Multinational Business Finance*. 5th ed. Reading, MA: Addison-Wesley, 1989.

Grosse, Robert, and John Stack. "Noneconomic Risk Evaluation in Multinational Banks." *Management International Review,* January 1984.

Hekman, Christine. "A Financial Model of Foreign Exchange Exposure." *Journal of International Business Studies,* Summer 1985.

Kobrin, Steven. *Managing Country Risk Assessment.* Berkeley, CA: University of California Press, 1982.

Mascarenhas, Briance, and Ole Christian Sand. "Country-Risk Assessment Systems in Banks: Patterns and Performance." *Journal of International Business Studies,* Spring, 1985.

Miller, Kent. "A Framework for Integrated Risk Management in International Business." *Journal of International Business Studies,* Second Quarter 1992, pp. 311–31.

Shapiro, Alan. *Multinational Financial Management.* 3rd ed. Boston: Allyn & Bacon, 1989.

NOTES

[1] A full set of the measures used in capital budgeting appears in basic finance texts, such as Brealey and Myers, *Principles of Corporate Finance,* 3rd ed. (McGraw-Hill, 1988).

[2] However, if the local-currency price goes up due to the currency revaluation and demand is price inelastic, the total revenue received may go up even if the quantity sold declines.

[3] Low-cost financing may be available locally even without government subsidy. In most countries, capital controls limit the ability of foreigners to borrow locally. Thus, in Japan, where interest rates are below those in the United States, a firm with local operations may take advantage of these rates.

[4] See, for example, "The ITT Affair," in Prakash Sethi, *Up Against the Corporate Wall* (Palisades, CA: Goodyear Publishing, 1976).

[5] See, for example, Shapiro (1989), chap. 14.

[6] *Eximbank Program Summary* (Washington, DC: Office of Public Affairs, Export-Import Bank of the United States, n.d.).

[7] See Alan C Brennglass, *The Overseas Private Investment Corporation* (New York: Praeger Publishers, 1983), and Economist Intelligence Unit, "Investment Guarantees," in *Financing Foreign Operations* (New York: Economist Intelligence Unit, current edition).

[8] See Economist Intelligence Unit, *Financing Foreign Operations,* for information about restrictions on financial transfers in over 50 countries.

[9] See, for example, Nick Gilbert, "Hedging Trims the Costs," *Euromoney,* February 1985, pp. 141–44, and Derek Bamber, "How SKF International Keeps a Grip on 18 Currencies," *Euromoney,* September 1982, pp. 341–51.

Bill Smythe & Company

Introduction

A firm from any country that decides to set up a foreign subsidiary for manufacturing, sales, shipping, or other business activity generally faces an important challenge in dealing with the foreign-currency aspects of the business. American firms in particular tend to have difficulty with this situation, because they often operate exclusively in dollars in their US operations. European firms, on the other hand, are typically used to working in at least two or three currencies, and in many cases with the European Currency Unit as well. Thus, especially for American firms, the need to understand and deal with foreign currencies is a fundamental business problem of the 1990s.

One industry that has long been associated with international business is the production of textiles, for example, men's and women's clothing. From the ancient silk trade that formed an important part of the activities of the British East and West India Companies to modern offshore assembly of blue jeans in Taiwan, trade in textiles has extended throughout the world. Even with this international component, the production of clothing in most countries remains primarily domestic; that is, due to differences in costs, tastes, and government regulations, clothes sold locally are generally also produced locally.

The clothing business in the United States historically has been a very inward-looking industry. Most clothing is made from domestically produced fibers, either natural (such as cotton or wool) or synthetic (such as nylon or polyester). Although a large percentage of the natural fiber is imported today, most clothing is still made of primarily domestically manufactured material. Very little US domestic production is exported; several American companies, however, have foreign subsidiaries that produce locally in various foreign markets.

One way domestic firms have been able to survive international competition is through successful lobbying for protection against imports. The US textile industry has been one of the most adept at gaining government protection, mainly through the international Multifibre Arrangement. This accord among producing and consuming nations gives the importing countries essentially unlimited power to restrict imports of both raw materials and assembled clothing to protect domestic producers. The Multifibre Arrangement is a major exception to the rules of the General Agreement on Tariffs and Trade (GATT), which promote freer trade among member nations such as the United States and its European trading partners. (The Uruguay Round of GATT concluded with an agreement to phase out the Multifibre Arrangement by the year 2004.)

This case was written by Professor Robert Grosse as a basis for class discussion. Revised 1994.

About the Company

Bill Smythe & Company was founded in 1961 by a Philadelphia shop foreman, Bill Smythe. Smythe had spent five years working for a small men's shirt manufacturer in Yeadon, Pennsylvania, which went out of business due to inadequate sales and rising costs. With his knowledge of the manufacturing process and his determination to succeed through better marketing than his former employer had practiced, Smythe set up his shop in a West Philadelphia industrial district and began to produce a line of high-quality men's shirts and women's blouses. His first customers were many of the same clients served by the previous company.

Within a year of opening the shop, Smythe decided to expand his marketing efforts. Sales were fairly stable but barely enough to pay the bills until he set up a licensing agreement with a leading designer of high-fashion women's clothing. This agreement enabled him to produce blouses under the designer's name and obtain access to several large department store clients. Even after paying the licensing fee, Smythe's earnings rose substantially.

By 1970, Bill Smythe & Company was selling over 200,000 shirts and blouses per year. The original 5 employees had grown to 11, and the shop now took up 4,000 square feet of operating space. At this point, Smythe had licensing agreements with three fashion designers to make both shirts and blouses. The branded lines made up over three-fourths of his total sales. In looking over the business, Smythe decided his next step should be to expand into additional product lines.

The process of growth continued during the 1970s. The firm added lines including handkerchiefs, underwear, and jackets; the last line was discontinued in 1978 when consistently poor sales led Smythe to drop it. By the end of the decade, Bill Smythe & Company had become a fairly large producer of shirts and blouses in the northeastern United States, with export sales into Canada. Despite the efforts to diversify, sales were dominated by Smythe's two original lines.

By that time, competition from foreign producers was beginning to affect sales. Smythe found that Italian and Spanish firms in particular were making unbranded shirts that undercut his prices by almost 30 percent, and some of these firms were producing brand-name shirts at a similar price advantage. By coincidence, Smythe discovered that one of the Italian firms was run by a high school classmate, Joe Todarello, who had returned to his parents' native country and entered the business there. When Todarello mentioned that his father wanted to sell the firm, Smythe quickly offered to buy it and keep his friend as general manager. This arrangement was concluded in 1987. It turned out very well, with the Italian subsidiary bringing in about 22 percent of total company sales within four years of the acquisition.

Although he had never thought about the problem in any detail, Smythe began to realize that changes in the lira/dollar exchange rate were seriously altering his costs and profits in the early 1990s. He was especially unhappy with the loan that he had used to finance most of the purchase of the Italian firm. The loan was made in dollars to the Italian subsidiary with Smythe & Company's guarantee, but the subsidiary was paying it off through profits earned. During the early 1990s, the lira had been devaluing in spurts against the US dollar (thus raising the financing cost with each devaluation). Figure 1 shows this situation. When the dollar began to decline relative to the deutsche mark and the Japanese yen in 1990–91, the lira had strengthened somewhat, but the downward trend continued in more recent years. Smythe found that his earnings in Italy declined precipitously from 1990 to 92 (due to depressed sales as well as currency devaluation). In 1993 sales rose, but operating profits remained weak. In 1994

FIGURE 1   Lira/Dollar Exchange Rates,* 1973–1993

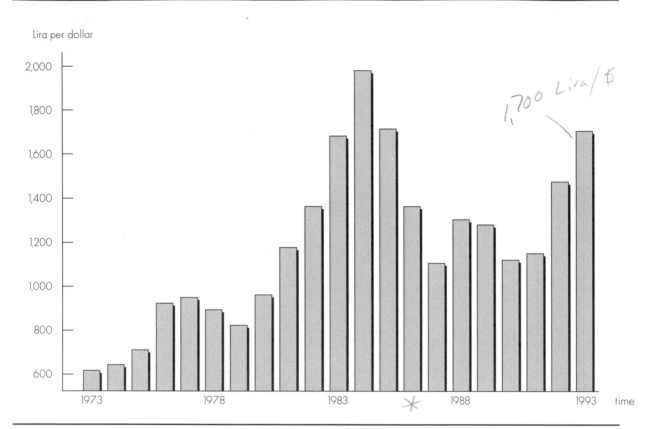

*Lira per dollar, end-of-year market rate.

earnings (counted in dollars) rose sharply as operating costs in Italy stabilized and the US dollar weakened.

Current Concerns

In December 94, Bill Smythe sat restlessly in his living room, looking over the projected earnings statement (Table 1) drawn up by Joe Todarello. While the numbers in lire appeared clear and justifiable, Smythe was unable to come to grips with the problems of exchange risk and projecting dollar values of the various cash flows. Moreover, he believed he should consider the possibility of restrictions on the firm's shipments of materials and finished shirts and blouses between Italy and the United States. He had asked Todarello to describe the currency situation in 1994 and 1995. Table 2 was Todarello's response.

The projections show a stable growth of lira earnings and cash flow. Dollar cash flows are negative, reflecting the continued purchase of materials and equipment from the US parent company. Profit remittances are *not* included in the calculations. Export sales to a German department store, which began in 1992, are listed as German mark cash inflows, which are also growing at a stable rate. Export sales from the Italian subsidiary to the US parent company are shown as lira cash inflows, since they are billed in lire by the subsidiary.

TABLE 1

SMYTHE ITALIA
Pro Forma Income Statement
1995 to 1999
(billions of lire)

	1995	1996	1997	1998	1999
Revenues:	21.2	27.0	36.4	45.9	60.4
Local sales	15.8	20.4	28.5	35.7	49.2
Export sales	2.3	3.9	4.5	6.8	8.2
Earnings on investments	3.1	2.7	3.4	3.4	3.0
Expenses:	18.4	22.9	29.3	37.3	47.8
Labor	5.2	6.8	8.8	11.5	14.9
Local materials	6.1	7.9	10.3	13.4	17.4
Imported materials	1.9	2.1	2.9	3.5	4.2
Licensing fees	0.9	1.1	1.4	1.8	2.4
Supervisory fees	0.7	0.9	1.1	1.4	1.9
Operating overhead	1.5	1.8	2.3	2.9	3.9
Interest expense	2.1	2.3	2.5	2.8	3.1
Net income before taxes	2.8	4.1	7.1	8.6	12.6
Corporate income tax (45%)	1.3	1.8	3.2	3.9	5.7
Net income after taxes*	1.5	2.3	3.9	4.7	6.9

*Tax of 30 percent is payable on any profit remitted to the US parent.

TABLE 2

SMYTHE ITALIA
Flow of Funds Statement
December 1994
(values in $US equivalents)

Accounts payable

	Currency		
Cash Flow	Lire	Dollars	Marks
	A/R lire→US		*A/R lire→D*
Next month	82,000	−39,000	8,000
In 2 months	79,000	−43,000	8,000
3 to 6 months	360,000	−195,000	34,000
7 to 12 months	540,000	−295,000	52,000
13 to 18 months	570,000	−295,000	57,000
19 to 24 months	580,000	−310,000	57,000
Year 3 and after (per year)	1,180,000	−600,000	120,000

Export to US Par A + sales

purchase of materials + equip from US parent

Exports to German depart store

16

Industrial Relations

Industrial relations are often regarded as place specific and therefore not especially relevant to MNEs and their competitive strategies. This perspective is inaccurate, however. MNEs possess internal strengths that they can use to improve their industrial relations management at the levels of both the parent and the subsidiary. Moreover, MNEs must consider the effects of industrial relations environments on some of their key strategic management concerns. This chapter examines these topics. The main goals of the chapter are to:

1. Explore the international aspects of industrial relations from the standpoints of MNEs, labor, and society.

2. Discuss the industrial relations systems approach to characterizing industrial relations environments.

3. Describe the international activities of trade unions.

4. Examine the management of industrial relations within MNEs.

5. Explain how industrial relations concerns affect certain strategic management decisions, such as those pertaining to production allocation, production smoothing, and disinvestment.

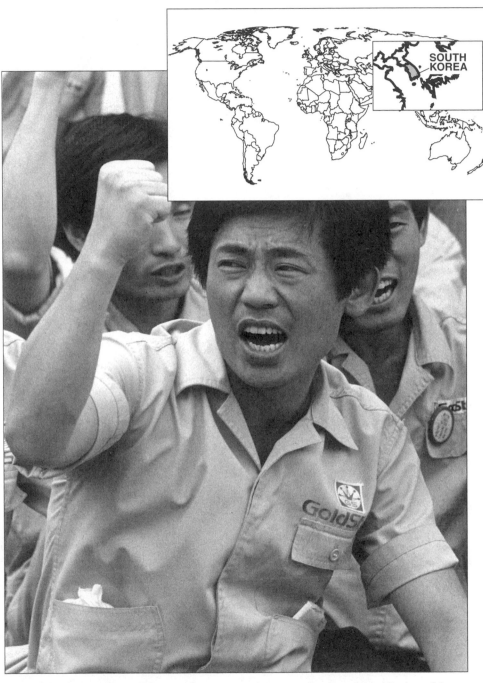

Labor turmoil in South Korea led to a strike among workers at an electronics assembly plant of the Goldstar Group in Changwon.

Reuters/Bettmann

WHAT ARE INDUSTRIAL RELATIONS?

The following chapter, "Personnel Management," focuses on the relationship of individual employees to their employers. This chapter deals with collective employee-employer relationships. Such relationships vary considerably country by country and industry by industry, and this variability can present the MNE with important problems and opportunities. We begin this chapter by reviewing some key aspects of **industrial relations,** especially in the United States. Knowledge of the US industrial relations system will provide us with a basis for understanding differences between industrial relations in the United States and other countries.

Industrial Relations in the United States

In the United States, we typically view industrial relations within the context of union-management relations and of a collective agreement or **labor contract.** Industrial relations, then, involve both substance (i.e., the terms of the contract) and procedure (i.e., determining and administering the contract).

Among the topics usually covered in labor contracts are job classifications, wages, wage supplements (such as shift differentials and overtime pay premiums), fringe benefits (e.g., health insurance and the retirement program), holidays, vacations, promotion and layoff procedures, a no-strike/no-layoff commitment, union recognition and security, and management rights. Other topics, such as cost-of-living wage supplements and the procedures to follow for plant closings, may also be covered. Typically, the contract includes rules regarding its administration. These rules identify the structure of the in-plant union representation and the procedure to be followed in handling complaints (or grievances) to resolve them in a timely fashion consistent with the substantive provisions of the contract.

Laws enacted by the US government have established rules regarding bargaining unit determination (whom will the contract cover?), union recognition, and the conduct of the parties during collective bargaining. The size or scope of the **bargaining unit** is usually decided by the National Labor Relations Board (NLRB) in an administrative ruling based on employee and employer petitions, historical precedents relating to the common interests of groups of workers, the nature of the tasks identified in the proposed unit, and so on. Voting by the employees in the proposed unit decides whether there will be a union and, if so, which union it will be. If there is strong employee support for a union and management concurs, the NLRB may determine a bargaining unit and then certify a union without an election.

US law also requires that both management and union bargain in good faith (this means, for example, that information necessary to the successful conduct of the bargaining must be shared and that there must be give-and-take during the negotiations) and that bargaining be conducted only over topics related to the terms and conditions of employment. Overall, the thrust of US labor law has been to lower the potential for labor-management conflict by establishing rational, democratic procedures related to union recognition; limiting the substance of collective bargaining to worker-related interests and issues; and requiring the parties to the collective bargaining process to be reasonably open, accessible, and forthcoming.

Perceptions of the Stakeholders

We see from this overview that industrial relations are important in several respects. From management's perspective, industrial relations determine labor costs, the ease with which work processes are changed, and the potential for conflict in resolving differences held by the union, the firm, or the employees.

From the union's perspective, industrial relations determine the extent of shared decision making on worker-related matters and on the level of income and financial security enjoyed by those whom the contract covers. Government and society also value successful industrial relations. Such issues as the frequency and duration of strikes that interrupt commerce, the cost-push pressures of wages on product prices, and worker participation in decision making typically relate to broader social interests in productivity, competitiveness, inflation, employment growth, and industrial democracy.

The following section discusses the international dimensions of industrial relations pertinent to MNEs and their operations, as well as important public policy issues regarding the effects of MNEs on employment and industrial relations. Subsequent sections cover key features of the industrial relations environment—worker representation, the nature of the labor-management agreement, wage determination, industrial conflict, and so on—that exist in several countries and the activities of unions and government-related organizations at the transnational level. The final section examines the management of industrial relations in an MNE context and the impact of industrial relations on strategic management.

WHAT IS INTERNATIONAL ABOUT INDUSTRIAL RELATIONS?

Ethnocentric, Polycentric, and Geocentric Views

Like industrial relations at the national or domestic level, industrial relations at the international level are important to companies, management, unions, workers, society, and government.

The ethnocentric MNE, which mandates the behavior of subsidiaries, typically has problems with industrial relations. The cultural, legal, and factual contexts that drive industrial relations are too crucial to be managed from the distance of the parent company. As a result, local management is usually given, perhaps begrudgingly at first, considerable autonomy in its industrial relations.

If one considered the multinational enterprise to be simply a collection of reasonably freestanding, national production and marketing units, industrial relations would, at a minimum, be as important to the MNE as they are to a purely domestic company. This is the polycentric view. Key elements in the competitive success and profitability of either type of firm—production wages, work methods, benefit levels, and so on—would be determined by means of the industrial relations process. But there is more to industrial relations than this for the MNE, as we will see later.

The mature multinational enterprise is more than a collection of freestanding, national subsidiaries. Because of its transnational linkages in terms of technological (including management expertise) and financial flows and its ability to identify and utilize product and resource markets advantageously, the geocentric MNE is quite different from the non-MNE in its industrial relations. Here are some illustrations:

- Opel (General Motors' German subsidiary) negotiates an *increase* in the basic workweek hours with Belgian unions as it adds a second shift at its Belgian assembly plant. The intent of management is to keep the costs of production there competitive with the costs of production at a similar Opel plant in Germany. The intent of the Belgian workers is to expand employment and enhance job security.

- A US electronics firm cuts back its US manufacturing output 10 percent by laying off a portion of its US workers. Its French subsidiary picks up the resulting product market slack. By cutting back employment in the United States, the firm avoids the large payments to workers that French law would have required had the cutback been made by the French subsidiary.

- Workers at a German company's British subsidiary go out on strike to support their demand for improved wages. Operations at the company's German plants continue, providing substantial cash inflows (revenues) to the entire MNE system. The British workers completely forgo their cash inflows—their wages—during the strike. The company is less severely pressed financially than these workers are and can sustain a long strike if need be.

- Ford of Europe integrates production among several European subsidiaries. For certain models of cars, the engines could be British-made, the power train and some stampings German-made, the wheels and other stampings Belgian-made, and so on. A strike by workers in Belgium could shut down assembly plants in Britain and Germany. This gives the Belgian workers operational leverage vis-à-vis management and enhances their power in collective bargaining. A similar conclusion would hold for workers in Britain or Germany.

These examples show how the multinationally distributed operations and markets of the MNE affect the economics and stability of the workplace and the relative bargaining power of the parties involved in industrial relations. These effects, in turn, can have a significant impact on unions and on worker-related social issues.

Labor's View of MNEs

Organized labor usually operates within the context of a nationally defined industrial relations system. It is the product of a specific cultural and legal heritage. As the above examples indicate, the MNE may determine or influence labor's interests transnationally, but unions and workers are less transnationally mobile than the MNE. They see the MNE, then, as having options that they lack. To them, the MNE has the potential to:

- Force workers in one country, faced by competition from workers in other countries, to "bid down" their wages and benefits to get or keep jobs.
- Take advantage of differences in legally required benefits for workers by adjusting operations in countries where the costs of such adjustments are lowest, thus imposing excessive dislocation burdens on workers in these low-benefit countries.
- Outlast workers in the event of a strike in one country because cash inflows to the MNE are at least partially maintained by operations in countries where no strike occurs.

In the Ford of Europe example above, the bargaining leverage gained by the unions because of transnational production integration may be only a short-run benefit, since the company might position future production facilities in worker and union environments that are less threatening to it.

Social Issues and MNEs

From a broad public policy perspective on the international dimensions of industrial relations, MNEs have been both criticized and praised. Critics contend that by opening plants abroad, MNEs have exported jobs from the United States and destroyed the diverse industrial base that it needs to sustain its economic well-being.[1] They argue that MNEs have compromised the national security of the United States by locating high-technology operations overseas and licensing foreign firms to produce high-technology products. They also claim that MNEs, by the very nature of their operations, negate the national interest expressed in the US National Labor Relations Act in maintaining the balance of power between management and unions that successful collective bargaining requires.[2] On the other hand, supporters of the MNEs contend that overall employment has grown faster in MNEs than in non-MNEs[3] and that workers in MNEs receive higher salaries than workers in non-MNEs.

A key issue in the public policy area arises from the ability of MNEs to respond quickly to new market opportunities wherever they arise, whereas workers are unable to suddenly relocate geographically or acquire newly needed skills. This is the adjustment problem. Most industrialized countries offer adjustment assistance funds to retrain and relocate workers affected by changes in products and markets. This suggests that these countries value the economic benefits they realize when firms develop new products and markets and that society in general should provide a "cushion" to workers adversely affected by such developments. As noted earlier, some countries penalize firms for laying off workers by requiring large severance payments. This implies that these countries do not want workers and society to be forced into a costly adjustment process unless the threshold value of the economic benefits realized in this way is above a legally defined minimum. A problem here is that marketplace competition may make adjustment compelling anyway. What could result from penalizing layoffs is "hidden unemployment" as workers are kept on the job in the face of declining production or as regulated product prices and state-provided subsidies keep firms afloat and jobs intact. This is a problem today in some of the state-owned enterprises in France and the United Kingdom. Finally, the more aggressive countries underwrite or legislate benefits to firms that invest in them or trade internationally so that they may get to keep jobs and earn foreign exchange. These benefits take such forms as tax rebates on exports, low-interest loans, government-funded R&D, and special purchase agreements. Policies of this kind distort comparative advantage and invite political retaliation.

THE DIVERSITY OF THE INDUSTRIAL RELATIONS FACING MNES

Since MNEs have generally concentrated their manufacturing investments[4] in the more industrialized countries, where larger markets and higher income levels exist, two of these countries—the United Kingdom and Germany—have been contrasted with the United States to illustrate the diversity among country-bound industrial relations systems. Japan's industrial relations system has also been considered because of the positive influence of its work force management techniques and industrial relations on its industrial prowess and its competitive successes. To help us focus on the business-related features of these industrial relations systems, our discussion is organized around selected key industrial relations issues evident in each system.

Worker Representation

United States In the United States, the union, if certified, becomes the exclusive bargaining agent for the employees in the bargaining unit. It negotiates with the company on the contract terms, and it monitors management's compliance with the contract. Depending on what the contract stipulates and on what state law requires, workers may or may not have to join the union or pay union dues as a condition for continued employment. Collective bargaining typically occurs at the company and plant levels, with some notable exceptions involving multicompany bargaining—for example, in trucking and the building trades, where the level is regional, and in the steel industry, where it is national.

United Kingdom   In the United Kingdom, work groups within a plant often express a sense of solidarity and negotiate with management on matters they believe are important. They elect someone from their ranks to be their chief spokesperson, or steward. Workers also often belong to a union, which is organized on a geographic basis and includes members at many firms in a local area. Collective bargaining is conducted with a company's representatives by a council of representatives of the unions in the area. It may also be conducted by a **steward's council** representing only workers at the company. This dualism, which is in sharp contrast to the exclusive jurisdiction that prevails in the United States, allows for conflict between the unions and the stewards. For example, the union council may accept an agreement with management and the company stewards may reject it. Major work stoppages have resulted in cases of this kind. Labor negotiations are conducted at the company level with the larger firms in an area or at the industry level for an area if the firms are fairly small.

Germany   In Germany, union membership is purely voluntary, and there is only one union for laborers in each major industry. Collective bargaining, conducted between the union and the employers' federation for the industry, covers major terms of employment, such as wages. Firms that are federation members apply the labor agreement to their workers. Nonfederation firms may or may not implement their industry agreements, depending on a variety of factors—the tightness of the labor market, the desires and solidarity of their workers, and so on. Secondary conditions of employment (such as scheduling of vacations and workshifts) are negotiated at the company and/or plant levels between management and legally established **works councils,** whose members are elected by the company's workers and may or may not be union members.

Works councils in Germany are legally empowered to "codetermine" with management issues related to worker safety procedures and other in-plant practices. These works councils are made up of management and employee representatives. Some employees are also elected to serve as employee representatives on **boards of supervision.** These boards, which in some respects operate like boards of directors, appoint and evaluate top management. Works councils and the presence of employees on boards of supervision are the results of the widespread German codetermination movement.

Japan   Unions in Japan are typically characterized as **enterprise unions.** There are over 70,000 of them, and they usually include all the hourly and salaried employees of the firm. Workers view themselves as employees first, and because they are employees, they belong to the enterprise union. Collective bargaining is accomplished at the enterprise level. Enterprise unions in the same industry affiliate to form industrial federations, which are generally loosely knit and do not engage in collective bargaining themselves. The federations typically coordinate the bargaining policies and timing of enterprise unions during *Shunto,* the so-called Spring Wage Offensive.

Labor-management relations in Japan reflect the often close, mutually supportive identification between the worker and the company. The larger firms, for example, offer "lifetime" employment (i.e., up to retirement age) and structure their operations and changes in operations to accommodate that commitment. Workers, on their part, dedicate themselves to the company and its competitive success.

The Labor Agreement

United States   In the United States, the **labor agreement** is a contract that can be enforced in court, if need be. It is in effect for a fixed period of time, and its terms and conditions apply to all workers covered by it. Therefore, the employees of an individual bargaining unit have no individualized right to bargain with management for their own wages and benefits. Legislation at the national level abolishes this right for such workers.

The content of the contract, which is typically fairly extensive, covers the various topics identified earlier. Disputes regarding the proper application of the contract's provisions are typically resolved by means of the grievance system specified in the contract itself. This usually means that binding arbitration, in which an impartial, outside party makes the final decision, is the last step in the grievance procedure.

United Kingdom   In the United Kingdom, the labor agreement is not a legally binding contract. It is an "understanding" among the parties that basically means, given the present circumstances, these are the acceptable terms and conditions of employment. Violations of the agreement by unions or stewards' groups carry no legal penalties, since these entities are not recognized in law. They have no legal status or identity.

The content of the UK labor agreement is generally less extensive than that of the US contract. Such agreements may contain provisions defining the structure of the relationships among the parties. Separate wage provisions are then negotiated; their duration is effectively open-ended. Procedures for handling complaints are often spelled out in the labor agreement, but there is no provision for arbitration. In fact, complaints are typically handled by the shop steward, who was probably not formally involved in the negotiations establishing these procedures, and resolved, if necessary, by industrial action (i.e., a strike) before the procedures have been completed.

Germany   In Germany, workers in an industry may be covered by several fixed-term contracts, each of which has a different expiration date. Typically a wage structure agreement spells out the job classifications and the relative wage levels for the different jobs. The tariff, or wage, agreement sets out the actual wages to be paid. Another agreement may specify the amount of indemnification paid to a worker who loses his or her job because of automation or a sales decline. Yet another agreement covers general working conditions, such as work times, personal leave, vacations, and overtime pay. The provisions of each agreement are limited to the issues that it alone addresses.

Conflicts over the application of an agreement can be negotiated between management and the individual involved, perhaps with the participation of a union representative and/or the works council. The final resolution of complaints is handled in German labor courts, if necessary. In contrast to the US system, individual workers covered by labor contracts may still negotiate individually or collectively with management to secure wages and benefits superior to those defined in the contract. By statute, their individual rights here are not preempted.

Japan   In Japan, union and company representatives review the labor agreement annually and change it if the parties agree that this should be done. Typically labor agreements cover wages, bonuses, working conditions, grievances, personnel affairs, and welfare issues. **Shunto,** the Spring Wage Offensive, is an annual, enterprise-level bargaining over wages and the summer bonus that is coordinated closely at the industry level. The practice of *Shunto* acknowledges that wage gains at the enterprise level are constrained by the labor costs of a firm's competitors. In effect, *Shunto* attempts to extend wage bargaining to cover all of the firms in an industry. There may be yet another round of bargaining when unions negotiate the year-end bonus.

The provisions of the Japanese labor agreement are often general and vague, and they even include employment conditions that are legally required. Disputes about the rights conveyed in such agreements are often settled between the parties in an amicable manner involving compromise. However, the disputes can be taken to an agreed-upon private third party for mediation and, if necessary, arbitration. Japanese labor law establishes labor relations commissions that can also mediate and arbitrate disputes, and the courts can do this too.

Industrial Conflict

The two most common forms of industrial conflict are strikes and lockouts. **Strikes** can result from two types of disputes: those relating to rights that workers believe are theirs because of contracts or past practices and those involving workers' interests regarding the setting of wages, benefits, and other terms and conditions of employment. **Lockouts,** in which employers close the plant and thus keep employees from working, don't occur nearly as often as strikes. Other forms of industrial conflict include "work to rule" (i.e., a slowdown, "going by the book"), industrial sabotage, and the occupation of plants by workers.

United States   As noted, most US labor agreements contain provisions barring strikes. The very existence of the agreement signifies that both management and the union have defined their mutual interests. The contract conveys certain rights to both parties (e.g., the wages to be received and the ability of management to reassign workers). The grievance system, which typically includes binding arbitration, is also defined in the contract. This procedure resolves whatever disputes over rights may arise.

Strikes and lockouts during the term of the contract are usually forbidden. One effect of all this is that once a contract is in place, strikes and lockouts are typically illegal and rare. Such actions, however, are not rare after a contract expires and when a new contract is being negotiated. They then involve the entire bargaining unit. At such times, the parties seek to define their interests. Typically "wildcat" strikes, strikes that occur during the term of a contract, result from allegedly onerous management practices or working conditions related to specific work groups and are not endorsed by the union. Such strikes are usually brief. Other forms of industrial conflict seldom occur.

Business unionism, which characterizes the pragmatic, enterprise-oriented focus of the US labor movement, acknowledges that an ongoing, hopefully profitable firm is in the best interests of the union and the workers. Likewise, socially accepted values, such as those relating to private property and the concept of the contract, help explain US labor's reluctance to destroy equipment, occupy a factory, or provide fewer labor services than the labor agreement calls for.

United Kingdom   Labor in the United Kingdom has historically been more strike prone than labor in the United States. The social philosophy of **voluntarism,** a keystone concept of the British labor movement, asserts that workers alone will define and pursue their self-interest. From this, it follows that the right to "industrial action," such as a strike or "work to rule," must be unconstrained (e.g., by law). Labor agreements do not prohibit the right to strike, and strikes have often occurred during impasses in bargaining and in support of workers' grievances. Such strikes were typically brief, and they often involved small work groups. More recently, arbitration is becoming increasingly popular for resolving disputes.

The dual worker representation structure (i.e., the shop stewards and the unions) in the United Kingdom has been known to complicate both collective bargaining and grievance handling and result in fragmented bargaining relationships and, in so doing, to enhance the propensity of workers to strike and to extend the duration of strikes. Lockouts, especially those involving company workers other than those in a work group that is out on strike, are not uncommon. Workers extend the idea of voluntarism to mean not only that they will take care of themselves but also that management will take care of itself. There is more class consciousness on the part of both labor and management in the United Kingdom than in the United States, and the work environment is probably less conducive to the efficient settlement of labor-management disputes.

Germany   Labor laws in Germany prohibit strikes and lockouts when an agreement is in effect. This means conflicts (such as strikes) over rights are illegal. Conflicts over interests, which occur when an old contract has expired and a new one is being negotiated, are legal. Collective bargaining brings focus and clarity to the issues and the potential for strikes is reduced by the fact that several labor agreements exist in an industry, with different termination dates and covering different terms and conditions of employment.

This structure is apparently consistent with Germans' preference for orderly, well-defined work relationships. Nevertheless, at times some strikes have occurred when an existing contract was in effect. These strikes were illegal. The issues, however, were usually not rights but interests. For example, in the early 1980s, unanticipated inflation was damaging workers' living standards, and strikes were conducted to increase wages accordingly, even though a wage agreement was currently in effect.

Japan   In Japan, strikes and lockouts at the enterprise level are rare. Strikes of exceedingly brief duration (perhaps a half-day or so) are typically scheduled during *Shunto* to demonstrate workers' support for their representatives' demands in industrywide negotiations. The issues over which industrial conflict may arise between management and the union are also fairly limited. For one thing, the provisions of the labor contract supersede an individual worker's terms and conditions of employment that are not equal to or better than what the contract mandates. For another, the law establishes standards for minimum wages, hours, overtime, rest periods, vacations, sick leave, sanitary conditions, and discharge notice that are set at the comparatively high levels of other advanced societies.

One result of all this is that the overwhelming majority of strikes concern economic issues, are brief, and, since they usually relate to *Shunto,* are anticipated. The Japanese social philosophy of *Wa* implies that individuals subordinate individual interests and identities to those of the group. Social harmony and teamwork are derived from this philosophy. Significant (i.e., other than ceremonial) conflict is the antithesis of *Wa.*

Cross-Country Comparisons

Management in the multinational enterprise is concerned with several aspects of the industrial relations systems in and across which it operates. These aspects are basically the same as those with which management in the domestic enterprise is concerned, but the MNE can treat them as variables in its strategic planning since its operations transcend typically place-bound industrial relations. This management perspective will be developed more fully toward the end of this chapter. However, some of the groundwork can be put in place now. The key question is: How do the countries compare on certain issues important to management, such as wages and benefits, the potential for productivity improvement, and production continuity?

Wages and Benefits   The importance of the level of wages and benefits is obvious. Major business decisions and significant financial commitments often turn on a comparative analysis of wage and benefit costs. But what about the propensity of these costs to change? What about the pace of these changes relative to inflation in general?

Wages in the United States have traditionally been among the highest in the world. Changes in basic wage rates, within the union-management context, are reflected in labor contracts. Such changes are programmed over a period of time, most often a three-year period. Cost-of-living wage increases must by definition lag inflation, and typically they do not fully offset the amount of inflation. Cost-of-living formulas defined in the labor contract define and control such increases.

In the United Kingdom, wages are almost constantly subject to scrutiny, and if workers or unions believe higher wages are necessary or desirable, a new round of wage bargaining can occur at any time. The structure of the work force representation may be a factor here too. In the United Kingdom, shop-level work groups can initiate new wage demands and attempt to make them effective. In comparable US industrial settings, the more broadly constituted union bargaining unit is the single collective bargaining entity. Wage escalation within that unit is not constantly at issue as it is in the United Kingdom, where a militant and aggressive work group may secure higher wages, which in turn leads to demands from other work groups within the firm for the reestablishment of the wage parity differentials that they have traditionally merited and enjoyed. The potential for a firm to be caught in a wage cost/product price squeeze appears to be substantially higher in the United Kingdom than in the United States.

In Germany, wages set in industrywide negotiations are paid by all firms in the industry. The firms also pay wage increments, depending on the labor market conditions they face, their profitability, or the intensity of their workers' demands. Strikes in support of wage increments are illegal when an industrywide agreement (which covers wage minimums at firms party to industrywide bargaining) is in effect. Moreover, the social and cultural environment usually does not support random strikes over economic issues by small, shop-level groups. German labor contracts do not contain provisions for cost-of-living wage increases. Wage increases lag inflation.

In Japan, industrywide wage bargaining occurs during *Shunto,* and the unions' wage increase targets reflect the recent inflation experience. Pattern-setting unions in each industry lead the way during *Shunto.* These unions are usually in firms with strong financial positions, and other unions in other firms push to imitate the wages they negotiate. Cost-of-living increases are part of *Shunto*'s wage targets. These increases lag inflation, but the pattern wage, which is based on the most profitable firm's ability to pay, may, if extended, put other firms at a cost disadvantage. **Pattern bargaining,** incidentally, is also common in some US industries (e.g., automobiles and aerospace).

Productivity Improvements   The use of new and better tools and equipment, changes in the way the work force is managed, and so on are intended to enhance productivity. A crucial element here is management's incentive to innovate, or take risks, for this purpose—for example, by spending large sums of money for new machinery that management believes will lower production costs. Here the prospects for increasing profits justify the cost of the new equipment. Management's right not to share decision making on such changes with unions becomes relevant, as do the timing and the methods by which the firm's workers come to share in the benefits of the productivity improvements.

In the United States and Germany, management can initiate process improvements, peg the affected workers' wages according to the prescribed job evaluation system, and benefit (profit) substantially from the new equipment. In Japan a similar situation exists, but wages, which to a greater extent reflect age and seniority considerations, are not likely to be increased because of a new job assignment. In all three countries, unions bargain for higher wages based, among other things, on the firm's profitability. But the profitability must be demonstrated first. The company does profit from productivity improvement, at least for a while—probably for a few years.

In contrast, in the United Kingdom, an equipment change may be accompanied by the negotiation of a **gain-sharing agreement** acceptable to the work group affected. A wage increase for this group can lead to demands for wage increases by other groups that seek to maintain parity, or customary wage differentials, among the firm's workers. The overall costs of these wage increases must be measured against the cost saving anticipated if new equipment is installed. In this case, the benefits of the productivity improvements are immediately shared with the workers, and the firm's incentive to innovate is dampened.

Strikes and Lockouts   Because they interrupt production, strikes and lockouts are costly. Whether or not a firm produces, its fixed costs, such as rent, interest on loans, and management salaries, continue. Without production, sales revenues are reduced (either immediately or eventually, depending on inventories). Industrial conflict per se has costs (to all parties) associated with it. If such conflict can be anticipated, these costs can sometimes be reduced by building up inventories of the firm's product or, if the conflict is expected at a supplier, by building up inventories of the supplier's product. Cross-country comparisons on strike experiences are difficult to interpret.[5] For example, when work stoppages per 100,000 employees in the United States and the United Kingdom are compared, it is found that the United Kingdom has twice as many work stoppages, but the number of lost workdays due to such stoppages in the United States is about double the number in the United Kingdom. The random or unplanned-for strike is, however, widely recognized as being more evident in the United Kingdom than in the United States.

Although the above data on work stoppages are not intended to malign the British industrial relations system, when compared to Japan, Germany, or the United States, the United Kingdom does appear less attractive to enterprises on three counts. This conclusion is not the purpose of our discussion, however. The point we wish to make is that industrial relations environments can vary substantially and can thereby affect a firm's profitability differently. The management challenge is to align the firm's operations with the industrial relations environment that offers the best fit.

Theories on Industrial Relations Systems

Industrial relations systems vary so widely country by country that it is difficult to see what commonalities exist among them. One of the first widely accepted attempts to conceptualize a cross-country theory of industrial relations was presented by Dunlop in the 1950s.[6] In his theory, Dunlop identifies elements common to all industrial relations systems and a schematic framework on the interactions among these elements. Figure 16–1 presents this framework. Dunlop identifies rules, or outputs, as common to all industrial relations systems. They have to exist, and they have to be determined by someone or some group, that is, the *actors*. In some societies, such as totalitarian states, government may unilaterally determine these rules. In others, such as the industrial democracies in the West, all three actors—workers, management, and government—participate. The influence of each actor may vary, however, depending on the rules at issue. For example, safety rules usually receive special attention by workers, management, and government alike. Installing new equipment and work methods will probably be management's prerogative.

The nature of the rules is also affected by the *contexts* within which they are expected to operate. Variations in product and process technologies, market structures relating to both product and resource markets, and ideology or culture relevant to the workplace may affect the kinds of *rules* as well as the intensity of

FIGURE 16–1

Dunlop's Industrial Relations System: Elements and Relationships

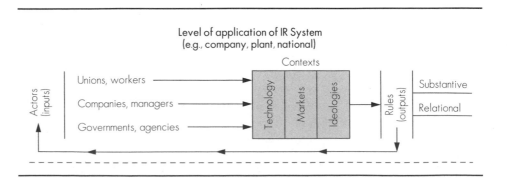

the actors' interests regarding them. Substantive rules define the nature of the outputs (wages, vacations, etc.). Relational rules define how the actors behave toward one another (e.g., no strikes or lockouts).

Dunlop's framework is a fairly static one, but it is useful in sorting out and developing an initial understanding of how any system operates and how changes might work their way through a system. Let's look at a few illustrations of recent sociopolitical changes and the structure of Dunlop's model.

During the 1980s, Poland's Solidarity Union represented a different ideology than that presented to workers by Poland's communist government. It persisted in developing and promoting this ideology, based on principles of political democracy and unionism free from government control (i.e., different relational rules). During 1989–90, Solidarity was at the forefront of social and institutional change in Poland as democratic pluralism replaced communist totalitarianism as the controlling sociopolitical ideology. The roles of all the actors changed dramatically as the adjustment to a more market-based context evolved.

The reunification of Germany in 1990 resulted in important changes in German industrial relations and the German economy. The communist-sponsored unions in East Germany were dissolved, and the industrial union structure of West Germany was applied to workers in the East. Wages accelerated in the East, but worker skills and other factors affecting worker productivity did not change so quickly. Unemployment expanded in the East, as did migration from the East to the West. In the 1990s, the German government is investing considerable sums of money in the East to rebuild the social infrastructure necessary for the expansion of private sector activities to expand productivity and employment. In Germany, ideology and market changes have resulted in adjustments by government, union, and company actors and changes in both substantive and relational rules.

Other theories have been presented, such as that by Clegg, who sought to identify trade union behavior within the context of a systematic behavior pattern.[7] His "trade unionism under collective bargaining" theory rationalizes such aspects of unionism as membership, structure, and governance in terms of the nature and scope of the collective bargaining in which the union participates. Clegg's theory is also useful in understanding the workings of an industrial relations system.

THE INTERNATIONAL STRUCTURE OF TRADE UNION ACTIVITIES

Trade unions are active internationally via three basic avenues: tripartite intergovernmental organizations, affiliation with unions from other countries, and an extension of their contacts with domestic firms and their home country governments.

Intergovernmental Organizations

ILO The **International Labour Office (ILO)** is a United Nations affiliate (located in Geneva) composed of government, industry, and union representatives. Through the years, the ILO has sought to define and promote fair labor standards regarding safety, health, and other working conditions and freedom of association and other workers' rights. Through its research and publishing programs, it reports on wages and working conditions by country and industry.

In the early 1970s, the ILO published a pioneering study on the social policy implications of the global activities of MNEs.[8] Among the topics covered by the study were investment concentration by area and industry, capital and technology transfers, international trade, labor effects, working conditions, and industrial relations effects. The study concluded by noting the different views and concerns of employers and workers and recommending that the social problems and benefits specific to MNEs, as opposed to those of national firms, be identified and studied further.

In the latter 1970s, the ILO conducted a series of industry-specific studies on US and non-US MNEs in Western Europe to document these views and concerns. In 1980–81, it published a series of country studies on the employment effects of MNEs, jobs lost and gained because of MNEs and the quality of jobs (e.g., skill levels) within MNEs.[9] It concluded that MNEs were important employers in many countries, and for a few countries, including the United States, the data implied that employment was growing faster in MNEs than in non-MNEs and the internal structure of employment was shifting more quickly toward white-collar workers in MNEs than in non-MNEs. The tendency of MNEs to be more R&D intensive than non-MNEs was seen as a key factor affecting the differences between them in employment growth and stability. The ILO sponsored a second study on MNEs' employment effects in the United States in 1989. This later study looked not only at the jobs issues but also at industrial relations and public policy effects.[10]

OECD   In 1976, the **Organization for Economic Cooperation and Development (OECD),** a government, industry, and union group located in Paris, established a set of voluntary guidelines for MNEs. These guidelines, which are still in effect, note that MNEs are obligated to respect the laws, regulations, and administrative practices of member countries and that countries are obligated to provide national treatment to MNEs within their borders. These mutual obligations of MNEs and countries appear simple, but they can become quite complex. The classic case in this regard, which occurred in 1976, involved a disagreement between the Belgian government and the Belgian subsidiary of Badger Company over whether Badger's parent, US-based Raytheon Corporation, was responsible for the legally required indemnification payments to Belgian workers who were laid off (permanently) when Badger's Belgian office was closed.[11] The government contended that Badger's Belgian subsidiary lacked sufficient funds for this purpose because of the parent's transfer pricing and transnational work allocation patterns. Here the obligation to respect national laws provided Belgium with a rationale for extending its influence to the parent company in another country.

Transnational Union Affiliations

Windmuller classifies international trade union affiliations into four categories: global, regional, specialized, and industrial internationals.[12] The global international category includes trade union organizations that cut across regional, specialized, and industrial groups. Such organizations, which can be found in nearly every country, are concerned mainly with political and missionary activities.

The International Confederation of Free Trade Unions (ICFTU) is the most important **global international** for MNEs, since its membership is heavily concentrated in North America and Western Europe, areas that are also significant to MNEs. Most of the **regional internationals** are subdivisions of the globals, and their activities are regional applications of globals' activities. **Specialized internationals**—for example, the Worker Group in the ILO, the Trade Union Advisory Committee in the OECD, and the European Trade Unions Congress, which represents workers' interests at the European Union level—function as components of intergovernmental agencies and lobby within those agencies.

The **industrial internationals** are also affiliates of the global internationals. In the ICFTU, they are termed the International Trade Secretariats (ITSs), and there is a separate ITS for each major industry group—for example, the International Metalworkers' Federation (IMF) in the metal trades. Unions at the country level in the metal trades belong to the IMF and to industry-specific departments in the IMF, for example, the Automotive Department.

Of special interest to the MNE, **worldwide company councils** have been formed under the auspices of the ITSs. A case in point is the General Motors Council in the IMF, which consists of union representatives from GM plants all over the world. The GM Council meets periodically to share information about working conditions, collective bargaining, and so on. Unions can use this information to push for comparable treatment in country-level bargaining. The international structure of the ITS provides a union vehicle that parallels the international structure of the MNE. On occasion, an ITS representative has sought to intervene at the global headquarters of an MNE on behalf of a member union that was having difficulty in its dealings with a subsidiary of the MNE at the national level.

During the 1970s, when the worldwide company councils were developed, there was considerable speculation that these councils would be vehicles for transnational collective bargaining with MNEs. However, transnational bargaining is precluded by such factors as the diverse legal and cultural environments affecting national unions. In the early 1990s, **industrial regionals** in Europe grew in importance as new industrial policies at the European Union were being debated and formed. The European Metalworkers' Federation, for example, seeks to influence EU policies affecting metalworkers' unions in the various European countries.

Extension of Domestic Contacts

Some US unions have responded to the US MNE by trying to bargain with it as a global, headquarters operation. The International Union of Electrical Workers (IUE), for example, invited union representatives from General Electric's foreign plants to participate with it in its collective bargaining. These representatives were only observers, however, and were not directly party to any negotiations. US labor law is the controlling factor here, since it limits collective bargaining to matters related to the US bargaining unit.[13]

Similarly, during collective bargaining several years ago, the IUE proposed that General Electric cease transferring work from its US operations to its foreign operations. The company contended that this proposal was without merit and refused to consider it or to provide the union with details on its foreign operations. The union then filed an unfair labor practice charge with the NLRB. The board's general counsel denied the charge and noted that the union had not substantiated its allegation that work transfers were in fact occurring.[14] Overall, unions have not been successful in their attempts to prohibit or limit, through collective bargaining, the foreign sourcing practices of MNEs (i.e., manufacturing abroad for the US market).

The AFL-CIO has been active in promoting US public policy changes that would limit the ability of US MNEs to export capital and technology and to import production. However, this effort has not been particularly successful.

The US-Canada situation is a special case in the extension of US union activities internationally. A Canadian region is an integral component of many US **international unions.** This binationalism in union structure has facilitated the binational coordination of collective bargaining with MNEs having US and Canadian operations and of subsequent contract administration activities. Canadian nationalism has resulted in some Canadian regions becoming autonomous unions, but close coordination with the US counterparts of these unions has been maintained. The 1989 US–Canada Free Trade Agreement has required unions on both sides of the border to coordinate collective bargaining even more closely. Unions' coordinated actions in light of the North American Free Trade Agreement (NAFTA) are a different matter, however. US unions will not be able to coordinate activities with Mexican unions as closely as they have with Canadian unions. The United States and Mexico do not share a common union heritage, nor do they have similar union structures as do the United States and Canada. Also, union members in the United States and Canada share a stronger sense of solidarity than they do with Mexican union members.

MANAGEMENT OF INDUSTRIAL RELATIONS IN THE MULTINATIONAL ENTERPRISE

Earlier the chapter substantiated the view that industrial relations systems differ considerably country by country and are place bound. Successful MNE management recognizes this and allows subsidiaries considerable autonomy in managing their worker relationships. This approach is consistent with generally accepted management principles regarding line/staff relations and decentralization of decision making that supports operating responsibilities at the subsidiary level. One MNE's view on the local autonomy experienced in industrial relations is provided by George McCullough, an industrial relations executive at Exxon:

My company operates in 137 countries. The variations in our labor relations processes, the manner in which we go about collective bargaining, and the differences in items included in collective agreements are staggering. Even in two countries like Holland and Belgium, where the proximity between Rotterdam and Antwerp has caused us to consolidate some management functions, the labor relations processes are totally independent of each other and the contracts bear little resemblance.[15]

Studies on the locus of decision making in MNE industrial relations operations invariably conclude that the local management makes the operating decisions and is responsible for implementing those decisions. Even in the Japanese multinationals, industrial relations, in the context of a union-management relationship, is the subsidiary's responsibility. Japanese management frequently defers to the expertise and opinions of local management. A single exception to such local autonomy is the handling of pension issues by MNEs. Approval of pensions, which may involve a future liability of the parent company, is often required at the parent level prior to acceptance at the subsidiary.

Most large MNEs have an **industrial relations staff** at the parent company level. The activities of this staff relate to both operational and strategic matters. These activities include advising and participating in personnel selection and development at both the subsidiary and headquarters levels.

Advising: The Subsidiary Level

The MNE industrial relations staff represents a pool of expertise that is available to subsidiary management. It is not only experienced in industrial relations per se but also knowledgeable about plant operations and workplace management. It can be called on for opinions and suggestions on such local matters as bargaining strategies and tactics or the development of a new job evaluation system.

The MNE industrial relations staff also monitors industrial relations at the subsidiary to ensure that wages, benefits, and working conditions relate solely to local labor market needs, thereby guarding against the emergence of a global settlement pattern, which would probably saddle the company with higher labor costs than those of its competitors. A related function of the headquarters staff is to provide information useful to subsidiary management during labor negotiations, especially when the local union supports its claims by citing ITS-generated data on company-specific conditions in other countries.

Advising: The Headquarters Level

The MNE industrial relations staff counsels the production, marketing, finance, and similar groups at the headquarters level. Budgeting and financial pro formas of subsidiary operations include estimates of labor costs. Forecasts of changes in these labor costs are often provided by the MNE industrial relations staff in consultation with local management. In the event of a strike or a lockout at a subsidiary, the industrial relations staff can provide advice to the MNE-level production, logistics, purchasing, and marketing groups on the anticipated duration of the conflict. If the MNE's production pattern is transnationally integrated, such advice is especially significant, since operations at other subsidiaries are affected by such a conflict. Alternatively, if headquarters management is weighing the possibility of replacing production at a struck subsidiary with production at another subsidiary, it will probably value an appraisal of the anticipated duration of the conflict.

Senior line management at the MNE level often solicits interpretations by the industrial relations staff of important events at the subsidiaries. Such interpretations prepare it to participate with and respond to subsidiary management in the making of line management decisions.

Personnel Selection and Development

Management personnel are usually selected by the person to whom they will report. Typically the person above the one who makes the selection approves or rejects the selection decision. The top industrial relations executive at a subsidiary would be selected by the subsidiary's managing director, and that selection would be approved or rejected by the headquarters-level executive to whom the managing director reports. Typically the head of the MNE industrial relations staff consults with senior line management at the MNE on such selection decisions.

The involvement of the MNE industrial relations staff is even more extensive than this, however. Career path and progression planning for key personnel is a fairly continuous process that includes individual development programs, identification of training needs, and so on. The MNE industrial relations staff participates in such planning as it affects key industrial relations personnel at the subsidiaries. Indeed, it may on occasion organize and conduct special training seminars for industrial relations managers from several of the MNE's subsidiaries.

THE INDUSTRIAL RELATIONS COMPONENT OF STRATEGIC DECISION MAKING IN THE MULTINATIONAL ENTERPRISE

Foreign Direct Investment

Strategic decisions are often regarded as those that establish the longer-run direction of the firm and provide the basis for operating decisions. From the industrial relations perspective, four strategic decision-making areas appear especially relevant: foreign direct investment, production allocation, production smoothing, and disinvestment.

Historically, the foreign direct investments of US MNEs (in the manufacturing sector) were defensive in nature. They were made to protect a foreign market presence originally obtained through exports. As foreign competition developed and profit margins were eroded, the firm sought to establish a plant within the market that it intended to continue serving. Its success often depended on its ability to transfer established management and production techniques from the parent to the subsidiary and to minimize overall production and marketing costs.

Of special importance, then, were those labor-related elements in the foreign environment that affected production costs and product availability. Critical assessments of alternative production sites typically included data on present and anticipated employee compensation costs and days worked per year (exclusive of holidays, vacations, and absenteeism). Wages and benefits are higher in Holland than in Hungary, for example. Days worked per employee per year may be lower in Germany than in the United Kingdom. All of these factors affect (product) unit labor costs. Potentially relevant factors are worker militancy and management's ability to initiate changes in workplace technology and work force organization. In these respects, Germany might be favored over the United Kingdom or France.

The key here is for management to identify all of the pertinent industrial relations factors and evaluate its foreign direct investment alternatives in light of those factors. The final outcome may well involve more than just a go or no-go decision. It may involve the nature of the work to be performed at the proposed plant or the kind and amount of production equipment that will be used. It may involve participation by the local government in securing attractive financial support or trade union concessions that will render the proposed facility more profitable. For example, when Ford Motor opened a plant in Belgium in the mid-1960s, the provincial government helped secure a written five-year peace commitment from the local trade unions. When Volkswagen decided to open a plant in Pennsylvania in the mid-1970s, the United Auto Workers (UAW) agreed that Volkswagen's wages could be lower than those of other US automakers. In the mid-1980s, the principals involved in the General Motors/Toyota NUMMI joint venture agreed to recognize the UAW as the plant workers' exclusive bargaining representative. The UAW, in turn, eventually negotiated an innovative contract to enhance productivity at the plant.

Production Allocation

With respect to industrial relations, **production allocation** decisions are similar to foreign direct investment decisions. Indeed, some might contend that the latter are, in effect, initial production allocation decisions. New product and equipment cycles, however, do afford MNEs the opportunity to reevaluate, and perhaps renegotiate, their industrial relations environments. In some instances, unions have effectively bargained down on wages and benefits to keep jobs, or governments have offered special incentives.

Offshore production decisions by MNEs are also production allocation decisions. However, such decisions are special in some ways. They are made largely because of labor cost differences, and they result from the MNE's unique resource market–scanning capabilities. The selection of the specific operations to be performed offshore turns substantially on the labor intensiveness involved. The parent-subsidiary logistics involved are usually inventory intensive and time consuming. Thus, the offshore production concept, including the labor element, is not especially flexible. Labor, which is usually the most flexible factor of production, is not so in this context. The firm that engages in offshore production may do well to also maintain a domestic production capability that can respond more quickly to demand changes and competitive conditions in the domestic product market.

ADDED DIMENSION

Who's the Culprit in This One?

When an economic recession recently occurred, a large MNE in the electronics industry had to cut back production in all of its major markets. It ordered a 10 percent employment reduction at all of its plants in those markets.

Some subsidiaries, however, were faced with paying large "redundancy" or discharge payments to workers who were let go. Management at these subsidiaries complained about this. The parent then changed its order and allocated cutbacks at the plants in different countries to minimize the total MNE system costs resulting from discharge payments. As a result, most of the cutbacks in employment were made in the United States, where no such payments were required. In Western Europe, where the required payments were quite high, there were small cutbacks or none at all. ∎

Before transferring production to an offshore facility, the firm is required by US labor law to negotiate with the union over the effects of the relocation decision on the workers who constitute the bargaining unit. Since that decision apparently turns on economic factors, and since collective bargaining is concerned with economic factors, enlightened management may well negotiate with the union over the relocation decision and not just over its effects. Negotiations of this kind could well result in the weakening or elimination of the relocation rationale.

It is interesting to note the historical differences here among the US, Japanese, and European MNEs. In contrast to US MNEs, Japanese MNEs are not required by law to negotiate with a union on the employment effects of transferring production to an offshore facility. But Japanese MNEs would not transfer such production without examining domestic employment effects, discussing the situation with the employees involved, and doing everything possible to reduce negative effects. Many European MNEs, on the other hand, have not favored offshore production. They have imported workers from nearby, low-wage countries instead. The interests of these workers and their effects on local, native workers have been addressed within the employee and union representation structures already in place.

Production Smoothing

Rutenberg identifies **production smoothing** as a special variation on production allocation and notes,

In each nation, production smoothing problems and opportunities are different. A unique feature of the multinational corporation is that headquarters can alter the flow of products between nations to smooth production . . . [that is, force a] reallocation of markets to factories to achieve optimal production smoothing for a multiproduct, multifactory corporation.[16]

Rutenberg identifies three types of factories that are crucial to a production-smoothing strategy and relevant to industrial relations: lowest unit cost factories, flexible multi-item factories, and seasonal factories.

The **lowest unit cost factory** produces standardized items and operates at full capacity. In such factories, productivity is the key consideration. Lowest unit cost factories can be either capital intensive or labor intensive. If they are capital intensive, the union enjoys some leverage vis-à-vis management, since comparatively high fixed costs will continue in the event of a strike. In such factories, one management strategy is to treat workers as salaried staff to encourage their closer identification with the company; another is to pay workers on a production output basis. If the factories are labor intensive, the offshore manufacturing plant becomes a viable consideration.

The **flexible multi-item factory** produces new items. The equipment in such factories is general purpose, and the work force is usually highly skilled. Job enrichment, Rutenberg suggests, appears appropriate to factories of this sort. Worker assignments and job categories cannot be rigidly defined. Some industrial relations environments, such as Japan, seem well suited to the flexible factory.

The **seasonal factory** probably operates a few months out of the year. In such factories, a work force buildup is followed by layoffs. Rutenberg suggests that seasonal factories be located in areas accustomed to seasonal work—in northern Finland, for example, where variations in weather conditions have preconditioned society to accept seasonal changes in labor demand. In such cases, even unions tend to accommodate the cyclical employment pattern.

Expanding on Rutenberg's scheme, there appears to be a fourth type of factory relevant to production smoothing. It is a variant on the flexible, multi-item factory model. In this instance, the flexible factory is so named because it can adjust output volume for any one product while experiencing low adjustment costs. To illustrate, Japanese car manufacturers such as Toyota limited exports to the United States during the 1990–91 recession rather than cutting back on US domestic production of Toyota cars manufactured in the United States. Toyota's workers in Japan were much more flexible than those in the United States in handling a drop in product demand. For example, it was not unusual for some of them to work at dealers selling Toyota products. American autoworkers are not that flexible.

This discussion on production smoothing can be best summarized via the labor flexibility/production variation matrix presented in Figure 16–2. Quadrants I and III are the ideal ones to operate in. Variations in production are most efficiently handled in locations where labor is highly flexible (quadrant I). For example, Japanese production is noted for its flexibility. Robots can be efficiently reprogrammed (preserving capital investment), workers have high skill levels and can perform effectively on various assignments, unions are not concerned with job demarcation systems, workers are willing to relocate if necessary, and so on.

FIGURE 16–2

Labor Flexibility/Production
Variation Matrix

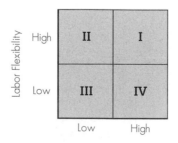

Where low variation is anticipated, low labor flexibility locations offer the best opportunity for low-cost operations (i.e., the low unit cost factory). Large amounts of fixed capital can be employed to secure scale economies, or production can be located in low-wage areas when skill needs are low.

In contrast, the firm is usually at a disadvantage costwise when production variation is low but labor is highly flexible (quadrant II). The high human asset (skill) levels of flexible workers generally sit idle when production is standardized and routinized. Yet the wage levels must be high enough to service these high human asset values. Similarly, high variation in production coupled with low labor flexibility results in high costs (quadrant IV). This could be the result, for example, of workers' low skill levels and the application of insufficient talents and/or knowledge to changing job demands or of institutional, worker-related barriers to worker flexibility, such as a requirement to pay overtime wage premiums when workers perform jobs outside of their permanent job classifications.

Production smoothing allows the MNE to implement competitive advantages, for example, by locating production facilities in environments characterized by quadrants I and III and then varying production in the quadrant I factory as demand varies over product and business cycles or during structural changes, while keeping production at the quadrant III factory level at optimal scale output.

Disinvestment

A **disinvestment** decision—that is, a decision to close or sell off a plant—is not easily or routinely taken. The prevailing wisdom, however, is that management should move swiftly and decisively in such matters, that it is best not to have a difficult situation linger. This wisdom must confront the reality that in many countries, especially Western Europe, legally constituted works councils have the right to be informed of the subsidiary's economic health and prospects and that substantial indemnification payments to laid-off workers are often legally required. Therefore, any disinvestment proposal should be carefully analyzed and its attractiveness discounted by the anticipated indemnification costs. The disinvestment procedure should be planned carefully, and the legal rights of workers to information must be addressed. Contingency plans should be developed to cover the adverse publicity that usually accompanies disinvestment decisions and even the possibility that workers may forcibly occupy the plant and attract additional headlines.

CONCLUSIONS

International industrial relations are more complex and diverse than industrial relations in a single country. Industrial relations are not necessarily more difficult to manage at the subsidiary level than at the domestic level, however, and the very diversity of international industrial relations may present opportunities to the MNE, especially in terms of strategic management.

The role and function of the MNE industrial relations staff require a special awareness and sensitivity. This staff must be knowledgeable about the different foreign industrial relations systems and the critical trends and events that affect subsidiary operations, and they must be sensitive to the effective allocation of authority and power between the MNE and subsidiary management levels. Sometimes only a fine line separates advising from controlling.

Different as industrial relations systems are, they all share a common general structure. All are concerned with the determination and application of workplace rules. The basic actors—management, union, and government—participate in this rule setting to varying degrees. Models such as those developed by Dunlop are useful starting points in learning about any specific industrial relations system.

QUESTIONS

1. Are industrial relations more or less significant to an MNE than to a purely domestic company?

2. What options or advantages not possessed by a purely domestic counterpart might the subsidiary of an MNE have in its industrial relations?

3. Compare the productivity incentives for management in the British and Japanese industrial relations systems.

4. Compare the productivity incentives for management in the British and American industrial relations systems.

5. If you could pick specific features (rules, practices, etc.) from the American, German, and Japanese industrial relations systems and put them into one "ideal" system, which would you pick? Why?

6. What purposes are served by an MNE industrial relations staff?

7. Why should industrial relations operating decisions be made by subsidiary-level management?

8. What do industrial relations imply for strategic management decisions regarding production allocation?

9. With regard to a plant location decision, what key characteristics of the industrial relations environment would an MNE take into consideration? Which of these characteristics would be of concern to an MNE but not to a purely domestic company?

10. How does industrial relations management in MNEs relate to the competitive advantages of MNEs?

REFERENCES

Bean, R. *Comparative Industrial Relations: An Introduction to Cross-National Perspectives.* New York: St. Martin's Press, 1985. See especially chap. 8, "Industrial Relations in Multinational Enterprises," pp. 184–207.

Commission of the European Communities. "Growth, Competitiveness, Employment: The Challenges and Ways forward into the 21st Century." Brunsek, December 5, 1993. See especially chap. 8, "Turning Growth into Jobs," and chap. 9, "Statutory Charges on Labour."

Dewling, Peter J; Schuler, Randall S; and Welch, Denice E. *International Dimensions of Human Resource Management.* 2nd ed. Belmont, CA: Wadsworth Publishing, 1994. See especially chap. 7, "International Labor Relations."

Ferner, Anthony. *Governments, Managers, and Industrial Relations: Public Enterprises and Their Political Environments.* Cambridge, MA: Basil Blackwell, 1988.

Harvey, Charles, and John Turner (eds.). *Labour and Business in Modern Britain.* Savage, MD: Rowan & Littlefield, 1989.

Kujawa, Duane. "U.S. Labor, Multinational Enterprise and the National Interest." *Law and Policy in International Business,* 1978 (no. 3), pp. 941–68.

_____ . *American Public Opinion on Japanese Direct Investment* (with Daniel Bob). New York: Japan Society, 1988.

_____ . "Technology Strategy and Industrial Relations: Case Studies of Japanese Multinationals in the United States," *Journal of International Business Studies,* Winter 1983, pp. 9–22.

Local Production of Japanese Automobile and Electronics Firms in the United States: The "Application" and "Adaptation" of Japanese Style Management. Tokyo: University of Tokyo, Institute of Social Science, Research Report No. 23, March 1990.

Sisson, Keith. *The Management of Collective Bargaining: An International Perspective.* Oxford, UK: Basil Blackwell, 1987.

Spalding, Hobart A. *Organized Labor in Latin America.* New York: New York University Press, 1977.

NOTES

[1]An early summary of these views is presented in Nat Goldfinger, "An American Trade Union View of International Trade and Investment," in *American Labor and the Multinational Corporation,* ed. Duane Kujawa (New York: Praeger Publishers, 1973), pp. 28–53.

[2]Duane Kujawa, "U.S. Labor, Multinational Enterprise, and the National Interest: A Proposal for Labor Law Reform," *Law and Policy in International Business,* 1978 (no. 3), pp. 941–68.

[3]For a general review of the evidence on these issues, see *Employment Effects of Multinational Enterprises in Industrialized Countries* (Geneva: International Labour Office, 1981).

[4]The reader should note that workers' and unions' interests in MNEs focus more heavily on firms in the manufacturing sector than on firms in the mining or extractive industries. The foreign situs of a mine may merely reflect the simple fact that that is where the ore is. Locating a plant abroad, however, is seen as a decision that turns on less absolute considerations.

[5]The observations on strike effects in this paragraph are based on data presented in Hugh Clegg, *Trade Unionism under Collective Bargaining* (Oxford: Basil Blackwell & Mott, 1978), p. 69.

[6]John Dunlop, *Industrial Relations Systems* (New York: Henry Holt, 1958).

[7]Clegg, *Trade Unionism,* passim.

[8]*Multinational Enterprises and Social Policy* (Geneva: International Labour Office, 1973).

[9]For the summary study, see *Employment Effects of Multinational Enterprises in Industrialized Countries* (Geneva: International Labour Office, 1981).

[10]Duncan C Campbell and Roger G McElrath, *The Employment Effects of Multinationals in the United States* (Philadelphia: Industrial Research Unit, Wharton School, University of Pennsylvania, December 1989).

[11]R G Blainpain, *The Badger Case and the OECD Guidelines for Multinational Enterprises* (Deventer, the Netherlands: Kluwer, 1977).

[12]John P Windmuller, "International Trade Union Organizations: Structure, Function, Limitations," in *International Labor,* ed. Sol Barkin et al. (New York: Harper & Row, 1967).

[13]Herbert R Northrup and Richard L Rowan, *Multinational Collective Bargaining Attempts* (Philadelphia: Industrial Research Unit, Wharton School, University of Pennsylvania, 1979), p. 120.

[14]Duane Kujawa, "Foreign Sourcing Decisions and the Duty to Bargain under the NLRA," *Law and Policy in International Business,* 1972 (no. 3), pp. 523–24.

[15]George B McCullough, "Comment," in *Multinationals, Unions, and Labor Relations in Industrialized Countries,* eds. Robert F Banks and Jack Stieber (Ithaca, NY: New York State School of Industrial and Labor Relations, Cornell University, 1977), p. 150.

[16]David P Rutenberg, *Multinational Management* (Boston: Little, Brown, 1982), p. 182.

Volkswagen of America (A)

Volkswagen of America (referred to hereafter as Volkswagen) is the US subsidiary of Volkswagenwerk, AG, headquartered in Wolfsburg, Germany. Volkswagenwerk is Germany's largest automobile manufacturer. Its worldwide production capacity is about 2.5 million units, about one-third of which it produces outside Germany.[1] In addition to its US operations, Volkswagenwerk has assembly plants in Nigeria, Belgium, and Yugoslavia and produces motor vehicles and components in Brazil, Mexico, Argentina, Peru, and South Africa.

During the 1980s, labor-management relations at Volkswagen of America were generally quiescent and constructive. But this was not always the case, especially in the start-up years. Let's take a look at what happened then.

Investment Considerations

Volkswagenwerk's first plant in the United States opened in 1969. It produced air conditioners for German-made VW "beetles" sold in the United States. In January 1976, Volkswagenwerk's supervisory board (analogous, to some extent, to a US firm's board of directors) authorized management to begin negotiations on establishing an assembly plant in the United States.

The issue of opening such a plant had been debated in the German company for several years. Worker representatives and others on the supervisory board were concerned about the employment effects in Germany if cars then being made in German plants and exported were assembled abroad.[2] The timing of the decision coincided with an investigation by the US Treasury Department of an allegation pressed by the United Auto Workers (UAW) that Volkswagenwerk had dumped cars in the United States in 1974 and 1975, that is, priced cars cheaper in the United States than in Germany. Commenting on both the decision and the Treasury Department's investigation, a spokesperson for the supervisory board noted,

We all realize that Volkswagens made in Germany are just too expensive, after repeated dollar devaluations, to meet the American and foreign competition in the United States. If we don't assemble there, we'll lose the American market. [Regarding the dumping complaint,] such a finding could force a reconsideration of the decision to go to the United States—and it would have enormous political repercussions in the Government too . . . If a special penalty duty were assessed on every Volkswagen, . . . the company would be forced to raise prices by so much that sales in the United States would collapse and our dealer network would fall apart.[3]

This case and the (B) case that follows were written by Duane Kujawa using information provided in discussions with Volkswagen company and union officials and collected from public sources. Revised 1994.

The deterioration of Volkswagen's US market position was also ascribed to higher fuel prices that were reflected in higher shipping costs associated with exporting from Germany, higher German labor costs, and the upward revaluation of the German currency during the 1971–75 period. Labor costs for Volkswagenwerk advanced 40 percent from 1973 to 1976.[4] This brought German labor costs, consisting of wages and benefits, up to parity with those of US autoworkers. Moreover, because of differences in vacations, holidays, and so on, German workers spent considerably less time on the job in a typical year than did their US counterparts. The result was that a US Volkswagen plant could operate with direct labor costs about 10 percent lower than labor costs in Germany.[5]

Later in 1976, Volkswagenwerk's supervisory board approved a decision to manufacture autos in Westmoreland County, Pennsylvania. The chairman of the management board stated that a US assembly plant would "lower manufacturing costs, neutralize the effect of international currency changes, and attain greater flexibility in supplying . . . American dealers."[6]

Obtaining a Labor Contract at Westmoreland

When Volkswagenwerk invested in the Westmoreland plant, it adopted a neutral approach toward the organizing of that facility by the UAW. The German parent had had a long-lasting, constructive relationship with the German union in the metalworking industry (I G Metall), and union members sat on its supervisory board. The parent had advised Volkswagen's management not to oppose the UAW's organizing efforts. The parent management did not deal directly with the UAW, however, and avoided giving further direction to Volkswagen's management on the conduct of its labor relations.

In May 1978, the UAW petitioned the National Labor Relations Board (NLRB) to conduct a representation election for hourly workers at Westmoreland. The hourly employment level was then about 900, and nearly 80 percent of the hourly workers had signed petition cards. No other union competed with the UAW, and Volkswagen's management did not oppose the UAW's organizing efforts. The election was held in June, and the UAW received 98 percent of the 885 ballots cast.[7]

Volkswagen immediately began collective bargaining with the UAW, and a tentative contract was soon agreed upon. A UAW spokesperson noted that the proposed contract included lower wage rates than those paid by the "Big Three" automakers, but most of the other items in the contract were "nearly identical to existing contracts with Detroit automakers."[8] The UAW president hailed the tentative contract as "an excellent example for other foreign auto manufacturers who may open manufacturing or assembly operations in the United States."[9]

But members of UAW Local 2055 at the Westmoreland plant rejected the proposed contract overwhelmingly. Moreover, they began a "wildcat" strike and moved immediately to picket the plant site. The key issue was that the wages called for would be substantially lower than those paid by the Detroit auto firms. The Westmoreland workers also reportedly believed that the proposed agreement shortchanged them on vacations, delayed for too long (one year) the start of Volkswagen's payments to a layoff fund, and denied workers the right to refuse heavy overtime.[10]

NOTES

[1]"Volkswagenwerk, AG," in *The World Directory of Multinational Enterprises,* ed. John N Stopford, John H Dunning, and Klaus O Haberich (New York: Facts on File, 1980), pp. 1126–27.

[2]"Inflation and Jobless Rate Stir West German Concern," *The New York Times,* May 19, 1976, p. 64.

[3]"Volkswagen Said to Plan Assembly Plant in U.S.," *The New York Times,* April 23, 1976, p. 1.

[4]"Volkswagen Is Investigating Two Sites in the Northeast for an Assembly Plant," *The Wall Street Journal,* October 6, 1976, p. 3.

[5]Ibid.; "VW Delays Start-up Date at Its Facility in New Stanton; Parts Problems Develop," *The Wall Street Journal,* January 8, 1976, p. 2; interview with the industrial relations director, Volkswagenwerk, AG, San Diego, California, June 1976.

[6]"VW Delays," p. 2.

[7]"Volkswagen Workers in Pennsylvania Pick UAW. as Their Union," *The Wall Street Journal,* June 12, 1978, p. 21.

[8]"VW's American Unit, UAW Agree to Terms of Tentative Contract," *The Wall Street Journal,* October 6, 1978, p. 31.

[9]Ibid.

[10]"Strike at VW Disturbs Foreign Auto-Makers Weighing U.S. Plants," *The Wall Street Journal,* October 13, 1978, p. 1.

Volkswagen of America (B)

In late 1987, Volkswagen of America announced it would close the Westmoreland County plant at the end of the 1988 model run. As with most major decisions, the rationale here was complex, but the proximate cause was quite simple: VW cars produced in America were not competitive; the plant was a money loser. Interestingly, some analysts called the decision a victory for the Japanese auto firms that had been fighting Germany in the United States for nine years.[1]

During the 1970s and 1980s, Volkswagen lost considerable market share in the United States—from 7 percent to 2 percent. By 1987, the Westmoreland plant was operating at one-third capacity and losing $120 million annually.[2] The reasons for Volkswagen's demise were many. Some observers contended the company just didn't have the right product. There were concerns too about product quality and product availability. Some believed Volkswagen's products were simply too expensive in light of the competitive prices of Japanese-made cars. Most likely each of these reasons had some impact on defining the company's competitive position and the decision to close the Westmoreland plant.

Interestingly, observers such as *Automotive News* concluded Volkswagen's relations with the United Auto Workers (UAW) did not affect the decision to close the Westmoreland plant.[3] Labor costs were an important issue, however. They were high (even with the comparatively "weak" dollar seen by most Western European countries and some Asian countries such as Japan) compared to costs at other Volkswagen plants located in low-wage countries such as Brazil and Mexico. The plan was to serve the US market with exports from these countries that would take up the slack occasioned by the closing of the Westmoreland plant.

Several points are worth mentioning here. One is that automotive assembly plants traditionally need a production volume of about 220,000 to 240,000 units per year to operate with optimal scale economies. These plants are of the prerobotics, preflexible production type. The Westmoreland plant was one of these. Production volume at Westmoreland had declined to 73,000 units per year in 1987. On a per-unit output basis, the capital costs at Westmoreland rendered total production costs uncompetitive. This is an example of the quadrant III type company illustrated in Figure 16–2.

In contrast to Volkswagen's situation, Japanese auto plants that use robots and other flexible production features need a plant output of only 80,000 to 120,000 units per year to operate at maximum efficiency. The Japanese plants fit into quadrant I in Figure 16–2.

How has the quadrant III approach affected plant workers compared to how a quadrant I approach would? Would workers still be "competitive?" Would they still have their jobs?

In the Volkswagen of America (A) case, production was transferred from the high-cost German environment to the more cost-competitive US environment. Now production was being transferred from the high-cost US environment to more cost-competitive environments in Brazil and Mexico. This had to be frustrating from the perspectives of American workers and American unions. What could the UAW and the Westmoreland plant's employees have done to deal with competition for jobs with workers in low-wage countries? Should they have lowered their own wages? Were there limits here? How about work rules? Could they have been changed to make the workers more productive? Did management need to play a leadership role here? Maybe the union and workers should have lobbied for a political solution, such as high tariffs on auto imports from low-wage countries. Who would be the winners and losers on this one?

In any event, Volkswagen sold the tooling and production equipment at the Westmoreland plant to First Automobile Works of Changchun, China, in mid-1989. In early 1991, Sony Corporation bought the plant in Westmoreland.

NOTES

[1]"Volkswagen Goes Back to the Drawing Board," *International Management*, February 1988, p. 43.

[2]Ibid.; "VW to Shut U.S. Plant by End of 1988 Run," *Automotive News*, November 23, 1987, pp. 1, 53.

[3]Matt DeLorenzo, "Anatomy of a Plant: Westmoreland Closing Holds a Lesson for All Transplants," *Automotive News*, November 30, 1987, p. 8.

17

Personnel Management

Personnel management within the MNE shapes the conduit through which the implementation of competitive advantages flows. The main goals of the chapter are to:

1. Describe how and why personnel management in MNEs differs from personnel management in purely domestic firms.

2. Examine the relationship between personnel management and the competitiveness of MNEs.

3. Examine statistics on the use of foreign nationals (expatriates).

4. Explain the criteria for choosing between local and foreign nationals.

5. Explore issues pertinent to expatriates, including selection, training, compensation, taxation, repatriation, and promotion.

6. Discuss the present demand for foreign assignments.

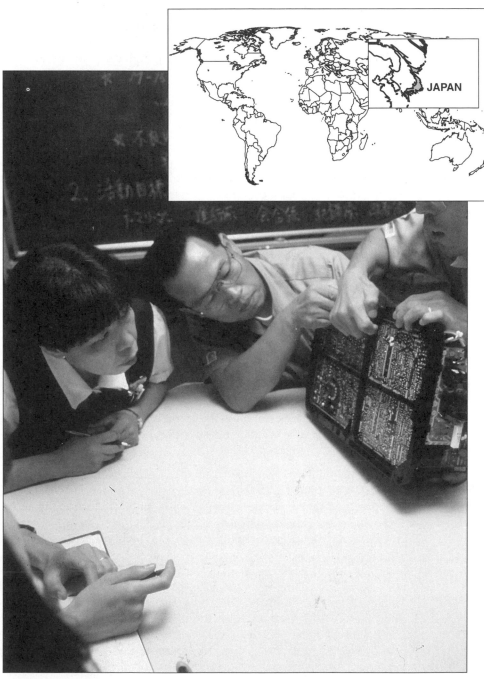

Japanese workers at a television factory participate in a quality control meeting with their manager.
© Tony Stone Worldwide: Charles Gupton

INTRODUCTION

All businesses function through people, and the effective management of people has become increasingly recognized as fundamental to business success. For the domestic, unicultural firm, people management embodies a varied set of activities. Typically it includes such personnel practices as recruitment, selection, compensation, career path planning, promotion, training, and performance motivation and evaluation. These practices are important to the multinational, multicultural firm too. But they are more complicated in the MNE setting, and other personnel practices are unique to MNEs.

Personnel Management Issues in MNEs

Consider personnel selection. For the MNE, selection involves questions at both the parent and subsidiary levels as to whether local nationals or home country nationals should be used. Should Nestlé, for example, rely primarily on Swiss nationals in its home office and on American nationals at its US subsidiary? Are there positions at the subsidiary for which Swiss nationals would probably be better suited? Are there positions from which Swiss nationals should be excluded? Compensation for persons assigned outside their home countries involves packages that cover the added costs of living abroad—costs for housing, taxes, and so on. People who accept overseas assignments are concerned about how the home office views such assignments and about the advancement opportunities that will be open to them upon their return. Is an overseas assignment an "out of sight, out of mind" situation? Training for a foreign post may involve an introduction to the cultural, social, and political conditions in the country of assignment. It may well involve training for the entire family of the assignee.

These and other differences between foreign and domestic assignments are the subject of this chapter. The topics covered include the relationship between the personnel function and the competitiveness of MNEs, the definition of expatriate management, the extent to and purposes for which expatriates are used, the use of local nationals versus expatriates, selection and training for foreign assignments, repatriation and promotion of expatriates, and, quite important, compensation and taxation issues pertinent to an overseas assignment.

PERSONNEL MANAGEMENT AND THE COMPETITIVENESS OF MNES

Challenge to the Traditional View

The traditional view has been that personnel management is a "facilitative" function, something that has to be done well to accommodate the more important success-related strategies pertaining to marketing, production, finance, and so on. Today this view is being seriously questioned. One challenge originates from the emergence of high-tech companies that value highly skilled employees as human capital assets. Another challenge stems from our growing understanding of and ability to adapt Japanese management practices that view employees as key ingredients in attaining low-cost, high-quality product strategies.[1] Indeed, several industries are totally revamping their personnel practices to utilize the brain power as well as the muscle power of their workers. General Motors' Saturn Plant, for example, departs radically from GM's historical management-labor relations in this regard. At Saturn, "operating teams" (workers) are responsible for defining and solving production problems and for achieving quality control as they work to assemble a car.

A third challenge to the traditional view originates from the emergence of the mature, *geocentric* MNE, which relies on the effective, transnational flow of information and directives—accomplished by people—that balances local competitive needs and strengths with those required or available elsewhere in the MNE system. Such information flows require personnel who are skilled in the company's operations, in the environments within and across which the MNE functions, and in the art of communication, including cross-cultural communication. Developing these personnel requires overseas assignments and responsibilities.

The New MNE Personnel Manager

Since personnel management in the MNE shapes the conduit through which the implementation of competitive advantages flow, it has a great impact on the effectiveness of the firm in the marketplace. The challenge of personnel management is to ensure effectiveness at minimum cost by finding the right balance between the parent's and the subsidiary's people needs and to staff these needs at both the parent and subsidiary levels with a continuous flow of knowledgeable, motivated personnel. Reaching these objectives is no easy task, and mistakes can be costly. The personnel manager in the MNE is thus seen as a special kind of person: a specialist in legal matters, such as equal employment opportunity and taxation related to foreign assignments; an expert regarding the personnel functions, such as recruitment, motivation, and compensation; and a highly knowledgeable person on company-specific matters, such as technology and competitive strengths and even the values and preferences of key executives.

DEFINITION AND USE OF EXPATRIATES

Parent company nationals, third-country nationals assigned to subsidiaries, and foreign nationals assigned to parent companies are typically referred to as **expatriates** and are the major focus of this chapter. Expatriates are generally found in technical and managerial assignments, and their numbers have historically been significant. For example, Hays reported that over 200,000 US citizens worked abroad in the early 1970s, and the US Department of Commerce's 1984 "benchmark" survey on foreign direct investment in the United States reported that an estimated 50,000 foreign citizens were employed by foreign firms in the United States.[2] While the numbers of expatriates working abroad are not tracked on a routine basis and there are no official figures regarding them, the rapid growth in foreign direct investment in the United States during the latter 1970s, the 1980s, and the early 1990s and the continued expansion of US MNEs abroad during this period suggest that the numbers of foreign nationals working outside their home countries probably increased during the 1980s. Indeed, Britain's ICI and Holland's Philips alone employed a total of 2,300 expatriates in the mid-1980s.[3]

Variations in the Use of Expatriates

Studies by Franko indicate that an MNE's use of expatriate personnel is high during the initial stages of foreign operations to accomplish technology transfers, including production and management technologies. The number of expatriates declines as the firm's local managers and technical staff assimilate this knowledge. It expands again as local operations become increasingly integrated into a global operational framework.[4] These views suggest that as a product's life cycle evolves, the need for expatriates expands (at the subsidiary level) in the early stage and then diminishes in the later stages. Finally, for the mature MNE, the need for expatriates arises at both the subsidiary and parent company levels. These views are also consistent with the staffing needs of those MNEs that develop from *ethnocentric* to *geocentric* as the intrafirm relationship evolves from a parent-to-subsidiary technology transfer process to an integrated, system wide need for the development and application of MNE-specific competitive advantages. These views also imply an expanding need for an awareness at the global management level based on country-by-country knowledge pertaining to a variety of employment-related concerns such as laws regarding race, age and sex discrimination, compensation practices, and taxes.

In a 1989 study, the Ashridge Research Management Group reported that many multinationals, such as Electrolux and ICI, were deliberately developing "international managers," people who could serve in any foreign location and also play a leadership role in determining future corporate strategy. Part of the development process for international managers involved short-term (i.e., for a few months to a few years) assignments at subsidiaries.[5]

Incidence of the Use of Expatriates

Studies of foreign MNEs in the United States have shed some light on the incidence of the use of expatriates. Of 100 foreign MNEs studied by the US Department of Commerce in 1975–76, about one-third reported that their CEOs were expatriates and that at levels below the CEO, expatriates often occupied only a few management positions. In addition, expatriates held technical positions. Moreover, mode of entry and parent nationality were found to be factors affecting the use of expatriates. Expatriates were more likely to be used in start-up cases than in takeover situations and at Japanese-owned subsidiaries.[6] In a study of Japanese multinationals in the United States published in 1986, Kujawa reported extensive use of Japanese expatriates. These expatriates—at Honda in Ohio and at Murata in Georgia, for example—were needed to implement and monitor Japanese management practices related to statistical quality control techniques and continued technology transfers from the Japanese parent to the US subsidiary.[7]

A 1989 study by Tung and Miller suggests US multinationals tend to use expatriates less than do European or Japanese multinationals. Their survey of US business executives found, for example, that only about 1 in 20 US executives believed an international assignment or experience was important for promotion into top management. Other studies, they noted, showed this perception was in stark contrast to the practices found in Japanese and European multinationals, where international experience was essential for promotion.[8]

We can conclude this section, then, by noting that the use of expatriates likely varies by product life cycle, the extent of the firm's geocentrism, the level of the (potential) expatriate position in the management structure, and the parent company's nationality. But there is also the question of balance. Where should the line be drawn between the use of local nationals and expatriates? We now turn to this issue.

LOCAL NATIONALS VERSUS EXPATRIATES

The question of whether to use local nationals or expatriates can be asked at both the parent company and subsidiary levels. The answer invariably turns on the perceived benefits to be gained by using expatriates balanced against the added costs required to maintain expatriate staff. Benefits are usually derived by bringing in technical or managerial expertise not available locally, including special knowledge about the firm itself. More effective communication and more consistent, trustworthy management behavior may be other objectives in assigning expatriates overseas. Measured against these benefits are different types of costs. Table 17–1 lists some of the pros and cons associated with choosing between local nationals and expatriates.

TABLE 17-1

Factors Affecting the Choice between Local Nationals and Expatriates

Factors Favoring Expatriates
Expatriates possess specific technical and managerial skills.
Using expatriates enhances communications between the parent and the subsidiary.
The presence of expatriates promotes the foreign or MNE image.
Parent-subsidiary relations are facilitated by the presence of expatriates familiar with the corporate culture.
The assignment of expatriates is part of their professional development program, and it improves senior management's decision making, as discussed in the context of the "international manager."

Factors Favoring Local Nationals
The total compensation paid to local nationals is usually considerably less than that paid to expatriates.
No host country cultural adaptation is necessary when local nationals are used.
Using local nationals is consistent with a promote-from-within policy.
No work permits are needed with local nationals.
Using local nationals promotes a local image.
Using expatriates with special employment contracts rather than using local nationals may block promotional opportunities for local nationals and thus run afoul of local equal employment opportunity regulations.

Cost Considerations

Studies have shown that using expatriates can be very expensive. Most firms use the rule of thumb that an expatriate costs at least three times as much as a local national. There are several reasons for the higher costs. Expatriates may be taxed twice on their income, especially their unearned income, in both the home and host countries. They may have home leave, family maintenance, and extra educational expenses. Also, and quite important, some areas simply cost more to live in than others, especially if the expatriate's consumption pattern is not consistent with local (native) supply patterns. For an expatriate, living costs among the different cities of the world are quite high and can vary substantially. Table 17-2 shows what it would cost for an American family of four to live in selected cities outside the United States. Not only do the overall costs vary considerably (at the limits), but the individual cost components also vary widely. For example, in 1990 the cost of housing ranges from $8,635 in Mexico City to $69,624 in Hong Kong, and taxes range from $10,770 in Hong Kong to $74,106 in Brussels! Clearly expatriates are expensive to put in place and to maintain. The contributions they make while on foreign assignments have to justify such expenditures.

In addition to out-of-pocket costs and the reasons suggested in Table 17-1, there are other reasons firms use expatriates only when necessary. These reasons and some of the positive aspects of overseas assignments are discussed in the sections that follow.

Effectiveness Considerations

We should note several final points regarding the use of local nationals versus the use of expatriates. First, when an expatriate is assigned overseas to fill a skill void, be it technical or managerial, it is often a prime responsibility of that person to train a local national to take his or her place. Second, some overseas positions are appropriate only for local nationals, since these positions are highly culture bound. Industrial relations management is an example. Other positions, such as the senior management position, seem to favor the use of an expatriate to facilitate communication and ensure control. Third, as MNEs mature into truly

TABLE 17-2

Living Costs of American Expatriates: For a Family of Four in Selected Cities, 1990

City	Housing	Transportation	Taxes	Goods and Services	Total
Hong Kong	$69,624	$21,113	$10,770	$16,904	$118,411
Tokyo	69,611	10,988	27,589	32,499	140,687
Geneva	45,788	11,461	40,367	35,143	132,759
Brussels	18,470	10,504	74,106	27,128	130,208
Frankfurt	23,844	10,657	50,197	28,253	112,951
Sydney	20,495	16,171	30,023	22,304	88,993
Paris	30,105	9,479	37,408	25,944	102,936
Amsterdam	20,794	9,592	37,237	25,503	93,126
London	27,979	11,640	19,572	25,371	84,562
Mexico City	8,635	3,056	13,183	10,710	35,584

Source: Baseline data prepared by Runzheimer & Company, Rochester, Wisconsin, and presented in *Business Week,* January 16, 1984, p. 99. Data adjusted to reflect inflation and changes in currency exchange rates during 1984–1990.

global enterprises, the need to integrate top management on a cross-national basis is expanding. Global firms need a global perspective at the top. The fact is, however, that top management and boards of directors have been slow to change and typically are not becoming multinational in their composition. This may change in the future as the "international manager" concept expands.

Host Country Considerations

Host countries, especially developing countries, generally favor the use of local nationals. Their reasons include increasing employment in general (jobs), advancing skill levels via on-the-job training and experience, and saving foreign exchange (where relevant). Nonetheless, these countries accept the use of expatriates when justified by legitimate business need. At times, though, MNE–host country friction can make securing local work permits for expatriates difficult and time consuming.

Even without such friction, regulations regarding the use of expatriates can be complex and costly to the MNE. The Bahamas, for example, will not approve the use of any expatriate until the position to be filled has been advertised and it can be demonstrated that no qualified person is available locally. Also, the MNE pays an annual work permit fee that can amount to thousands of dollars for each expatriate on assignment in the Bahamas.

To cite another situation, Brazil requires that the MNE document the need for an expatriate with the Ministry of Labor and submit to the ministry a copy of the expatriate's résumé, university diploma, and employment contract (between the MNE and the expatriate). Moreover, Brazil limits the number of foreign nationals employed to one-third of the total number of employees and limits the compensation paid to foreign nationals as a group to one-third of the compensation paid to all employees.

SELECTION AND TRAINING OF EXPATRIATES

An overseas assignment that ends traumatically for an expatriate hurts both the individual and the firm. A valued employee may be demoralized. Crucial time may be lost. Important supplier, customer, or governmental relations may be soured. Recognizing that an expatriate's job is likely to be more demanding than a similar job at the home base, the firm usually takes extra care in the selection and preparation of an expatriate for a foreign assignment. Nonetheless, a study reported in *The Economist* in 1984 noted that one in three American expatriates assigned abroad returned home sooner than originally planned. For European expatriates, the ratio was one in seven.[9] A 1981 study of 80 American MNEs found that at half of these companies, 10 to 20 percent of the expatriates were called home or fired because of their inability to perform effectively on a foreign assignment.[10] A similar study, focusing on expatriates in 35 Japanese MNEs, reported that at over three-quarters of these companies, fewer than 5 percent of the expatriates were called home.[11] It appears that some companies, especially American MNEs (and perhaps others), have something to learn.

The talents and skills needed in an overseas assignment include those typically identified with a domestic assignment: technical competence, educational achievement, initiative, creativity, independence, emotional maturity, ability to communicate, and so on. In an overseas assignment, several other talents and skills can be added to this list—for example, knowledge of a foreign language, cultural adaptability and empathy, and social flexibility (of the expatriate and his or her spouse and family). When the talents and skills required for a foreign assignment are lacking, special training programs are used. Studies generally confirm these points, but, as Tung reports, the selection and training of expatriate personnel depend on their precise overseas positions—chief executive officer (CEO), other manager, technical specialist, or operative.[12]

Selection

In her benchmark 1981 study of 80 US MNEs, Tung found that the importance of certain key attributes related to the selection decision varied considerably, depending on the position being filled at the subsidiary.[13] Selected data regarding these findings are presented in Table 17–3. In the selection decision for a CEO, the criteria emphasized managerial talent, maturity and emotional stability, initiative and creativity, experience in the company, adaptability and flexibility in a new environment, and technical knowledge. For managers other than CEOs, maturity and emotional stability, technical knowledge of the business, managerial talent, initiative, and creativity were emphasized over other criteria.

The criteria were considerably less extensive for technical specialists where technical knowledge and initiative and creativity were emphasized and for

TABLE 17–3

Selection Criteria for Expatriate Personnel: Survey of US MNEs (*n* = 80)

Criterion	CEO	Other Manager	Technical Specialist	Operator
Experience in company	83%	68%	58%	37%
Managerial talent	96	86	16	18
Initiative and creativity	84	82	82	52
Technical knowledge of business	79	91	89	68
Maturity and emotional stability	94	98	75	86
Knowledge of language of host country	26	42	25	46
Adaptability and flexibility in new environment	83	76	46	62
Spouse's and family's adaptability	61	63	40	49

Note: The percentages reflect those respondents who believed the criterion was used and was very important in the selection decision.
Source: Data abstracted from Rosalie L Tung, "Selection and Training of Personnel for Overseas Assignments," *Columbia Journal of World Business*, Spring 1981, p. 75.

458 PART III MANAGING THE MNE

operators where only maturity and emotional stability were stressed. In general, CEOs and other managers were more often seen as needing managerial experience and skills, personal and family flexibility, company experience, and communicative ability. Technical specialists and operatives were generally scored less frequently on all of these points. All four categories were scored quite frequently (that is, in over 70 percent of the MNEs surveyed) regarding technical skills, maturity, and emotional stability. Except for technical specialists, expatriates were required to display an interest in overseas work by a majority of the companies studied.

How does gender affect the selection outcome? Some societies and cultures, such as Japan and many of the Latin American countries, have traditionally been male dominated. Multinationals have been sensitive to this tradition, but in many instances have selected women to serve on expatriate assignments. But there is a long way to go on this issue. Part of the problem is that more women need to be included in the upper management and technical support positions at home from which the multinationals draw to fill expatriate slots abroad.

Training

Training programs seek to prepare potential expatriates for the situations and problems unique to an overseas assignment. For this reason, such programs are country specific and are quite often tailored to individual needs and time constraints. Among the topics typically covered are a cultural orientation, the social and religious setting, political and social issues, language training, home country–host country relations, and the legal environment.

In Tung's aforementioned benchmark survey of 80 US MNEs, responses were collected on the training activities pertaining to a foreign assignment. Of the firms surveyed, only 32 percent were found to have formal training programs.[14] The types of programs reported are shown in Table 17–4. About half of the companies with programs noted environmental/cultural orientation programs for CEOs and other managers. For these personnel, language training was often provided. Recall that language competence was discussed earlier as being unimportant in the selection decisions of many firms. Apparently firms do view language competence as important, but other criteria in the selection process override this criterion. Firms will train the selected expatriate in the needed language. Note too that the incidence of special training drops off sharply for technical specialists and operatives. This may reflect an anticipated brief duration of foreign assignment for the technical specialist (the "troubleshooter") and a somewhat company-confined assignment for operatives and thus, generally speaking, a lesser need for relational skills. In contrast to her findings on the low incidence of formal training in US MNEs, Tung reported that over half of the 35 Japanese MNEs she studied had formal programs stressing environmental and language training.[15]

TABLE 17–4

Frequency of Training Programs: Survey of US MNEs (n = 26)

Type of Training	CEO	Other Manager	Technical Specialist	Operative
Environmental	52%	54%	44%	31%
Cultural	42	41	31	24
Language	60	59	36	24

Source: Adapted from Rosalie L Tung, "Selection and Training of Personnel for Overseas Assignments," *Columbia Journal of World Business*, Spring 1981, p. 76.

Larger firms, in which the frequency of moving personnel into expatriate positions is high enough to sustain the costs of developing training programs, are more often involved in training activities. Smaller firms, which use expatriates less often, are more likely not to be involved in developing and conducting special training programs. Moreover, in smaller firms, the geographic diversity of overseas assignments, the pressures of time and money, and a lack of knowledge of their training needs at a given point in time generally preclude extensive training of expatriates by companies specialized in such training.

Studies have shown that failures on overseas assignments can often be traced to difficulties encountered by spouses and other family members in adapting to local environmental/cultural nuances.[16] In this regard, training can be especially beneficial. Again, larger firms are the ones that can afford such training. They are also the ones that define their career path programs for key personnel far enough in advance to incorporate such training into their expatriate assignments. General Motors, for example, maintains "management progression and succession charts" for key managerial employees in both domestic and foreign positions. These charts identify future positions for such employees and the further developmental activities required for promotion into those positions. The positions may be anywhere in the world where General Motors operates. Dow Chemical, British Petroleum, and other large MNEs maintain similar information on key executives.

COMPENSATION AND TAXATION

Motivation and performance on the job are closely related to the reward structure. "Pay for performance" is perhaps more evident in more companies today than ever before, given the trend toward increasingly competitive markets. How does an overseas assignment relate to one's income needs? How does it relate to one's performance on the job and to one's potential for visibility and preparation for advancement? This section addresses the first question. Overall, however, it is linked with several other questions. What special considerations affect the compensation paid expatriates? What currency-related problems might exist? How about income taxes for expatriates? These and other questions are addressed next.

ADDED DIMENSION

Welcome, Motorola University!

Motorola University (MU) was established in 1990. It doesn't offer degrees, but it trains over 100,000 Motorola employees worldwide every year. Everyone from the chairperson on down is now required to complete 40 hours of education annually. Motorola's training budget is about $50 million per year, and the company figures its return on this educational investment is about $30 for every dollar spent. Courses are taught in the company's training facilities in Phoenix, Austin, Singapore, London, and Schaumburg, Illinois.

MU's training mandate is to provide global education programs to support the company's worldwide business plan, that is, to give "strategic direction" to the company's worldwide training activities. How important is it that MU's leadership have international experience? ■

Source: Brian S Moskal, "Just a Degree of Confidence," *Industry Week*, February 19, 1990, pp. 65–66.

Compensation: Labor Market Factors

Several important factors, some obvious, others more subtle, influence the total compensation package pertinent to expatriate personnel.

The base salary paid an expatriate must be competitive with what that person would receive on a domestic assignment. The salaries paid expatriate personnel must reflect the labor markets in which they participate. For example, an American expatriate engineer on assignment in Singapore has alternative employment opportunities in the United States. The salary paid this person has to be competitive with the salaries paid engineers in the United States (not engineers in Singapore). Otherwise, the MNE would not be able to hire or retain expatriate engineers. For similar reasons, the major fringe benefits provided expatriates, such as retirement benefits and medical and life insurance, must be competitive with those afforded domestic personnel in the home country.

If the salaries and benefits of expatriates are competitive with salaries and benefits at home, they will probably differ from and typically be better than those obtained by local nationals on assignment at a subsidiary. This does not disrupt local pay and benefit scales, since the expatriate is recognized as providing special services to the company that are typically unavailable locally, that is, services for which there is no local labor market counterpart and therefore no locally established, comparative compensation level. Where expatriate assets of this kind are less apparent, the fact of being an expatriate is sufficiently distinctive, and on this ground alone local personnel generally accept the necessity of "special" salaries and fringes. In contrast, if the subsidiaries of MNEs pay local nationals salaries higher than those that local companies pay local nationals in comparable positions, labor market problems can develop as other local employers move to match the compensation levels at the MNEs and as the MNEs subsequently respond by establishing yet higher total compensation costs and thus reestablishing pay differentials. The labor cost spiral benefits no one. To ward off that possibility, MNEs have been especially deliberate in setting salaries for local personnel that are essentially responsive to local labor market conditions.[17]

Compensation: Cost-of-Living Considerations

Cost-of-living considerations are a second set of factors influencing the compensation levels of expatriate personnel. To be competitive in securing personnel for expatriate assignments, the MNE must offer a compensation package that reimburses expatriates for the added costs associated with living abroad. Otherwise, the net compensation of an expatriate assignment would be lower than that of a domestic assignment.

What are these cost-of-living considerations? Taxation at the foreign locale is certainly one. Others relate to bona fide additional personal expenses arising from an expatriate assignment. Examples are the travel costs associated with an expatriate's need to manage personal investments in the home country; the cost of hiring someone to manage such investments, such as a real estate agent in the case of a home rental; and the cost of attending to other important personal matters, such as the care of an elderly parent.

Some added costs of living arise not from a geographic relocation per se but from lifestyle values and needs. For example, overseas housing, education, recreation, security, and so forth must meet the expatriate's home country expectations and alternatives. There are also the home leave requirements of the expatriate and his or her family. The cost of living abroad may also be affected by a spouse's inability to secure professional employment in a foreign country or the inability of older children to obtain part-time employment and the income thus generated. Such forgone family income requires indemnification. To encourage expatriates to accept assignments abroad and to complete the terms and conditions of the contracts governing such assignments, especially time-on-the-job provisions, bonuses may be included. This practice is apparently more common in construction (turnkey) projects and in natural resource development projects than in manufacturing operations.

All of these cost-of-living requirements add up. Shehzad reports, for example, that the total cost of an American manager on assignment in Tokyo and in Ireland will be, respectively, six times and three times the cost of a manager in the United States.[18] Tung and Miller note that the costs of expatriates run two to three times their base salary levels and can be justified only for "fast-track" managers and technical specialists.[19]

Compensation: Currency Factors

The currency of compensation is an important concern too. Expatriates "live" in two countries. They have to meet day-to-day living expenses in the currency of the country of assignment, but they also have expenses they must meet in the currency of the home country—expenses for savings and investments, life insurance premiums, a child's education, and so on. For these reasons, expatriates' compensation packages are typically split into local-currency and home-currency payments. The latter are deposited by the parent company in the employee's account in the home country; the former are typically paid by the subsidiary.

What happens in the event of exchange rate changes? If local inflation pushes up the local-currency cost of living and the exchange rate does not reflect this deterioration in the value of the local currency, the home country cost of maintaining an expatriate's local standard of living will rise. This will necessitate an adjustment in the compensation package provided by the expatriate's home country. On the other hand, if the local currency devalues on foreign exchange markets to reflect the internal inflation, the home-currency costs borne by the expatriate will not rise and the compensation package will not require adjustment. For example, expatriates' employment contracts with US MNEs are dollar based. Their dollar value is a constant. They have cost-of-living provisions, however, to compensate for situations where inflation increases local living costs in the absence of offsetting exchange rate changes.

Taxes

Income taxes, which exist in nearly every country, are always paid by expatriates in the countries where they work. However, special tax considerations may significantly affect individual cases. Some countries, for example, tax expatriates only on the income they receive in the host country. When salaries are split between local and home currencies, local taxes are paid only on the former. In the United Kingdom, 50 percent of the income earned by a non-British citizen working for a foreign company is exempt from British income taxes. Some countries, such as the United States, require that the unearned income of expatriates (e.g., interest and dividend income) be taxed as if it had been earned in their own countries.

Tax policy affecting US expatriates is governed by US tax law, as most recently amended by the **Tax Reform Act of 1986.** Beginning in 1987, for example, a US citizen has been allowed to exempt the first $70,000 of income earned abroad from federal income tax. This income deduction comes off the top of the expatriate's reportable income and may put the expatriate in a lower marginal tax bracket than would otherwise be the case. Of course, if the effective foreign income tax rate is higher than the US rate, the US national on assignment overseas derives no benefit from the deduction.

Unearned income, as noted earlier, is taxable income in full. It benefits from no foreign income exclusion. If there is a tax treaty between the United States and the host country where the expatriate works, however, the foreign income taxes paid on unearned income are creditable against US taxes due on this income. The net effect is that the expatriate pays the higher of the US and the foreign tax rate.

To qualify for the foreign earned income credit a US taxpayer overseas must meet certain residency requirements. The taxpayer must have a tax home that has shifted to the foreign country and must be a **bona fide resident** of the foreign country for an entire year or *physically present* overseas for a minimum of 330 consecutive days. The tax home is the place of employment, and the shift to the foreign location must be indefinite, that is, for a duration of at least two years. For a person to qualify as a bona fide resident of a foreign country, US tax law requires an indefinite period of employment and the establishment of a permanent family residence outside the United States. Of course, the residency requirements of the foreign country must also be met. A bona fide resident of a foreign country can travel into and out of the United States at will. There is no minimum number of days per year over which the person must stay out of the United States, as with the physically present overseas category.

The income taxes expatriates pay reflect a complicated set of laws and personal as well as corporate considerations. Advance planning is important, and the use of tax counsel is not unusual. In fact, many of the larger MNEs routinely provide such counsel to expatriate personnel on a periodic basis. Dow Chemical, for example, provides such counseling to both US nationals on assignment at foreign subsidiaries and foreign nationals on assignment in the United States.

IB ILLUSTRATION

Can You Figure This One Out?

Jesse Jones, an American citizen, is employed by the American firm Patriotics, Inc. He is assigned to its French subsidiary, Ex-Patriotics, SA. Jesse's salary is $240,000 per year. Jesse also earns $8,000 annually on bank interest on his savings accounts in France.

Assume that in this hypothetical case, France taxes Jesse's earned and unearned income at an effective rate of 50 percent. Also assume that France allows no income deductions and thus taxes Jesse's entire income at this rate. In the United States, Jesse qualifies for the $70,000 earned income exclusion. For simplicity, assume that there are no deductions here too and that Jesse's effective tax rate in the United States is 28 percent.

What are Jesse's taxes in France? (Answer: $124,000.) What is Jesse's US taxable income? (Answer: $178,000.) What are his US taxes payable before the foreign tax credit? After the foreign tax credit? (Answers: $49,840; zero.) If France dropped its income tax rate to 20 percent, what US taxes would Jesse pay after applying the foreign tax credit? (Answer: $240.) ■

REPATRIATION AND PROMOTION

Repatriation occurs when the expatriate returns from an assignment at the parent or subsidiary located in a foreign country. It is a major event in any person's career, and it would be expected to occur during a period of high personal expectations for promotion and solid career-path progress. Such expectations are especially likely to be held by expatriates who are parent country nationals. The extent to which expectations of this kind have been met is a matter of record, and the record shows that the pattern has changed as the MNE has grown and matured.

The Early Experiences

During the late 1960s and the 1970s, a period of rapid growth in the number of MNEs, many parent-level expatriates on assignment at subsidiaries found the going rough. One reason was that many of these assignments were responses to problems at the subsidiaries that required expertise available only at the parent. The assignments arose too quickly to allow for adequate preparation of either the expatriate or the expatriate's family.[20] The result was frustration. Moreover, little consideration was given to the position the expatriate would hold upon returning to the parent company. The literature of the period identified several problems or concerns pertinent to the repatriation of expatriates:

1. "The career path holiday."[21] Expatriates on foreign assignments are on a career path holiday. Little or no concern is expressed for how they will fit into the organization upon their return.
2. "The isolation syndrome."[22] The expatriate feels isolated, personally and professionally. Communication with the home office is difficult, since no one (or few) appreciates the difficulties of operating abroad.
3. "Missing the management progression mainstream."[23] Advancement relates to exposure and significance. The foreign assignment isolates the assignee, and often the employer judges overseas experience as irrelevant to what is important for advancement.
4. "Play it again, Sam!"[24] Repatriated expatriates are often placed in a holding pattern upon their return home, since no appropriate positions have been defined for them. In some cases, this means having to prove oneself to the parent organization all over again.
5. "And now, the letdown!"[25] Senior-level foreign assignments generally require a lot of autonomous, almost entrepreneurial decision making and interactions with others, such as high-level government officials. The new job at home is likely to be more constrained both in external contacts and in the scope of management responsibility. The personal adjustments required can be difficult.
6. "The high opportunity cost of staying on."[26] Repatriated executives put into a parent company holding pattern find that they can earn more money and be challenged again by taking positions at other companies.

These concerns, which could themselves be costly, along with the (US) tax disincentives of the latter 1970s and early 1980s, which greatly reduced the foreign earned income exclusion, resulted in a substantial curtailment of the use of expatriates by US MNEs.

**ADDED
DIMENSION**

Taxes and Timing: The Inevitable Can Be Minimized!

Tax analysis and planning can be a tedious exercise at best. Yet it is important, especially for the expatriate. For example, some countries have a de minimus rule requiring a minimum period of assignment during any tax (typically calendar) year. If the expatriate's minimum period of assignment is 60 days, effecting patriation prior to March 1 would save paying foreign taxes that year. Moreover, if the income earned abroad then were less than $70,000, no US income taxes would be paid on that amount either.

Stock options provide another example. If the expatriate participates in a qualified incentive stock option plan (ISO), US tax law may allow for deferral of a capital gain when the option is exercised (obviously at a market price above the option price). Deferral is not allowed in Germany, Mexico, and many other countries. The gain is taxable, often at high foreign marginal tax rates. The expatriate may be better off converting that option after arriving home! A third example pertains to the four-year deferral of capital gains resulting from the sale of a US residence. If a new home is not bought within these four years, the gain is taxed. The employer (which would likely have to reimburse the expatriate for these taxes) may be well advised to bring the expatriate home before the time limit expires. ∎

Source: Jeffrey M Kadet and Robert J Gaughan, Jr., "Oversee Expatriate Returns to Curtail Taxes," *Personnel Journal,* July 1987, pp. 71–76.

The Changing Rationale

The role and treatment of the expatriate have changed dramatically as the structure and operations of MNEs have evolved. During the emergent years of the MNE, management could generally be characterized as fairly ethnocentric and certainly as inexperienced in the handling of overseas personnel assignments. Foreign subsidiaries were seen as appendages, conduits through which flowed products, technical expertise, financial resources, and marketing prowess generated by the parent company. Expatriates were in fact operating downstream with regard to the development of competitive advantages. Their positions were not as important or powerful as those at home. Moreover, a tight competitive environment accompanied the onset of defensive foreign direct investment. Firms had to set up plants overseas, and do so quickly. This time compression exacerbated the already difficult situation that expatriates were experiencing because of their firms' inexperience in handling them. A lot of mistakes were made that complicated the role, if not the lives, of expatriates. Family problems, for example, led many expatriates to want to return home. Also, as discussed earlier, the professional experiences of those on assignment overseas often led to personal frustration and to a questioning of the desirability of expatriate assignments.

In the polycentric structures, where considerable autonomy was exercised at local levels, the expatriate's role, if any, was quite limited. For example, prior to the integration of automobile production between the United States and Western Europe and within Western Europe, Ford Motor Company's subsidiaries were substantially autonomous. They used few, if any, expatriate personnel. Indeed, at one time in the 1960s, the only managerial personnel link between Ford of England and the US parent was the presence of Henry Ford II on the former's board of directors. Nonetheless, expatriates could be found in polycentric MNEs. Some were located in the finance and treasury functions. Others were holdovers from an ethnocentric period. In fact, some expatriate managers worked deliberately to isolate the subsidiary from parent company control.[27] These managers liked to be their "own boss" and enjoyed working and living abroad.

Historically, subsidiaries of European MNEs were fairly autonomous from their parent organizations. Expatriate managers were schooled over long periods of time, however, and were substantially conversant with corporate values and methods. Little ongoing communication occurred between these managers and the managers at the parent.[28] This was especially evident with Europeans in senior management assignments at the US subsidiaries of European MNEs.[29]

The Recent Experiences

Today's mature MNEs have expatriate policies and programs that are more established and effective than those of earlier times. For example, career path planning, which is routinely offered to executives in the larger MNEs, identifies postexpatriate placement alternatives prior to an expatriate assignment. The larger firms are also more likely to have special training programs for personnel who accept expatriate assignments and for their spouses.

The enhanced concern of the MNE for the expatriate reflects, to some degree, the expatriate's increased importance to the competitive success of the enterprise. Since the mature MNE seeks competitive advantages that result from, among other factors, the integration of information and expertise across geographic

---

**IB
ILLUSTRATION**

A Global Product Brings People Together at Bank of America

Bank of America's System Engineering group (BASE) is responsible for aligning technical expertise with overall business strategies and is providing the bank's World Business Division with managerial and technical support in the development of International Banking Systems (IBS), an on-line computer system that supplies current financial information to account officers and corporate customers, facilitates electronic global monetary transfers, provides treasury department support for foreign exchange and money market activities, and so forth.

The IBS was originally developed in England, Germany, Holland, and Belgium. It is now operational in all overseas divisions and in the United States. Bank of America regards its implementation of the IBS as one of its "most significant strategic decisions." The IBS allows the bank to deliver comprehensive, integrated electronic banking services to customers worldwide.

BASE is headquartered in San Francisco and coordinates closely with the bank's strategic planning and control functions there. The IBS was originally developed in only a few European countries and was extended to cover global operations. Applications specialists who were already using the IBS were instrumental in implementing it elsewhere. BASE and IBS personnel with experience in the new system assisted colleagues in other countries in getting on-line while streamlining their own operations. IBS allows bankers around the world to coordinate activities with a single global customer, such as an MNE. ∎

Source: BankAmerica Corporation, 1984 *Annual Report*, pp. 2–8.

boundaries, the people who embody multinational knowledge are especially valuable to it. Where these people originally came from is perhaps incidental to their value. It is their experiences and expertise that enhance their value.

Some examples might be useful here. In the global MNE, R&D may be conducted in various national centers and then pooled at the corporate level. National Semiconductor, for example, conducts research in the United States, Japan, and Israel. It coordinates projects among centers in these three countries to integrate their findings and come up with product and process improvements that are applicable worldwide. The personnel at these centers are more project oriented than location oriented and may or may not be local nationals.

Marketing research is handled on a geographically decentralized basis but is pulled together at some central point as product definition is evaluated in terms of manufacturing processes and production allocation. Honda, for example, conducts marketing research on motorcycles in numerous countries. This work involves both local nationals and Japanese expatriates. Honda pulls its findings together to decide on a specific motorcycle design and subsequently defines which organizational units worldwide will be responsible for production.

Operations management or industrial engineering in different geographic segments can pool expertise and develop, for example, operating systems with global applicability. Ciba-Geigy, a large Swiss chemical company with major operations in the United States and Europe, routinely integrates operations technology between the two areas. Process engineers and managers in both areas communicate continuously, and often US personnel are on assignment in Europe and European personnel are assigned to the United States.

The point here is that people from different countries with different experiences are valuable at the global level of the MNE. The situation today is very different from what it was in the earlier years, when subsidiaries were appendages. The globally integrated MNE is a different entity and thus has different personnel needs.

ADDED DIMENSION

Traits of the Modern International Manager

Jacques Maisonrouge, president of IBM World Trade Corporation, expressed some fairly strong beliefs about today's international manager:

One major consequence of this internationalization of business has been the increased need for international managers; that is, for managers who, aside from having all the qualities that make good managers of national companies, are also mobile, adaptable, and at ease in cultures other than their own. In addition, because they will undoubtedly work outside their home countries at some point in their careers, they should have one or two foreign languages; an understanding of the sociopolitical environment in which they will be working; and a world view that inhibits the growth of chauvinism.

. . . tomorrow's managers will have to demonstrate more awareness of the world around them [and] more flexibility of mind . . . than ever before. In a world where new knowledge continues to accumulate rapidly, the most valuable managers of all will be those who have learned *how* to learn. ∎

Source: J G Maisonrouge, "Education of a Modern International Manager," *Journal of International Business Studies*, Spring–Summer 1983, pp. 143–44.

Foreign Assignments in High Demand

People are certainly aware of the increasing potential for professional success associated with overseas assignments. The expatriate assignment is becoming increasingly attractive to many executives. Kenny, Kindler & Hunt, a New York executive recruiting firm, reports that fast-track executives are seeking overseas assignments to show that they can operate effectively at the general management level. In a survey that it conducted in 1983 in which 37 percent of the 125 managers polled were willing to take overseas jobs—up from 10 percent a decade earlier[30]—Heidrick & Struggles, another executive recruiter, reported that managers who in the past had shunned overseas jobs that got them "two-years into oblivion," or forgotten at the parent, were now seeking such jobs.[31] These findings comport well with a statement by the vice president of PepsiCo's international division that "his group is the primary farm team for top company talent."[32]

Business schools in America, Europe, and Asia are increasingly concerned with educating the international manager. MBA and specialty degree programs, such as the Master of International Business Studies (MIBS) degree at the University of South Carolina and the Master of International Management (MIM) degree at Thunderbird (the American Graduate School of International Management in Arizona), are becoming increasingly popular. Enrollments in these programs are expanding, and more universities (e.g., Wharton, UCLA, Miami, etc.) are developing academic programs geared toward education for international business. These programs and their expanding enrollments support the thesis that international business employment opportunities are increasing.

CONCLUSIONS

Many important personnel management issues are pertinent to the MNE. One issue is the use of expatriate managers and technical specialists.

Benefits/Costs

Many pros and cons are associated with the use of expatriates. Two pros seem especially relevant, however. Expatriates can provide special expertise that is not otherwise available at a specific location, and they can often provide it quickly and in a manner consistent with company practices. However, using expatriates, is very costly. Obviously the benefits derived from their special expertise must exceed the added costs of using them.

Historically, a fairly large percentage of expatriate assignments have ended in failure, with the expatriate returning home prematurely. This expensive experience raises questions as to the adequacy of the standards that have been used to select and train these expatriates.

Selection

The criteria used in selecting expatriates have varied considerably depending on the overseas position involved. CEOs and other managers have been required to possess managerial experience and skills, personal and family flexibility, company experience, and communicative ability. Highly valued traits of technical specialists and operatives have included emotional stability and maturity. Training for expatriates has often been country specific, with topics including cultural, religious, political, and social issues; language proficiency; home country–host country relations; and the legal environment. Training for CEOs and other managers has been more extensive than that for technical specialists and operatives. Larger firms have typically employed more sophisticated selection procedures and training programs than those used by smaller firms.

Compensation

The compensation paid expatriates must be competitive with what they would receive if they were employed at home. It must also cover the added costs of living abroad and maintaining both a domestic and a foreign presence. Examples of the former are housing, educational expenses, forgone income that a spouse or children might have earned, and security expenses. Examples of the latter are travel expenses, the extra costs of maintaining investments at home, and extra taxes. The compensation of expatriates is also complicated by split payroll policies that result in partial compensation payments in both home- and host-country currencies, by inflation in the country of assignment, and by changes in exchange rates.

Taxes

Expatriates always pay income taxes where they work in the countries that have income taxes. Special considerations derived from their expatriate status may lower their tax bills, however. A US national on assignment abroad is allowed a substantial foreign earned income exemption by the Tax Reform Act of 1986. An expatriate's unearned income is never exempt from US taxation. Foreign taxes paid on such income by an expatriate, however, can be credited against any US taxes due. To be eligible for the foreign earned income credit, an expatriate must meet certain residency requirements.

Repatriation

In the early days of the MNE, expatriate repatriation was often a disappointing experience. Firms were inexperienced in dealing with expatriates, and the competitive pressures of the times necessitated moving needed people overseas quickly. Mistakes were made. Those who had been on assignment overseas often fared miserably upon their return to the home operation. For these and other reasons, especially reasons related to the taxation policies then in effect, the incidence of expatriate assignments declined.

The Increased Importance and Attractiveness of Expatriate Assignments

As MNEs matured and their operations and marketing became more globally integrated, the status and value of the expatriate were enhanced. The future even for US MNEs seems especially promising in this respect. Career path planning and other MNE activities reduced the uncertainties associated with expatriate assignments, especially the uncertainties related to repatriation. Perhaps more important, the attractiveness of expatriate assignments increased as MNEs became more dependent on personnel with multinational experiences that would contribute to strategies of global competitive effectiveness. Consequently, larger numbers of executives and technical personnel have come to view overseas assignments as positive aspects of their professional development.

QUESTIONS

1. Identify the links between personnel management and the competitiveness of MNEs. How do expatriate personnel relate to the transfer of management-based technologies, such as those pertaining to experience curves, and product and process technologies?
2. What is an expatriate? Does the use of expatriates correlate with the product life cycle? If so, how? How would the use of expatriates vary among ethnocentric, polycentric, and geocentric MNEs?
3. What are the main pros and cons of using expatriates compared to using local nationals?
4. What are the most important selection criteria for selecting expatriates for overseas positions? How and why do these criteria vary with the nature of the overseas position?

5. What special training programs might be beneficial for expatriates and their families pending an overseas assignment? What is the likelihood that such programs would be found in a US multinational? Why?

6. What major factors affect the compensation paid expatriates? How do expatriates differ from local personnel with regard to influences on compensation?

7. How are exchange rate changes accommodated in the compensation packages of expatriate personnel? How might such packages be administered in cases of currency nonconvertibility?

8. Describe the provisions of the US tax law that pertain to foreign earned income and unearned income. What is the rationale for these provisions?

9. Why did US MNEs have difficult early experiences in the handling of their expatriate personnel?

10. Compare the role and significance of the expatriate in the competitive strategies of emergent MNEs and mature MNEs. What role do expatriates play in the competitiveness of MNEs today? What effect does this role have on their desire to include overseas experiences in their career ladders? Why?

REFERENCES

Adler, Nancy J. *International Dimensions of Organizational Behavior.* Boston: PWS–Kent Publishing, 1991. See especially chap. 5, "Multinational Teams"; chap. 8, "Cross-Cultural Transitions: Expatriate Employee Entry and Reentry"; and chap. 9, "A Portable Life: The Expatriate Spouse."

Dowling, Peter J, and Randall S Schuler. *International Dimensions of Human Resource Development.* Boston: PWS–Kent Publishing, 1990.

Edstrom, Anders, and Jay Galbraith. "Transfer of Managers as Coordination and Control Strategy in Multinational Organizations." *Administrative Science Quarterly,* June 1977, pp. 248–63. (A classic.)

Gerber, Beverly. "A Global Approach to Training." *Training,* September 1989, pp. 42–47.

Grub, Phillip D; Fariborz Ghadar; and Dara Khambata, eds. *The Multinational Enterprise in Transition.* Princeton, NJ: Darwin Press, 1986. See chap. 5, "International Personnel Management."

Kiggundu, Moses N. *Managing Organizations in Developing Countries: An Operational and Strategic Approach.* West Hartford, CT: Kumarian Press, 1989.

Maisonrouge, J G. "The Education of the Modern International Manager." *Journal of International Business Studies,* Spring–Summer 1983, pp. 141–46.

Ronen, Simcha. *Comparative and Multinational Management.* New York: John Wiley & Sons, 1986. See chap. 12, "Staffing the MNC Foreign Subsidiary."

Rossman, Marlene L. *The International Businesswoman of the 1990s: A Guide to Success in the Global Marketplace.* New York: Praeger Publishers, 1990.

Tung, Rosalie L. "Career Issues in International Assignments." *Academy of Management Executive,* August 1988, pp. 244–47.

NOTES

[1] For evidence, see Duane Kujawa, "Technology Strategy and Industrial Relations: Case Studies of Japanese Multinationals in the United States," *Journal of International Business Studies,* Winter 1983, pp. 9–22; and Duane Kujawa, *Japanese Multinationals in the United States: Case Studies* (New York: Praeger Publishers, 1986), pp. 40–88.

[2] Richard D Hays, "Expatriate Selection: Insuring Success and Avoiding Failure," *Journal of International Business Studies,* Spring 1974, p. 25; US Department of Commerce, *Foreign Direct Investment in the United States,* vol. 1 (Washington, DC: US Government Printing Office, 1976), p. 20.

[3] As reported in "Mad Dogs and Expatriates," *The Economist,* March 3, 1984, p. 69.

[4] Lawrence G Franko, "Who Manages Multinational Enterprise?" *Columbia Journal of World Business,* Summer 1973, pp. 30ff.

[5] Kevin Barham and Clive Rassam, *Shaping the Corporate Future* (Ashridge, CO: Ashridge Research Management Group, 1989).

[6]US Department of Commerce, *Foreign Direct Investment,* vol. 5, appendix 1, "Management and Employment Practices of Direct Foreign Investors in the United States," pp. I-63–I-64.

[7]Kujawa, *Japanese Multinationals,* pp. 40–59.

[8]Rosalie L Tung and Edwin L Miller, "Managing in the Twenty-first Century: The Need for Global Orientation," *Management International Review* 30, 1990/1, pp. 5–18.

[9]"Mad Dogs and Expatriates."

[10]Rosalie L Tung, "Selection and Training of Personnel for Overseas Assignments," *Columbia Journal of World Business,* Spring 1981, pp. 68–78.

[11]Rosalie L Tung, "Human Resource Planning in Japanese Multinationals: A Model for US Firms?" *Journal of International Business Studies,* Fall 1984, p. 141.

[12]Tung, "Selection and Training," p. 69.

[13]Ibid., p. 75.

[14]Ibid., p. 76.

[15]Tung, "Human Resource Planning," p. 142.

[16]See, for example, Hays, "Expatriate Selection," pp. 30–36.

[17]Ehrenfried Pausenberger, "The Conduct of International Enterprises in Developing Countries," *Intereconomics,* November–December 1980, p. 297.

[18]N Shehzad, "The American Expatriate Manager's Role and Future in Today's World," *Human Resource Planning,* 1984, pp. 55–61.

[19]Tung and Miller, "Managing," p. 10.

[20]Llewellyn Clague and Neil B Krupp, "International Personnel: The Repatriation Problem," *Personnel Administrator,* April 1978, pp. 29–33; Cecil G Howard, "Integrating Returning Expatriates into the Domestic Organization," *Personnel Administrator,* January 1979, pp. 62–65.

[21]Ibid.

[22]Lee Smith, "The Hazards of Coming Home," *Dun's Review,* October 1975, pp. 71–73.

[23]Howard, "Integrating Returning Expatriates."

[24]"How to Ease Reentry after Overseas Duty," *Business Week,* June 11, 1979, pp. 82–83.

[25]Smith, "Hazards of Coming Home."

[26]D W Kendall, "Repatriation: An Ending and a Beginning," *Business Horizons,* November–December 1981, pp. 21–25.

[27]Published evidence on such a point is difficult to find. However, the authors have conducted a considerable number of company-specific case studies in which expatriate executives have attested to these views. One example, involving expatriate management at Chrysler Corporation's then Spanish subsidiary and the parent's desire to wrest managerial control from a local team consisting of both local nationals and expatriates, is briefly reported in Duane Kujawa, *International Labor Relations Management in the Automotive Industry* (New York: Praeger Publishers, 1971), p. 31.

[28]For evidence, see Lawrence G Franko, *The European Multinationals* (Stamford, CT: Greylock Publishers, 1976), pp. 187–98.

[29]US Department of Commerce, *Foreign Direct Investment,* pp. I-60–I-65.

[30]"Overseas Work Appeals to More US Managers as a Wise Career Move," *The Wall Street Journal,* July 19, 1983, p. 1.

[31]Ibid.

[32]Ibid.

Ernesto Gracias por Nada

Ernesto Gracias por Nada had served as president of Ace Synthetics Caribbean (ASYNCA) for two years, and today was his "big day." He was resigning his position with Ace to join Plasticos, SA, as executive vice president, strategic planning. Ernesto had been working on this move for over a year.

Plasticos was Ace's major customer in the Caribbean and Central America. It bought petrochemical-based feedstocks from Ace that it molded, extruded, or otherwise fabricated into plastic piping, conduit, and sheet used in the construction industry. Both ASYNCA and Plasticos were subsidiaries of US multinationals long active in Latin America. Both were known to be progressive companies. But how often does the president of a major subsidiary resign? What happened at Ace that made Ernesto want to leave? What could Plasticos do for him that Ace couldn't?

Ernesto joined Ace in 1975, nearly 20 years ago. He had just completed his MBA at ESAN, a graduate business school in Lima, Peru. He was 28 then. Ernesto also held a bachelor's degree in chemical engineering from a university near his boyhood home in Rosario, Argentina. Prior to attending ESAN, he had worked for several engineering consulting firms on projects in Argentina, Ecuador, Jamaica, the Dominican Republic, and Peru. The people he worked with were quick to recognize his technical competence and his strong interest in management. Most of them believed a distinguished career lay ahead of him.

Ace's Organization Structure

Ace Synthetics organized its Latin American division in 1965 to enhance its focus on several growing, important markets in that region. During the latter half of the 1960s, Ace Synthetics Latin America (ASYNLA) was essentially a marketing organization selling intermediate products produced in upscale, highly capital-intensive plants in the United States. Its marketing success resulted in local production where market size—from a regional, multicountry perspective—could justify direct investment. During the 1970s, Ace put up plants in Brazil, Mexico, Argentina, Chile, and Colombia.

In the early 1980s, ASYNLA "spun off" several operating companies whose responsibilities included both producing certain products locally and marketing all Ace products within their respective countries. Hence, Ace Synthetics Brazil (ASYNBRA), Ace Synthetics Mexico (ASYNMEX), Ace Synthetics Argentina (ASY-

This case is based on a real person and real companies and events known to the case writer, Duane Kujawa. However, fictitious names have been used for all the parties for purposes of anonymity. Revised 1994.

NAR), Ace Synthetics Chile (ASYNCHI), and Ace Synthetics Colombia (ASYNCO) came into being. ASYNCA was also formed then and was given marketing responsibilities for all Ace products in all the Caribbean and Central American countries. ASYNLA was restructured to perform as a regional headquarters organization responsible for all of Latin America and as a marketing organization covering those Latin American countries where no other subsidiary had responsibility, for example, Ecuador, Bolivia, Uruguay, and Peru. At this time, ASYNLA was relocated from its New Jersey–based parent company office to Coral Gables, Florida.

Ace relied on a matrix structure to provide it with operational flexibility and market continuity. Its major organizational units were product based as well as geographically based. The Organic Chemicals Group, for example, had worldwide responsibility for organic chemical production, and it was also responsible for the sale of all Ace products (regardless of their production sites) wherever organic chemical plants were located. (Recall that plants were located in major markets.) Area-specific marketing groups such as ASYNCA handled all of the Ace products marketed in their regions.

In this structure, business plans were developed via a committee process involving those responsible for the production of certain products and those responsible for the territories in which those products were marketed. Decisions on production level, production allocation, and pricing, for example, were recognized as interdependent and requiring diverse managerial inputs. The matrix structure also allowed for the ongoing close coordination among all the organizational subunits, including production, marketing, R&D, and finance, that was required for maximum long-term profitability.

Ace's Key Personnel Policies

Ace's matrix structure required the internal development of managerial/technical personnel. Committee decisions rested not only on accurate inputs from each member but also on knowledge of the broader, systemwide considerations on which decisions were ultimately based. These considerations, in turn, required personnel who were knowledgeable about Ace's overall operations and committed to maximizing returns at the overall corporate level.

For these reasons, Ace hired in only at the lower-level entry positions. Individuals needed to grow within the organization by accepting diverse and increasingly responsible positions that expanded their knowledge of how Ace operated overall, while allowing for progressively stringent testing of their technical and managerial competencies.

Every year, Ace evaluated the performance of its key personnel and forced a rank-ordering of these people reflecting their performance effectiveness. The top 20 percent were given substantial merit pay increases and positioned for subsequent promotion into even more responsible and rewarding positions. The middle 60 percent were given average raises. The bottom 20 percent got no raise and were often encouraged to leave. Ace's compensation policy was to reward performance while encouraging performance improvement.

Ace preferred to use cash compensation as much as possible. It believed this was a stronger performance motivator than indirect payments such as fringe benefits. Many viewed Ace's retirement bonus as the ultimate cash reward. Key employees received a cash bonus equal to three years' salary when they retired. This typically amounted to several hundred thousand dollars and was in addition to the regular retirement program benefits.

Ernesto's Case

Ever since Ernesto joined Ace, he had received superior performance ratings. He was always in the top 20 percent, and he had progressed fairly rapidly up the company's hierarchy. He was initially a technical sales representative in an Argentina-based group responsible for polymer sales. He was appointed head of the polymer marketing group in Peru within two years, and two years after that appointment, he was put in charge of polymer sales for all of Argentina. He moved to the Coral Gables regional office in 1987 as director of polymer sales at ASYNLA. In 1989, he was promoted to director of marketing, Organic Chemicals Group, at ASYNLA. As before, his performance was outstanding.

By 1992, Ernesto had spent five years at Coral Gables. Company policy now required that he return to Latin America since he was not on the Ace-US payroll. During his five years at Coral Gables, he was treated like all Ace-US management personnel in terms of pay scale and basic benefits. In addition, as an expatriate manager, he was given extra compensation to cover schooling costs for his children, travel during an extended annual home leave, and so on.

The five-year limit was imposed for several reasons. One reason was that five years seemed more than adequate from a professional development standpoint. A second was that expatriates were expensive, so there had to be good grounds for continuing to pay the added costs associated with their status. Yet another reason was that such expatriates from Latin American countries were ultimately more valuable to the company if they returned to Latin America, where their assets, including their linguistic and cultural affinities, could be put to optimal use.

Ernesto was first offered a position as executive vice president at ASYNVEN (the Venezuelan subsidiary). He turned it down, claiming hardship on his family if he were to relocate just then. A month later, he requested advancement into the Ace-US organization. His request was denied. Shortly thereafter, Ernesto was offered and accepted the president's position at ASYNCA. Within three months, he and his family had relocated to San José, Costa Rica.

Ernesto believed he had been treated unfairly by Ace. Other Latin American executives confided that they too thought Ace had treated them as "second-class citizens," since their career paths had been essentially confined to Latin America. Ernesto and others like him were highly results oriented and had been compensated handsomely over the years. They had all developed substantial investments in the United States. (These investments reflected a variety of concerns, not the least of which was the long-term currency hedge that such investments provided in the face of nearly continuously declining Latin American currency values.) Moreover, a Latin American on assignment in a Latin American country did not receive the special three-year salary bonus upon retiring.

Ernesto arrived in San José determined to recover what he believed was a financial loss occasioned by Ace's failure to recognize him on an equal basis with parent country nationals. It took him about two years to identify Plasticos as his "target" and to negotiate his salary and benefit package.

Export-Import Management

This chapter describes how export-import transactions are carried out and demonstrates how a firm can benefit from being involved in international trade. The perspectives of small firms, large MNEs, and importers are presented in separate sections to show the opportunities available to each. The main goals of the chapter are to:

1. Explain how relatively simple export-import transactions, including documentation, work.

2. Show how domestic and multinational firms can benefit from exporting.

3. Demonstrate the gains available to the firm from using imports in its business strategy.

4. Explain a wide variety of the most important trade financing procedures.

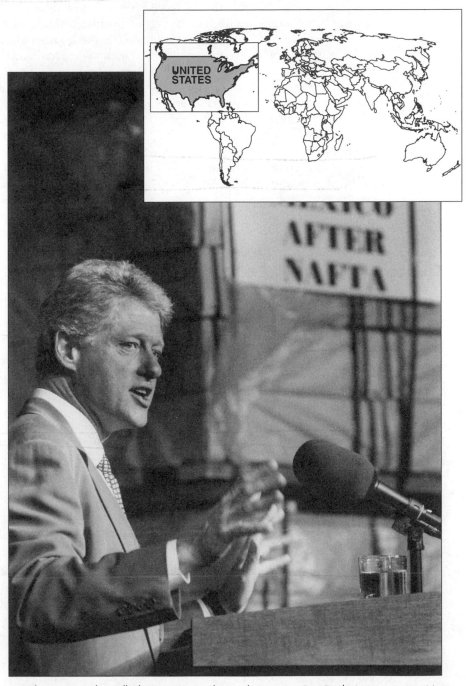

United States President Bill Clinton promotes the North American Free Trade Agreement in a New Orleans, Louisiana, warehouse.
Reuters/Bettmann

INTRODUCTION

International trade was probably the first form of international business, and it certainly involves the largest number of participants in international business today. The value of international banking transactions far surpasses that of trade, whose value in turn exceeds that of foreign direct investment, foreign portfolio investment, contractual arrangements such as licensing, intergovernment transfers, and other forms of international business. The participants in many of these business activities tend to be large, established companies and banks. The area of exports and imports, on the other hand, has a huge variety of participants, ranging from one-person companies that buy products from manufacturers for export to major multinational enterprises such as General Electric, which constructs nuclear power plants and a great variety of other products and exports them to many countries.

Exporting can be used as a marginal activity by a company that sells some product in one country and agrees to ship that product overseas on request. Similarly, importing may be used to obtain an input needed for manufacturing when domestic supplies are inadequate. In each case, the international aspect of the business may be relatively unimportant to the firm, but it exists anyway. Then, if the firm discovers that overseas sales (or imported parts) begin to account for a major part of total sales, it may specifically focus on developing a strategy for exports and imports.

This entry into international business through exporting or importing is not a necessary condition, since a firm may just as well decide to invest overseas in a low-cost location to maintain its market share for a product facing serious price competition. In this case, initial international business occurs through foreign direct investment. The key point is that, generally speaking, exporting or importing is a type of international business open to virtually any size or kind of firm, whereas other types of international activity, such as foreign direct investment and overseas franchising, tend to demand greater capital, management time, and other company resources.

Multinational firms have the potential to use exports and imports to both move products among their affiliates in different countries and deal with outside customers and suppliers. MNEs that do this enjoy many opportunities to benefit from low-cost overseas suppliers (including their own affiliates), sell excess inventories from an affiliate in one country to customers in another, and even to ship some products to a subsidiary that produces others to offer a full product line to local customers. On the whole, MNEs can use international trade to pursue many business goals more efficiently and effectively than can purely domestic firms.

Many companies fail to consider *imports* as a means of supplying their needs for parts, components, and even finished products. Perhaps this bias is due to the managers' main focus on sales (and hence on potential exports). Or perhaps it follows the typical government-led emphasis on exports to improve a country's balance of trade. Since imports as well as exports may contribute to a company's business success, they should not be ignored. Reducing the cost of production inputs (through importing) adds to the bottom line, just as increasing the volume of sales does.

In this chapter, we first illuminate the main participants, instruments, and practices in international trade and then explore managerial issues. In the next section, we examine the basic export-import transaction. Then we consider the perspectives of small firms, MNEs, and importers. Next, we look at the specific issue of financing exports and imports. Finally, we reconsider the ways exporting and importing can utilize (or create) the firm's competitive advantages.

A BASIC EXPORT-IMPORT TRANSACTION

The Participants

Although there is probably no such thing as a "typical" **export-import transaction,** we can consider a number of frequently used instruments and features of such transactions as a basic model to which other alternatives can be attached or compared. Figure 18–1 depicts a transaction in which an importer and an exporter agree on a sale and each uses a bank to handle the financial arrangements. Other intermediaries—an insurance company, a transportation company, and customs in the importing country—are also shown.

The transaction would probably take place somewhat as follows. First, the exporter would look for a foreign buyer for its products. (Alternatively, a foreign buyer might come to the exporter and request a shipment.) When the exporter finds a buyer—not necessarily an easy task—the transaction can proceed. The two firms negotiate for terms such as the price, the quantity to be delivered, the delivery date, and the payment date. When an agreement is reached, some kind of bill of sale can be drawn up, depending on what the two parties determine. The negotiations will probably include a demand by the exporter for some guarantee of payment made on the importer's behalf, for example, a letter of credit from a bank the exporter chooses. (The financial aspects are discussed at length in the "Trade Financing" section.) These negotiations, if successful, result in an export-import transaction.

In addition to the payment documents, the transaction usually involves an insurance contract on the goods shipped (to protect against losses from damage in shipping) and a contract with some transportation company to ship the goods from the exporter to customs in the importer's country. The goods must be cleared by customs inspectors in the receiving country, after which the importer or another transportation company may pick them up for delivery to the importer's facility.

FIGURE 18–1

A Simple Export-Import Transaction

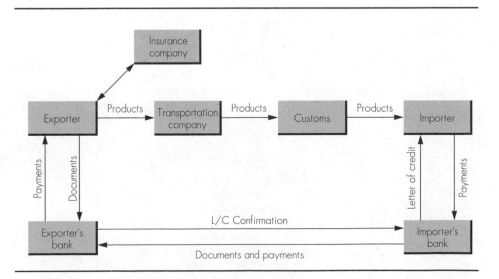

This highly simplified transaction illustrates some central concerns of the parties involved in international trade. The exporter wants to ensure payment as soon and as firmly as possible. The importer wants to make sure that the goods arrive on time and in good condition. Each bank wants to make sure that payment takes place on time and, of course, that it earns its fees for providing the letter of credit or other services (in addition to interest on any financing it offers). The insurance company wants to make sure that the cargo is delivered as contracted in the sale. Finally, the transportation company wants to make sure that the exporter (or importer) pays for the shipment as contracted. These concerns are summarized in Table 18–1. Notice the concerns are more or less inverse for the exporter (who wants earlier payment and later shipment) and the importer (who wants later payment and earlier delivery). The other parties mainly want to see the transaction completed as contracted, since their incomes generally come from fees based on the value of the shipment.

The Documentation

Carrying out the export-import transaction just described requires a substantial amount of documentation. The documents most often used include the letter of credit, the bank draft, the bill of lading or combined transport document, the commercial invoice, the insurance certificate, and the certificate of origin. Let us consider each document in turn.

An (export) **letter of credit (L/C)** is a contract between an importer and a bank that transfers liability for paying the exporter from the importer to the (supposedly more creditworthy) importer's bank. From the issuing bank's point of view, the L/C represents a contingent liability: if the terms stated in the letter of credit are met, the bank agrees to pay the exporter. As Figure 18–2 shows, the terms of the L/C specify the presentation of appropriate documents (in this case a commercial invoice, a customs invoice, a packing list, a bill of lading, and a 60-day bank draft) but do not refer to the quality (i.e., acceptability) of the merchandise.

TABLE 18–1

Export-Import Participants and Their Concerns

Participant	Concerns	Items Affecting Income	Risks
Exporter	Early payment, guaranteed payment	Revenues, production costs, transport costs, financing costs	Nonpayment, delays, damage to goods
Importer	Timely arrival of goods, safe arrival of goods, latest payment allowable	Product cost, import-related fees and expenses, financing costs	Delays, fraud, damage to goods
Exporter's bank	Documents in order, payment received from importer's bank	Fees, contract-processing costs	Nonpayment, incorrect documents
Importer's bank	Documents in order, payment received from importer	Fees, contract-processing costs	Nonpayment, incorrect documents
Insurance company	Payment of premiums, safe arrival of goods	Premiums, contract-processing costs	Damage to goods, incorrect documents
Transport company	Payment of shipping charges	Fees, contract-processing costs	Damage to goods, delays

FIGURE 18-2 A Letter of Credit

**APPLICATION & AGREEMENT
FOR IRREVOCABLE COMMERCIAL
LETTER OF CREDIT**

L/C No _____
(For Bank Use Only)

DATE __June 19,19__

To: MARINE MIDLAND INTERNATIONAL BANK
777 Brickell Avenue, Suite 1201
Miami, Florida 33131

Please issue for our account an irrevocable Letter of Credit (herein called Credit) as set forth below by:

☐ AIRMAIL   ☐ AIRMAIL, WITH SHORT PRELIMINARY TELEGRAPHIC ADVICE   ☒ FULL TELEGRAPHIC ADVICE

Advising Bank (Please leave blank unless Advising Bank has been specified)	For Account of
The Hongkong & Shanghai Banking Corp. 18 Rue de la Paix 75002, Paris France	ABC Company 100 Madison Street New York, New York

In Favor of (Beneficiary)	Amount
XYZ Trading Co., Ltd. P.O. Box 260-09 Paris, France	In Numbers US$45,000.00 In Words Forty-five thousand and 00/100 U.S. Dollars
	Drafts must be presented for negotiation or presented to drawee on or before Expiration Date September 1, 19

Available by drafts at _____60 days sight_____ drawn, at your option, on you or your correspondent
(Please indicate Sight or Tenor)
for ___100___ % of the invoice value.

When accompanied by the following documents, as checked:

☒ Commercial invoice ___1___ original and ___2___ copies.
☒ Customer invoice ___1___ original and ___2___ copies.
☐ Insurance Policy and/or Certificate _____
☐ Including War Risk _____
(If other insurance is required, please state risks)

☒ Other documents __Packing list in duplicate__
_____
_____

☐ Air Waybill consigned to _____
☒ On Board Ocean Bill of Lading (if more than one original has been issued all are required)
Issued to Order of **MARINE MIDLAND INTERNATIONAL BANK** _____
Marked: Notify: ABC Company, 100 Madison Street, New York, N.Y.
_____

Freight: ☒ Collect ☐ Paid

Covering: Merchandise described in the invoice as (Mention commodity only in generic terms omitting details as to grade, quality, etc.) Purse accessories

Shipping Terms
(Check One)   ☐ FAS   ☒ FOB   ☐ C&F   ☐ CIF   ☐ OTHER
(Specify City, Port or Airport)

Shipment From: Paris, France To: New York, USA Latest: August 21, 19	Credit Transferable ☐ Yes ☒ No	Partial Shipments ☒ Permitted ☐ Not Permitted	Transshipments ☐ Permitted ☒ Not Permitted

☒ Documents and/or Draft(s) must be presented to negotiating or paying bank within __10__ days after the date of issuance of documents evidencing shipment but on or before the expiration of the Credit. *(Note: If number of days left blank it will automatically be considered 21 days.)*

☒ Insurance effected by ourselves. We agree to keep insurance coverage in force until this transaction is completed. All banking charges outside the U.S.A. are for ☒ Beneficiary's account ☐ Our account

☐ Other instructions _____

Disposition of Documents: ☒ To Us ☐ Other _____
Unless Otherwise Instructed You May Authorize Your Correspondent To Forward All Drafts and Documents In One Airmail.

MMIB-60 (Rev s8 85)

As long as the bank that issues the L/C (Marine Midland International Bank) is presented with the required documents before the L/C expires, it is obligated to pay the exporter. If the importer fails to pay the bank, the bank must deal with that problem as a separate contract. Similarly, if the importer fails to receive acceptable merchandise for any reason, that problem must be dealt with as a separate contract not involving the bank (e.g., damages to merchandise are covered by insurance, and fraud by the exporter is a failure to uphold the initial commercial contract). Multiple contracts are involved in the simple export-import transaction; the L/C in particular requires only that the specified documents be in order for the exporter to receive payment from the bank; all other contractual obligations are generally separate from this one.[1]

Notice that the document shown in Figure 18–2 is called an *irrevocable commercial letter of credit*. The word *irrevocable* refers to the fact that, once drawn up for the importer and accepted by the exporter, the L/C may not be amended by either party without prior approval by both. The L/C is also *commercial,* because it refers to a commercial transaction. This type of L/C is called *documentary,* because it requires that documents be presented in order to carry out payment. It is the most commonly used means of guaranteeing payment in international trade between unrelated firms. If the paying bank is not located in the exporter's country, the exporter may demand that a bank in that country offer a "confirmation" of the L/C. In that event, the responsibility for paying the exporter falls on the confirming bank, which in turn will seek payment from the importer's bank, which in turn will seek payment from the importer. (In this example, the Hongkong & Shanghai Banking Corporation offers only "advice" to the exporter, XYZ Trading Company. This bank could be asked to confirm the transaction and take responsibility as noted.)

The **bank draft,** also called a *bill of exchange,* is similar to a simple check in its use as the means of payment for an export-import transaction. If the transaction is payable on sight, the draft becomes a check when the exporter presents it (plus the L/C and other documents). If the transaction is payable at some fixed time after acceptance of the documents, the draft is akin to a postdated (delayed-reaction) check, cashable only at the specified date. The latter is called a **time draft** and the former a **sight draft.** Figure 18–3 is a time draft, payable in 60 days from the account of ABC Company at Marine Midland International Bank.

When a letter of credit is used to guarantee payment to the exporter, the draft remains the vehicle through which payment is made, but it becomes relatively unimportant because the bank issuing (or confirming) the L/C has taken responsibility to pay the exporter, whether or not the importer's account contains sufficient funds. If the draft is used alone (i.e., without a letter of credit), it becomes all-important as the means of payment. (Payment by draft alone, of course, is less expensive for the importer than using an L/C as well.)

When a draft is used without a letter of credit, some form of instructions must accompany it to explain to the various parties involved what other documents and goods are involved in the transaction. This type of transaction is called a **documentary collection.** If the draft is payable on sight, the instruction letter specifies that the documents will be released to the importer upon payment of the draft (abbreviated D/P). If the draft is payable at a later date (i.e., a time draft), instructions will specify that the documents will be released to the importer upon acceptance of the draft (abbreviated D/A). Notice that in the case of a sight draft,

FIGURE 18-3

A Commercial Draft

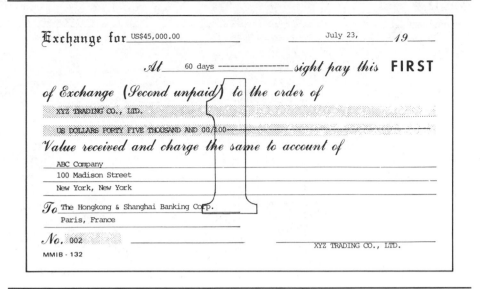

$$Exchange\ for\ \underline{US\$45,000.00} \qquad \underline{July\ 23,} \quad \underline{19}$$

At _____ 60 days --------------- *sight pay this* **FIRST**

of Exchange (Second unpaid) to the order of

XYZ TRADING CO., LTD.

US DOLLARS FORTY FIVE THOUSAND AND 00/100────────────────

Value received and charge the same to account of

ABC Company
100 Madison Street
New York, New York

To The Hongkong & Shanghai Banking Corp.
Paris, France

No. 002

XYZ TRADING CO., LTD.

MMIB - 132

the importer actually pays the exporter before receiving the goods; thus, the exporter's main risk is that it may ship the goods to customs in the importer's country and subsequently need to retrieve them if the importer fails to complete the transaction by paying the draft. (Payment on sight occurs when the importer receives the documents after the exporter ships the goods and sends the documents to the importer.) In the case of a time draft, once the importer accepts the draft (it becomes a "collection"), the exporter surrenders the merchandise, leaving only the draft as its claim on future payment. Both sight and time drafts accompanied by instructions and other documents (but no L/C) are called **documentary drafts.**

A **bill of lading** issued by a shipping company or its agent is used as evidence of a contract for shipping the merchandise and as a claim to ownership of the goods. The exporter owns the goods until the importer accepts the documents, at which point ownership shifts to the importer. The bill of lading serves as a receipt for the exporter, showing that it delivered the merchandise to the shipping company for transportation to the importer. The bill of lading does *not* require the carrier to inspect the merchandise; it requires only that the carrier accept the containers stated by the exporter as containing the specified merchandise.

If the goods are shipped by airplane or by more than one means of transport, alternative documents may replace the bill of lading. An **airway bill** is used in shipment by air. A **combined transport document** is used for shipments that involve more than one mode of transportation (e.g., a truck to the port, then a ship).[2]

Another document usually included in an export-import shipment is the **commercial invoice,** which the exporter writes to precisely describe the merchandise and terms of the sale. This document resembles the shipping invoice used in domestic shipments.

Some proof of *insurance* is generally included. The **insurance certificate** explains what type of coverage is being used (e.g., fire, theft, water) and names the insuror and the exporter whose property is being insured.

TABLE 18–2

Common International
Trade Documents

Instrument	Seller or Issuer	Buyer	Reason for Use
Letter of credit (L/C)	Commercial bank	Importer	To guarantee payment to the exporter
Bank draft	Drawn on a commercial bank	Payable to exporter	To serve as the means of payment
Bill of lading	Shipping company	Exporter	To prove the exporter delivered the goods as agreed
Combined transport document	Shipping company	Exporter	To prove the exporter and each transport company delivered the goods as agreed
Commercial invoice	Exporter	Importer	To describe precisely the merchandise and terms of sale
Insurance certificate	Insurance company	Exporter	To prove the shipment is insured and on what terms
Certificate of origin	Government of shipping country	Exporter	To verify the country where the merchandise was produced for customs purposes

To assess tariffs and other government-imposed restrictions on trade, the shipment may require a **certificate of origin** stating the country in which the goods were produced. This document is necessary when shipping to European Union countries, where tariffs are charged on goods originating outside the Union but not on goods produced in member countries.

Table 18–2 summarizes the documents just discussed, noting the parties involved and the reasons for the document's use. The preceding discussion is not intended to cover all the documents used in export-import transactions; rather, it points out the ones most widely used. In every transaction of this kind, it is necessary to check with each country's government before shipping, to verify what documents are necessary.

EXPORT MANAGEMENT FOR THE DOMESTIC FIRM

This section examines exporting as a part of the business of a nonmultinational firm. Such a firm may be large or small, but it does *not* do substantial international business; that is, its competitive advantages do not include experience in foreign markets. This type of firm must consider exports to be a kind of new business, just like production of a new product or entry into a new market segment in the domestic market. The appropriate products must be selected, buyers must be found, production and transportation costs must be estimated, promotional strategy must be created, and the business must be incorporated into the organization effectively. While each of these matters deserves detailed study, they are discussed here only to point out some of the most important considerations.

Exporting within Corporate Strategy

Figure 18–4 offers a view of *exporting* in a corporate strategy context. It depicts exporting as a means of entry into foreign markets. Other alternatives include foreign direct investment and contractual arrangements such as licensing and franchising. The company can set its strategy by assessing its competitive

FIGURE 18-4

Foreign Business Strategy

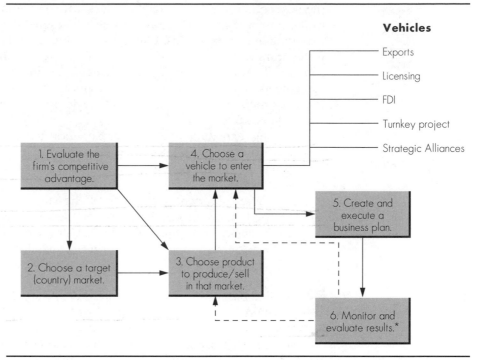

*The dashed lines show that performance evaluation may lead to changes in the products selected or in the market entry vehicle (or even to exit from the market) if the results justify such strategic shifts.

advantages and disadvantages (step 1), then proceeding to explore foreign markets that offer a potential for sales.

The target markets can be chosen on the basis of expected sales, competition from other suppliers, government restrictions, costs of getting the product to those markets, and any other relevant factors. Although there are over 180 countries in the world, the firm will most likely be able to narrow its initial search to a very small number of markets, probably based not only on incomes but also on proximity and cultural affinity.

Once a country has been chosen (step 2), the strategy must be developed for selecting products and a market entry vehicle. If the firm makes only one product or a narrow product line, product selection is not an issue. For the diversified firm, it may be appropriate to introduce different products into different national markets. Product selection is based on competitive conditions in the chosen market for the range of products the firm makes, the costs of making and transporting the products, and the risks involved (step 3). In any event, once a product has been selected, the firm can proceed to explore ways of getting that product to the foreign market.

Depending on the firm's set of competitive advantages and the conditions in a given national market, each market-serving alternative can be evaluated (as discussed in Chapter 2). Assuming the firm has no experience with other international business, and because the costs and risks of exporting are usually low, it will most likely choose exporting (step 4).

Nevertheless, the other market-serving alternatives should be considered carefully. Direct investment certainly can give the firm a greater local visibility in the host country, and it avoids the risk that the government will impose barriers to imports in the future. However, direct investment is much more costly than exporting in most situations. Likewise, licensing should be considered, especially if the firm's technology is capable of being protected and import restrictions are substantial. And, of course, other strategic alliances such as joint marketing agreements or joint production ventures should also be evaluated in terms of their impacts on costs, revenues, and the strategic position of the firm relative to key competitors.

Assuming exporting does appear superior to the other choices and the company does decide to pursue the given market (rather than eliminate it from consideration), the firm can create and execute a detailed business plan (step 5, discussed below).

Finally, after observing the results of the strategy for some period of time (step 6), the firm can make adjustments or reject the strategy in favor of another. Altogether, Figure 18–4 presents a logical structure for thinking about foreign market entry, through exports or other means available to the firm.

The Business Plan

The detailed business plan mentioned as step 5 should cover the usual marketing considerations such as pricing, promotion, and distribution, as well as the organization of the firm to handle this new business.

Pricing may be aimed at covering the incremental costs of producing extra products for export,[3] covering the full costs of production (including fixed costs), or equating marginal revenue to marginal cost. Other goals, such as revenue maximization or loss minimization, could be sought too. The point is that pricing for overseas sales may be based on criteria different than those used in pricing for domestic sales.

Another consideration is that if the exchange rate changes, prices in the domestic currency will change in terms of the foreign currency. Such a change may help or harm the firm, but it definitely should be taken into account when setting a pricing strategy for export sales. For a target country whose currency is devaluing relative to the home country currency, the firm's export prices will need to be lowered to maintain the same host country prices. For a country whose currency is revaluing relative to the home country currency, the firm's product will become less expensive unless export prices are raised to offset the exchange rate change.

A firm exporting to several foreign markets would like to price separately in each market, charging higher prices in markets that will bear them. This strategy can create problems, however, since customers in a low-price country may try to resell the product in high-price countries, thus competing with the firm itself! Also, this type of price discrimination may lead the authorities in high-price markets to penalize the firm for using monopolistic practices.

Promotion may be extended abroad or adapted to the host country environment, as discussed in Chapter 13. If exports are solicited from abroad, no promotion is required initially. If the firm wants to expand its export business, some promotional effort will be required. If the market entry mode chosen is exporting through distributors, promotion must be done among potential distributors rather than focusing only on final customers.

Distribution to the foreign market will require making new arrangements with transportation companies, insurers, and so on, because the transactions will cross national borders and thus cross national legal jurisdictions. While no single distribution method can be singled out as best for all cases, the pros and cons of each method can be evaluated just as in the domestic market. The key differences are that costs are generally higher because distances are longer and risks are greater because of the additional national economies and legal jurisdictions involved.

Organizational issues relate to the fit of international sales into the company's total business (as discussed to some extent in Chapter 12). Generally, exports are handled by an existing division when they are small in value. As exports grow, it may make sense at some point to assign responsibility for foreign sales elsewhere by establishing an international division or otherwise reorganizing the firm. Basically, the goals are to communicate with prospective customers in the host country about product availability and to control the export activity so that it does not disrupt other company business.

EXPORT MANAGEMENT STRATEGY FOR THE MNE

Once the company has become multinational or is willing to consider establishing overseas operations, a new set of alternatives arises. Now it may be possible to export some products from the home country to the target country and to produce other products in the target market. When the MNE introduces new products at home, it may simultaneously introduce them in the host market, through either exports or local production in the existing facility there. When cost or regulatory difficulties arise in one country, it may be possible to move production to the less-constrained country, resulting in either imports or local production for each market served. The MNE may also export parts or other production inputs from an affiliate in one country to another affiliate in another country for assembly, in this case serving the host country market only indirectly, through products manufactured by the host country affiliate. In general, the MNE possesses a greatly expanded set of choices in comparison with the domestic firm in any country.

Returning to Figure 18–4, the MNE again begins with an inventory of its competitive advantages and disadvantages to see what products and markets are worth exploring. Now it can divide target markets into those where it already has some operations—and thus where additional products can be introduced—and those that are new to it. In a market in which the MNE already has operations, it has a competitive advantage (relative to other foreign firms without local operations) in its knowledge of demand conditions and of the legal, cultural, and cost barriers to serving that market. In a market in which the MNE does not yet have operations, it faces barriers similar to those confronting the non-MNE, except that the MNE has had experience in dealing with new entry in other markets (such as dealing with tariffs and import licensing) that may be transferable to the new market. The knowledge advantage from previous international business gives the MNE an edge over other firms in market entry in both situations. Thus, the MNE's choice of a target market depends on both market characteristics in potential host countries and the firm's existing array of foreign affiliates.

The MNE's choice of products to sell in the target market once again depends on the firm's previous activities in that market. Some products may have already been introduced there. Others may be appropriate for local production rather than for export from the home country (or from an affiliate in another country).

Having considered such factors, the firm can choose products based on expected demand in the target market, the costs of getting the products to customers, and the risks involved.

The choice among exports, local production, and other market-serving alternatives has already been discussed. For the MNE, it is important to note that some products may be supplied to a particular country through one vehicle and other products through other vehicles.

When the MNE manager arrives at step 5 of the decision-making process, a specific business plan must be designed, once again recognizing the interrelations between the new project and the firm's existing activities. The new export venture must be evaluated on the basis of its _incremental_ contribution to the firm's sales and profits. If the exports simply replace products previously manufactured by the company in the target country, they are justified only if they lower the costs or risks of producing and delivering the products to customers. If the exports represent entry into a new market, they may be evaluated as in the case of the non-MNE.

If the exports are sold from one affiliate to another in the same firm, the issue of **transfer pricing** arises. By pricing intrafirm shipments higher or lower, the firm may transfer more or less funds to the shipping affiliate. While this issue does not necessarily affect the decision to export, it does constitute a vehicle for moving funds to desired locations within the MNE, a strategic consideration that may be very important when exchange controls and other restrictions on company financial dealings exist.

Organizationally, the export function in the MNE is often assigned to an international division or added onto each product division as needed. The need for internal control over export decisions becomes more and more important as exports, local production, and other alternatives are used to serve markets in various countries. The key concern is that export sales must not simply replace existing company business (e.g., through local production or licensing) but must generate additional profits to the firm by raising revenues, lowering costs, or lowering risks.[4]

IMPORT MANAGEMENT

While attention generally is focused on exporting as the relevant aspect of international trade for the firm to pursue, there is no reason _importing_ cannot be equally important. In fact, some firms do their entire business as import intermediaries, finding suppliers overseas and customers domestically for various products. Both the MNE and the non-MNE can utilize importing to obtain lower-cost or unavailable products from abroad.

Both the MNE and the domestic firm can make importing part of the purchasing function. Simple product availability may be the initial reason for seeking a foreign supplier; if the needed product is not available from domestic suppliers, imports must be used. The decision to import may also be based on comparative cost differences between domestic and foreign suppliers and on the risk-reducing goal of obtaining multiple suppliers, including one or more from abroad. In general, the use of imports in the firm's total business can serve a variety of goals, each of which improves the firm's position in the market.

The multinational firm can not only use imports as a source of supplies from other firms; it can also import from affiliates abroad. Very important for many MNEs today is the use of **offshore assembly** (for example, of televisions, stereos, and other electronic products), which requires import into the home country from an assembly plant overseas. Also important for MNEs is the possibility of supplying the home market from a foreign affiliate in the event of a strike, machinery breakdown, or other production problem in the home country. Thus, MNEs need to consider the risk-reducing aspect of importing at least as much as the cost-reducing aspect.

TRADE FINANCING

In the simple export-import transaction discussed earlier, **trade financing** was included when the importer used a letter of credit, allowing payment to be postponed for some period of time, such as 180 days. Realistically, both the importer and the exporter may need pretrade and posttrade financing. The importer may need **pretrade financing** if it is required to make partial or total prepayment to the exporter or required to place a deposit with the government before receiving permission to import. Even after shipment, the importer may need credit during the period before it is paid for sale of the merchandise. The exporter may need pretrade working capital financing. Later, if the exporter accepts payment via a time draft or any other future means of payment, it may also need financing for the period after shipment but before payment by the importer. Table 18–3 shows common means of financing these needs.

The exporter may obtain pretrade financing by requiring the importer to prepay the shipment. Alternatively, the exporter may seek a working capital loan from a commercial bank or some other financial institution. One type of working capital loan, called a **back-to-back L/C,** uses the letter of credit issued by the importer's bank as security for a loan made to the exporter. A second letter of credit is issued by the exporter's bank, drawn on the exporter's account, and paid to its supplier. The exporter's bank may offer this type of credit more readily than a straight loan because the importer's L/C provides evidence of a reasonable likelihood that the exporter will be able to pay back the credit.

The importer may not need to worry about pretrade financing unless the shipment is prepaid or the government requires a deposit before issuing an import license to permit the transaction. In either case, the likely means of financing (other than using internal sources of funds) is a bank loan.

For **posttrade financing,** the exporter has various alternatives. It can seek another bank loan to cover the period until it receives payment from the importer. Often it can discount the receivable through the creation of a **banker's acceptance.** Many L/Cs are drawn up to conform to the rules for creating banker's acceptances that can be discounted at a Federal Reserve bank in the United

TABLE 18–3

Simple Trade Financing Techniques

	Pretrade Financing	Posttrade Financing
Exporter	Prepayment Back-to-back L/C Working capital loan	Sale of receivables (e.g., banker's acceptance) Bank loan Sight draft and letter of credit Documentary collection payable on sight
Importer	Bank loan to cover prepayment	Letter of credit and time draft Bank loan Sale on consignment Sale on open account

IB ILLUSTRATION

Pyrotek Goes International

Pyrotek Corporation is a small, family-run company based in Dallas, Texas, that manufactures and sells fire extinguishers for use in office buildings, hotels, and industrial settings. The firm has been in business for over 10 years, and it has established a viable market niche with a dozen fairly large clients and about 100 smaller clients. Three members of the Wyler family and five other employees constitute the entire work force of Pyrotek. In 1993, the company had sales of about $12 million, virtually all of which were made in the United States. Only three rival firms are perceived as providing competition for Pyrotek, although several larger suppliers produce fire extinguishers for major hotel chains, restaurants, and other potential Pyrotek customers.

Pyrotek's main competitor recently reduced its prices on the basic carbon dioxide and foam extinguishers that make up most of the market. Facing this challenge, Wyler began to look for new suppliers of the metal tubing, valves, and fittings that the firm uses to make fire extinguishers. In addition, sales were increasing to the point where Pyrotek could not continue to expand without installing new manufacturing capacity of its own. Based on these two pressures, Wyler was able to find a brass foundry in Birmingham, Alabama, that agreed to contract on a long-term basis to produce much of the needed valves and fittings and assemble the fire extinguishers. The deal included an option for Pyrotek to buy 25 percent of the stock in the foundry over a period of five years.

This step solved the problem of expansion for the firm, but it left the cost/price issue unchanged. At almost the same time the foundry deal was closed, Wyler was contacted by a Taiwanese firm that manufactured brass and copper casings. This firm was trying to attract American customers for its products. It offered a price of $US 0.65 per casing (the shell of the fire extinguisher), a considerably lower price than the $US 1.20 Pyrotek was paying its existing suppliers. With no experience in international business, Wyler was extremely hesitant to enter into a contract. However, he was also aware of the "Asian challenge" American manufacturers faced and of the successes several US auto and electronics firms had had in dealing with Asian suppliers.

Wyler decided to "hedge" his bet by purchasing only about 10 percent of his needs from this new supplier. After an initial order of 3,000 casings, Wyler was totally satisfied with the quality and delivery conditions of the shipment. Today Pyrotek imports approximately one-half of its supplies from Taiwan and is actively seeking additional Asian suppliers for its other components. ■

States.[5] If the L/C meets these rules, many banks will be willing to purchase the L/C and draft from the exporter at a discount, at which point the documents become a banker's acceptance. (The discount rate for banker's acceptances varies all the time; the current rate can be found daily in the "Money Market Rates" column of *The Wall Street Journal*.) To avoid having to deal with posttrade financing, the exporter can push the problem onto the importer by demanding payment on sight (i.e., at shipment).

The importer will generally use a letter of credit plus a time draft for posttrade financing. If this financing lasts until the importer receives payment from its customers, all of its financing needs are satisfied. If not, the importer will seek other means, such as a bank loan. Perhaps the importer can push the problem onto the exporter by demanding sale on **consignment** (in which payment is made to the exporter only when the importer sells the goods to a final customer) or on **open account** with no fixed date required for payment. This last option is usually available only to importers that are legally tied to their exporters, such as subsidiaries of the same company.

These means of financing export-import transactions are not the only ones available, but they do account for most of the business of this kind that is done today. Additional financing is available from an array of nonbank institutions that offer services that complement or substitute for bank lending. Four of the most important sources are (1) government loans and loan guarantees, (2) factoring, (3) forfaiting, and (4) countertrade.

Government Loans and Loan Guarantees

In one form or another, every country today offers *government support* to its exporters. Japan offers low-interest loans to exporting firms, France rebates part of the taxes exporters have paid on exported products, Brazil allows exporters to exchange foreign-currency earnings at a favorable exchange rate, and other governments do one or more of these things.[6]

The United States offers its exporters two of the above types of support. First, it allows firms that incorporate an overseas export sales subsidiary as a **foreign sales corporation (FSC)** to reduce the taxes paid on their export earnings by as much as 50 percent.[7] Although this is not a "loan" in strict terms, it is a means of reducing the cost of export sales that affects the exporter in a manner similar to that of a low-interest loan. Second, the United States offers exporters support through the loans and guarantees provided by the Export-Import Bank of the United States (Eximbank).

Broadly speaking, **Eximbank** offers US exporters a variety of programs that reduce their costs and risks in dealing with foreign clients. Short-term loan guarantees (actually provided by the Foreign Credit Insurance Association under Eximbank's supervision) enable exporters to obtain credit in cases where commercial banks would not offer it. Similarly, Eximbank offers medium- and long-term loans and guarantees that enable exporters to finance their foreign sales, generally in cases where bank financing would be difficult or impossible to obtain. Eximbank also provides a program of insurance against the political risks that could confront an exporter (e.g., war, government policy changes, currency inconvertibility). Each of these programs is discussed in detail in Eximbank's publications.[8]

Factoring

For financing the period between the shipment of its merchandise and payment by the importer, an exporter may turn to a factoring company, or factor. This arrangement is a direct alternative to acceptance financing. A factor will buy the exporter's receivables at a discount and assume the risk of nonpayment by the importer, as well as the right to payment of the receivables.

Factoring involves a greater commitment from the exporter than does acceptance financing, because a factoring contract generally calls for the exporter to sell *all* receivables to the factor during the contract period. Since factoring is a contractual arrangement between the exporter and the factor, the terms of the contract may include virtually anything the two parties agree to do. Typically, the factor agrees to buy all export accounts receivable from the exporter at a specified discount and to assume all responsibility for collecting from the importer. In return, the factor receives the discounted receivables, on which it gains effective interest when it is paid their full value by the importer. The factor also charges a fee for performing this service.[9]

The choice to an exporter between use of a factor and use of a bank as intermediary in the export-import transaction depends on (1) the cost of using each intermediary, (2) the amount of business being committed, and (3) the degree of flexibility desired.

Forfaiting

Another method of trade financing that is quite similar to factoring and the use of banker's acceptances is forfaiting. **Forfaiting** was developed to handle large capital goods exports from Western firms to former Eastern-bloc countries. Like factoring, forfaiting is a means of nonrecourse export finance. Also as with factoring, the exporter sells its receivable (for an export shipment) at a discount to a forfaiting firm, which accepts the risk of nonpayment by the importer and the right to payment under the exporter's sales contract. However, the forfaiting firm obtains a guarantee (or *aval*) from the government of the importing country, which accepts responsibility for payment as contracted.

Forfaiting originally gained acceptability among some Western European banks, especially in Switzerland, during the 1960s. For export sales to communist countries, these banks (through their forfaiting subsidiaries) began to purchase the payment contracts from exporting companies when suitable guarantees of payment by the host governments could be arranged. The banks agreed to purchase these contracts *à forfait*, that is, without recourse to the exporting firm. Thus, full nonpayment risk was shifted to the forfaiter, which accepted the guarantee of the host government (or a government bank) as sufficient to justify the transaction. Since the forfaiter operated regularly as an analyst and acceptor of host government risk, it was presumably better able than the exporter to assess and manage that risk. This kind of trade financing is now more broadly available for large transactions involving medium- and long-term payment by the importer. Figure 18–5 depicts the relationships involved in forfaiting.

FIGURE 18–5

Forfaiting

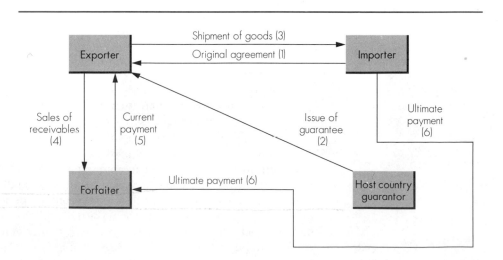

The costs of forfaiting to the exporter are multiple and generally are justifiable only if the transaction is too complex to be handled through the banker's acceptance method. These costs commonly include (1) a charge for country and transfer risks, about 0.5 percent to 5 percent per year; (2) a charge for the use of money and for the covering of interest rate risks—generally the eurocurrency rate, LIBOR; and (3) a charge for administrative work, about 0.5 percent per year.[10]

Countertrade

Finally, the exporter may be able to use **countertrade**, the exchange of goods for goods. Due to the unavailability or very high cost of foreign exchange, many importers are constrained from making purchases from abroad. Countertrade eliminates this bottleneck. (Of course, since the exchange of goods for goods is merely barter, countertrade is characterized by all of the inefficiencies and bottlenecks associated with barter.) However, it transforms the exporter's problem of financing the sale into a problem of using or selling the goods received in payment. Moreover, this problem is often complicated by the fact that the goods received in countertrade may be shipped later than the original exports, causing the exporter to require financing during the interim.

Though no standard form of countertrade has yet been developed, two broad categories of countertrade transactions can be distinguished. The first category, often called **counterpurchase,** involves commercial compensation by the importer in the short or medium term. For example, the former Soviet Union purchased construction machinery from the Japanese firm Komatsu in return for Komatsu's agreement to buy Siberian timber. Also, Occidental Petroleum contracted to sell phosphate rock in exchange for molten sulphur with Poland. (Many more East-West counterpurchase agreements appear in Chapter 21.) The second category, a **buy-back agreement,** involves long-term repayment and often compensation with industrial products. The compensation may be raw materials or intermediate goods (i.e., industrial products), or it may be output from the technique or installation that was sold by the Western exporter. For example, Fiat, SA built an automobile plant in the Soviet Union and received payment in a number of shipments of finished cars. Similarly, after the US government forced US suppliers out of the market in 1980, the German, French, British, and Italian governments subsidized companies from their countries to construct a $US 4 billion natural gas pipeline in the Soviet Union; the Soviet Union paid for this project with natural gas. Transactions in both of these categories involve all goods and no money; hence the term *countertrade* or *barter* conveys the appropriate idea.

Countertrade imposes serious constraints on the exporter relative to other means of trade financing. First is the problem of trying to value the products to be received in payment. Second is the problem of disposing of these goods. Third, if payment is not simultaneous with the exporter's shipment, some other form of financing will still be necessary (even if it is generated internally by the exporter). Fourth, the exporter assumes all of the country risk of dealing with the importer. These difficulties may outweigh the value of the possible export sale. The value of countertrade transactions has been estimated to be less than 15 percent of exports to Eastern Europe and a much smaller percentage of the exports among other countries.[11] Countertrade involving US firms was estimated to constitute less than 6 percent of total exports and 0.1 percent of imports in 1984; 80 percent of this trade was related to US military sales to foreign customers.[12]

ADDED DIMENSION   Why Countertrade Is Increasing

Countertrade grew rapidly during the 1980s and appears to be flourishing in the mid-1990s. The reasons for this persistence of an apparently suboptimal business activity are numerous. First and foremost, when many countries continue to face balance-of-payments problems, specifically deficits that use up available foreign exchange reserves, these countries look to means of obtaining desired imports without having to pay with foreign currency; countertrade fits the bill. Second, given that firms from many countries lack experience in selling overseas, countertrade requirements can force foreign MNEs to do the overseas marketing for them and thus gain access to new markets. Third, when goods are sold in countertrade deals, they may not be priced explicitly in currency terms. This fact may permit a country to sell goods at discount or dumping prices, when they would otherwise be restricted or when direct selling would force cartel (e.g., oil, sugar, coffee) prices down. Fourth, because of protectionist pressures in many countries, countertrade can be used to force importers to accept the country's exports, thus (supposedly) maintaining jobs and incomes in the host country. These and other factors are resulting in increased countertrade at the same time international business is becoming more open around the world. ■

CONCLUSIONS

Exports and imports accounted for about $3,775 billion worth of sales in 1992, clearly a huge portion of total international business. Companies ranging from very small intermediaries to giant multinational enterprises participate in export-import transactions, though of course large firms dominate in terms of the value of their shipments.

Even a simple export-import transaction generally requires a large number of participants, ranging from the exporter and importer to transportation companies, insurers, and banks. The mechanics of such a transaction were described in the chapter, but the actual documents and participants may differ from the description given depending on the countries (i.e., national laws) involved, the type of shipment, and many other factors. It is fair to say, however, that most export-import transactions are variants of the process described here.

Like FDI (and local production), licensing, franchising, and so on, exporting can be viewed as a means of foreign market entry. Exporting can be selected to achieve least-cost supply for the foreign market, or to reduce the risk of having all sales in one country, or to establish a base for further production, such as offshore assembly. All in all, exporting can be a dynamic strategic activity that affects even domestic competitiveness rather than simply a means for disposing of excess production that a firm may be stuck with in its home country.

Domestic firms can utilize exports to both absorb products that cannot be sold locally and expand business in new markets. For the domestic firm, probably the key problem in international trade is finding buyers abroad; when that has been done, the problems of financing, distribution, and organization can be dealt with.

Compared to domestic firms, multinational firms have many more possibilities for using exports. In addition to exporting to outside buyers, MNEs can export to their own subsidiaries overseas. An MNE can produce the same product in two countries; then, if any difficulty that constrains production occurs in either country, the MNE can import from the other country. An MNE can have an affiliate in one country produce some products and then fill out that affiliate's product line with shipments from another affiliate in another country.

Importing is an often neglected part of international trade strategy. Any firm may find it can obtain production inputs from abroad more cheaply or when suppliers are not available locally. Also, by sourcing abroad (using foreign suppliers) and at home, a firm can diversify its suppliers and avoid dependence on local firms only. Each of these possibilities provides a competitive advantage for the importing firm.

While not necessarily the most important part of an export-import transaction, financing does play an important role in such transactions. Traditionally, commercial banks have offered most of this financing, in the form of letters of credit and banker's acceptances. Recently, forms such as countertrade and forfaiting have come into greater use. Factoring also continues to play a role in trade financing. MNEs gain a useful competitive advantage over local firms in any country through their export financing, because they can use high or low transfer prices to move funds wherever desired, can delay or advance payment to move funds at a desired time, and face no risk of nonpayment by their importing subsidiaries (although the host country may restrict the affiliate's ability to pay).

QUESTIONS

1. Describe a basic export-import transaction, including the various participants and types of documentation.

2. When trying to enter a new national market, how would you choose among exports, FDI (plus local production), licensing, and other market-serving possibilities? That is, what criteria would you use?

3. Explain how a letter of credit works. Who is responsible for paying the exporter? What happens if the importer does not pay as contracted, even though all other parts of the transaction were performed as stipulated?

4. What competitive advantages does a multinational enterprise gain by operating a network of affiliates that export among themselves?

5. What benefits does the domestic firm gain from exporting? How do these benefits differ from the benefits an MNE gains?

6. What benefits does the domestic firm gain from importing? How do these benefits differ from the benefits an MNE gains?

7. Explain how forfaiting works. Why would a firm use forfaiting rather than other means of financing an export sale?

8. Countertrading has become quite popular in trade with Eastern European countries. Why is it *not* likely to replace traditional bank financing as the main source of trade finance?

9. Create a market entry strategy for RJR-Nabisco, Inc., which wants to enter the market for cookies in Japan. Assume that the company has no affiliates in Japan. Discuss the choice of entry mode, product selection, and business plan.

10. What reasons might a US company have for exporting its electronic products to customers in Mexico even though production costs are lower and tariffs are fairly high there?

REFERENCES

Aggarwal, Raj. "International Business through Barter and Countertrade." *Long Range Planning,* June 1989.

Crédit Suisse. *Forfaiting.* Zurich: Finanz AG, 1986.

Eiteman, David, and Arthur Stonehill. *Multinational Business Finance.* 5th ed. Reading, MA.: Addison-Wesley, 1988.

Guild, Ian, and Rhodri Harris. *Forfaiting.* London: Euromoney Publications, 1985.

Haar, Jerry, and Marta Ortiz-Buonafins. *Import Marketing*. Lexington, MA.: Lexington Books, 1989.

International Chamber of Commerce. *Guide to Documentary Credit Operations*. Paris: ICC, 1992.

Khoury, Sarkis. "Countertrade: Forms, Motives, Pitfalls, and Negotiation Requisites." *Journal of Business Research,* June 1984.

Morgan Guaranty Trust Company. *Financing Exports and Imports*. New York: Morgan Guaranty, n.d.

Root, Franklin. *Entry Strategies for International Markets*. Lexington, MA.: Lexington Books, 1987.

NOTES

[1] Letters of credit are frequently subject to legal action by parties involved in the export-import process. Much of the terminology and conditions in L/Cs has been standardized and codified in *Uniform Customs and Practices 400,* published by the International Chamber of Commerce.

[2] Examples of each of these and other documents can be found in International Chamber of Commerce, *Guide to Documentary Credit Operations* (Paris: ICC, 1978).

[3] Pricing to cover only marginal costs may be viewed as *dumping* by the host country; thus, the firm may be required to select a price higher than this.

[4] Exports can lower risk by replacing local production in a country that experiences political or economic upheaval. They can also supplement local production, providing a portfolio of supply sources and thus again reducing risk.

[5] The banker's acceptance is considered "eligible" if it matures in less than 270 days. That is, the acceptance may be discounted at any Federal Reserve bank by the paying bank or any secondary purchaser of the acceptance.

[6] An overview of federal export subsidy programs appears in Business International Corporation, *Financing Foreign Operations,* "Commercial Banks" (New York: Business International Corporation, latest edition). Also see Robert D Frazer and Associates, *International Banking and Finance,* vol. 1 (Washington, DC: R&H Publishers, latest edition), and Burke Dillon and Luis Duran-Downing, *Officially-Supported Export Credits* (Washington, DC: International Monetary Fund, 1988).

[7] See the Foreign Sales Corporation Act of 1984, which appears in the *Internal Revenue Code* (Washington, DC: US Government Printing Office, 1984), sections 921–27.

[8] See, for example, *EXIMBANK Program Summary* (Washington, DC: Export-Import Bank of the United States, current edition).

[9] The factor's fee can be viewed as a charge for accepting the risk of nonpayment, and the discount can be viewed as a charge for making funds available immediately to the exporter. However, both charges really contribute to the total cost, which the factor receives to cover the two needs of the exporter.

[10] All costs are as estimated by Crédit Suisse, *Forfaiting* (Zurich: Finanz AG, 1986).

[11] Organization for Economic Cooperation and Development, *East-West Trade: Recent Developments in Countertrade* (Paris: OECD, 1981), pp. 10–11.

[12] US International Trade Commission, *Assessment of the Effects of Barter and Countertrade Transactions on U.S. Industries,* publication no. 1766 (Washington, DC: USITC, October 1985).

ACME Rockets, Inc.

James King, president of ACME Rockets, Inc., recently returned to his hometown of Milwaukee from a model toy exhibition in Toronto. There he had talked extensively with several other company presidents about their common problem of stagnant sales in North America. One of his new Canadian acquaintances from the exhibition had presented a strong case for pursuing sales in foreign markets, especially in the European Union. This person reasoned that she had successfully and relatively easily entered the US market by exporting her wooden toys, so extending this experience to other foreign markets should be manageable. Since trade barriers were declining in most of the world, opportunities were opening up for both small and large exporters. All of the participants in this discussion were running companies with fewer than 100 employees and sales in the range of $US 10–75 million per year, so they faced similar problems of limited managerial time and financial resources.

King saw the possibility of selling in Europe as a very desirable alternative to beefing up his advertising efforts in the United States to boost sagging sales. His company's model rockets, ranging from $3 toys to $250 intricately designed models for science projects, were producing an adequate income for the company, but the market seemed to have become saturated in the past three years after an initial rapid growth during the first five years of operation. (ACME's financial statements are presented at the end of the case.)

King had founded ACME after working for several years for a large consumer goods manufacturer. Originally he had studied mechanical engineering and planned to work for a company such as Lockheed or Boeing. When he discovered his greatest interest was in sales and business administration rather than industrial design, he took the position in sales of consumer goods. Realizing that he wanted to pursue a business of his own and had six years of experience under his belt, King decided to take the plunge. Using his engineering background, he decided to try making higher-quality model rockets than those commonly available in toy and hobby stores. Remembering Wile E Coyote's zany gadgets for outracing the Road Runner, he named his company ACME Rockets, Inc.

The day after the toy exhibition, King met with his management team of four department heads in their regular weekly strategy session. He raised the issue of pursuing export markets in Europe as well as expanding ACME's efforts in Canada. The sales manager, Jan Vlcek, was enthusiastic about this idea, since he

This case was written by Professors James Sood and Robert Grosse as a basis for class discussion. Revised 1994.

liked the thought of traveling through Europe to examine the markets. Sandy Rogers, the financial manager, reacted in almost the opposite manner. She saw spending lots of money chasing foreign markets as imprudent, when US opportunities could still be pursued much more aggressively. (While ACME certainly did not sit on a pile of cash for this purpose, the company was far from broke.) Klaus Schneider, the production manager saw the idea as a possibility for unloading the excess inventory that currently sat in ACME's warehouse, as well as an outlet for more rockets that could push the plant toward fuller capacity. The personnel manager, José Romero, was somewhat concerned about the cultural differences in Europe that might create a barrier to ACME's products or advertising methods. Nevertheless, he thought the idea should be examined in more detail.

In the following week's meeting, King brought up the idea of exporting to the European Union again. He asked each of his managers to suggest points that should be studied in deciding on the feasibility of this new direction for ACME. The first point raised was about customers: Where would they be, and how could they be approached? With the resources available to ACME, it would not be possible to mount a large-scale project evaluation effort. Sandy Rogers suggested that talking with other members of the Milwaukee Chamber of Commerce would give them some ideas about how other local firms did their overseas marketing. She also thought someone from the Chicago World Trade Center might be able to offer more insights.

Jan Vlcek felt somewhat overwhelmed about the prospect of leading the new marketing effort. He was already fully occupied with ACME's existing promotional efforts in the United States, and he did not relish the thought of expanding his hectic schedule. On the other hand, he wanted to explore the prospect of selling in Europe, so he faced a difficult situation. José Romero recognized Vlcek's reticence and proposed that an outside consultant be hired to help with the newly labeled "European Marketing Plan." By giving Vlcek the authority to approve the consultant, he would be able to maintain his control over the marketing function while benefiting from the consultant's work. This proposal brightened Vlcek's outlook considerably.

When the meeting concluded, James King was quite pleased with his colleagues' support for the new venture. He subsequently asked Vlcek to check around Milwaukee for a consulting firm to carry out the marketing study. This effort resulted in the venture's first setback: All the large, well-known management consulting firms wanted more than $50,000 to conduct the study, even before getting down to the details of ACME's needs. Vlcek then recommended that they ask a marketing professor at the local business school for help, since he had a friend in another company who had used this method before to get a marketing survey done. Sandy Rogers immediately thought of her favorite marketing professor, Bruce Madison, from the executive MBA program she had taken last year.

Professor Madison was happy to offer his help, and at a much lower cost than that required by the large consulting firms. Given his teaching duties at the university, he offered to carry out an initial market study that would identify potential types of customers, rules on importing, and channels of distribution in Europe. He would then recommend steps for ACME to take so that a more detailed plan could be created. This effort would cost the company $10,000, which included the final report and four weeks of research by Madison and a research assistant.

Madison recommended that ACME get in touch with one or more market research firms in London for a more detailed analysis of the European Union market for the firm's model rockets. Without hesitation, James King agreed to the proposed market study and asked Madison to get started.

Professor Madison's Market Study

Madison first decided to determine ACME's production capacity. Klaus Schneider, the production manager, explained to him that ACME had been operating during the past year at about 80 percent of capacity with its one eight-hour shift of workers in the Milwaukee plant. The capacity of the plant could be expanded by asking the existing production workers to work overtime or by beginning a second shift.

Next, Madison looked at ACME's financial condition. The income statement (Table 1) indeed portrayed a stagnant situation for the past several years, though fortunately ACME was earning a solid profit each year. The balance sheet (Table 2) was a bit weak, with more than $3 million in short-term liabilities and a fairly large balance of uncollected receivables. In Madison's view, the company was solvent but not in a position to pursue any major expansion activities.

Finally, Madison talked with Jan Vlcek about ACME's current marketing strategy. Not surprisingly, Vlcek was rather reluctant to discuss the situation, given both the recent leveling off of sales and his lack of experience in international marketing. Madison tried to defuse Vlcek's evident antagonism toward an outsider who was trying to impose a marketing strategy on ACME. After complimenting Vlcek on the marketing success ACME had achieved under his leadership, Madison asked why the firm had encountered a slowdown in growth over the past several years. Vlcek explained that he had indeed tried to stimulate a new upswing in US sales, but competition from other established makers of model airplanes and rockets, such as Mattel and Lionel, had frustrated the effort. The domestic market was quite saturated. This led Madison to conclude that overseas markets could very well be an appropriate focus for ACME at this time.

Based on these pieces of information, Madison reasoned that an effort to push ACME's sales into Europe would definitely be an appropriate strategy (though he also saw room for improvement in the firm's domestic marketing efforts). He assigned his student assistant to search the international trade information available in Milwaukee to identify firms that could export for ACME to Europe. He also asked the student to try to find names and addresses of distributors in Europe who would be able to sell the model rockets in those countries.

A review of the rules applicable to imports into the European Union showed no apparent limitation against the model rockets, and it appeared that a tariff of at

TABLE 1

ACME's Simplified Income Statements, 1988–94 ($US millions)

	1988	1989	1990	1991	1992	1993	1994
Net sales	4.16	6.47	8.30	10.13	12.54	12.98	13.25
Cost of goods sold	2.87	4.66	5.81	6.98	8.90	9.10	9.54
Gross profit	1.29	1.81	2.49	3.15	3.64	3.88	3.71
Operating expenses	1.17	1.54	2.02	2.52	2.88	3.18	3.08
Profit before taxes	0.12	0.27	0.47	0.63	0.76	0.70	0.63
Federal income taxes	0.04	0.09	0.15	0.19	0.27	0.23	0.20
Net profit after tax	0.08	0.18	0.32	0.44	0.49	0.47	0.43

TABLE 2

ACME's Balance Sheet,
December 31, 1994
($US millions)

Cash	0.316
Accounts receivable	2.748
Inventory	1.958
Plant and equipment	2.933
Total assets	7.955
Accounts payable	0.861
Notes payable	1.163
Accrued taxes	0.410
Short-term debt	0.812
Long-term debt, current portion	0.237
Long-term debt	1.453
Shareholders' equity	3.019
Total liabilities and shareholders' equity	7.955

most 7 percent *ad valorem* would be encountered in any of the EU countries. Madison put this information into his report, along with a recommendation for ACME to consult with a law firm in the chosen target country to make sure no other restrictions existed. He did not recommend a particular European country as the target market, since he viewed this as a decision for James King to make. He did suggest that the United Kingdom would be a logical choice because of its language and cultural similarities to the United States. He also suggested that ACME give careful consideration to Germany, because it is the largest economy in Europe.

Regarding channels of distribution, Madison found that no large toy store chains (similar to Toys "R" Us or Lionel Toy World) existed across Europe. Thus, sales of model rockets would have to be either to individual toy or hobby stores or to distributors who would seek out retail stores as clients. Clearly, at this point the only viable way for ACME to proceed was to consider wholesale distributors who would act on ACME's behalf to contract with retail stores.

Also regarding European distribution, ACME would have to create new promotional materials and instructions for the model rockets in several languages, assuming sales were to be pursued in France, Germany, Italy, and elsewhere in Europe. This problem could be ignored initially until buyers were identified, but ultimately it would require significant expense to redo the printed materials that accompanied ACME's products.

At the end of the month, Madison delivered his report to James King, along with his recommendation that ACME begin immediately to look for European distributors for the model rockets. King was happy with the optimistic outlook of the report, but he still did not see clearly how to proceed.

19

Technology and the MNE

This chapter focuses on technology—the single most important competitive advantage in business today. Most of the chapter is devoted to demonstrating how technology can be a competitive advantage and how firms can obtain, utilize, and protect a technological edge. The main goals of the chapter are to:

1. Define *technology* and *technology transfer.*

2. Show how firms can benefit from the use of product, process, and management technology.

3. Analyze the choice of whether to exploit technology within the firm or sell or license that technology to other firms.

4. Explain how a firm can protect its proprietary technology.

5. Discuss the concerns of governments in industrial and less developed countries with respect to the use of technology by MNEs.

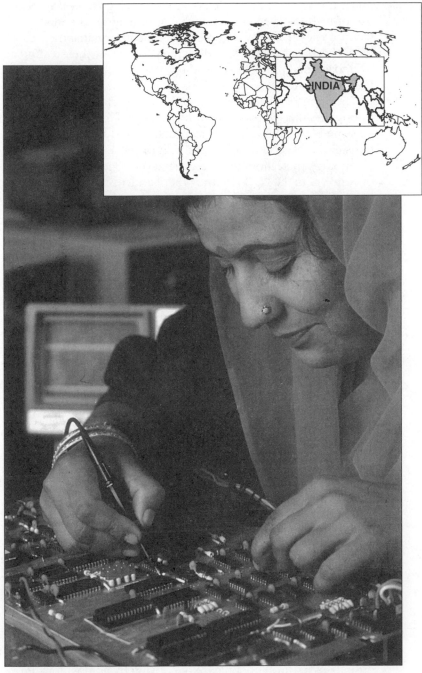

In New Delhi, an Indian woman uses an electric soldering iron during the manufacturing process of a computer board.
©Dilip Mehta/Contact Press Images

INTRODUCTION

Technology is the single most important competitive advantage of firms in the world today. From new products, to knowledge of markets, to industrial processes, technology is fundamental to the success of both domestic and international firms. We begin this chapter by defining *technology.* Then we explore the use of technology as a competitive advantage of the MNE. Firms need to select technologies that provide optimal competitive gains, then decide how to implement those technologies, and then try to protect their technological advantages. A fundamental problem is deciding how to obtain desired technology—through R&D or through acquisition from another firm.

The transfer of technology among countries within the MNE network and through markets outside the firm is a second focus of our analysis. Dealing with governments in both industrial countries and LDCs on the issue of technology transfer has become a major problem for MNE managers. In industrial countries, technology protection and the generation of new technology are the main areas of concern. In the LDCs, on the other hand, restrictions on technological transfers through limits on royalties, lack of patent protection, and other legal constraints on company activities compel MNE managers to seek strategies that overcome or at least recognize these constraints and incorporate ways to accommodate them.

Definition[1]

The business literature generally refers to at least three types of technology: product, process, and management.[2] **Product technology** is the knowledge used to produce any product—the information that specifies the product's characteristics and uses. **Process technology** is the knowledge used in production to organize the inputs and operate the machinery; it relates to the techniques and process by which a given product or service is produced. **Management technology** is the knowledge used in operating a business, the managerial skills that enable a firm to compete by using its resources effectively. Each type of technology can create a competitive advantage for the firm that possesses it. In other words, although all firms possess each type of technology, an advantage accrues to firms that are able to obtain *superior* technology.

Given that technology is industrial knowledge, we will consider its creation, introduction into markets, and spread into different markets and applications. These three stages of technology development are known as *invention, innovation,* and *diffusion.* **Invention** is the creation of new knowledge that may have application to business or industry. An invention may be as extraordinary as the lightbulb or as commonplace as a new type of laundry soap. **Innovation** is the introduction of the new knowledge into the marketplace. A fairly recent innovation is the CD ROM data storage disk, which enables microcomputers to hold literally libraries of information on each disk. Most inventions never become innovations, that is, never reach the stage of commercialization. For every successful innovation, there are thousands of inventions that never become commercialized. **Diffusion** is the spread of the new knowledge throughout the market, including markets in different countries, and to different product applications. It may take place through a company's affiliates in different locations and businesses or through purchase or copying by competitors. Proprietary drugs, for example, are typically diffused by the initiating firm's sale of the product through its affiliates and distributors around the world.

An aspect of technology that we should note at the outset is its nature as a **public good,** a good that can be used repeatedly without being used up. Technology is a form of knowledge that is not destroyed when it is transferred among people or firms. This aspect of technology is the source of both competitive strength for a firm that successfully innovates and of social concern for countries that wish to reap the benefits of innovation made available to their populations at as low a cost as possible. The cost of creating a technology is not zero, and that cost is borne by the innovating firm;[3] the cost of diffusing that technology is often relatively low, and innovating firms do not like to let their hard-earned technological gains be given away to the public without earning a good return. This issue of social versus private valuation of technology is discussed shortly.

Technology Transfer

Technology transfer is the diffusion of technology from the place of its introduction to other markets around the world. This diffusion may take place through market transactions, with one firm selling a product, process, or skill to another, or it may be carried out within a firm through its network of affiliates. Since technology has become recognized as an extremely important base for competition worldwide, governments are quite concerned with obtaining up-to-date technology at the lowest possible cost. Innovating companies, on the other hand, wish to protect their technology as much as possible so that they can reap its benefits. Clearly, the interests of firms and governments may diverge in this matter, and technology transfer has become a major issue of debate with respect to the MNE.

Within the multinational firm, technology transfer is also an internal managerial concern. Informing managers, technical staff, and workers in different locations about new technologies is far from costless. Moreover, the firm must carry out such transfers efficiently and adjust structurally and operationally to derive maximum benefits from the exploitation of these technologies. Corporate strategy must include the determination and effective transmission of key technology to the people, subsidiaries, and locations that can use it best.

Technology Appropriability

Technology may well represent the key competitive advantage that the innovating firm possesses. After having invested human and financial capital in developing proprietary technology, such a firm will naturally seek to protect it. Looking at the effort of the innovating firm to maximize its returns from proprietary technology (namely, knowledge possessed by the innovating firm that is unavailable to other firms in the marketplace), Magee (1977) coined the term *appropriability*. **Appropriability** is the ability of the innovating firm to protect its technology from competitors and to obtain economic benefits from that technology. For example, the knowledge required to construct a nuclear power plant is very specialized and therefore highly appropriable. On the other hand, the knowledge required to produce a certain food flavor is often quite simple once the ingredients are known; thus, the innovating firm seeks protection such as a patent or, as with Coca-Cola, tries to keep the "formula" a secret from competitors. Such knowledge is appropriable only if it can be hidden from rival firms or denied to them through legal means such as patents. The more appropriable the technology, the better able the innovating firm will be to guard it and transfer it internally (that is, to *internalize* the technology).

TECHNOLOGY AS A COMPETITIVE ADVANTAGE

The success of multinational firms during the 20th century has very often depended on a base of **proprietary technology.** In this section, we first look at some empirical evidence on the importance of technology in international competition. Second, we consider the problem of obtaining technology that could give the firm competitive advantages. Third, we examine ways in which a firm can utilize the advantages generated by proprietary technology.

Success of MNEs Based on Technological Advantage

Technology was demonstrated to be a key production factor in international business through a large number of research efforts conducted during the 1960s. The search for an explanation of the Leontief paradox (namely, that although the United States was relatively capital rich, its manufactured exports were less capital intensive and more labor intensive than its import-competing goods) led several investigators to focus on the **technology intensity** of U.S. exports. The studies of Gruber, Mehta, and Vernon (1967) and Hufbauer (1966), were discussed in Chapter 3. Those studies concluded that technology intensity was an important explanatory variable for US exports; that is, technology was highly positively correlated with US exports, and thus US exports were technology intensive and not paradoxically labor intensive.

Studies of US foreign direct investment have produced similar results: US firms with a higher degree of technology intensity (measured, for example, as R&D expenditures relative to sales or as the number of scientists and engineers employed relative to the total number of employees) tend to establish more affiliates abroad than do less technology-intensive firms. Gruber et al. (1967), Horst (1972), Caves (1974), and others have lent support to this point. Hence, greater technology intensity seems to lead to greater multinationality. (This correlation was shown clearly in Chapter 2, Table 2–2, which lists top-performing US-based firms, almost all of which are highly multinational and most of which are more or much more technology intensive than the US industry average.)

Each of the preceding measures of the importance of technology in international business supports the general principle that technology is a fundamental "factor of production" that enables firms to compete successfully against foreign and domestic competitors. This does not mean all firms must be technology intensive to succeed; rather, it means technology is one factor that can create a sustainable competitive advantage for its possessor. The next step is to explore when and how technology can be used in competition. This is something the studies mentioned above failed to do, since their emphasis was macroeconomic. We want to know how to obtain the technology that leads to an advantage and how to utilize that advantage in business activities. Our next step, therefore, is to focus on these microlevel (company-specific) concerns.

How to Acquire a Technology Advantage

The basic decision for a firm considering the acquisition of any needed input is whether to make that input internally or buy it from an outside supplier (or do both). When the input is a known machine or a component, the choice will be whether or not to manufacture it. When the input is a skill, such as knowledge of a particular market, the choice will be whether to hire a specialist or sell to an intermediary firm that deals with final customers. When the input is process or product technology, the choice will be whether to try to create the knowledge by carrying out R&D or buy the knowledge from another firm through a license or some other contractual form.

The last choice is much more difficult than the first two because it involves so much uncertainty. If the firm chooses to undertake R&D to create product or process technology, it has no way to ensure that the result will meet the need. R&D is risky by its very nature, since it requires creativity on the part of the research person or team and leads to output that may be very efficient, very inefficient, or of no use at all in dealing with the problem at hand. Thus, while the **make-versus-buy decision** can be made on a fairly concrete basis for inputs whose technology and costs are known, the decision to produce technology by carrying out R&D has a much less concrete basis and necessarily leads to substantial uncertainty.

Moving a step further, when a firm depends on technology as a key competitive advantage, the need to generate new technology on a continuing basis becomes paramount. In industries such as pharmaceuticals, computers, and telecommunications, R&D is a critical function in each firm. In these kinds of industries, the question becomes: How much R&D should the firm do? Since no simple, direct relation exists between R&D expenditure and successful new-product development, there is no simple answer to this question. However, since products in these industries do become obsolete, the firm that does not introduce new products will in all likelihood be unable to compete. Then what level of R&D is in some sense "optimal"?[4]

The best answer is "It depends." It depends on how large the firm is, how diversified its products and markets are, how financially sound the firm is, how appropriable its technology is, and many other factors. A small firm that competes on the basis of its ability to create new products must carry out extensive R&D. A very large MNE, on the other hand, may be able to use a comparatively small research team aimed mainly at learning about new technology developments and deciding whether to incorporate them into the firm's business. If such a firm chooses to acquire a particular innovation, the decision becomes whether to buy it from the producer, undertake R&D in an effort to copy it, or even try to buy the innovating firm. This kind of **follow-the-leader strategy** has been pursued successfully by many firms in a variety of industries. Of course, a firm that pursues the follower strategy loses the opportunity to take full advantage of innovations achieved by other firms. Hoffmann–La Roche, for example, would have earned far less had it depended on another firm to develop its highly successful tranquilizers Valium and Librium. Also, spillover effects of R&D efforts may lead to the creation of additional new products or processes. These benefits would be lost to a firm that chose not to carry out the basic research and pursued the follow-the-leader strategy. (3M uses internal "new-venture teams" to carry out R&D on projects proposed by company employees. These projects are then pursued as relatively independent efforts until results are achieved and the decision to go to market is made.)[5]

Notice that the multinational firm gains an advantage in R&D because of its ability to spread its R&D expenses over a global market rather than having to depend solely on domestic sales to recoup them. Also, the MNE has broader access to technical talent in many countries.

How to Utilize a Technology Advantage

Each firm differs from every other firm, if only because it employs different people with different skills. At the simplest level, **technology advantage** is any superior business knowledge that is held by people in one firm and not held by

IB
ILLUSTRATION

Pfizer's R&D Strategy

Pfizer, a US-based pharmaceuticals firm, chooses to invest in its own R&D to create new ethical drugs (i.e., proprietary pharmaceuticals). Pfizer's choice is to internalize the entire process of R&D, production, and sale as much as possible and thus reap maximum revenues and profits. This firm sets limits on its research spending by comparing the expected costs of research projects with the size of the potential market for the new product being sought.

In the area of antiarthritic drugs, for example, Pfizer sought to develop a product that could be administered once a day rather than every few hours. In the pharmaceuticals industry, the process of R&D plus product testing and submitting to regulatory approvals until a new drug is commercialized is generally believed to cost at least $100 million. Only after forecasting that its expected sales would substantially exceed this amount did Pfizer choose to undertake the research that led to the product Feldene. Pfizer does not undertake R&D for a product whose potential market it judges to be smaller than $100 million. (Notice that the R&D being considered is fairly well targeted at a potential product rather than open-ended as in the case of university research, which depends largely on the preferences of the individual researchers.)

From Pfizer's perspective, a second limitation on R&D spending is the shortage of highly qualified research scientists to work on possible projects. Even if dozens of the new products that Pfizer is considering for development appear viable, the number of people—inside the firm, in universities, and in other firms—who are qualified and available to do the necessary research is quite limited. This also restricts the amount of R&D spending by Pfizer.

For these two practical reasons (expected market size and availability of research scientists), an optimal amount of R&D can be approximately established despite the claim that research results are unpredictable. That overly simple claim of unpredictability obviously fails to come to grips with the problem, whereas pragmatic reasoning defines the problem clearly and focuses on the real limitations that exist on R&D. ∎

people in another firm. As discussed in detail in Chapter 2, each firm should try to take maximum advantage of its technological edge over other firms. How can this be done? (The problem of *protecting* the firm's technology is discussed later.)

Consider Hoffmann–La Roche & Company, the Swiss-based multinational pharmaceutical firm.[6] This firm innovated the two drugs chlordiazepoxide and diazepam (whose Hoffmann–La Roche brand names are Librium and Valium, respectively) in the early 1960s. Librium and Valium became two of the most successful tranquilizers in history. To protect the proprietary technology embodied in these drugs, Hoffmann–La Roche took out patents in each country where it sold them. The patents gave the firm long-term legal protection against competitors that might seek to copy the patented products. In most countries, patent protection lasts well over 10 years. (In the United States, for example, it lasts 17 years.) By registering Valium and Librium for patent protection around the world, Hoffmann–La Roche effectively gained a period of time in which it was the sole producer of the drugs. Thus, the firm was able to sell enough Valium and Librium at a high enough price to repay the research costs of developing them (and many less successful drugs), as well as to pay for additional research to create new drugs for future sales. Because patent protection lasts for only a fixed period of time, additional R&D (and hopefully the creation of more successful products) must be part of the firm's strategy.

Hoffmann–La Roche sells Valium, Librium, and its other products through its own network of affiliates around the world. In a small number of cases, generally under government pressure, the firm has also licensed local companies to produce its proprietary drugs. Most of its sales, however, take place through subsidiaries that it manages and owns. This is an example of internalized technology. (Also, the technology is *embodied* in products, which are then sold to customers.)

As a second example, consider Arthur Andersen & Company, the US-based multinational accounting firm. This firm's knowledge of accounting rules and practices and of business strategy is superior to that of many US firms and many firms in other countries. Its proprietary technology is not in product or process technology but in management knowledge.

Arthur Andersen is organized as a partnership, with individual accountants and consultants acting as both owners and managers. A legal entity called a *société coopérative* was formed in Switzerland and functions as a legal link among Arthur Andersen's widespread affiliates throughout the world and to the home office in Chicago. The main strategic links among Arthur Andersen affiliates are partners from affiliates in one country who are made partners in affiliates in other countries. By linking firms across countries through individual partners, Arthur Andersen is able to transfer its technology as embodied in its people. Thus, in its overseas activities, Arthur Andersen usually operates as a linked set of partners, although the legal entity is sometimes a corporation in which the parent firm owns some or all of the shares. In 1985, for example, Arthur Andersen acquired the Philippine firm SGV Group, with over 3,000 employees, via the Swiss Société Coopérative. (The Philippine firm itself has affiliates in Thailand, Taiwan, Malaysia, and Indonesia.)

Arthur Andersen sells its knowledge as a service to other firms and to individuals. Its main businesses are auditing and tax accounting. Each service is sold to outside clients, a number of which are multinational firms, that can benefit from Arthur Andersen's knowledge of tax and other accounting rules in many countries.

These two examples show that there are numerous means for taking advantage of proprietary technology and that these means are very dependent on the kind of business involved. The possibilities include internalizing knowledge through a network of subsidiaries, working through partnerships (as discussed above), licensing local producers, and selling the use of the company name through a franchise. Let us examine these alternatives to see which company and product characteristics best suit each.

Internalizing   The first strategy is to internalize all technology. This translates into international business by requiring the firm to use local affiliates around the world to sell its products or services, and perhaps use exports for some smaller or less important markets. **Internalization** tends to work best under these conditions:

1. The firm makes new *products* that competitors cannot copy easily.
2. Important economies of scale that the firm achieves on *products* would be lost if outside firms also used the technology and served part of the total market.

3. The *firm* depends greatly on the sale of the product or service that uses the technology.

4. The *firm* is so small that it lacks the personnel to both use the technology internally and sell it to outsiders; or the firm is so large that it can easily exploit the technology through its own affiliates.

5. The firm considers its *technology* more valuable than do potential buyers of the technology.

6. The *technology* is costly to transfer from one firm to another.

These conditions illustrate the kinds of situation-specific issues a firm must take into account to properly utilize its technology advantage. They point out some of the company-specific, product-specific, and knowledge-specific considerations that (in these cases) would justify internalizing technology.

Recall the example of Polaroid Land cameras from Chapter 3. The key technology in that case was the knowledge necessary to produce high-quality, instant-developing film. Because no other firm was able to recreate equivalent technology, Polaroid gained a lasting competitive advantage in the photography market. There is no doubt that such firms as Eastman Kodak, Agfa-Gavaert, and Fuji have better distribution networks worldwide and perhaps other advantages over Polaroid. However, as long as Polaroid can keep the instant-developing segment of the photography market to itself, it will be able to compete successfully. By continuing to innovate and improve its film, Polaroid has been able to keep patent protection on its best technology over the years. The particular characteristics of this case, taken from the preceding list, are that (1) the product cannot be copied by competitors, (2) the firm is highly dependent on its technology for its success, and (3) the firm is large enough to exploit the technology through its own affiliates around the world. These conditions justify the internalization of instant-developing film technology in Polaroid Corporation and the sale of only the final product (i.e., *not* the knowledge by itself) to customers.

Externalizing   As a second possible strategy for utilizing proprietary technology, the firm could contract with other firms under a licensing agreement, management contract, or other income-producing arrangement that involves the sale of the technology rather than the sale of a final product that embodies the technology. This strategy of **externalization** would be appropriate under these conditions:

1. The firm's *products* are easily copied, but rival firms would still be willing to buy its product- or process-specific knowledge.

2. The firm's *products* are not central to its ability to survive in competition.

3. The *firm* has greater skill in creating the technology than in producing and marketing the final products.

4. The *firm's* financial and personnel capabilities make it desirable to let another firm incur the cost of producing the products.

5. The firm cannot protect its *technology* with a patent, and it could lose the benefits of that technology unless it contracted for the technology's use by rival firms.

6. The *technology* is not costly to transfer between firms.

Each of these conditions tends to justify the sale of proprietary technology to other firms rather than (merely) internalizing it in final products. Broadly speaking, these product-, firm-, and technology-specific conditions relate to situations in which the technology is embodied in products that are not the lifeblood of the firm or to situations in which the technology itself, rather than the final product, is the most valuable factor.

The sale of "intermediate goods"—either components that embody proprietary technology or knowledge in the form of plans, blueprints, books, or other technical information formats—is common practice in many industries. The entire industry of management consulting is a form of externalizing business knowledge and skills. The management consultant possesses skills useful for running a firm, but chooses to sell those skills contractually to various firms without actually joining any of them. (Often such a consultant *is* eventually hired by one of the client firms when the skills are perceived as sufficiently valuable to justify this step!) Similarly, public accounting and economic forecasting businesses sell knowledge for further use by firms producing final products or services. Arthur Andersen is an example of such businesses. Even in manufacturing, there are many consultants and capital equipment manufacturers that work independently from companies, selling their knowledge on one-time or repeated contractual terms to different firms.

Franchising   Another interesting example of technology transfer through intermediate goods rather than final products is **franchising.** Many hotel chains, restaurants, and other service firms create a company or brand name that comes to connote good quality, rapid service, and so on. Once the name becomes established, its possessor can sell its use to other firms. This contractual arrangement is called *franchising.* McDonald's, Burger King, Hilton, Holiday Inns, Avis, and Hertz are just a few of the best-known franchisors.

The franchisor generally sells the franchisee the right to use its name plus some array of products and services. For example, franchisees contract with Burger King to buy plastic packaging, napkins, some food ingredients, and kitchen equipment used in cooking the hamburgers and other products sold in the restaurants that bear the Burger King name. Burger King maintains the right to control the quality of the franchise (e.g., through quality control of products and pricing strategy) so that franchisees cannot tarnish the company's image. In return for the use of Burger King's name and for these services, the franchisee must pay the company a fee based on the volume of sales. In this arrangement, the technology being transferred includes some production (of hamburgers) technology, some marketing skills, and some management policies.

A Continuous R&D Process

A general method of targeting research that avoids the dilemma of huge uncertainty in new-product development, and one that many firms have selected, is to build incrementally on proven technology through a **continuous R&D** process. That is, the firms follow a strategy of developing modifications for the basic product or process, without undertaking major basic research in areas unrelated to the successful original innovation. Clearly this is the strategy IBM has followed in the development of its personal computer. Virtually all of the components used in making the first IBM PC were innovations that IBM or other companies had made in other applications. The PC itself is thus an amalgam of

The International Product Cycle

Another way to look at the use of technology as a competitive advantage comes from Vernon's international product cycle analysis. By studying the stage of any product in the cycle in a given country, the firm can select a strategy that exploits its advantages. For example, when personal computers became extremely popular in the United States (around 1982), competition became fierce and these computers advanced quickly from the new-product to the maturing-product stage. At that time, the personal computer was still in the new-product stage in Argentina. Thus, IBM or Apple Computer had opportunities to operate as new-product producers in the Argentine market, selling with very little competition and facing a very price-inelastic demand. In the United States, on the other hand, these firms had to lower their prices and work on new software and hardware developments to maintain their market positions. The maturing-product stage of the cycle required these actions, as well as increasing efforts to lower production costs. In fact, both IBM and Apple have turned to offshore, low-cost supply sources for such components as memory chips and peripheral equipment.

The international product cycle offers insights not only for high-tech industries but also for standardized products. Once production technology has become standardized, the firm must search for low-cost production sites and low-cost distribution channels. By taking a global perspective, a firm in an industry whose technology is fairly standardized, such as shirt or shoe manufacturing, can select production sites that offer cost advantages *and* markets in which particular shirts or shoes can compete. ■

existing technologies, packaged in a valuable way and marketed very successfully. (IBM's competitive advantages in reliability and service, as well as its huge capital resources, enabled it to apply known technology to the product and to market the product with phenomenal success.)[7]

Dow Chemical Corporation is another MNE that follows the incremental approach to developing technology. Dow uses what are called **skunk works** (a term coined at Lockheed Aircraft Corporation in California), or small project teams that work on new applications of existing technologies or on the development of new technologies for specific uses. The skunk works are viewed as separate from the mainstream of the firm's production and sales activities, but the firm supports them to maintain an active presence in R&D. By remaining small, the skunk works allow the project teams to function more or less as entrepreneurs, though with potential substantial backing from the corporation in the event of a promising development. Because the skunk works generally focus on clearly defined new products or processes, they can be viewed as incremental builders on existing technology.

Using Strategic Alliances   Another means of utilizing a technological advantage is through a strategic alliance such as a coproduction agreement, joint research project, or turnkey venture. Both Westinghouse Electric Company (USA) and Siemens, AG (Germany) possess advanced technology in factory automation; they formed a joint production agreement in 1988 to manufacture more than 20 such products, including robots. This strategic alliance is intended to give each company greater access to the other's home market, while leaving both free to compete in other product areas.

Joint research projects have proliferated in the computer industry in recent years as firms increasingly choose to pool R&D resources to reduce the in-house cost of designing new memory chips, processor chips, and other equipment. For example, IBM, AT&T, and MIT formed a research consortium to explore the field of high-temperature superconductivity. Turnkey ventures are less frequent, though they similarly leverage the technology of the possessor firm by contracting with an outside supplier of some other key ingredient to the business. Exxon's coal project in Colombia is a venture in which Exxon supplies the technology and international marketing of the coal, while Colombia provides access to the natural resource, labor for local facilities, and an agreement to take over the entire project in 30 years.[8]

All of these strategic alliances enable a firm that possesses technology to enjoy some benefit from that technology, while allowing the partner access to it, in exchange for some key input such as funding, additional technology, or market access. The crucial consideration in such alliances is to avoid jeopardizing the firm's competitive advantages through sharing the technology. If the partner gains enough from the joint project, that firm may in the future become a competitor against the original partner, unless the technology is protected adequately.

CONTROL OF PROPRIETARY TECHNOLOGY

So far, we have examined the use of technology as a competitive advantage in international business. An important aspect of this advantage is its ability to be dissipated, that is, to be acquired by other firms and thus reduced in value to the original possessor. The next problem we will consider, therefore, is the *protection* of proprietary technology.

Whether the knowledge in question is production or management technology, potential exists for rival firms to copy it. In some cases, the rival firm may assimilate the technology by simply looking at the innovation. In other cases, the technology may be complex or difficult to transfer, so the rival firm needs to spend substantial money to obtain it. In any case, the technology can be dissipated and the competitive advantage lost. A protection method is thus needed.

Methods for Protecting Technology

Once again, the appropriate strategy depends on the type of technology. If the knowledge the firm possesses is a manufacturing process that produces a new product, that process and the product can be protected with a **patent** in most countries. If the knowledge is embodied in a book or manual that can be sold, a **copyright** will protect the document against copying, although the knowledge itself will need patent protection as well. If the knowledge is embodied in the product and implies a high standard of quality or service, often a **trademark** can be obtained for protection. Each of these legal devices is formally defined below.

Patent "Patent law represents a balancing of society's interest in promoting free competition against its interest in encouraging innovation by rewarding inventors with temporary monopoly rights. . . . A patent may be granted to any person on any new and useful invention of (1) a process, (2) a machine, (3) a product, (4) a composition of matter, (5) a new and useful improvement of a prior patented invention, (6) a growing plant, or (7) a design." (Note the Hoffmann–La Roche example presented earlier.)

Copyright   "A copyright protects literary, musical, dramatic, pictorial, audio, and audiovisual works, but it is only the form of the work that is protected rather than ideas, concepts, or methods of operation. . . . The copyright holder is given exclusive right to reproduce, perform, or display the work, subject to what is known as 'fair use.' . . . The life of a copyright under [U.S. law] is 50 years beyond the death of the last surviving author."

Trademark   "A technical trademark is a distinctive mark, word, design, or picture which is affixed to goods so that purchasers may identify their origin. In general, a trademark must be fanciful, arbitrary, unique, and nondescriptive."[9]

The trademark, copyright, and patent laws offer protection to innovating firms if their technology fits into one of the above categories. They do not protect all kinds of innovation, and in different countries the rules and their enforcement vary widely even for these three types of technology.

Other methods for protecting technology include *hiding* it from competitors. This strategy works especially well when the key aspect of the technology is simple to understand but embodied in the product in a complex manner. Then, unless competitors can obtain the "formula" for using the technology, the proprietor can preserve its advantage. Another method is to require employees developing new products to sign an agreement prohibiting their use of the new technology outside the firm so that they cannot leave the proprietor firm and use their knowledge of the technology to compete against it.

Yet another method for protecting technology is to simply exploit it quickly, gain a large market share where it is used, and thereby discourage market entry by other firms. This strategy enables the firm to move quickly along the experience curve, lowering costs and creating a larger entry barrier over time.

Problems in Protecting Technology

Despite the methods of protection just discussed, there are still many situations in which adequate protection may not be available. For example, the Four Tigers of Asia (Hong Kong, South Korea, Singapore, and Taiwan) are notorious for producing imitations of branded, patented, copyrighted, and otherwise protected products.[10] From computers to videodiscs, from audiocassettes to textbooks, a huge market exists in every country, particularly since interpretation of the law is required to judge whether or not an imitation is legal.

A problem that often thwarts the firm's efforts to protect its technology is **industrial espionage.** This method of obtaining technology from the possessor firm is also illegal and also occurs frequently. In a highly publicized case, IBM successfully sued Hitachi Corporation for stealing IBM documents containing proprietary information about a new mainframe computer introduced in 1981.[11] A scientist who had left his employment at IBM enabled Hitachi to obtain extensive documentation about the computer, thus placing Hitachi in a substantially better competitive position. In another very visible case, General Motors sued Volkswagen for illegally obtaining secret company documents in 1993. The case resulted from Volkswagen's hiring of a key GM senior executive, who took documents and several colleagues along with him to the competitor firm. While the espionage was detected and prosecuted in these cases, much undetected espionage undoubtedly takes place.

A problem with which multinational firms in particular have to deal is the *difference in rules on technology use and technology transfer in different countries*. Less developed countries often afford foreign MNEs less protection on their technology than do industrialized countries. The Andean Pact countries in Latin America, for example, did not allow patents for many proprietary products brought in by MNEs during the 1970s and 1980s, and these countries did not allow local subsidiaries to pay royalties to parent companies for the use of technology. These restrictions were dropped in 1987.

A problem for firms involved in joint ventures or other contractual links with other firms is the *difficulty of constraining partners* to apply shared knowledge only to the application under contract. In this type of situation, the firm supplying its technology to a joint project often finds that the partner is able to appropriate the technology for uses the supplier cannot control or profit from. Thus, some of the value of the technology is lost to the supplier firm.

A final problem related to the protection of proprietary technology is the *mobility of employees*. Even if a firm successfully uses patents and copyrights on its technology, its competitive advantage may be lost if key employees (such as the scientists or managers who introduced the technology) leave the firm to work elsewhere. Since these people cannot leave their brains behind when they leave one company to join another, job mobility causes a tremendous amount of technology transfer to take place at relatively low cost.

COUNTRY-SPECIFIC CONCERNS IN TECHNOLOGY USE AND TRANSFER

In Industrial Countries

The generation and use of technology in industrialized countries tends to be very market based, with the government playing the role of referee and rulemaker. Table 19–1 lists a few government rules related to technology in a selected group of developed nations. Note that patent life is fairly consistent among these countries (in the range of 17 to 20 years), as is the lack of limitations on intercountry transfer of technology. In fact, the main "limitation" is on the use of royalties to pay for technology transfer; these are limited to 6 to 10 percent of the firm's sales in a few countries. Perhaps a more important restriction is the immigration laws in most developed countries, which make it difficult to transfer skilled employees to different countries.

Despite the tendency of the governments in developed countries to allow market activity to determine technological advancement and diffusion, as Table 19–1 shows, another factor needs to be considered. The governments in each country shown spend billions of dollars each year on military and other government-sponsored research. In fact, the US government accounts for (i.e., finances) approximately 46 percent of R&D spending in the United States today (though industry carries out 73 percent of the actual R&D).[12] Viewed in this light, governments are clearly major players in the creation and diffusion of technology.

Companies doing business in industrial countries find that R&D is subsidized either through tax benefits or through direct government spending on company research. R&D is seldom restricted, except in cases where public health or safety is perceived to be at risk, for example, recombinant DNA research ("gene splicing") or research on nuclear reactions.

When transferring technology between countries, a firm can usually choose among exporting, direct investment, and local licensing on the basis of market

TABLE 19-1   Industrial Country Rules Relating to Technology Use and Transfer

Selected Countries	Limits on Royalties	Unpatentable Items	Patent Duration	Trademark Duration	Highest Tax Bracket on Royalties (%)
Canada	None	Chemicals for food and medicine, theories	20 years	15 years, renewable	25%
France	6% of sales, unless technology is approved to have tax deduction	Nonindustrial items, animal and plant varieties, computer programs, medical treatments.	20 years	10 years, renewable	33.3
Germany	None, fair rate to have tax deduction	Nonindustrial items, medical treatments, computer programs	20 years	10 years, renewable	25
Italy	None	Theories, nonindustrial items	20 years	10 years, renewable	21
Japan	None, but generally 5% of sales	Nuclear transformations, nonindustrial items	20 years	10 years, renewable	20
United Kingdom	None, but generally 7% of sales	Nonindustrial items, scientific discoveries, artistic creations, medical treatments, animal and plant varieties	20 years	7 years, renewable	25
United States	None	Noncommercial items	17 years	10 years, renewable	30

Source: Economist Intelligence Unit, *Investing, Licensing, and Trading Conditions* (New York: Economist Intelligence Unit, 1993–94).

conditions, without concern for government intervention. In that case, the decision can be based on the factors just discussed, such as the technology's importance to the firm, its ease of transferability to other firms, and the size of the host country market.

Legal protection of proprietary technology is widely available in industrial countries, although industrial espionage and some illegal copying still take place in many industries. The countries of the European Union have standardized most of their rules on technology usage and transfer, and these rules differ fairly little from the rules in Japan and the United States. One major difference is in the amount and targeting of government spending on R&D in each country.

Another factor that firms operating in industrial countries need to consider is the level of competition and the length of product cycles. As modern telecommunications and transportation have virtually eliminated the distances between developed countries, innovations in any one country tend to be copied or transferred within MNEs very rapidly. In the 1990s, firms are increasingly introducing new products into several markets simultaneously, without waiting for the traditional international product cycle to follow its course. One can conclude that the diffusion process of proprietary technology is becoming increasingly rapid and that innovating firms must be aware of the shortening life spans of their products.

In many cases, R&D by firms from industrial countries has become international. Large MNEs such as General Electric and IBM operate research facilities in several countries, benefiting from breakthroughs that take place in each country and spreading them to affiliates elsewhere. Several studies over the past few years have demonstrated the increasing internationalization of the R&D function within MNEs.[13]

Pfizer Corporation carries out basic research on new chemical entities in the United States, the United Kingdom, and Japan. It also has a large product development laboratory in France and numerous development facilities in other countries for the local product testing their governments require. The Pfizer strategy is to maintain key research facilities in locations that have concentrations of research scientists and a relatively high likelihood of new-product developments by many firms. Minor product adaptation is done when needed in Pfizer's plants around the world, but major research work is concentrated in the three large centers.

In Less Developed Countries

The generation and transfer of technology are far more restricted in less developed countries than in industrial countries. Less R&D takes place in LDCs, and more government policies constrain the use and transfer of proprietary technology. Table 19–2 shows some of the important government policies that

TABLE 19–2 Less Developed Country Rules Relating to Technology Use and Transfer

Selected Countries	Limits on Royalties	Unpatentable Items	Patent Duration	Trademark Duration	Highest Tax Bracket on Royalties (%)
Argentina	None	Pharmaceuticals, nonindustrial items	5, 10, 15 years	10 years, renewable	30%
Brazil	1–5% gross sales	Pharmaceuticals, foods, chemicals, metallic mixtures	15 years	10 years, renewable	25
Egypt	None	Any substance used as food or medicine; only production processes are patentable	15 years, renewable	10 years, renewable	32
India	5% domestic sales or 8% exports	Foods, drugs, chemicals, optical glasses, semiconductors	14 years*	7 years, renewable	30
Korea	Prior approval required if > 3% net sales	Nuclear transformations vital to national defense or public interest	15 years	10 years, renewable	25
Mexico	None	Animal and plant species, genetic material, inventions based in human tissue	20 years	10 years, renewable	15
Nigeria	1% of sales, otherwise prior permission required	Animal and plant species, biological processes, scientific principles	20 years	7 years, renewable	15
Singapore	2–3% sales	Ideas, scientific principles	17 years	20 years	35
Venezuela	None, but no payments for unused technology	Materials of human body or genetic makeup, nuclear or fusionable materials, scientific theories, math methods, computer programs, medical methods.	20 years	10 years, renewable	30 (60 for mining royalties)

*India allows patents for five years from date of sealing or seven years from date of granting, whichever is less, on food processes and medicines, plus five years renewal.
Source: Economist Intelligence Unit, *Investing, Licensing, and Trading Conditions* (New York: Economist Intelligence Unit, 1993–94).

**IB
ILLUSTRATION**   IBM in Mexico

IBM has operated in Mexico as an importer of mainframe and minicomputers since the 1950s. Manufacture of minicomputers was begun near Guadalajara in 1981; at the time, all IBM facilities abroad were wholly owned by the company. Mexico is a relatively small market for IBM, accounting for annual sales of only 90,000 PCs in 1986, valued at approximately US $200 million. On the other hand, Mexico's proximity to the United States and the availability of low-cost labor presented an important opportunity to IBM for reducing production costs of its computers that are sold elsewhere.

Mexico has, since 1973, required that all FDI projects accept a minimum of 51 percent local ownership. But, as with IBM in Guadalajara, this rule has been broken when the government found compelling reasons to permit greater foreign ownership (typically due to the investment's introduction of new technology, creation of many jobs, and/or generation of significant exports). Nonetheless, the Mexican government has largely held to the minority joint-venture law, even during the 1980s foreign debt crisis.

Mexico passed legislation in 1981 to require foreign computer manufacturers to meet the 1973 rule on 51 percent minimum local ownership and to increase their Mexican local content beyond rules established for most other industries. The stated goal was to achieve 70 percent local supply of the nation's computer needs by 1986. In addition, computer manufacturers were required to meet minimum export requirements to generate foreign exchange for Mexico.

In 1984, IBM proposed to construct a PC plant at the site of its existing minicomputer facility near Guadalajara, to invest about U.S. $40 million, and to produce about 100,000 personal computers per year, 75 percent of which would be exported. The firm sought 100 percent ownership of the plant, presenting its case that the project would create many major benefits for Mexico (namely, about 80 direct new jobs and over 800 indirect ones; transfer of high-tech job skills into Mexico; new direct investment of US $7 million; and exports of 75,000 personal computers per year). The government initially

Source: Taken from Jack N. Behrman and Robert Grosse, *International Business and Governments* (Columbia: University of South Carolina Press, 1990).

influence technology use by multinational firms in LDCs. Compared to industrial countries, LDCs offer less patent protection, place more limitations on international transfer of technology, and present greater demands for participation in the process of technology creation and diffusion. This should not be surprising, since these countries face a "technology gap" between their economies and the economies of industrial countries and see a need to catch up. Among the ways they attempt to catch up is to get MNEs to engage in greater local R&D activity and to transfer skills to local people; both policies are widely used today.

For their part, multinational firms generally find that local R&D in less developed countries is relatively inefficient (or not even viable) because there are far fewer skilled scientists, engineers, and managers in such countries than in industrial countries. Therefore, MNEs tend to concentrate their basic research in developed nations and to carry out a minimum of product development (often adaptation to local conditions) in the LDCs that require it. Moreover, as emphasized in Vernon's international product cycle, firms prefer to undertake R&D in or near their large markets so that they can respond to customer preferences and rejected the proposal, on the grounds that IBM did not propose to use sufficient local content in the plant, and thus would be importing too much in parts and materials. It appears as well that the other foreign firms that were producing PCs locally successfully lobbied the government to refuse 100 percent ownership to IBM, since they all had accepted minority positions.

A year later, with Mexico increasingly hobbled by its more than US $100 billion indebtedness to foreign banks and other foreign lenders, IBM twice more resubmitted the proposal, each time increasing its commitment to purchase local inputs, to increase investment more than tenfold, and to raise the level of exports, but to retain 100 percent ownership. On the third occasion, with the enhanced offer and the promise of more technology and the establishment of secondary and tertiary enterprises, the Mexican government found itself much less able to resist the clear balance-of-payments and employment benefits to be produced by the project, and agreement was reached.

The final agreement called for IBM to invest a total of US $91 million. This money was distributed among expansion of the Guadalajara plant ($7 million), investment in local research and development ($35 million), development of local suppliers ($20 million), expansion of its purchasing and distribution network ($13 million), contribution to a government-sponsored semiconductor technology center ($12 million), and the remainder to begin local university partnerships and other linkages to local computer-related activities. Also, IBM agreed to achieve 82 percent local content by the fourth year of operation and to export 92 percent of the PCs produced in Mexico. The firm retains 100 percent ownership of the plant.

This example demonstrates both the importance of technology transfer to the host country and the bargaining relationship between the LDC government and the foreign MNE. ■

government policies. This is another reason for the small amount of MNE research done in LDCs.

The choice among exporting, direct investment, and licensing is sometimes mandated by the less developed countries. Often they simply do not allow direct investment in a particular industry or require licensing of local firms. In other situations, they require local investment (i.e., FDI) and do not permit imports. Thus, the MNE manager's choice of market entry method, and consequently of the technology transfer method, is often forced by the host government. Similarly, operating conditions often include continued pressures to increase technology transfer into the country, as the box "IBM in Mexico" shows.

Even after the firm brings a new product or process into an LDC, the legal protection for proprietary knowledge is often either unavailable or less assured than in industrial countries. Many LDC host countries refuse to grant patent protection for some products, reasoning that the technology is not new, it should not be proprietary, or the MNE has already earned a reasonable return on its patent in industrial countries. Any of these arguments may lead to less protection for the technology than that available in industrial countries.

The competitive situation is far less pressing in many LDCs than in developed countries; thus, in LDCs technology tends to diffuse more slowly, and a technological advantage can be maintained for a longer period of time. Even when patents expire, local firms are often slow to acquire the technology and compete with the originating firm. Because of a lack of competitive pressure, MNEs often continue to use production processes in LDCs even after those processes have been replaced by modernized processes in the MNEs' facilities elsewhere.

Finally, for the past two decades, governments of LDCs have been pressuring the MNEs to use **appropriate technology.**[14] This is generally considered to mean less capital-intensive and more labor-intensive technology in LDCs with an overabundance of labor and a scarcity of capital. Long and heated debates have taken place between companies and governments, and the United Nations has even tried to create a Code of Conduct on Technology Transfer that would push MNEs into using technology that offers maximum benefits to LDC host countries. There has been no clear outcome as yet, but at least a better definition of *appropriate technology* has been developed. It is now defined as product, process, or managerial knowledge that is optimally adapted to local conditions (rather than just labor intensive).[15]

CONCLUSIONS

Technology is knowledge that has application in an industrial (business) setting. Such knowledge may be created through research and development or simply through experience in doing business from which the firm develops managerial skills. It can also be purchased from innovating firms. Technology may be used through internal transfer and deployment within the firm or through sale to outside firms via licensing or some other contractual means. Ultimately, the competitive advantage obtained from technology may be dissipated due to copying by other firms or their creation of comparable knowledge.

Technology is at the heart of the multinational enterprise. Whether it be product, process, or managerial technology, the MNE usually depends on it for competitive advantage. This kind of firm benefits from technological advances made by an affiliate in one country that can be transferred within the firm to affiliates in other countries. Production technology can be created through R&D in several countries, benefiting from the spillover effects of the activities of other firms there. The knowledge of market and supply conditions in many countries is itself a technological advantage MNEs possess.

Control over the use and diffusion of proprietary technology is a difficult task for the multinational manager. There are many protection measures, and these are sometimes effective in preserving the competitive advantage of proprietary technology. Eventually, however, all technology becomes diffused or outmoded, and the proprietor firm needs to develop or acquire new technology to create new competitive advantages.

Each country has established rules governing the use and transfer of technology by firms operating there. Developed countries tend to offer relatively few restrictions on the creation and dissemination of technology. LDCs generally limit MNEs' use of technology by imposing restrictions on licensing agreements, limiting patent protection, and otherwise trying to restrict the competitive advantage MNEs derive from technology.

QUESTIONS

1. What is technology? How do multinational enterprises use it in competition?

2. Explain the concept of a "public good." Why does this concept cause problems for innovating firms? How do governments view this issue? How does management?

3. By what methods can technology be transferred internationally? What are the key costs and benefits to an MNE of using each transfer method?

4. How can an MNE create a technological advantage over other firms? Give several examples.

5. What is R&D? What is the optimal level of investment in R&D for a multinational firm?

6. Explain several methods a firm can use to protect its proprietary technology.

7. What are the main kinds of problems that make it difficult for a firm to maintain its competitive advantage based on proprietary technology?

8. How do industrial countries and LDCs differ in their approaches to regulating technology use and transfer?

9. How can an MNE best deal with the regulatory structure technology faces in the less developed countries?

10. What would be a viable strategy for a firm in international competition such as Hoffmann–La Roche, given that its key proprietary pharmaceuticals have passed the period of patent protection?

REFERENCES

Behrman, Jack N, and W A Fischer. *Overseas R&D Activities of Transnational Companies*. Cambridge, MA.: Oelgeschlager, Gunn, and Hain, 1980.

Caves, Richard. *Multinational Enterprise and Economic Analysis*. Cambridge: Cambridge University Press, 1982, chap. 7.

Contractor, Farok. *International Technology Licensing: Compensation Costs and Negotiation*. Lexington, MA.: D C Heath, 1981.

———. Inter-firm Technology Transfers and the Theory of Multinational Enterprise." *The International Trade Journal*, Fall 1989, pp. 21–48.

Davidson, William, and Donald McFetridge. "Key Characteristics in the Choice of International Technology Transfer Mode." *Journal of International Business Studies*, Summer 1985.

Emmanuel, Arghiri. *Appropriate or Underdeveloped Technology?* New York: John Wiley & Sons, 1982.

Guile, Bruce, and Harvey Brooks (eds.). *Technology and Global Industry*. Washington, DC: National Academy Press, 1987.

Magee, Steven. "Information and Multinational Corporations: An Appropriability Theory of Direct Foreign Investment." In *The New International Economic Order*, ed. J Bhagwati. Cambridge, MA.: MIT Press, 1977.

National Science Foundation. *National Patterns of Science and Technology Resources*. Washington, DC: National Science Foundation, 1990.

Organization for Economic Cooperation and Development. *Appropriate Technology*. Paris: OECD, 1976.

Teece, David. *The Multinational Corporation and the Resource Cost of International Technology Transfer*. Cambridge, MA.: Ballinger, 1976.

Tinnin, David. "How IBM Stung Hitachi." *Fortune*, March 7, 1983.

NOTES

[1]Technology is "industrial science, the science or systematic knowledge of the industrial arts, especially of the more important manufactures" (*Webster's New International Dictionary*, 2nd ed.). *Webster's* identifies two key points in this definition. First, technology relates to industry; that is, it is the application of science to business. Second, it relates to systematic knowledge of the various parts of industry such as production, but also distribution, R&D, and even marketing and finance.

[2]Jack Baranson, *Technology and the Multinationals* (Lexington, MA.: D C Heath, 1978), defines three types of technology: product, process, and managerial. Walter Chudson, in *The International Transfer of Commercial Technology to Developing Countries* (New York: UNITAR, 1971), similarly defines technology as having three forms: product design, production techniques, and managerial functions.

[3]See, for example, David Teece, *The Multinational Corporation and the Resource Cost of International Technology Transfer* (Cambridge, MA.: Ballinger, 1976).

[4]See, for example, Henry Grabowski and Dennis Mueller, "Industrial Research and Development, Intangible Capital Stocks, and Firm Profit Rates," *Bell Journal of Economics,* Autumn 1978, and E L Reynard, "A Method for Relating Research Spending to Net Profits," *Research Management,* July 1979.

[5]Thomas Peters and Robert Waterman, *In Search of Excellence* (New York: Harper & Row, 1980), pp. 223–34.

[6]Thomas Gladwin and Ingo Walter, *Survival of the MNE,* pp. 300–304; and the Harvard Business School case "Hoffmann–La Roche A.G."

[7]"IBM: Colossus of Armonk," *Creative Computing,* November 1984, pp. 298–306.

[8]Examples such as these, along with useful descriptions of the projects, appear regularly in the bimonthly magazine *Mergers & Acquisitions.*

[9]Harold Lusk, Charles Hewitt, John Donnell, and James Barnes, *Business Law and the Regulatory Environment,* 5th ed. (Homewood, IL.: Richard D Irwin, 1982), pp. 984, 987, 990.

[10]See, for example, "Where Trademarks Are Up for Grabs," *The Wall Street Journal,* December 5, 1989, p. B1.

[11]David Tinnin, "How IBM Stung Hitachi," *Fortune,* March 7, 1983.

[12]National Science Foundation, *National Patterns of Science and Technology Resources* (Washington, DC: NSF, 1990), p. 3.

[13]See, for example, Robert Ronstadt, *Research and Development Abroad by U.S. Multinationals* (New York: Praeger Publishers, 1977), and Jack N Behrman and William A Fischer, *Overseas R&D Activities of Transnational Companies* (Cambridge, MA.: Oelgeschlager, Gunn, and Hain, 1980).

[14]See, for example, Henry Norman and Patricia Blair, "The Coming Growth in Appropriate Technology," *Harvard Business Review,* November–December 1982.

[15]Organization for Economic Cooperation and Development, *Appropriate Technology* (Paris: OECD, 1976), chap. 1.

Miracle Corporation

Introduction

Staring out the window of his room in a downtown Washington hotel at the jets taking off and landing at National Airport, Dirk Roberts pondered tomorrow's presentation to the executive committee. Dirk was Miracle Corporation's coordinator of international investments and strategic planning and had lately been working on one of the most challenging projects he had seen in his eight years with the firm. Roberts had just returned from a meeting with Mexico's assistant undersecretary for economic development, Dr. Roberto Estaphan, and was returning to Miracle's St. Louis headquarters the following morning. That afternoon, he was to make a presentation to the Executive Committee for Strategic Development on the details of the meeting with Dr. Estaphan and offer recommendations as to how Miracle should organize itself vis-à-vis its proposed Mexican investment.

Company Information

Miracle Corporation was in the business of manufacturing electronic test equipment for the automotive repair industry. Miracle had annual sales in the $300 million to $350 million range and employed 130 employees at its plant in St. Louis. It also had a 20-person research center in Michigan to track technological developments in the automotive industry.

Electronic test equipment is the auto industry equivalent of the diagnostic equipment found in hospitals and doctors' offices. Without some means of accurately measuring the performances of automotive engine components, valuable repair time would be lost speculating on the reasons an engine is running incorrectly. As automotive technology advanced with the advent of semiconductor technology, a need arose for more sophisticated testing equipment to track faults in vehicles' electrical, carburetion, fuel injection, and ignition systems. Vehicle emissions regulations also created a demand for measurement equipment. Fifty percent of Miracle's sales were exhaust emissions analyzers to automotive service establishments. This segment of its business had taken off as a result of Miracle being the first manufacturer to have an analyzer certified for use in California (home of the most stringent emissions control laws in the United States) in 1984. As "green" awareness rose, other states and communities had since followed California's lead in adopting strict vehicle emissions controls, and this business segment was growing rapidly.

This case was written by Professor Frank Dubois as a basis for class discussion. Revised 1994.

The firm also sold and leased highly sophisticated engine test and measurement equipment to automotive dealerships and other repair shops. This represented about 30 percent of sales. The final 20 percent of sales was composed of sales of hand-held test equipment such as timing lights to check engine timing, multimeters to check electrical faults, and dwell and RPM meters.

Miracle's customers for emissions analyzers and engine test equipment were split into two segments. The primary market was auto dealerships. Dealers' service departments required state-of-the-art test equipment, since they needed to diagnose new models brought in for warranty claims. Since repairs were made under warranty and generated no revenue to the car's manufacturer, dealers were given various forms of incentives (in the form of low-interest loans and discounts) to minimize the warranty costs that were reimbursed to the dealer as part of the franchise agreement. Having the latest test equipment allowed dealers to track faults and make repairs quickly. Dealers were generally allowed to trade in their old equipment for new equipment as new car technology came on line. Often the old equipment was returned to the factory for refurbishment and then sold to Miracle's other major market: general-service auto shops.

The general-service shops owed their existence to a reluctance on the part of a large segment of the driving population to have postwarranty service done at dealerships. These repair shops typically offered lower repair costs and personalized service. Mechanics in general-service shops, generally worked for independent entrepreneurs who were not required to do low-margin warranty work and were under less pressure to generate revenue. Because of their focus on repairs to older vehicles, these shops did not have to invest in state-of-the-art test equipment and could make do with older equipment.

Miracle also had a distribution arrangement with the leading automotive equipment vendor in the United States, Pop-Off Corporation. This arrangement had been quite lucrative for both parties, and as a result Miracle had an 80 percent share of the US market for this equipment. Miracle produced equipment for sale under its own brand name in the United States and Canada and was an original-equipment manufacturer for Pop-Off, manufacturing products under the Pop-Off label. Pop-Off distributed automotive tools and other products through independent franchisees who were given exclusive rights to sell products to automotive service establishments using a showroom-on-wheels concept. Pop-Off vendors owned large panel trucks stocked with a large assortment of tools and equipment. These trucks made the rounds of automotive service establishments in every city in the United States and Canada. Most vendors carried at least two or three of Miracle's lower-priced hand-held test items, including battery testers, timing lights, mini–engine analyzers, and multimeters. More costly items, such as integrated engine analyzers costing as much as $10,000 and emissions test equipment, had to be special ordered with delivery times of two to six weeks, depending on the backlog and the degree of customization the customer wanted.

In addition to sales to Pop-Off, Miracle had a contract with a major retail chain to manufacture hand-held test equipment for the do-it-yourself consumer market. This contract represented about 10 percent of Miracle's sales revenue. Export sales were dominated by the emissions analyzers and were growing rapidly as a result of international efforts to control vehicle emissions. Miracle also had export sales through its relationship with Pop-Off and hoped to increase this component of its business.

The auto test equipment industry was quite small, with only three other major competitors in the United States. Competition was generally on product performance and after-sales service rather than on price. Miracle believed it was the market leader as a result of its early entry into the emissions analyzer market. Sales revenue from this segment provided funds to improve the performance capabilities of its equipment and keep up with changes in automotive technology. The major competitive threat Miracle faced was competition from the Far East, which offered comparably priced products specifically designed for the high-performance, small displacement engines used in Japanese imports. The less expensive hand-held items, such as battery testers and timing lights, were taking a beating from imports from Taiwan, Hong Kong, South Korea, and Singapore. As a result, Pop-Off was putting pressure on Miracle to either reduce costs or increase product performance. In addition, the small test equipment account for the retail chain was coming up for renewal next year. The executive committee was worried that unless quick action was taken to reduce manufacturing costs and lower prices while maintaining profit margins, both the Pop-Off and retail accounts would be lost, and Miracle's future would be in peril. Miracle's stock price was already starting to show weakness as a result of a financial analyst's sell recommendation on cable TV's "Nightly Business Report."

Investment in Mexico

Miracle's executive committee had decided the time was right to explore investment in a manufacturing platform in Mexico. They were interested in a Mexican location because of US tariff regulations and the possibility of the two countries negotiating a free-trade agreement sometime in the 1990s. Many other US companies were shifting operations to Mexico in response to competitive pressures. Even Japanese and European firms were setting up operations across the border to serve the US market. There was a consensus among Miracle's executive committee that the best way to maintain market share and remain competitive during the economic slump of the early 1990s was to shift a portion of production to a site in northern Mexico into a facility known as a *maquiladora*. Mexico was chosen as a site because the company was worried about losing control over the operation and had relatively little experience in the international environment. Most *maquiladoras* were located less than a one-day drive from the border, and the corporate Lear jet would facilitate one-day trips for upper management.

Maquiladoras are offshore manufacturing facilities that operate under terms of US tariff laws 806.3 and 807.0. Under the terms of these laws, a firm can export from the United States to Mexico parts and components for further processing and assembly and pays duty upon import back into the United States only on the value-added in Mexico. In other words, the value of the product for US customs purposes is the difference between its value leaving the United States and its value upon return to the United States. In addition, labor rates in Mexico averaged approximately $1.50 per hour versus $7.80 per hour in the United States.

The problem with the project from Dirk Roberts's perspective involved the location of the project, the characteristics of the products that would be produced there, and the type of processing technology that would be transferred to the *maquiladora*. Roberto Estaphan had remarked that the Mexican government did not look favorably on the transfer of less than state-of-the-art equipment into

Mexico unless it was absolutely necessary. The Mexican government was proud of the accomplishments of Ford's automotive manufacturing plant in Hermosillo and wanted as many new investments as possible to follow Ford's lead in transferring modern technology. Modern technology contributed to spin-offs in terms of training and development of supporting industries. Estaphan also stated that the Mexican government was willing to offer lower tax rates to those firms that used modern equipment in their Mexican facilities. The government would lower tax rates even further for firms that chose manufacturing locations some distance from the border. There were serious social and environmental problems along the border, and the Mexican government was trying to encourage new *maquiladoras* to set up in the underdeveloped interior.

Characteristics of the Manufacturing Process

Miracle's main plant was in St. Louis. All manufacturing took place in this plant. As a result of automation of most of the major process functions, the plant's capital-to-labor ratio was very high, and Dirk Roberts was worried that transferring some of the production process technology might be inappropriate at a low-wage site. The assembly line for the hand-held test equipment relied on a significant investment in plant and equipment to support a very high output rate. There was, however, a hand assembly component to the production process. For much of this work, Miracle relied on low-skilled, hourly labor.

An exception was the manufacturing line for the integrated engine analyzers and emissions test equipment. Since production volumes for this product were quite low, Miracle had in place a much less sophisticated production process. Products were assembled using relatively standardized components such as printed circuit boards and power supplies that were sourced internally. Workers assembled the final product in batches using general-purpose equipment. At this stage of the process, Miracle needed very highly skilled employees because of the different variations of the product that could be manufactured. Most of the employees working on this line had been with the firm for over 10 years, and the company had invested heavily in their training as technology grew more sophisticated. Management was pleased that various attempts to unionize its direct labor force had not been successful.

Notwithstanding the impact on the St. Louis work force, Roberts was also worried about the effects of Mexican manufacturing on the firm's ability to meet delivery commitments. Miracle prided itself on its ability to ship 99 percent of its engine analyzers on schedule. Since the cost of the engine analyzers precluded keeping a very large inventory, the ability to meet due dates reliably was critical to winning orders. Because of the lower investment in hand-held test equipment, large stocks of finished-goods inventory were kept to ensure a steady supply of distributors. The company found that demand for these products was inversely related to business cycles. Demand increased during downturns, because people kept their cars longer and had a greater need for repair services. (However, the 1990 recession, coupled with Operation Desert Shield, had hit Miracle's business hard, particularly in communities surrounding major military installations. Many auto repair shops noticed a reluctance on the part of military wives to take over the traditionally "male" job of automotive upkeep.)

With this information in mind, Roberts proceeded to sketch out recommendations to the executive committee.

QUESTIONS

1. What arguments should Dirk Roberts make in his presentation to the executive committee with respect to the technology transfer question?

2. What considerations should Miracle Corporation take into account in deciding between locations on the border or in inland Mexico? What locations would you suggest?

3. What types of products are most amenable to production in a *maquiladora*? Which of Miracle's products or components might be most efficiently manufactured in Mexico?

4. Do you think US tariff regulations should provide incentives for firms to move manufacturing outside of the United States?

PART

IV

DOING BUSINESS IN . . .

Industrialized Countries

This chapter discusses some general characteristics of industrialized countries and common problems and opportunities that occur when doing international business there. The main goals of the chapter are to:

1. Demonstrate important characteristics of industrialized countries.

2. Show what kinds of international business are common and strategically appropriate in industrialized countries.

3. Examine the role of governments in industrialized countries and show how firms can deal with them.

4. Consider entry and operating strategies that international firms can use in industrialized countries.

5. Illustrate the general issues with the case of Japan.

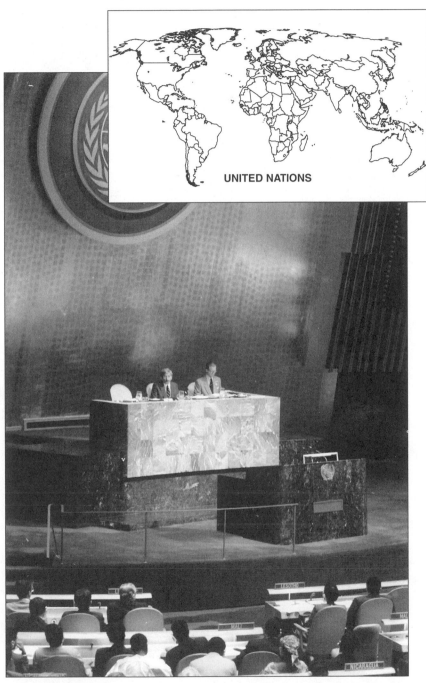

The United Nations chambers in New York house representatives from 177 member countries around the world.
AP/Wide World Photos

INTRODUCTION

Definition of Industrialized Countries

The countries we consider in this chapter are the developed nations of Western Europe and North America, plus Japan, Australia, and New Zealand. They are called **industrialized countries (ICs)** because their economies have become dominated by industrial production (and services) rather than agriculture. All have high standards of living relative to the rest of the world, and all have been using market-based economic systems (as opposed to communism) for decades. Table 20–1 lists the countries that are considered industrialized today and provides several measures of their economic performance, such as per capita incomes, unemployment, and real economic growth rates. Notice that Scandinavia, the United States, and Switzerland have the highest incomes and Japan (which was substantially behind the others after World War II) has had the highest growth rates. The economic performances of the industrialized countries are dramatically better than those of the less developed countries (LDCs), although such individual LDCs as Hong Kong, Korea, and Singapore have achieved very impressive economic records during the past decade or so, and several oil-exporting LDCs with small populations, such as Kuwait and the United Arab Emirates, have high per capita incomes. (In 1991, per capita GNP averaged $US 350 in low-income LDCs, $US 2,480 in middle-income LDCs, and $US 21,530 in industrialized countries.) More detailed comparisons can be made by looking at Table 20–1 along with its counterpart in the next chapter, Table 21–1.

In addition to the macroeconomic indicators shown in Table 20–1, many other measures of development distinguish the industrialized countries from the rest of

TABLE 20–1   Selected Characteristics of Industrialized Countries

Country	GNP per Capita ($US, 1991)	Growth Rate of GNP per Capita*	Average Annual Inflation (%/yr.)*	Average Unemployment, 1991 (%)	Current Account BOP, 1991 ($ millions)	Manufacturing as % of Total GDP, 1991
Canada	20,440	2.0	4.3	10.2	(25,529)	—
United States	22,240	1.7	4.2	6.6	(3,690)	—
Australia	17,050	1.6	7.0	9.5	(9,853)	15
Japan	26,930	3.6	1.5	2.1	72,905	25
New Zealand	12,350	0.7	10.3	10.3	(920)	18
Austria	20,140	2.1	3.6	3.5	(252)	25
Belgium	18,950	2.0	4.2	9.3	4,731	22
Denmark	23,700	2.2	5.2	9.1	2,167	19
Finland	23,980	2.5	6.6	7.5	(6,685)	24
France	20,380	1.8	5.7	9.3	(6,148)	21
Germany†	23,650	2.2	2.8	5.5	(19,497)	23
Ireland	11,120	3.3	5.8	15.7	921	3
Italy	18,520	2.2	9.5	10.8	(21,454)	21
Netherlands	18,780	1.6	1.8	7.0	8,760	20
Norway	24,220	2.3	5.2	5.5	4,939	14
Spain	12,450	2.8	8.9	16.0	(15,954)	—
Sweden	25,110	1.7	7.4	2.7	(3,243)	22
Switzerland	33,610	1.6	3.8	1.2	9,847	—
United Kingdom	16,550	2.6	5.8	7.9	(22,876)	—

*For the period 1980–91.

†Data in the first three columns refer to the Federal Republic of Germany before unification.

Sources: World Bank, *World Development Report, 1993* (Washington, DC: World Bank, 1993.) Unemployment data: Organization for Economic Cooperation and Development, *Labour Force Statistics, 1971–1991* (Paris: OECD, 1993), p. 32.

the world. For example, all the industrialized countries have well-developed securities markets in which private sector and government borrowers and lenders participate. While the markets in the United States and the United Kingdom are the largest and most influential in international financial dealings, even tiny Luxembourg has stock and bond markets and other financial markets. Broad financial systems of this kind are usually lacking in less developed countries and in the formerly communist countries of Eastern Europe.[1]

Industrialized countries generally possess an advanced system of *distribution*: roads, railroads, airports, and navigable waterways. These pathways for the transportation of products and people enable companies to get their products to customers and to move raw materials and intermediate goods to processing locations. Similarly, advanced *communications* networks allow rapid and efficient transmission of information through telephone, fax, television, radio, and print media. Also, the systems of *education* in industrialized countries generally offer high-level training in the skills needed to function in an industrial setting, particularly engineering, sciences, and business administration. Each of these types of infrastructure exists in less developed countries as well as industrialized ones. The key difference is their very wide availability and high quality in the developed countries compared to those in the LDCs.

Main Forms of International Business in Industrialized Countries

Not surprisingly, the main forms of international business discussed throughout this book are those used among the industrialized countries. As noted earlier, about two-thirds of world exports and imports take place among developed nations (which comprise one-sixth of the world's population), and an even larger portion of total foreign direct investment occurs among them. International banking activity likewise involves mostly banks and clients in North America, Europe, and Japan, despite the emphasis of public debate on LDC debt during the economic crisis (especially in Latin America) of the 1980s. Table 20–2 shows some aggregate measures of the international business that occurs in the developed country members of the **(OECD) Organization for Economic Cooperation and Development.**[2] Note that by far the bulk of international business worldwide occurs among industrialized countries and that foreign direct investment is more concentrated among these countries than is international trade (or lending).

TABLE 20–2 International Business among Industrialized Countries and LDCs

From ICs to	Exports 1992 ($US billions)	FDI In Flow 1992 ($US billions)	Commercial Bank Loans Outstanding, 1989* ($US billions)
ICs	1960.6	102.4	1,925.8
Latin America	130.9	17.7	117.8
Africa	58.9	3.0	18.5
Asia	299.5	30.1	96.4
Eastern and Central Europe	—	4.5	—

*Liabilities of borrowers in each group of countries owed to foreign commercial banks.
Sources: International Monetary Fund, *Direction of Trade Yearbook* (1993); Bank for International Settlements, semiannual international lending report (1989); United Nations, *World Investment Report 1994* (Geneva: UNCTAD, 1994).

With this base of information, we can proceed to discuss major factors that company managers should consider when doing business in industrialized countries. In the next section, we examine a variety of attributes of industrialized countries as they pertain to international firms. Then we focus specifically on the regulatory structure and government policies that affect international firms in these countries. Next, we consider entry and operating strategies for multinational firms, followed by some strategies for dealing with the host and home country governments. Finally, we examine current international business activities and concerns in a particular industrialized country: Japan.

KEY CHARACTERISTICS RELATING TO MNEs

The Concept and Function of the Marketplace

All industrialized nations use the free market as one acceptable means of organizing economic activity, subject to fewer or greater government constraints, depending on the country. This assertion is more or less a definition; the only countries that have high per capita incomes, well-developed economic infrastructures, and other characteristics similar to those of the industrialized nations are a few formerly communist countries, such as Russia and the Czech Republic. Those countries have begun to move to a **market-based economy.** While these distinctions are intended primarily to distinguish countries on the basis of economic development, in fact the formerly communist countries vary considerably between high-income and low-income countries, between industrial and agricultural countries, and so on. Nonetheless, we will retain the common classification of industrialized countries as those that use a market-based economy and have achieved relatively high levels of per capita income and other measures of development.

Even the industrialized countries vary fairly widely in their degree of private sector and public sector (i.e., government) participation in business. France and Italy continue to place ownership and control of a large number of companies and industries in the hands of government managers. In contrast, in the United States and Germany, very few government-owned companies exist except for some public utilities.

Recall that economic activity can be organized by markets, by governments, *and* by large firms that internalize business activities. As noted in Chapter 2, the MNE is itself a means of organizing economic activity internationally, because it carries out production, resource transfers, distribution, and consumption. Sometimes large firms operating internally can carry out business activities more efficiently than small, competitive firms; thus, they add an element of efficiency to the market. Since the vast majority of multinational enterprises are headquartered in ICs and both earn their income and employ their staffs there, these countries do not view MNEs nearly as critically as do many LDCs. Consequently, MNEs as well as markets are allowed to function with substantial freedom in ICs compared to some LDCs.

Although these generalizations are reasonably accurate, many differences still exist in the degree of freedom of markets and MNEs in different ICs. As mentioned, France's government owns and operates numerous corporations, whereas the United States owns and operates almost none. The Japanese economic system favors private ownership of firms but tends to limit competition in favor of company-government cooperation to avoid extensive layoffs of employees or company failures. In contrast, the British government owns a substantial portion of industry but permits fairly open competition, with much less company-government cooperation. The Western European countries have generally allowed corporate mergers and acquisitions to create large companies capable of competing with American and Japanese firms, whereas the United States has followed a strong antitrust policy for most of the 20th century. In sum, although all the ICs utilize the marketplace as a base for their economies, each follows a somewhat different model for doing so.

Cultural Differences   Despite the many similarities in the economic systems of developed countries, major differences due to cultural factors still exist among them. For example, doing business in Japan may appear to parallel doing business in the United States, but many US companies find it much more complicated. Although consumers in the United States and Japan have similar levels of income and education, huge differences exist in tastes, business practices, and many other aspects of business. US firms trying to enter the Japanese market have often found a need to obtain some "inside" help from a Japanese company that knows the local distribution system and can get products to customers. Numerous stories about the problems of US firms trying to do business in Japan appear in *The Wall Street Journal* every year. These stories generally point out that the traditional inward-looking Japanese business system makes it very difficult for foreigners to enter. Many other cultural factors, not the least of which is language, effectively limit the access of foreign firms to the Japanese market. Each of these factors raises a barrier to business among industrialized countries, which thus cannot be viewed as homogeneous markets despite their similarities.

IB ILLUSTRATION   Privatization in Europe

During the 1980s, a massive sweep of privatizations took place in most of the Common Market countries. Begun by the Thatcher administration's sale of British Telecom and a dozen other high-profile, state-owned companies, privatization has become a signal of European governments' willingness to use the free market to build the region's economies.

Once the bastion of protectionism in Europe, France has moved aggressively into the privatization mainstream with the sales of several major state-owned firms. Saint-Gobain, a diversified company with a concentration in glassmaking, was sold in 1987 through a widely promoted campaign to attract small investors from all parts of France. This company had been nationalized in 1982 under the socialist government that also nationalized the banking system. After several years of losses and low profits, Saint-Gobain began to improve profitability in 1986 and was then sold to the public in 1987 for $US 1.9 billion.

France's government followed this sale with the denationalization of several banks and other major industrial and service firms. Although the initial steps into privatization were taken by the Conservative government of Premier Jacques Chirac, this policy continues to be followed in the 1990s. As the European Union drops more of its restrictions on internal business, all the national governments will have to consider more ways to assist their national firms to compete in the regional market. Privatization is one vehicle that permits firms to pursue market-based strategies without being subjected to the noneconomic demands placed on government-owned companies. ■

Government Involvement in Business

Governments in every country own some or many companies, particularly in such industries as electric and telephone utilities, banking, and petroleum. For the most part, IC governments own fewer companies than governments in LDCs. During the 1980s and early 1990s, the tendency was toward even less government ownership in ICs, as shown by the sales of shares in the following national companies:

Great Britain: British Telecom, British Petroleum, British Gas, British Airways

Japan: Nippon Telephone and Telegraph, East Japan Railways

France: Banque National de Paris, Elf Aquitaine (oil), Rhone-Poulenc, (chemicals), Saint-Gobain (industrial equipment), Assurances Générales (insurance)

Italy: Montedison (a very large chemical company), Alfa-Romeo, Credito Italiano

Germany: the government-owned portion of Volkswagenwerk, Lufthansa, Deutsche Telekom

Despite this trend, many companies with total or partial government ownership still exist in Western Europe. A measure of overall government participation in the economy appears in Figure 20–1. This measure shows aggregate government spending on defense, education, health, social security, economic services, and general administration. On average, the government sector accounts for less than one-third of economic activity in industrialized countries. On top of this, government-owned companies account for another 10 percent of GDP in most Western European countries.

Perhaps the most important issue raised by the existence of government-owned (or state-owned) companies that compete with privately owned ones is the nature of competition. How can a private firm compete with a company that is backed by the resources and rulemaking power of a government? In another light, how can a government-owned company compete with a private company when it must serve both political and economic goals and hence must usually sacrifice some efficiency for political reasons? As global competition increases among firms from many countries, concern about the practices of state-owned companies that are not limited by profit considerations (because governments can subsidize them) will continue to intensify. During the 1990s, **privatization** of state-owned firms has become a truly global phenomenon.

A second form of government involvement in business is subsidization of local firms and/or restriction of foreign firms. In every country, governments show some sort of favoritism to local firms and institutions and discriminate against foreign firms. From limits on deposit taking by foreign-owned banks to government purchasing practices that favor local over foreign suppliers (such as the "buy American" policy in the United States), antiforeign bias exists everywhere. In the 1990s, increasing efforts are being made to force governments to treat foreign firms fairly in business, following a principle, established in 1976 by the OECD, that calls for "national treatment of non-nationals."[3] That is, the OECD called on its member countries to give equal treatment under the law to foreign and domestic firms. Although a trend toward more equal treatment exists, antiforeign rules and practices still occur in the business systems of industrialized countries.

FIGURE 20-1

Government Participation in the Economy (central government expenditures as a percentage of GDP)

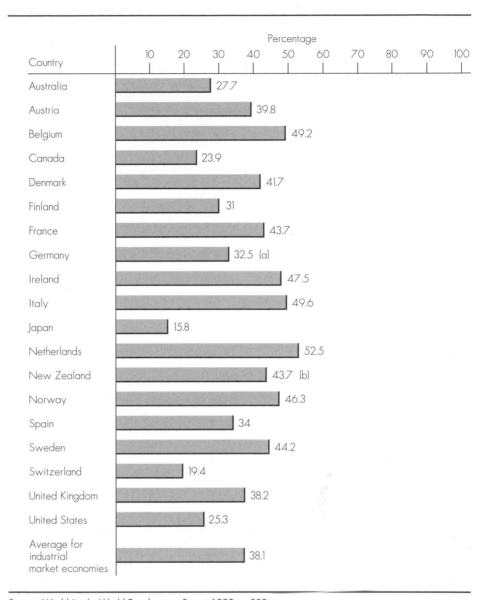

Country	Percentage
Australia	27.7
Austria	39.8
Belgium	49.2
Canada	23.9
Denmark	41.7
Finland	31
France	43.7
Germany	32.5 (a)
Ireland	47.5
Italy	49.6
Japan	15.8
Netherlands	52.5
New Zealand	43.7 (b)
Norway	46.3
Spain	34
Sweden	44.2
Switzerland	19.4
United Kingdom	38.2
United States	25.3
Average for industrial market economies	38.1

Source: World Bank, *World Development Report 1993*, p. 223.

GOVERNMENT CONCERNS AND POLICIES RELATED TO MNEs

Except for IC policies that have been established to protect local businesses against foreign competition, most of the IC policies that affect MNEs are aimed at regulating business in general. For example, antitrust rules seek to maintain competitiveness in the economy and limit monopolistic practices such as unfair pricing by MNEs and local firms alike. Similarly, pollution control is a major concern in most countries; in dealing with this concern, the ICs have established rules that limit company practices regardless of the nationality of the firm. The following sections discuss several major concerns of IC governments that relate to MNEs, beginning with the concerns that tend to be most significant to the government-business relationship. In each case, the concern has led to some policy responses, which are discussed as well. Table 20–3 lists these concerns and

TABLE 20–3   Industrialized Country Concerns and Policies toward MNEs

Concern	Company Activities	Government Policies	International Agreements
Employment	Importation of products and people, antiunion behavior, production switching	Immigration limits, labor protection laws, investment incentives	OECD Code of Conduct, ILO Tripartite Agreement
Balance of payments	Importing and exporting, transfer pricing, remittances, loans	Tariffs, nontariff barriers, requirement of arm's-length pricing, taxes on transfers	GATT, OECD Code, regional integration agreements
Taxation	Transfer pricing, arbitrary booking of sales and expenses	Corporate income tax, remittance taxes	OECD Code, bilateral tax treaties
Antitrust	Dumping, overpricing, collusion	Sherman and Clayton Acts in the United States	EEC Treaty articles 85 and 86, OECD Code, UNCTAD Code on Restrictive Business Practices
Sovereignty	Overseas decision making, production shifting	Attempts to extend jurisdiction extraterritorially	OECD Code, European Union and NAFTA accords
Information disclosure	Multicountry operations, transborder information transfer	Information on foreign operations demanded	OECD Code

policies. The listing in the table is intended to be in order of importance, with the most important concern at the top. However, the actual priority of any concern depends on the country and its economic/political situation at a particular time.

Employment

Employment, and its consequent impact on national income, is generally the single most important concern of home and host governments dealing with MNEs. If MNEs hire local people when they enter a country and produce output that raises GNP, they are viewed positively by the host government. If they displace local workers through imports of their products or through layoffs at their local plants, offices, and so on, they are viewed negatively. If MNEs move their production out of a country because of labor problems or high costs, they are certainly viewed negatively.

It is often very difficult to measure the overall impact of an MNE on employment in a given country. Since one cannot turn back time and see what would have happened had the MNE been absent from a given situation, generally no precise measure of that "what if" result is possible. Thus, employment impacts tend to be measured in the manner stated above, and when a company changes its employment pattern, it is scrutinized carefully by both home and host governments.

Government policies that deal with employment include a variety of limitations on employment practices. The most common rules relate to immigration. Every country restricts foreign nationals from receiving visas to enter the country for employment (because this would presumably keep a local person from being employed). The United States is among the strictest in limiting entry by foreign nationals for employment purposes. The European Union, on the other hand, has established rules permitting nationals of any member country to freely seek employment in another member country to create a single EU-wide labor market.[4] (Nationals of other countries still face substantial restrictions on entry into any European Union country for employment.)

MNEs are greatly affected by the limitations on hiring and firing imposed by most countries. Throughout Europe, national laws require payment of substantial severance benefits to employees who are laid off by a firm. In addition, most countries require demonstration of a just cause for terminating employment rather than allowing employers the power to lay off workers or managers for any reason. Even the United States has been increasing such restrictions.[5] Rules of this kind raise the cost of layoffs in general and raise the cost to MNEs of moving operations from one (national) location to another if layoffs are involved.

At the multilateral level, both the International Labour Office (ILO) and the OECD have enacted guidelines for the treatment of workers by multinational firms. The ILO's "Tripartite Declaration" and the OECD's "Guidelines" describe acceptable behavior for MNEs. The prescriptions in these documents are so general that they have had very little impact on company decisions. However, since both documents call for fair and reasonable treatment of workers and for the upholding by MNEs of the labor laws in the countries where they operate, they reinforce the efforts of countries to ensure that MNEs engage in the desired labor practices.

The Balance of Payments

The *balance of payments* impacts of MNE activities are another top concern of IC governments. MNEs transfer funds repeatedly between parent and affiliates and among affiliates in different countries. Every transfer of this kind has a different impact on the sending versus the receiving country and, of course, raises a different concern for each of their governments. MNEs ship products and services among affiliates, again giving rise to BOP impacts that concern national governments. Virtually every link between MNE affiliates in different countries, even down to transborder telephone calls, leads to direct or indirect BOP impacts.

Industrialized countries use a wide variety of limitations on imports and subsidies for exports, as discussed in Chapter 9. While the GATT negotiations have reduced tariff protection on manufactured goods to very low levels over several decades, nontariff barriers and restrictions on imports of agricultural goods and services still limit trade in many ways. For example, due to a tremendous bilateral trade deficit with Japan over the past decade, the US government has "jawboned" (threatened to set up tariff or quota barriers if foreign importers do not "voluntarily" limit their sales to the United States) the Japanese into reducing their sales of autos and televisions in this country. This tactic has stimulated such Japanese MNEs as Toyota, Honda, Sanyo, and Toshiba to avoid **de facto protectionism** by establishing manufacturing subsidiaries in the United States.

Limitations on funds transfers are much fewer among the ICs than among the LDCs. Even so, each industrialized country has on occasion limited its residents' ability to take funds abroad through some form of exchange controls. The countries with the largest trade deficits, such as France and Italy, have been most prone to using such controls, though in the late 1960s the United States limited funds transfers by MNEs to their foreign affiliates. In the early 1990s, with a huge

US trade deficit, no exchange controls were enacted, though the Federal Reserve was accused by some foreign governments of allowing interest rates to remain high to attract foreign capital into the United States.

At the transnational level, the GATT has become a substantial forum for reducing barriers to the exports and imports of MNEs (and other firms) and for harmonizing the treatment of trade. The GATT does not, however, attempt to guide trade in any particular direction, as do national laws in each country. Concerning financial flows, the OECD guidelines call for MNEs not to undertake transactions that destabilize national balance-of-payments positions. Adherence to this guideline is particularly difficult, since any cross-border financial transaction has opposite effects on the countries involved (i.e., it may be good for one country and bad for the other). In sum, no clear international accord exists with regard to financial flows, though some analysts have called for a GATT-type organization to deal with them.

Taxation

Taxation is a third major concern of IC governments in dealing with MNEs. Each government would like to tax MNE activities in its jurisdiction, but MNEs are able to move funds around through a variety of financial transfers. The home country would like to tax earnings of foreign affiliates that are based on value added by the parent firm, but host governments have first access to those earnings. Host governments worry about parent companies charging their affiliates high transfer prices, royalties, and other fees so that little profit is shown in host countries and little tax is paid there. To the governments, this is largely a zero-sum game due to treaties that reduce **double taxation** of company income; if one firm receives more tax payments from an MNE, the other receives less. The central issue is fairness; each government should be able to tax the company activities within its jurisdiction based on the **fair value** of those activities. Even apart from the fact that each government would probably prefer to receive as much tax as possible, admittedly measures of fair value are arbitrary at best.

The main tax policies used in industrialized countries are national corporate income taxes that apply to all firms within the jurisdiction, that is, parent companies and local affiliates of foreign firms. When profits are remitted to parent companies abroad, the home country allows some kind of tax reduction (credit or deduction) to account for taxes paid abroad. Profit remittances (dividends) are generally taxed by the host country, as are payments of royalties and fees to the parent company. The MNE usually has substantial leeway to place available funds in such instruments as eurocurrency deposits, so funds transfers are not the central concern of governments. It is the MNE's ability to declare more (or less) taxable income in selected jurisdictions that creates the tension with governments; for example, a firm can book more sales in low-tax jurisdictions and more costs in high-tax jurisdictions.

The taxes MNEs actually pay vary widely from country to country and across industries. Because of government incentive policies, the United States taxes such industries as oil exploration and capital-intensive manufacturing less than it does other industries.[6] Due to similar incentives, companies that locate their plants and offices in specified zones in Great Britain, France, and Italy pay lower taxes than other firms in those countries. For the most part, such policies are not directed toward MNEs alone, but they do alter the tax environment MNEs face.

The OECD guidelines call for MNEs to use arm's-length transfer prices and otherwise fairly value their transactions so that taxes are properly determined and paid to the governments concerned. Double-taxation treaties between countries try to avoid overtaxing MNEs relative to local firms in each country by allowing for coordinated taxing of earnings by the home and host governments. As yet, no single policy for taxation of MNEs has been established in multilateral agreements.

Antitrust Regulation and Competition

Antitrust (or, viewed from the other side, *competition*) is another major concern of IC governments. Historically, the most restrictive legislation to limit monopolistic practices, that is, to ensure competition in the market, has been enacted by the United States. European countries and Japan have tended to encourage company combinations that lead to larger firms, which are then expected to be better able to compete in oligopolistic markets. While these countries usually do not object to large company size, they do seek to limit abusive practices such as discriminatory pricing and collusion among firms to monopolize a market.

The principal legislative vehicles of antitrust regulation include the Sherman and Clayton Acts in the United States, the Antimonopoly Law of 1947 in Japan, and Articles 85 and 86 of the European Community Treaty (plus individual national laws in Europe). **Dumping** is a particular monopolistic practice that has led to government action in the 1980s and 1990s, when Japanese firms took leading market positions in many industries and countries. To constrain Japanese MNEs from dumping their products at prices below cost, the US and Western European governments enacted penalty tariffs, fines, and so on. If additional industries become dominated by groups of MNEs, the industrialized countries will undoubtedly pay increasing attention to antitrust problems.

Other Concerns

The four concerns just considered are not always the most important, but they arise repeatedly in discussions about regulating MNEs and are often central to both company and government interests. Additional concerns, such as the protection of local firms and the involvement of government-owned companies, were discussed in the previous section. A handful of other concerns merit mention here.

First, we should note the issue of **sovereignty.** While this concern is much more prominent among the LDCs, it has important implications in ICs as well. Canada, for example, has traditionally pursued a very difficult path between allowing US-based MNEs to dominate the economy and limiting their activities, thus creating economic tensions with the United States. In the late 1970s and early 1980s, Canada used the Foreign Investment Review Agency to evaluate foreign direct investment proposals, and the agency rejected a large number of them. In 1985, this protectionist policy was replaced by the Investment Canada program, which sought to attract more direct investment (and consequent jobs and income) and allowed more foreign control of the economy.[7] Although not going to Canada's earlier extreme, all industrialized countries limit foreign ownership and other forms of participation in key industries such as national defense, telecommunications services, and the postal service. Each of these limitations can be viewed as an attempt by the national government to preserve sovereignty over the national economy.

A second concern is **information disclosure.** Each country requires disclosure of some types of information by firms doing business there. MNEs are constantly being asked to provide information about foreign operations to national governments that want to assess taxes, limit unfair practices, and even protect consumers and investors. MNEs often argue that the information requested is overly expensive to collect and report and/or that it could be used by competitors if disclosed. A related concern is **information transfer** across national borders. National governments are seeking to judge the importance of transborder data flows, especially within MNEs. Such transfers place information that could be sensitive to national interests in the hands of company decision makers in other countries; the full implications of this concern remain to be seen.[8]

Additional concerns such as pollution control, consumer protection, and labor protection sometimes present major hurdles for MNE managers, but they are usually not aimed specifically at MNEs; rather, they are directed at all firms operating in the given country.

ENTRY AND OPERATING STRATEGIES FOR MNEs

Entry Strategies

General entry strategies were presented in Chapter 2 and specific strategies for exporters in Chapter 18. This section raises a few additional points with respect to entry into industrialized countries. While conditions differ to some extent across industrialized countries, the main factor in determining an **entry strategy** is usually *competition*. That is, the choice of a country, a product, and an entry mode (see Figure 18–1) depends on the kind of competition the firm faces in each country.

In the television industry, for example, competition takes place among a half-dozen or so major manufacturers, whose plants are located in countries or regions with low-cost labor, plus many additional firms that buy televisions from the primary manufacturers and sell them through retail outlets, sometimes under their own brand names. Entry into the market of, say, Belgium, would most likely be through exports from a low-cost factory in another country. Whether the exports will be sold by the manufacturer itself or through a secondary firm and its retail network must still be determined. Sony, Panasonic, General Electric/RCA, and Siemens have entered through the establishment of sales offices and through direct sales to retailers, in both cases under their own brand names. Other firms sell televisions to retail stores, which place their own brands on the TVs and market them through their own channels. Virtually no manufacture of televisions takes place in Belgium.

There are no restrictions on foreign-owned television manufacturers that want to enter the Belgian market. Such firms must follow the same rules as local firms and must compete with imports or local production. Since competition is very strong in this industry, a firm might consider setting up local production in exchange for some form of government protection. Such a strategy would probably be wasted, however, because the European Union countries would continue to have free access to the Belgian market and any subsidy offered to one firm would be protested by other suppliers. Since the principle of free competition is clearly established in Belgium, a television maker would be concerned mainly with minimizing the delivered cost of getting the TVs to the market and with maintaining the quality of the product relative to the others that are available. Seeking government protection would most likely not be a viable strategy in this case.

The choice between entering with an owned affiliate and contracting with another firm to make the product or deliver the service raises another interesting problem. If we assume the firm is from North America or Japan, then producing in, say, the French market constitutes an entry into the European Union. If the firm does not specify the contract carefully enough, the French contractee may be able to use the product or service in other EU countries in ways detrimental to the supplier firm's overall strategy.

For example, if a small Japanese manufacturer of computer circuit boards chooses to produce and sell in France through a licensee, that licensee may want to serve the entire European Union. Unless the contract is written restrictively enough, the licensee may have the right to do so, even if the Japanese manufacturer wants to set up its own plant in Italy or elsewhere in the EU for a similar purpose. The initial manufacturer may find that France's participation in the EU requires an "EU strategy" rather than a strategy for the French market alone.

In fact, for the competitive reasons just discussed, the OECD countries can be usefully divided into North America, the European Union, and Japan (ignoring Australia and New Zealand). Within each of these areas, few legal barriers to trade and other transborder business activities exist, and transportation costs are very low compared to the costs of interregional transport. In addition, there are few cultural barriers between the United States and Canada in North America, though often substantial cultural barriers exist among countries in Europe. Another barrier to interregional business that should be noted is the difference in time zones: North America crosses six time zones, and the European Union crosses three. Japan, in contrast, is in only one time zone, and that one has very little overlap of business hours with the other two regions. None of these points is an absolute barrier to interregional business, but they all tend to make firms view North America, Europe, and Japan as three separate markets.[9]

Operating Strategies

Assuming the entry strategy chosen is an owned affiliate, the firm must next consider the operating details. Given that government protection is not likely to be a viable option in many cases, the firm will need to compete on the basis of cost, product differentiation, or market segmentation. All three of these strategies were discussed previously: following are examples to illustrate them.

Cost minimization strategies have been widely followed by domestic firms as well as MNEs. During the past half-century, many US firms have moved production from the industrial Northeast to lower-cost locations in the South. During the late 1970s and the 1980s, dozens of European and Japanese firms set up manufacturing in South Carolina, Georgia, and other Southern states, because these states had a cost advantage over Michigan, Pennsylvania, and other Northern states but still offered access to the entire US market.

For similar reasons, Monsanto, Dow, Ciba-Geigy, ICI, and several other multinational chemical companies have chosen to manufacture basic chemicals in Northern Ireland. This politically risky location has the advantages of low-cost labor (relative to the rest of the EU) and a government incentive program that further reduces costs. In this case, where production costs are the key competitive variable, firms have been able to operate a European strategy with a supply of basic chemicals from their plants in Northern Ireland. Of course, other costs such as transportation and communication are also low compared to what they would be from production sites outside the EU.

The strategy of *product differentiation* plays a very important role in the industrialized countries, where consumers have relatively large amounts of discretionary income to spend on both necessities and luxury items. Not only can

McDonald's, Burger King, and Wendy's succeed as fast-food outlets, but, with different food items and pricing strategies, so can Wimpy's, Kentucky Fried Chicken, and Arby's. Entry into the US market for this type of store still offers possibilities to additional participants as long as they can sufficiently differentiate their menus and other characteristics to attract customers. The fast-food concept swept the United States first, but the other ICs have accepted it as well hence opportunities exist in Tokyo and Rome too.

Product differentiation by country or region is a strategy followed by automobile manufacturers such as General Motors and Ford. These two companies have introduced different models in their European affiliates than those they sell in the United States and Japan. Both Ford and GM have introduced "world cars" that they sell in both Europe and North America, but they also produce many models that they sell within only one or a few countries. In fact, they sell virtually all of their North American models only in the Western Hemisphere, and GM imports none of its Opel and Vauxhall models into this area.

Finally, *market segmentation* is a useful strategy in industrialized countries, whose markets are generally much larger than those in LDCs. Even when large competitors dominate markets for thousands of products, smaller firms or competitors not yet in the market can often find a niche for their sales.

DEALING WITH THE GOVERNMENTS OF INDUSTRIALIZED COUNTRIES

Much of the discussion in this chapter has focused on the central importance of competition in determining business opportunities and problems in the industrialized countries. It is also true, however, that the governments of industrialized countries impose highly detailed rules on some industries (such as defense-related ones) and operate companies in others (such as utilities). Also, the government sector typically constitutes more than one-fourth of the total economy; thus, the government is a huge consumer in each industrialized nation. In this section, we look at some of the central issues of government-business relations during the current decade.

Probably the most contentious issues in the 1990s in government-MNE relations are:

- MNE decisions to locate production facilities, often made to minimize costs, that shift production and jobs away from high-cost countries.
- MNE financial policies that affect a country's BOP and taxes, such as transfer pricing and other funds transfer strategies.
- MNE allocations of markets to affiliates, which are then limited to serving only some markets and thus may not respond to national efforts to stimulate exports or restrict dealings with specific countries.
- Overshadowing all of the above points, the multinationality of MNEs versus the uninationality of governments, which some governments argue creates unequal bargaining power in favor of MNEs.

Successful dealings with host and home governments require careful consideration of both sides of these issues. The MNE manager, while needing to pursue the goals of the firm, must be aware of the government's goals as well and recognize the government's sovereign right to set rules that seek to achieve those goals.

The MNE's decision to move production to low-cost locations has become an increasingly crucial issue in the 1990s. US-based firms have faced substantial criticism for using *offshore production* in the electronics, clothing, automobile, and many other industries. Because MNEs can consider many national locations for production while governments can regulate only one, there is an essential imbalance in positions between the two. A fundamental step for MNEs is to demonstrate clearly either (*a*) that employment is not lost through offshore manufacture but merely shifted into other tasks (e.g., the production of other products or more white-collar activities in the firm) or (*b*) that the employment would have been lost anyway due to less costly foreign production by firms of other countries. Both of these contentions are difficult to prove; thus, the tension between government and MNE remains.

On the issue of *financial transfers*, for example, the MNE manager typically wants to minimize the tax burden paid on transfers and to take advantage of the ability to move funds where the firm needs them. But when a country faces a balance-of-payments problem due to a trade deficit and/or capital outflows based on expectations that the currency will devalue, the MNE's funds transfers may add to the problem. There is no simple solution to this conflict, although the MNE can seek to improve government relations by exporting to other affiliates, importing less into the country, reducing funds outflows, and generally looking for ways to help the country's BOP. Such a strategy might ward off government policies that would constrain the MNE much more significantly.

Market allocation by MNEs limits a government's ability to push companies into greater exporting or other domestic or overseas activities. Typically, the MNE uses a local subsidiary to supply the local market but not to supply its operations in other countries. For example, if the Canadian government wants to stimulate exports, it would probably find it difficult to convince the affiliates of US companies that they should ship products to the United States, whose needs the parent firm is already supplies. This problem becomes especially acute when the affiliate is a joint venture and the partner firm perceives itself as constrained from exports that would add to the joint venture's profitability. Again, the issue is not simple to manage. Perhaps the best alternative for the MNE is to consider ways the affiliate could export without too greatly affecting the firm's global strategy. Then government relations might be enhanced at a low cost to the firm.

Finally, the basic issue is *multinationality*. An MNE is bound to follow the rules in any country where it does business. However, it is not tied down by the laws and conditions in one country, because it also does business in other countries. When difficulties arise in one country, the MNE may be able to shift some or all of its business activities to another. Since a government cannot pursue an MNE into another nation's jurisdiction, a situation of unequal power exists. However, as Vernon (1977), Behrman & Grosse (1990), and others have noted, MNEs are not free to ignore governments; if an MNE wants to do business within a government's jurisdiction, it will have to follow the demands of that government. Sovereignty is not at bay. As additional questions about the transnational dealings of MNEs arise, MNE managers will need to develop responsive strategies to government demands rather than utilizing multinationality as a tool to avoid them.

EXAMPLE: COMPETING IN JAPAN

Overview

Since Japanese and American firms will continue to become more directly competitive in the years ahead and both Japan and the United States are highly desirable target markets in terms of size and per capita incomes, managers from both countries will benefit from a better understanding of the functioning of each other's business system. This section lays a simple foundation for starting to understand the Japanese system; additional insights about human resource management in Japanese firms were offered in Chapters 16 and 17, and several excellent references on the issues are cited at the end of this chapter.

Since a detailed analysis of Japan's business system is not possible here, our approach is to discuss several key aspects of Japanese business that confront foreign firms seeking to operate in Japan. First, we discuss the largest and most important companies and industry groups; next, we note key aspects of Japan's indicative planning process (i.e., the government-business relationship); finally, we consider some competitive strategies for foreign firms.

Major Local Competitors

Major local competitors for virtually any foreign firm operating in Japan are the six largest trading companies, the **sogo shosha,** and their related networks of firms. These few firms account for about one-fifth of Japan's GNP and for about one-third of Japan's imports and exports. Table 20–4 lists the six *sogo shosha* and some of their characteristics. These firms follow in the tradition of the pre–World War II **zaibatsu,** Japanese holding companies that owned or otherwise controlled hundreds of affiliated firms in manufacturing, finance, and other business areas. The *zaibatsu* dominated Japanese business at that time, but they were forcibly dissolved as a result of the war and the subsequent Allied occupation. While many of the *zaibatsu* were effectively split up, a few retained business ties and in the 1950s redeveloped some of their ownership ties. This led to the reconstitution of the two largest groups around their original core firms, Mitsubishi and Mitsui.

Additional networks of firms formed around a number of large industrial corporations, such as C Itoh and Marubeni in textiles and Nissho-Iwai in metals, as well as around banks, such as Fuyo (Fuji) and Sanwa. All of these groups once again established their **keiretsu,** affiliating large numbers of suppliers, intermediaries, and other related firms into industrial power centers. A distinguishing characteristic of the postwar groups has been their extensive expansion into international business through the creation of trading companies, the *sogo shosha*. Today the dominant form of business entity in Japan is the industrial

TABLE 20–4 The Six Largest Sogo Shosha in Japan

Name	1992 Sales ($ million)	Major Industries
Mitsui & Co. Ltd.	153,737	Chemicals, energy, steel, food products
Mitsubishi Corp.	145,476	Oil, industrial products, financial services, computers, communications
C Itoh & Co.	157,106	Banking, electronics, textiles, oil, metals
Sumitomo Corp.	147,631	Steel, chemicals, precious metals, communications, oil
Marubeni Corp.	144,282	Textiles, machinery, steel, food products
Nissho Iwai Corp.	100,825	Banking, steel, aircraft, machinery, ships, lumber, rolling stock

Source: *Business Rankings Annual,* 1993, p. 210; Dun & Bradstreet, 1992, p. 93.

group, linked by ownership and business ties to a *sogo shosha* rather than to a family-related *zaibatsu.* The *sogo shosha* function as marketing arms for the affiliated firms of the *keiretsu,* seeking sales at home and abroad as opportunities are uncovered. Figure 20–2 sketches some of the relationships among members of the largest *keiretsu,* the Mitsubishi group of companies. Note that the central components of the chain are the trading company, which provides markets and information for the group; the banks, which provide financing for the group; and a large number of manufacturing companies, which provide the main products sold by the group.

The Japanese trading companies and their associated *keiretsu* pose a very real threat to potential foreign competitors, since they control a large portion of Japan's distribution channels and operate cooperatively among many of the country's manufacturers, banks, and so on.

Government-Business Relations

Relations between the government and private sector firms have developed far more cooperatively in Japan than in the United States. While the private sector does own and operate most of Japan's business system, government policy is often used to support chosen industries and firms. Historically, government policy has been inward looking as far as production is concerned and outward looking with respect to sources of supply. (Since Japan is not blessed with many fossil fuels or other minerals, oil, coal, iron, and so on must be imported, and export markets must generate funds to pay for these imports.)

The government agency responsible for implementing Japan's industrial policy is the **Ministry of International Trade and Industry (MITI).** After World War II, this agency was given responsibility for instituting a plan of economic development focusing on four major industries: electric power, steel, shipbuilding, and fertilizers. By setting up a system of incentives to prompt investment in these industries and assist the successful firms in entering export markets, as well as a strict system of protection against competitive imports, MITI contributed substantially to Japan's "economic miracle" after the war. During the 1950s and 1960s, GNP grew about twice as fast in Japan as in the most dynamic of the other industrialized countries.

In more recent years, MITI has maintained its role as a primary agent of indicative industrial policy, offering incentives to push business into desired activities, especially to stimulate investment in targeted industries such as chemicals and computers. The policies of protectionism have been largely dismantled; today Japan is no more protectionist than other industrialized nations.

MITI has historically dealt with business as a partner in development rather than as an antagonist. (There is frequent movement of managers from private sector corporations into MITI and from MITI back to the private sector.) MITI tends to be highly supportive rather than distrustful of the private sector. This cooperative relationship has been noted widely as a reason for Japan's superior ability to put national economic resources into leading ("sunrise") industries and to avoid overcommitment to declining ("sunset") industries. MITI officials frequently meet with company managers in selected firms and industries to discuss business needs, government goals, and ways to cooperate. All in all, Japan's system of indicative planning has functioned very successfully during the past 40 years.

FIGURE 20-2 The Mitsubishi *Keiretsu*

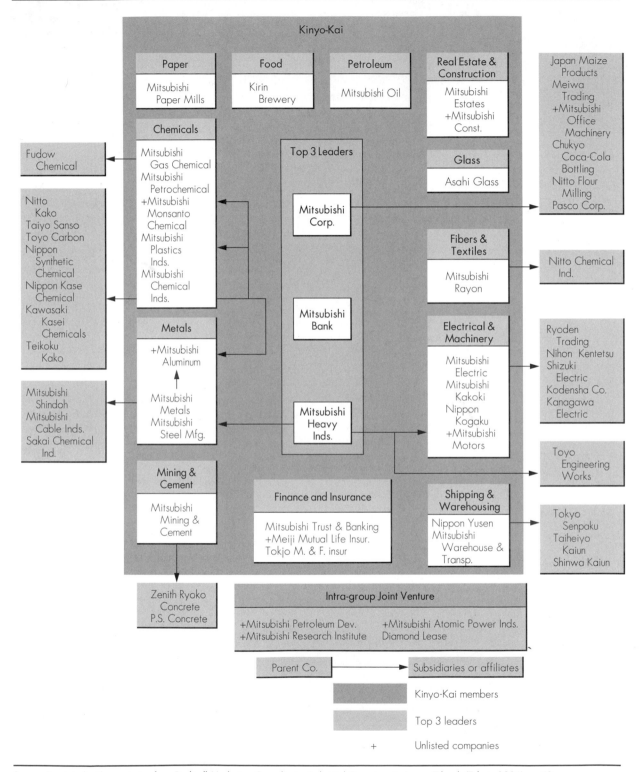

Source: Reprinted with permission from Dadwell Marketing Consultants, *Industrial Groupings in Japan*, 7th ed. (Tokyo, 1986), p. 48.

Successful Competitive Strategies

In the 1980s, foreign firms entering Japan found that the legal restrictions were not overwhelming, but the cultural barriers were. The language is a major hurdle—Japanese is only remotely related to the Indo-European languages such as English, French, and German—and the highly homogeneous society is quite inwardly biased. Japanese consumers tend to prefer to buy from domestic suppliers and to reject foreign goods in general. This presents a huge barrier to the foreign exporter or direct investor.

One extensively used strategy has been the **joint venture** with a Japanese partner. By linking up with a local firm that belongs to one of the key *keiretsu,* a foreign firm can obtain distribution and promotion support that would be totally unavailable to the independent firm. By taking on a Japanese name, the foreign firm may avoid the negative customer reaction that prevails throughout the country. Finally, by working really closely with a Japanese partner, the foreign firm may be able to absorb some of the managerial and technical expertise that has enabled many Japanese firms to succeed around the world in recent years.

Another strategy that has proven successful in Japan is the **licensing** of a Japanese firm to use the foreign firm's proprietary technology. After World War II, when the Japanese government restricted domestic industries to local participants, this was the only way (except for exporting) the Japanese market could be entered. Foreign direct investment has been permitted increasingly freely since the 1960s, but licensing continues to offer a low-cost alternative. The main advantage of licensing is that it allows immediate market entry without the start-up costs of setting up production, distribution and so on. The main disadvantages are that earnings are limited to the licensing fee and the proprietary technology must be given up to the licensee.

A **sequential entry strategy** might offer better results. In this strategy, the firm uses licensing to gain some knowledge about the Japanese market and subsequently sets up its own local manufacturing or service facilities. (IBM initially entered the Japanese market through licensing agreements with various local firms in the 1950s. When the prohibition on FDI was lifted, IBM was able to enter with its own operations, and today it is one of the most successful foreign firms in Japan.)

Another strategy that has become very common during the past decade is the formation of **strategic alliances** with Japanese firms to gain market entry. These agreements include joint marketing accords, in which the foreign company sells its (branded) products through the Japanese partner and the Japanese firm sells its products in Europe and/or North America through the foreign partner. This kind of arrangement has been followed by a number of pharmaceuticals companies, including Eli Lilly (with Fujisawa), Merck, and SmithKline. Similarly, Nissan markets Volkswagens in Japan, while Volkswagen sells Nissan four-wheel drive vehicles in Europe. Other strategic alliances include joint production facilities (PPG and Asahi Glass), joint research projects (GE with Toshiba and Hitachi), and other associations that can be devised and organized.

In sum, all of the basic market entry strategies discussed in this book are now generally possible in Japan. The difficulties most foreign firms have encountered lie much more in the areas of product acceptability, distribution, promotion, and so on—fundamental business considerations—than in the area of government regulation. Japan's market, while very large and very affluent, presents major barriers of cultural and geographic distance from the experience of European and American firms.

CONCLUSIONS

Doing business in industrialized countries is the main concern of most MNEs today. Problems in LDCs or formerly communist countries may be more visible and more difficult, but most of the international business carried out today is between industrialized nations. These countries have market-based economies that permit many MNE activities. In fact, the main problem generally faced by firms in the industrialized countries is competition from other firms.

While government-owned companies exist in every IC, the private sector plays a very large role in the economy. Government policies tend to be procompetition; they limit the activities of business mainly to ensure that both local firms and MNEs deal fairly in matters of employment, pricing, taxpaying, and so on. In industrialized countries, dealing with governments is largely the same for both local and foreign firms. A key concern in government relations is that MNEs are multinational, while governments are only uninational. This concern has led governments to share information about MNEs among themselves, harmonize some of their policies that relate to MNEs, and require that MNEs provide more information about their operations.

Strategies for doing business in ICs focus mainly on creating solid competitive positions. The basic strategies include cost minimization, product differentiation, and market segmentation.

QUESTIONS

1. Define *industrialized country*. Does Norway fit into your definition? Does Spain? How about Kuwait? What would be an appropriate definition of industrialization?

2. Which countries are the most developed today? Which ones do you think will be the most developed by the year 2000? Why?

3. What are the general differences between the French and US business systems? What are the particular differences between these systems with respect to the treatment of MNEs?

4. How do IC governments participate directly in business? What implications does this situation have for the MNE manager?

5. Name four main concerns of IC governments in dealing with foreign multinational firms. What can the firms do to minimize tensions with the host governments with regard to each concern?

6. Name four main concerns of IC governments in dealing with MNEs based in their own countries. What can the firms do to minimize tensions with the home governments with regard to each concern?

7. What problems would arise for multinational firms if transborder transmission of information were restricted, as has been proposed in recent government discussions? How could MNEs cope with these problems?

8. Present three broad operating strategies for MNE affiliates in industrialized countries. Which of these strategies would have been appropriate for Monsanto Chemical Corporation when it sought to enter the European Union?

9. Explain the imbalance of power between MNEs and national governments due to the fact that the MNEs can operate in several countries, whereas the national governments are limited to their own jurisdictions.

10. Create a market entry strategy for a small German textile manufacturing company that wants to enter the US market for synthetic fabrics. Make necessary (reasonable) assumptions so that your answer covers the organizational form of the venture, the channels of distribution, the structure of decision making in the firm, financial concerns, and any other issues you believe are important.

REFERENCES

Behrman, Jack, and Robert Grosse. *International Business and Governments*. Columbia, SC: University of South Carolina Press, 1990.

Bergsten, C Fred; Thomas Horst; and Theodore Moran. *American Multinationals and American Interests*. Washington, DC: Brookings Institution, 1978.

Boyer, Edward. "How Japan Manages Declining Industries." *Fortune,* January 10, 1983.

Gladwin, Thomas, and Ingo Walter. *Multinationals under Fire*. New York: John Wiley & Sons, 1980.

Grosse, Robert. *Foreign Investment Codes and the Location of Direct Investment*. New York: Praeger Publishers, 1980.

Hirschmeier, J, and T Yui. *The Development of Japanese Business*. 2nd ed. London: Allen & Unwin, 1981.

Ohmae, Kenichi. *The Borderless World*. New York: Harper Business, 1990.

Organization for Economic Cooperation and Development. *Declaration on International Investment and Multinational Enterprises*. Paris: OECD, 1976.

Safarian, A E. *Governments and Multinationals: Policies in the Developed Countries*. Washington, DC: British–North American Committee, 1983.

United Nations. *National Legislation and Regulations Relating to Transnational Corporations*. New York: UN Center on Transnational Corporations, 1983.

Vernon, Raymond. *Storm over the Multinationals*. Cambridge, MA: Harvard University Press, 1977.

NOTES

[1] Until recently, it also was possible to distinguish the industrialized countries from the other groups because of their freely elected, democratic governments. Since the international debt crisis of the early 1980s and the fall of the Berlin Wall, most of the countries in all three groups are democracies today.

[2] The OECD is an organization that groups the industrialized countries of the world plus a few LDCs, such as Turkey and Portugal. The organization provides a forum for the rich countries to cooperate on issues of concern: improving education and social services, harmonizing policies such as those on MNEs, and so on. The OECD was founded in the early 1950s and is headquartered in Paris.

[3] Organization for Economic Cooperation and Development, *Declaration on International Investment and Multinational Enterprises* (Paris: OECD, 1976), sec. 2.

[4] This, of course, is easier said than done. Language and other cultural differences hinder the creation of a true EU-wide labor market.

[5] See "Beyond Unions," *Business Week,* July 8, 1985, pp. 72 ff.

[6] See *The Miami Herald,* May 26, 1985, p. 3F, for a listing of the taxes paid by 200 of the largest US corporations in 1984.

[7] See the "Investment Canada Act," *Investment Canada Regulations*. Ottawa: Government of Canada, 1986 [S.C., 1985, c. 20.]. This issue has been further shifted since Canada joined the United States and Mexico in NAFTA, which reduces restrictions on MNEs operating across all three countries.

[8] The issue of regulating transborder transfers of information has led to OECD and United Nations efforts to establish a code of conduct. See, for example, the United Nations Center on Transnational Corporations, *The CTC Reporter* (latest issue).

[9] The overwhelming concentration of international business in these three groups of countries is analyzed in Kenichi Ohmae, *Triad Power* (New York: The Free Press, 1985).

Case

Morioka Manufacturing Company

Introduction

During the 1970s and 1980s, worldwide attention focused on the successes of Japanese firms doing business in the United States, Europe, and elsewhere. Nissan, Toyota, Honda, NEC, Sanyo, Panasonic, and numerous other Japanese brand names have become household words throughout the world. Only two or three decades ago, the largest and most successful international firms came almost exclusively from the United States and Western Europe. How have the Japanese attained such an impressive position in world markets?

As we already saw in "The US Steel Industry" case, the Japanese steel manufacturers are currently exceeding their American and European competitors in labor productivity and in reducing production costs. In addition, in many industries the quality of Japanese products is perceived to be better than that of firms from other countries. Companies that want to compete successfully against the Japanese will need to achieve similar results in their own business activities. This case focuses on the issue of labor productivity, using the Japanese model as a basis for the discussion.

Japanese-style management has been widely analyzed, from its emphasis on long-term employment to its concept of consultative decision making. The central issue in all of the analyses is that Japanese firms appear to pay more attention to *human resources* (i.e., the people who work in the firm) than do firms from other countries. Among the policies Japanese firms use for human resource management are these four key elements:

1. Long-term employment
2. Slow performance evaluation and promotion
3. Generalist career paths
4. Consultative decision making

Since World War II, large industrial corporations in Japan have followed a practice of hiring their employees and managers directly from high school or college, then keeping them employed throughout their careers within the same firm. Very little mobility exists between companies, since Japanese society has come to expect that a person will remain with the same employer until retirement. A very positive aspect of this practice is that it provides job security for

---

This case was written by Professor Robert Grosse as a basis for class discussion. Revised 1994.

everyone in the firm; thus, individuals tend to identify their own interests more closely with those of the company, which must perform well if their jobs are to be protected. Also, the company can justify expenditures on employee training, knowing that employees will remain and benefit the company with their increased skills. The negative aspect (from a Western point of view) is that few socially acceptable choices exist for someone who wishes to change companies during a career, regardless of the reason.

By giving careful evaluation to each employee and manager, Japanese firms demonstrate a sense of caring for the person. Also, by promoting managers through the ranks of management very slowly, the firm conveys to all that long-term performance is what counts. Even after the long initial period, ranks tend to be equal among people with similar seniority, although tasks and compensation become differentiated according to performance. People "save face" by maintaining equal rank with others in their cohort through the years, while the firm is managed capably by assigning the key decisions to those who demonstrate the greatest ability to handle them.

A third characteristic of Japanese human resource management is the use of a generalist career path. That is, Japanese workers and managers are trained in one area of specialization when they join the firm, then rotated among assignments and specializations during their careers so that everyone learns several job skills. Someone hired as a financial analyst may be shifted into the personnel department after four or five years and into government-business relations after that. A worker who spends all or most of his or her time on an assembly line may be moved into repair work and subsequently into another type of assembly-line activity. This policy enhances the flexibility of the firm, because people can be shifted from job to job. It also enables the firm to operate more efficiently by imparting more skills to managers and workers. Thus, no one becomes overspecialized, and everyone spends some time in areas outside the initial area of specialization, although a worker or manager may return to a preferred specialty after spending time working in other areas.

Finally (in this brief sketch), Japanese firms use a system of consultative decision making, which attempts to pass information about important company activities from the top managers all the way down to the lowest-ranking workers. In particular, decisions that will affect employees in any area of the firm are discussed with those people *before* the decision is made; thus, the affected workers and managers can voice their opinions and concerns before a problem arises. (For example, an auto company will distribute information about a proposed new assembly line so that workers affected by the change will be able to see its impact on them and discuss it with their superiors before the change is made.) Because top managers have been rotated through several functional areas of the company, they tend to understand the concerns of people at lower levels and to be responsive to them. Because all employees involved in the decision have the opportunity to raise concerns about potential problems, the firm can avoid errors that would otherwise occur. Ultimately, top management must take responsibility for decisions. Therefore, this process does not imply that everyone has equal say in decision making. It is the conscious effort to create communication from bottom to top and from top to bottom in the firm; this information flow enables managers to make better decisions that are so crucial here.

Other aspects of Japanese human resource management could be noted, but those already discussed give a good idea of the basic differences between those firms and their competitors from other countries. One major subject of discussion by managers in the United States during the past few years has been the possibility of transferring some of the Japanese style to US firms. Are people from different countries and cultures similar enough that Japanese practices can be used elsewhere? An illustration of these issues follows.

The Case

Morioka Manufacturing Company (also known as 2M) is a fairly typical large Japanese corporation that makes abrasives for automobile and industrial clutches, grinding and sanding machines, and specialized polishing equipment. In 1985, the company had about a 70 percent market share in Japan and had gained almost 25 percent shares in most Western European countries and in North America. Total worldwide sales were over 250 billion yen in 1984.

2M was evaluating a proposal to acquire a factory formerly operated by Bendix Corporation in California. The factory produced industrial clutches, which Bendix sold to a variety of companies for use in industrial machinery. Because the factory shut down only last year, almost half of the 300 workers formerly employed there would be available to work for 2M. Yoshi Hajima, the director of 2M's International Division, was wondering about the advisability of investing in the United States at all. He knew the political pressure on Japan to import more US goods and to invest in the United States to provide more American jobs was strong and most likely would continue through the rest of the decade. 2M could face limitations on its exports to the US market at any time. Since that market now provided about 40 percent of the company's worldwide sales, maintaining US business was critical.

The Bendix factory was not completely outmoded, but it would require substantial investment to upgrade the machinery. The location in California was not a problem for US sales because of the excellent transportation system in the United States. In fact, the whole idea had only one negative aspect. Hajima had seen various studies that showed an enormous productivity gap between output per worker in Japan and in the United States. He was not excited about the prospect of dealing with Americans, even though there was no current threat of a union fight (that is, an effort by workers to organize a union to demand better treatment by management). Other Japanese firms had successfully invested in the US market, though very few had achieved anything near the productivity levels of their Japanese operations.

Hajima was most concerned about the need to establish a positive, enjoyable atmosphere in the workplace. He had grown up in such an environment and felt complete loyalty to the company that had supported him. He wondered if the US workers, with their average annual turnover rate of almost 10 percent in the chemical industry, could possibly achieve a harmonious relationship with managers and staff that would lead to some degree of company loyalty at 2M in California. He was somewhat encouraged by the telephone conversation he had with a friend at Mitsui's office in San Francisco. The friend had found that the American workers at Mitsui were generally very happy to try many of the Japanese practices, and indeed turnover there was much lower than in comparable US firms. Still, Hajima was skeptical.

Perhaps the largest difference between the Americans and the Japanese workers with whom Hajima was familiar was the American social preference for rugged individualists versus the Japanese emphasis on commitment to the team (or company) and group achievement. He did not think the American workers would readily join company-sponsored social groups or do group exercises before work, as in Japan. Though quality circles had shown some promise of acceptance and positive results in American firms, Hajima did not believe this was enough to generate the needed level of commitment to the firm. With only a fair understanding of English, he felt quite uncomfortable trying to assess the situation and reach a decision.

21

Less Developed and Formerly Communist Countries

This chapter examines business conditions and opportunities for international firms that seek to operate in less developed countries (LDCs) and in the formerly communist countries. First, we present the characteristics of LDCs; this is no simple task, since LDCs include countries ranging from relatively high-income Korea and Singapore all the way to very low-income Bangladesh and Ethiopia, with governments ranging from elected socialist and capitalist regimes to military dictatorships. Second, we examine the former Soviet bloc countries; this task is complicated by the unsettled state of both economic and political affairs in the region. The main goals of the chapter are to:

1. Demonstrate important characteristics of less developed and formerly communist countries for international firms.

2. Describe the kinds of international business that are common and appropriate in these countries.

3. Examine concerns and government policies that relate to foreign MNEs.

4. Consider the entry and operating strategies that international firms can use in these countries.

Hundreds of Muscovites waited to order food from the first McDonald's restaurant that opened in the former Soviet Union in 1990.
©Reuters/Bettmann

INTRODUCTION

While no brief discussion of business conditions, policies, and opportunities in less developed countries (LDCs) can hope to offer detailed insights into particular countries, this chapter aims to raise the key issues facing foreign firms that want to do business in Latin America, Africa, and Asia. Business conditions are far from uniform in these countries, which range from newly industrializing nations such as Singapore and Taiwan in Asia to the poorest, least developed African nations such as Ethiopia and Uganda, with most of Latin America somewhere in between. International firms in these countries engage in the full range of business activities, though a large part of their activities involves extractive industries and manufacturing assembly operations for exporting products to the industrialized countries.

This section provides a definition of less developed countries and a brief commentary on the main kinds of international business found in such countries. The next section presents similar information about the former Soviet bloc countries. The third section discusses key aspects of LDC and former communist countries' political and economic environments that particularly relate to MNE activities. The fourth section focuses on government policies and practices in dealing with foreign MNEs. The fifth and sixth sections present company strategies.

Definitions of Less Developed Countries

In principle, a **less developed country (LDC)** is one that is at a lower level of economic development than some other countries. This oversimplified definition simply recognizes that some countries are poorer than others and classifies them according to such measures as per capita income, average life expectancy, and average level of education. Since economic development continues to occur in all countries, the absolute measures of poverty, health, education, and so on continue to improve, though some countries remain in the bottom part of the distribution and others in the top part. That is, the measures of economic development themselves change as standards of living rise worldwide, but some countries must still be below the world average.

The World Bank uses a classification scheme that groups countries into four categories: low-income, lower-middle-income, upper-middle-income, and high-income economies. Table 21–1 describes selected countries from all three LDC categories along several dimensions.

Another classification scheme has been used by the United Nations, which grouped countries into developed economies, socialist economies, and developing countries. These categories group low- and middle-income countries together, with the exception of Eastern Europe and China, which were listed as socialist economies. The developed economies here are equivalent to the high-income economies in the World Bank grouping. This scheme simplifies the categories, but it also obscures the different situation of the key group of oil-exporting developing countries by placing them together with all other LDCs. It also fails to reflect the democratization of Eastern Europe.

Finally, the classification of **newly industrializing countries (NICs)** has arisen to describe the LDCs that have moved farthest along the road to industrialization. Most of these are Southeast Asian countries that have succeeded in attracting large amounts of foreign investment in manufacturing. MNEs from Japan, Europe, and North America (as well as locally based MNEs) use facilities in these countries to assemble electronic equipment, clothing, machinery, and

TABLE 21–1   Selected Countries Classified as LDCs by the World Bank

Country	GDP per Capita, 1991 (US $)	Growth Rate of GDP per Capita*	Average Annual Inflation (%/year)[†]	Average Unemployment (%), 1991	Current Account BOP, 1991 ($ millions)	Manufacturing as Percentage of Total GDP, 1991
Low-Income						
Ethiopia	110	1.4	2.4	N.A.	−222	9
Uganda	150	N.A.	N.A.	N.A.	−182	4
India	260	3.2	8.2	N.A.	−3,026	12
Kenya	290	1.9	9.2	N.A.	−231	12
China	320	9.4	5.8	2.3	13,272	38
Nigeria	350	1.9	18.1	N.A.	1,203	N.A.
Haiti	400	−0.7	7.9	N.A.	−11	N.A.
Egypt	570	4.8	12.5	N.A.	2,404	N.A.
Indonesia	640	5.6	8.5	N.A.	−4,080	21
Lower-Middle-Income						
Bolivia	690	0.3	263.4	7.3	−262	N.A.
Philippines	710	1.1	14.6	9	−1,034	26
Bulgaria	880	1.9	7.8	12	−718	N.A.
Romania	1,200	0.1	6.2	N.A.	−1,184	N.A.
Nicaragua	1,830	−1.9	583.7	14	−5	19
Poland	2,040	1.1	63.1	N.A.	−1,282	N.A.
Czechoslovakia	2,110	0.6	3.5	N.A.	947	N.A.
Upper-Middle-Income						
South Africa	2,340	1.3	14.4	8.6	2,664	25
Brazil	2,740	2.5	327.4	N.A.	−3,071	26
Hungary	2,990	0.6	3.5	6.6	403	29
Russia	3,220	N.A.	N.A.	0.04	5,100	N.A.
Mexico	3,390	1.2	66.5	2.6	−13,282	22
Argentina	3,500	−0.4	416.4	N.A.	−2,832	N.A.
South Korea	6,500	9.6	5.6	2.3	−8,726	28
Libya	N.A.	N.A.	0.2	N.A.	N.A.	N.A.
High-Income						
Saudi Arabia	7,060	−0.2	−2.4	N.A.	−25,738	7
Israel	12,790	1.7	89	10.6	−822	N.A.
Kuwait	N.A.	N.A.	−2.7	N.A.	N.A.	29
Singapore	14,280	6.6	1.9	1.9	4,208	29
United Arab Emirates	20,140	−6.3	1.1	N.A.	N.A.	N.A.

*Average annual rates during the period 1980–91.
[†]Average annual inflation during the period 1980–91.
Sources: World Bank, *World Development Report, 1993* (Washington, DC: World Bank, 1993); United Nations, *Statistical Yearbook, 1990/91* (New York: United Nations, 1993).

various other products. The attraction of these countries lies in their relatively high levels of education, low wages, and industrious work forces, all of which make local manufacturing profitable for domestic and foreign firms. Indeed, the phenomenal success of such ventures has led some people to contend that these countries, which they call the "Asian Challenge," will rival the United States and Japan for supremacy in manufacturing during the coming years.[1] Table 21–2 illuminates some key characteristics of the NICs.

TABLE 21–2   Development Indicators for NICs

Country	Indicator			
	GDP per Capita, 1991 (US $)	Annual Growth Rate of GDP per Capita, 1980–91	Exports as Percentage of GDP, 1991	FDI Inflow, 1992 (US $ millions)
Brazil	2,740	2.5	10	1454
Hong Kong	11,650	6.9	141	1918
Singapore	14,280	6.6	185	5635
South Korea	6,500	9.6	29	550

Sources: World Bank, *World Development Report, 1993* (Washington, DC: World Bank, 1993); International Monetary Fund, *Direction of Trade Statistics Yearbook, 1993* (Washington, DC: IMF, 1993); International Monetary Fund, *Balance of Payments Statistics Yearbook, 1993* (Washington, DC: IMF, 1993); United Nations, *World Investment Report,* (New York: United Nations, 1994).

Each classification scheme has useful aspects. Which scheme is best really depends on the type of presentation desired. For our purposes, we should note that important differences exist among oil-exporting LDCs, NICs, and other less developed countries and that one should be aware of these differences when using World Bank, United Nations, or other sources of information.

Definition of Eastern European Countries

When Mikhail Gorbachev began his program of *perestroika* (economic opening) in the Soviet Union in 1985, the process of transition toward market-based economic system in Eastern Europe began. In 1989, with the decisions of several Eastern European countries to form elected governments and break away from the Soviet bloc and the Soviet Union's decision not to interfere in this process, the "privatization" of the region began. The fall of the Berlin Wall, which separated East and West Germany, in November 1989 symbolized the full-scale opening of Eastern Europe to elected governments and to market-based economies in which MNEs can play a much wider role than before. The break-up of the Soviet Union in 1991 completed the initial process of opening.

The nations of concern in this section are the countries that formerly belonged to the Soviet bloc, plus the People's Republic of China. The definition of these countries is clear in this sense, though a lot of debate has occurred over whether the countries should be called Central Europe or Eastern Europe. Since the Soviet Union indeed formed most of what could be labeled Eastern Europe, the former label makes sense. Since the Cold War terminology of East/West division is such an accepted part of our vocabulary, this chapter continues with the label "Eastern Europe" for discussing the former Soviet bloc countries: Russia, Bulgaria, the Czech Republic, Hungary, Poland, Romania, and the others.

Selected countries in Eastern Europe plus China are listed in Table 21–1, along with some broad characteristics of their economies. While China alone comprises almost one-fourth of the world population, notice that it accounts for less than 5 percent of world GDP; China clearly is a less developed country. Also notice that the economies of the Eastern European countries have macroeconomic characteristics similar to those of their Western European neighbors, though with lower levels of per capita income, lower levels of international trade, and generally lower growth rates; these are clearly industrial countries.

During the period of the Cold War, business operated through government-owned and managed companies, with decisions on pricing and production levels largely determined by the central planning organs rather than by consumer demand. Free enterprise remains substantially limited in these countries even today, since the government sector still owns most business, and the transition to greater private sector participation is slow. However, this broad picture of the formerly communist countries fails to give an idea of the real possibilities that exist to carry out business with them. For that purpose, some evidence about the kinds of business that have taken place between MNEs and Eastern European countries in recent years will be useful.

Main Kinds of International Business in LDCs and Formerly Communist Countries

The international business activities carried out in LDCs are at least as varied as those performed in developed countries. These activities include exporting and importing, foreign direct investment, such contractual arrangements as licensing and franchising, and international banking. The most striking characteristic of much of this business is that it is generally far more *regulated* in LDCs than in industrialized countries. The limitations placed on foreign business in LDCs far surpass those imposed by industrialized countries. This point will be discussed in some detail in the section "Government Policies."

Another striking characteristic of international business in less developed countries is its relatively small size. LDCs comprise more than 80 percent of the world's population but only about 25 percent of international business. Tables in Chapters 2 and 3 illuminate this issue to some degree, showing that LDC exports and imports each constitute slightly less than one-third of the world total. (This measure can be divided between oil-exporting countries and other LDCs. In the early 1990s, the former had a substantial trade surplus and the latter faced a large trade deficit.)

As far as foreign direct investment is concerned, Table 21–3 shows the distribution of FDI in the countries listed previously. Probably not surprisingly, the largest amounts of FDI go to the largest economies, although the Southeast Asian NICs have attracted a disproportionate amount to their relatively small countries. Of total worldwide FDI, just under 25 percent is in LDCs, and about one-third of that is in manufacturing. The service sector has become the second largest recipient of FDI in LDCs. It replaced mining after the wave of nationalizations of oil properties and other mining ventures of MNEs during the 1960s and 1970s.

Until 1990, very few examples existed of Eastern European countries allowing foreign firms to hold controlling ownership of business ventures within their borders. Prior to this time, and even today in terms of the bulk of ventures, most international business involving Eastern European countries is carried out through nonequity methods such as exports and imports, licensing agreements, management contracts, countertrade, and turnkey ventures or through minority joint ventures.

While historical data about most business activities in Eastern Europe remain difficult to obtain, export and import information is relatively accessible. Until the end of the Cold War, most of the exports and imports in this region were shipped between Soviet bloc members; today trade with the rest of the world has opened up substantially, though principally with Germany and other European Union members.

Much of the imports into Eastern Europe consists of manufactured goods, especially high-tech electronics, instruments, chemicals, and the like. Grain shipments from the United States and Canada are also an important part of such

TABLE 21–3   Flows of Foreign Direct Investment in Selected Less Developed Countries (in millions of SDRs)

Country	1966–1971	1972–1977	1978–1983	1984–1989	1990–1992
Ethiopia	65	83	—	—	—
Uganda	24	–2	—	—	3
India	–42	–29	—	—	—
Haiti	0	33	48	38	22
China	226	—	—	9,575	13,266
Kenya	—	142	327	135	82
Bolivia	28	52	171	19	167
Indonesia	308	1,054	1,331	2,169	4,349
Egypt	—	130	2,922	5,707	1,368
Nigeria	683	1,822	1,021	3,781	2,197
Nicaragua	134	61	15	2	15*
Romania	—	—	—	—	92
Poland	—	—	—	28	1,052
Bulgaria	—	—	—	—	102
Czechoslovakia	—	—	—	—	1,846
Hungary	—	—	—	—	2,941†
South Korea	136	419	–15	1,849	–843
Brazil	922	6,155	11,181	6,985	1,502†
Mexico	1,466	2,746	7,444	9,230	12,656
South Africa	1,240	448	–1,529	–309	–18
Israel	178	375	–366	475	–565
Singapore	299	2,350	4,681	5,870	11,434
Libya	383	–1,631	–3,250	–50	—*
Saudi Arabia	–3	–1,730	17,207	4,210	2,024†
Kuwait	—	—	–438	–1,214	–539

*Data through 1991.
†Data 1991–1992 only.
Source: International Monetary Fund, *Balance of Payments Statistics* (Washington, DC: IMF Publications Unit, 1969, 1977, 1981, 1986, 1989 and 1993).

imports. Much of the exports from Eastern Europe consists of raw materials such as oil and natural gas (from the former Soviet Union) and a variety of relatively low-tech, low-cost manufactures. In recent years, exports of chemicals, food, textiles, and wood products from Eastern Europe to Western Europe have become very significant.

Although the use of **offshore assembly** to reduce production costs is becoming more and more common, such manufacturing counts for only a small part of total FDI at present. Even if we assume that all US FDI in Hong Kong, Singapore, South Korea, and Taiwan is for offshore assembly, it constitutes only about $4.2 billion of the total $US 29 billion in LDC manufacturing. The trend is dramatically upward, however, as shown by the fact that as recently as 1970, US manufacturing FDI in those countries was less than $US 270 million out of an LDC total of $US 5.5 billion.[2]

International bank lending to LDCs also grew dramatically during the 1970s and early 1980s. During the 1982–92 period, lending grew much more slowly as many LDCs moved through an external debt crisis and Eastern Europe restarted the process of market-based development. Table 21–4 shows the change in commercial bank loans to developing countries from 1976 through 1992. Notice

TABLE 21-4 Commercial Bank External Claims on Borrowers in LDCs, Selected Years (millions of US dollars of loans outstanding)

Country	December 1976	June 1982	December 1986	December 1989	December 1992
Ethiopia	18	41	135	163	269
Uganda	7	57	62	66	61
Nigeria	284	6,714	—	7,302	4,154
India	571	1,577	6,705	10,571	11,101
Kenya	102	830	828	1,365	1,316
China	506	1,295	6,552	17,977	30,198
Haiti	39	59	64	105	16
Indonesia	4,010	8,155	15,944	18,808	28,417
Bolivia	448	1,053	590	278	220
Philippines	2,953	—	13,857	9,666	6,873
Egypt	1,264	5,350	6,525	6,084	4,129
Nicaragua	634	796	503	388	832
Romania	—	—	3,059	194	1,361
Poland	—	—	10,246	10,039	12,363
Bulgaria	—	—	3,516	7,795	7,638
Czechoslovakia	—	—	3,197	5,377	5,037
Hungary	—	—	9,569	11,925	8,843
Mexico	17,885	64,395	70,840	59,746	53,866
Brazil	18,461	55,300	69,400	60,944	51,404
South Africa	7,624	14,125	15,618	13,854	13,283
Argentina	3,260	—	31,063	27,054	30,260
South Korea	3,701	19,994	15,618	23,291	38,812
Libya	148	830	698	910	465
Saudi Arabia	1,053	5,268	5,392	5,852	9,652
Singapore	9,168	33,690	87,545	108,806	147,814
Kuwait	939	6,274	5,840	5,683	8,309
Israel	2,033	6,126	5,243	3,507	3,061
United Arab Emirates	1,172	4,449	4,201	4,129	2,456
Hong Kong	7,485	34,003	99,051	136,968	163,523

Source: *Bank for International Settlements,* "Maturity Distribution of International Bank Lending" (Basel, Switzerland, June 1977, December 1982, June 1987, July 1990, and July 1993).

that the most internationally indebted countries are the large Latin American borrowers, followed by the newly industrializing countries. (This is somewhat misleading, because Hong Kong and Singapore are offshore banking centers, where large volumes of eurocurrency transactions take place separately from borrowing for domestic uses.) The countries that are least economically developed have attracted the least commercial bank financing (given their relatively low ability to generate foreign exchange to repay such loans). The Latin American countries experienced huge decreases in foreign credits during the 1980s, as they were unable to service that debt incurred earlier. Finally, note that the Arab OPEC countries incurred substantial foreign debt during 1982–92. This was certainly associated with the decline in the price of oil since 1981.

Joint ventures are another category of international business that has been growing between Eastern European partners and multinational firms from Western Europe, North America, and Japan. McDonald's restaurant in Moscow, which opened in 1990, is a good example of the new wave of foreign business entries that have begun to operate as foreign owned (in this case, 49 percent owned by

McDonald's Corporation). While full or majority ownership is still not commonly permitted to foreign firms, joint ventures are proliferating in Eastern Europe. A few examples of such ventures are listed in Table 21–5. Like the technology transfer agreements, these joint ventures tend to involve very large, experienced MNEs. Most of the joint ventures are very large, since the Eastern European governments have tended to prefer attracting a small number of foreign participants that can generate large amounts of production of known quality. This situation is changing as the countries open their economies to more foreign as well as domestic, private sector business under more kinds of agreements.

General Electric Company carried out one of the major joint ventures in Eastern Europe during the early 1990s with its purchase of 50 percent of the Hungarian lighting manufacturer, Tungsram. This $US 150 million investment gave GE a major foothold in the European market for lightbulbs, which GE has not served through local production for several decades. General Electric is using

TABLE 21–5   Joint Ventures between Western Companies and Eastern European Countries plus China

Company	Country	Name and Date of Joint Venture	Ownership (West/East)	Product
Agfa-Gevaert & Vienna Trade	Hungary	Asi (1990)	50/50	Market and service business equipment
Avibras Aerospacial (Brazil)	China	INSCOM (1989)	N.A.	Market communication satellite launching
Bouygues (France)	Bulgaria	Interstroy (1989)	N.A.	Commercial construction
Central Cooperative Bank (Austria)	Czechoslovakia	Gestin (1989)	N.A.	Tourism
Ciba Geigy	China	No name (1988)	N.A.	Pharmaceuticals
Fiat (Italy)	USSR	No name (1989)	30/70	Automobiles
GEC Plessey (Grt. Britain)	USSR	Comstar (1989)	N.A.	Telecommunications
Highmed System (Canada)	Hungary	Rolitron (1989)	N.A.	Dialysis equipment
Hyundai (South Korea)	USSR	No name (1990)	N.A.	Lumber production and ship repair
IKEA (Sweden)	Poland	No name (1989)	N.A.	Furniture
J L Forklift Tryk (Denmark)	Bulgaria	No name (1990)	50/50	Forklift trucks
Johnson & Johnson (US)	China	No name (1988)	N.A.	Bandages
Kiser Research (US)	Hungary	CompuDrug USA (1988)	N.A.	Computer software
Levi Strauss (US)	Hungary	No name (1988)	50.6/49.4	Clothing
McDonald's (US)	USSR	No name (1988)	49/51	Restaurants
Minolta (Austria)	USSR	Minolta Trading Ukraine (1990)	33/67	Service office equipment
Minolta Camera (Japan)	USSR	No name (1990)	N.A.	Copiers
Northern Telecom (Canada)	China	No name (1988)	N.A.	Communications equipment
Occidental Petroleum (US)	China	No name (1988)	55/45	Coal plant
Pepsico & McCormick (US)	China	No name (1988)	N.A.	Seasoning manufacturing
Philips (Netherlands)	Czechoslovakia	Avez (1989)	N.A.	VCRs
Rhone-Poulenc (France)	Hungary	Rhone Poulenc Agro Borsod (1990)	50/50	Plant production agent
Samsung (South Korea)	Hungary	No name (1988)	N.A.	Color TVs
Schwinn (US)	Hungary	No name (1989)	51/49	Bicycles
Senetek (Denmark)	Czechoslovakia	Tessek (1989)	N.A.	Chemicals
Siemens (Germany)	Yugoslavia	No name (1989)	N.A.	Telecommunications
Siemens (Germany)	Poland	No name (1990)	49/51	Digital exchanges
US West (US)	Hungary	No name (1990)	49/51	Cellular telephones
Valmet Paper (Finland)	China	No name (1988)	N.A.	Machinery
Warner Lambert (US)	China	No name (1989)	N.A.	Pharmaceutical capsules

Source: Paul Surovell (ed.), INTERFLO, 1988–1990.

the venture to serve both the domestic Hungarian market and the European market for lightbulbs from Tungsram's 12 manufacturing plants, adding to GE's European lighting business. Although the means of payment of dividends from Hungary was not known, it is likely that payment in lightbulbs that can be sold elsewhere in Europe would suit both GE's and Hungary's interests.

KEY CHARACTERISTICS RELATING TO MNEs

Government Involvement in Business

As in the industrial countries, the government sector in LDCs and formerly communist countries constitutes a substantial percentage of the total economy. Figure 21–1 shows estimates of the size of the public sector in selected LDCs. In fact, on average the government's activities account for a *smaller* portion of GDP than in the industrial countries (even when state-owned companies are included). This situation needs to be contrasted with the *regulatory* environment that confronts private sector firms in DCs and LDCs.

While such industrialized countries as France and Sweden have a very high degree of government participation in business through government-owned companies and highly regulated industries, most industrialized countries allow firms substantial freedom to operate as the market dictates. Among LDCs, in contrast, the exceptions are the few Asian and Latin American nations that allow broad competitive freedom to the market, while the rule is that LDC governments place many limits on company activities and participate actively in the market through government-owned or controlled companies. In most LDCs, a national oil company controls that industry (for example, PDVSA in Venezuela, National Iranian Oil Company in Iran, and Nigerian National Petroleum Corporation in Nigeria) and a national bank (in addition to the central bank) controls or greatly influences local financial markets (for example, Banco de la Nación and Banco Continental in Peru; Arab Banking Corporation in Kuwait, Libya, and the United Arab Emirates; and the Bank of Korea and Korea Development Bank in Korea), all in addition to government-controlled postal service and electric and water utilities.

Even beyond these industries, the government in an LDC often operates through an owned or controlled company that competes with private firms in other industries. A national automobile company (for example, Hindustan Motors in India) may compete with General Motors, Toyota, Ford, and others in the local market. A national food-processing company or cooperative (such as Food Corporation of India and the National Cereals and Produce Board of Kenya) often competes with Borden, Kraft, United Brands, and others both domestically and in other countries. The list may extend to dozens of industries, depending on the country.

In Eastern Europe, government participation in business is moving from state ownership of virtually all business to a more regulatory environment, as in the countries of Western Europe. China is obviously the exception, with a communist government still in power in the mid-1990s. Except for China, then, the Eastern European countries are reducing the role of the state as owner of industrial enterprises and replacing that ownership with regulation. Market transactions are permitted and even encouraged, with the state retaining the role of overseer, promoter of selected sectors, and still part owner of many businesses. (The process of change after many decades of operating communist economies is not quick and easy; hence, foreign firms must not expect to find the opportunities for market access and "normal" {capitalist} business practices to be anything other than time consuming and arduous.)

FIGURE 21–1

Government Participation in the Economy (central government expenditures as a percentage of GDP, 1991)

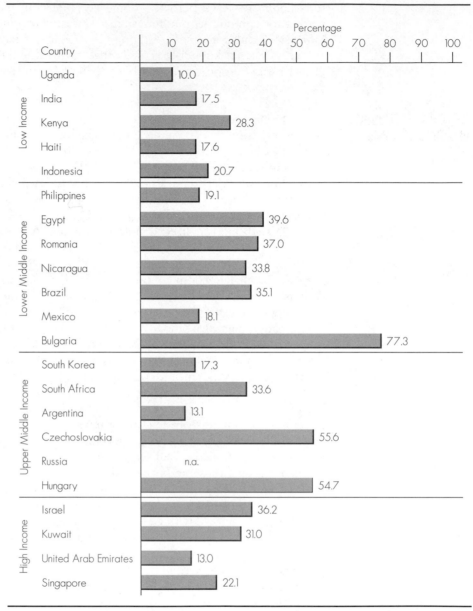

Source: World Bank, *World Development Report 1993* (Washington, D.C.: World Bank, 1993).

Social and Cultural Differences

Social and cultural differences unquestionably play a major role in business between Eastern European and outside partners, whether from Western Europe, North America, or Japan (the main sources of ventures in Eastern Europe today). Business practices in the formerly communist countries remain highly bureaucratized, since the managers of newly developing firms were largely trained in running state-owned enterprises. In addition, the government remains the largest business owner and operator in all of these countries for the near future.

In addition to the differences in business practices, the problems of language, social practices, and ethnic preferences must be faced in doing business with Eastern Europe and China. Overcoming the substantial hurdles involved in doing business in these countries requires both an ability to deal with the rapidly changing business systems and an ability to cope with language differences, consumers who formerly had little experience in market transactions, and ethnic groups that make a country such as the former Soviet Union really a group of markets rather than one homogeneous one.

One study examined the factors that influence success in business negotiations with the Chinese.[3] The study found that knowledge of Chinese business practices was very important to success but knowledge of Chinese social customs and language was relatively unimportant. The Chinese were apparently more interested in the characteristics of the product or service than in the supplier's ability to communicate well in Chinese or to "fit in" socially. (This finding may be biased, however, because only Western firms were polled, not Chinese partners.) The conclusion to draw here is that social and cultural differences do matter, and in particular that the issues related to differences in business practices are most important.

Dual Economies

Much has been said in the literature on economic development about the existence of **dual economies** in LDCs.[4] That is, the economic environment in many LDCs contains two separate and distinct groups: people who belong to a traditional society and do not participate in international business or even in the national market economy and people who belong to the market economy, which includes manufacturing and other modern industry, with its links to foreign business.

In Latin America, the Indian populations of the Andean and Central American countries typify the traditional societies, having very low per capita incomes, often living in remote areas far from cities, and having few ties to the market economy, which predominates in a few cities in each country. In political science terms, these people represent the **periphery,** which fails to benefit substantially from the economic development of the **center,** that is, the cities. The populations of Latin American cities (of both European and Indian descent), while far from a wealthy class overall, include a wealthy elite group as well as middle-income and poor groups. The entire urban area generally has access to foreign products and to a functioning market economy; hence it is the center of economic development.

The multinational enterprise usually deals only with the **market sector** of a dual economy, that is, with the urban centers and more specifically with the middle and upper classes (which have sufficient purchasing power to buy foreign goods or sufficient education to work in the factories or offices of foreign firms). This presents quite a difficult social problem for the MNE to deal with, since the government officials who determine policy toward business generally come from the urban centers, while a large percentage of the population may exist on the periphery. The response of most MNEs has been to operate in the market sector and let the government worry about the **traditional sector.** This response has subjected MNEs to great criticism by LDC analysts and policymakers. Unfortunately, these firms are expert at producing and selling goods and services but not at redistributing income or choosing a country's economic development strategy. Because MNEs are a part of economic development, however, their managers must come to grips with such problems. Possible strategies are discussed next.

Political Risk

A third key characteristic of both LDCs and formerly communist countries that tends to affect foreign firms is the high degree of political risk. Broadly speaking, less developed countries tend to present foreign companies with much more frequent and greater shifts in policy than do developed countries. While a shah is not overthrown or a president deposed every day, the amount of political instability tends to be far higher in LDCs than in industrialized nations. Also, the frequent changes in political orientation, from leftist to conservative to centrist, tend to result in policy changes ranging from nationalizations to tax holiday incentives. The often unstable political environments lead MNE managers to perceive greater political risk in LDCs than in industrialized countries even if the instability does not have substantial effects on business activities.[5] This uncertainty is multiplied in the formerly communist countries of Eastern Europe, where national boundaries are still being redrawn and both political and economic systems are being restructured.

GOVERNMENT POLICIES

Important Government Concerns

Whereas industrialized countries seek to ensure a fair distribution of the benefits of MNE activities through taxation and antitrust rules, the Eastern European, Latin American, African, and Asian countries look in addition for access to technology, capital, and managerial skills. In another view, the industrialized nations are concerned largely with sharing the benefits of MNEs fairly, whereas the LDCs and formerly communist countries are concerned with gaining more of those benefits and minimizing the costs of doing so. (It must be recognized, of course, that most of the world's multinational enterprises come from the industrialized countries and thus are "foreign" elsewhere.)

The result of these concerns is a range of policies that attempt to extract as much value as possible from MNE activities without driving away the firms that provide the benefits. Table 21–6 lists important concerns of LDCs in dealing with foreign firms and notes some of the policies that LDCs currently use. Each concern is discussed next.

Sovereignty   Since the 1960s, a fundamental concern of LDCs, especially those that are former colonies of European countries, has been the demonstration of **sovereignty,** that is, control over the national economy. Many of the most serious problems for foreign companies arose during the late 1960s and early 1970s,

TABLE 21–6

LDC Relations with MNEs

Issues of Concern to the Government	Policy Reactions of LDCs
Sovereignty	Require joint ventures "Unbundle" capital, technology, management, distribution, etc.
Lack of financial capital	Capital controls
Lack of technology	Technology controls Incentives for local R&D
Lack of infrastructure	Local content requirements
Lack of access to developed-country markets	Stimulate offshore assembly Encourage countertrade
Unemployment	Local labor requirements
All the concerns of the developed countries	

when LDC governments expropriated a number of oil, copper, and other raw materials investments and demanded that other investments be partially sold to local investors. Chile, for example, expropriated the copper mines of Anaconda, Kennecott, and Cerro de Pasco in 1969 and several other foreign (primarily US) investments during the Allende regime from 1970 to 1973. Even more striking were the oil company nationalizations during the mid-1970s following the OPEC embargo and price hike in 1973. Most of the Middle Eastern countries national-ized the properties of foreign oil companies during that period, as did Venezuela and Ecuador in Latin America.[6] (**Expropriation** implies forced loss of MNE property with inadequate or no compensation. **Nationalization** refers to forced sale of MNE property to local purchasers with compensation.) Very few expro-priations have occurred worldwide since 1980. In fact, Chile began following a free-market policy in 1973 and has welcomed MNE participation in the economy since then.

Another policy that became widely used to gain more local ownership of MNE activities was the requirement of a **fadeout** of foreign ownership over some time period. Instead of demanding that the MNE sell its local affiliate to nationals immediately, a number of LDCs set rules requiring the sale of 51 percent or more of foreign-owned businesses over a period of 10 to 20 years. The Andean Pact countries utilized this policy up until 1987. A somewhat similar policy, imple-mented by India and Nigeria, requires new investments to take joint venture partners with some prescribed minimum ownership (60 percent local ownership in India and 40 or 60 percent in Nigeria, depending on the industry). Each of these policies could be considered a partial nationalization, since the intent is to have local investors gain control over the affiliate.

Expropriation and nationalization have not been the only responses of LDCs to their concern about controlling the national economy. Many of the policies enacted by LDCs in the past two decades have aimed at **unbundling** the MNE into components that have value to the host country. For example, to force MNEs to transfer managerial skills to local people, LDCs have limited the use of expatriate managers in MNE affiliates and required local nationals to be em-ployed. Similarly, to gain access to technology, LDCs have tried to force MNEs to sell their proprietary technology to local firms and have disallowed the payment of royalties to parent firms so that the country will not pay (through transfer of funds abroad) for technology developed by the MNE elsewhere. Without totally disallowing the entry of MNEs, many LDCs have sought to obtain the valuable pieces of the firm separately.

Lack of Financial Capital Another concern of LDCs is a relative lack of financial capital for investment in productive activities. More specifically, this refers to a shortage of foreign currencies that could be used to buy foreign products needed to support the local economy and to a lack of domestic long-term capital markets that could provide financing as well. While a government can print as much money as it wants, it cannot print the dollars or deutsche marks needed to buy machinery to run local factories. Nor can a government simply create long-term financial markets without substantial private sector participation and support, both of which are generally lacking in an LDC.

No simple solution exists to this problem. Many countries try to implement **capital controls** to limit transfers of funds abroad (which drain the country of foreign exchange). When capital controls are implemented, a black market typically arises for the purchase of foreign exchange, and the problem continues.[7]

Transfers of funds abroad are also taxed by host governments, thus reducing their profitability. This policy has some usefulness, though it does not stop the capital from moving. Many efforts have been undertaken to stimulate the development of capital markets in LDCs; thus far, successes have been limited largely to offshore eurocurrency markets such as those in the Bahamas and the Cayman Islands, neither of which has provided any major local access to the markets for local development. On the other hand, Singapore and Hong Kong are examples of offshore financial markets that *have* significantly aided local development, and some larger LDCs, such as Brazil and Mexico, *are* operating sizable local stock and bond markets.

The real basis of the problem is that investors, domestic and foreign, try to move their funds to safe and high-yielding investments. When an LDC demonstrates an unstable political climate or a debt crisis that makes foreign exchange very scarce, these investors will try to place their funds abroad, and they occasionally cause such a massive **capital flight** that the crisis is exacerbated.[8] In addition to seeking funds from MNEs, less developed countries go to the private credit markets for international bank loans and bond issues, and they attempt to raise their borrowing needs from international organizations such as the IMF and the World Bank.

Lack of Technology   All countries have come to view technology as a critical factor of production.[9] That is, no country is willing to follow simple comparative advantage and specialize solely in the production of raw materials, even if cost conditions dictate such specialization. Rather, every country seeks access to current technology in manufacturing so that the economy can be diversified and not be dependent on a narrow range of products (especially raw materials). Consequently, LDC governments want to obtain a continuing flow of current technology from suppliers such as MNEs at the lowest cost and to the greatest degree possible.

The policies used to achieve this goal range from refusal to recognize patents (which is intended to gain access to technology without paying for it) to incentives for local R&D. The Andean Pact countries do not allow payments to parent firms for technology transferred to local affiliates, although they still maintain patent protection. Most LDCs offer one or another form of subsidy to attract MNEs to do some local product development (the *D* of R&D), recognizing that basic research is usually centralized in one or two locations in the firm. In late 1984, Brazil required that all computers (except mainframes) sold in the country be produced locally by local firms. This attempt to force the development of a domestic capability in such a key high-tech industry has led to great turmoil in the Brazilian computer industry, with IBM, Burroughs, and other MNEs still not certain of the full implications for their activities in Brazil.[10]

Lack of Infrastructure   Not only do most LDCs lack major domestic companies in manufacturing industries; they also lack the necessary **infrastructure**—that is, good roads, accessible electric power, good telephone service, up-to-date educational institutions, and other utilities and public services—to support such industries. These facilities tend to be extremely sensitive politically, and foreign firms are often not permitted to provide the services such facilities render, though they may supply equipment and other inputs to construct the facilities.

The most common strategy LDCs use to create the necessary infrastructure is to contract with MNEs to set up the telephone system, port, or power plant and then either buy the project under a turnkey arrangement or let the MNE remain as an adviser and perhaps licensor of the government-owned project. During the past several years, more and more LDCs have been *privatizing* some of their utility firms, often selling ownership to foreign MNEs.

Another tactic governments use is to require MNEs and other firms that operate locally to obtain a substantial percentage of their inputs locally. In this manner, MNEs are compelled to carry out as much of the production process as necessary to reach the local content limit and/or to buy inputs from local suppliers. Thus, other local businesses are stimulated and a larger industrial sector is created. The supplier firms form part of the local infrastructure MNEs need to produce locally. The Venezuelan government, for example, requires that automobile firms obtain at least 40 percent of their sales value from local sources, either their own local production or purchases from local suppliers. General Motors, Toyota, and Jeep have expanded their local assembly operations to achieve the necessary level of local content under this rule.

Lack of Access to Developed-Country Markets   Even when LDCs make products that can be competitive in world markets, they face another disadvantage relative to MNEs. LDC firms generally lack the knowledge of market conditions in the industrialized countries that they need to build distribution networks there. The enormous competitive advantage gained by an MNE that operates a distribution network in several countries and passes information among its affiliates cannot be overemphasized. Without such networks, the LDC raw material supplier or manufacturer faces little chance of success in competing with the MNEs.

In response to this problem, a number of policies have been tried. One interesting example during the 1980s, a result of the Latin American debt crisis, was Colombia's requirement that any firm importing specified products into the country also had to find some product or service of equal value to export. This effort to balance trade and reduce the dollar outflow from Colombia was a form of barter or countertrade that attempted to gain the country better access to the markets of other countries.[11] Another example is the attempt made by many countries, especially in Southeast Asia and Mexico, to attract offshore assembly by MNEs. By positioning itself as a location for assembly of manufactured goods, the LDC gains not only new production and employment but also access to the developed-country markets via the MNE that takes the assembled goods and sells them abroad.

Unemployment   Unemployment is the last concern of LDCs that we will discuss here, though certainly not the last of the many difficulties LDCs face in seeking to improve their economic conditions. Rates of unemployment and underemployment in LDCs are estimated to be anywhere from a manageable 2 to 3 percent in such countries as Korea and Singapore all the way to 25 percent or more in such countries as Jamaica, and these rates are not even available from Ethiopia and Uganda. Thus, most LDCs experience far more unemployment than industrialized nations.[12] This issue represents a continuing critical problem for most LDCs, which look to MNEs as one source of additional jobs.

The main policy tool LDCs utilize to push MNEs to hire as many locals as possible is the local labor requirement, under which limits are set on the use of expatriate staff. Typically, labor is required to be all local and management is required to be 90 to 95 percent local, depending on the country. Also typically, the MNEs have no trouble achieving these targets because they seldom transfer production workers overseas and because the high cost of using expatriates makes hiring local managers very desirable. The use of expatriate managers was a serious point of contention in the 1960s and 1970s, when MNEs used far more of them, but most MNEs now have enough local managers in most countries to avoid conflict on this score.

A criticism of MNE employment practices in LDCs is that they are too capital intensive in countries where the abundant supply of labor calls for more labor-intensive production. This issue was discussed in Chapter 11 and will not be treated again here. In the present context, we are concerned with the fact that LDC governments are interested in stimulating MNEs to utilize more labor-intensive production and other activities. No specific policies to carry out this task are in wide use, probably because no one has been able to decide what "appropriate technology" really is. (For instance, more labor-intensive technology and production often leads to costlier products, which are not competitive in international markets.)

The Concerns of the Developed Countries   The previous categories covered only problems peculiar to LDCs. In addition, the less developed countries, like the industrialized countries, are concerned with their balances of payments, the distribution of the costs and benefits of MNE activities, and tax issues. Rather than repeat what was already discussed in Chapter 20, this section concludes with the reminder that the problems presented there also concern the LDCs.

Table 21–7 reviews the categories of problems specific to LDCs by presenting a selected listing of policies in 14 countries.

ENTRY AND OPERATING STRATEGIES FOR MNEs

Entry Strategies

The possible **entry strategies** for doing business in LDCs do not differ from those for entering industrialized countries, as they were presented previously. This section looks at some strategic considerations that may be important due to the relative political and economic instability of LDCs compared to industrialized countries. Because a change in government or any number of other factors can change the "rules of the game" rapidly and significantly, the MNE manager should consider measures to protect against risk at every stage of a project in an LDC. Government policies enacted to improve the balance of payments could cut off exports from some foreign affiliate of the MNE to its local LDC affiliate, which might affect the MNE drastically by eliminating its perhaps substantial imports. Foreign direct investment is, of course, subject to many more possibilities of adverse policy or other environmental changes, ranging from nationalization to a national depression caused by a worldwide decline in the prices of primary goods. Before entering into business in a less developed country, the MNE manager needs to plan for such potential problems.

The Obsolescing Bargain

Before deciding what protection plan for the business to carry out in an LDC, the MNE manager should consider the firm's bargaining position relative to that of the host government. The firm is in a much different position *before* investing or setting up its other business activity in that country than afterward, when assets have been deployed and are committed to a particular use. For example, before

TABLE 21–7   Selected Policies in 14 LDCs and Formerly Communist Countries

Country	Ownership Rules	Financial Controls	Technology Controls	Local Content Requirement	FDI Incentives
Brazil	Foreign ownership prohibited in some industries, restricted in others	Foreign exchange and remittance controls	Technology transfer regulated	Only in capital goods industry with government-subsidized financing	For investment in selected regions and industries
Chile	Some limitations	Foreign exchange and remittance controls	None	None, except in auto industry	Few; for mining, oil technology
Czech Republic	None	Some exchange controls	No approval necessary	None	None
Egypt	Few legal limits in select sectors; few 100% foreign firms exist	Some exchange controls	Some controls	Requirements for certain industries exist	Substantial
Hungary	Few limitations on foreign ownership in selected sensitive industries	Foreign exchange controls; favorable to foreign capital inflows	Technology import fostered	None	Numerous and varied
India	No majority ownership in select industries	Foreign exchange controls; remittances scrutinized	Close scrutiny	Maximum use encouraged	Numerous and varied, designed to promote selected industries and regions
Indonesia	Foreign firms must fade out to 49% in 20 years	None	Foreign ventures must bring technology and training	None, except automotive industry	Few; for investment in selected industries and regions
Korea	Foreign ownership restricted but not prohibited	Foreign exchange controls	Liberal licensing rules; technological imports encouraged	None	Few; for investment in selected industries and regions
Mexico	Limited to 34%, 40%, or 49% foreign in select industries	None	None	Since NAFTA "North American content" rules exist instead of local content rules (according to GATT)	For export-oriented ventures
Nigeria	In some industries, foreign ownership prohibited or restricted	Foreign exchange controls; remittance limits	Approval required	Tax incentives	For pioneer industries
Poland	None; except gambling activities	Decreasing foreign exchange controls; transfer of capital abroad restricted	None	None	Since January 1994 a halt on special incentives for FDI
Russia	Legal limits exist only in banking and insurance industry	Foreign exchange controls	Technology imports unrestricted; restrictions on some technologies for export	Imposed on state-sponsored construction contracts (70%)	For investment in selected areas
South Africa	None	Foreign exchange controls; remittance restrictions	Licenses easily obtained	In auto industry	Area incentives
Venezuela	Majority ownership in select industries	None	Must be registered	In autos, some other industries	Numerous incentives, especially for select regions exist

Source: Economist Intelligence Unit, *Investing, Licensing, and Trading Conditions* (New York: Economist Intelligence Unit, 1994).

setting up an oil refinery, an oil company possesses several desirable characteristics from the viewpoint of the host government. The company will bring in money, machinery, people who can train local workers and managers, access to foreign oil customers, and so on. With such a favorable set of components, the FDI project generally looks very desirable to a host government, and it can often be used to obtain very favorable tax treatment and other incentives for the MNE. Once the refinery is in place, however, the bargaining advantage shifts somewhat to the host government. Now the company has physical assets present in the country and links to its other operations elsewhere. The government can now raise taxes and impose other costs on the company, which is to some extent captive in the country. The MNE's bargaining power has faded away to some degree, or obsolesced. The **obsolescing bargain** is the "contract" between company and government that includes the rules under which the affiliate operates. Very often those rules become much less favorable to the company once it has committed its assets and the government has gained a stronger position.

Operating Strategies

Once the firm has chosen an entry strategy and protected itself as well as it can against the problem of the obsolescing bargain, it must adopt an **operating strategy.** One consideration will continue to be the maintenance of a strong bargaining position relative to the host government. This can be accomplished through maximizing the use of the firm's competitive advantages, such as proprietary technology and its international information and distribution networks and other links to affiliates in other countries. The more ties the firm maintains to inputs and markets in other countries, the less the host country in question can constrain the MNE without facing a reduction in the benefits it obtains from the MNE's local operations. A clear example is that of offshore assembly. An MNE's local television assembly plant in Taiwan is probably fairly safe from the vagaries of government policy shifts, since any adverse regulation could cause the firm to shift its assembly to Singapore, South Korea, or Hong Kong. In addition, the main production inputs usually come from the home country, and the market to be served is usually a developed country or countries. Each of these aspects of the business of offshore assembly gives the firm bargaining strength relative to that of the host government even after the plant has been established.

As in developed countries, the firm's operating strategies in LDCs may focus on cost minimization, product differentiation, or market segmentation. In the less developed countries, there is often a much greater possibility of market segmentation through government protection. That is, in LDCs, where governments play a much larger role in the operation of the economy, firms may gain protected market positions by obtaining government contracts or by receiving government protection against competitors in exchange for setting up a local affiliate. Thus, although competition still plays a large role in LDC business, government policies can create profitable market niches for firms that plan carefully and negotiate skillfully for them.

In dealing with the particular risks inherent in LDC operations, the firm has many options. As with other risks, the firm may eliminate or reduce these risks by avoiding LDCs, insuring the project with some public or private insurer, or hedging the exposed assets with local liabilities. In addition, the firm can diversify its international activities into other countries so that a particular LDC does not affect too much of its total operations.

The hedging strategies for both political and exchange risks were discussed previously. The governments of many industrialized countries offer commercial and political risk insurance to exporters and direct investors doing business with LDCs. In addition to the common financial hedges to offset exposed local-currency assets, such as local borrowing, MNEs have employed a variety of other strategies for dealing with this risk. When assets must be kept in the local currency, firms have generally tried to place investments in assets that tend to keep pace with local inflation, such as real estate, government-backed securities with values tied to inflation or the US dollar, and the local operation itself.

Countertrade and Other Efforts to Obtain Credit

Credit is a major concern of Eastern European countries. There is far more demand for Western products in Eastern Europe than the reverse. Because foreign exchange markets are in the process of opening, foreign currencies are generally scarce and expensive. China's yuan remains inconvertible at this time. In sum, access to acceptable means of payment will continue to be a problem in these countries in the near future.

One method that is used to avoid immediate payment in dollars or other hard currency is to finance imported purchases with bank credit or **supplier credit.** Another method is to force Western exporters to accept payment in products rather than money (i.e., *countertrade*). Both of these methods are widely used in East/West trade and other East/West business arrangements.

Some of the countertrade agreements that have been made over the years are quite colorful. Pepsi-Cola agreed to sell its soft drink in the Soviet Union and to receive payment in Stolichnaya vodka. Fiat set up an automotive plant also in the Soviet Union, and received payment for the plant in cars. The German manufacturer, Krupp, sold industrial machinery to Hungary in exchange for canned ham, steel wool, and several other products. Other, more prosaic and more recent ventures are listed in Table 21–8.

Bank financing for importers in Eastern Europe was fairly widely available for many years, due to the countries' histories in creditworthiness. During the international debt crisis of the early 1980s, several of the Eastern European countries were forced into rescheduling of their foreign bank loans, with Poland and Romania facing the most difficult situations, which have not yet been

TABLE 21–8 Selected Countertrade Deals between Eastern and Western Partners

Company	Country	Date	Products Involved
Agresco (Israel)	USSR	1990	Israeli fruits and vegetables for Soviet goods to be determined
Asahi Tsushin (Japan)	China	1989	Swap TV shows and movies between the two countries
Imar & Brital (Italy)	USSR	1988	Italian building for Soviet souvenirs
Israel Citrus (Israel)	Yugoslavia	1988	Israeli fruit for Yugoslav wood
Leyland Daf (Great Britian)	China	1988	British trucks for frozen prawns and human hair
Miju (South Korea)	USSR	1990	Korean shampoo for Soviet vodka and beef tallow
Nippon (Japan)	China	1989	Japanese switchboards for Chinese circuits
Philips (Netherlands)	Albania	1988	Dutch electronic components for Albanian cement and tobacco
Pig Improvement Co. (Great Britain)	Cuba	1988	British breeding pigs for Cuban sugar
Sov Nor Shipping (Norway)	USSR	1989	Soviet ships, US fast food, and Bermudan and Norwegian shipping
World Class Products (United States)	USSR	1989	Taiwan sewing machines for Soviet handicrafts through U.S. company

Source: Paul Surovell (ed.) INTERFLO, 1988–1990.

resolved. In the late 1980s, commercial bank lending to the region began to expand again. While acceptance financing for exporters to Eastern Europe is not commonly available, receivables can often be discounted through forfaiting companies, most of which are affiliated with large banks anyway. (*Forfaiting* is discussed in Chapter 18.)

Western exporters frequently offer trade credit to their Eastern European buyers. Such terms are common, since sales tend to be large and competition from other Western firms is often substantial.

Even with all of these methods for dealing with financing problems, difficulties remain. The weak economies of this region (and China) make exporting difficult, and thus paying for imports remains a problem. Frequent hard-currency shortages put pressure on Western exporters to arrange complex countertrade transactions. In sum, financing is a key problem in business with Eastern Europe and China today.

DEALING WITH LDC GOVERNMENTS

The government is a much more important participant in the economies of most LDCs than in the economies of industrialized countries. For that reason alone, MNE managers in LDCs need to be extremely sensitive to the issue of government-business relations. In addition, because most MNEs are headquartered outside LDCs, they are viewed as "foreign" in the LDCs where they do business. Thus, relations with the government (and the public) generally play a much more important role in LDC business than in IC business. **Foreignness** may be the most important issue in dealing with LDC host governments.

Other central issues that create tensions in the relations between MNEs and LDC host governments include

- MNE financial policies, especially remittances of earnings that contribute to capital outflow.
- MNE employment practices that result in fewer host country employees than the government would like and MNE use of technology that is more capital intensive than the government would like.
- The size of MNEs relative to the economic size of host countries, which gives MNEs substantial economic power.
- The multinationality of MNEs, which enables the home country parent to make decisions on activities in the host country and to transfer people, money, and other resources into and out of the host country—decisions that the government of the host country is unable to control.

To successfully deal with LDC governments, MNE managers need to understand both sides of these issues and take steps that reduce the tensions they cause. The bargaining model presented in Chapter 22 goes some way toward generating an understanding of this crucial relationship. A few specific issues are noted here.

Company *financial policies* often focus on minimizing company assets in LDCs with rapidly devaluing currencies and unstable economic conditions. Host governments, of course, do not want to see funds outflows of this type, which exacerbate the capital flight problem, so they regularly look for ways to constrain firms from transferring their earnings abroad. The MNE manager needs to find ways to either reduce outflows or generate funds inflows (for example, through exports) that will reduce BOP pressure on the host government. This is often a very difficult task for the affiliate manager, since the MNE home office would prefer to see as much of earnings as possible remitted from high-risk, rapid-devaluation countries. It might be argued that the MNE would be best off if it reinvested its earnings in the host country as wisely as possible and remitted some funds on a regular basis. Local asset values can often be maintained against devaluation, and by not contributing to capital flight, the MNE would create goodwill for its continuing activities in that country. This is by no means an ultimate solution for the MNE, but it may enable it to operate in an LDC on a continuing basis, with better government relations than it would have otherwise.

The *employment practices* of MNEs tend to be criticized mainly because of the high unemployment in LDCs and the high visibility of MNEs. In fact, several studies show that MNEs tend to offer better compensation and training to their LDC employees than do local firms.[14] The "appropriateness" of the technology used in the LDC operations of MNEs can always be debated, but if that technology enables the firm to operate efficiently and competitively, it can be viewed as contributing to the country's ability to maximize use of its available resources. In many cases, MNEs perhaps need to make public the number of people they employ so that host governments and pressure groups will be forced to recognize their contributions on this score.

The *economic power* MNEs possess can appear quite overwhelming to an outside observer. Many firms' annual sales are larger than the annual GDPs of many countries. The amounts that firms spend to construct facilities surpass the investment capabilities of many governments. Recall that each government has the power to set the rules of the game for business in its jurisdiction. So if any firm exercises economic power in some fashion unacceptable to the host government, that government can easily intervene to constrain the firm. Nonetheless, firms do possess bargaining strengths relative to host governments, and a government that wants to keep a firm operating locally cannot raise restrictions indefinitely. The result is a recurring set of negotiations and bargaining between the two sides over how the benefits and costs of the MNEs' activities should be distributed between them.

Multinationality is the final focal point of tensions between MNEs and LDC governments. A firm with access to funds, people, markets, inputs, and so on outside the host government's jurisdiction has a clear advantage over that government. This advantage cannot be completely negated, though international codes of MNE conduct creating a multinational government policy structure toward MNEs have been debated (and some have been enacted). At present, however, MNEs still occupy a position of strength on the basis of their multinationality, since the codes of conduct have not been able to limit their practices very much.[15]

CONCLUSIONS

Much more attention to government-business relations is required in LDCs than in industrialized nations. A wealth of government-owned companies, strict limitations on company activities, and frequent rule changes make the path of the MNE difficult in many LDCs. Given the active roles that most LDC governments play in business, MNE managers need to pay close attention to these governments both as regulators and as customers.

At present, international business in LDCs accounts for less than a third of total international business. Since LDCs have most of the world's population and a large portion of its natural resources, they constitute valuable target markets and sources of production inputs. Thus, despite the difficulties of underdeveloped economic infrastructures and often changing regulations, LDCs present many opportunities to MNEs.

The MNE manager can gain important insights into the treatment that the MNE is likely to receive in a particular LDC by studying that country's process of economic development. An LDC that follows the path of import-substituting growth is likely to impose trade barriers and protect local industry against foreign competition. An LDC that uses an export promotion strategy is likely to foster a much more open business environment. These two broad approaches to development give only a macro perspective on the LDC. The examination of other aspects of economic development theory and policy as they apply to the LDC may offer additional useful insights into the environment there.

MNE managers in LDCs and formerly communist countries will always face the problem of foreignness. No matter how responsive to host government rules and preferences the MNE is, it still represents foreign owners and decision makers. The MNE manager must be aware of the tension that this foreignness may engender and be prepared to minimize it when possible.

Regardless of the strategy that it adopts to do business in a less developed or Eastern European country, the MNE needs to consider methods of protection against political risk, exchange risk, and commercial risk. Those methods, which were discussed in other chapters, should form a part of the total strategy for ongoing business. Since the firm's ability to gain an advantage in dealing with the host government declines once it has committed real resources in the host country (and thus faces the problem of the obsolescing bargain), it requires both entry and operating strategies for risk protection.

Business in Eastern Europe and China will become increasingly important throughout the 1990s as these countries become more a part of the industrial world and their markets become more accessible to MNEs from Western Europe and elsewhere. Because of the drastic government policy changes consequent to the decision of most of these countries to pursue market-based economies, political risk related to the rules changes is a dominant concern in the years ahead. This fact, plus the highly bureaucratic regulatory environments that now exist, make these countries potential targets mostly for large, multinational firms that can forgo profits on such ventures for several years of negotiations and during early start-up periods.

The main products that appear in trade with Eastern European countries are lower-tech manufactures and raw materials coming from Eastern Europe and higher-tech manufactures and some consumer goods going to Eastern Europe. Customers in Eastern Europe typically are government-owned firms for industrial goods, though final consumers for consumer goods are becoming accessible to MNEs.

QUESTIONS

1. Define *less developed country.* Does Nigeria fit into your definition? Does Singapore? How about Portugal? Kuwait? What is an appropriate measure of economic development for an LDC?

2. Present a strategy that AT&T or L M Ericsson could use to compete in the Indian market for telecommunications. Use information from the chapter about rules on foreign business in India.

3. What risks does an MNE encounter if it agrees to accept a local partner and enter an LDC market with a joint venture manufacturing plant? Assume the company produces chemicals. How can the MNE deal with these risks?

4. Name four main concerns of LDC governments in their dealings with foreign multinational firms. What can the firms do to minimize tensions with the host government with regard to each of these concerns?

5. Considering the obsolescing bargain, what can a company do to maintain its bargaining power even after it has committed resources to a plant or other facility in an LDC host country?

6. Explain how offshore assembly could be a viable strategy for a US-based machinery manufacturer that wishes to enter the Jamaican market.

7. Why are there so few Eastern bloc investments in Western countries in contrast to the fairly substantial number of Western joint ventures, turnkey ventures, and licensing projects in Eastern countries?

8. Explain how a Western company that exports to an Eastern European country can finance the accounts receivable from its customer if the terms of the deal call for payment partly in money and partly in products, payable one year from the exporting date.

9. As part of your company's strategy for sourcing production in more than one country, you have been considering producing electric motors in Hungary for sale in Western Europe. You already have a plant in France, but the lower cost of production in Hungary would offer a valuable cost advantage in competing with other European firms. What are some of the key costs and benefits of such a strategy?

10. How can a firm deal with the political risk inherent in any venture in an Eastern European country? (Assume the venture is a partially owned factory in the Czech Republic.)

REFERENCES

Economist Intelligence Unit *Business Eastern Europe* and *Business Latin America*. New York: Economist Intelligence Unit, biweekly newsletters.

China Business Review.

Cline, William. *International Debt and the Stability of the World Economy.* Washington, DC: Institute for International Economics, 1983.

Grosse, Robert. *Multinationals in Latin America.* London: Routledge, 1989.

Hagen, Everett. *The Economics of Development.* 4th ed. Homewood, IL: Richard D. Irwin, 1986.

Hofheinz, Roy, and Kent Calder. *The Eastasia Edge.* New York: Basic Books, 1984.

Kobrin, Steven. *Managing Political Risk Assessment.* Berkeley, CA: University of California Press, 1982.

Manufacturers Hanover Trust Corporation. "Eastern Europe: Review and Outlook." New York: Manufacturers Hanover Trust Corporation, May 1990.

Samuels, Barbara. *Managing Risk in Developing Countries.* Princeton, NJ: Princeton University Press, 1990.

Surovell, Paul. *Interflo.* Monthly East-West business newsletter, Maplewood, NJ.

Tung, Rosalie. "U.S.-China Trade Negotiations: Practices, Procedures, and Outcomes," *Journal of International Business Studies,* Fall 1982.

World Bank. *World Development Report, 1990.* Washington, DC: World Bank, 1990.

NOTES

[1]Roy Hofheinz and Kent Calder, *The Eastasia Edge* (New York: Basic Books, 1984).

[2]US Department of Commerce, *Survey of Current Business,* August 1971 and August 1990.

[3]Rosalie Tung, "U.S.-China Trade Negotiations," *Journal of International Business Studies,* Fall 1982.

[4]See, for example, Everett Hagen, *The Economics of Development,* 3rd ed. (Home-

wood, IL: Richard D. Irwin, 1980), chap. 15, and I M D Little, *Economic Development* (New York: Basic Books, 1982), chap. 6.

[5]See Steven Kobrin, *Managing Political Risk Assessment* (Berkeley, CA: University of California Press, 1982), concerning empirical measures of political instability leading to loss outcomes for firms.

[6]See Kobrin, *Managing Political Risk Assessment,* concerning expropriations in the international oil industry.

[7]For example, see Michael Nowak, "Black Markets in Foreign Exchange," *Finance & Development,* March 1985.

[8]Capital flight is considered to be a central cause of the continuing Latin American debt crisis. See, for example, Donald Lessard and John Williamson, *Capital Flight and Third World Debt* (Washington, DC: Institute for International Economics, 1987).

[9]See, for example, Michael Porter, *The Competitive Advantage of Nations* (New York: Free Press, 1990), chaps. 3, 4.

[10]Economist Intelligence Unit, *Investing, Licensing, and Trading Conditions* (New York: Economist Intelligence Unit, January 1985), Brazil section, p. 7.

[11]Economist Intelligence Unit, *Investing, Licensing, and Trading Conditions* (New York: Economist Intelligence Unit, December 1984), Colombia section, p. 29. Only some specific products are subject to this countertrade requirement, although the list has been expanding since its initiation in 1984.

[12]Unemployment rates are taken from International Labour Office, *Yearbook of Labor Statistics* (Geneva: ILO, 1983).

[13]See, for example, Norman Gall, "How the Chicago Boys Fought 1000% Inflation," *Forbes,* March 31, 1980.

[14]See, for example, Jerry Ingles and Loretta Fairchild, "Evaluating the Impact of Foreign Investment," *Latin American Research Review* (1978), and Robert Grosse, "The Economic Impact of Foreign Direct Investment: A Case Study of Venezuela," in Grosse (1989).

[15]See Robert Grosse, "Codes of Conduct for Multinational Enterprises," *Journal of World Trade Law,* September–October 1982.

Volkswagen Heads East (or Skoda Heads West)

Introduction

Competition in the global auto industry has become increasingly fierce among the dozen surviving major manufacturers in the mid-1990s. (See the Appendix for more details). With the dramatic successes of the Japanese leaders (Toyota, Nissan, and Honda), Both the North American and European industries have become subject to intense rivalry among US, Japanese, and European automakers. Table 1 shows the positions of major competitors in Western Europe during 1990. These conditions have led to calls for protection in the European Union against outside producers, as well as responses by the European car companies looking to solidify their positions.

The increasing intensity of competition in Europe appears to be due to several factors. First and perhaps foremost, the Japanese firms expanded their local production aggressively in North America during the 1980s, and now they are looking to the European market as the last major target in the global industry where their positions are weak. The leading Japanese firms, with their high-quality and low-cost cars, produced growing profits and market shares during the late 1980s at the same time their US and European rivals (broadly speaking) faced declining shares, low profits and/or losses and generally difficult conditions. Second, the opening of Eastern Europe that began with Soviet President Gorbachev's policy of *perestroika* has led to aggressive strategies by several firms to build business in Eastern Europe. Third, the European Union's goal of achieving much greater economic integration by the end of 1992 led Japanese and US automakers to pursue more extensive local production in Europe. These firms wanted to both benefit from regionwide economies of scale that the reduced commercial barriers would allow and avoid being excluded by whatever protectionism would occur against non-European firms after 1992.

One of the most active responses of the European firms has been to pursue business in Eastern Europe in the countries of the former communist bloc. Of course, the most rapid expansion has been into the region that was formerly East Germany. There Volkswagen negotiated a joint production agreement with IFA Kombinat Personenkraftwagen to make Polos and Golfs (to replace the infamous two-stroke East German Trabant), Opel (part of General Motors) agreed to build a new assembly plant in Eisenach (to replace the East German Wartburg), BMW invested in machine tools and parts manufacturing, and Ford established an extensive dealer network—all by the end of 1990.

This case was written by Professor Robert Grosse and Professor Vendulka Kubalkova as a basis for class discussion, 1991.

TABLE 1

Western Europe's Auto
Market in 1990
(January–October)

Company	Sales in $US Millions	Percentage Change versus Year Earlier	Market Share
Volkswagen	1,739	+1.9%	15.2%
Fiat	1,624	−4.9	14.2
Peugeot Citroen	1,483	+1.0	13.0
General Motors	1,344	+2.7	11.7
Ford	1,324	−3.7	11.6
Renault	1,117	−5.0	9.8
Mercedes-Benz	373	+2.8	3.3
Rover	344	−5.8	3.0
BMW	314	−5.4	2.7
Volvo	204	−10.3	1.8
Japanese	1,339	+6.1	11.7
Others	235	−5.0	2.0
Total	11,440	−0.9	100.0

Source: *The Economist,* December 15, 1990, p. 74.

In addition, the European majors have been pursuing investments and alliances in other Eastern European countries, from Poland to Czechoslovakia. For example, Fiat agreed to form joint ventures in Poland and the former Soviet Union for auto production. Opel agreed to assemble cars and components in Hungary and the former Soviet Union. Ford agreed to produce auto parts in Hungary. By the end of 1990, more than a dozen major investment contracts had been signed by the automakers.

This set of conditions provides the background to the decision of Czechoslovakia's Skoda autoworks to sell part ownership to an outside automaker so that Skoda could survive the opening of the Czechoslovak economy in the 1990s.

Skoda Automobile Company, Mlada Boleslav

Skoda has been the main automobile manufacturer in Czechoslovakia and Eastern Europe. It was spun off in 1945 from the Skoda Industrial Works, which was established in 1859. Skoda Works, a top-caliber engineering company, competed on level terms with the finest German and American companies of the day. General Electric, Krupp, and Siemens were then its peers, not its superiors. Skoda cars were popular on European roads between the two world wars. Even under communism, Skoda was known as the most efficient auto producer in the Soviet bloc, though its plants and cars were no longer competitive compared to Western European vehicles. The Soviet Union used a primitive form of protectionism when it simply ordered Skoda's management to completely halt the development of new cars and the modernization of production.

Skoda's three assembly plants were producing about 185,000 cars per year in 1989. Only one model, the Favorit, based on the eight-year-old design of the Italian Bertone, was in production at that time. The firm employed about 21,000 workers, of which 1,600 were Soviet-style gulag prisoners, and sold $US 588 million of cars in 1989. With output of 10 cars per worker per year, Skoda's productivity was at least three times lower than that of auto companies in the West. The firm has been accumulating losses at a rate of 200 million Czech crowns per month since the opening of the economy.

The Czechoslovak government, as owner of Skoda, faced a daunting task when the country became independent of the Soviet Union in 1990. Because the cornerstone of reform was the establishment of a market-based economy, competitive firms would be necessary for the future. This implied that some of the main state-owned companies, which provided many jobs and very substantial income, would likely have to be privatized in some form or other. The government realized the hopelessness of Skoda's entering directly into competition with well-established European rivals such as Volkswagen and Fiat, not to mention General Motors and Ford. Thus, it was decided to look for a Western partner that could provide up-to-date technology and market access outside of Czechoslovakia in return for part ownership of Skoda that would allow the acquirer immediate access to the Czechoslovakian market and to existing distribution channels there.

The Czechoslovak government's main concern in selling Skoda to a foreign buyer was that production in Czechoslovakia would not be reduced or terminated; on the contrary, it would be expanded and jobs would be guaranteed. Also, the government wanted to ensure that the Skoda name would be maintained as a Czechoslovakia-based automaker. These points imply that Skoda would remain a large employer in Czechoslovakia and would continue to generate large income there. Since the local market would take several years to build up purchasing power relative to Western European countries, it was expected that the foreign buyer of Skoda would export a significant amount of the locally produced cars through its international dealership network. While the government wanted to maintain majority local ownership over Skoda, this concern apparently was not an overriding one.

The Competition between Volkswagen and Renault/Volvo

In 1990, with the assistance of Price Waterhouse, the Czechoslovak government formally opened a bidding process for foreign purchase of part ownership in Skoda. Twenty-four foreign automakers examined the Skoda offer. These included General Motors and Ford, as well as the main Europe-based firms. Almost all of them withdrew from the process before submitting final bids, leaving Volkswagen and a team of France's Renault and Sweden's Volvo as the only potential buyers. Apparently there were two reasons most of the possible bidders withdrew: the truly daunting cost of upgrading (or simply replacing) Skoda's production facilities and the expected limited market within Czechoslovakia for several years into the future.

Renault and Volvo, both in fairly weak financial condition at the time, offered to invest about FF 14 billion (just under $US 3 billion) in Czechoslovakia over 10 years. They reluctantly agreed to maintain the Skoda name and export cars into the European Community market.

The Renault/Volvo offer was dwarfed by Volkswagen's bid. VW agreed to invest DM 9.5 billion (about $US 6.5 billion) over 10 years, guarantee jobs in Czechoslovakia, and preserve Skoda as a separate division in Volkswagen (as had been done with the acquisition of Spain's SEAT in 1986). VW's stated intent was to place Skoda at the inexpensive end of its product line and expand market share in that segment (along with sales from SEAT). Volkswagen planned to expand production in Czechoslovakia to double the current level of output by 1995.

The bidding was not as one-sided as it may appear, since VW had to overcome the Czechoslovak government's concern about selling Skoda to a German buyer. (German direct investors constituted about 70 percent of total Western foreign investment in Czechoslovakia by 1991.) Traditional Czechoslovak opposition to German firms had to be transcended to convince the government to accept the VW bid.

Skoda's trade union, concerned about proposed drastic layoffs by the Renault-Volvo consortium, demanded that Volkswagen be chosen as the partner, contending that VW clearly offered better employment guarantees and fringe benefits. The Czech government denied this was a factor in its final decision and stressed the generosity of the VW offer, which in financial terms was equal to one-tenth of total Czechoslovakian GNP! The Czech prime minister, Peter Pithart, listed as the main reasons for choosing Volkswagen the proposed technology investments, the impact on employment, the willingness to respect the Skoda brand name, and VW's leading position in the European auto market. The Czechs, distrustful of socialist economic practices, apparently also disliked the fact that Renault was state owned. In addition, Volkswagen agreed to maintain in production the existing Favorit (with a new engine) for consumption in the former Eastern Germany and in Czechoslovakia as one of the cheapest cars available.

Implictions for Volkswagen

Volkswagen committed itself to a huge capital investment in a politically unstable country with greatly limited purchasing power. In addition, VW agreed to preserve the jobs of the existing Skoda workers and to expand production (and presumably employment) during the 1990s. This commitment came at the same time as the growth of competition in the European auto market and when VW had very limited market shares in North America and Japan.

In exchange for the costs of this agreement, Volkswagen received 31 percent ownership of Skoda in 1991 and an increasing share up to 70 percent ownership by 1995 as VW's capital investment increases. Tax treatment and other incentives are not publicly available at this time, but one might assume that the government offered some favorable treatment.

This strategy creates a huge risk for Volkswagen during the 1990s. If Skoda cannot be turned into a competitive international firm, VW will have used up precious resources at a time when the firm is already subject to serious competitive pressures in its traditional European domain.

Postscript

The Skoda joint venture and the acquisition of the East German Trabant's manufacturer are by no means the only VW initiatives in its quest to establish itself as the leader in the Eastern European automobile industry. Since the Skoda bid, Volkswagen has also gained a majority stake in another Czechoslovakian automobile manufacturer for which it bid in competition with General Motors. The Slovak Bratislava Auto Works (BAZ) will become the second VW enterprise in Czechoslovakia and its 19th production facility in the world when the investment is completed. With an initial investment of $US 35 million in 1991, Volkswagen will acquire an 80 percent stake in BAZ. The remaining 20 percent will belong to the Czechoslovak government. From its Slovak BAZ plant, Volkswagen will produce 3,000 Passats annually, increasing production to 30,000 cars or more by 1993.

PART

V

A Look to the Future

22 Multinational Enterprises and the World Order: A Look to the Future

This chapter attempts to project the key concerns of international business managers to the end of the century. It looks at government policies, internal company activities, the economic environment, and the political environment. The main goals of the chapter are to:

1. Describe the importance of technological change in determining business patterns.

2. Discuss possible shifts in government policy toward MNEs.

3. Consider the likelihood of the MNE's survival.

4. Project likely shifts in competitive conditions in international industries.

5. Project likely shifts in relationships between managers and workers, between managers and company owners, and among managers within the MNE.

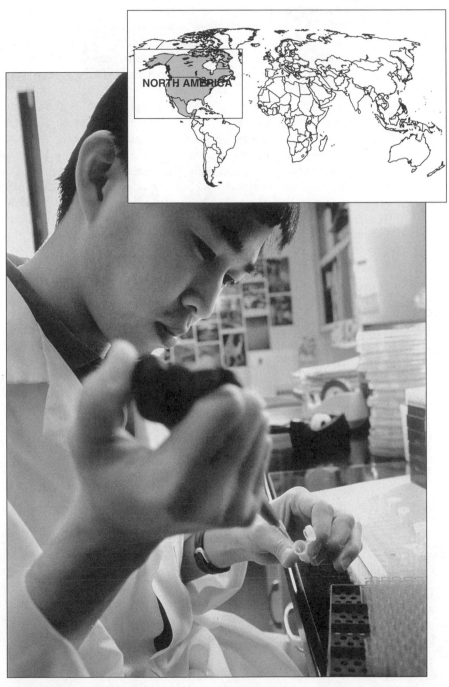

Biotechnology is emerging as one of the fastest-growing industries in today's world of international business.
©Tony Stone Worldwide: David Joel

INTRODUCTION

This chapter looks to the future. What will be the key concerns of MNE managers in the year 2000 and beyond? How will MNEs deal with home and host governments and societies as the number of MNEs grows and national priorities shift? What will be the major characteristics of international business a decade from now? The answers to these questions cannot be known for certain, but some of the broad outline of future conditions can be read from today's circumstances. Without speculating too extensively, we will look at some important issues managers in international business are likely to face during the next 10 years.

In the next section, we discuss a range of issues that will present major challenges to managers in international firms in the future. Then we look at a perspective on the sometimes rocky, sometimes smooth, but always important relations between international firms and governments. It is argued that as a reaction to competitive conditions and external pressures such as government demands on firms, companies will increasingly become **international contractors,** using contractual relationships rather than ownership in many international business situations. Next, we examine key aspects of the structure and conduct of competition in global markets. Finally, we look at important developments in internal company relations among workers, managers, and owners.

MAJOR MANAGERIAL CONSIDERATIONS FOR INTERNATIONAL FIRMS

Technology

Technology is arguably the most important input in the production of goods and services, since it determines the manner in which capital, workers, and other factors are utilized. Since it is not possible to know what inventions will be made in the future, it is likewise impossible to know what key innovations will transform the workplace.

In the industrialized countries, we have seen a continuing trend toward the production of such services as recreation, government, and computer programming during the past half-century. *Employment* in agriculture, fishing, and other sources of food products has been declining, while the *production* of food products has continued to grow (due to labor-saving advances in production technology). Similarly, employment in manufacturing has ceased to grow substantially and has even been declining in some countries—again while output has continued to rise due to greater efficiency and increased use of other production factors. The trend toward greater employment in the provision of services will probably continue in the industrialized countries, though not to the complete exclusion of manufacturing and the production of raw materials.

One important reason for continuing to manufacture in industrialized countries, despite the lower production costs that often exist in LDCs, is the importance of **spillover benefits** from manufacturing. When a firm produces automobiles in Detroit, that production leads to related production of tires, steel, glass, and so on to supply the automakers, which in turn leads to the development of new products and processes through the experiences of the various manufacturers. Such spillover benefits help maintain the technological advantages of the innovating countries, which would be lost if manufacturing were fully transferred to other countries.[1]

There are other important reasons for continuing to manufacture. First, some products can be produced only where technical knowledge is available; these products include high-tech electronics, specialty chemicals, and aerospace vehicles. Second, firms do not want to subject all of their manufacturing to "country risk" problems (which are particularly prevalent in LDCs); thus, they typically diversify production into both DCs and LDCs. Finally, some products are simply cheaper to produce and distribute in industrialized countries, which are the main markets. All of this implies that manufacturing will continue to be a very significant base of the economies of industrialized countries.[2]

An important aspect of technological development is its impact on the workplace. The clearest tendency in technological change is that such change generally leads to a reduced need for production inputs, changes in the amounts of certain inputs needed, or greater satisfaction of consumer demands, in each instance raising the economic welfare of society. Based on this reasoning, we can expect future technological change in industrialized countries to reduce the amount of time required for work and increase the amount of leisure time. Though the tendency is the same in less developed countries, high levels of unemployment and highly skewed income distributions (dual economies) will continue to limit the benefits of technological change in such countries compared to industrialized countries.

A specific change in workplace activity that is underway and promises to continue into the future is office computerization. Microcomputers have revolutionized the performance of many business tasks—from typing to copying, to mailing, to financial forecasting—and this trend has led to greater decentralization of work. More people carry out office activities at home, with fewer trips and more telecommunication to the office. Since more and more people are employed in office-type activities, in manufacturing firms as well as service providers, and in government as well as the private sector, computer-related changes in the office environment are radically altering how people do their jobs. From the perspective of the MNE manager, those firms that carry out this transition most effectively will gain a competitive advantage over rivals.

Government-Business Relations

Due to the very low likelihood of a war among major industrial powers, which could dramatically alter government-business relations, changes in government policies are likely to be incremental during the next decade. That is, national governments recognize the benefits and costs of allowing MNEs to operate. Therefore, these governments will continue to impose policies that constrain MNEs from undertaking what they view as undesirable activities (e.g., massive destabilizing currency transfers, production switching to avoid labor disputes, pollution-causing production, electronic transfer of "sensitive" information across national borders), and they will continue to try to attract MNE activities that they view as desirable (e.g., local R&D, manufacturing, transfer of knowledge). This broad agreement that MNEs are "legitimate" actors in business was truly confirmed by the fall of the Berlin Wall and the Eastern European countries' efforts to attract MNEs there.

At the transnational level, intergovernmental agreements on policy toward MNEs remain very elusive. The attempts of several organizations to formulate codes of conduct and other transnational policies have been relatively unsuccessful. Aside from further agreements to share information about company activities and some standards on corporate behavior, such as nonintervention in government affairs, major transnational policies that would affect the investment or major operating decisions of MNEs appear unlikely.

The United Nations began an effort to create a **Code of Conduct on Transnational Corporations** soon after the call in 1972 for a **New International Economic Order** that would redistribute wealth to give the less developed countries a greater share. The aim of this code is to prescribe guidelines or rules whose observance will ensure that multinational firms more fully serve national goals in the countries in which they operate. Issues such as technology transfer, international financial transfers, labor relations, and information flows constitute the core of the proposed code. Although the United Nations members have been negotiating for more than 20 years, several major disagreements still block the final passage of the code. However, the United Nations members fairly closely agree on the main provisions of the code, most of which are noted in the accompanying "IB Illustration" box.

At the multilateral level, other initiatives besides the UN Code of Conduct have taken front stage in the past several years. Certainly the European Union's EC-1992 and Maastricht Treaty efforts to advance regional integration through a wide-ranging set of common rules and policy harmonizations is creating a European policy environment that will become increasingly uniform among the member countries. This will result in a much more important role for the European Union in dealing with MNEs—on antitrust, taxes, labor relations, and many other issues—and a situation in which those MNEs that operate without European affiliates may face less favorable treatment than those operating from within the EU. Essentially a code of conduct will be produced through common, *multilateral* legislation in the EU that gives the European governments more leverage in dealing with the *multinational* firms.

A similar phenomenon is occurring in North America with the establishment of the North American Free Trade Agreement. This trading bloc can be expected to harmonize more of its member countries' treatment of MNEs, primarily on trade issues but potentially on other economic concerns too. The bold steps by Mexico to link itself more closely to the United States beginning in 1989 have generated a wholesale scramble by other Latin American countries to forge economic ties and potentially move into a Western Hemisphere trade alliance. This possibility is greatly limited by the huge differences in the levels of economic development of the potential member countries, but the global wave of pro-market policy that is under way could very well lead to a significant trade partnership in the Americas.

The regional groupings could include an Asian component, either if Japan is able to join other countries there to form a trading bloc or if the other Asian countries (led by Korea and Taiwan) industrialize rapidly enough and integrate their economies sufficiently to create a major market there. Whether or not the Asian countries join North America and Europe as regional economic blocs, the blocs that do develop will offer greater opportunities for MNEs to realize scale economies within each region, along with greater challenges from the firms that are attracted to try to serve the huge regional markets.

The less developed countries moved toward much more favorable regulation of MNEs in the late 1980s and early 1990s compared to the two previous decades. They have turned away from the strategy of inward-looking development, characterized by heavy emphasis on import substitution, to a more outward-looking view that permits greater participation by foreign firms. As LDC government managers become more expert in dealing with MNEs, however, they are tending to follow the industrialized countries in demanding more from these firms. Nevertheless, the broad sweep of openness is quite clear from Latin America to Asia and in between.

IB ILLUSTRATION

The United Nations Code of Conduct on Transnational Corporations*

In mid-1994, final agreement on this code still faced a number of hurdles. However, the overriding structure of the code was in place and was broadly accepted. Major sections of the code cover the following subjects:

Policy toward MNEs

1. *Observance of domestic laws in host countries.* Local subsidiaries, branches, and other affiliates of MNEs are to be subject to the national laws of the country in which they operate.

2. *Settlement of disputes between MNEs and countries.* The host government has the right to choose the court or other legal arbiter of disputes involving firms within its jurisdiction.

3. *Noninterference in domestic political affairs.* MNEs should not engage in activities that undermine the host country's political, social, and constitutional systems.

4. *Respect for national sovereignty.* MNEs must respect the national sovereignty of host countries and the right of host countries to exercise sovereignty over their natural resources and wealth.

Policy toward Governments

5. *Fair and equitable treatment.* MNEs should receive fair and equitable treatment from host governments.

6. *National treatment.* Subject to needs for national security and other government policy goals, MNEs should receive treatment similar to that received by domestic enterprises in similar circumstances.

7. *Nationalization and compensation.* States have the right to nationalize assets of MNEs, and compensation is to be paid according to applicable legal rules.

8. *Funds transfers by MNEs.* MNEs are entitled to transfer all payments legally due. Transfers are subject to relevant legislation of the host country, such as foreign exchange laws.

The bilateral assignment of responsibilities to companies and governments follows the structure of the OECD Code (1976) and is intended to create a stable business environment conducive to foreign direct investment and other company activities that stimulate economic development. ■

*See, for example, United Nations Center on Transnational Corporations, *CTC Reporter,* Spring 1990, which discusses the code effort from several perspectives.

Very important exceptions to the basic trend are firms in raw materials industries whose ownership LDC governments took or kept in the 1960s and 1970s. These governments show every sign that they will continue to own and control many such state-owned firms without private sector participation. On the other hand, a strong trend toward **privatization** clearly is under way in other industries, from manufacturing to public services. As a result, opportunities are growing for MNEs to enter directly in formerly restricted industries and work with raw materials industries via licensing, management contracts, and other creative "strategic alliances" with the state-owned firms.[3]

The phenomenon of privatization has become a very important worldwide signal of governments' willingness to permit the private sector a greater role in economic development. From the sale to the public of British Airways, to the sale of the Argentine telephone company to foreign investors, all the way to the denationalization of many industries in the Eastern European countries, the number and value of privatizations in the past decade is truly awesome. This process is continuing today and portends increasing MNE/host government *ownership* links as state-owned firms are partially sold to MNEs and the public-private joint ventures then make their way forward.

Company-Society Relations

While market-oriented government policy has become more widely accepted in recent years, so too has the demand for greater corporate responsiveness to national concerns such as pollution control, fair labor relations practices, and so on. International firms undoubtedly will face growing demands for accountability for their actions worldwide. Union Carbide's need to meet claims due to the industrial accident in 1984, when its joint venture plant in Bhopal, India, leaked deadly gas that killed more than 2,000 people,[4] is one striking example in which corporate responsibility was essentially forced on the firm, and such demands can be expected to increase in the future. The joint venture itself, a limited liability company, had far too few assets to settle those claims, and the parent company stepped in to meet the costs.

Despite popular movements that favor smaller firms (promoted, for example, by E F Schumacher's *Small is Beautiful*) and a less bureaucratic society, large MNEs with competitive advantages, including scale economies and international information transfer, play an increasing role in business worldwide. This is not to say that all business is becoming more concentrated; rather, more firms are becoming multinational. In the United States, the rate of growth of small firms is far greater than that of large MNEs, but so too is the rate of failure of the small firms.[5] On balance, one may conclude that small local firms and large MNEs will continue to coexist, with no trend toward either smaller or larger average firm size.

Industry Structure

The 1980s witnessed a dramatic rise in very large corporate mergers in the industrialized countries. From Bridgestone's purchase of Firestone, to CGE's purchase of ITT's telecommunications operations, to Hoechst's purchase of Celanese Corporation, these "megamergers" have become almost commonplace. Such cross-border mergers have continued apace in the 1990s, with Sony's purchase of CBS, the acquisition of Gerber Products by Sandoz AG (of Switzerland), Hoffman-LaRoche's purchase of Syntex (US), Hong Kong Bank's purchase of Midland Bank, and many more. At the other end of the size spectrum, thousands of tiny firms have become multinational in the same industries in which the megamergers have occurred. Even the largest firms have either chosen or been forced to contract out some of their activities rather than internalizing, again adding to the number of competitors. Industry structure is perhaps becoming more changeable, though no more or less concentrated on average.

One result of this merger and acquisition activity is that newly formed competitors often shake up previous industry structures. When a chemical company buys an oil company, for example, the vertical linkages involved affect competitive conditions in both the oil and the chemical industry. The chemical company (e.g., Du Pont) obtains a guaranteed source of supply of raw material at a relatively low price, and the oil company (e.g., Conoco) gains a customer for a substantial part of its output. This kind of competitive positioning is sure to continue, resulting in major realignments of firms in each industry. (Note that such realignments are due to the acquisition strategies of firms rather than to technological changes, which are another factor that tends to remake industry structures.)

Perhaps the most striking shift in international industry structure that has developed in the past few years is the use of **strategic alliances.** These cooperative agreements between firms that often are competitors in other contexts are remaking industry structures in numerous ways. First, in the auto industry, direct competitors such as Toyota and General Motors have formed joint ventures to produce cars together to benefit from the management skills of one partner (Toyota) and the market access of the other (General Motors). Dozens of additional ventures have been formed, involving all of the major competitors in this global industry. Chrysler, which owns 12 percent of Mitsubishi, jointly produces cars with Mitsubishi in Illinois; Renault and Volvo each own 45 percent of the other's truck- and bus-producing subsidiaries; a full listing of these auto industry alliances would take more than this entire page. While certainly all of the cooperative ventures will not last, the key question is whether they contribute to industry stability or disintegration. Thus far, market shares have varied significantly, but the major players in the industry have not.

In other industries, such as computers, alliances for the purpose of developing new products such as memory chips or new technologies such as risc-based logic chips and superconductors have sprouted up in the United States and Europe. Even competitors as fierce as IBM and Apple have formed alliances, in this case for the purpose of developing a new operating system and for other software development. These ventures often group half a dozen or more competitors that pool funds for research on the new products, hoping to take away knowledge that will enable each to survive in this very capital-intensive business. Thus far, these ventures have been highly unstable (e.g., US Memories, which was disbanded in 1989), leaving the competitors mostly to develop their technologies separately.

Strategic alliances have the potential to remake industry structures as they redefine the boundaries of competitiveness and cooperation. At present, there is no clear picture of what kinds of alliances in which industries can survive for long periods of time; this picture may become more focused as we move through the 1990s.

Company Internal Relations

One of the most intractable problems of industrial society has always been the **alienation** of workers from their jobs.[6] When jobs consist of carrying out a few functions within a large, impersonal assembly line or a complicated production process, such alienation is commonplace. Over time, industrial psychologists and other investigators have developed ways to reduce the severity of this problem. One way is to move workers into different kinds of work during the day to maintain their mental alertness. Another is to involve workers in company decision making, whether through worker representation on plant councils or boards of corporate supervision (as in Germany's codetermination), through quality circles, or through the Japanese *ringi* system of consultative decision making. The goal of all these techniques is to create a more productive, more satisfied work force. As the problem of alienation has become more widely recognized, solutions are being implemented more extensively.

The problem is far from solved, as demonstrated by the occurrence of strikes and demonstrations from time to time in all of the industrialized countries. However, as manufacturing and raw materials production become more mechanized and as more workers function in office environments rather than in factories or fields, the severity of the problem is being reduced to some degree. The future human relations problems of companies will tend to relate to fair treatment and participation in decision making. As noted above, many methods of increasing worker participation have been tried, and more are being developed all the time. One key source of future competitive advantages will be the skill to manage human relations within the firm so that employees are motivated and productive and the human capital investment they embody is challenged and tapped.

Relations between Developed and Less Developed Countries

The political environment plays a part in the MNEs' future, not only through dealings with individual host and home countries but also through broader political relations among blocs of countries. The powerful blocs of North America and Europe (plus Japan) will play a continuing dominant role in dealing with MNEs. As less developed countries and the countries of Eastern Europe become more integrated into the international market system, substantially greater MNE activity will develop in those countries.

Because each LDC faces a different level of economic development, different resources, different political goals, and so on, no grouping of such countries appears likely to confront the MNEs in the future. Barring the emergence of successful interest groups such as OPEC in the 1970s, the LDCs will probably continue to cooperate with the industrialized countries, seeking financial aid and other assistance and not opposing the basic market economy that is used. This does not mean that relations between the two groups of countries will proceed smoothly in the future but that the disputes between them will probably not lead to fragmentation of the international economic system. In fact, what appears more likely is the integration of countries such as those in Latin America with the North American industrial nations, the integration of the "newly industrializing" nations of Eastern Europe with the European Union, and possibly the integration of some of the Asian countries with Japan.

SURVIVAL OF THE MNE?

Concerns and Bargaining Strengths

Previous chapters have discussed the relative bargaining positions of MNEs and governments in industrialized, less developed, and formerly communist nations. Drawing from those discussions, a list of significant factors that should determine future bargaining positions is shown in Table 22–1. As long as a country can supply raw materials used in production or offer a market significant enough to attract MNE business, that country will possess a bargaining capability vis-à-vis MNEs that enables it to channel their activities in return for allowing them access to the materials or market. On the other side of the coin, as long as an MNE has some proprietary capability that governments see as desirable, such as product technology or distribution channels into foreign markets, plus the ability to move to another country if a government is not sufficiently cooperative, that MNE will possess a bargaining capability relative to the governments. (MNEs are limited in

TABLE 22-1

Bargaining Chips of MNEs and Governments

Governments	Companies
Control over access to raw materials	Control over technology
Control over market access	Control over international transmission of information
Setting the rules of the game (e.g., the role of private enterprise, the operation of state-owned firms)	Production-switching capability
	Access to export markets
Setting specific rules on MNEs—taxes, permissions, etc.	Flexibility to change strategy and activities limited only by preferences of owners
The obsolescing bargain	Economies of scale and scope
	Control over financial resources

their choice of strategies by their owners' preferences for management of the firm, while governments are limited by their constituents' preferences, as expressed through either a voting process or some more authoritarian method of control.)

The relationships between MNEs and governments will continue to operate as bargaining situations, favoring one or the other as political, technological, competitive, and other conditions change. The obsolescing bargain will continue to characterize business-government negotiations, requiring company managers to plan their entry and operating strategies to recognize the "hostage" effect of placing fixed assets in any government's jurisdiction (including that of the home country). While governments are continuously discovering new methods of obtaining benefits from MNE activities, there is no tendency to eliminate MNEs as actors in international business, since many of their bargaining advantages remain proprietary and highly "appropriable" (i.e., capable of being protected by the firms).[7]

Relations between MNEs and governments are not necessarily antagonistic; in fact on many occasions the two seek largely the same goals. In contexts such as offshore assembly, operation of research laboratories, exploration for raw materials, and many other areas, the interests of firms and governments are quite similar. Thus, the bargaining relationship does not imply only competition between firms and governments, but cooperation as well. These cooperative situations may be seen as strategic alliances, to be fostered when conditions favor them, but to be managed carefully to ensure that goals do remain consistent and that the company's best interests are being served.

The New MNE: The International Contractor

Due to the bargaining situations described above and to increased competition from other firms, MNEs are experiencing more and more pressure to externalize their activities. Whether it be the demand of a host government to take on a local partner or the enticement of a joint research project with a rival firm to reduce R&D costs, pressures are mounting toward increased contractual arrangements between firms. Simultaneously, the previous reliance on wholly owned affiliates, especially preferred by US-based firms, has shifted toward a greater willingness to utilize nontraditional methods such as joint ventures, licensing or service contracting, turnkey ventures, and combinations of these arrangements as managers realize their relative profitability and strategic viability.

As additional small firms become multinational (by establishing affiliates in three or more countries), the tendency again is to externalize some activities, especially when the firm's resources or skills do not permit it to go beyond its core activities. What we are seeing, in essence, is that even small firms are looking at multiple countries as their markets rather than being constrained by national borders in their strategy making. Then, as corporate expansion occurs, and given low international transportation costs and easy communication, they seek new markets or products in different countries. Just as small domestic firms often contract out for parts of their business, so too do the new small multinationals, which face similar constraints on their activities.

In sum, large MNEs are utilizing more externalized contracting due to regulatory constraints, and both small and large firms are using externalized contracting due to their internal economic and managerial constraints. Both of these trends foreshadow the rise of the **international contractor (INC),** as discussed in Chapter 2. The INC is defined as a firm that carries out business activities in at least two countries, but without necessarily owning affiliates in both. The INC operates from a home office that controls the use of its key competitive advantages, such as its proprietary production technology and international information network. The home office also decides when to utilize the INC's competitive advantages through internalized operations such as local and foreign subsidiaries and when to sell knowledge or some other intermediate goods to potential customers. The INC is still a multinational firm in the sense that it possesses multinational operations; its difference from the MNE lies solely in its lack of dependence on *ownership* of affiliates as the main vehicle for using its competitive advantages in different national environments. (The MNE, in fact, is a subset of the INC.)

The international contractor, like the MNE, may be a small or a large firm. The INC is, in principle, more open to nontraditional means of doing business around the world. For example, when Citibank discovered that its data-processing skills were in demand by clients and competitors around the world, it chose to sell more than just its banking services. Now Citibank sells dozens of services to outside clients: access to a global, computerized information network, technical support to clients that want to use the system, the software for recordkeeping in such banking activities as customer deposit and loan accounts, technical support for use of that software, and so on. Rather than internalizing these services completely, Citibank has chosen to contract out for their use and expand its sales into markets that the bank itself cannot enter and into services that it previously limited to internal use.

Many other examples of international contractors exist. General Electric Company, the US-based diversified electrical products manufacturer, has added a trading company to its portfolio of businesses. The trading company seeks outlets for GE products in most countries of the world and tries to dispose of products it has received in payment from customers unable to pay in hard currency. GE has even used the trading company to sell the products of other firms in international markets, functioning somewhat like the Japanese *sogo shosha* as an intermediary between a producer and the ultimate purchaser.

Conflicts between MNEs and Governments

The management of conflicts with home and host governments is already a crucial MNE task, and that task will become even more important in the future. Gladwin and Walter (1980), for example, found evidence of 650 such conflicts involving a sample of only five multinational firms during the period 1969 to 1978. Behrman and Grosse (1990) examined in detail the areas of potential and actual conflict between MNEs and governments, areas ranging from transfer pricing to interference in domestic political affairs and from employment practices to technology transfer.

Behrman and Grosse have developed a framework that offers useful insights into the key strategic considerations. This framework is shown in Figure 22–1. They reason that corporate strategy for managing a conflict (or cooperation) situation with a government should be based on an evaluation of (1) the bargaining resources held by the government and the company; (2) the stakes each party has in the situation; and (3) the goal congruence, or similarity of interests, between government and company in the particular situation. All three dimensions contribute to the MNE's bargaining power relative to the government, and strategy for dealing with the government should be based on an accurate assessment of the firm's bargaining strengths and weaknesses.

For example, a firm that finds itself in position M in Figure 22–1 will have a very valuable opportunity to receive desired treatment by the government, since all three bargaining dimensions favor the firm. This kind of situation occurs

FIGURE 22–1

The Bargaining Relationship between MNE and Host Government

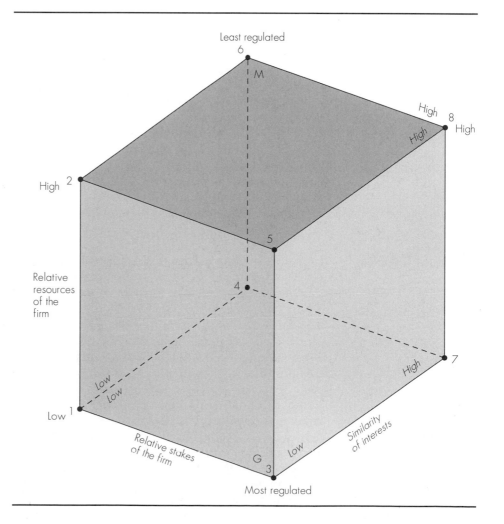

when, for example, a high-tech firm seeks to do offshore assembly in an LDC. The firm offers employment and technology transfer, plus exports from the country; the firm has other, alternative locations to carry out the offshore assembly; and the country is (typically) interested in attracting this kind of business. Contrast this example with point G in Figure 22–1, where the government is likely to have a much stronger bargaining position than the firm. This situation can be illustrated by a country with a large market dealing with a low-tech, relatively small MNE, for example, the Brazilian government negotiating with US consumer products firms. In this context, the government has a relatively large bargaining resource, namely control over access to the desirable market. The government has little at stake in the situation, since other consumer products from various industrial and less developed countries presumably offer similar products to those available from our example firm. Finally, the firm is assumed to be interested in serving the local market rather than exporting, so the government will probably not improve its balance of payments from this firm's activities. In sum, a strong bargaining position results for the government when the firm does not offer major help in pursuing national goals, when the firm has more at stake, and when the goals of each actor are somewhat divergent. Any situation of government-company bargaining can be analyzed in this framework, leading to a better understanding of the firm's options in seeking favorable treatment. Figure 22–1 indicates that the MNE can improve its relations with the government through strategies that move the relationship toward point M.

COMPETITIVE CONDITIONS

The structure and intensity of competition in market-based economies is subject to major changes when technological advances take place, when mergers or divestitures occur, when governments alter the rules of the game, and when other unanticipated events occur (e.g., the OPEC cartel's successful oil price hikes in 1973 and 1979, the breakups of AT&T in 1984 and NTT [Nippon Telephone & Telegraph] in 1985, the Latin American debt crisis of the 1980s, and the fall of the Berlin Wall in 1989). This section comments on the kinds of competitive impacts that can be expected from each type of major change in conditions.

Changes in Technology

Technological innovations undoubtedly will continue to cause drastic upheavals in industry structure. Each new type of transportation vehicle has either replaced its predecessor or created a separate market for a new kind of transportation service. Each advance in communications technology has resulted in new firms and new interrelationships in the communications industry. Even innovations in such low-tech areas as restaurants (e.g., the fast-food restaurant chains and the diversification of single-food providers) and recreation (e.g., the shift to high-tech running shoes) have greatly reshuffled industry structures. International restaurant chains were almost unknown 25 years ago, but McDonald's and Burger King now span much of the world. One or two brands captured most of the athletic shoe market in the 1950s and 1960s, but today dozens of competitors make exotic and often quite expensive running shoes (e.g., Etonic, New Balance, Reebok, and Nike, in addition to the longer-established Adidas, Pumas, and Keds).

These technological shifts portend major industry restructurings, many of which cannot be foreseen. On the other hand, some likely focal points of such restructurings *can* be identified. For example, the future competition in computers, telecommunications, and transportation vehicles will surely differ tremendously from that of today; the expected change is readily anticipated. However, it is difficult to judge which of the existing firms will survive and how the new industries will be structured.

Mergers, Acquisitions, and Divestitures

A second major cause of industry restructuring is company growth or decline via the purchase or sale of parts of the business. As we have noted repeatedly, vertical integration is often accomplished through acquisition of upstream or downstream firms. Similarly, reduction in firm size is often carried out through divestiture of divisions or subsidiaries. Each time an acquisition or divestment occurs, the competition in the industries involved changes to some degree. When the players are large (e.g., Nabisco and R J Reynolds, Du Pont and Conoco, General Motors and Electronic Data Systems on the expansion side; on the contraction side, ITT's sale of Continental Baking and even its telecommunications division and International Harvester's sale of its farm equipment business), the impact on the industries is substantial. When the players are small, the impacts are less extensive, but the industries are affected nonetheless. And, of course, today's small firms may evolve into tomorrow's major competitors through acquisition strategies.

Government-Owned Firms

Among the less developed countries, the euphoria of the 1960s and early 1970s, when many LDCs viewed government-owned firms as the answer to foreign-owned multinationals, has ended. State-owned companies do not automatically use more "appropriate" technology or possess the competitive advantages of MNEs. (Specifically, they have neither the multinational information networks nor the access to foreign markets of MNEs.) Based on this reasoning and on the relatively scanty economic success of state-owned firms during the past two decades, such firms are being privatized in droves during the 1990s. This is not to imply that state-owned companies will disappear from the competition; rather, their limitations are being recognized, and LDCs are in many cases finding a place for MNE participation in the same industries.

Among industrialized countries, the economic costs of operating state-owned firms led to many privatizations in the 1980s. Conrail (in the United States), NTT (in Japan), British Telecom (in the United Kingdom), the chemical giant Montedison (in Italy), and many other government firms have been partially or totally sold to private sector buyers. These sales were followed by the privatizations of most of the major telephone companies and airlines in Latin America during the early 1990s. All this implies mainly that future competition will be dominated not by state-owned firms but by MNEs and local firms that can develop sustainable competitive advantages, such as those that result in economic efficiency.

LDCs versus Industrialized Countries

The differences between conditions in the developed, industrialized countries and conditions in the less developed countries should not be underemphasized. The changes in competitive conditions just discussed are likely to be accompanied by much greater upheaval in the LDCs than in the industrialized countries. For example, even though state-owned companies are seen as being relatively inefficient in competition with private sector firms, many LDCs will (for "political" reasons) continue to bear the economic costs of operating some of them. Also, the changes in technology and in company size that will reshape industrial markets will not necessarily pass on to the LDCs in the same manner. The main result of the telecommunications revolution will probably be their use of different suppliers of communications and data-processing equipment, since almost all of the competing firms are from industrialized countries. By the same token, the major mergers and divestitures that will redefine industry structures in global industries will in most cases probably only replace one foreign supplier with another in LDCs. On the other hand, domestic firms in such LDCs as the newly industrializing countries may become competitive in world markets. This appears to be happening in South Korea, Singapore, Hong Kong, Taiwan, and Brazil and has already happened in Japan.

COMPANY INTERNAL CONDITIONS

A look to the future of international business should focus not only on external, environmental conditions but also on internal (labor and personnel) issues related to the international firm. In this section, we consider these latter issues and the relationship between owners and managers.

Labor-Management Relations

As industries become more mature, especially extractive and manufacturing industries, their labor requirements tend to decline. Greater efficiency in production often leads to a reduced need for factors of production, particularly labor but also capital and other inputs. This tendency does not portend declining overall employment, because it is offset by growing employment in new industries and perhaps by shifts to higher employment in the service sector, as discussed previously. Given the declining labor requirements of maturing and standardized industries, the political and collective bargaining power of unions in those industries (as such unions are now constituted) is bound to decline too.

These unions will disappear completely or will be replaced in importance by new unions in the new industries or by some alternative form of labor-management relations. That is, the United Auto Workers, the United Steel Workers, the textile unions, and several other unions will continue to decline in membership and in importance. (It is not unthinkable that the International Ladies' Garment Workers' Union [ILGWU] will cease to exist a decade or two from now.) These unions will be replaced by other (perhaps new) organizations of workers in, for example, electronics manufacture and biotechnology production and by worker groups in the service sector (many of which already exist). The trend away from employment in manufacturing will not eliminate conflicts between labor and management; however, those conflicts will be altered from shop floor to office concerns.

Current trends toward worker participation in management and/or ownership of firms in the industrialized countries may succeed in reducing the conflict between workers and managers to a very low level. Efforts to achieve Japanese-style worker productivity and commitment to the firm are likely to continue as long as the Japanese model appears to yield superior results. Apart from the Japanese model, the "excellent" firms recognized by Peters and Waterman (in *In Search of Excellence*) demonstrate the kind of focus on maintaining a satisfying, stimulating work environment that seems to succeed in many companies. Thus, it is conceivable that labor-management relations will generally improve due to the widespread recognition of the value of such improvement.

Personnel Relations

One trend that is becoming increasingly clear in large MNEs is that the future international contractor will employ people of many nationalities and many ethnic groups, because the corporation obtains benefits from employing locals in some countries and the benefits of the geocentric approach to management fosters global recruitment of personnel. The competitive advantage gained from hiring the best people available, regardless of nationality, is evident in the large, successful MNEs even today.

For example, in recent years Dow Chemical Corporation named as head of its Latin American headquarters a North American, a Latin American, a Greek, and then a Frenchman. Each of these executives has had experience in senior positions in the company elsewhere in the world (e.g., in the European headquarters, the Asian headquarters, and corporate headquarters in Michigan), and each has continued to move up the corporate ladder. The personnel strategy of Dow Chemical is to hire the most qualified people available in the locations where they are needed and then move them, regardless of their nationality, to new posts as their skills and the firm's needs dictate.

Management-Owner Relations

Today large industrial corporations are generally owned by large numbers of shareholders, none of whom control sizable percentages of the total stock of the firm. The separation of management from ownership is a fundamental characteristic of free-market development in the 20th century. This basic separation will probably continue, though more and more ways are being discovered to channel managers' efforts to serve owners' interests. (The popularity of leveraged buyouts in the late 1980s appears to have been due to the ability of outside investors to locate firms in which a divergence arose between company capabilities, based on owners' interests, and the market value produced by managers' actions and reflected in share prices.)

Some interesting variations on this theme occur in the state-owned companies, in which management is often government appointed and the sole shareholder is the government itself. This relationship between owner and manager is quite different from that existing in large, private firms, and it leads to different corporate goals and strategies.

Small firms may have closely held shares that belong to the managers themselves. In such firms, there is no separation of owner and manager, and the managers presumably always make decisions that are in the owners' interest. This eliminates the problem of suboptimal performance (and the pursuit of personal rather than corporate goals), which can plague large, widely held firms.

CONCLUSIONS

The future is unknowable. Hopefully, the discussion in this chapter has offered some idea of the kinds of environment, external and internal, in which the international firm will operate during the next decade.

Probably the most visible characteristic of multinational enterprises 10 years from now will be the much larger number of such firms. As transportation and communication become even cheaper in the future, more and more firms will view their markets as multicountry regions or even the whole world. The names of some of the largest firms will change, and many new products will emerge, but the overriding feature will be the global nature of competition.

In this context, the *international contractor* will become the model for successful competitors. That is, firms that can adapt their ownership structures and strategies to accommodate differences in national rules, conditions, and preferences will prevail. No longer will ownership of subsidiaries be the basic building block of growth; control over business activities in different locations will also be achieved through such means as management contracts, supply agreements, and joint ventures. Flexibility in dealing with government negotiations, supplier-customer relations, internal human resource management, and business rivalries will become an even more important competitive advantage than it is now.

In government negotiations, the international contractor will face much more rigorous bargaining in which it will have to demonstrate the social benefits of its operations to receive continuing government approval of its activities. Governments in less developed countries as well as in industrialized nations have become aware of their strengths in bargaining, and they will assert those strengths in dealing with INCs.

In supplier-customer relations, the INC will find many more "foreign" suppliers of goods and services in every country. Hence, the need for a competitive strategy based on some sustainable advantage (such as proprietary technology, differentiated products, or government protection) will become increasingly important.

Internal human resource management within the INC will become a greater concern as competition increases and firms seek such competitive advantages as higher worker productivity and peace between labor and management. Many Japanese firms today are perceived as having an advantage in human resource management. In the future, firms in other countries (Korea and Singapore, for example, but also possibly the United States and Germany) will attain a similar advantage, and that advantage will become more indicative of good management than of cultural background.

Business rivalries will not become more severe in all industries in the future, but they will likely become more international. That is, firms from many countries will compete in multiple national markets, resulting in greater multinationality of competition. As always, the more competitive firms will tend to drive out the less competitive ones, and barriers to market entry and exit will preclude huge numbers of firms from competing in many key sectors, but the competitors that do participate in each market will come from a greater number of countries.

Managers will continue to need the technical tools they obtain in business schools and the practical experience they acquire in the business world. Seeing the environment clearly and defining and carrying out competitive strategies effectively will continue to be the keys to successful management in international business.

QUESTIONS

1. What is the international contractor? How does it compare with the multinational enterprise?
2. What important bargaining strengths of INCs will enable them to negotiate successfully with governments in the future?
3. What important bargaining strengths of national governments will enable them to negotiate successfully with INCs in the future?
4. How will changes in technology affect the business environment of the remainder of the 1990s? Specifically, how will new telecommunications technology affect competition in the computer industry?

5. How will the INC justify its legitimacy in the eyes of host governments? That is, what social benefit generated by INC activities will make it valuable to host governments?

6. What role will government-owned firms play in the competition of the 1990s? In what industries will such firms be prevalent?

7. List and explain major conflict areas between INCs and national governments that will cause tensions and perhaps crises between them. How can managers deal with these conflict areas?

8. What characteristics of small INCs will enable them to compete internationally in particular products or market segments during the 1990s?

9. What kinds of international business activity can be expected to occur in less developed countries during the 1990s?

10. What industry or business would you choose to be in when the year 2000 arrives? What are the international business aspects of that industry or business? How will you try to compete with rival firms?

REFERENCES

Behrman, Jack N, and Robert Grosse. *International Business and Governments*. Columbia, SC: University of South Carolina Press, 1990.

Boddewyn, Jean J. "Political Aspects of MNE Theory." *Journal of International Business Studies,* Fall 1988.

Gladwin, Thomas, and Ingo Walter. *Multinationals under Fire*. New York: John Wiley & Sons, 1980.

Ohmae, Kenichi. "The Global Logic of Strategic Alliances." *Harvard Business Review,* March–April 1989.

————. *Triad Power*. New York: The Free Press, 1985.

Organization for Economic Cooperation and Development. "Declaration of OECD Member Governments on International Investment and Multinational Enterprises." Paris: OECD, 1976.

Perlmutter, Howard, and David Heenan. "Thinking Ahead." *Harvard Business Review,* March–April 1986.

Porter, Michael. *The Competitive Advantage of Nations*. New York: The Free Press, 1990.

Root, Franklin. "Some Trends in the World Economy and Their Implications for International Business." *Journal of International Business Studies,* Winter 1984.

NOTES

[1] See Porter (1990), chapter 4, for a compelling argument about the dynamic competitiveness produced for core and supplier firms that benefit from these spillovers.

[2] This conflicts with the view presented by Norman Jonas in "The Hollow Corporation" (*Business Week*, March 3, 1986), which argued that major US firms are becoming "hollow corporations," conducting their manufacturing abroad or contracting it out to foreign suppliers.

[3] Even in the highly visible petroleum sector, some moves to privatization have occurred, such as the sale of the Argentine oil company YPF to private investors in 1993.

[4] See Paul Shrivastava, *Bhopal: Anatomy of a Crisis* (Cambridge, MA.: Ballinger, 1987).

[5] See monthly data in "General Business Indicators" in the *Survey of Current Business*.

[6] P J D Drenth, H Thierry, P J Willems, and C J de Wolff, *Handbook of Work and Organizational Psychology* (New York: John Wiley & Sons, 1984).

[7] This bargaining process is analyzed in detail in Behrman and Grosse (1990).

Industry Profiles

This appendix contains extensive case studies of four major industries—petroleum, automobiles, banking, and telecommunications—in which international competition is involved. Each section explores industry characteristics such as locations of production and consumption, recent history, and industry structure. In addition, individual firms and their competitive strategies are discussed.

INTRODUCTION

This appendix provides a view of four major industries that have figured prominently in international business in the 20th century: petroleum, automobiles, banking, and telecommunications. It explores the international aspects of these industries, from competition among multinational firms to international structure of production, and looks at the various stages of production from initial processing to consumer sales. More specifically, it presents basic information about the industries and then examines the implications of current conditions and expected changes for international business managers.

While one cannot become an industry expert after reading these few pages, it is possible to gain from them a better understanding of the pressures firms in these industries face and the relative positions of some of the largest firms. By examining four distinctive types of industry (natural resource, high-tech, service, and smokestack), we are able to gain insights that have application to a wide variety of additional industries and firms.

Four Industries

The *petroleum* industry is arguably the single most important industry of the past 50 years. Oil is the most important energy source used in the 20th century, as well as being the base of the petrochemical industry. Oil is a relatively scarce natural resource, and supplies of oil are located largely in less developed countries (especially the Middle Eastern countries). The cartel of less developed oil-producing countries shifted the balance of economic power somewhat away from the industrial nations and toward the oil-producing nations during the 1970s. Finally, in the present context, trade and direct investment in the oil business constitute a major portion of total international business. Beginning with the Arab oil embargo and the OPEC (Organization of Petroleum Exporting Countries) price hikes in 1973 and 1974, crude oil prices went from about $US 2 per barrel to almost $US 40 per barrel by 1980, and then back to around $US 20 per barrel by 1985, then again up to $US 30 in 1990, and down to $US 16 in 1994.

After numerous nationalizations in LDCs during the mid-1970s, the petroleum industry has evolved from a fairly small number of vertically integrated MNEs (the "Seven Sisters" and a handful of others) to myriad firms and contractual arrangements. These changes have had an enormous impact on consumers, governments, and firms in other industries. Inflation in the industrialized countries rose from an average of around 6 percent per year in the early 1970s to well over 12 percent by 1980. (One reason for inflation was expansionary government monetary and fiscal policies in industrialized countries to mitigate the negative effects on employment and income of the huge transfers of financial wealth to the oil-exporting countries.) Worldwide recessions occurred in 1975–76 and 1980–83 after major hikes in oil prices. The ripples from these changes are still being felt today.

The *automotive* industry is a traditional "smokestack industry" that involves large-scale, capital-intensive production facilities with assembly lines, a heavily unionized work force, and fairly standardized (or at least mature) products and emphasizes price competition in the final product market. Unlike the petroleum industry, this industry is not based on a single raw material but is a heavy user of a number of industrial inputs, including steel, glass, rubber, and oil. Competition in the production aspect of this industry remains the province of firms in industrial countries, with strong competitors in the United States, Europe, and Japan. However, the actual production of components, assemblies, and even full automobiles has been shifting more and more to low-cost locations around the world. This is the youngest of the four industries, having first come into existence at the end of the 19th century.

Banking contrasts sharply with the petroleum and automotive industries. Banking is a service that requires few raw materials. The provision of domestic banking services is highly regulated in every country, though the eurocurrency market is relatively unrestricted in a few countries (primarily the industrialized nations). Banking has been closely tied to the oil industry, not only as a source of loans and deposits but also as the major vehicle through which "recycling" of the money ("petrodollars") earned by OPEC countries in the 1970s took place. Both the banking and petroleum industries supply fairly standardized products. Competition in banking is often based on nonprice factors, such as service or regulatory conditions. Banking is by far the oldest of our four industries.

The *telecommunications* industry differs greatly from the other three. This industry has existed since the advent of the telegraph in the 1840s, and it has continually faced dramatic competitive shifts as new technology has been developed. From telegraph to telephone to television, the industry has repeatedly led technological advancement in the modern world. In the 1980s, the advances were related primarily to the integration of the computer industry with telecommunications. Building on the use of tiny transistors embodied in silicon chips, both computers and telecommunications switching equipment became almost infinitely complex and at the same time relatively inexpensive and widely available to consumers during the past decade. The competition among firms in the telecommunications industry has changed rapidly with each new generation of computer technology, from memory increases to communications advances and improvements in processing speeds. During the past decade or so, the telecommunications industry became characterized by the use of offshore assembly in Southeast Asia for the production of telephones, televisions, computer chips, and many other products. In the 1990s, telecommunications has generally been regarded as the epitome of the high-tech industries.

International Aspects

Our intent in this appendix is to highlight the international aspects of each of the four industries covered. The next four sections look at the cross-country structures of each industry, the history that has led to its current competitive environment, and its major firms and some of their competitive strategies. Particular emphasis is placed on the ownership arrangements that pervade each industry, for example, banking in most countries is fragmented geographically and primarily locally owned, whereas telecommunications equipment is produced globally by a small number of multinational firms. A wide variety of contractual agreements arose in the petroleum industry as governments nationalized oil production, but these governments still need the MNEs for technical assistance, access to foreign markets, and other services. Automobile manufacture remains the province of a small number of MNEs, but marketing, service, and parts production all involve thousands of smaller competitors in many countries. Although the examples presented focus on MNEs, the following sections also demonstrate the involvement of smaller firms in each industry.

OIL

Sources of Production and Consumption

Most of the world's proved oil reserves are located in the Middle East, as shown in Figure A–1. Saudi Arabia alone has proved reserves totaling about 259 billion barrels, compared to the 24 billion barrels of the United States and the 57 billion barrels of Russia.[1] The numbers in Figure A–1 portray the results of a major shift

FIGURE A–1

World Distribution of Proved Oil Reserves (billions of barrels as of January 1, 1994)

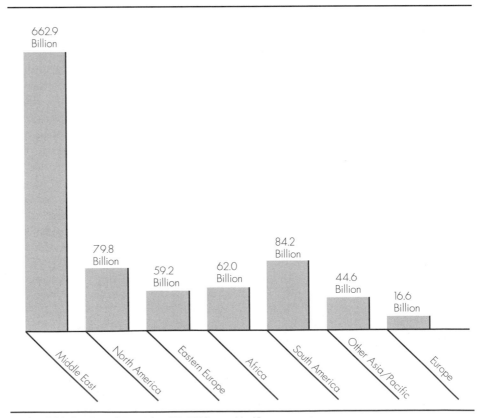

Source: *Oil & Gas Journal,* December 27, 1993, pp. 44–45.

in oil reserves since World War II. Before that time, the United States was the largest oil-producing nation, supplying over half of the world's demand. (Most of this US production went to serve US consumption.) Major discoveries in the Middle East during the late 1940s catapulted Saudi Arabia ahead of all other oil producers. The Ghawar oil field alone had proved reserves of 60 billion barrels.

On the demand side, as may be expected, the industrialized countries account for most of the world's oil use. The United States leads the consuming nations, with annual consumption of about 6 billion barrels of oil out of a total world consumption of about 22 billion barrels per year.

Recent History

The oil industry has been dominated by US-based firms, plus Shell and British Petroleum, during most of its existence. Since the founding of Standard Oil of New Jersey in 1882, that firm (the core of which became Exxon) has been the industry leader. (In 1986, however, Royal Dutch/Shell took over the position of industry leader when the parent firm purchased the 49 percent of its US subsidiary that was not already owned.) During the first half of the 20th century, a group of vertically integrated firms in the United States and Great Britain achieved substantial positions in all phases of the industry in the noncommunist world, from exploration to the operation of gasoline stations. These firms (Exxon, Mobil, Texaco, Socal, Shell, Gulf, and British Petroleum) were labeled the **Seven Sisters** because of the similarities in their size and strategies.[2] With the merger of Gulf into Socal (or Chevron) in 1985 and the increased importance of Amoco (Standard Oil of Indiana), plus the truly global nature of the oil business today, perhaps the leading oil industry firms should now be called the **"Major Multinationals."** Table A–1 lists the largest oil multinationals and a few of their characteristics.

TABLE A–1 Competitive Strengths of 13 Major Oil Companies

Company	Annual Sales, 1993 ($US millions)	Competitive Advantages
1. Royal Dutch/Shell Group*	95.134	Similar to those of Exxon
2. Exxon*	92.825	Worldwide distribution network, access to multiple sources of crude, proprietary technology, financial strength, and cash flow
3. Mobil*	56.576	
4. British Petroleum (including Sohio)*	52.485	
5. Total Compagnie Française des Petroles	37.016	Government protection in France
6. ENI (Italy)	34.791	
7. Texaco*	34.359	Marketing strength and ability, multiple sources of crude, proprietary technology
8. Chevron*	32.123	
9. Petróleos Méxicanos	26.573	Inexpensive oil and built-up cash
10. Amoco*	25.336	
11. Aramco (Saudi Arabia)	N.A.	Inexpensive oil and built-up cash reserves, ability to produce lots or little oil and force the market to adjust, greatest crude reserves
12. Petróleos de Venezuela	21.275	Inexpensive oil and built-up cash
13. Kuwait Petroleum Corp.	N.A.	Inexpensive oil and built-up cash

*Major multinational.
Source: "The International 500," *Fortune*, July 25, 1994.

Early Oil Producers The United States was the largest producer of oil during the first half of this century. As exploration in other countries grew during the 1940s, discoveries in the Middle East quickly led that region to surpass the United States as an oil producer. The companies involved in oil exploration and production in the Middle East were the Seven Sisters plus a few foreign competitors. Exploration in Algeria, Nigeria, Venezuela, Indonesia, and several other LDCs also led to expanded worldwide oil production, which reached about 18 million barrels per day in 1960.

Throughout this period, the multinational oil companies operated through **concessions** in oil-producing countries (i.e., agreements with governments to extract and sell oil in exchange for paying taxes, fees, and other charges) and controlled most of the oil produced. The governments of the producing countries gained substantial revenues through fees and royalties on oil sales. The oil companies used land under concession from host governments, and these governments were paid fixed per-barrel royalties on the oil produced. It was not until the early 1950s that Middle Eastern countries began charging income tax (at a 50 percent rate) on sales of oil. Since the oil companies sold most of their oil to their own downstream affiliates for refining and subsequent processing, they were able to keep wellhead prices low and thus keep taxes to host governments low. In September 1960, five of the LDC host countries joined together to form **OPEC (Organization of Petroleum Exporting Countries)**, specifically to protect their interests in obtaining stable and higher returns on oil production. Since then, OPEC has expanded to 13 members, which at one point controlled about two-thirds of the world's oil supply. During the 1960s, the OPEC countries chipped away at the oil companies' control of the oil industry, mainly by raising royalties and taxes.

By 1970, the balance of power in the oil industry had shifted dramatically in favor of host governments. According to Exxon Corporation "Whereas oil had accounted for about 10 percent of the total energy consumed in Western Europe in 1950, its share was more than 55 percent by 1970. In Japan over the same period, oil's share rose from 9 percent to 33 percent. Imports accounted for virtually all the oil consumed in both areas."[3] Even the United States began to import a substantial quantity of oil from OPEC suppliers. Not only did global demand create a seller's market for petroleum, but by 1970 supply conditions had shifted to the point where OPEC provided about 60 percent of noncommunist output. Finally, through the education of increasing numbers of students from Saudi Arabia, Iraq, Venezuela, and other countries in the world's leading universities, a base of managerial skills was being developed to manage OPEC oil for the specific benefit of these countries rather than for the benefit of the oil companies. Each of these shifts pushed the obsolescing bargain farther in favor of the oil-producing countries.

The Role of Arabian Gulf Oil Looking back at this period, two events appear to have set the stage for the incredible upheavals of the 1970s. First, the Arab-Israeli war in 1967 led to the closing of the Suez Canal, through which much of the Arabian Gulf oil was transported to Europe. This event highlighted the growing dependence of the industrialized countries on Arabian Gulf oil, and it also focused attention on US support for Israel, which created very serious tensions between the United States and the Arab countries. Second, a construction accident in 1970 caused the temporary shutdown of the Trans-Arabian Pipeline, requiring all Arabian Gulf oil to be shipped much farther away—around the Cape of Good

Hope in South Africa—to reach European buyers. This event led to increased oil prices and a successful demand for higher taxes by OPEC members, thus reinforcing the oil-producing nations' awareness of their bargaining strength.

In 1971, the Arabian Gulf countries and Libya successfully forced negotiations with the oil companies to set oil prices through agreements between the governments and the companies and to raise taxes on the oil sold. These agreements, signed in Tehran (Iran) and Tripoli (Libya), marked the first time producing countries had achieved dominant influence over crude oil pricing. Following this success, the members of OPEC began pressing for ownership of the oil production facilities. By the end of 1972, Saudi Arabia, Abu Dhabi, and Qatar had negotiated to buy 51 percent of the oil-producing facilities within their borders over a 10-year period.

The **nationalization** of oil companies and the control of pricing by OPEC members jumped ahead again in September 1973, when another Arab-Israeli war broke out and the Arab countries unilaterally raised their oil prices and embargoed oil shipments to the United States and the Netherlands (because these two countries showed support for Israel in the war). Crude oil prices (at $US 2.70 per barrel in early October) were raised 35 percent on October 16, 1973, and 131 percent on January 1, 1974. The OPEC governments raised taxes on the oil companies to 85 percent of income and royalties to 20 percent of the list price of crude oil. Greater government ownership of oil companies operating within the OPEC nations was also demanded, and by the end of 1974 most of the OPEC nations had achieved 60 percent ownership.

Since 1974, the nationalization of oil companies within the OPEC nations proceeded to complete local ownership in most cases. Crude oil prices are now set by OPEC governments without negotiations with the companies. After a few years of price increases that approximately kept pace with inflation, the Iranian crisis of 1978, which led to the overthrow of the shah's government, disrupted the supply of oil from that country. OPEC raised prices accordingly throughout 1979. By year end, consumers' fears of a new oil shortage and OPEC's reaction to panic buying had enabled OPEC to increase oil prices 95 percent to $US 26 per barrel. This second oil price shock was followed by two years of steadily increasing OPEC prices, which peaked at $US 34 per barrel in October 1981.

Oil consumers reacted to the continuing upward spiral of oil prices by trying to conserve energy in their existing activities, switching to alternative energy sources, and simply cutting down on energy-intensive activities. The effects of these reactions were slow to be felt, but by 1982 the fuel efficiency of US automobiles had been raised to over twice the 1972 level (mileage of over 30 miles per gallon was common for new cars, compared to about 15 miles per gallon in the early 1970s), coal and nuclear power were replacing oil in many electric utilities, and both residential and commercial electric power use (per customer) had dropped noticeably. These reactions, as well as a worldwide recession and the emergence of major new oil supplies in the North Sea and North America, had created an oversupply of oil by the end of 1982.

By the mid-1980s, world oil sales had shifted away from the OPEC countries, which now sell only about 40 percent of the world total, to other suppliers such as Norway, Mexico, the United Kingdom, and Canada, countries that do not follow OPEC market-sharing practices. Also, sales of oil on the "spot" market, which, unlike OPEC sales, are not tied to long-term contracts, rose in the mid-1980s to almost one-third of total crude oil sales. Some OPEC (and other) producers have placed substantial amounts of their production into this market, and many oil companies are increasingly making their purchases without long-term contracts (i.e., on the spot market). Finally, the OPEC countries themselves discounted their prices substantially during the 1980s oil glut, so the posted price published by OPEC countries is no longer a good measure of actual sales prices. In fact, in late 1985, OPEC abandoned attempts to control its members' oil-pricing policies. The cartel has failed to maintain its monopoly control over oil supply, though only after more than a decade of successful operations that led to huge transfers of wealth from industrial countries to OPEC members.

Renewed efforts to fix crude oil prices succeeded to some extent in 1987, when OPEC agreed to a price of $US 18 per barrel. This agreement was achieved despite the all-out war between Iran and Iraq and the widespread use of discounts and other efforts of OPEC members to sell more than their production allocations in the cartel. Prices soared again when Iraq invaded and annexed Kuwait in 1990. The price of oil futures rose above $US 40 per barrel before the market settled back to prices in the $US 20–30 range. Price volatility is now a regular feature of the oil market, while consumption remains fairly stable. The price of Saudi Arabian light crude was $US 16 per barrel in mid-1994.

Industry Structure

The ownership of companies producing *crude oil* shifted from almost exclusively the Seven Sisters and other private firms during the first half of this century to almost exclusive host government ownership (in the LDCs) by 1980. Figure A–2 bears out this point. Both exploration for new oil and downstream processing of

FIGURE A–2　International Oil Companies' Equity Interest in Middle Eastern Crude Oil Production, 1965–1987

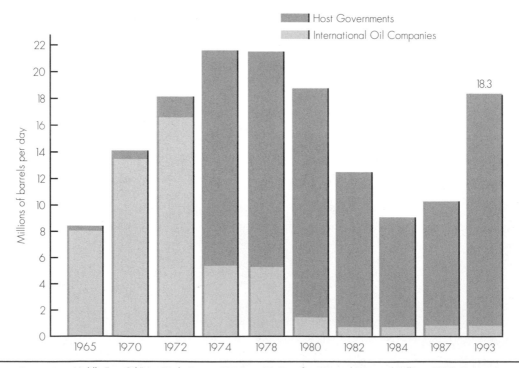

Sources: Exxon Corporation, *Middle East Oil* (New York: Exxon, 1994), p. 35. Data from *Annual Statistical Bulletin, 1987,* Organization of the Petroleum Exporting Countries, and Exxon Corporation estimates.

crude oil, however, are still dominated by the oil companies. One would expect the OPEC governments to be interested in downstream production, and indeed in 1993, refining capacity within OPEC was about 6.8 million barrels per day compared to worldwide refining capacity of about 73.0 million barrels per day. Unfortunately for the OPEC refineries, oil demand dropped sharply during the early 1980s, and refining became an unprofitable or marginal venture in many cases. Several OPEC countries had begun to process farther downstream, into petrochemicals,[4] but petrochemical demand has stagnated over the past several years. While it appears that OPEC-based firms will supply substantial amounts of downstream products to world markets in the long run, their progress thus far has been curtailed by weak demand worldwide.

We can conclude that upstream oil production in LDCs has been very largely taken over by governments, in contrast with the production and distribution of all stages of oil-based products, which are owned and controlled largely by private companies, though even at the downstream stages many independent companies are major competitors along with the Major Multinationals. Figure A–3 depicts the present structure of the petroleum industry, which is in marked contrast to that of the pre-1970 period when vertically integrated companies dominated the entire industry. Notice specifically that the *refining* stage of the industry is the only one that is still dominated by the Major Multinationals and that many independent firms exist in the stages of exploration, transportation of both crude and final

FIGURE A–3

A Sketch of the Global Structure of the Petroleum Industry, 1994

Company	Stage	Key Competitive Factors
Major Multinationals, hundreds of independent exploration companies, national oil companies	**Exploration** ↓	Technology, funds, legal access to the area
Major Multinationals, Aramco, National Iranian Oil Company, Petroleos de Mexico, other national oil companies, other private oil companies	**Crude oil production** ↓	Access to oil and funds
Major Multinationals, Greek and other shipowners, independent pipeline owners	**Transportation of crude** ↓	Access to ships and pipelines
Mostly the Major Multinationals; also national oil companies and some private ones	**Refining** ↓	Supply of crude, funds, access to markets
Major Multinationals, independent truckers	**Transportation of final products** ↓	Ships, trucks, access to markets
Dow, Du Pont, ICI, Bayer, BASF, and thousands more, including the Major Multinationals	**Petrochemical production** ↓	Access to refined oil products, technology, access to markets
Thousands of owners and franchisees in most countries	**Gasoline stations**	Access to gasoline, good location

products, and marketing. The Majors are vertically integrated throughout the industry, so they can benefit from shifts in market conditions that favor firms in one stage or another. At various times in the history of the industry, transportation of crude (when John D Rockefeller built Standard Oil), ownership of crude (when OPEC successfully raised prices in the 1970s), and access to final markets (at times of weak demand conditions) have been the keys to the competitiveness of large firms in the industry.

The number of major participants in the crude oil production and refining stages has increased since government-owned companies from OPEC have entered these stages of the industry. In the LDCs, the vertically integrated private companies such as the Major Multinationals have been forced to take small minority ownership positions or to sell their technology and management services through contractual agreements. However, the very first stage in the industry, exploration, and the activities farthest downstream, such as the manufacture of petrochemical products, are generally dominated by the vertically integrated private companies, which possess knowledge of markets and distribution channels plus proprietary production and exploration technology. The **obsolescing bargain** (see Chapter 21) has enabled oil-producing LDCs to wrest control of the raw material almost completely away from the MNEs, but those parts of the petroleum industry that demand sophisticated technology or access to marketing channels in other countries remain the province of the MNEs.

One would expect OPEC oil firms to extend their activities throughout the industry as they develop the necessary expertise and market access. However, the notable lack of success of government-owned companies in international competitive markets to date does not portend the emergence of new Exxons from among the OPEC countries. Even so, several of the state-owned firms, such as Petroleos de Venezuela, have expanded overseas into downstream businesses.

The *technical* structure of the petroleum industry is such that independent firms can compete in one or more stages of Figure A–3 without full **vertical integration.** The refining stage, however, does require specialized equipment for handling different grades of crude oil; thus, each refinery is constructed to process a particular type of crude (e.g., Saudi Arabian light or Venezuelan heavy). A major advantage therefore exists for a firm that integrates *crude oil production* and *refining.* On the other hand, gasoline, fuel oil, and other distillates can be purchased from many different refineries without important differences in quality. Thus, gasoline station operators can do business without owning refineries or other upstream installations. Such independent operators are at a disadvantage, however, when the supply of gasoline is limited (as in 1974 and 1979). During such times, vertically integrated firms or firms with guaranteed (contractual) access to gasoline possess a major competitive advantage.

Numerous manufacturers compete at the petrochemical production stage of the industry without owning supplies of crude oil or distillates. In petrochemical production, the key competitive advantages are proprietary technology and market access, neither of which requires upstream ownership of supplies. This is not to deny that all of the Major Multinationals actively compete in petrochemicals and that some chemical firms have chosen to obtain guaranteed supplies of oil through upstream integration (e.g., Du Pont's purchase of Conoco in 1983).

Firms

Some of the major competitors in the global petroleum industry today are listed in Table A–1. The table shows some important competitive advantages of the Major Multinationals and several of the national oil companies. Notice the clear contrasts between the government-owned firms, which possess large quantities of proved crude reserves (and money), and the privately owned Major Multinationals, which possess worldwide distribution systems, marketing knowledge, and proprietary technology. In the mid-1990s, Exxon and Shell were the most powerful firms in the industry, though the other Majors had strong competitive advantages relative to all other firms and were dominant in particular market segments as well. Useful additional details on the competition among these firms can be found in a number of recent accounts of this key industry.[5]

AUTOMOBILES

Distribution of Activity Worldwide

The motor vehicle industry is the world's largest manufacturing industry. Its activities spread throughout the globe, with over 85 percent of production and a similar portion of consumption taking place in North America, Western Europe, and Japan. While substantial natural resources are used in the production of cars and trucks (and other motor vehicles), that production is still located primarily in the major industrial markets. Figure A–4 shows the distribution of automobile production and consumption worldwide over the past half-century. Notice that although production in North America had fallen to about one-fifth of the global total by 1982, consumption in that region still accounted for about one-third of total world consumption. This implies, of course, that North America was the major net importer of automobiles in the world during the 1980s. Among the

FIGURE A–4A   Global Automobile Production

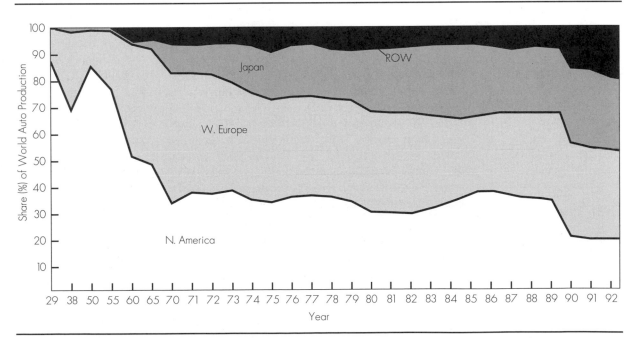

Share of world automobile production by region, 1929–92.
Source: Roos and Altshuler (1984), p. 20; *Automotive News*, 1992 market data book issue.

FIGURE A-4B   Global Automobile Consumption

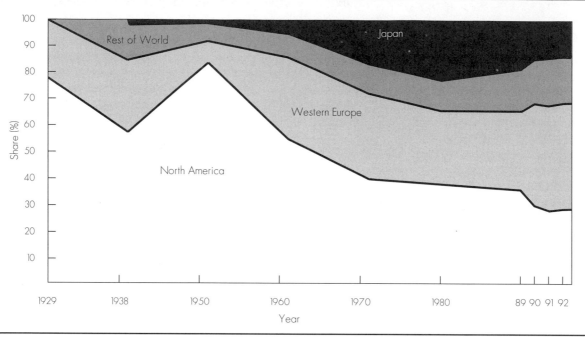

Share of world automobile market by region, 1929–92.
Source: Roos and Altshuler (1984), p. 23, and *Automotive News*, 1992 market data book issue.

reasons for North America's position as an importer of automobiles are lower production costs and greater precision in production in Japan (and Europe), the easy access foreign producers have to the North American market, a frequent higher quality ranking of Japanese and German cars relative to their American competitors, and the huge size of the North American market relative to other markets around the world. These and other reasons for this situation are explored shortly.

Because automobiles are composed of fairly standardized components, there has been a tendency to place greater reliance on low-cost locations for the production of components and the assembly of automobiles. In the 1970s and 1980s, Brazil, Mexico, and Korea in particular became important sources of supply of parts and assemblies to the auto industry. Brazil alone assembled almost 1 million autos (in addition to producing auto parts) in 1980, when about 27 million autos were produced worldwide. The increasing use of low-cost locations has continued in the 1990s.

Recent History

Historically, the automobile industry has been dominated by American firms, particularly General Motors and Ford. This dominance began in the early 1900s, when Henry Ford's company brought standardized parts and mass production, plus the use of a continuous assembly line, into operation. Prior to 1900, for the first 20 years of the industry's existence, German and French manufacturers produced most of the automobiles in use. By 1923, Ford and General Motors (GM) together accounted for 91 percent of world auto production, and their combined share remained above two-thirds of the world total until after World War II.[6]

Through strategies of foreign direct investment, Ford and GM obtained strong market positions in Europe and North America. During the 1930s, Ford set up manufacturing facilities in England, Germany, and France. GM chose acquisitions of existing European firms, buying Vauxhall in England and Opel in Germany in the late 1920s. (Both firms were denied permission to establish manufacturing in Italy, where they would have competed with state-owned Fiat.) Both Ford and GM also operated manufacturing facilities in Canada.

After World War II, competition from non-US firms began to heat up. High tariffs on imported autos, support for state-owned manufacturers, and rapidly growing European economies led to a boom in European production by such companies as Renault, Volkswagen, and Fiat. (The Ford and GM affiliates in England and Germany also grew rapidly in this environment.) When the European Common Market was established in 1958, European producers were able to take advantage of economies of scale that resulted from serving the six-country market instead of the relatively small national markets. By 1973, the European Community market was about the same size as the North American market, and European automakers were beginning to enter the US small-car market very successfully.

At the beginning of the postwar period, auto production in Japan lagged far behind that in Europe and North America. Japanese auto production was less than 1 million vehicles per year until the late 1960s. By 1970, however, it had hit 3 million, and Japanese auto exports to the United States had reached a market share of more than 4 percent. By 1980, Japanese exports accounted for almost 23 percent of the US auto market. Like the European autos, the Japanese autos were smaller than their US counterparts and offered a low-cost alternative to US buyers.

The success of Japanese cars in the US market led to pressure from the domestic companies for protection. By 1981, **voluntary export restraints (VERs)** were negotiated between Japan and the United States that limited the number of Japanese cars imported. (The limit was 4.2 million cars per year in 1994. See Chapter 9 for more discussion.) To avoid losses of market share, the Japanese auto firms made substantial investments in production facilities in the United States during the 1980s. By 1990, the Japanese "transplant" factories were producing over 2 million cars per year in the United States.

Industry Structure

In most countries, the automobile industry is dominated by models designed and produced elsewhere. A small number of manufacturers in a handful of industrial countries make virtually all of the cars and trucks used in the world's almost 200 countries. (Six firms produce over two-thirds of world auto output.) From a different perspective, the three major markets for autos are North America, the European Union, and Japan. All of the six largest auto firms manufacture vehicles in at least two of these areas in dozens of plants. In sum, the industry is highly concentrated among six firms, in descending order of size, General Motors, Ford, Toyota, Nissan, Renault, and Volkswagen. (Fiat and Peugeot-Citroen are not far behind Volkswagen in size, though they are far less multinational outside Europe than any of the six largest firms.) Table A–2 depicts some features of the 10 main competitors in the world auto industry.

Like the petroleum industry, the automobile industry includes thousands of additional firms that are involved in various stages of operations, from the production of components to the final sale of cars and trucks to retail customers.

TABLE A–2

Major Competitors in the
International Automobile
Industry

Firm	Home Country	Annual Sales, 1993 (in $ millions)	Competitive Advantages
General Motors	US	$133,622	Largest size and largest distribution network
Ford	US	108,581	Large size and diversification, innovative skills
Toyota	Japan	85,283	Low-cost production, good labor relations, best financial situation, high-quality image
Daimler-Benz	Germany	59,102	Reputation for very high quality
Nissan	Japan	53,760	Low-cost production, good labor relations, high-quality image
Volkswagen	Germany	46,312	Government support
Chrysler	US	43,600	Relatively low costs and recent good image
Honda	Japan	35,798	Good labor relations, high-quality image
Fiat	Italy	34,707	Government support
Renault	France	29,975	Government support

Source: "*The International 500,*" *Fortune,* July 25, 1994.

What distinguishes the six (or eight) major multinational auto firms is their control of the *final assembly* stage of production. These final assemblers produce less than half of the total value added in the industry. The rest comes from suppliers, such as tire firms (e.g., Goodyear, Michelin, Bridgestone) and drivetrain manufacturers (e.g., TRW, Borg-Warner, Dana); distributors, such as the thousands of independent new-car dealers in the industrial countries; and financiers, such as the major commercial banks.

Among the six largest firms in the industry, General Motors and Ford are more vertically integrated than the others, while Toyota and Nissan are much less integrated. Also, the Japanese firms have traditionally specialized in smaller, less expensive cars and achieved a much better quality record than their foreign competitors. These positioning strategies have brought the Japanese firms greater success during the past two decades, when customer preferences have favored more differentiated and less expensive vehicles. In particular, the competitive edge of the Japanese firms has resulted from their ability to adapt models to changes in consumer tastes and serve the low-cost end of the market with relatively high-quality products.

The Six Major Multinational Automotive Firms

The six largest multinational auto firms have somewhat different corporate strategies and structures. This section points out some characteristics of these firms that are relevant to global competition with their rivals. The firms are presented in declining order of size (i.e., annual sales).

General Motors has been the largest auto company in the world for most of the auto industry's history. In 1993, GM's annual sales were almost one-third larger than those of its nearest competitor. GM has traditionally made a wide variety of large autos that constitute over half of its total production, while filling out its product line with medium, compact, and subcompact vehicles. Among GM's main competitive advantages are its financial capacity to respond to problems and opportunities around the world with massive funds when needed, its highly diversified portfolio of production facilities in the industrial countries and in LDCs, and its base in the United States, the largest national market for motor vehicle sales. Recently GM also demonstrated a willingness to cooperate with foreign rivals in production and research (see the NUMMI case in Chapter 11), thus benefiting from those firms' skills as well as its own.

Ford Motor Company has been the second largest manufacturer in the auto industry for most of its existence. Ford's product line is similar to that of GM, though Ford has only three-quarters of GM's worldwide volume. Historically, Ford has been somewhat more vertically integrated than any of the other major auto firms, with its own very large steelmaking operation and its greater in-house production of other inputs. Ford's major competitive advantages include its long and successful experience operating in foreign markets, its base in the United States, and its innovative capacity, as shown (for example) by its introduction of the compact Mustang model in 1965, its importing of the Fiesta model from Europe in the late 1970s, and its introduction of the Taurus, the world's best-selling car in 1993.

Toyota is the larger of the giant Japanese auto producers, both of which have become multinational competitors only in the past two decades. Toyota's growth rate has far surpassed those of the American and European firms since 1970, and it has been one of the best examples of the "Japanese challenge" to world business in the 1980s and 1990s. That is, with its advances during this period in competition with the other major firms in many national markets, Toyota has demonstrated most of the attributes of successful Japanese MNEs. Its competitive advantages include far lower production costs and greater production efficiency than those of any of the non-Japanese firms, harmonious labor-management relations, excellent quality control, vehicles with relatively low gasoline consumption, a successful focus on smaller cars, and great financial stability (with zero long-term debt).

Fiat became the third largest European auto producer (after Daimler-Benz and VW) by pursuing a strategy of diversification into all major automobile segments. Beyond the traditional, economical small to intermediate-size Fiats, the firm now owns Alfa-Romeo (producer of high-performance, sporty cars), Lancia (large, classic luxury cars), and Ferrari (high-performance sports and race cars). With its protected domestic market, in which it has a 60 percent market share, the company has expanded throughout Europe and into North America with overseas production and sales. Fiat's broad strategy emphasizes styling and high performance, especially in the acquired divisions.

Nissan, Japan's second largest automaker, presents much the same success story as Toyota. The company became a major multinational competitor during the 1970s and 1980s, and its competitive advantages largely parallel those of Toyota. That is, Nissan benefits from low production costs, highly productive labor, and consistently high-quality products. While Nissan rode the wave of Japanese success in the US auto market by selling small, inexpensive models during the past two decades, its growth has been slower than that of either Toyota or Honda. Nissan's most recent strategic direction in the United States has been to position itself as the high-fashion, high-performance Japanese producer. The introduction of cars such as the Maxima (rated the most trouble-free car sold in the United States), the luxury model Infiniti, and the Altima has established Nissan in this market position relative to its Japanese rivals.

Volkswagen is the most multinational of the European auto producers, with plants in the United States, Mexico, and Brazil. The Beetle, Volkswagen's initial entry into the American market (in the 1950s), was tremendously successful and led Volkswagen to dramatic growth throughout the 1960s. Since that time, the firm has not enjoyed such strides ahead of its rivals. Volkswagen became the first major foreign automaker to set up production in the United States with its Westmoreland, Pennsylvania, plant, purchased in 1974. Although this venture was only moderately successful and was later sold, similar direct US investments have been made by Volkswagen's major non-US competitors. Volkswagen's major competitive advantages include its reputation for reliability (established by the Beetle), its protected base in Germany, and its focus on the small-car market segment.

This overview of six of the largest automakers is offered as a sketch of the competitive conditions in the automobile industry rather than as a precise definition of the capabilities or difficulties of these firms. It is intended to give some insights into the current and future shape of the industry around the world.

BANKING

Worldwide Distribution of Activities

The fundamental services rendered by banks are the lending of funds and the taking of deposits. The "raw materials" of the banking industry are deposits and other sources of funds, and the main "output" of the industry is credit in the form of loans and other instruments. In addition, banks offer many other financial services that generate income, such as issuing guarantees of performance on behalf of clients, serving as intermediaries for the purchase and sale of financial instruments other than deposits and loans, and making a market in such instruments as foreign exchange. Finally, banks provide nonfinancial services such as *information*—information about market trends for various products, economic and political conditions in various countries, financial market conditions at home and abroad, and other matters of interest to clients. In some countries, commercial banks participate directly in markets for stocks and bonds (i.e., in investment banking) and in markets for real estate, insurance, and other financial services. Our discussion will focus primarily on the two traditional banking functions—taking deposits and lending—and more specifically on these functions in the international context.

Every country has a domestic banking system that is regulated by a domestic monetary authority (typically a central bank) and involves participation by locally owned financial institutions. In this sense, banking activities are distributed across the globe, in rich and poor countries. Many countries limit participation in domestic financial markets to locally owned institutions, with foreign banks allowed only to have representative offices or to operate only indirectly through relations with local banks. Such limitations exist in the formerly communist countries, and they are also fairly extensive in less developed countries. This means that much of international banking takes place through "correspondent banking relations," that is, through transactions in which a bank in one country deals at arm's length with its counterpart in another country. It also means that there are far fewer multinational banks than multinational industrial corporations.

In the industrialized countries and in a handful of LDCs (Panama, Hong Kong, Bahrain, the Bahamas, the Cayman Islands, and a few more), international banking transactions are relatively open to foreign-owned financial institutions and free of most limits (other than those intended to ensure prudent banking practices) on the lending and deposit-taking practices of participating banks. The eurocurrency markets flourish in this environment, as do dealings in foreign exchange and other internationally transferable financial instruments.

Table A–3 depicts the international spread of bank affiliates outside their home countries. Notice that the main centers of foreign bank activity are the primary countries involved in eurocurrency transactions: the industrialized nations plus a handful of LDCs that offer legal incentives to attract foreign bank activity.

Recent History

In general, banking offices and services have followed industrial clients into new types of business and into new countries over the years. In the 18th and 19th centuries, this meant that British, French, Spanish, and Dutch banks established overseas networks of affiliates to support the business taking place within the colonial systems of their respective countries. Even today, the presence of British banks (e.g., Barclays and Lloyds) in former British colonies, French banks (e.g., Crédit Lyonnais and Banque Nationale de Paris) in former French colonies, and so on is greater than one might expect considering the small markets of many of these nations and their distance from their former home countries.

In the first half of the 20th century, when Great Britain and the United States were the largest industrial powers, banks from these two countries extended their overseas activities as British and American multinational industrial firms spread their mines, factories, and offices throughout the world. By 1960, there were about 5,000 foreign branches and agencies of commercial banks headquartered in major industrialized countries (still dominated by the more than 4,000 affiliates of British banks in the British Commonwealth, mainly throughout Africa and Asia).[7] American banks in particular faced a regulatory structure that encouraged overseas expansion, since domestically all banks were limited to expansion within one state only, and then often only on a restricted basis. The "money center" banks from New York aggressively extended their activities into Europe and elsewhere during this time.

During the 1970s, international banking was struck by the dramatic shift in wealth between industrialized nations and OPEC developing nations that resulted from the two oil crises. The banking industry responded by recycling the "petrodollars" generated by this shift. As we saw in the section on the oil industry, this recycling led to a very large increase in lending to nontraditional borrowers, such as governments in less developed countries. It also led to the establishment of new multinational banks in the oil-exporting countries and to the creation of a financial center in the Middle East (in Bahrain).

The structure of international financial dealings with LDCs changed remarkably during the 1970s. In the two preceding decades, most of the lendings to governments in less developed countries came from official sources, such as foreign government departments (e.g., the US Treasury) and international agencies (e.g., the International Monetary Fund and the World Bank). During those decades, approximately two-thirds of the loan financing provided to LDC governments came from official sources and the remaining third from commercial banks. By the late 1970s, financing of this kind had grown dramatically and had shifted toward the private sector so that commercial banks now provided about two-thirds of such financing (particularly to large LDCs such as Brazil and Mexico) and official agencies the remainder.[8]

Among the industrialized countries, competition among banks has developed in line with changes in the competitiveness of manufacturing firms. That is, as US (and British) firms have lost market share to competitors in Europe and Japan, so have US (and British) banks faced increasing competition from German, Swiss, and Japanese banks in many countries. Also, as national governments have

TABLE A–3   Banks' Global Network of Overseas Branches, Affiliates, and Subsidiaries

Country of Origin	Host Area								
	USA	UK	France	Germany	Switz.	Neth.	Argen.	Brazil	Mexico
USA		47	14	12	7	3	8	3	1
Japan	48	28	14	3	1	0	2	1	0
UK	21		3	3	3	3	1	1	0
Brazil	16	4	2	3	0	2	4		1
France	15	16		6	4	1	2	1	0
Germany	13	14	3		0	0	1	1	0
Canada	12	9	1	4	1	1	1	0	0
Italy	12	12	2	4	1	1	2	0	0
South Korea	11	6	1	1	0	1	0	0	0
Spain	11	7	10	2	0	1	0	3	0
Hong Kong	9	5	1	0	2	1	0	0	0
Australia	7	12	0	1	0	0	0	0	0
Venezuela	7	0	1	0	0	0	0	1	0
Mexico	6	4	0	0	0	0	0	0	
Switzerland	6	12	1	2		1	0	0	1
Netherlands	5	8	0	1	0		1	0	0
Bahrain	3	3	0	1	0	0	0	0	0
Argentina	2	1	1	0	0	0		2	0
Others	95	107	26	10	5	1	0	6	0
Total	299	295	80	53	24	16	22	19	3

Sources: USA data: *Institutional Investor*, September 1987; UK data: *The Banker*, November 1987; all other countries; data: *The Bankers' Almanac and Yearbook, 1987.*

permitted greater participation by foreign banks in their economies, the competition among banks has become much more international.

Industry Structure

The banking industry is structured somewhat differently in each country. In the United States, there are over 10,000 commercial banks. Federal law substantially limits an individual bank's activities in more than one state. Nonetheless, about 20 of the largest banks, with assets of over $US 20 billion apiece, carry out almost half of the value of US banking transactions. In Great Britain, where nationwide banking is permitted, a group of eight very large banks (Barclays, National Westminster, Abbey National, Midland, Lloyds, Trustee Savings Bank, Royal Bank of Scotland, and Bank of Scotland) dominate the domestic market and own most of the 13,000 bank branches throughout the country. Over 400 foreign banks participate in the international segments of the market. In Venezuela, seven local banks hold 60 percent of the banking deposits and control most of the international segment as well. Foreign banks are limited to ownership of 20 percent of the equity in a Venezuelan bank.[9] All in all, domestic banking activities are much less concentrated in the United States than in other countries, but international banking activities are fairly concentrated everywhere.

The *eurocurrency* market, the largest financial market in the world, is located mainly in the financial centers of the industrialized countries,[10] plus a handful of offshore sites such as Hong Kong, Panama, and Bahrain. The banks participating in this market at any location generally belong to the group of multinational banks noted in Table A–4. (The eurocurrency market is discussed in some detail in Chapter 7.)

Table A–3   *concluded*

					Host Area						
Vene.	Japan	Hong Kong	Bahrain	Egypt	Nigeria	South Africa	Bahamas	Cayman Islands	Panama	Singap.	Malasia
1	22	20	9	2	1	0	59	67	7	18	3
0		15	1	0	0	0	1	4	5	18	1
0	5	8	7	1	2	0	5	22	1	11	1
1	2	1	2	0	0	0	3	10	3	2	0
0	7	8	8	1	0	0	1	4	6	11	0
0	6	7	0	0	0	0	0	4	1	4	1
0	5	7	2	1	0	0	5	3	2	5	1
0	2	4	0	1	0	0	1	1	0	4	0
0	3	3	2	0	0	0	0	0	1	2	0
2	1	1	1	0	0	0	2	4	1	0	0
0	1		2	0	0	0	1	0	0	4	2
0	3	3	0	0	0	0	0	2	0	4	0
	0	0	0	0	0	0	0	0	3	0	0
0	0	0	0	0	0	0	2	3	0	0	0
0	2	2	2	0	0	0	6	5	3	3	0
0	3	3	0	0	0	0	0	1	1	3	1
0	0	0		0	0	0	0	1	1	1	0
0	0	0	0	0	0	0	0	1	3	0	0
0	14	29	16	10	1	1	6	24	5	31	6
4	76	111	52	16	4	1	92	156	43	121	16

Participation by government-owned institutions is especially important in banking, since governments establish the rules of the game in each country and can pursue goals other than profit as part of their banking strategies. Typically, the largest and most important commercial banks in less developed countries are state owned, and this situation also exists in a few industrialized countries, such as Sweden and France. The major French banks, which are mostly government owned, provide an excellent example of such institutions, dominating the domestic market and competing actively in the euromarkets. The services offered by state-owned banks do not differ from those offered by their private sector competitors; in international banking, the only noticeable difference between state-owned and private sector banks is that the state-owned banks serve some captive clients (namely government agencies and companies).

Major Banking Competitors

Table A–4 lists the 50 most important commercial banks in the world according to their rankings by assets. Notice that the dominance of US-based banks has disappeared over the past decade and there is a fairly even distribution of leading banks among the United States, Japan, Canada, Germany, France, Great Britain, and a few other European countries.

The particular competitive advantages possessed by the multinational banks listed in Table A–4 are somewhat difficult to assess. If we use the number of foreign affiliates as a measure of experience in international business, the British banks have a large advantage. If we consider the diversity of financial services offered, the Japanese banks with ties to large trading companies are probably the most active outside the realms of deposit taking and lending. To some extent, the

TABLE A–4   The World's Largest Commercial Banking Corporations, 1993

Bank	Shareholders' Equity ($ million)	Total Assets ($ million)	Net Income ($ million)
1. Sumitomo Bank	19,772.01	454,639.81	183.45
2. Dai-Ichi Kangyo Bank	18,573.37	462,285.71	404.74
3. Fuji Bank	18,061.77	460,926.84	507.21
4. Sanwa Bank	17,829.67	451,585.99	828.57
5. BankAmerica Corporation	17,144.00	186,933.00	1,954.00
6. Sakura Bank	16,503.84	443,518.61	502.58
7. Mitsubishi Bank	16,185.57	479,741.69	546.56
8. HSBC Holdings	16,104.75	304,438.88	3,056.95
9. Credit Agricole Group	15,054.80	281,541.33	929.73
10. Union Bank of Switzerland Group	14,060.10	209,101.11	1,523.64
11. Citicorp	13,953.00	216,574.00	2,219.00
12. Industrial Bank of Japan	12,160.13	340,506.52	356.32
13. Deutsche Bank	12,085.73	318,534.66	1,289.95
14. Bank of China	11,814.48	280,065.86	2,160.91
15. Chemical Banking Corporation	11,164.00	149,888.00	1,604.00
16. Nationsbank Corporation	9,979.00	157,686.00	1,501.00
17. Tokai Bank	9,963.94	274,031.85	182.78
18. JP Morgan	9,859.00	133,888.00	1,586.00
19. ABN Amro	9,827.88	252,139.28	1,039.32
20. Credit Lyonnais	9,544.12	337,208.38	1,074.92
21. Credit Suisse Group	9,477.08	155,985.91	980.83
22. Swiss Bank Corporation	9,340.04	139,041.10	917.01
23. Groupe Caisse d'Epargne	9,315.99	161,231.10	349.32
24. Long-Term Credit Bank of Japan	9,300.13	268,656.27	227.16
25. Compagnie Financiere de Paribas	9,300.00	228,892.80	469.26
26. Asahi Bank	9,288.41	250,172.88	314.04
27. National Westminster Bank	8,708.39	225,853.61	950.03
28. Caisse des Depots et Consignations	8,502.30	260,496.00	651.24
29. Banque Nationale de Paris	8,269.17	249,230.50	164.07
30. Société Générale	8,178.87	258,902.57	657.64
31. Chase Manhattan Corporation	8,122.00	102,103.00	966.00
32. Rabobank	7,885.31	130,034.63	576.66
33. Barclays Bank	7,848.48	245,276.82	462.46
34. Bank of Tokyo	7,761.61	216,418.90	375.64
35. Mitsubishi Trust & Banking	7,602.93	141,633.31	240.84
36. Sumitomo Trust & Banking	7,451.83	133,910.54	216.26
37. Dresdner Bank	7,339.60	218,972.49	612.71
38. Banc One Corporation	7,003.64	79,918.56	1,139.98
39. Westdeutsche Landesbank Girozentrale	6,684.39	191,286.31	276.62
40. Banco de Brasil	6,452.39	71,187.75	388.74
41. CARIPLO	6,075.86	71,910.92	186.74
42. People's Construction Bank of China	6,069.43	141,071.67	5,483.81
43. Banca di Roma	5,982.32	88,799.21	180.44
44. Canadian Imperial Bank	5,962.32	100,618.81	547.21
45. Royal Bank of Canada	5,944.33	118,915.79	224.88
46. National Australia Bank	5,837.71	75,744.34	735.92
47. Mitsui Trust & Banking	5,629.97	125,993.23	100.31
48. Agricultural Bank of China	5,583.17	150,927.34	335.38
49. Halifax Building Society	5,498.53	101,199.03	865.26
50. Daiwa Bank	5,409.23	144,181.48	257.82

Source: "The Euromoney 500," *Euromoney*, June 1994.

banks that can minimize their costs of providing financial services show the greatest profitability, since the cost of obtaining funds is fairly similar for all of the banks in question. In this case, it is the diverse group of banks that show the greatest returns on assets that possess a cost advantage. (Clearly, the multinational banks that have access to funds in a number of countries have a probable cost-of-funds advantage over local banks in any one market that offers limited borrowing sources.) The advantage of a well-known brand name is possessed by all of the banks listed; indeed, any bank with over $US 40 billion in assets is generally considered trustworthy! A final competitive advantage worth noting is an existing customer base in one country that can be extended overseas as clients establish operations in other countries. Banks based in the United States, home of the largest number of multinational enterprises, should have an advantage in this regard with their access to more clients in the domestic market.

An interesting aspect of competitive advantage in banking is the positioning of large, multinational banks in competition with smaller local banks in national markets. Since such competition usually occurs for domestic banking activities, it will not be discussed here. However, a number of useful analyses of the subject are available in the literature.[11]

TELECOMMUNICATIONS

Telephone Service and Production Worldwide

In every country, telephone *service* is provided by a local company (typically owned by the government), regardless of the skills needed to operate the system or the source of the equipment used. The *production* of telephone equipment, on the other hand, is dominated by half a dozen firms worldwide. Because the provision of telephone service is viewed as a strategic issue in the national economy, this industry is influenced by political as well as economic factors. While historically companies such as ITT (International Telephone & Telegraph) operated telephone systems in some less developed countries, by 1985 the ownership of national telephone systems virtually everywhere except the United States had become the province of national governments or their chosen domestic companies. A reverse trend began in the early 1990s with the privatization of telephone companies in many countries.

Producing the high-tech equipment that is used to transmit and receive telephone and other telecommunication signals requires huge capital and technological resources. Therefore, the production side of telecommunications still remains in the hands of corporations, though often with strict contractual arrangements between these corporations and governments to disallow corporate activities perceived to be against the national interest.

The production of telecommunications equipment ranges from sophisticated manufacture of incredibly tiny integrated circuits to assembly of the telephone units used in homes and offices. While most of the really technology-intensive work is done in a few industrialized countries by very large MNEs, assembly of telephones and some components, such as silicon chips, is now done in a wide variety of countries, especially in the low-cost NICs of Southeast Asia (namely Taiwan, Singapore, Hong Kong, and South Korea). Because of the pervasive nationalism in the provision of telephone service, equipment standards have never become standardized and a wide variety of standards still exists among countries.[12]

Recent History

The recent history of the provision of telephone *service* largely follows the pattern of raw materials production around the world. That is, less developed countries declared the telephone service industry to be a "national resource," and in the 1960s and 1970s such countries nationalized their telephone systems. Then, in the late 1980s and early 1990s, several of th same countries and some industrial nations moved to *privatize* their telephone service provision (for example, the United Kingdom, Chile, Mexico, and the Philippines).

On the other hand, telephone *equipment production* has followed the spread of new technology, with competition among a few large firms supported by their national governments and fewer than 10 major competitors dominating production worldwide since World War II. The most important technological changes during the past 40 years have been the development of satellite transmission, the use of optical fibers in telephone cables, and the introduction of silicon chips of increasingly tiny dimensions to replace first vacuum tubes and then transistors for information storage and switching. As these changes occurred, the competitors in the industry remained mostly the same, but their competitive positions shifted depending on the extent to which they took advantage of the new technological opportunities.

The most important recent events that have altered competition in the telecommunications industry have been the denationalization of telephone companies in some less developed and industrialized countries and the opening to competition of telephone equipment production. These events are discussed in more detail shortly.

Industry Structure

This discussion focuses on the production side of the telecommunications industry and on international telecommunication service. Domestic telecommunication service, which is either government owned or greatly government controlled in all countries, will not be discussed here.

The telecommunications industry is now in a state of rapid transition. Due to the "information revolution," microelectronics has become the focal point of the communications business. Tiny silicon chips that can store more than 4 million bits of information per chip are being widely produced, and 16 megabit chips are coming into large-scale production. Such chips are used in typewriters, telephones, electronic games, and even in the equipment that switches telephone calls from one location to another (i.e., telephone exchanges). Manufacturers of telephones and other telecommunications equipment must act quickly to master the new technology and create products that utilize it. The companies that modernize their products rapidly will survive. Those that do not will be pushed out of the market.

Perhaps even more important than the technological factors that influence competition in the telecommunications industry are national technical standards. No universally accepted standards exist that would allow companies to standardize their products worldwide. In addition to technical differences in the provision of electricity (e.g., 120-volt versus 220-volt power), there are government-imposed standards for telecommunications equipment that differ even among the closest European neighbors, let alone countries as far apart as Japan and the United States. Such standards favor domestic companies over their foreign competitors and lead to a fragmenting of competition internationally. This problem has been reduced significantly in Europe through negotiation of common standards as part of the EC 1992 initiative.

Despite these problems, the providers of telecommunications equipment are mostly large, diversified MNEs. Although many components are produced by smaller firms in various industrialized countries and some LDCs, the bulk of telecommunications switching gear, satellites, and other equipment used internationally is made by fewer than a dozen firms worldwide. Each of these firms has a large share of its home country market and competes actively in dozens of other countries.

Firms

Telecommunications is an international industry. The telephone systems of virtually every country in the world have been installed and supplied by a handful of companies. The most important are American Telephone & Telegraph (AT&T), based in the United States; Northern Telecom, based in Canada; Siemens, based in West Germany; L M Ericsson (LME), based in Sweden; and Nippon Electric Corporation (NEC), based in Japan. Each of these companies has diversified into other industries, though telecommunications is a multibillion-dollar part of each company's annual sales. Table A–5 presents some basic background information about these companies.

The strategies of the five companies diverge to some extent. Ericsson has focused most of its corporate resources on development of the so-called office of the future, in which data processing, telephone conversations, and word processing will all operate through an electronic system. (IBM, which entered the telecommunications market from the data-processing business, has also chosen to place substantial company resources into the development of an electronic office.) On the other hand, Siemens has been moving more cautiously in the telecommunications market, while also using its resources to support expansion in many other businesses, such as power-generating equipment and electrical machinery. The following paragraphs offer a brief commentary on the competitive strategies of the five companies.

Until January 1, 1984, *AT&T* operated the local and long-distance telephone systems in most parts of the United States. (A few areas were served by General Telephone & Electronics Corporation.) About 80 percent of AT&T's more than 1 million employees worked in operating telephone companies that provided service to firms and individual households. On January 1, 1984, AT&T divested all of its local telephone operating companies, retaining only long-distance and international service, plus telephone manufacturing, telecommunications research, and corporate headquarters. Because of its history as the highly regulated near-monopolist supplier of telephone services in the United States, AT&T is viewed as being at a great disadvantage in terms of knowledge of how to market its products to potential customers. Currently AT&T appears to be focusing on the creation of the "office of the future," based on the telecommunications technology that it has developed and its purchase of NCR. It has entered the market for desktop computers with machines that use its very advanced operating system, UNIX. Within the United States, it has been mounting an effort to provide full office automation to its numerous clients. For several years, it has offered satellite communications to private users as well as telephone companies. In general, AT&T is aiming to produce and market products and services across the full range of the telecommunications industry.

Northern Telecom has been the most internationally diversified of the telecommunications competitors, due largely to its relatively limited home market in Canada. The company has private branch exchange (PBX) manufacturing operations not only in North America but widely spread throughout Europe (France, Ireland) and Asia (China). Northern Telecom is largely focused on the telecom-

TABLE A–5

Five Telecommunications
Companies

AT&T

Founded in 1885
Headquarters in New York
Employs 312,200 people worldwide
1992 sales—$64.9 billion
Main business segments:
  Western Electric
  Communications information systems
  Computers (NCR)
  International
  Bell Labs
Major recent product:
  System 85 private branch exchange
Important competitive advantages:
  Best R&D (Bell Labs)
  Well positioned for "electronic office" because of long US experience

Northern Telecom, Ltd.

Founded in 1914
Headquarters in Mississauga, Ontario
Employs 58,000 people worldwide
1992 sales—$8.4 billion
Main business segments:
  Telecommunications
  Cables
  Semiconductors
  Other
Major recent products:
  Meridian PBX
  Sonet (synchronous optical network)
Important competitive advantages:
  Reputation for high-quality products
  Experience in international competition

L M Ericsson

Founded in 1876
Headquarters in Stockholm
Employs 66,000 people worldwide
1991 sales—SKr 52.2 billion
Main business segments:
  Public telecommunications   SKr 22.5 billion
  Information systems   SKr 2.7 billion
  Cable   SKr 8.0 billion
  Defense systems   SKr 2.4 billion
  All other   SKr 17.6 billion
Major recent products:
  AXE central switching unit
  MD 110 digital subscriber exchange
Important competitive advantages:
  Quality of products
  Experience in production of telephone exchanges

Nippon Electric Corporation

Founded in 1899
Headquarters in Tokyo
Employs 104,000 worldwide
1992 sales—$30.9 billion

TABLE A–5
concluded

Main business segments:	
Communications	37%
Computers and industrial electronic systems	24%
Electronic devices	24%
Home electronics	10%
Major recent product:	
NEAX digital switching system	
Important competitive advantages:	
Reputation for high-quality products	
Major semiconductor producer	

Siemens

Founded in 1847
Headquarters in Munich
Employs 418,000 people worldwide
1992 sales—$49.4 billion

Main business segments:	
Telecommunications and security systems	$5.8 billion
SNI computers	
Energy and automation	7.2 billion
Nuclear power	7.1 billion
PBX and data systems	5.8 billion
Medical equipment	3.0 billion
Electrical and automotive systems	2.4 billion
Major recent product:	
EDX-C stored-program control switching system	
(for telex)	
Important competitive advantages:	
"Systems manufacturer," focuses on selling complete systems	
Manufactures own semiconductors	
Reputation for high-quality products	

munications equipment manufacturing business and is much less diversified across industries than its key international competitors. This firm has demonstrated its technological leadership and its ability to compete internationally by being the first (and by 1990 the only) non-Japanese supplier to Nippon Telephone and Telegraph, the Japanese telephone company. By positioning its recent PBX, the Meridian system, as an "open system," Northern Telecom has entered the "global" telecommunications market of the 1990s with a product that can meet local standards in most countries and has a greater number of data and voice lines than most other PBXs at this time.

L M Ericsson's approach to the office of the future is to coordinate the word-processing, telephone, and data-processing functions through switching equipment such as the PABX that the firm already produces. This approach differs from that of IBM, which appears to be basing its office of the future on a central computer, with telephone switching and other functions coordinated through the computer. LME gained expertise in office equipment through its acquisitions of Datasaab (computer company) and Facit (typewriter company) in 1981. Information systems became a major part of LME's business, with sales equal to those of its telecommunications division in the mid-1980s. As the second largest supplier of telecommunications equipment in markets other than the United States (behind CGE, the French firm), LME has a substantial experience advantage over

AT&T, NEC, and Siemens. After failing to achieve a significant position in computers, Ericsson sold its data-processing division in 1988 and refocused on telecommunications.

Nippon Electric Corporation has a far smaller overseas marketing network than the other four companies. Therefore, one aspect of its strategy is to expand the international part of its business, focusing especially on the United States. NEC relies on its image as a supplier of high-quality electronic products, though many critics view its after-sale service as poor. Much like AT&T, until recently NEC sold much of its equipment directly to the Japanese telephone company, a related firm. Since NEC began to look for outside customers, its approach has been weak in the marketing area. Its strengths lie in its ability to produce very reliable equipment and in its low costs due to the use of efficient Japanese and Asian labor. Its present strategy is to merge its activities in the computer and communications areas toward the emerging industry of information technology. NEC expects to lead this industry in technology development.

Siemens is the second most diversified of the five companies. Its products range from lightbulbs to nuclear power plants, with about a third of its sales in telecommunications. Except for its telecommunications division, Siemens is quite similar to US-based General Electric Company. As the largest private sector company in Germany, Siemens plays a very important role in that country's economy. Its competitive advantages appear to lie in its reputation for reliable, well-designed products and after-sale service. A major criticism of the company is that it moves very bureaucratically, reacting to competitors' advances rather than leading the market. In the telecommunications market, the ability to introduce products that use the latest technology has become more and more important during the past decade. Thus, Siemens will probably have to become more innovative to compete effectively in this market in the future. Through licensing and joint ventures with two California firms, it has entered the market for computer chips. The acquisition of Nixdorf made Siemens an immediate major player in computers. This strategy is expected to help Siemens design state-of-the-art telecommunications products.

No one can know the future. It is not possible to forecast exactly which of the five companies will produce the best results in the 1990s. Nonetheless, based on the companies' competitive advantages and current strategies, it is possible to gain some useful insights into the likely direction of future competition.

CONCLUSIONS

Each of the four industries examined in this appendix has been very important internationally during the 1980s and the 1990s. All four are linked through financial transactions and information networks, though no individual firms own businesses in all four. Each of these industries also involves competitors ranging from the largest multinational enterprises all the way down to the smallest local bank, gas station, or telephone vendor. While the discussion focused on large firms that participate in several segments of the market, the activities of thousands of smaller firms play an important role in the total picture, especially when the large MNEs are excluded from market segments that are protected for local, typically smaller competitors.

Despite the great importance of government regulation and participation in these industries, the dominant firms in the international parts of the industries are mostly private sector corporations. During the 20th century, government-owned enterprises have not gained the level of international diversification that their private counterparts have achieved. This fact does not deny the growing activities of firms such as Petrobras (based in Brazil), Crédit Lyonnais (based in France), or Nippon Telephone & Telegraph (based in Japan). In the future, a much greater share of global business may very well be held by public sector corporations, depending on how firms, both public and private, respond to future competitive challenges. Many of the leading state-owned firms, such as British Petroleum and NTT, are being privatized to some degree, and this change is creating partially state-owned MNEs.

While only the telecommunications industry is necessarily based in the rapidly changing electronics field, the banking industry has clearly become more and more dependent on international communications and data processing, and the petroleum industry utilizes sophisticated electronic equipment for information processing, production machinery controls, and even exploration. Companies in the automobile industry are moving to "factories of the future," which feature extensive use of industrial robots. The nature of competition in each of these four industries is changing as such technological shifts occur and as government policies toward foreign private sector enterprises change.

QUESTIONS

1. Explain the importance of *technology* in the petroleum, automobile, banking, and telecommunications industries.

2. What firms are major competitors in the oil-refining business in the United States, Europe, and the Middle East? What firms are major competitors in the gasoline sales business? Why is there a substantial difference between the two?

3. What are the key factors that determine the competitiveness of banks in domestic markets in (*a*) the United States and (*b*) Latin America?

4. What are the key factors that determine the competitiveness of banks in international financial markets in the United States and Europe?

5. Describe the competitive positions of AT&T, LME, and NEC in the production of global telecommunications equipment production. Which strategy do you think will work best in the next five years? Why?

6. The oil industry is based on a natural resource that many governments nationalized in the past two decades. Why does the telecommunications industry, which uses almost no natural resources, face similar government restrictions?

7. Do you expect to see more or fewer international banks in the next 10 years? Why?

8. Which countries are the main producers of crude petroleum? Which countries are the main consumers of oil-based products? What can multinational oil companies do to benefit from this situation?

9. How would you expect IBM's entry into the telecommunications industry to affect competition in that industry? What will be the probable impact of IBM's entry on the other firms mentioned in the text?

10. Describe a set of market segments in the petroleum, automobile, and telecommunications industries that would be appropriate ones for small firms to enter. Explain why each of these segments would be potentially viable for a small firm.

REFERENCES

American Petroleum Institute. *Oil & Gas Journal*. Various issues.

Anderson, Robert. *Fundamentals of the Petroleum Industry*. Norman, OK: University of Oklahoma Press, 1984.

Bradley, Stephen; Jerry Hausman; and Richard Nolan, eds. *Globalization, Technology and Competition: The Fusion of Computers and Telecommunications in the 1990s*. Boston: Harvard Business School Press, 1993.

Crane, Dwight, and Samuel Hayes. "The Evolution of International Banking Competition and Its Implications for Regulation," *Journal of Bank Research*, Spring 1983.

The Economist. "International Banking" (annual supplement in March issue).

Exxon Corporation. *Middle East Oil*. New York: Exxon, 1984.

Fortune, "The International 500" (annual August issue).

Odell, Peter. *Oil and World Power*. 8th ed. Middlesex, UK: Penguin Books, 1986.

Roncaglia, Alessandro. *The International Oil Market*. Armonk, NY: M E Sharpe, 1985.

Sampson, Anthony. *The Seven Sisters*. New York: Basic Books, 1979.

_____ . *The Money Lenders*. New York: Penguin Books, 1983.

Smith, Roy C. *Global Financial Services*. New York: Harper Business, 1990.

Walter, Ingo. *Global Competition in Financial Services*. Cambridge, MA.: Ballinger, 1988.

Womack, James; Daniel Jones; and Daniel Roos. *The Machine that Changed the World*. New York: Rawson Associates, 1990.

World Motor Vehicle Data. Detroit: World Motor Vehicle Association, various editions.

Yoffie, David, ed. *Beyond Free Trade: Firms, Governments, and Global Competition*. Boston: Harvard University Press, 1993.

NOTES

[1] *Oil & Gas Journal,* December 27, 1993.

[2] The firms competed actively against one another in many contexts, but not in pricing. The US firms often have sought US government support for their mutual interests.

[3] Exxon Corporation, *Middle East Oil* (New York: Exxon, 1984), p. 24.

[4] See *Oil & Gas Journal.*

[5] Anthony Sampson, *The Seven Sisters* (New York: Basic Books, 1979); Robert O Anderson, *Fundamentals of the Petroleum Industry* (Norman, OK: University of Oklahoma Press, 1984); Peter Odell, *Oil and World Power.*

[6] *World Motor Vehicle Data.*

[7] Dwight Crane and Samuel Hayes, "The Evolution of International Banking Competition and Its Implications for Regulation," *Journal of Bank Research,* Spring 1983, p. 41.

[8] Data calculated from World Bank, *World Debt Tables,* various issues, and Bank for International Settlements, *Lending by Group of 10 Banks to Nonresident Borrowers,* various issues.

[9] Data on United States, Great Britain, and Venezuela are from Business International Corporation, *Investing, Licensing, and Trading Conditions* (New York: Business International Corporation, 1989 country issue for each country).

[10] Bank for International Settlements semiannual data on nonresident deposits in a group of 10 commercial banks, June 1990.

[11] See, for example, R Alton Gilbert, "Bank Market Structure and Competition," *Journal of Money, Credit, and Banking,* November 1984, pp. 617–45; also see Gerald Hanweck and Stephen Rhoades, "Dominant Firms, 'Deep Pockets,' and Local Market Competition in Banking," *Journal of Economics and Business,* 1984, pp. 391–402.

[12] See, for example, *Business Week,* March 31, 1986, pp. 68–70.

Glossary

Absolute Advantage or **Absolute Cost Advantage** The production cost advantage that one country may have over another when one (or both) of two products is cheaper to produce in the first country.

Accidental Exports Exports undertaken in response to unsolicited customer requests or otherwise in an unplanned manner.

Accounting System A numerically based method for keeping track of assets, how assets are funded, sales, expenses, and so on.

Accounts Receivable Management The strategy used by some MNEs to adjust their A/R to reduce exchange risk and to optimally time funds transfers.

Achievement Motivation People behave as they think. If they think about achievement, they will tend to be achievers.

Affiliate A firm linked to the parent through some degree of ownership (from joint venture to wholly owned subsidiary) and control. The legal form may be subsidiary, branch, or other.

Airway Bill A document analogous to the bill of lading but used for air transport.

Alienation The problem in industrial societies that some workers become dissatisfied with their jobs due to boredom, lack of stimulation, and impersonality.

American Depositary Receipt (ADR) A derivative financial instrument which is based on an overseas stock issue in a foreign company that is held by a banking intermediary which in turn issues ADRs in the US market. The ADRs are issued in dollars and correspond to the overseas shares issued in local currency.

Andean Pact A regional integration group formed in 1967 that today includes Bolivia, Colombia, Ecuador, Peru, and Venezuela.

Antitrust The concern of governments that a firm or firms may gain excessive market power and act to monopolize markets and potentially harm consumer interests. Antitrust policy, often called competition policy, is used by governments to deal with this issue.

Appropriability The nature of a technology that enables the innovator to protect it from use by competitors and to obtain economic rents from it.

Appropriate Technology Technology that is suitable for the distribution of factors of production in the country where it is used. In countries where labor is relatively abundant, for example, appropriate technology would be relatively labor-intensive.

Association of Southeast Asian Nations (ASEAN) A regional integration group formed in 1967 that includes Indonesia, Malaysia, the Philippines, Singapore, and Thailand.

Automatic Adjustment Mechanism The economic response that occurs when a BOP imbalance arises. When a trade deficit exists under flexible exchange rates, a currency devaluation usually occurs to stimulate exports and reduce imports. Under fixed exchange rates, domestic inflation is expected to be lower than foreign inflation, leading to relatively lower domestic prices and again increased exports and reduced imports.

Availability of Natural Resources This is a source of advantage to a company/country in international competition. The possessor of the natural resource has an advantage over the country or company without such availability.

Back-to-Back Letter of Credit A form of pretrade financing in which the exporter uses the importer's letter of credit as a basis for seeking credit from a bank, which in turn backs its letter of credit to the exporter with the demonstrated likelihood of ability to repay that the importer's L/C represents.

Balance of Payments (BOP) The financial record of all transactions between residents of one country and the rest of the world for some given time period.

Balance of Payments Accounting A double-entry bookkeeping system that is used to record transactions that appear in the balance of payments.

Balance of Payments Adjustment The automatic response of an economy to an imbalance in a country's international transactions. If a trade deficit occurs, it usually leads to a currency devaluation and/or reduction of domestic prices relative to prices in other countries.

Balance Sheet Hedging The MNE strategy of using financial hedges (such as forward contracts) to avoid translation risk that would potentially adversely affect the firm's balance sheet.

Bank Draft The means of payment for an export/import transaction. The draft may be a *sight draft*, i.e., payable when received, or a *time draft*, payable at the time specified on the document itself.

Banker's Acceptance A form of posttrade credit for the exporter, in which the exporter sells the account receivable to a bank at a discount in exchange for immediate payment.

Bargaining Unit   All employees in a group that are covered by the same labor contract.

Basic Balance   A balance of payments that measures all of the current account items plus the country's net exports of long-term capital during some time period.

Bill of Lading   A shipping document that is used as evidence of a contract for shipping merchandise and as a claim of ownership of the goods.

Board of Supervision   A group of employee-elected and shareholder-elected representatives that has major control over management decisions and that appoints the top managers. Usually found in Germany, Benelux, and Northern Europe.

Bona Fide Resident   A person who resides in a country as a legitimate local resident for tax or other legal purposes. This is a classification used often for determining tax liability.

Branch   An office or extension of the parent company in a foreign country that is not incorporated in the foreign country.

Brand or Trade Name   A name, often protected by a trademark, used by a firm for its product(s). The name may, over time, come to connote high quality, good service, or some other favorable attribute that attracts purchasers away from similar products made by other firms.

Broadline Global Competition   The competitive strategy that implies production of a wide range of products in one or more industries with sales in many countries.

Brokers' Market   The market for exchange of financial instruments between any two parties using an intermediary (broker) similar to an auctioneer to unite buyers and sellers. The foreign exchange brokers' market in the United States makes up a large part of the trades that involve two banks as buyer and seller.

Business Unionism   A union philosophy stressing maximizing economic returns to union members rather than social or societal reforms to advantage working classes.

Buy American   This is a program under which US government agencies may be required to purchase their supplies from domestic firms. The idea relates also to publicity campaigns that try to encourage US consumers to buy from domestic suppliers.

Buy-Back Agreement   A form of countertrade in which the initial export sale is for a capital good that is used to produce products which are subsequently used as payment by the importer.

Call Option   An option contract that entitles the purchaser to *buy* a fixed amount of foreign exchange at a fixed price in the future.

Capital Controls   Limits on access to foreign exchange. These controls limit not only capital outflows but also imports, which cannot be paid for if capital controls disallow the payments.

Capital Flight   The export of financial resources by residents of a country, typically in response to a situation of economic or political crisis.

Caribbean Basin Initiative (CBI)   A US government policy begun in 1983 that attempts to stimulate private-sector business in the Caribbean and Central America through tariff reductions and other incentives.

Caribbean Common Market (Caricom)   A regional integration group formed in 1973 that includes former British colonies in the Eastern Caribbean.

Cartel   A group of producers of a product that attempts to monopolize the product and fix prices and quantities to maximize their gains. OPEC is the most successful cartel of countries in history.

Center   In the literature of economic development, cities, regions, or countries in the 'center' are those with greatest economic development. This contrasts with the 'periphery' of less developed regions.

Centralized Cash Management   By using this strategy, a MNE can reduce the level of cash balances in individual affiliates and hold and manage key cash resources in one optimal location.

Certificate of Origin   A shipping document that states the country of origin of the merchandise.

Code of Conduct on Transnational Corporations   An intergovernmental agreement sponsored by the United Nations that is intended to spell out rules of good corporate behavior for MNEs in host and home countries. The Code still was not approved within the United Nations by the end of 1987.

Combined Transport Document   A document analogous to the bill of lading but used for shipping when there is more than one form of transport involved.

Commercial Invoice   The exporter's bill of sale that describes precisely the merchandise and terms of sale.

Common Market   A customs union which additionally allows freedom of movement of capital and labor (i.e., factors of production) between member countries.

Comparative Advantage (or Cost) Theory   The trade theory that demonstrates how, based on relative factor supplies and comparative production costs, countries will maximize their welfare by specializing in production of products where they are efficient and trading to obtain products where they are less efficient.

Competitive Advantage   Any characteristic possessed by a firm that enables it to achieve lower costs, higher revenues, or lower risk than its competitors.

Competitors   Rival firms. Companies based domestically or overseas that compete against the firm in question in a given market.

Concession   A legal agreement between a host country and a firm in which the country gives the firm the right to explore for, extract, and sell oil in exchange for specified taxes, fees, and other charges.

Consignment   A legal form of sale in which the recipient of a producer's goods takes possession of the goods but does not own them. Payment is made for sale to customers when the goods are sold rather than upon shipment from the producer to the consignee.

Consolidated Report   A financial report such as an income statement or balance sheet that presents an international firm's total (global) including overseas subsidiaries, licenses, and other activities.

Consolidated Statement   An accounting statement showing the combined operations of parent and subsidiaries.

Consolidation   The process of preparing a consolidated statement whereby line-by-line summations of parent and subsidiary accounts are ultimately presented.

Contingent Liability   A contractual commitment that requires the issuer to deliver whatever instrument is specified (for example, foreign exchange) if the buyer chooses to exercise it.

Continuous R&D   A strategy under which the firm develops new technology incrementally, based on extensions of its existing technology. This can be contrasted with R&D in new areas where the firm is not already active.

Control   Monitoring operations, taking decisions to conform to plans and, when necessary, taking decisions to change plans or behaviors to eliminate variations from plans in any organization.

Controlled Foreign Corporation   A foreign corporation 50 percent or more owned by US shareholders, that is, US citizens or corporations holding at least 10 percent of the common stock each.

Conversion Loss   Receipt of lower revenues than expected because the exchange rate has changed and the foreign-currency receivable was originally worth more of the home-country currency than was ultimately received. Conversion losses may also arise from an increase in foreign currency payables and are realized losses.

Copyright   A legal contract under which a government agrees to protect the originator of a literary, musical, dramatic, or other work from unauthorized use by outsiders.

Cost Method   A method used in preparing a parent company's non-consolidated accounting reports that treats income at the affiliate's level as being received by the parent only when the affiliate's dividends are actually received by the parent.

Cost Minimization   An operating strategy under which the firm or SBU attempts to compete based on low prices and low costs.

Council for Mutual Economic Assistance (CMEA or Comecon)   The regional integration group led by the Soviet Union and comprised primarily of Eastern European countries, though also including Vietnam, Cuba, and Mongolia. This group is also called the Soviet Bloc.

Counterpurchase   A form of countertrade in which the initial export sale is paid for by later shipments of goods by the importer.

Countertrade   A means of posttrade financing that involves payment in goods rather than money for an export sale. Barter of one product for another is the simplest form of countertrade.

Country Risk   The probability that some country-specific factors such as government policy changes or economic events will affect the firm's business activity unexpectedly and importantly.

Cultural Risk   The probability that the firm will face unexpected problems due to differences in culture between its managers and its customers or workers (or even managers) from other cultures.

Culturally Adaptive   Management decisions must accommodate the cultural environment.

Culture   Acquired or learned values and behaviors which characterize a group of people and distinguish one group from the other.

Culture-Based Products   Products distinctively suited for use by and sold to a specific culture.

Currency Diversification   The strategy of reducing the impact of unexpected currency fluctuations by undertaking activities in a variety (portfolio) of different currencies.

Currency Inconvertibility   The situation that arises when a firm is unable to gain access to foreign exchange in the normal market(s) of a country. This is generally the case in communist countries and often occurs in LDCs when economic crises arise.

Current Account Balance   A balance of payments that measures a country's exports of goods and services, minus its imports of goods and services, plus its net receipts of unilateral transfers during some time period.

Customs Union   A regional economic integration group that uses both unrestricted trade between member countries *and* a common policy toward trade with outside countries.

De Facto Protectionism   Non-tariff forms of protection used by countries to restrict imports. The United States uses "voluntary" quotas on Japanese autos and has tried to "jawbone"other countries to reduce their exports to the United States and to increase their imports of US goods.

Debt/Equity Ratio   The capital structure of a firm. The average debt/equity ratio differs from country to country.

Delivered Cost   The cost of producing and shipping a product to the target market. This includes total production cost, cost of insurance and freight, tariff cost, and any other cost involved in getting the product to the market.

Demand Patterns   Measures of the characteristics of goods and services purchased by consumers in different countries. Demand patterns tend to be similar in countries at the same stage of economic development.

Differentiation Advantage   A competitive advantage obtained by a firm that is able to successfully convey the quality or cost differences of its products or services compared to those of rival firms.

Diffusion   The spread of new technology throughout the market.

Disinvestment   Divestiture. Disinvestment occurs when a firm sells or otherwise disposes of a foreign direct investment.

Diversification   Entry into a different business activity outside of the firm's traditional business. This may be a different product, stage of the production process, or country.

Documentary Collection   A means of paying for an export/import transaction that uses only a draft and other informational documents, but *not* a letter of credit.

Documentary Draft   A sight or time draft that is accompanied by instructions and other documents but no L/C.

Double Taxation   Taxation of the earnings of a multinational firm by two countries. This occurs when a foreign subsidiary pays tax in the host country, and then the same profits are taxed (usually with a credit or deduction) by the home country of the parent firm.

Dual Economy   The economy in a less developed country in which some of the firms and households (for example, in cities) participate in the market sector with links to other countries. The other part of the economy is isolated from the international economy (on the periphery) and often operates at a subsistence level (for example, in rural areas).

Dumping   Selling at an unfairly low price in an import market. The US Government has defined dumping as selling below the cost of production or selling below the price in the firm's domestic market.

Eclectic View   Dunning's theory of international business that explains MNE activities based on their ownership advantages, their use of internalization, and on locational factors.

Economic Integration   Expansion of commercial and financial ties among nations. It is expected that greater economic integration of the world will lead to more efficient production and greater output, thus potentially making all countries better off.

Economic Risk   The foreign exchange risk that future cash flows of the firm will be unexpectedly affected by future changes in exchange rates.

Economic Union   An advanced stage of economic integration in which member countries establish common monetary and fiscal policies, as well as policies to achieve a common market.

Embargo   A quota with maximum imports of zero units. That is, a total disallowance of imports of the product being embargoed (or on all imports from the country being embargoed).

Enterprise Union   A union comprised of employees at a single company. Typical to Japan.

Entry Strategy   A method used by an MNE for entering a foreign market. These include exports, direct investment, licensing, franchising, turn-key ventures, and other contractual forms.

Equity Method   A method used in preparing a parent company's nonconsolidated accounting reports that treats income at the foreign entity's level as being received by the parent (for reporting purposes) when it is earned by the foreign entity.

Ethnocentrism   Evidenced in multinational enterprises via centralized decision making and control.

Eurobond   A bond denominated in any currency other than that of the country where it is issued.

Eurobond Market   The market for bonds denominated in any currency other than the local one in any country. Most eurobonds are dollar-denominated bonds issued outside of the United States.

Eurocurrency Market (or Eurodollar Market)   The market for short-term foreign-currency-denominated instruments such as bank deposits in any country. The bulk of the eurocurrency market involves dollar-denominated bank deposits outside of the United States.

Eurodollar   A US dollar-denominated bank deposit located outside of the United States. Most eurodollars are time deposits or certificates of deposit.

Euroequities   Shares of stock issued in multiple countries, typically in the European Union.

Euromarkets   Markets for short- or long-term financial instruments in any country in which the instruments are denominated in currencies other than the local one.

European Community (EC, or Common Market) The association of Western European countries formed in 1957 that has eliminated most tariffs among members, established a common external tariff, harmonized some fiscal and monetary policies, and broadly attempts to increase economic integration among the member countries.

European Currency Unit (ECU) A composite currency similar to the SDR, whose value is based on a weighted average of the currencies of the European Community. Although it is only an accounting convention (i.e., an ECU bill does not exist), the ECU is being used increasingly to denominate international bond issues and other large international financial transactions.

European Monetary System (EMS) A mini-IMF organized by the members of the European Community. The EMS observes exchange rate fluctuations between member-country currencies and makes loans to member governments, primarily to serve the goal of balance of payments stability.

Exchange Controls Government-imposed limits on use of foreign exchange, generally used to restrict outflows of funds from a country. They include limited access to foreign currency at the Central Bank, and multiple exchange rates for different users, among other methods.

Exchange Rate The price of one currency in terms of another.

Exchange Risk The possibility that a firm will not be able to adjust its prices and costs to exactly offset exchange rate changes. Not only must exchange rates be able to vary, but the variations must not be fully anticipated.

Exchange Risk Adaptation The strategy of adjusting the firm's activities to reduce the potential impact of unexpected exchange rate changes. This may be done through financial hedging or other adjustments in the foreign currency activities of the firm.

Exchange Risk Avoidance The strategy of avoiding dealings in currencies that are viewed as having high exchange risk, and/or charging higher prices when exchange risk appears to be higher.

Exchange Risk Transfer The strategy of eliminating or reducing exchange risk by contracting with insurance providers to cover possible exchange rate-induced losses.

Exercise Price The price at which an option may be used to buy/sell foreign exchange.

Eximbank The Export-Import Bank of the United States, the main US Government agency responsible for assisting US exporters via loans and loan guarantees.

Expatriates Nationals of one country who work abroad in another country.

Experience Curve Effect Declining production costs due to the benefit of prior learning as (repetitive) output occurs.

Export Commission Agents Those who buy on behalf of a foreign client and then export directly to that client from the country of purchase.

Export Department An organizational unit within a company that handles exports.

Export/Import Transaction The basic activity of international trade.

Export Management Companies Companies which handle other firms' exports, essentially often acting as an export department for these firms.

Export Merchants Exporters who buy from domestic suppliers and sell to foreign customers.

Export Promotion A strategy for economic development that focuses on increasing a country's exports to generate foreign exchange and stimulate domestic production. This is an outward-looking development model.

Export Trading Company A company, authorized by US law, which combines the export and export support operations of companies which are domestically competing companies.

Expropriation The forced takeover of a company's assets by the host government without compensation (or with inadequate compensation).

Externalization The opposite of internalization. A market or production process is externalized when the firm stops carrying out the activity itself and contracts with an outside firm or agent to do it.

Extractive FDI Direct investment used by the MNE to obtain raw materials such as oil, copper, or other metals, agricultural products, etc.

Factoring Selling an account receivable at a discount to an intermediary company called a factor. The exporter receives immediate (discounted) payment, and the factor receives eventual payment from the importer.

Fade-out A policy sometimes used by national governments that requires a foreign investor to sell partial or total ownership of its affiliate over time. Typically, majority local ownership is sought by the governments.

Fair Value The portion of a firm's activities that can be determined to be carried out in a given jurisdiction. The fair value is crucial to efforts by governments to tax MNE activities.

Financial Accounting Disclosure   The presentation of the consolidated statements, showing both income and balance sheet accounts.

Financial Transfers   Methods used by MNEs to move funds internationally, such as profit remittances, fee payments, payments for intracompany shipments, and loans.

Flexible Multi-Item Factory   A factory that is usually labor intensive and thus capable of producing several different products without large capital costs.

Follow-the-Leader Strategy   The strategy of oligopolistic reaction. It implies that the follower waits to see how an industry leader operates (e.g., in introducing new technology), and then pursues a copycat strategy in areas that appear profitable.

Foreign-Base Company   A *controlled foreign corporation* that derives a substantial portion of its income from investments, sales, services, or shipping.

Foreign Corrupt Practices Act   A US law that prohibits certain kinds of bribes and questionable payments, requires internal accounting control procedures regarding such payments, and the imprisonment of company officials guilty of evading these requirements.

Foreign Currency Option   An option contract that gives the holder the right but not the obligation to exercise it to purchase a given amount of foreign currency at a fixed price during a fixed time period. Contract specifications are similar to those of futures contracts, except that the option requires a premium payment to purchase (and it does not have to be exercised).

Foreign Direct Investment   The extension of controlling ownership by a firm from one country over a firm in another country through new investment or acquisition.

Foreign Exchange   A financial instrument that carries out payment from one currency to another. Common instruments of foreign exchange include bank drafts, wire transfers, forward and futures contracts, and cash.

Foreign Exchange Arbitrage   A business in which a foreign exchange trader buys and sells foreign currency simultaneously in two markets or at two maturities to profit from differential exchange rates without taking exchange risk.

Foreign Exchange Hedging   Financial methods used to protect a firm against unexpected changes in exchange rates that could affect the firm's cash flows.

Foreign Exchange Market   The market(s) in which financial instruments denominated in one currency are traded for instruments denominated in other currencies. Typically, a country's main foreign exchange market is carried out through the commercial banking system.

Foreign Investment Controls   Government-imposed limits on the ability of firms to undertake foreign direct investment. These typically restrict FDI *inflows,* though they have been used to try to limit the outflow of FDI as well.

Foreign Sales Corporation   A legal entity through which a firm can channel exports and derive special income tax benefits.

Foreign Sales Corporation (FSC) Act   A US Government law that replaces the Domestic International Sales Corporation (DISC) legislation. The FSC is a foreign company that exports for a U.S. firm, which may show its export profits in the FSC and avoid U.S. taxation on a percentage of the earnings until they are remitted to the parent US firm.

Foreign Sourcing   Producing or purchasing products or production inputs from a foreign location, typically to lower costs. Many electronics firms source their memory chips in their own plants or through contracts with local firms in Taiwan or Singapore to lower the costs.

Foreign Subsidiary   An overseas company owned by a parent company in the home country. The subsidiary legal structure implies local incorporation of the affiliate in the foreign country.

Foreignness   The characteristics of a firm or person that cause it to be viewed as different from domestic firms or people. Foreignness is often associated with foreign ownership, foreign styles, and different languages.

Forfaiting   A means of posttrade financing analogous to factoring. Forfaiting is used primarily for large capital goods exports to Eastern European countries.

Forward Foreign Exchange Market (Forward Market)   The contractual form used by commercial banks to offer their clients the opportunity to fix an exchange rate for future delivery of one currency for another.

Four P's   product, price, promotion, and place.

Franc Area   The group of former French colonies that continue to use the French franc as an acceptable currency and/or tie their currency values to the franc.

Franchising   A legal form in which a firm (e.g., a hotel chain or restaurant) sells the right to use its name to a buyer, which then produces a final product or service using that name. Generally the franchisor (owner of the name) provides assistance to the franchisee and imposes standards of quality control and other restrictions on use of the franchise.

Free-Trade Area   A regional economic integration group that implements policy for unrestricted trade between member countries, but leaves each country free to set its own policy with outside countries.

Functional Currency The "home country" currency of the parent or the subsidiary which is used in preparing and presenting accounting reports at the operations level.

Functional Structure An internal organizational structure in which the firm divides responsibilities at the highest level according to functions such as marketing, finance, production, human resources, and R&D.

Futures Foreign Exchange Contract (Futures Contract) A legal contract similar to a forward contract, except that it is traded on a securities exchange and has fixed specifications such as maturity date, contract size, and trading limitations during the contract's life.

Gain-Sharing Agreement An agreement between management and labor (typically in the United Kingdom) to share economic gains, usually because of new equipment being installed.

GATT The General Agreement on Tariffs and Trade, the world's main intergovernmental organization that seeks to reduce barriers to international trade. GATT currently has 90 member governments.

Geocentric Organization An organizational management style in which the firm views the whole world as its relevant market for decisionmaking, and in which no one country dominates these decisions.

Global Focus A generic competitive strategy in which the international firm sells in one market segment in multiple countries.

Global International An organization of trade unions from countries around the world.

Global Logistic Network Product and component flows among subsidiaries, between parent and subsidiaries, between the company and vendors, and between the company and customers.

Government Protection A corporate strategy in which the firm builds competitive advantage based on protection offered by the government, such as subsidies or barriers to entry of other firms.

Government Relations The part of a firm's activity that involves dealing with home and host governments.

Grossed-Up Dividend The dividend received by the parent, plus the withholding tax on the dividend plus the amount of income taxes paid by the subsidiary on the income that generated the dividend.

Group Identification People within a group think first of the group, before thinking of themselves.

Hierarchical Relationships Reporting, power, and control relations between people at different (vertical) organizational levels.

Home Country The country in which the MNE is headquartered, and usually where most of the shareholders live.

Horizontal Integration Entry by a firm into a similar business activity in a new location. Restaurant chains, for example, are horizontally integrated providers of food service.

Host Country Any other country, except the home country, where the MNE does business.

Human Resource Management The management of people. Includes hiring, compensating, evaluating, motivating, training, and so forth.

Imperfect Competition Theory An economic theory of the firm in which firms are not viewed as homogeneous, and thus where competitive advantages exist and can be achieved.

Import Substitution A strategy for economic development that focuses on creating domestic industries to replace imported products and services. This is an inward-looking development model.

Income-Based Products Product whose consumption patterns are highly correlated with income levels. High-income products are generally luxury goods, for example.

Indirect Exporting Exporting through an intermediary company such as an export trading company.

Industrial Espionage The effort by an outsider to illegally obtain protected technology from its originator.

Industrial International An affiliate of a *global international* representing workers' interests within a specific industry.

Industrial Regionals Confederations of trade unions based on industrial identification and geographical location. For example, the European Metalworkers' Federation.

Industrial Relations Employer-employee relationships where employees are treated as groups rather than individuals.

Industrial Relations Staff The company's management group concerned with labor-management affairs.

Industrial Relations System An overall perspective on how the interests of workers, managements, and societies come together in determining employment terms and conditions.

Industrialized Countries (ICs) Nations whose economies are dominated by industrial production rather than agriculture or raw materials, whose per capita incomes are high relative to the rest of the world, and who use market economies.

Information Disclosure   Provision of data about company activities to governments in countries where the firm operates.

Information Transfer   The transmission of information from one country to another within an MNE. This issue is important in government relations, since some types of information being transferred are considered sensitive by the governments.

Infrastructure   Basic economic underpinning of a business system such as roads, accessible electric power, telephone service, and other utilities, that are important to a firm that wants to operate locally.

Innovation   A technology change that is successfully introduced into the marketplace, that is, a new product.

Insurance Certificate   A shipping document that demonstrates insurance coverage for the merchandise, naming the exporter and the insuror.

Interbank Market   The market for exchange of financial instruments between commercial banks. Most foreign exchange in the United States is traded in the interbank market.

Interest Parity   The condition that investment in a domestic financial instrument or hedged investment in a foreign-currency instrument of similar risk, maturity, and other characteristics yields the same return.

Internalization   Extension of ownership by a firm to cover new markets, new sources of materials, and new stages of the production process. Internalization is the business strategy counterpart to the economics terms *vertical integration* and *horizontal integration.*

International Contractor   A firm that does international business; that is, a firm involved in exports, direct investment, international licensing, or any other form of business that crosses national boundaries.

International Distribution   The shipment of products or services between countries. This is a source of potential competitive advantage for multinational as opposed to domestic firms.

International Diversification   An ability that exists for MNEs to reduce the firm's risk by operating facilities in more than one country, thus lowering the risk of problems in any one country.

International Division   An organizational decisionmaking structure in which overseas activities are grouped into a single division for management purposes, rather than spread across products or functions.

International Fisher Effect   The condition that an interest rate differential on similar instruments between two countries is eliminated by an offsetting exchange rate change between their currencies.

International Labor Office   A United Nations affiliate with representation from employers, unions, and governments concerned about employment terms and conditions.

International Monetary Fund (IMF)   The organization of 146 national governments that seeks to maintain balance of payments stability in the international financial system. The IMF observes exchange rate regimes and fluctuations (but does not set rates), lends funds to member governments to help in balance of payments crises, and performs other functions toward achieving international financial stability.

International Monetary System   The system of international financial transactions between governments that is operated through the International Monetary Fund.

International Product Cycle   The theory of international trade and investment developed by Vernon to explain international business based on technology and marketing elements as well as comparative costs.

International Trading Companies   Specialist companies that provide export/import service to manufacturers and customers, as well as other intermediaries. Such companies often find overseas markets for manufacturers and conversely find overseas suppliers for end users.

International Transaction   A purchase or sale that involves a seller and a buyer in different countries.

International Union   A union with regionals or locals in more than one country.

Intertemporal (or Interest) Arbitrage   Exchange arbitrage that involves buying foreign exchange in the spot market, investing in a foreign currency asset, and converting back to the initial currency through a forward contract. This is done when interest parity does not hold.

Invention   The creation of new knowledge that may have application to business or industry.

Inventory Management   The strategy used by some MNEs to reduce inventories by pooling different affiliates' stocks and to reduce political and/or exchange risk by holding inventories in less risky countries.

In-Country Distribution   Movement of products through domestic distribution channels such as shipping and warehousing, as contrasted with international distribution.

Joint Venture   A strategic alliance in which the two or more partners each own part of the venture, typically a corporation. The joint venture is legally separate from the parent firms.

Keiretsu   Networks of large numbers of suppliers, intermediaries, and other related firms that have formed industrial power centers in Japan after World War II.

Labor Agreement   Same as the *labor contract*.

Labor Contract   The terms and conditions of employment as negotiated between management and a union.

Lead Market   A country in which the firm introduces its product innovations first, in order to test the market reaction and to use as a base for further introductions in other countries.

Leontief Paradox   The surprising finding by Wassily Leontief that the United States in 1947 had a higher capital/labor ratio in production of import-competing products than in exports. That is, US exports are relatively more labor-intensive, and imports more capital-intensive, despite the relatively greater availability of capital in the U.S. than in other countries.

Less Developed Country (LDC)   A country in the third world. The LDCs are countries primarily in Africa, Asia, and Latin America with relatively low per capita incomes and relatively high dependence on primary materials industries.

Letter of Credit (L/C)   A contract between an importer and its bank that transfers liability for paying the exporter from the importer to the importer's bank.

LIBOR   The London interbank offered rate. This interest rate is a daily average of those quoted by major banks in London to accept deposits of at least $US 1 million from other banks or high-quality clients.

Licensing   A contractual form in which the firm possesses technology that it chooses to sell to other firms for their subsequent use in production, distribution, etc. The initial firm typically charges a royalty for selling the technology and thus benefits from the buying firm's use of that technology.

Lockout   Management not allowing a group of employees to work.

Long-Term National Financial Markets   Capital markets in different countries, that is, markets for long-term financial instruments such as stocks and bonds in different countries.

Low Cost Unit Factory   The production location with lowest costs, either because of low wages or large capital investment (and production scale economies).

Macrorisk   The political risk that exists for all firms (or all foreign firms) in a particular country.

Major Multinationals   The world's largest oil companies. They include: Royal Dutch Shell, EXXON, Mobil, British Petroleum, Texaco, Chevron (Socal), and Amoco.

Make-Versus-Buy Decision   The choice for a firm either to produce a product or input for itself or buy it from an outside supplier. By producing them within the firm, internalization of those inputs' production takes place.

Management Information System   The accumulation and presentation of data and information pertinent to the effective management of the multinational enterprise.

Management Technology   The knowledge used to operate a business, that is, the managerial skills that enable a firm to compete by using its resources efficiently.

Manufacturer's Export Agents   Companies which handle other firms' efforts, essentially often acting as an export department for these firms.

Market Absorption Curves   Graphs depicting the relationship between a product's time in the market and the percent of the potential market that has bought the product.

Market Allocation   The strategy used by MNEs to restrict activities of each affiliate to specified markets, to avoid competition among these units.

Market for Goods and Services   The final market that is served by functioning of financial markets. The financial markets provide transfer of funds from savers to purchasers of goods and services as well as conversion of funds today into funds for future purchases.

Market Sector   That part of a dual economy that is market-based and is connected to international business with the industrial countries.

Market Segmentation   An operating strategy under which the firm or SBU attempts to compete based on defining and pursuing a niche or segment of the total market, such as the highest quality segment, or the smallest size segment, and so on.

Market-Serving FDI   Direct investment used by the MNE to produce and sell its products or services in the host country.

Marketing Mix   The various components of marketing that are used to sell a product: the product itself, brand name, advertising, packaging, pricing, distribution, etc.

Market-based Economy   A country which uses private-sector markets as the base for functioning of the economy, as opposed to central planning in a communist country.

Master Strategy   A company's basic plan on how to accomplish its strategic objectives.

Matrix Structure   A managerial decisionmaking structure in which decisions at the highest level of the firm are made through a combination of functional, product, and sometimes regional lines of authority.

Mature MNE   An organization which has developed internationally, and has geographically distributed assets and knowledge of both resource and product markets literally around the world.

Maturing Product   A product which is produced by several firms, whose technology is no longer monopolized by the innovating firm, and which faces increasing price elasticity of demand.

Microrisk   The political risk that exists for a particular firm or industry in a given country.

Mission Statement   The fundamental aim of an organization, based on which all strategy is developed.

MITI   A Japanese government agency; the Ministry of Trade and Industry.

Monopoly Power   The economic strength that MNEs possess relative to other firms and relative to governments because of their size, their availability of information, and their multinationality.

Most-Favored-Nation   A principle in international trade regulation that is used by members of GATT. If a trade barrier is reduced between any two members of GATT, that same benefit is automatically extended to all other GATT members under the most-favored-nation principle.

Multifibre Arrangement (MFA)   The international agreement among major textile producing and consuming countries that establishes quotas on imports into the main (industrial country) markets. This arrangement is scheduled to be phased out by the year 2004.

Multilateral Netting   The strategy used by some MNEs to reduce international funds flows between affiliates by canceling redundant cash flows and transferring only the net amounts necessary.

Multinational Access to Technology   A competitive advantage available to international firms because they are able to obtain new technology in one country and apply it in their business in other countries.

Multinational Company (MNC) also called **Multinational Enterprise,**   Transnational Corporation and other names. This is a firm with owned operations in at least three countries. The term MNC is often used to refer to the very-large international firms such as EXXON and Toyota.

Multinational Diversification   A competitive advantage that exists for international firms that can spread their risks of supply of inputs and demand for their products across multiple national markets and thus reduce those risks.

Multinational Marketing   Selling the product in several different country markets.

Multinational Marketing Capability   A competitive advantage that derives from the firm's ability to spread the risk of fluctuations in demand across several national markets and also spread the costs of product development and production across several national markets.

Multinational Sourcing   A capability that exists for MNEs to find or set up production sources in more than one nation, thus enabling the firm to lower its costs relative to firms that produce or buy in only one country.

Multinationality   The essence of the MNE. By operating simultaneously in several countries, the MNE is able to transfer information about prices and demand conditions, move funds and products to safer or otherwise preferable locations, and generally escape the limitations imposed by the environment in a single country.

National Capital Markets   Markets for long-term financial instruments such as stocks and bonds that operate mainly domestically. This contrasts with the less-regulated and more-international euromarkets.

National Focus   The competitive strategy that implies adaptation of products to each national market in which the firm operates.

National Money Markets   The short-term financial markets in individual countries. These include markets for instruments such as treasury bills and short-term bank deposits as well as commercial paper, banker's acceptances, and other instruments that mature in less than one year.

Nationalization   The forced takeover of a company's assets by the host government *with* compensation. Sometimes this is achieved by requiring sale of controlling ownership to local investors, still leaving the MNE with some partial ownership.

New International Economic Order   An idea created in the United Nations in the early 1970s that intended to develop mechanisms for redistribution of income between rich and poor countries. The effort was essentially dropped after the oil crisis of 1973–74, though the concept remains in discussion.

New Product   A product in the first stage of Vernon's international product cycle. The product has characteristics of embodying new technology and facing relatively price-inelastic demand in the market.

Newly Industrializing Country (NIC)   Among the LDCs, one of the rapidly-growing countries that have proceeded farthest along the road to industrialization. NICs include South Korea, Hong Kong, Taiwan, Singapore, and Brazil.

Nontariff Barriers (NTBs)   Government-imposed restrictions on imports other than tariffs which also limit imports. They include licensing requirements, prior deposits, bureaucratic delays, and many more restrictions.

Obsolescing Bargain The situation that exists *after* an MNE commits its capital and human resources to an investment project in a host country. The MNE's bargaining position relative to the host government diminishes (obsolesces), since it has important resources at risk in the host country. Over time, the government typically gains even greater ability to force the firm to follow its desired goals as the firm becomes more integrated into the local economy.

Official Settlements Balance The "bottom line" balance of payments when all private sector transactions have been accounted for and all that remain are official exchanges between central banks (and the IMF). This balance measures the country's new inflows of official holdings of foreign exchange, SDRs, gold, and the country's borrowing position at the IMF.

Offshore Assembly The overseas production of goods whose inputs are fabricated in one country, typically done to reduce labor costs. That is, basic materials are made in one country, they are shipped abroad for assembly or processing, and then the final products are shipped to the target market for sale.

Offshore Production Either offshore sourcing or offshore assembly.

Open Account A means of selling exports in which the buyer does not pay the seller until some future date, often upon sale of the products to final customers. This arrangement is common within multinational firms, but not common between independent firms.

Operating Plan Defines where the company intends to go in the short term. Is concerned with monthly sales targets, quarterly budgets, and similar items.

Operating Strategy The day-to-day method of doing business that an MNE must tailor to conditions in each host country. Operating strategy is dependent on the degree and kind of government regulation, competitive conditions, and other factors.

Opportunity Cost The potential gain foregone in any business activity that is given up by hedging against the risk of loss on that activity. The opportunity cost of a forward contract is the lost foreign exchange earnings that would have occurred if the contract were not used and the exchange rate had changed favorably to the firm. For a country the opportunity cost of using resources in one activity is the cost of foregoing the next best alternative use of those resources.

Orderly Marketing Agreement An intergovernmental agreement to limit imports of a product(s). These agreements are usually made when imports are visibly hurting the domestic industry and the importing country cannot demonstrate that the importing firms are dumping or otherwise operating illegally.

Organization of Petroleum Exporting Countries (OPEC) The multinational cartel of oil producing countries that successfully raised the price of oil by over 400 percent in 1973–74 and again by over 200 percent in 1979.

Organization for Economic Cooperation and Development An intergovernmental organization that has as members the industrialized countries (the first world). The OFC is concerned with economic and social issues.

Overall Objectives The broad goals of a firm at the highest level. This could also be called the mission of the firm.

Patent A legal contract under which a government agrees to protect a possessor of proprietary technology from use of the technology by unauthorized outside users.

Pattern Bargaining An industry-wide bargaining strategy characterized by a contract settlement with one company that establishes a basis for other firms in the industry to follow.

Periphery That segment of a country's population that is least advantaged economically. Also, the periphery countries of the world are the LDCs.

Personal Selling Efforts by individuals to sell specific products to specific customers.

Personnel Evaluation Measurement of performance of company employees done for the purpose of salary determination, job assignment, and other uses.

Place The fourth 'p' of marketing, referring to the location of production and distribution of the product.

Political Union A type of economic integration that calls for full political integration between countries, that is, creation of a single political jurisdiction (country).

Polycentric Organization An organization that is managed in a relatively decentralized manner, with local affiliates having a high level of autonomy in decisionmaking and consequently often being very responsive to local market conditions.

Portfolio Investment The purchase of financial instruments such as stocks, bonds, bank deposits, and so forth, by an investor; in our context the investor would be from one country and the investment in another country.

Posttrade Financing Credit extended to the exporter or importer after shipment but before this firm receives its payment for the goods.

Pretrade Financing Credit extended to an exporter to enable that firm to produce the goods that will be exported. This is a form of working capital financing.

Price Controls   Limits established by governments on the price charged by a firm for selling its product. Controls usually limit the maximum price allowed, especially for basic goods such as foods, public utilities, and pharmaceuticals.

Price Escalation when Exporting   A simple strategy of charging a higher price for exported goods than for those sold domestically, presumably to account for the added risks of exporting.

Pricing   The third 'p' of marketing, which refers to the selection of a price to suit market and cost conditions facing the firm.

Privatization   The change in ownership of state-owned firms when they are sold to private-sector buyers. In recent years, numerous partial privatizations have resulted in national telephone companies and airlines becoming partly privately owned and managed.

Process Technology   Technology that applies to the way that products or services are made, that is, to the production process, as opposed to the characteristics of the product itself.

Product   The first 'p' of marketing, which refers to the choice of which product and what characteristics to sell in a given market.

Product Allocation   Assigning specific quantities of specific products to specific markets.

Product Differentiation   An operating strategy under which the firm or SBU attempts to compete based on non-price factors such as quality, service, and other product characteristics.

Product Modification   Slight changes made to a product to respond to marketing and/or competitive needs.

Product Structure   An organizational decisionmaking structure which places decisions at the highest level in the hands of managers with product (as opposed to functional or area) responsibility.

Product Technology   The knowledge used to produce any product, that is, the information that specifies the product's characteristics and uses.

Production Allocation   Assigning production that is needed globally to various subsidiaries.

Production Smoothing   Allocating production to various subsidiaries with the intention of maintaining relatively steady output levels at all locations.

Promotion   The second 'p' of marketing, which refers to the advertising of the product, as well as branding and packaging.

Proprietary Asset   A competitive advantage that accrues due to some firm-specific attribute such as proprietary technology or access to a scarce natural resource.

Proprietary Technology   Knowledge about how to make a product (or service), how to operate a production process, or how to run a business, that one firm possesses and that other firms do not. The innovating firm is able to protect this technology for itself, either through legal means (e.g., patent or trademark) or by secrecy.

Protected Niche   The competitive strategy that implies obtaining government protection for the firm's activities in the countries where it operates.

Protestant Work Ethic   The ethic which believes that work is prayer, is commanded by God, and is an end in itself.

Public Good   A product that can be used repeatedly without being used up. Technology is a public good, because using it does not deplete it.

Purchasing Power Parity   The condition that an inflation differential between any two countries is eliminated by an offsetting change in the exchange rate between their currencies.

Put Option   An option contract that entitles the purchaser to *sell* a fixed amount of foreign exchange at a fixed price in the future.

Quota   A quantity restriction on imports. The number of Japenese cars imported into the United States has been limited by a "voluntary" quota during much of the 1980s.

Regional Economic Integration   Expansion of commercial and financial ties among countries in a regional group, leaving the rest of the world outside of the group. Five forms of regional economic integration have been identified during the post-World War II period, ranging from free trade areas to full economic and political unions.

Regional International   An organization of trade unions from a specific region of the world, for example, Western Europe.

Relative Productivities   The comparative abilities of two firms to use given resources to produce greater or lesser output. The more productive firm will be more competitive.

Repatriation   The return of a person or money or other assets from an overseas affiliate or use back to the home country.

Reporting Currency   The parent company's currency used in preparing and presenting accounting reports at the parent level.

Rugged Individualist   The characteristic attributed to Americans, asserting that they have an innate desire for independence and for individual pursuit of goals.

Scale Economies in Advertising   The condition where the incremental costs of each unit of advertising expenditure are declining, for example, where fixed costs of advertising copy preparation can be allocated to an increasingly large total market as additional ads are placed in different markets.

Scale Economies in Distribution   Cost reductions achieved by shipping large quantities of products, thus lowering the unit shipping costs relative to competitors that ship lower quantities.

Scale Economies in Financing   Cost reductions gained by borrowing large quantities of funds at lower interest and other cost than charged to borrowers of smaller quantities.

Scale Economies in Production   Cost reductions achieved by a large size production facility. When large-scale output is achieved, low unit costs result (relative to competitors operating smaller-scale facilities).

Scale Economies in Purchasing   Cost reductions gained by buying large quantities of inputs at lower unit costs than those paid by buyers of smaller quantities.

Seasonal Factory   A factory that can handle large variations in employment and capacity usage over the year, for example, at Christmas time.

Self-reference Criterion   The imposition of our own standards or expectations when judging or observing the behavior of others.

Sequential Entry Strategy   An MNE strategy that implies market entry through a relatively inexpensive step such as exports or licensing, and a buildup of commitment into joint venture ownership and/or full subsidiary ownership.

Seven Sisters (or the Major Multinationals)   The world's largest oil companies. In the late 1980s they included: Royal Dutch Shell, EXXON, Mobil, British Petroleum, Texaco, Chevron (Socal), and Amoco.

Shunto   The "spring wage offensive" in Japan characterized by coordinated collective bargaining by *enterprise unions* seeking wage increases that mainly pertain to cost-of-living and industry productivity concerns.

Sight Draft   A means of payment for an export contract in which the draft (essentially a check) is payable upon delivery to the exporter. The draft is often used in conjunction with a letter of credit.

Skunk Works   A think-tank environment used by some MNEs to encourage researchers to pursue new projects in small teams without excessive bureaucracy from the mainstream business of the firm.

Social Benefit/Cost Ratio   The sum of all social benefits generated by a potential project divided by the sum of all social costs generated by the project. If the ratio is greater than one, the project should be undertaken, from the host country's perspective.

Social Darwinism   Survival of the fittest.

Sogo Shosha   The Japanese trading companies, such as Mitsubishi Shoji and Mitsui Bussan.

Sourcing FDI   Direct investment used by the MNE to produce its products or inputs overseas for eventual sale back in the home country (or in other countries).

Sovereignty   Control over the national economy.

Special Drawing Right (SDR)   The official currency of the IMF. The SDR is a composite currency based on the weighted values of the dollar, yen, mark, French franc, and the British pound. New SDRs are issued infrequently by the IMF, and this currency is used as the unit of account for transactions with the IMF.

Specialized International   A component of an intergovernmental agency which represents workers' interests and views within that agency.

Spillover Benefits   Positive externalities. To a country, spillover benefits accrue when a business activity is undertaken and it has positive impact beyond the success of the venture itself (such as additional employment, improved balance of payments, etc.). To a company, spillover benefits accrue when an activity is undertaken that has a positive impact on the rest of the firm's business in addition to the activity's own success.

Standardized Product   A product that is produced by many firms, whose technology is well known, and which faces very price-sensitive demand. Commodities are generally standardized products.

Sterling Area   The group of former members of the British Commonwealth that continue to use the British pound as an acceptable currency and/or tie their currency values to the pound.

Stewards' Council   An elected group of worker representatives, not a union, to negotiate with management on labor agreements and the solving of workers' problems. The Stewards' Council is more commonly found in the United Kingdom.

Strategic Alliance   A cooperative agreement between two or more firms. Such alliances range from joint ventures with mutual part-ownership of a venture to cross-licensing, joint marketing, joint research, and other types of contractual arrangements.

Strategic Business Unit (SBU)   An organizational subdivision that generally has profit/loss responsibility and groups like products and activities together for determining competitive strategy.

Strategic Management   The determination of SBU goals, design of strategy to pursue them, and responsibility to control and redefine this process.

Strategic Objectives   Those goals established in the process of strategic management.

Strike   A group of employees' refusal to work.

Subpart F Income   Income received from a *foreign-based* company.

Subsidiary   A foreign corporation whose stock is more than 50 percent owned by the parent company and is therefore controlled by the parent company.

Subsidy   As refers to international trade, a subsidy is some cost-reducing privilege offered by the government to domestic firms to stimulate their competitiveness so that they may be more successful against imports.

Tariff   A tax placed on imports that thereby raises the price and restricts the quantity of imports.

Tariff Reform Act of 1986   A recent amendment of the US international trade policy, establishing among other things a right for the US President to impose sanctions on foreign countries that dump goods in the US market at unfairly low prices.

Technology Advantage   A competitive advantage gained from creation or obtaining of proprietary technology.

Technology Intensity   The amount of technology used relative to capital and labor in production of a product or service.

Technology Intensive   Depending more on research and development (i.e. technology) than other firms in the same or other industries. A technology intensive firm is generally one that spends more on research and development or has more scientific and technical staff than other firms in a given context.

Technology Transfer   The passage of product or process technology, or management skills, from one firm to another, or between affiliates of a multinational firm.

Three-Way (or Triangular) Arbitrage   Exchange arbitrage among three currencies which involves beginning in one currency, passing through each of the other two, and ending in the initial currency.

Time Draft   A means of payment for an import/export transaction. The time draft is payable after delivery at the time stated on the draft. It is often accompanied by a letter of credit guaranteeing the payment.

Time Orientation   The importance of time—punctuality and lateness.

Trade Adjustment Assistance (TAA)   A US government policy that offers aid to workers laid off because of competition from imported goods. This mechanism attempts to alleviate the burden on people who are hurt by the operation of comparative advantage in international trade, which leads to contraction of some domestic industries and expansion of others.

Trade Balance   Comparison of the value of merchandise exports minus the value of merchandise imports for a given country for a given time period. A surplus trade balance implies exports greater than imports; a trade deficit implies imports greater than exports.

Trade Creation   Generation of new exports between members of an economic integration group, due to lowering of trade barriers between them.

Trade Deficit   A situation in which a country's imports exceed its exports for a given period of time such as one year. The deficit may lead to consequences such as currency devaluation, capital movements, government policy shifts, etc.

Trade Diversion   Replacement of exports from non-members of an economic integration group because of increased internal trade among the members.

Trade Financing   Credit extended to an importer by the exporter, or a commercial bank or some other intermediary, that enables the importer to pay for the merchandise, presumably until it is sold and the importer receives funds to pay.

Trademark   A legal contract under which a government agrees to protect the originator of the distinctive mark, word, design, or picture, from unauthorized use by outsiders.

Trading-with-the Enemy Act   A U.S. government law that forbids US firms from doing business with countries that are from time to time listed as enemies; for example, North Korea, Cuba, and Vietnam.

Traditional Sector   The poorer part of a dual economy that is based on traditional agriculture, hunting, or fishing, and is weakly connected to the market sector.

Transaction Efficiencies   The gains of economic welfare generated by operation of MNEs because they are (sometimes) more efficient than smaller, uninational firms.

Transaction Risk   The possibility that a foreign currency-denominated transaction will be worth less (or more) than expected in local currency when the transaction is completed in the future.

Transfer Price   The price for products, components, and so forth, traded among units within the same multinational enterprise.

Transfer Pricing   The establishment of prices to charge on goods and services sold between affiliates of the same company. These internal prices may be managed by the firm to shift tax burdens and to move funds between affiliates.

Translation Loss   An accounting loss reflected in adjustments to accounting statements at the end of an accounting period to record changes in home-country currency values caused by changes in foreign currency based receivables, payables, or other assets or liabilities.

Translation Risk   The possibility that a firm's balance sheet entries will be changed in domestic currency due to changes in exchange rates that affect foreign-currency accounts.

Transnational Corporations   See Multinational Corporations.

Trigger Price Mechanism   A system used by the United States during 1978–82 to limit imports of steel products. The trigger price was the estimated cost of producing each steel product in Japan, the world's low-cost producer of most steel products. Firms attempting to import at prices below the trigger prices faced penalties for dumping in the US market.

Turnkey Venture   A strategic alliance in which the initiating firm sells a product or project (e.g., a coal mine or power plant) to a typically-government buyer. The initiating firm keeps the right to own and manage the venture for a fixed period of time, after which the keys are turned over to the buyer.

Two-way (Exchange) Arbitrage   Simultaneous purchase and sale of a foreign currency or another financial instrument in two different markets to take advantage of different prices in the two markets.

Unbundling   A strategy of governments to try to force MNEs into sharing more of their benefits with the local country; for example, through shared ownership, required technology transfer, local content requirements, and so forth.

Universal MIS   A management information system that is common to all operations, whether at the parent or subsidiary levels.

Value-Added Tax   A tax applied on the value added by each manufacturer or distributor during the production and marketing of a product.

Vertical Integration   Entry of a firm into a different stage of production in its own industry. The auto company, Ford, not only produces cars, but it is vertically integrated into steel production.

Voluntarism   A tradition among British workers that their interests in unions is a fundamental right, and that they will respect each individual's right to work or not work to secure benefits from management.

Voluntary Export Restraints (VERs)   A trade policy used by the United States in place of a quota. Such restraints have been used to limit Japanese auto exports to the US, by demanding that the Japanese auto firms 'voluntarily' limit their exports to the US to a fixed annual maximum.

Voluntary Quota   An orderly marketing agreement under which the exporting country agrees to limit exports to some predetermined level or some percentage of the importing country's market.

Weighted-Average Cost of Capital   The firm's cost of funds, measured as the cost of each source of funds weighted for that source's part in total funding.

Weighted-Average Exchange Rate   The exchange rate used in translating income and expense accounts at the end of an accounting period. It takes into account the relative movement of exchange rates during the period and adjusts the consolidated statement to reflect some weighted mean rate.

Works Council   An elected group of employee representatives that have legal rights to certain company information and to co-determine with management certain issues, especially those pertaining to safety. The Works Council is more commonly found in continental Europe.

Worldwide Company Councils   An organization comprised of trade union representatives from different countries who work for, or represent workers at, a single multinational enterprise.

Zaibatsu   The pre-World War II Japanese holding companies that controlled major industrial empires.

靴化 販兒

Name Index

Index